SEASONAL FLORIDA

A TASTE OF LIFE IN NORTH FLORIDA

Jo McDonald Manning

All rights reserved,
Copyright 1994

Yardbird Productions, Ponte Vedra Beach, Florida

Cover designed by Randy Taylor,

Gloria Norton, Food Stylist
Photography by McElwee & McElwee

No part of this book may be reproduced in any form.
ISBN: 0-9640567-5-5

Copies of Seasonal Florida may be obtained from:
Seasonal Florida, P.O. Box 1694,
Ponte Vedra Beach, Florida 32004

Or by mailing an order blank from the back of the book to the above address.

seasonalfloridacookbook.com

SEASONAL FLORIDA TABLE OF CONTENTS

FOREWORD	4
NORTH FLORIDA COOKERY	7
TOURING THE BACKROADS	11
OLD TIMEY FAVORITES	19
BISCUITS, BREAKFAST AND BRUNCH	49
APPETIZERS AND TAILGATE FOOD	83
SAVORY SOUPS, GUMBOS AND CHOWDERS	113
SIMPLY SCRUMPTIOUS SALADS	147
SEAFOOD, FISHES AND POND CRITTERS	171
YARD BIRDS AND OTHER FOWL	211
WILD GAME, CRACKER CATTLE AND PINEY WOODS ROOTERS	233
FINGER LICKIN' DEEP SOUTH BARBECUE	261
PERLOS, RICE DISHES AND PASTA	283
SOUTHERN GARDEN VEGETABLES AND SWAMP CABBAGE	303
DESSERTS AND SWEET THANGS	327
FAMILY AND FRIENDS	375
BED N' BREAKFAST INNS AND BOUTIQUE HOTELS	411
SEASONAL FLORIDA MENUS AND GLOSSARY	424
FOOD FESTIVALS, U-PICK-EMS AND FARMERS' MARKETS	432
INDEX	440

FOREWORD

Welcome to Seasonal Florida, one of the best kept secrets in the Deep South. North Florida has a climate much like the southern parts of its neighboring states of Alabama and Georgia—with many, many miles of coastline on both the Gulf of Mexico and the Atlantic Ocean.

The climate here is mild but has distinct seasonal changes unlike the rest of the state. Spring features flowering dogwoods, redbuds, azaleas, daffodils and fragrant narcissus. Humid summers are accented with pastel oleanders, crept myrtles, daylillies, and the fragrance of gardenias, tea olives, orange blossoms and the southern magnolia. In the fall, the woods and swamps turn bright orange, yellow and red as the maples, birch, gums, and cypress change colors and begin the dormant season. Winters are short and mild with occasional light freezes and maybe a rare blast of snow to tease the children. But almost like magic, as the sasanqua and camellia blooms begin to fade, azaleas begin to bud, signaling that spring is just around the corner, repeating the colorful cycle.

The Stuart Knox Gillis House (featured on the cover) has been a landmark in our hometown of DeFuniak Springs since it was built in 1901. The house had been vacant for years and was in need of many repairs. When my five sisters and I bought it in 1989, we thought it would be a great place for all our families (I am one of nine children) to congregate on holidays and maybe later open a bed and breakfast. We quickly discovered that it needed more work than we had thought! Woodpeckers and other birds had moved into the twenty-foot columns and capitals. We were able to restore the cypress columns, but the terra cotta capitals were unfortunately beyond repair. Luckily we were able to match the originals with new ones from Atlanta. The heart of pine exterior, after intense scraping, soaked up over 100 gallons of paint. Six live oaks were planted to represent the six sisters, and during holidays we began installing a sprinkler system, trees, shrubs and sod. In less than two years, we had spent almost as much on the outside of the house as we had initially paid for the house and lots. Estimates keep coming in. And the inside—have you ever tried to get six sisters to agree on anything?

S. Knox Gillis House located in DeFuniak Springs, c 1989.

FOREWORD

Well, we knew we had to raise some big time money, so my sisters and I formed GARTEC, which is an acronym for Genny, Anna Jo, Ruby, Tawee, Elizabeth and Carolyn.

Gartec girls, c 2000.

We had some awe-inspiring garage sales and started a cottage industry making Christmas ornaments to sell to folks vacationing at the nearby "Emerald Coast." We were doing pretty well, but we needed to keep thinking of new ways to raise money to restore the house.

Then one day my loving husband said, "Honey, why don't you take all the recipes we have and write a book on the food and fun things we enjoy in North Florida? It would help to raise money for the restoration of "The Big House." And I said, "All right, it might take six months, a year tops." Well, it's been way over three years and we're still working away.

This book is a joint effort representing both my family and my husband's family recipes; the Granny's, Grandpa's, Mother's, Daddy's, Aunt's, and Uncle's are from both families.

Since our grandparents and great-grandparents lived close by, we often stayed with them learning about the "old-timey" days. This included preparing and eating unique foods like clabber, gopher and hominy. For both my husband and myself, this probably marked the beginning of our development as "foodies."

After moving away from home to attend college (ending up together at the University of Florida), we married and have spent the last thirty-five years in Northeast Florida, in Duval and St. John's Counties. Of course, we have been traipsing back and forth to our hometowns on holidays and vacations.

We've also explored the backroads of most of North Florida (stopping at every promising restaurant, cafe and truck stop along the way). Over the years we have collected a fair amount of regional recipes, from friends, family and a few friendly chefs. Some recipes we have created ourselves from fondly remembered meals.

New recipes are very rare—most are simply variations of existing recipes from other areas. The famous Huguenot torte from Charleston has been attributed to a pudding from the Midwest, which probably originated somewhere in Europe. Many of our soups, gumbos and stews are adaptations from the early settlers' use of the local game and seafoods to the recipes from the old country. A lot of our desserts originated in Europe and have been altered to use our local ingredients. Sometimes it's an improvement to the original, sometimes not.

So next time someone gives you one of their original "secret" recipes, thank them warmly and give them one of yours. It just might be one from *Seasonal Florida*.

FOREWORD

Growing up in a small southern town was a wonderful experience. We had no televisions, video games or cell phones. But we did have bicycles, tree forts, swimming holes and were entertained by skeeter hawks and lightening bugs at twilight.

Many of our fondest memories revolve around seasonal events and highlight some of our favorite foods. Shrimp boils and beach parties at Grayton Beach marked the beginning of summer. Crabbing trips to the bayous yielded the main ingredient for our crab boils. Flounder gigging down at the Choctawhatchee Bay provided fish and fun. Sometimes we'd "borrow" a watermelon from a nearby farmer and let it chill in the natural springs while we swam and played gator.

When the mountain laurels and honeysuckles were in full bloom, spring picnics, with fried chicken, favorite sandwiches and deviled eggs were enjoyed down in Euchee Valley. Dinners on the ground, with chicken and dumplings and egg custards, were featured at many church socials. When the mayhaws were ripe, we'd pick them with our cousins and have the mayhaw jelly on granny's hot biscuits the next morning.

Hog killings occurred in winter and yielded bacon, sausage, hams, for the smokehouse and the pork shoulders so delicious barbecued. Fish fries with hushpuppies were the reward after a successful day fishing in the creeks, bays, or Gulf of Mexico.

You will find these and more childhood adventures sprinkled all throughout *Seasonal Florida*. We hope these fond memories will entice you to try some of our classic recipes--and create fond memories for your family and friends.

Drawing of early DeFuniak Springs by David Butler.

IN PURSUIT OF FRESH FLAVOR

The first serious cooking in North Florida has been contributed to the Indians who populated the state prior to the 1500's. These Indians perfected the art of barbecuing and grilled their game and seafood over hot coals. Primitive farming enabled them to grow vegetables to supplement their game, seafood, nuts, berries and palm hearts. Recent archeological finds have shown that Florida Indians were growing maize (corn) and beans prior to 450 B.C.

In the 1500's Spanish, French and English explorers came seeking the gold of the New World, as well as the elusive Fountain of Youth. These early explorers settled the coastal cities of Fernandina, St. Augustine, and Pensacola. They brought with them seasonings and cooking techniques from their cultures and began to meld these with the local ingredients of the New World. Life here was hard, but probably no worse than in the old country where they had been persecuted for religious and other reasons. They grubbed out a meager existence in the New World by farming, hunting and trading.

Emigrants from Europe moved here via the Carolinas and became known as "Crackers" their meals had little variety. Meat was typically smoked pork such as fatback, which was fried to season hominy, grits, or corn bread and greens from the garden. Wild game was prepared when available. A trip to the coast might yield some fish or shellfish to break the monotony.

As time went on, new vegetable and fruit seeds were planted and more variety was available for the table.

New crops were planted and cultivated by plows pulled by mules or oxen. Sugar cane from the islands was introduced and supplemented the nectar of the honey bees. Citrus trees from Spain were planted in the warmer areas. Fruit and nut trees were planted in the fertile farms around the river valleys. New varieties of fowl, swine and cattle became available and were a welcome addition to early farms.

So the North Florida cooks introduced a Southern cuisine that had hints of Creole, Spanish, African, Indian, Minorcan and other European influences. This cuisine continued through the 1800's, and improved as it passed through each successive generation.

The invention of refrigeration in 1851 by Dr. John Gorrie, of Apalachicola had a major impact on cooks. The icebox, and later the refrigerator, kept foods, meats and seafoods fresh for much longer periods of time.

At the turn of the century, a railroad was completed through North Florida, connecting the Gulf of Mexico at Pensacola with the Atlantic Ocean at Jacksonville. Many new towns sprang up along those tracks.

Florida's oldest confederate monument, located at the Walton County courthouse. It was moved from it's original location in Eucheeanna.

Early lumber train, salvaged from the Suwannee River, now located at the Agricultural Lab in Tallahassee.

The railroad provided much needed jobs and daily mail service to North Florida. Cookware, preservatives, vegetable seeds, fruit and nut trees and many products not available in local stores could now be ordered through mail order catalogues. Cooks utilized these new products to improve the local cuisine. During the Great Depression in the 1930's and World War II in the 1940's, there was rationing and shortages, but the innovative cooks of North Florida were used to making substitutions and continued to fill their tables with good tasting and wholesome meals.

After the war, our government decided to get involved in local cuisine via home demonstration agents and home economic teachers. These well-meaning agents held meetings in the various communities and brought local cooks and homemakers up-to-date on what was happening elsewhere.

Those favorite dishes everyone had loved were suddenly deemed old-fashioned. Everyone was excited with the "nouveau cuisine." These new dishes were typically some sort of congealed salads made with various artificial flavors of Jell-o, bing cherries, fruit cocktail, crushed pineapple, nuts, cottage cheese, and "Co-Cola."

The dish was then often topped with sour cream, miniature marshmallows and store bought mayonnaise.

As if this wasn't enough, then came the endless parade of casseroles. These were typically made with some left-over cooked vegetable nobody liked anyway, like broccoli, brussels sprouts or canned asparagus, with 2 or 3 cans of various creamed soups. Water chestnuts, cranberries, Brazil nuts, dehydrated parsley, niblet corn, canned fried onion rings, Ritz cracker crumbs, a generous sprinkling of MSG, topped with a half inch layer of Velveeta cheese often yielded "this week's" casserole. Those delicious homemade cakes were replaced by the ready mixes from Mr. Hines and Mrs. Crocker. Pies and puddings soon appeared in instant form. My God, what's that in Granny's hand surely not a can of store bought biscuits. This is a bad dream and we'll wake up soon!

Oxen were utilized to drag the heart pine logs to the nearest stream where they were floated down to the sawmills at the mouth of the rivers, c 1930's.

S. Knox Gillis House, DeFuniak Springs, c 1994.

Then came the television and with it those memorable T.V. dinners. A choice of turkey, chicken or salisbury steak. Each with a glob of mashed potatoes (we think), gravy like library paste, peas the size of marbles and a dessert previously unknown on Earth.

The man on T.V. said convenience was what's happening and boy, did we have convenience; instant potatoes, instant grits, instant coffee, instant tea, instant pudding, instant oatmeal, instant biscuits, instant milk, you name it. If it could be instantized, we got it.

Church and social dinners became a disaster. Our favorite cooks were ashamed of their old dishes and began bringing tutti-fruity salads instead of peas and butter beans. Fresh greens were replaced with canned green beans and Cheese Whiz casserole. At least there was our favorite, a banana pudding-yuk, what's this? Instant pudding and Cool Whip? The vanilla wafers were real—or were they?

Regional favorites began disappearing from local cookbooks sold by churches and schools. They were replaced by the endless variations of congealed salads and casseroles, as well as desserts copied from the boxes of cake mixes. Would this nonsense ever end?

Fortunately—and not surprisingly—after too many years of this "convenience" food there has been a strong return to the cuisine of the old days. Nothing fancy, just good solid cooking made with fresh vegetables, meats and seafood, seasoned with smoked meats, herbs and spices.

Seasonal Florida represents many years of verbal and written research to present as accurately as possible old and new recipes that utilize local food products.

Many of our contributing cooks have passed on and we are very fortunate to have documented their experience and knowledge of our regional cooking. We are sure many recipes have been lost forever because someone didn't take the time to write them down. If you have someone who cooks your favorites, please write them down and pass them on to be shared. Who knows? One day you might get a hankering to write a cookbook. It happens.

Restored columns and capitols, S. Knox Gillis House, DeFuniak Springs, c 1994.

Touring the Backroads

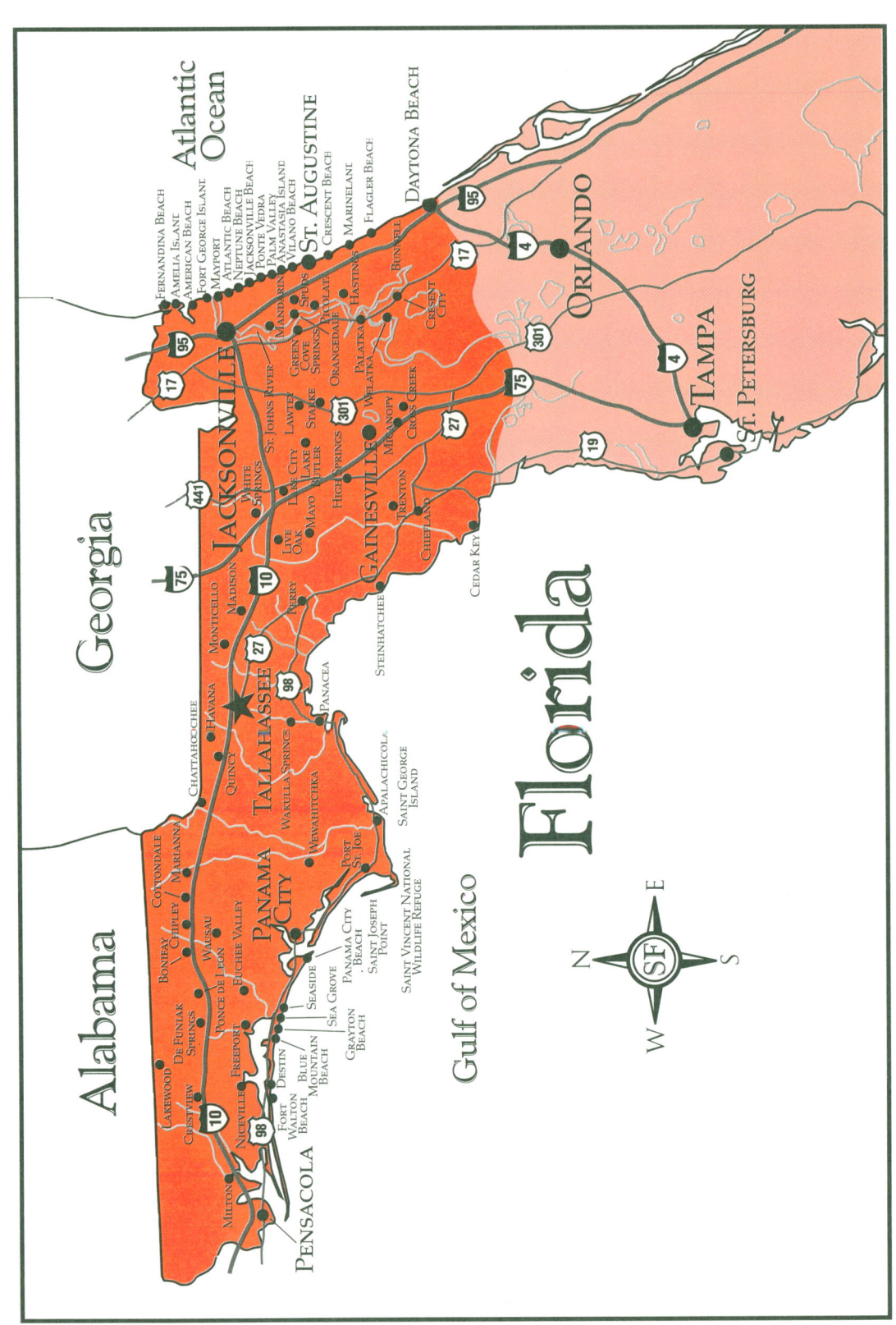

Touring The Backroads

*Former Florida Governor W.S. Jennings at the gates of
St. Augustine, riding unique Florida transportation, c 1901.*

Pensacola
Milton
Fort Walton Beach
Destin
Niceville
Miramar Beach
Inlet Beach
Blue Mountain Beach
Grayton Beach
Seagrove Beach
Seaside
Freeport
Portland
Euchee Valley
DeFuniak Springs
Lakewood
Ponce de Leon
Bonifay
Chipley

Marianna
Wausau
Panama City Beach
Panama City
Port St. Joe
Wewahitchika
Apalachicola
Panacea
Wakulla Springs
Quincy
Havana
Tallahassee
Monticello
Madison
Perry
Steinhatchee
Mayo
Live Oak
White Springs

Lake City
High Springs
Trenton
Chiefland
Cedar Key
Gainesville
Stark
Lawtey
Micanopy
Cross Creek
Welatka
Palatka
Spuds
Hastings
Crescent City
Bunnell
Flagler Beach
St. Augustine
Crescent Beach

Anastasia Island
St. Augustine Beach
Vilano Beach
Ponte Vedra Beach
Palm Valley
Jacksonville
Jacksonville Beach
Atlantic Beach
Neptune Beach
Mandarin
Orangedale
Picolata
Green Cove Springs
Mayport
Fort George Island
Amelia Island
American Beach
Fernandina

When Juan Ponce de Leon landed near St. Augustine on Easter morning in 1513, his arrival touched off an almost 300-year-struggle for control of Florida. He eventually returned to colonize Florida eight years later, only to die in Cuba from a wound suffered in a battle with Florida's Indians. Still, Spaniards, lured by tales of treasure and the promise of discovering new land, kept coming. In 1528, Panfilo de Narvaez landed at Tampa Bay with more than 300 men, marched north into the Panhandle, and was never seen again. Hernando de Soto followed in the late 1530's and met a similar fate on the Mississippi River. Twenty years later, Tristan de Luna failed in his attempt to establish a colony in Pensacola.

It is Pedro Menendez de Aviles who finally founded St. Augustine, the first permanent European settlement in the United States. The city was established in 1565 as a fort and base of operation against the French. Thus began a struggle between the Spanish and the British for control of Florida and its valuable trade route for the next 200 years. By 1700, both had established thriving settlements.

It wasn't until 1763, however, that Spain was forced to cede Florida to the British to regain Cuba, which the British had recently captured. Under British rule, Florida grew into a thriving colony, with the British concentrated in the west and the Spanish still dominating in the east. Loyal to England during the American Revolution, the colony became a pawn in negotiations leading up to the wars end. The Treaty of Paris, signed in 1783, caused the British to return all of Florida to Spain.

Spain's second attempt to control Florida was no more successful. Andrew Jackson invaded Spanish Florida twice during the 1800's, first during the War of 1812 and again a few years later during the Seminole War. Finally in 1819, Spain gave Florida to the United States, who formally took possession of East and West Florida in 1821 with Jackson serving as governor.

While the state had been unified with the new capital at Tallahassee, the state of Florida was still wrought with unrest between white settlers and local Seminole Indians, and three bloody wars ensued. In 1858, Seminole Chief "Billy Bowlegs" was captured, and the Seminoles were sent to reservations in the West. Three hundred Seminoles escaped into the Everglades, where their descendants still live today.

Just as Florida began to recover from its Seminole Wars, the 1860's brought another conflict. Florida became the "Breadbasket of the Confederacy" during the Civil War, thanks to its rich agricultural industry. When the war ended in 1865, Tallahassee was the only Confederate state capital east of the Mississippi that had not fallen.

As more and more of North Florida grows into urban landscapes, it's comforting to know there's plenty of the old and natural Florida still left. The Panhandle is an area most non-Floridians aren't even aware of—they think the state begins in Jacksonville and ends in Key West. The Northwest region offers lots of the "old" along with the "new" and breathes a certain kind of peace.

TOURING THE BACKROADS

Canopy-treed roads, rolling hills and stately plantations offer a stark contrast to the sugar-white sand beaches, towering beach front resorts and tourist attractions.

To discover part of this "Old Florida," tour the area stretching from Pensacola (Mardi Gras Street Festival) to Panama City (Seafood Festival). Pensacola, Florida's westernmost city, is steeped in history (the area was first settled by the Spanish in 1559) and rich in its eclectic architectural heritage. While you are there, visit Pensacola Beach, Fort Pickens and the Navy Museum and stop by Hopkins' Boarding House to sample the home-style cooking.

Santa Rosa County lies to the east. Drive along Santa Rosa Island and enjoy the picturesque view of the sugar-white sand and emerald-green water. To the north lies the city of Milton (Scratch Ankle Festival), which was once a thriving outpost of sawmills visited daily by four-mast schooners and shipping steamers.

Okaloosa County encompasses the shore side towns of Fort Walton Beach (Seafood Festival), Destin (Gumbo Cook-Off Festival), and the deep blue 100-square-mile Choctawhatchee Bay where wind-surfers and sailboats challenge the waves, and millions of mullet, blue crabs and oysters are harvested annually. In Niceville (Boggy Bayou Mullet Festival), tree-shaded campgrounds in Rocky Bayou State Park make for a great escape. While most everyone who visits the beaches of South Walton County leaves sporting a tan, there is more to do along this 26-mile sun swept expanse between Miramar Beach and Inlet Beach than just soak up the sun. Exploring area nature trails by foot or on horseback is an activity for all ages. Cassine Gardens' nature trails meander through three miles of scenic marshland, forest and beaches. Take the side roads along route 30-A and visit the secluded jewels of Blue Mountain, Grayton and Seagrove Beaches, some of the first beach communities developed along the Gulf of Mexico. Next stop off at the new town of Seaside (Wine and Jazz Festival). This world-class community, barely a dozen years old, has received many awards for its planning and architecture. West of Seaside visit Eden Gardens, the restored home and grounds of an early lumber baron.

While traveling north through the old port towns of Freeport and Portland, it's hard to imagine that vast forests once covered the state. These virgin pines and cypress were cut into boards and beams and shipped on schooners from ports like these all over the world. To the east is Euchee Valley, where Scottish immigrants settled around 1820. Historic DeFuniak

Wilson Cypress company men measuring 3,000 year old cypress in North Florida. c 1910.

Springs, (Chautauqua Festival), located ten miles northwest, boast of the perfectly round Lake DeFuniak. Be sure to visit the Chautauqua Auditorium, and the Walton DeFuniak Library, established in 1886.

Chautauqua Auditorium, DeFuniak Springs, c 1911.

A 1.3 mile sidewalk and drive around the lake has homes featuring lacy gingerbread, columns, turrets, and towers. Our S. Knox Gillis House is located at 772 Circle Drive. A few miles north of DeFuniak Springs is Lakewood, the highest point in Florida at 345 feet above sea level.

Ponce de Leon (Collard Festival), located 9 miles east of DeFuniak Springs, is the home of the now famous Ponce de Leon Springs, which some say has "magical powers which retain youth" and is a favorite swimming hole for local folks. My husband grew up in Ponce de Leon, swam in the springs regularly, and says the only magical powers that it has is the ability to turn your lips blue if you stay in the water more than two minutes!

Morrison and Vortex (Blue) Springs are also located here, and are open for scuba diving. These springs are so refreshingly cold that people often rest watermelons in the water to chill.

On the fourth Saturday in November, many locals and visitors come from all over to congregate in Ponce deLeon and pay homage to the lowly collard green. There are many events, including the crowning of the Collard Queen, but the main reason people drive from miles around is to visit with old friends and relatives and to enjoy dinner (the noon feast). If you are fortunate enough to be there when they are serving, you will be dining on fried country ham, old-fashioned collards, sweet potatoes, potato salad, hot cracklin' corn bread, and dessert.

Travel east on U.S. 90 crossing the Choctawhatchee River and swamp that once had millions of large cypress trees, some with trunks over a dozen feet in diameter. This river swamp now grows the Tupelo Gum trees which helps the bees produce our unique honey.

Most of the towns along U.S. 90 sprang up after the railroad was completed at the turn of the century. DeFuniak Springs, Bonifay (All Night Gospel Sing) and Chipley (Historic Day) were named for prominent men who ran the railroads.

Large Live Oak tree, Miller Homestead, Holmes County.

TOURING THE BACKROADS

In Marianna, visit the Florida Caverns State Park and take a long cool walk into the caverns and explore the various underground tunnels.

To the south are the sand hills with their many lakes and ponds teaming with bass, redbreast brim, shellcrackers, warmouth, bluegills and stumpknockers. Nearby is Wausau (Annual Possum Festival). Wausau has a statue commemorating the lowly possum that provided many a meal for the hard hit Panhandle residents during the depression days of the 1930's.

Panama City Beach (Seafood Festival) offers many reasons for a visit to Florida's Northwest—billions of them. The sugar-white sand of its beaches (99% pure quartz) is the result of Appalachian Mountain quartz crystals that have been broken down, washed, bleached, ground and polished into millions of grains of sand, stretching 27 miles along the turquoise-green waters of the Gulf of Mexico. The Emerald Coast is widely regarded as one of the world's most beautiful beaches. Check out the fresh seafood of Capt. Anderson's Restaurant on Grand Lagoon.

The waters in and around Panama City and Destin are alive with a wide variety of fish, including red snapper, grouper, king mackerel, cobia, scamp, pompano and amberjack. Anglers can fish, not only from charter boats, but from piers, jetties, and the shore. You can also snorkel, dive, parasail, jetski, and windsurf in the bays and the Gulf of Mexico.

To the southeast is Port St. Joe (Seafood Festival), said to be a company town once controlled by the notorious Ed Ball, and Wewahitchika (Tupelo Honey Festival), simply called "Wewa" by locals.

Further to the southeast is the historic town of Apalachicola (Florida State Seafood Festival). Be sure to visit the Dr. John Gorrie Museum—Dr. Gorrie invented refrigeration in 1851. Visit a local oyster bar and have some delicious Apalachicola oysters.

Then continue your travel along scenic Highway 98 across the coast and up through Panacea (Blue Crab Festival). Panacea, situated on the Gulf of Mexico, is known as "The Blue Crab Capital of the World."

Nearby is Wakulla Springs, one of the world's deepest fresh water springs. It is open to the public for swimming, diving and glass bottomed boat trips which travel down the picturesque Wakulla River. Try some of the Southern cuisine at the restaurant adjacent to the Springs.

To the northwest are Quincy and Havana (Old Time Havana Days), once the world's largest producers of shade tobacco. This area now produces millions of mushrooms and vine-ripe tomatoes for shipment to Northern markets. Don't miss the Nicholson Farmhouse, located between Quincy and Havana. Created by moving several old farm houses together, it's an excellent steak house. They feature aged steaks cooked in an open-air kitchen.

Tallahassee (Heritage Festival), Florida's capital, sports a landscape of canopied roads and Southern plantation homes and is frequently referred to as "The Other Florida" for good reason. Areas of interest include The Florida State Museum, The Florida Agriculture Museum and the Maclay Gardens, home to thousands of camellia and azalea plants.

Cracker cattle at Agricultural Museum in Tallahassee.

Monticello (Watermelon Festival), and Madison (Down Home Days), are located to the east. They feature quaint homes, architecturally significant courthouses and storefronts of years ago.

To the south is Perry (Florida Forest Day), home to several large sawmills. Perry features an annual free fish fry. Nearby is Steinhatchee, known by Southeastern sportsmen for many years as a favored retreat for game and fishing.

Travel northeast through Mayo (Pioneer Day Festival), and Live Oak (Clabber Girl Cookoff), and visit the Stephen Foster Center at White Springs (Florida Folk Festival). Nearby is the Osceola National Forest, where you might spot some black bears.

Travel south through Lake City, home of Florida State Farmer's Market and on through High Springs (Pioneers Day Festival), an important railroad town around the turn of the century. It has a historic district offering a panorama of architectural styles. Then travel through the small communities of Trenton, (Down Home Days) and Chiefland (Watermelon Festival).

Next visit Cedar Key (Seafood Festival), a settlement with a history built around oysters, timber (the cedars were cut for pencils), turpentine, salt and sponges. Try some seafood at the local restaurants built over the water. If you are lucky, stone crab claws may be in season.

As you are heading into Northeast Florida, travel through the farming communities of Alachua and Columbia counties. South of Gainesville, home of the "Fighting Gators"(Hoggetowne Medieval Faire), is Paynes Prairie State Reserve, a wildlife sanctuary featuring American bison, alligators and a variety of birds. To the north you will find the communities of Starke and Lawtey, known for their delicious strawberries. A short distance from Gainesville to the southeast is the historic town of Micanopy (Fall Harvest Festival) which has become a mecca of antique shops. To the east is Cross Creek, the location of Marjorie Kinnan Rawlings State Historic Site. Her orange groves and house are maintained as they were when she lived there and are open to the public.

The area along the St. John's River near Welatka and Palatka (Blue Crab Festival), is well known for its bass fishing. Nearby are Spuds and Hastings (Cabbage and Potato Festival), which supplied the Flagler Hotel system with fresh vegetables. Crescent

City (Catfish Festival), to the south, was built during the citrus boom.

Now travel east through Bunnell (Cracker Day) on to Flagler Beach, which has six miles of unspoiled beaches and one of the longest piers in Florida. Fridays in Flagler Beach bring an old-fashioned theme to the center of town with its Farmer's Market selling farm fresh vegetables, fruit, baked goods, nuts, seafood and plants.

Alligator Farm, in St. Augustine, c 2002.

St. Augustine (Minorcan Fromajardis Serenade Festival), south of Jacksonville in St. John's County, brings history to life. Founded in 1565, it is the oldest European settlement in the United States. St. Augustine's Restored Spanish Quarter is a living museum. Plan to spend the night in one of the many bed and breakfasts located in the historic district, and enjoy some famous St. Augustine fried shrimp and Datil pepper sauce at O'Steen's or Barnacle Bill's.

St. John's County also takes in the oceanfront communities of Crescent Beach, Anastasia Island, St. Augustine Beach, Vilano Beach and Ponte Vedra Beach, nicknamed the "Pebble Beach of the East" because of the high concentration of championship golf courses located in the area. Be sure to try one of the unique restaurants along the Intracoastal Waterway in Vilano Beach and Palm Valley. Some feature local oysters, gator tail and and heart of palm.

Often referred to as Florida's First Coast, the northeast region provides a glimpse of the past—large expanses of wilderness, antebellum homes, and preserved hamlets of a Florida that once was. Jacksonville (Jazz Festival), is the hub of Florida's First Coast. This booming city of the 90's blends historic architecture and modern skyscrapers: it's a metropolis laced with 20 miles of beaches, and divided by the waters of the St. Johns River. Jacksonville sprawls over 840 square miles and stands as America's largest city in land area. While there try some of the older barbecue restaurants. Have some of Harvey's pork at the original Bono's on Beach Boulevard or try Lucille's rib sandwich plate at Cotton's on Main Street.

Some 12 miles east of downtown, the beaches of Jacksonville—spanning the communities of Jacksonville Beach, Atlantic Beach, and Neptune Beach—offer offshore fishing, excellent dining and nightlife.

Cotten's Bar-b-que, Main Street, Jacksonville, c 1995.

TOURING THE BACKROADS

To the south of Jacksonville are the old communities of Mandarin (winter home of Harriet Beecher Stowe), Orangedale, location of early citrus groves. Picolata, which featured a steamboat landing to St. Augustine and Green Cove Springs (Ham Jam), which was a tourist haven before the railroads continued south.

Mayport Lighthouse, c 1995.

North of Jacksonville is the sleepy fishing village of Mayport (Kingfish Tournament and Seafood Festival). Have some fresh seafood at one of the riverfront restaurants and take a leisurely trip across the St. John's River on the ferry to Fort George Island to visit the Kingsley Plantation where slaves grew indigo and Sea Island cotton.

Then travel along the coast to Amelia Island, where you might want to take a horseback ride at Seahorse Stables on one of the few unspoiled beaches left in Florida, and see it as the Spanish saw it in 1565. American Beach (Kuumba Festival), remains almost the same as it did in the 50's during segregation.

Like most of the historical areas in this region, Amelia Island, just north of Jacksonville, has a story to tell. It is called the "Isle of Eight Flags," a reference to its rich history of 400 years under eight flags. At its center is Fernandina (Shrimp festival), and its 50-block historic district.

Tour the shops on Centre Streetand have lunch at the Marina Restaurant which has been serving Southern style seafood, three meals a day, seven days a week for 24 years.

However, its beaches, 13 miles of sweeping Appalachian quartz shores and towering 40-foot sea oat-speckled dunes are undeniably the most mesmerizing attractions. Whispering salt marshes harbor more than 250 types of birds. Ancient live oaks with shaggy beards of Spanish moss guard sun-dappled canopied paths. Lush coastal hammocks thick with sabal palms and wind-gnarled trunks of oaks and cedar are enveloped in blankets of American yaupon, palmetto, and morning glories. This environment teems with diverse wildlife, from bobcats and red foxes to alligators and manatees. Amelia Island's Lighthouse stands out as the oldest structure on the island.

Barbara Zuber and John Baker enjoying the surf at Seahorse Stables, c 1970's.

This completes our tour of seasonal Florida. Unfortunately, millions of visitors zip through our beautiful state on their way to Disney World or South Florida, staying on the Interstate highways and missing out on all the picturesque towns, country roads, parks and local cuisine. Hopefully, our book will inspire a few to stop and smell the magnolias.

Old Timey Favorites

Cracker House

Stocks, 22
Gravies, 24
Cane Syrup, 25
Milk Cow, 26
Yard Eggs, 27
Grits, 28
Rice, 28
Garden Vegetables and Fruits, 29
A Mess of Greens, 29
Pot Likker Dumplings, 29
Old-Fashioned Collard Greens, 30
Rooster Spur Pepper Sauce, 30
Black-Eyed Peas with
  Hog Jowls, 30
Sand Pear Relish, 31
Tomato Relish, 31
Datil "Bottled Hell"
  Pepper Sauce, 31
A Pot of Lima Beans, 32
Dried Beans, 32
Fresh Field Peas and
  Butter Beans, 32
Roast-Neers, 33
Corn and Tomatoes, 33
Skillet Fried Corn, 33
Steamed Cabbage, 34
Rutabaga, 34

Fried Green Tomatoes, 34
Okra and Tomatoes, 34
Fried Okra, 34
Pickled Okra, 35
Lime Pickles, 35
Zucchini/ Squash Pickles, 35
Marinated Cucumbers, 35
Sweet Dill Pickles, 35
Homemade Mashed Potatoes, 36
Garlic Mashed Potatoes, 36
Old-Fashioned Potato Salad, 36
Fried Sweet Potatoes, 36
Baked Sweet Potatoes, 36
Hogs Head Cheese, 37
Chit'lins, 37
Back Bone and Rice, 37
Brains and Eggs, 38
Old-Fashioned Fresh Ham, 38
Link Sausage, 38
Boiled Peanuts, 39
Parched Peanuts, 39
Peanut Brittle, 39
Sugar Peanuts, 39
Breads, 40
Cracker Hoecake, 40
Lacey-Edged Corn Cake, 40
Daddy's Crusty Cornbread, 41

Cracklin' Cornbread, 41
Skillet Cornbread Cake, 41
Skillet Cornbread Dressing, 42
Southern Hushpuppies, 42
Sweet Potato Biscuits, 43
Lunchroom Yeast Rolls, 43
Perfect Pie Crust, 44
Cookie Crumb Crust, 44
Graham Nut Crust, 44
Meringue, 45
Half Moon Pies, 45
Old-Fashioned Cane
  Syrup Teacakes, 45
Old-Fashioned Rice Pudding, 46
Gingerbread with Cream
  Cheese Icing, 46
Gingerbread Persons, 46
Divinity, 46
Ambrosia, 46
Southern Iced Tea, 47
Black Tea, 47
Sassafras Tea, 47
Lemonade/Limeade, 47
Eggnog with Busthead Rum, 47
Grandmother's Liniment
  Recipe, 48

OLD TIMEY FAVORITES

It's been said that to be a good Southern cook you need only five things: a cast-iron skillet, bacon drippings, cornmeal, buttermilk and fresh-grown ingredients. But the truth is, it usually takes a knowledgeable and experienced cook to turn out a memorable meal.

Like so many who grew up in small Southern towns in North Florida, we took the delicious fresh food we ate for granted. Whether it was prepared at home, at Grandmother's house, at a church dinner or a family reunion, the food was always really good and there was plenty of it. Nothing was elaborate, just good, fresh ingredients prepared with simple seasoning and love.

After we left home, we quickly discovered that if we wanted some of that home cooking, we had to go back home because we had failed to pay much attention to food preparation while growing up. Fortunately, we still had family and friends who were happy to share the basics of Southern cooking. We discovered that some cooking techniques which appeared simple could sometimes be very difficult to master.

Now that we have children who have moved away, the cycle is repeating itself. We're including this chapter for our children and others who want to learn the basics of good Southern cooking so they can recreate the dishes enjoyed during childhood.

Our grandmothers cooked on wood burning stoves that are no longer practical. We're sure the aroma of the burning wood flavored the breads, biscuits, etc., much like it flavors the meat in a wood burning barbecue smoker. But who wants to chop and fetch the wood? Not to mention the heat in the kitchen and fire hazard. Our practical choices today are gas and electric stoves. We prefer a gas range because it gives more heat control, but many Southern cooks prefer electric.

Give some thought to size when choosing your oven. A large oven is helpful if you plan to bake often and in large quantities.

Early refrigeration was a wooden icebox serviced regularly by the ice man, who sometimes gave us children slices of ice to savor. Then one day our first "Frigidaire" arrived, complete with a little light inside and a freezer, where we could keep popsicles and nickel cups of ice cream we were sometimes given if we were good. Later on, we got an even larger freezer that could hold all the extra vegetables, fish and game to be eaten year round.

Log House Miller Homestead Holmes County built in 1848.

OLD TIMEY FAVORITES

Today's refrigerators, with the large freezing compartments, are adequate for our needs. We do have a small separate icemaker since we prefer hard, clear ice cubes for our iced tea and cold drinks.

Most of our favorite cooks prefer cast-iron skillets. Some have been handed down through several generations. These pans have been well seasoned and some are as smooth as a baby's bottom. Old brands such as Griswold, Wagner and Martin are considered the best and are pretty pricey, if you can find them.

The Martin Foundry is located in Florence, Alabama. They also made a cast-iron wood-burning stove. We have one at our pond house in Eucheeanna. It makes wonderful biscuits and breads.

Our pond house in Eucheeanna was originally the kitchen of the house built by Johnny McDonald my grandfathers brother around 1920.

We relocated it adjacent to our catfish pond and built a dock so the grandchildren can catch the catfish.

Log Barn Miller homestead Holmes County.

We just can't imagine trying to cook our favorite Southern dishes without our cast-iron skillets. These skillets absorb heat slowly, distributes it evenly and browns food well. We often take the skillet straight to the table and serve from it. Chicken Valdosta, Chicken Piccata, Spanish Chicken and Rice, Veal Camille, Corned Beef Hash, and Breakfast Frittata just to mention a few.

Thanksgiving turkeys at Eucheeanna, pond house and dock in background, c 2004.

If your skillets have a build-up of grease, soak in a mixture of Red Devil Lye (1 can) for every 5 gallons of water for 2-3 days. This will clean the iron without damage. Rinse in a solution of baking soda and water to remove all lye, dry completely, lightly grease inside and out with bacon drippings and set in a 300 degree oven for 1-2 hours. If proper care is taken the skillets will blacken and develop a silky smooth patina.

STOCKS

Stocks can turn an ordinary dish into a memorable meal. One of the most important techniques and secrets of the professional cook is the preparation and reduction of stocks. Stocks are essential to good cooking, inexpensive, and easy to make. Roasting beef and veal bones with vegetables until brown and caramelized will give your stock extra color and rich flavor. We prefer stocks that are not seasoned with herbs.

Freeze stocks in different sized containers, in ice trays, cups or quarts for more convenient use. Frozen stocks begin to lose their flavor after a few months, so be sure to date them.

Chicken Stock

Place 6-7 pounds chicken backs, necks, and wings, 2 medium onions, peeled and quartered, 2 large cloves garlic, 2 celery ribs, chopped, with leaves and 4 quarts of cold water in a 8-10 quart cooking pot. Bring to a boil, reduce heat and simmer, skimming any gray foam that rises to the top. Cook 4 hours, adding hot water to maintain 4 quarts of liquid. Simmer an additional 3-4 hours, or until liquid is reduced by half. Strain through cheesecloth, cool to room temperature and refrigerate overnight. Remove and discard the layer of fat that has accumulated on the surface. Freeze any stock not being used immediately. Reduce the stock by half for a richer flavor. If frozen, the stock should be used within a month. Makes 2 quarts.

Fish Stock

Snapper heads, grouper heads and backbones are our preference for making fish stock. We often double this recipe. Place 2 pounds of fish heads and backbones in 8-10 quart cooking pot with 1 medium onion, peeled and quartered, 1 large clove garlic, and 1 rib of celery, with leaves, chopped. Cover with cold water by 2 inches and bring to a boil, reduce heat to simmer and skim off any gray foam that comes to the top. Cook four-eight hours for a rich stock, replenishing water as needed to keep fish bones covered. Reduce stock by half. Strain through cheesecloth, cool to room temperature before putting into containers to store. Freeze until ready to use. Makes approximately 2 quarts.

Crab Stock

Fill a stock pot with 2 quarts of water. Add crab shells, legs, two onions, quartered and bring to a boil. Reduce heat to low and simmer until liquid is reduced to one quart. Strain and discard crab and onion. Use this stock the same day as made. Makes one quart.

Shrimp Stock

Place 2 pounds shrimp shells and heads in a large cooking pot, add 1 peeled and quartered medium onion, 1 large clove garlic, 1 chopped celery rib with leaves, and cover with cold water by 2 inches. Bring to a boil, reduce heat to simmer and skim off gray foam that comes to the top. Cook 1-2 hours, replenishing water as needed to keep shells covered. Reduce by half for a richer stock. Strain through cheesecloth and cool completely before storing in containers. Freeze until ready to use.

Ham Stock

Ham stock is an absolute must for flavoring many Southern vegetables. This amount of stock is enough for 1 pound of fresh peas, butter beans, green beans, dried peas or beans. Have your butcher cut the ham hocks or ham bone into fourths. Use the stock within a day or two after making; ham stock doesn't freeze well. Place 2 smoked ham hocks or left-over ham bone, cut in pieces, in a large pot and cover with cold water by 2 inches. Bring to a boil, reduce heat and let simmer uncovered. Cook 1 to 2 hours. Remove fatty skin. Cool and refrigerate if not using immediately.

Beef Stock

Spread 3 pounds beef bones and 2 pounds stew beef in a roasting pan. Cook in a 400 degree oven for a half hour, add 2 unpeeled onions, quartered, and 2 carrots, halved and roast, stirring once or twice, for a half hour or until thoroughly brown. Transfer it with a slotted spoon to a large stock pot. Pour off any fat from the pan, add 2 cups water, and deglaze the pan over high heat, scraping up any brown bits. Add the liquid to the pot with three and one half quarts cold water and bring to a boil, skimming the froth. Add 1 teaspoon salt, a half teaspoon thyme, 1 bay leaf, 2 ribs celery, 4 unpeeled garlic cloves, and 6 parsley sprigs and simmer the mixture for 4 hours. If a more concentrated stock is desired, continue to cook until desired concentration is reached. Strain the stock through a fine sieve into a bowl and let cool. Chill the stock and remove the fat.

Demi-glace

In a large saucepan cook 7 cups beef stock over moderate heat until it is reduced to about 4 cups. Let the demi-glace cool completely, pour into ice trays and freeze, when frozen remove cubes, wrap individually in plastic wrap and place in a large freezer container or place in very small freezer containers. Demi-glace keeps frozen, indefinitely. Makes 4 cups.

GRAVIES

Most people in the deep South love gravies. We have them at breakfast, dinner and supper. Our gravies begin with pan drippings left from frying meats and are thickened with flour, then stock, cream or water is added. Serve gravies over biscuits, meats, grits, rice, mashed potatoes, on vegetables or as a side dish.

Meat Gravy

Pour grease off after frying meat, reserve 2 tablespoons pan drippings, keeping the brown sediment. Return pan to medium-low heat, sprinkle 3 tablespoons all-purpose flour in pan and stir to keep lumps from forming. Stir and scrap until roux is a light caramel color. Slowly add one and one half-two cups of stock(cream, stock or water for fowl, water or stock for red meat), stir constantly and bring to a full boil. Reduce heat and cook until smooth, slightly thickened and raw taste of flour is gone. Season with salt and pepper to taste. Makes one and one half- two cups.

Milk Gravy or White Sauce

Melt 2 tablespoons unsalted butter in a heavy bottomed saucepan over medium-low heat. Add 3 tablespoons all-purpose flour stirring constantly for 2-3 minutes, making sure not to brown. Add 1 cup hot milk, whisking constantly to avoid any lumps. Add a half cup whipping cream, continuing to whisk until sauce becomes smooth and has thickened. Remove from heat, stir in white pepper and salt. Taste and correct seasoning. Makes one and one half cups.

ROUX

Roux is a thickening agent that adds wonderful flavor, color and consistency to sauces, gumbos, gravies and stocks. It is simply oil or butter mixed with flour and cooked at a low temperature for several hours, or at a high temperature for a matter of minutes.

Brown Roux

Place one cup vegetable oil in a cast-iron skillet over medium-high heat. Whisk in one and one fourth cups all-purpose flour slowly. Whisk rapidly and continually until smooth, being very careful not to let roux splash on you. If the roux burns it will give your dish a bitter taste. Use a wooden spoon and continue to stir until desired color is reached, a peanut butter color or nutty brown.

Remove roux from heat and stir until mixture cools. Excess oil will rise to the top after roux has cooled and can be removed by laying paper towels over the top.

CANE SYRUP

Seed sugar cane saved from last years crop would be planted in the spring and harvested in the fall. Syrup making was a fairly common custom a few years ago. After sugar cane was harvested, it was squeezed in a cane mill operated by a mule or later by a "Massey Ferguson" tractor. A fat-lightered fire was then started under the syrup kettle. The juice would be boiled in large, 80 gallon cast-iron kettle for hours until it was reduced to cane syrup. It takes over 10 gallons of cane juice to produce one gallon of syrup.

The skimmings were removed and fed to the hogs or allowed to ferment and used in home brew. The rendered cane stalks were fed to the live stock. The syrup was poured into metal syrup buckets which many times were later recycled for lunch pails. These pails, taken to school, sometimes contained leftover biscuits with a hole punched in them and filled with cane syrup.

The cane stalks were run through a cane grinder mill to render the juice.

The syrup was stored in the syrup house until needed. Many times the farmers would trade the syrup to their neighbors for products they had produced on their farms.

In the kitchen syrup was used as a sweetener in cooking pies, cakes and cookies. The syrup was poured into a syrup pitcher which was placed on the dining table at every meal.

At breakfast it was enjoyed over oatmeal, biscuits, pancakes, and hoecake. At dinner (noon meal) it sweetened leftover breakfast bread as well as hominy and grits.

At supper my grandaddy would mix cane syrup with granny's homemade butter and sop up the mixture with hot biscuits.

Syrup kettle used in the production of cane syrup.

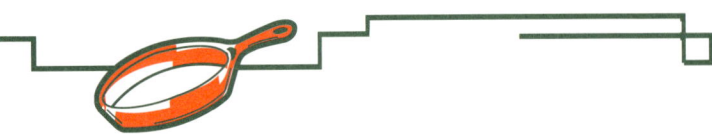

MILK COW

Her name was Peggy and she was black and white. Since we didn't have a pasture she had to be walked to a neighbor, Mrs. Biddle's pasture.

I was too young to walk her so the job went to my older brother and sisters. I remember the milk daddy brought into the kitchen in a pail. He was always encouraging us to drink it while it was warm but I just couldn't. Carolyn was the only one that loved that warm fresh milk from Peggy. I thought she could have all she wanted, too.

Homemade Butter

Place 2 gallons of whole milk in refrigerator until the cream separates from the milk (3-4 hours). Skim the cream from the milk and place cream in a churn. The butter should "make" within 15-40 minutes. Skim off the butter and place in cheese cloth to drain. Place in refrigerator wrapped in parchment paper or place in butter mold.

Great Grandma Baker's Buttermold, c 1940's.

Clabber

Place remaining liquid from making butter in a glass container and in a day or two it will form clabber.

Clotted Cream

Turn milk from the evening milking into a deep, narrow kettle holding about one gallon. Let stand in refrigerator over night, In the morning place in a warm place for eight hours. By evening the cream maybe lifted off in a solid layer. Place in a covered bowl in the refrigerator. It may be eaten the next morning for breakfast. Serve with fresh fruit.

Cream Cheese

Cream cheese is made from clabbered milk. The clabber is placed in a long bag of muslin, tied tightly and hung in a cool dry place to drip overnight with a bowl under it. When it is ready to use the cheese is taken out of the muslin and beaten until light. It is then placed in a perforated mold.

In a small bowl beat the softened cream cheese, confectioners' sugar and vanilla until fluffy. Gradually beat in enough cream to achieve a spreading consistency. Cover and chill for at least 2 hours.

OLD TIMEY FAVORITES

YARD EGGS

Years ago, just about everybody had their own chickens, White Leghorn, Rhode Island Red, "Dominickers" or perhaps even some feisty "bannys." These chickens roamed around the yard clucking, pecking and scratching up bugs and plants. They kept the family supplied with tasty yard eggs, sometimes giving a bumper crop which could be sold. Granny kept this "egg money" hidden away and used it for special purchases.

These eggs were rich in taste and color and had a distinct flavor. When a new batch of chickens was needed, sometimes a glass egg was placed into the nest to fool the old hen into setting. Hens were very protective of their eggs and were the source of the phrase "mad as a wet setting hen".

Country Fried Yard Eggs

Heat a cast-iron skillet over low heat for several minutes. Add enough bacon drippings to cover bottom. Break egg into bowl and gently slip into hot skillet. When white part of egg becomes set, lightly salt and pepper. Use a slotted spatula to gently flip the drippings over the egg. Cook until white is firm but yolk is still runny. Serve at once.

Creamy Scrambled Eggs

Heat cast-iron skillet over medium heat for several minutes, add one half tablespoon bacon drippings. When oil is hot enough to sizzle a drop of water, add 3 beaten and salted eggs to skillet. When eggs begin to set on bottom of skillet, stir with a wooden spoon until eggs form soft curds. Remove from heat and stir in 2 tablespoons of whipping cream. Serve on heated plates. For a change, stir in 1 chopped green onion with 2 tablespoons softened cream cheese and omit whipping cream or add a third cup sautéed onions, a third cup smoked mullet, flaked and a third cup Swiss cheese, grated. Serves 1-2

Perfect Poached Eggs

Eggs should be at room temperature for best results. Place 1-2 quarts of water in a large 12 inch shallow skillet. Add 3 tablespoons of white vinegar and bring water to a simmer. Break egg into small bowl and slip into water, continue until desired number of eggs are in water. Cook until whites are set and yolks are still runny, about 3-4 minutes. Remove with a slotted spoon and place on paper towels to drain.

Place cooked eggs in a bowl of cool water when preparing a large number and then reheat by placing in hot poaching water just before serving.

Easy Boiled Egg

Place four large eggs in medium sauce pan, cover with one inch of water, and bring to a boil, over high heat. Remove pan from heat, cover, and let stand ten minutes. Transfer eggs to ice water bath, let stand five minutes.

OLD TIMEY FAVORITES

GRITS

Old-Fashioned Speckled Heart Stone Ground Hominy Grits are essential, especially in the winter for a true Southern breakfast. Use coarse stone-ground grits if available. These grits may take a little longer to cook, but the flavor and texture are far superior to instant grits.

Bring 4 cups of water to a boil in a 2 quart saucepan. Add a half teaspoon salt, 1 tablespoon unsalted butter and slowly stir in 1 cup coarse stone-ground grits. Return to boil, cover, and reduce heat to low. Cook 45 minutes and stir often. If grits become too thick, add small amount of water and stir. If grits are runny, remove the lid last 15 minutes of cooking. Remove from heat, let sit covered for 5-10 minutes, stir and serve. Serves 4

Cheddar Cheese-Pepper Grits

Simply stir in one-one and a half cups grated extra-sharp cheddar cheese. Stir in one to two seeded and finely chopped peppers into cheese grits, mix thoroughly and serve.

Fried Grits

Pour cooked grits into a buttered 9"x12" pan. Spread and smooth the top. Cool and refrigerate overnight. Cut the grits into rounds using a biscuit cutter, about two and one half inches in diameter. Lightly dust both sides with cornmeal. Place a cast-iron skillet over medium heat, add 2 tablespoons of oil and fry the grits until golden. Drain on paper towels and keep warm. Add additional oil as you fry, if needed.

75 Year old Grist Mill, Escambia County, c 1945.

RICE

Rice has long been an important ingredient in Southern cooking. It was widely planted along the Southeastern Coast and used extensively with soups, gumbos, perlos, stews, seafood dishes, gravies and even desserts. It help to extend dishes when more food was needed for the table. The age and brand of rice dictates the amount of liquid it will absorb.

White Rice

Measure 3 cups of water into a saucepan and bring to a boil. Add 1 teaspoon of salt and 1 tablespoon butter, stir in 1 cup of long-grain rice. Bring to a boil. Cover with a tight fitting lid and reduce the heat to low. Cook 15 minutes, taste rice for tenderness, rice may need 2-3 minutes longer to cook. Pour rice into colander, run cool water over rice and drain. Return colander with rice to pan and cover with lid until ready to serve. Makes 3 cups of cooked rice.

GARDEN VEGETABLES AND FRUITS

The freshest fruits and vegetables are usually found in roadside vegetable stands, farmers' markets or, better yet, directly from the farmer who grows them. The U-Pick' em operations springing up around the South give the discriminating cook the opportunity of fresher produce without having to grow and maintain a garden. A list of North Florida U-Pick' em (U-Gather) and Community Farmers' Markets are listed in the back of this book. Take your family and friends along to the fields and markets so they too can take advantage of freshness and quality.

A Mess of Greens

Greens in the South specifically refers to turnips, mustard, collards or kale. The deeply flavored broth in which the greens are cooked is called "pot likker" and is savored by many Southerners. Corn bread can be dunked into the "pot likker" as is the custom. We sometimes add a teaspoon of sugar, especially if the greens have been picked more than a day before.

In a large pot, bring 4 cups of water to a boil. Add a half pound smoked or fresh pork neck or bacon, cut in several pieces. Cover and reduce heat to simmer for 45 minutes to an hour. Select 3 pounds fresh turnips or mustard greens with no yellow leaves. Remove tough stems and roots of turnips. Wash greens several times, draining each time until all sand is removed. Peel and cube roots, if desired, and set aside. Add 2-3 tablespoons bacon drippings to pot with greens, pressing and packing into pot since they wilt when heated. Lightly salt, reduce heat and simmer greens covered for 20-30 minutes. Stir occasionally. Add roots and additional water if needed and cover. Continue to cook for 15 minutes or until tender. Remove from heat, taste for seasoning and let sit in stock until ready to serve. To serve, remove greens from stock with a slotted spoon and place in a serving dish. Use a fork and a sharp knife to cut greens in several places. Serve with "potlikker" on the side. Serves 6

Pot Likker Dumplings

Combine 2 tablespoons of minced onion, two and a half cups cornmeal, and a half teaspoon salt, in a bowl. Add enough boiling pot likker from turnips to make a stiff dough. Cool slightly. Stir in 1 well beaten egg. Shape into small patties about a half inch thick. Lay patties gently on top of simmering turnips, cover and cook 10-15 minutes.

Old-Fashioned Collard Greens

Mother always told us that collards would be more tender after the first frost. When collards are tough, dip a large wet cooking fork into a box of soda, using only the soda that adheres to the fork and stir into collards. This will make them more tender. Select fresh tender collards with no yellow leaves. Serve with Rooster Spur Pepper Sauce.

Place a fourth pound lean smoked bacon, cut in 2 inch pieces into a large pot and fry until drippings appear. Cover with water by 3-4 inches and bring to a boil, cover and reduce heat to low and cook about 30 minutes. Wash 2-3 pounds of collards (one large bunch) several times to remove all sand. Remove and discard part of the tough stem. Stack leaves, roll and cut into 1 inch strips. Add collards, and additional water if needed. Bring to a boil, cover and reduce heat to a simmer; stir occasionally. Cook greens 30 minutes, add salt to taste, 1 teaspoon of sugar and additional water if needed. Continue cooking until greens are tender. Add 2 tablespoons of bacon drippings to a 4 inch deep cast-iron skillet over medium-low heat. Remove collards from pot, using a slotted spoon, and place in skillet with bacon drippings. Fry and toss collards until mixed with drippings. Cover and cook, about 5 minutes, and serve. Serves 6-8

Rooster Spur Pepper Sauce

This vinegar type pepper sauce can be found in just about every pantry in the South, especially in the fall when fresh turnip greens and collards are most available. It is great on perlos, too. Choose a clear glass jar to put the peppers in so the different colors of the peppers can show through. Jars with an enamel lid and rubber washer are best. Metal lids will rust. Your pepper sauce will be ready to serve in three weeks. These peppers do not stay crisp, but get nice and soft and keep almost forever.

Wash and drain 1 pint fresh Rooster Spur peppers(red, yellow and green) or Bird's Eye peppers. Dry with paper towels, remove stems and pack in a clean pint jar. Heat enough distilled white vinegar, to cover peppers, over medium heat until hot. Pour over peppers and seal. Store in dark area. Makes 1 pint

Black-Eyed Peas With Smoked Hog Jowls

Wash 12 ounces dried black-eyed peas, remove any small stones and soak overnight. The next day, place three fourths pound smoked hog jowls in cast-iron Dutch oven, cover with water and bring to a boil. Reduce heat to low and cook 1 hour or until jowl is tender. Remove jowl and set aside. Drain peas and add to stock. Add 1 tablespoon sugar, 1 whole medium onion and salt to taste. Bring to a boil, reduce heat, cover and simmer peas 30 minutes or until tender. To avoid excessive breaking of peas, do not stir during cooking. Cut jowl into small pieces and mix with peas. Correct seasoning and serve. Serves 6

Sand Pear Relish

Even if you have only one pear tree, it will usually produce more fruit than you can possibly use. We make this relish with sand pears, which give it a nice texture. Spoon a tablespoon of this relish beside a serving of fresh field peas to liven them up and create a beloved Southern dish.

Peel and core 1 peck of sand pears. Use a meat grinder to grind pears and 5 medium onions, peeled. In a large heavy bottomed pot, add pears, onions, 3 green bell peppers, seeded and finely chopped, 3 red bell peppers, seeded and finely chopped, 2 pounds of sugar, 5 cups apple cider vinegar, 1 tablespoon salt, 1 tablespoon pickling spice tied in a cheese cloth and 1 tablespoon tumeric. Bring to a slow boil, cook 30 minutes. Remove spice bag. Ladle into sterilized jars, wipe rims with a damp cloth, seal and screw bands on tightly. Makes 8-10 pints

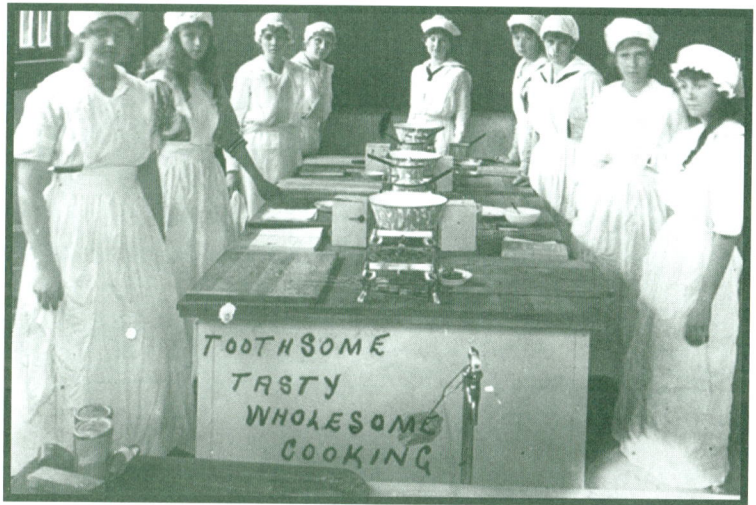

Cooking School, c 1920.

Tomato Relish

Peel 1 quart ripe tomatoes and chop them up. Place in a heavy-bottomed pot. Add 1 cup chopped onion, 1 cup chopped celery, a half cup chopped green bell pepper, three-fourths cup sugar, 4 teaspoons salt, 1 cup white vinegar, 2 tablespoons mustard seeds and stir thoroughly. Cook on low heat 40-50 minutes. Place in sterilized jars and seal.

Datil "Bottled Hell" Pepper Sauce

This is the Datil pepper sauce served in most seafood restaurants in St. Augustine. Simple, but effective and delicious.

Place 2 cups Datil peppers, stemmed and seeded, 2 small cloves garlic, peeled and one half cup apple cider vinegar in food processor or blender and purée. Put mixture into a large saucepan, add 64 ounces of ketchup and two and a half additional cups of apple cider vinegar. Bring to a boil, reduce heat and simmer 10 minutes. Cool mixture and pour into jars with non-metallic lids or Grolsch's beer bottles.

A Pot of Dried Lima Beans

For a "down-home" style of eating on a cold winter day, nothing is better than a pot of lima beans simmering slowly in rich ham stock. Smoked ham hock, cut in fourths, is our preferred seasoning for all dried beans and fresh peas. It is one of our very favorite meals when served with fresh green onions from the garden and the crunchy, crispy outer crust of Daddy's Crusty Pone Corn Bread.

Cover 12 ounces of washed dried lima beans with water and soak overnight. The next day, place 1 pound of smoked meaty ham hocks in a large pot and cover with water by 2 inches. Bring to a boil, cover, reduce heat and simmer for at least 1 hour. Add drained beans and cook 45 minutes to 1 hour or until beans are tender (adding more water to cover beans if necessary). Mash some of beans on side of pan to thicken stock. Season with salt, if needed, and serve. Serves 4-6

Dried Beans

Place 2 cups dried navy or pinto beans in 8 cups of water. Soak for 8 hours, rinse well and drain. Place 2 smoked ham hocks into a large saucepan with 1 quart of water or more, bring to a boil, cover and simmer for 1 hour. Add beans, 1 large onion, chopped and 2 cloves minced garlic. Add additional water to slightly cover beans, bring to a boil and cook for 1 hour uncovered over medium-low heat. Add more water if necessary. Bring to a boil, reduce heat to simmer and cook covered one-one and a half hours more or until tender. Taste beans and add salt if needed.

Fresh Field Peas And Butter Beans

It used to be an all-day affair to pick, shell and cook peas and butter beans. Today we have electric pea shellers, but some folks refuse to use them. Like most vegetables, peas and butter beans can be frozen, but unfortunately it alters the taste, so we eat them often when they are in season. Left over peas and butter beans should be refrigerated and reheated immediately after taking them out, to keep them from souring. Fresh okra pods or corn on the cob can be added during the last 10 minutes of cooking, if desired. Serve with Sand Pear Relish and Datil (Bottled Hell) Pepper Sauce.

Place 1 pound smoked meaty ham hocks, cut in quarters, in large pot with water to cover by 1-2 inches. Bring to a boil, cover and reduce heat to simmer for 1 hour. Wash 1 pint of field peas and 1 pint speckled butter beans, and add to ham stock. Return to boil, making sure water covers vegetables by one and one half inches. Cover and reduce heat to simmer. Cook for 45 minutes to 1 hour or until peas and butter beans are tender, adding more water if needed. Taste for salt and serve. Serves 6

Roast-Neers

Once a Northern guest was visiting a Southern boarding house and asked the proprietor why people from the South put their elbows on the table. The proprietor replied, " I guess it comes from eating all those roast-neers."

The minute corn is cut from the stalk, the sugar in it begins turning to starch. The sooner it's cooked after picking, the sweeter it will taste. When the first corn is available, we usually feast on a simple lunch of roast neers, or boiled corn on the cob. This is served with nothing but real butter, salt, freshly ground black pepper and a large pitcher of iced tea. Add sugar to the boiling water if your corn has not been picked that day.

Shuck 6 ears of corn and remove any silks. Bring 3-4 quarts of water to boil in a large pot. Add the corn and 1 tablespoon of sugar (if needed). Return water to boil and cook 3-5 minutes. Remove corn from water and drain. Serve corn immediately with lots of butter, salt and pepper to taste. Serves 2-6

Corn and Tomatoes

Cut the kernels from the cobs of 20 ears of corn, scrape a knife down the cob to milk it. Heat 2 sticks of butter in a large skillet over medium-high heat. Add 2 medium minced onions, 2 bell peppers, minced and 6 large tomatoes that have been peeled, seeded and chopped and cook until onions are translucent, about 15 minutes. Stir in the 2 teaspoons salt and 1 teaspoon freshly ground black pepper, then add the corn and milk and stir well. Reduce heat to medium and cook for 20 minutes. If the corn begins to dry out add cream and a little more butter. Serves 6-8

Skillet Fried Corn

Someone came out with a corn cutter a few years ago—a simple wooden plank with an adjustable blade. It greatly speeds up the process of cutting corn from the cob. Of course, several of my sisters refuse to use it and still insist on using a knife.

Shuck one and one half dozen ears of fresh corn and remove the silks. If using a corn cutter, place a 9x13 inch pan in your sink, to catch the cut corn. Run corn down the angled corn cutter, or use a sharp knife and cut the corn from the cob by slicing about half the kernels from the top to the base. Then scrape downward on the cob to get remaining corn and milk. Heat a large 12 inch cast-iron skillet and add a third cup bacon drippings. When hot, add the corn, stirring constantly for 2 minutes. Reduce heat to low, stir often for 5-7 minutes. Add salt to taste and 1 tablespoon sugar if needed. Corn should be thick and creamy. Taste and correct seasoning. Serve piping hot. Serves 4-6

Steamed Cabbage

In a large heavy bottomed pot cook 3 slices of thick sliced smoked bacon, cut into 1 inch pieces until most of the fat is rendered. Add a half cup of water, salt to taste and bring to a boil. Add one head of cabbage that has been cut into 2 inch chunks. Cover and reduce heat to low. Cook until desired doneness, about 15-20 minutes.

Rutabaga

In a large heavy bottomed pot cook 2 slices of lean bacon, cut into 1 inch pieces, until fat is cooked out but not brown. Add 2-3 cups of water to the pot and bring to a boil, reduce heat, cover and cook 15-20 minutes. Add 6 cups of peeled and cubed rutabaga, cover and bring to a boil, reduce heat and simmer for 25-30 minutes. Stir in 2-3 tablespoons of sugar, salt and pepper to taste, simmer 15 minutes longer. Test with the tip of a knife for tenderness. Reduce liquid if needed and serve.

Fried Green Tomatoes

Wash 2 pounds fresh green tomatoes and dry with paper towels. Cut into one-fourth inch slices. Mix a half cup self-rising cornmeal and a half cup self-rising flour with 2 teaspoons of salt in a large bowl. Add 1 egg and 1 cup of buttermilk, mixing thoroughly. Add tomatoes and toss to coat. Place in colander with bowl beneath to catch batter. Heat a large, deep, cast-iron skillet over medium-high heat and add peanut oil for deep frying. Drop tomatoes into hot oil, piece by piece, and fry until golden brown. Drain on a metal wire rack or brown paper bags and cook remainder of tomatoes. Serve immediately. Okra and squash may also be cooked this way. Serves 6

Okra and Tomatoes

The combination of okra and tomatoes is an old Southern favorite. This boarding house version is popular with customers who keep coming back, time and again, for that good Southern cooking.

Combine 2 pounds fresh okra, sliced in a half inch pieces, three 16 ounce cans of stewed tomatoes, 1 cup chopped onion, a fourth cup bacon drippings and salt and pepper to taste in a large pot. Simmer on top of the stove in a covered saucepan or skillet, or bake in a 350 degree oven in a tightly covered casserole for 30-45 minutes. Check okra for desired tenderness. Serves 8-10

Fried Okra

Wash 2 pounds of fresh okra and dry with paper towels, slice okra into half inch pieces. Place in a bowl and almost cover with buttermilk, let stand 15 minutes. Place 1 cup self-rising cornmeal into a large ziplock bag. Drain okra in a colander and place in the ziplock bag. Shake to coat okra with cornmeal. As you remove okra from the bag, shake off excess cornmeal. Heat 1 cup of peanut oil in a large cast-iron skillet. When oil is hot add okra, making sure not to crowd the pan. Remove okra to paper towels to drain and fry remaining okra.

OLD TIMEY FAVORITES

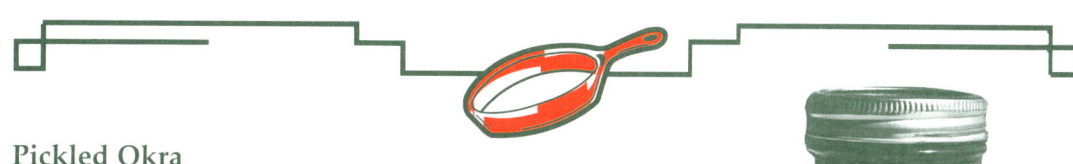

Pickled Okra

Wash 3 pounds small, tender okra pods leaving top cap to pod and remove excess stem. Pack in eight sterilized canning jars. Place 1 small clove of garlic, 1 hot red pepper, a half teaspoon dill seed, 1 teaspoon mustard seed, a half teaspoon celery seed to each jar. Bring 1 quart apple cider vinegar, 1 cup of water and 6 tablespoons of salt to a boil. Reduce heat and simmer 5 minutes. Pour over okra and seal jars immediately. Store for 6 weeks before serving. Makes 8 pints

Lime Pickles

Cut 7 pounds cucumbers into slices or a half inch chunks. Cover with 1 cup lime to 1 gallon water and let stand 24 hours. Rinse several times and let stand in cold water 3 hours. Let stand overnight in 2 quarts vinegar, four and a half pounds sugar, and 1 teaspoon whole cloves, 1 teaspoon pickling spice, 1 teaspoon tumeric and 1 teaspoon salt. Boil 35 minutes and can in sterilized jars. Makes 6-8 quarts

Zucchini Squash Pickles

Wash 2 pounds zucchini squash, slice thin. Peel and thinly slice 2 small onions cover with water, add a fourth cup salt and let stand 2 hours. Bring 2 cups white vinegar, 2 cups sugar, 1 teaspoon each of celery seeds, mustard seeds, and tumeric to a boil, stirring until clear. Drain zucchini and onions and place in jars. Pour vinegar mixture over zucchini to cover. Screw lids on and refrigerate. Makes 6 pints

Marinated Cucumbers

Years ago, before air conditioning, it was a custom to turn the clean plates upside down and cover the leftover food with a tablecloth to keep the house flies off. These cucumbers were one dish that was often found under the tablecloth for the next meal. The best part was that the cucumbers improved in flavor after several hours in the marinade. If cucumbers are watery, sprinkle with a little salt and let sit 15 minutes.

Place 2 cups peeled and sliced cucumbers in a shallow glass container with a tight fitting lid. Add a half cup chopped white onions and sprinkle with a third cup sugar. Pour a fourth cup white distilled vinegar over all and stir to distribute sugar. Cover and refrigerate at least 2-3 hours before serving. Cucumbers will keep 2-3 days refrigerated. Serves 4

Sweet Dill Pickles

Add 2 cups sugar and 1 cup of water to a small boiler, bring to a boil, stirring until syrup is clear. Cut 46 ounces dill pickles in four inch lengths. Place pickles in colander, rinse and drain well. Pack pickles in same jar and pour syrup over them. Add 1 teaspoon mustard seeds and 1 teaspoon celery seeds. Screw lid on tightly and refrigerate 24 hours before serving. Great with fried fish.

POTATOES

Homemade Mashed Potatoes

Homemade Mashed Potatoes are sometimes made with an electric mixer and served as a soupy mess. We think a few lumps give the potatoes a little character, so invest in a manual potato masher and forget the mixer on this one.

Peel 2 pounds of Irish (Idaho) potatoes, wash and cut into 1 inch chunks. Place in a large pot and boil in lightly salted water for 20 minutes, covered, or until potatoes are tender. Drain, reserve 2-4 tablespoons of liquid and return potatoes to pot. Add 3 tablespoons unsalted butter, a fourth to a half cup hot whipping cream, and salt to taste. Use a fork or potato masher to mash potatoes, add reserved liquid if needed, leaving the potatoes slightly lumpy. If not serving immediately, cover pot and set in a warm place until ready to serve.

Garlic Mashed Potatoes

Cover 1 head of garlic in aluminum foil and roast in a 400 degree oven for 1 hour. Remove from oven. When cool cut tip of garlic head with a sharp knife and squeeze garlic to remove pulp. Mix the garlic pulp with mashed potatoes and serve.

Old-Fashioned Potato Salad

Peel and cube 4-6 large potatoes and place in saucepan. Place 6 eggs on top of potatoes and cover with water. Bring to a boil, salt lightly, reduce heat to low and cook 10-12 minutes or until potatoes are tender. Remove eggs and place in cool water. Drain the potatoes and place in a large bowl. Peel eggs, chop and add to potatoes while potatoes are still warm. Add three fourths to one cup cubed sweet pickles (preferably homemade), 2-4 tablespoons St. Augustine Sweet onion, minced, a half cup celery and bell pepper, each chopped, 1-2 cups homemade mayonnaise, 1 teaspoon fresh lemon juice and mustard, salt and pepper to taste. Mix thoroughly, mashing most of the potatoes. Sprinkle with paprika and serve warm. Garnish with pimento and sliced hard boiled eggs. Serves 6-8

Fried Sweet Potatoes

Peel and slice sweet potatoes a half inch thick, place in a pan and pour salted water over them. Bring to a boil, reduce heat to low and cook 10 minutes. Drain and pat dry with paper towels. Heat a large cast-iron skillet, add 1 cup vegetable oil. When oil is hot, fry the potato slices until thoroughly cooked. Drain on paper towels and serve hot, topped with butter and lightly sprinkle with Lowery's Seasoned salt.

Baked Sweet Potatoes

Preheat oven 350 degrees. Wash potatoes and pat dry with paper towels. Place on foil covered pan and bake one and a half hours or until easily pierced with a sharp knife. The potato skin will collapse. Butter and serve hot.

HOG KILLINGS

Hog killings were special events in days gone by. The men would kill, scrape, clean, and cut up the hogs and the women would make preparations for sausage and rendering lard. Virtually every part of the hog was utilized, including the head, which would be boiled and made into souse.

Hog's Head Cheese (Souse)

Since hog heads are not readily available, we have adapted Daddy's recipe using Boston butts. The ears are optional. Add more pepper flakes if you like it Cajun style.

Place 2 pounds pork roast (Boston Butt) and 6 hogs ears in a large pot. Add enough water to cover meat by 1 inch. Bring to a boil, cover and reduce heat to simmer, replenishing water if needed. Cook 2 hours or until tender. Remove meat and ears and let cool to room temperature. Cut into small pieces and put through a sausage grinder. Place in a large bowl and season with 1 teaspoon salt, 1 teaspoon freshly ground black pepper and 1-2 teaspoons red pepper flakes. Taste to make sure seasoning is correct.

Form into a ball and place in center of cheese cloth. Gather ends of 2 feet of cheesecloth and twist. Hang the cheese so it can drip overnight. When the cheese has stopped dripping, wrap it in plastic, leaving the cheesecloth on. Refrigerate overnight or until completely chilled. Will keep refrigerated at least a week.

Chit'lin's (Small intestines of the hog)

We can't think of a Southern dish that divides food advocates more than chit'lin's. Granny and several uncles dearly loved them. The rest of us made no bones about it—-we hated them. When she cooked chit'lin's the whole house smelled like a pigpen. "Try it—-You'll like 'um" worked only once. After that we made sure we had other plans on chit'lin' day. We are including this recipe for historical reasons only.

Wash 2 pounds chitterlings thoroughly under cool running water. Place in Dutch oven and cover with water. Add 2 cups chopped onion, 1 tablespoon salt, and 1 teaspoon red pepper flakes. Bring to a boil, cover and reduce heat to low. Simmer until chitterlings are tender, about 2 hours or until most of the liquid has evaporated. Correct seasoning and serve. Serves 4-6

Back Bone N' Rice

This is an old dish our grandparents enjoyed after a hog killing. It's getting hard to find fresh backbones but this dish is worth the trouble.

In a heavy-bottomed pot place 4 pounds pork backbones and two and a half quarts of water, bring to a boil, cover and reduce heat to low. Simmer 45 minutes and stir in one and a half cups rice, 1 cup chopped onion, 1-2 minced Datil peppers, 1 large clove garlic, minced, freshly ground black pepper and 2 teaspoons salt. Return to boil, cover and reduce heat to low. Cook for 20 minutes. Garnish with a half cup chopped green onions. Serves 6

OLD TIMEY FAVORITES

Brains and Eggs

Wash 1 pound of fresh pork brains in cold water. Remove membranes, place in bowl and cover with water. Add 1 tablespoon lemon juice, cover and soak in the refrigerator for 2 hours. Drain and dry. Heat 1 tablespoon bacon drippings in a cast-iron skillet, add brains, salt and pepper and cook 20 minutes. Break brains in small pieces, the size of a pecan. Add more bacon drippings and 8 beaten eggs. Cook until soft scramble. Correct seasoning and serve.

Old-Fashioned Fresh Ham

Place 1 fresh ham in a large container of water. Add 4 tablespoons salt, 2 tablespoons black pepper and 6 dried red peppers. Bring to a boil, remove foam, reduce heat and cook 4-6 hours or until tender. Remove from pot and when cool enough to handle remove skin. Serve with a Mess O' Greens and hot cornbread.

Hog Killing, c 2000.

SMOKEHOUSE

In the old days most large farms had a smokehouse. The smokehouse typically was a small wooden frame building with a dirt floor. The coldest day of winter was when they had the hog killing. The hogs were cut up into hams, middling (bacon) and loins. The rest was ground-up and stuffed into the hog guts for sausage. The hams, middling and loins were tied with a strips of bear grass and hung from poles along with the sausage and smoked with hickory and oak sawdust until preserved. The smoked meat was taken out as needed, sliced and fried for breakfast or supper.

NOTE: After frying smoked meats place 4 or 5 slices of tomatoes in the pan. The tomato juice deglazes the pan and the glaze flavors the tomatoes.

Link Sausage

Prepare batch of sausage (see page 71). With a sausage stuffer stuff the meat into casings, about 4 feet long. Hang sausage in the smoke house along with hams and bacon.

Log Smoke House at Miller Homestead, Holmes County, built in 1849.

Shortcut: Stop by Thriftway Supermarket in DeFuniak Springs and pick-up a package of Register's or Kelly's smoked link sausage.

PEANUTS

During the Civil War peanuts were known as "goober peas". Before the war these tasty legumes were not known by the Yankee soldiers.

Green peanuts are freshly dug and are suitable for boiling. When dry, peanuts can be parched and used to make peanut butter, cakes, pies and cookies.

Boiled Peanuts

These boiled peanuts are a family favorite, especially if Daddy picked them from his garden and boiled them. He just loved to make boiled peanuts and gave them to anyone who dropped by. Select nicely filled-out peanuts. Wash 2 pounds green peanuts and put them in a large pot. Add enough water to cover by 2 inches. Add 1 tablespoon salt to each quart of water. Cover and cook over high heat until peanuts come to a rolling boil. Reduce heat to medium-low and continue to cook for two and a half -three hours, adding additional water if needed. After the initial cooking time, bite into a peanut every 15-20 minutes to check for doneness. The peanut should be soft. Allowing peanuts to stand in salted water after cooking will increase their saltiness. Drain and cool to room temperature. Refrigerate any leftover peanuts.

Parched Peanuts

Spread raw shelled peanuts in a single layer in shallow pan. Heat in slow oven (300 degrees) for 30-45 minutes. Peanuts are done when brown. Check periodically by removing skins from a few nuts.

Peanut Brittle

Cook 2 cups white sugar, a half cup water and one and a half cups light corn syrup until it boils good. Then add 3 cups of raw shelled peanuts. Cook until peanuts are brown. Remove from burner. Add 1 heaping teaspoon baking soda and a half teaspoon salt. Pour on buttered platter. Spread out thin. Then break up into pieces.

Sugar Peanuts

Preheat oven 300 degrees. Place 4 cups of shelled raw peanuts with red husk, 2 cups sugar and 1 cup water in a large cast-iron skillet. Bring to a boil over high heat. Stir with a wooden spoon to coat peanuts with syrup. Cook until all water boils out and syrup turns to a dark pink color. Pour peanuts and syrup into a buttered cookie sheet that has edges, spreading peanuts out evenly. Place in oven and bake for 15 minutes. Remove from oven, salt top of peanuts lightly, and return to oven. Bake another 15 minutes. Remove from oven and immediately place peanuts on wax paper. Store nuts in glass jars with tight fitting lids.

Harvesting peanuts on the Spears farm in Holmes County, c 1947.

BREADS

All the great cooks we knew prided themselves on their hot, straight from the oven, homemade breads. Flour made from wheat was used for making biscuits, yeast rolls and desserts. Bread was served at each meal and came to the table directly from the oven. The trick was to get it buttered without burning your fingertips. Cornmeal was used to make the daily cornbread which was eaten nearly every day in the South.

Corn was the grain most popular for the North Florida farmers. It was often eaten when fresh, or green as it was sometimes called, or used when dried. When harvested dry, the stalks and shucks were fed to the livestock along with some of the dried corn. The rest was stored in cribs for later use.

Dried corn was sometimes shelled and taken to the local grist mill to be milled into grits and cornmeal. Mill stones were powered by water from local creeks. The owner of the mill would keep a percentage of the corn for his fee. Corn was ground between the large mill stones, yielding hominy grits. The powder or meal was then scraped from around the stones.

Like most other things today, mass production of grits and cornmeal has lowered the price a little, but at the same time lowered the taste too. We find that the old-fashioned stone-ground grits and cornmeal are far superior to types mostly found today in supermarkets. A few of the old mills are still in existence. We have found that Fink's Mill located north of Ponce de Leon makes a reliable product and use it in all our recipes calling for plain cornmeal. Some mills still offer their products through the mail.

Cracker Hoe Cake

Spread 1 cup water-ground cornmeal in a shallow pan and heat it in the oven to make it crisp. Pour into a bowl and add three-fourths teaspoon salt and enough boiling water to make a batter that just holds the cornmeal together. Grease a cast-iron skillet or griddle with bacon drippings (you can grease the blade of a clean hoe, if you want to do it right), and heat. Spread the batter in one big cake or three or four small cakes about a half inch thick. Cook slowly, turning when bottom is well brown.

Lacey-Edged Corn Cake

Sift 2 cups cornmeal, 1 teaspoon baking soda and 1 teaspoon salt into a bowl. Add 1 egg and 3 cups buttermilk, stirring to blend. Batter should be thin. Heat a cast-iron griddle over medium-high heat. Add a teaspoon bacon drippings. Swirl the girdle to coat the bottom and drop the batter by spoonfuls. Edges of cakes should be lacy. Turn and continue to cook until brown and crisp.

Daddy's Crusty Pone Cornbread

If we had to choose a favorite bread for our family, it would have to be Daddy's Crusty Pone Cornbread. Daddy could transform the simple ingredients of stone-ground cornmeal, salt, water and oil into a mouth watering, crispy, crunchy bread. It becomes a delectable piece of heaven when cooked in a cast-iron skillet. Our family is adamantly divided between salty or unsalty cornbread therefore, two pones are an absolute must. The salty pone got Daddy's large thumb print.

Different cornmeal absorbs different amounts of water so adjust accordingly. The batter should be stiff enough to form a patty.

Preheat oven 450 degrees.

Combine 2 cups of medium cornmeal, one and one half-two teaspoons salt, and one and one half to one and three fourths cups water. Mix until batter is smooth and has the consistency of stiff cake batter. Heat a 12 inch cast-iron skillet over medium-low heat. Add one third cup vegetable oil to skillet. When oil is hot, scoop half the cornmeal into your hands, pat until smooth and form into an oval patty. Place in skillet and gently press to fill one-half of the skillet, form the remainder of batter and place in skillet. Use a tablespoon dipped in oil to smooth and form pone, making sure the pones do not touch in center. Place on lowest rack of oven and bake 20 minutes. Turn pones over and bake 20 minutes more or until golden brown. Best if eaten immediately. Serves 6

Cracklin' Pone Cornbread

To prepare cracklins, place a fourth pound of finely chopped salt pork or fatback in cast-iron skillet over moderate heat, stir frequently until bits are crisp and brown and have rendered all their fat. Remove with a slotted spoon and drain. Add cracklins to batter of Daddy's Crusty Pone Cornbread before baking.

Skillet Cornbread Cake

The skillet and oil should be hot enough to sizzle when corn bread batter is poured in. Remove bread from skillet as soon as it is baked to keep the crust crunchy.

Preheat oven 375 degrees.

Sift one and one half cups medium cornmeal, 1 cup all-purpose flour, 1 tablespoon sugar, 1 teaspoon salt, 1 teaspoon baking soda and 2 teaspoons baking powder into a large bowl. In a small bowl beat 2 eggs with 2 cups buttermilk and 3 tablespoons melted butter or oil. Combine liquids with dry ingredients and mix until smooth. Heat a cast-iron skillet on low heat for at least 5 minutes, add 2 tablespoons bacon drippings or oil. When oil is hot, add batter. Bake 30 minutes or until golden brown. Makes one 9 inch cake.

Skillet Cornbread Dressing

This is a Deep South tradition at our Thanksgiving feast. And oh, is it good! The corn bread used for the dressing should be baked the day before. Preheat oven 400 degrees.

Place one 9 inch crumbled cornbread cake and 2 cups crumbled stale white bread in a large mixing bowl. Add 2 eggs, 5 cups rich chicken stock and mix on low speed of mixer until thoroughly mixed. Sauté 1 cup chopped celery and onions in one half cup unsalted butter until softened. Add mixture to bread with 1 tablespoon sage, or to taste, 1 teaspoon salt, lots of black pepper and mix thoroughly. Batter should be a little thinner than cake batter. Taste for additional seasonings. Pour into buttered 9x13 inch baking dish. Bake 45 minutes-1 hour or until center is set and top is lightly browned. Serves 10-12

Southern Hush Puppies

Hush puppies are another bread favored in the South. You only have to use your imagination to figure out how the name of this Southern dish originated. We have heard several versions, from the Civil War, Tallahassee turpentine stills, St. Marks' fish fries, you name it. Everyone claims to have discovered this popular bread that obviously originated as dog food.

It seems there are as many variations of hush puppy recipes as there are claims of creating it. All of them start with cornmeal, but that is where the similarity ends. Some have as much flour as meal, and ingredients such as cream-style corn, frozen corn kernels, bell peppers, English peas and various other vegetables. Most are mild, but others call for enough hot pepper to cook the bread without the hot grease. The mixing liquid for the dry ingredients ranges from water, milk, buttermilk, to flat beer, grapefruit or tomato juice. We suspect these ingredients have been included out of necessity, since hush puppies are often cooked at fish and hunting camps where "what you have is what you get. "This is our favorite hush puppy recipe.

In a large bowl, mix 2 cups fine cornmeal, one and one half tablespoons all-purpose flour, 3 teaspoons baking powder, a half teaspoon baking soda, 2 teaspoons salt, 3 tablespoons sugar, a half medium bell pepper, minced, and 1 medium onion, also minced. Mix 2 eggs, 2 tablespoons vegetable oil, two-thirds cup beer with 1 cup buttermilk and stir into dry ingredients. Heat enough peanut oil to deep fry over medium-high heat (350 degrees). Drop by tablespoonfuls into the hot oil. Hush puppies will float to the top when done. Drain on a metal rack or brown paper bags and serve immediately. Serves 10-12.

Sweet Potato Biscuits

Preheat oven 400 degrees. Cut 4 tablespoons shortening into 1 cup all-purpose flour, add 3 teaspoons baking powder and two-thirds teaspoon salt which have been sifted together. Stir in 1 cup mashed baked sweet potatoes and add a half cup milk, maybe a little more to make a dough stiff enough to roll. Roll on floured board and cut with a biscuit cutter. Bake for 25 minutes.

Lunchroom Yeast Rolls

These rolls "hot from the oven" definitely say lovin', loving those yeasty rolls. Our sister, Ruby, is a trooper and sometimes will pass the second batch around the table as soon as the rolls are taken from the oven. The first batch is long gone by this time. These are a family MUST at our Thanksgiving and Christmas dinners, or any time of the year we can persuade Ruby they are absolutely necessary.

Dissolve 2 packages of active dry yeast in 1 cup lukewarm water. Place 1 cup Crisco, three-fourths cup sugar and 2 teaspoons salt in a large bowl. Pour 1 cup boiling water into bowl and stir until Crisco has melted. Add 2 slightly beaten eggs and yeast mixture and stir. Add 3 cups all-purpose flour and mix until smooth. Add remaining 3 cups all-purpose flour and mix until all flour is incorporated. Place dough in a lightly greased bowl and turn it to coat lightly with oil. Cover with a kitchen towel and let rise in a warm place for an hour and 15 minutes or until double in bulk. Punch dough down, cover with plastic wrap and refrigerate overnight. Preheat oven 400 degrees. Divide dough into thirds. Dust work area and rolling pin lightly with flour. Roll the dough one fourth-one half inch thick. Cut into 2 inch rounds with biscuit cutter. Dip half of one side of roll in 1 cup melted lightly salted butter. Fold dough in half and place on baking sheet with sides just touching. Let rolls rise in warm place for 30 minutes- 2 hours or until double in bulk. Bake for 15 minutes. Rolls are best if eaten straight from the oven and buttered. Makes about 48 rolls.

Apalachicola cook churning butter, c 1925.

DESSERTS

Perfect Pie Crust

The difference between a good pie and a great pie is the top and the bottom. Once you've mastered the meringue and crust, the rest is easy.

We find that a mixture of solid vegetable shortening and butter produces a tender, flaky crust, but you must work quickly. During very dry weather, dough often needs a little more water. Try to use the least amount of water necessary to hold the dough together. A glass pie pan gives you an evenly brown, flaky crust. Preheat oven 425 degrees.

Combine one and one-third cups all-purpose flour, 1 teaspoon sugar, and a half teaspoon salt in large mixing bowl. Blend in a fourth cup solid vegetable shortening and a fourth cup butter, with pastry blender until flour resembles a coarse meal. Sprinkle dough with 3-5 tablespoons ice water, a little at a time, and stir with a fork until dough can be formed into a ball—all water may not be needed. Gather the dough and turn out on lightly floured sheet of wax paper. Form into disc, about 4 inches across and one and one half inches thick, being careful not to handle dough more than necessary or the crust will be tough. Lightly flour wax paper and rolling pin. Working quickly, roll dough with light even strokes from the center of the dough to the edges. Lift dough and lightly dust paper and rolling pin with flour if needed. Rotate dough and roll until dough is uniformly an eighth inch thick and the circumference is larger than pie pan. Lift edge of wax paper, and roll the dough onto your rolling pin. Unroll the dough over your pie pan and press dough to fit pan. Trim off excess dough, leaving a fourth-a half inch overhang. Patch any thin areas by lightly moistening dough with water and press, patching with excess dough. Fold the overhanging dough under to form a rim and make decorative edging with fingers or fork. Prick sides and bottom of pie crust with fork at a half inch intervals if crust is to be prebaked. Chill pastry at least 30-45 minutes before baking to keep sides from collapsing. Bake in middle of oven 12-15 minutes or until lightly browned and crisp. Cool crust before filling. Makes one 9 or 10 inch pie crust.

Cookie Crumb Crust

Place 11 graham crackers or 22 Oreos, or 22 Vanilla Wafers, or 22 ginger snaps in a plastic bag and beat with a rolling pin until cookies become fine crumbs. Add 4 tablespoons sugar, 4 tablespoons melted unsalted butter and a half teaspoon vanilla. Press into a 9 inch pie pan. Bake 8 minutes in a 350 degree oven.

Graham/Nut Crust

Mix 1 cup graham cracker crumbs, a half cup chopped Pecans or almonds with 2 teaspoons sugar, and 4 tablespoons unsalted butter. Press into the bottom of pie pan and bake at 370 degrees for 10 minutes. Fill with your favorite pudding.

OLD TIMEY FAVORITES

Meringue

To produce a really fluffy meringue it is essential to have egg whites at room temperature (75 degrees), absolutely no egg yolk in the whites and clean utensils that are grease free. Cream of tartar reduces the risk of over beating or watery meringue. Preheat oven 350 degrees.

In a large bowl, beat 3 egg whites with an electric mixer, about 1 minute. Add a pinch of cream of tartar and beat on high speed until soft peaks form. Add a third cup sugar just before whites are fully whipped, a tablespoon at a time, and beat until it holds stiff glossy peaks and sugar has dissolved. Add a half teaspoon vanilla, if desired. Spread meringue over hot pie filling, making sure meringue touches crust to prevent meringue from shrinking back while baking. Bake in center of oven 10-12 minutes or until meringue is golden brown.

Half Moon Pies

Do not confuse half moon pies with whole moon pies, which are traditionally consumed with R.C. Colas. Half moon pies were made in the winter with dried fruit. Dried peaches, apples, pears or apricots were reconstituted, seasoned and put into pastry, shaped into half moons, then fried or baked golden brown. When baking the pies, brush each with an egg wash and cut two steam vents in the top of each pie.

Place one and a half cups dried fruit with a half-three fourths cup of sugar, 1 teaspoon lemon juice a fourth teaspoon cinnamon, a half teaspoon nutmeg, and cover with 4 cups water, bring to a boil, reduce heat and stir until fruit is mashed and all liquid in pan is absorbed. Set aside to cool. Roll the pie crust dough until it is an eighth inch thick. Use a 5 inch saucer as a guide and cut as many circles as you can. Place two-two an a half tablespoons fruit filling in center of each circle. Lightly wet outside a fourth of dough, fold over and seal with the tines of a fork. Dip tines in flour to prevent it from tearing the dough. In a large cast-iron skillet, heat an inch of oil to 375 degrees. Fry pies until golden brown, turning once and drain on a metal wire racks, or bake in 425 degree oven for 15-20 minutes. Serve while hot.

Old-Fashioned Cane Syrup Tea Cakes

Grandmother made these tea cakes and always kept them in the pie safe. Sometimes she would let us get by with having them for breakfast because we needed something sweet to dunk in our forbidden coffee.

Cream 1 cup of the sugar with three-fourths cup unsalted butter (room temperature). When fluffy, add 1 egg and 2 tablespoons cane syrup or molasses. Stir in 1 teaspoon cinnamon and ginger, one and one half teaspoons soda, a half teaspoon cloves and salt. Add 2 cups all-purpose flour and mix thoroughly. Chill until firm. Form into small balls, about the size of a nickel. Roll balls in sugar. Place on cookie sheet and press with bottom of glass to flatten. Bake at 350 degrees for 6-7 minutes

Grandma Baker's syrup pitcher, c 1930's

Old-Fashioned Rice Pudding

In a medium saucepan bring two and a fourth cups of whole milk almost to a boil. Add a half cup long grain rice and a fourth teaspoon salt. Cover and simmer 20 minutes or until most of the milk is absorbed, stirring occasionally. In a medium bowl beat 3 egg yolks until thick, about 2 minutes, beat in a fourth cup sugar and a fourth teaspoon ground cinnamon. Stir in three-fourths cup heavy cream, a half cup raisins and a half teaspoon orange zest and a half teaspoon lemon zest. Gradually stir in cooked rice mixture. Transfer to a one and one half quart casserole. Bake in a 350 degree oven for 10 minutes. Carefully stir mixture and sprinkle with additional cinnamon. Bake 15 minutes more or until center seems set when shaken. Cool 45 minutes before serving. Serves 6-8.

Gingerbread with Lemon-Cream Cheese Icing

Cream a half cup of butter and 1 cup of sugar thoroughly; add 2 beaten eggs. Dissolve 2 teaspoons of baking soda in 1 cup of buttermilk and add to mixture. Stir in 1 cup of molasses. Sift 3 cups of all-purpose flour, 1 teaspoon salt, one and a half teaspoons ground ginger, 2 teaspoons ground cinnamon, a fourth teaspoon ground nutmeg and 1 teaspoon ground cloves together and add to molasses mixture. Pour into a 13x9 inch baking pans Bake 350 degrees for 20-25 minutes. Spread with Lemon-Cream Cheese Frosting: 4 ounces of cream cheese softened, a fourth cup butter, softened, 2 cups powdered sugar, 1 teaspoon lemon zest and a half teaspoon lemon juice. Combine all ingredients, mixing until smooth.

Gingerbread Persons

Sift together three and three-fourths cups all-purpose flour, 1 teaspoon baking soda, a half teaspoon salt, 1 teaspoon cinnamon, 2 teaspoons ground ginger, and a half teaspoon ground nutmeg. In another bowl, beat 1 cup softened unsalted butter until creamy, add three-fourths cup sugar, and a fourth cup packed brown sugar, beat for 5 minutes. Beat in 1 egg, and a half cup unsulfured molasses. Add flour mixture and stir until thoroughly mixed. Refrigerate until chilled. Preheat oven to 350 degrees. Roll out portions on lightly floured surface, a fourth inch thick, and cut in desired shapes. Brush flour from cookies and bake for 8-10 minutes.

Divinity

Boil a half cup water, 2 cups sugar and a half cup white corn syrup until it turns brittle when a little is dropped from your stirring spoon into a cup of cold water. Pour syrup slowly over two egg whites that are beaten stiff, beat as you pour. Add 1 cup chopped pecans and 1 teaspoon vanilla. When pretty and fluffy looking and starting to set up, spoon it out into balls onto a buttered platter.

Ambrosia

Peel and cube 6-8 Florida navel oranges in a bowl. Taste oranges for sweetness and sprinkle with sugar if needed. Add 1 cup of freshly grated coconut. Cover with plastic wrap and set aside for one hour before serving. Maraschino cherries and 1 cup coarsely chopped pecans may also be added. Serves 6

BEVERAGES

Southern Iced Tea

Most of the tea drinkers in the world prefer their tea hot, therefore most of the blends are created for hot tea. Folks in the South like their tea ice cold, drink it at every meal and in between, too. Our climate calls for lots of cool drinks and iced tea is the drink of choice.

Add 1 commercial tea bag to 6 cups boiling water, remove from heat and allow tea to steep as long as possible. The longer it steeps, the more flavorful it becomes. Add one and one third cups sugar to a gallon container along with the tea and enough water to make almost a gallon.

Pour tea into a tall glass filled with ice, garnish with lemon or lime slices and a sprig of mint if you feel real special. Mint is one of the easiest herbs to grow. Plant a clump of mint under an outdoor water faucet and it will supply you with all the mint you need for Southern iced tea.

Black Tea

Place Youpon (Ilex Vomitoria) leaves on a cookie sheet and bake in a slow oven (250 degrees) until light brown, about 2 hours. Bring 1 gallon water to boil, add a fourth cup baked youpon leaves and remove from heat, let steep 5 minutes. Strain through sieve and serve hot or cold. Add 2 tablespoons of honey for sweet tea.

Sassafras Tea

Bring one and a half quarts of water to a boil. Add a half cup dried, chopped sassafras roots. Simmer for 30 minutes and strain. Add honey for sweet tea.

Lemonade/Limeade

Mix 2 cups lemon juice or lime juice, 3 cups water, and 2 cups simple syrup (see page 373). Stir well and serve over ice with a fresh sprig of mint. Add cherry juice for pink lemonade.

Eggnog with Busthead Rum

The counties along the Choctawhatchee River had to be the wettest dry counties in Florida. Many gallons of "shine" were produced in those swamps along the river and turned up in "Jook Joints" all over the state.

Granny was friends with the local sheriff and each year a mason jar of "White Lightnin" appeared on her porch a couple of days before Christmas for her traditional eggnog. Once I asked her why she put that stuff in the eggnog and she replied, "Honey that's what cooks the eggs."

In a deep bowl beat 12 egg yolks and 1 cup sugar until mixture is thick and smooth. Use a wooden spoon to stir in 4 cups or more of bourbon, one and a half cups rum and 2 cups half and half. Beat 1 quart of whipping cream until soft peaks form and fold into egg mixture. In a separate bowl beat egg whites until stiff and fold gently into the egg mixture until no white remains. Sprinkle with freshly grated nutmeg and serve in chilled cups. Serves 12

MEDICINE

Grandmother Ingram's Liniment Recipe

Grandmother Ingram was a women to be reckoned with—intense, wise, and strongly opinionated about the rights and wrongs of the world. She wore her white hair coiled into a braided bun, and when she let it down, it fell all the way down her back. Sometimes she let me brush it and I felt very special.

Growing up, we often went to spend the night with her. Her house was spotless, and when you went to visit, you helped it stay that way. She went to bed before dark and was up again before daylight. When you visited, you followed the same regimen. Sitting around wasn't allowed, and neither was whining or complaining. Spending the night sometimes meant shelling peas on the front porch, airing out and sunning her quilts and feather tickings, working in the garden and watching Lizzie (Grandmother Ingram) wring the neck of a chicken, then hack it off with a hatchet.

Three huge magnolia trees towered over her house providing cool shade, a thick sensuous fragrance when the magnolias were in bloom, and a perpetual supply of leaves for us grandchildren to rake. Staying with Grandmother Ingram meant a little dose of (hardworking) independence, and some special time for one of a family of eight children.

The most comforting time to be at Grandmother's was when you needed doctoring. She made homemade liniment and stored it in a dark place on the back porch. It had a strong medicinal aroma, and when she rubbed it on your chest, it opened the world. You had to be sure to get your pajamas in the wash the next day. Our treat for enduring the old-timey medication came at breakfast the next morning when we were served bread pudding with delicious, forbidden black coffee.

Liniment

1 dozen eggs
6 ounces ammonia
1 pint turpentine
2 ounces sassafras
2 ounces peppermint
6 blocks camphor gum

We found her recipe for ingredients, but unfortunately, she didn't write down the instructions. In the old days, camphor gum could be found at almost any drug store in the glass jar next to the asafetida.

Sarah Elizabeth Davis Ingram, c 1960.

Biscuits Breakfast and Brunch

Brunch in the garden, c 1925.

Mother's Skillet
   Buttermilk Biscuits, 52
Daddy's Hoecake, 53
Rise and Shine Biscuits, 54
Fromajardis, 55
Tupelo Honey
   Bran Muffins, 56
Wild Blueberry Muffins, 57
Orange Fig Muffins, 58
Hypocrite Rolls, 59
Tupelo Honey Butter, 59
Cinnamon Rolls, 60
Sunflower Bread, 61
Simmon Bread, 62
Banana Bread, 63
Libby's Heavenly Hots, 63
Gabby's Flapjacks, 64
Whole-grain Griddle Cakes, 64
Orange Blossom Special, 65
Tomorrow's Waffles, 65

Nassau Grits, 66
Country Ham and
   Red-eye Gravy, 67
Smoked Ham Biscuits
   with Jezebel Sauce, 67
Country Fried Steak n'
   Tomato Gravy, 68
Corned Beef Hash, 69
Breakfast Casserole, 69
Smothered Fried Rabbit, 70
Hog n' Hominy, 71
Pork Sausage, 71
Sawmill Gravy, 72
Mullet Roe, 73
Shrimp Paste, 73
Bodacious Brunch Dishes, 74
   Eggs Chautauqua, 74
   Eggs Nassau, 74
   Eggs Lafitte, 75
   Crab Lafitte, 75

Hollandaise Sauce, 75
Bearnaise Sauce, 75
Creole Sauce, 75
Breakfast Frittata, 76
Toad-in-the-Hole, 76
Ode to the Omelet, 77
   Seafood Filling, 77
   Asparagus Filling, 77
   Creole Filling, 77
   Pesto Filling, 77
   Florentine Filling, 77
Daddy's Fig Preserves, 78
Freezer Jam, 79
Chickasaw Plum Jam, 79
Mayhaw Jelly, 80
Sand Pear Preserves, 81
Scuppernong Jam, 81
Corncob Jelly, 82

BISCUITS, BREAKFAST AND BRUNCH

One of my fondest childhood memories is climbing out of bed in the morning to the smell of breakfast cooking. We didn't have to be called twice. Mother was a prize-winning biscuit maker, and we found it fascinating to watch her prepare those melt-in-your-mouth buttermilk biscuits from scratch. She never used a recipe. Flour was bought in 24 pound sacks and she kept hers in a special cabinet stored in a tin canister with sifter and biscuit bowl. To make biscuits, Mother sifted the perfect amount of flour needed into an enamel bowl used only for that purpose, made a well in the center of the flour, added the bacon drippings and buttermilk and the show began. Using the tips of her fingers, she would begin mixing, going around the wall of flour until she had the amount of dough she wanted. A heated cast-iron skillet with bacon drippings was waiting on the stove. She pinched off a section of dough about the size of an egg, hand shaped it (being careful not to handle it too much) and gently placed it in the skillet. When the skillet was full, she'd pat each one with some extra bacon drippings before putting them in the oven to bake.

Mother always had wonderful homemade preserves and jellies on hand. Sometimes we even churned our own fresh butter. Tupelo honey came from Daddy's bee hives kept in the river swamp, and a family friend supplied country cane syrup. We often heard the story of "in the old days," children punched a hole with their thumbs in any left over biscuits, filled the hole with cane syrup and stuck them in their pockets to be enjoyed at school for lunch.

Our hoecake was another treat, usually made with cornmeal in most homes, but made with flour for my family's breakfast. Daddy cooked it on top of the stove. He said his mother made them because it wasn't as time consuming as biscuits. Hoecake is more like a huge biscuit that has two crisp, nutty brown sides.

In the days when people did a lot of physical work, breakfast was the most important and largest meal of the day. It could consist of soups, several types of meats, grits, eggs, vegetables, biscuits, syrups and preserves. Today's style of living has changed breakfast to a more modest meal. Still, certain Southern favorites are enjoyed almost every morning at our table.

Grits, of course, were another favorite. Not just any grits but the ones that were coarse ground and cooked until they were thick and held a form. Grits are easy to prepare. I've never understood why people would want to buy instant grits when they could have delicious, textured grits. Grits alone have a very mild taste and are usually served with gravies or mixed with cheese or peppers. They are cheap and plentiful. In some North Florida homes, grits are still served with fried fish and squirrels.

BISCUITS, BREAKFAST AND BRUNCH

For many years now we've had a very special Christmas breakfast at Mother and Daddy's. As you walk up the porch and open the squeaky screen door, the aroma of country smoked bacon, sausage and "really good" coffee welcomes you. Christmas breakfast means seeing everyone in the family gathered in Mother and Daddy's kitchen for the first time since the Christmas season began (of course, we've all just seen each other 4 weeks earlier at Thanksgiving). Those greetings usually go on until someone notices the first pot of coffee has given out. It's early morning and there is always laughter and the excitement of Christmas in the air. Mother and Daddy had been up for hours, preparing, knowing how to tempt us with what we all love for breakfast. Mother, finishing her last batch of perfect buttermilk biscuits and Daddy, flipping his last mouth-watering hoecake, are never too busy to stop for a quick hug. A large pot of flavorful, coarse, thick grits simmer away on the back burner and fresh yard eggs from Daddy's chickens sit nearby on the counter waiting to be cooked.

As soon as the biscuits and hoecake are taken from the oven they are passed around to be buttered from the crock of homemade butter. The sweets are already on the table--a pitcher of cane syrup, from our neighbor, Tupelo honey from Daddy's bee hives, black berry jelly from the summer crop, Ruby's plum jam, and Daddy's fig preserves.

Plates are always piled high because you have to have a little of everything, and we know from experience that there might not be any seconds. It's generally considered bad manners to take the last biscuit, but that doesn't apply in our large family.

As contentment and warmth spreads through the rooms, our first thoughts are: "I'm not ready to move and I wonder who made this mess!" With breakfast dishes washed, and the house straightened, each family returns to their homes to put away wrapping paper, bows and Christmas goodies. Christmas Dinner is only a few hours away. Somehow the time zips by, and we are amazingly ready to feast again.

Nieces, nephews and grandchildren patiently waiting for Christmas breakfast at the Big House . Top to bottom: Elizabeth, Karley, Garrett, Ruby, Alex, Amelia, Dalton, Madison, Emily, Sara Liz, Kelton, Aubrey, Ashleigh, Jake, and John, c 2004.

MOTHER'S SKILLET BUTTERMILK BISCUITS

Feeding a family of ten was almost a full time job. Mother was up early preparing breakfast which always included her buttermilk biscuits. Hot buttermilk biscuits were served with every meal. The biscuits would be baked in a cast-iron skillet and turned upside down on a plate to reveal their crisp golden crust.

Mother somehow managed to cook three large meals a day, seven days a week, do the laundry and keep the house clean for a family of 10. I think it's because she knew how to organize us. I can remember her finishing breakfast just to jump right in and start on the noon meal. I don't remember her sitting down to eat with us though. I asked her about this once and she said it was because she wasn't hungry. She definitely had that knack of getting you to do the jobs thoroughly the first time. You didn't even realize you had a chore. Complaining didn't even enter the picture. She did it through praise, and I don't mean the gushy kind. There was no hesitancy or pause in her decisions and directions. As busy as Mother was she always found time to bake these delicious biscuits for us.

Leola Ingram McDonald, c 1942.

Serves 6-8

2½ cups self-rising flour
6 tablespoons bacon drippings
1¼-1⅓ cups buttermilk

Preheat oven 450 degrees.

Place a 10 inch cast-iron skillet over low heat while you prepare the biscuits. Place a half cup of flour on sheet of wax paper. In a medium bowl, place 2 cups of the flour, making a well in the center. Add 4 tablespoons of the bacon drippings and all the buttermilk. Mix lightly until thoroughly combined. Drop a heaping tablespoon (size of an egg) of dough onto the flour and roll around to lightly coat all sides. Place 2 tablespoon bacon drippings in heated skillet, place biscuits side by side, with edges touching. Pat a little bacon drippings on the top of biscuits, and bake in middle of oven until golden brown, about 15-20 minutes. Serve hot from the oven with butter, homemade jam and jelly.

Mother's biscuit bowl and Grandmother's pie safe. These are a few of my favorite things, c 2004.

DADDY'S HOECAKE

This isn't the typical hoecake that's made with cornmeal. It's more like a huge biscuit that's cooked on top of the stove until both sides are a crispy, nutty brown.

Hoecake made this way takes a bit of trial and error to perfect. For years I watched Daddy mix the dough, gather it in his hands and then place it in a hot cast-iron griddle, cooking it to perfection. Now that I've tried it many times, I realize you must have the right consistency, the right skillet (griddle), very large hands and lots of patience to prepare it his way. I continue to wrestle with the dough each time I make it, but once in a while it turns out perfect and that makes me feel almost as tall as Daddy.

Serves 6

1¾ cups self-rising flour
1-1 ¼ cups buttermilk

6 tablespoons vegetable oil plus 4-6 tablespoons more

Heat a #8 cast-iron, round griddle with a half inch lip over low heat. Place one and a half cups flour in bowl, make a well in center, add the buttermilk, oil and combine to form dough. Raise heat to a medium-low heat, add 2 tablespoons of oil. Use remaining flour to dust dough, and hands and gather dough into a ball. Place dough in center of skillet and gently press to within 1 inch of edge of skillet. Reduce heat to low and cook until light brown crust forms. Gently lift edge of dough with spatula in 3-4 places and add a 1 teaspoon of oil and cook until darker crust forms, rotating skillet to brown evenly, about 10-12 minutes. Slide hoecake onto plate, invert plate and slide uncooked side of hoecake into skillet. Add 2 teaspoons of oil, lift hoecake with spatula to let oil flow underneath and continue cooking 10-15 minutes, lifting edges of hoecake and adding 1 teaspoon of oil as needed. Cook until hoecake is a nutty brown. Serve at once with lots of butter, Tupelo honey, cane syrup, figs or your favorite preserves.

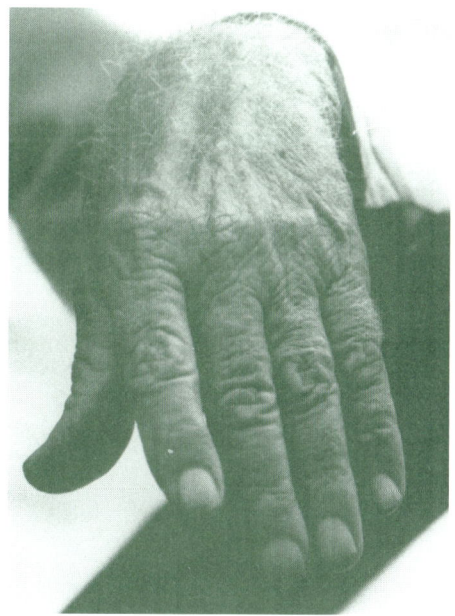

Daddy's hand, c 1982.

RISE AND SHINE BISCUITS

"Chicken in the bread pan, scratchin' out dough, Granny will your dog bite? No child no."

Granny often woke us in the mornings saying, "Rise and shine, and meet the sun halfway." Rise and Shine Biscuits are ready to bake almost immediately with little fuss. Let them rise in a warm place until doubled in size. These biscuits don't have to be baked all at once. The dough will keep in the refrigerator for 2-3 days.

Makes 14-16 large biscuits

2 packages active dry yeast
½ cup warm water
5-6 cups self-rising flour
¼ cup sugar
1 teaspoon soda
½ cup shortening (Crisco)
½ cup butter, softened
2 cups buttermilk

Preheat oven 350 degrees.

Sprinkle yeast over warm water and let stand until dissolved. Mix flour, sugar and soda in a large bowl. Cut in shortening and butter with a pastry blender. Add buttermilk and dissolved yeast and mix well. Place desired amount of dough to be baked on a lightly floured surface. Cover remainder with plastic wrap and refrigerate until needed. Pinch off a piece of dough about the size of a lemon and roll into a ball. Place in lightly greased cast-iron skillet. Brush tops lightly with melted butter. Bake 10-15 minutes and serve straight from the oven.

Dough bowl, carved from Black Gum tree by our great grandfather, Thomas Jefferson Garrett, c 1910.

FROMAJARDIS

These are a St. Augustine Minorcan favorite, traditionally served on the night before Easter. Years ago, young men went about town serenading at homes, singing Fromajardis Minorcan folk songs and were rewarded with these cheese pastries or turnovers.

These tasty, cheesy delights make a great breakfast dish and are still served at the St. George Pharmacy and Luncheonette on St. George Street in St. Augustine's Historical District.

Juan Ponce de Leon

Makes 12 turnovers

2½ cups all-purpose flour
Pinch of nutmeg
½ teaspoon salt
½ cup cold unsalted butter cut into bites
¼ cup Crisco
½ cup ice water

1 pound extra-sharp Cheddar cheese, grated
6 eggs, beaten
⅛ teaspoon salt
½ teaspoon cayenne pepper
¼ cup evaporated milk

Preheat oven 350 degrees.

Mix flour, nutmeg and a half teaspoon salt in large bowl. Blend butter and Crisco into flour mixture until mixture resembles meal. Add ice water and form dough into ball, roll dough into a 10x5 inch rectangle on a floured surface. Fold the top third of the rectangle over the center and the bottom third over the top. Turn the folded dough so that the open end faces you. Roll the dough into a rectangle about 10 inches long. Fold into thirds, roll and make three more turns, always starting with the open end facing you. Fold into thirds and chill dough for 1 hour. Place cheese and eggs in a large bowl with an eighth teaspoon salt and cayenne pepper and mix thoroughly. Roll dough into a 10x30 inch rectangle on a floured surface. Cut dough into twelve 5 inch rounds, about the size of a small saucer. Place one and a half tablespoons of cheese-egg mixture on the uncut side of round of dough. Brush edges of dough lightly with ice water. Fold to make half circle, press edges together, cut an X in the top to vent, and crimp edges with the tines of a fork. Brush with milk and bake 10 minutes on lowest oven rack, raise to upper rack and bake 10-15 minutes longer, or until golden brown. Best when served warm.

TUPELO HONEY BRAN MUFFINS

*T*upelo honey is produced by honey bees from the Tupelo Gum Tree which grows along the Chipola, Apalachicola and Choctawhatchee Rivers of Northwest Florida. Here in the river swamps, honey is produced in a unique fashion. Bee hives are placed on elevated platforms along the river's edge. During April and May, the bees fan out through the surrounding Tupelo blossom-laden swamps and return with their precious treasure. These river valleys are the only place in the world where Tupelo honey is produced commercially.

Real Tupelo honey is light gold with a greenish cast. The flavor is delicious, distinctive and choice table grade honey. Good clear Tupelo honey, unmixed with other honeys, will not granulate. Diabetics can eat this honey because of the low dextrose ratio. We think it's the best honey available. Apparently we aren't alone, judging from the current price. Gallberry and Palmetto honey are good, too, if you can't find Tupelo. Honey makes baked goods more moist and dense than sugar.

1 cup boiling water
1 cup 100% Bran
1¼ cups Tupelo honey
½ cup unsalted butter
2 eggs
2 cups buttermilk
½ cup orange juice
1 cup carrots, grated
1 cup flaked coconut

2 cups whole wheat flour
½ cup cornmeal
2½ teaspoons soda
½ teaspoon salt
2 teaspoons grated orange rind
2 cups All-Bran
1 cup raisins (optional)

Preheat oven 375 degrees.

Pour boiling water over bran and set aside. If using raisins, soak them in hot water for 30 minutes. In a large mixing bowl, cream the honey and butter. Add the eggs, beat well, add the soaked bran, buttermilk, orange juice, carrots, coconut and mix. Sift together the flour, cornmeal, soda, salt and add to mixture with orange rind. Stir in the All-Bran. Drain raisins and pat dry with paper towels, and add to mixture. Spoon into greased muffin tins, filling them three-fourths full, sprinkle with additional coconut if desired and bake 15-17 minutes.

Ingram McDonald, our brother robbing his bee hives in the Choctawhatchee River Swamp.

WILD BLUEBERRY MUFFINS

Native blueberry, plum, persimmon and mayhaw plants are more resistant to disease than the new hybrids. We think the fruit has a better flavor. We transplant these plants in the winter. Prune back by one half.

In 1893, Moses Asberry Sapp, a farmer and logger, transplanted the Rabbits-eye variety of blueberries from Northwest Florida wetlands to a three-fourths acre plot and thus established the first domestic production of blueberries. The high price paid for blueberries soon led opportunist to dig up most of the native plants in Okaloosa, Walton and Santa Rosa Counties.

Blueberries, mayberries, and juneberries still grow wild in the woods around North Florida. Recently, the blueberry has become widely planted as a u-pick-'em product. New varieties grown nowadays use irrigation and fertilizers which produce more berries than the wild bushes. These muffins are the first thing we make when fresh blueberries come in. (That is, after we have eaten a handful or two.)

Makes 16 muffins

- 2 ⅓ cups all-purpose flour
- 1 cup sugar
- 2 teaspoons cream of tartar
- 1 teaspoon soda
- ½ teaspoon salt
- 6 tablespoons unsalted butter, softened
- ½ cup milk
- ¼ cup whipping cream
- 1 egg, beaten lightly
- ½ teaspoon vanilla
- 1 pint fresh blueberries

Preheat oven 350 degrees.

Place 2 cups of the flour, sugar, cream of tartar, soda, salt and butter in food processor and process until mixture resembles meal. In a large bowl, whisk together the milk, whipping cream, egg and vanilla. Place berries in a sieve and sprinkle with a third cup flour. Gently shake berries until all are coated with flour. Lightly combine flour mixture with liquids. Muffins will be tough if over mixed. Fold in floured blueberries. Use paper liners in muffin tins and fill two-thirds full with batter. Bake 25-30 minutes.

These blueberry muffins, hot from the oven, were made with native blueberries from our farm in Eucheeanna.

ORANGE FIG MUFFINS

In 1539, conquistador Hernando de Soto planted the first sour oranges in Florida. By 1579, the St. Augustine colonists had planted citrus groves for their own use, but it was during the British period when oranges were first exported. By 1835, St. Augustine growers sold 2.5 million barrels annually. Today Florida growers, each year, are shipping over 150 billion boxes of oranges world wide.

Orange trees were planted on the plantations in St. Augustine and along the St. Johns River in Ft. George Island, Mandarin and Orange Park. The citrus was wrapped in Spanish moss, packed in barrels, and shipped north on the many boats that docked in Jacksonville. Later, severe freezes wiped out these groves and the citrus production moved farther south down around the Indian River.

These muffins are great on cold winter mornings. Use juice from a fresh Florida orange and fill your kitchen with the aroma of citrus.

Makes 12-14 muffins

- 1 medium orange
- ½ cup dried figs
- ½ cup orange juice
- 8 tablespoons unsalted butter, cut into 8 pieces
- 1 large egg
- 1½ cups all-purpose flour
- ¾ cup sugar
- 1 teaspoon soda
- 1 teaspoon baking powder
- 1 teaspoon salt

Preheat oven 375 degrees.

Remove rind from orange and place in food processor, process until pieces are pea-sized, add figs and process until finely chopped. Remove white pith from peeled orange, cut into chunks, and remove seeds. Add figs, orange, orange juice, butter and egg to processor, process until combined. Transfer orange mixture to a large bowl. Sift flour, sugar, soda, baking powder and salt together and add to orange mixture. Stir batter until just combined, batter should be lumpy. Place paper liners in 14 muffin pans. Spoon batter into prepared tins, filling them two-thirds full and bake 20 minutes, or until done.

HYPOCRITE ROLLS

"When the roll is called up yonder, I'll be there."

We believe this bread got its name because of the way it looks. The outside is crisp and the inside is hollow. Serve this delicious bread hot with Sand Pear Preserves or Tupelo Honey Butter (below).

1/3 cup lukewarm water (110 degrees)	3½ cups all-purpose flour
1 package active dry yeast	1 teaspoon salt
2 teaspoons sugar	1 cup lukewarm milk
	Vegetable oil for frying

Place lukewarm water and a half teaspoon of the sugar into a small bowl, and stir in the yeast. Let mixture rest for 3-5 minutes or until the mixture foams. Combine flour, salt, the remaining sugar and sift into a large, deep bowl. Make a well in the center of flour and pour in the milk, and yeast mixture. Use a wooden spoon to mix and stir until smooth. Turn the dough out on a lightly floured surface, and knead by, pushing the dough down with the heel of your hand, pressing forward and folding it back on itself. Add more flour as necessary and knead for 7-8 minutes or until dough is smooth.

Place in a greased bowl, turn once to grease top, and cover with plastic wrap. Let rise in a warm place until doubled, about one-one and a half hours. Punch dough down and place half the dough on a lightly floured surface. Roll dough one fourth-one half inch thick, cut into 2 inch x 3 inch strips and fry in hot oil until golden brown. Roll remaining dough and cook, or place excess dough in a bowl, cover with plastic wrap, and refrigerate for yeast rolls or pizza crust the next day.

TUPELO HONEY BUTTER

½ cup unsalted butter, softened
¼ cup Tupelo honey
½ teaspoon orange rind, grated

Blend butter, honey and orange rind together and serve.

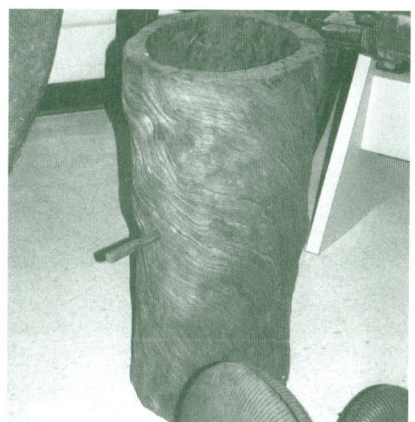

Hollow Black Gum trees were the source of early bee gums (hives), c 1920.

CINNAMON ROLLS

*T*he best country style restaurant in North Florida might just be over the state line in Thomasville, Georgia. The Market Place Diner located at the Farmer's Market puts out a fantastic, all you can eat spread. Always fried chicken and several other meat dishes but we go for the vegetables. Turnips, mustard and collard greens, seasoned to perfection, string beans and new potatoes, okra and tomatoes, perfect rutabagas, lima beans like my Daddy used to cook and the line goes on and on. Cornbread, yeast rolls and homemade desserts and oh yes, the fabulously tasty cinnamon rolls. Unfortunately we are always too full to enjoy the desserts. The sign says you're not supposed to take any food home, but my sister Tawee (she's the one that makes the great pies) and I just have to stick a cinnamon roll in our pocket or purse and sneak them out to enjoy later.

Makes 2 dozen rolls
Sweet dough:
½ cup milk
½ cup sugar
1½ teaspoons salt
¼ cup shortening
2 packages dry yeast
½ cup shortening

2 eggs, beaten
5 cups all-purpose flour
1½ cups brown sugar
2 teaspoons cinnamon
⅔ cup raisins

Scald milk and stir in sugar, salt, and shortening. Cool to lukewarm. Dissolve yeast in very warm water. Stir until dissolved, then stir into the lukewarm milk mixture. Add beaten eggs and 3 cups of the flour. Beat until smooth and stir in the additional 2 cups of flour. Turn dough out onto lightly floured board and knead until smooth and elastic. Place in a greased bowl and brush the top with soft shortening. Cover and let rise in a warm place, free from draft, until double in bulk (about 1 hour). Punch down and turn out on to lightly floured board. Divide sweet dough in half. Place on floured surface and roll each half into an oblong 14x9 inches, a fourth inch thick. Spread generously with melted butter. Sprinkle each oblong with three-fourths cup brown sugar, 1 teaspoon cinnamon and a third cup raisins. Roll dough a jelly roll and cut into 1 inch slices. Place on greased pan 1 inch apart. Cover and let rise in warm place for a half hour, or until doubled in bulk. Bake 350 degrees for 30-35 minutes.

Icing: Thoroughly mix 1 cup xxxx sugar and 1 tablespoon heavy cream, if mixture looks too thick add cream by drops until pourable consistency. Drizzle over warm buns.

Butch and Sundance.

SUNFLOWER BREAD

Daddy's summer garden always had sunflowers. He kept some of the seeds to plant the next year and some he dried for the song birds.

Sunflowers are now grown as a crop on some North Florida farms and the seeds are processed into vegetable oil. Doves love to visit these fields, so I guess it's still sort of bird food.

Makes one 9x 5 inch loaf

1¼ cups warm water
1 package active dry yeast
2 teaspoons sugar
¼ cup Tupelo honey
2 teaspoons molasses
½ cup buttermilk
5 tablespoons butter, softened

1½ teaspoons salt
4 to 4¼ cups whole wheat flour
½ - ¾ cup sunflower seeds, toasted
1 egg yolk
1 tablespoon milk

Pour lukewarm water in a large bowl and sprinkle the yeast and 1 teaspoon of the sugar over it, mix and let stand about 5 minutes. Add remaining sugar, honey, buttermilk, 4 tablespoons of the butter and salt, stirring to dissolve. Add 4 cups of the flour and toasted sunflower seeds, mixing well.

Spread one tablespoon of softened butter over the inside of a large bowl. Turn dough out on a lightly floured surface. Knead for 10 minutes - dough will be sticky, work in a fourth cup more flour, sprinkling it over the dough and adding only the amount needed. Shape into a ball and place in buttered bowl, turning about to butter the entire surface. Cover with a towel and set in a warm, draft-free place for 20 minutes. Knead dough again briefly, form into a ball and let rise, covered, for 40-50 minutes. Shape the dough into a loaf, mix egg yolk and milk, and paint top of the dough with pastry brush.

Place in greased loaf pan, cover loosely with plastic wrap and let rise 45 minutes, or until dough doubles in bulk. Remove plastic wrap and bake bread in a 375 degree oven for about 40 minutes. Remove from pan immediately and rap the bottom with your fingertips, if it does not sound hollow, return to pan and bake 5 minutes more. Cool on a wire rack and serve warm or at room temperature with Tupelo Honey Butter (see page 59).

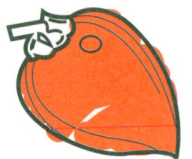

'SIMMON BREAD

*'Possum up a 'simmon tree,
Raccoon on the ground,
Raccoon says,"Mr. Possum
shake them 'simmons down".*

We have a large Japanese Persimmon tree at the Big House on Circle Drive. The fruit gets ripe in the late fall, so Genny gets to enjoy fresh persimmons during the Thanksgiving holidays. Sometimes she will be generous and give us a few for this bread.

If you are fortunate enough to live close to some wild persimmon trees, use these, but make sure they are ripe.

Makes 2 loaves

- 3 cups ripe persimmon pulp
- ½ pound unsalted butter, softened
- 2 cups sugar
- 1½ teaspoons baking soda
- ½ teaspoon cream of tartar
- 4 cups all-purpose flour
- ¼ teaspoon almond extract
- 2 cups roasted pecans, chopped
- ½ teaspoon salt

Preheat oven 350 degrees.

Purée enough peeled persimmons through a food mill to measure 3 cups. Into a large bowl cream the butter and sugar together until light and fluffy. Into a bowl sift the soda, cream of tartar and flour together. Blend into the creamed butter and sugar. Fold in the persimmon pulp, almond extract, pecans and salt. Pour the batter into two buttered loaf pans 9x5x2 inches and bake for 1 hour, or until a cake tester inserted in the center comes out clean.

ROASTED PECANS

Preheat 400 degrees.

Spread pecans halves or pieces on a cookie sheet and roast pecans 8-10 minutes, stirring occasionally. Pecan pieces cost less than halves so check your recipe before buying.

BANANA BREAD

*T*he aroma of this bread baking always brings back many childhood memories. This bread is best when very ripe bananas are used. It also makes a great dessert. We felt very fortunate when our Aunt Velora found Granny's hand written recipe for Banana Bread and sent it to us.

Makes two 9x 5 inch loaves

- ½ cup unsalted butter, softened
- 1 cup sugar
- 1⅓ cups ripe bananas, broken into chunks and mashed
- 2 eggs, separated
- ½ teaspoon vanilla
- ½ teaspoon lemon juice
- 1 teaspoon baking soda
- ¼ teaspoon salt
- 1½ cups all-purpose flour
- 1½ tablespoons hot water

Preheat oven 350 degrees.

Cream butter and sugar in a large bowl. Add bananas, egg yolks, vanilla, lemon juice, soda and salt. Mix thoroughly with mixer. Stir in flour with a wooden spoon. Beat egg whites until stiff. Gently fold egg whites into batter, add hot water and gently stir. Bake in buttered pans 45 minutes-1 hour or until done. Cool in pan for 10 minutes, then turn out and cool completely or serve warm.

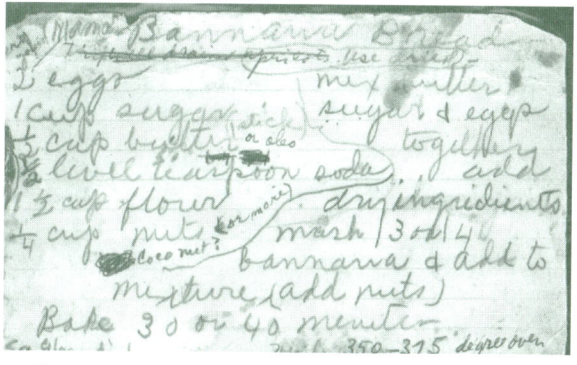

Granny's handwritten recipe for banana bread, c 1935.

LIBBY'S BRIDGE CREEK HEAVENLY HOTS

How could something so delicious be so simple to prepare. Libby said they would melt in your mouth and she was right.

- 2 cups sour cream
- 4 eggs
- 3 tablespoons sugar
- ½ teaspoon salt
- 5 tablespoons cake flour
- 1 teaspoon baking soda

Blend all ingredients and cook silver dollar size cakes on greased skillet. Flip with a fork.

GABBY'S FLAPJACKS

One of our favorite games as youngsters was cow persons and Native Americans, (my daughter made me do it). We would often ask Mother to please make us some "Flapjacks" for breakfast so we could take them outside and sit around the ol' chuck wagon (cardboard box). Then we would have an authentic cowboy breakfast just like Roy and Dale.

Makes 18-20 four inch FlapJacks

2 cups all-purpose flour
4 teaspoons baking powder
2 tablespoons sugar
1 teaspoon salt
2 cups buttermilk

2 eggs, lightly beaten
¼ cup unsalted butter, melted
¼ cup vegetable oil for greasing griddle

In a large bowl add the flour, baking powder, sugar, and salt. In a separate bowl add the buttermilk and stir in the eggs and butter. Add the wet mixture to the dry ingredients, do not over mix, there should be some small lumps. Add additional buttermilk if batter is too stiff. Heat griddle over medium heat. Grease griddle lightly with vegetable oil, and pour batter to form flapjacks. Cook until small bubbles form, add sliced bananas, blueberries or roasted nuts before turning if desired. Flip over and cook another 2 minutes. Stack on heated platter placed in 200 degree oven until all flapjacks are cooked.

WHOLE GRAIN GRIDDLE CAKES

Serves 6

⅔ cup old-fashioned oatmeal
1⅓ cup whole wheat flour
1 cup cornmeal
⅓ cup all-purpose flour
4 teaspoons baking powder
2 teaspoons soda
2 teaspoons salt

2 teaspoons salt
1⅓ sticks of cold unsalted butter
4 cups buttermilk
4 eggs, lightly beaten
⅓ cup maple syrup

Place oatmeal in food processor and process until it becomes a coarse powder. Add remaining dry ingredients and process until well mixed. Remove half of the mixture to a large bowl. Cut butter into 1 inch chunks and add to processor. Process until butter is incorporated, add to flour mixture in large bowl. In another bowl add buttermilk, eggs and maple syrup. Mix together thoroughly and add to dry ingredients, mixing until combined; let stand 5 minutes. If necessary, thin with a fourth-one half cup buttermilk. Cook same as flapjacks.

ORANGE BLOSSOM SPECIAL

"It's the Orange Blossom Special, coming on down the line."

French toast, in the old days, was simply a slice of light bread, drug through a beaten egg, fried and covered with cane syrup. This was a nice change for breakfast, but nothing like this version which we discovered later in life. The addition of brandy and orange-flower water makes it a special treat.

Serves 4

5 eggs
½ cup granulated sugar
3 tablespoons brandy
½ tablespoons orange-flower water
⅛ teaspoon salt
1 teaspoon lemon rind, grated
1 loaf day old French bread
Vegetable oil to measure 1 inch depth in large skillet
Powdered sugar, or Tupelo honey

Slice bread into 1 inch slices. In a large deep bowl, beat the eggs and sugar with a wire whisk until frothy. Beat in the brandy, orange-flower water, salt and lemon rind. Add bread slices, turning to moisten evenly. Heat a heavy 12 inch skillet with oil over medium heat. Fry the bread, making sure not to crowd the pan, for about 2 minutes on each side, or until golden brown. Drain on paper towels and serve immediately sprinkled with powdered sugar, or Tupelo honey.

TOMORROW'S WAFFLES

Makes 8 waffles

One 7 grams package dry yeast
2 cups warm milk
8 tablespoons melted butter
1 teaspoon salt
1 teaspoon sugar
2 cups all-purpose flour
2 eggs
¼ teaspoon baking powder
Powdered sugar, or Tupelo honey

Dissolve yeast in a half cup warm milk in a large bowl until foamy, 8-10 minutes. Add milk, butter, salt and flour and beat until well combined. Cover with plastic wrap and set aside at room temperature overnight. The next day whisk eggs and baking powder into batter until combined. Pour a half cup of batter into hot waffle iron (preferably cast-iron) and let set 30 seconds then lower lid and cook until golden brown. Repeat process until waffles are cooked. Batter will keep several days in refrigerator.

NASSAU GRITS

One of our favorite morning meals begins in the ocean. We take our seine net out in the surf and drag it along the shore until we have enough fish for breakfast. The catch is always different and might include mullet, trout, croaker, mackerel, pompano, drum or several varieties of pan fish. We select the ones for cooking and release the rest along with the crabs, sting rays and baby sharks. The fish are quickly cleaned and pan fried, and accompanied with a generous helping of Nassau Grits, fresh fruit and hot Banana Bread(see page 63).

Legend has it that this recipe was created in the islands and later made its way to Pensacola where it's still served in several restaurants.

Serves 6

- 3 cups water
- ½ teaspoon salt
- ½ teaspoon unsalted butter
- ¾ cup Old-Fashioned Stone-Ground Hominy Grits
- 3 slices thick cut smoked bacon
- 2 cups onion, chopped fine
- ½ teaspoon garlic, minced
- ½ cup bell pepper, chopped fine
- 1 cup smoked ham, finely chopped
- ¾ cup crushed plum tomatoes
- ¼ teaspoon cayenne
- 1 tablespoon parsley, chopped

Add water and salt to a large saucepan and bring to a boil, add butter and slowly stir in grits, stir constantly to prevent lumps. Cover, reduce heat to low and, stirring frequently, simmer 30-40 minutes. Fry bacon until crisp in a cast-iron skillet, remove bacon and set aside. Pour bacon drippings out of pan and reserve. Return skillet to medium heat with 2 tablespoons of the reserved drippings, add onions, garlic and bell pepper and cook until softened. Place in bowl and set aside. Add 1 tablespoon remaining bacon drippings to same skillet, add ham and cook for 5 minutes over medium heat, stirring occasionally. Add crushed tomatoes, cayenne and onion mixture to ham, stir until mixed, and simmer for 30 minutes, stirring occasionally.

Combine the cooked grits and tomato mixture and cook 10-15 minutes. Crumble bacon on top, sprinkle with parsley and serve.

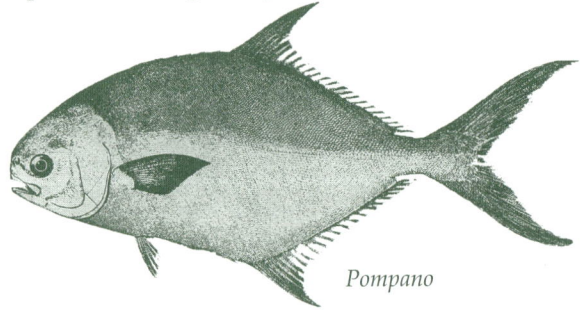

Pompano

COUNTRY HAM AND RED-EYE GRAVY

According to local legend, a Confederate general acquired a cache of bourbon with which he rewarded his troops after winning a battle. The next morning his cook asked him what he wanted for breakfast and he replied, "ham and gravy the color of your eyes." While we doubt the authenticity of this story, it is an old Southern dish and is still enjoyed by many.

Serve with Country Fried Eggs, Old-Fashioned Stone Ground Grits and Shrimp paste.

Serves 4

4 large slices country ham, cut ¼ inch thick
3 tablespoons strong coffee

Trim fat from ham, cut into small pieces and place in a large cast-iron skillet. Fry over medium heat until crisp and pieces have rendered all their fat. Remove and discard. Place the ham slices in the skillet and fry until ham is evenly brown on both sides. Transfer ham to a heated platter and pour desired amount of coffee into skillet. Bring to a rapid boil, scraping up any brown bits. Pour over ham and serve with grits and biscuits..

SMOKED HAM BISCUITS WITH JEZEBEL SAUCE

Place butt half of precooked ham in smoker stoked with Oak and Pecan wood. Smoke 4-5 hours at 220 degrees until meat thermometer registers 160 degrees. Remove ham and let rest. Add wood and open vents to increase smoker temperature to 350 degrees. Prepare 3 batches biscuits (see page 52). Cook in smoker until brown. Slice biscuit in half and place slices of ham on biscuit and cover with honey mustard or Jezebel sauce.

JEZEBEL SAUCE

One 10 ounce jar apple jelly **One 12 ounce jar pineapple preserves**
One 5 ounce jar horseradish **One 5 ounce jar mustard**

Mix well and heat in a small saucepan until melted. Keep leftover refrigerated.

COUNTRY FRIED STEAK N' TOMATO GRAVY

This is an old family recipe. It's one dish where canned tomatoes are almost as good as fresh. Granny used to tenderize her steaks by beating them with the top of an empty 6 ounce "Co-cola" bottle. She claimed the king sized Cokes were "watered down" and wouldn't buy them.

We like this for a late breakfast in the winter. Serve this tasty gravy over grits or Mother's Buttermilk Biscuits.

Old coke bottles required a 1 cent deposit. According to the writing on the bottom these bottles came from the Hygenia Bottling Company in Defuniak Springs, c 1950.

Serves 4-6

1¼ pounds round steak
Salt and freshly ground
    black pepper, to taste
¼ teaspoon cayenne pepper,
    or more
1 tablespoon garlic, minced
2 tablespoons flour, or more

2 tablespoons bacon drippings
    or oil
1 cup onions, chopped
1 cup plum tomatoes,
    seeded and chopped
¼ cup demi-glace
1 cup beef stock

Trim all fat from the meat and remove any bones. Cut meat into 2 inch square pieces and pound until thin. Rub salt, peppers, and garlic into both sides of meat, then rub in the flour. In a large cast-iron skillet, add the bacon drippings over medium heat and brown the meat on both sides. Lower the heat and add the onions, tomatoes, demi-glace (see page 23), and stock. Bring to a simmer, cover loosely and cook over low heat for 30-45 minutes. Uncover and turn meat over. A rich brown gravy will form during cooking. If it appears too thick, add additional stock. If not thick enough, remove lid and cook until gravy is desired thickness. Correct seasonings and serve with grits and biscuits.

Trey, picking green and vine-ripe tomatoes at Padgett's Farm, Ponce de Leon, c 2004.

CORNED BEEF HASH

When we first published *Seasonal Florida* in 1994 we had to eliminate a few recipes for lack of space. We did our best to drop the ones we thought no one would miss. Imagine our surprise when both our children lambasted us because we left out the corned beef hash. Over the years it had become one of their comfort foods. So the next Christmas we made each of them a personal cookbook with all the recipes we had left out. Now that we have the opportunity we're including the recipe in the revised *Seasonal Florida*, because it might become someone else's comfort food too.

Serves 4
- 1¼ cups onions, minced
- 1 tablespoon butter
- 1 tablespoon olive oil
- 1½ tablespoons plain flour
- ½ cup chicken broth
- 2 cups new potatoes, cooked and diced
- 12 ounce can of Hormel corned beef
- ¼ teaspoon oregano
- ¼ teaspoon thyme
- 3 tablespoons parsley, minced

In a large cast-iron skillet sauté the onion in the butter and olive oil over medium heat until transparent, then raise the heat and let them slightly brown. Lower the heat and sprinkle the flour in, stir to make a paste; cook 1-2 minutes. Slowly add the broth, and let the mixture come to a boil. Mix in the potatoes, corned beef, oregano, thyme and half the parsley. Taste for seasoning adding salt and freshly ground black pepper if needed. Firmly press the hash down with a flat spatula. Reduce heat to low, cover and cook for 10-15 minutes. Stir the hash to get the crust mixed into the hash. Press the hash down again and pat the edges away from the sides of the pan. Let the hash continue to cook, uncovered, and form another crust. The hash can become as crusty as you desire. Sprinkle with remaining parsley and serve with poached eggs, toasted English muffins and Mayhaw jelly.

BREAKFAST CASSEROLE

Makes 10 Servings
- 1 pound mild ground pork sausage
- 1 pound hot ground pork sausage
- 1 (30-ounce) package frozen hash browns
- 1½ teaspoons salt, divided
- ½ teaspoon freshly ground black pepper
- 1 cup extra-sharp cheddar cheese, grated
- 6 large eggs
- 2 cups milk

Cook sausage in a large cast-iron skillet until crumbly and no longer pink. Drain well. Prepare hash browns according to package directions, using a half teaspoon salt and pepper.

In a large bowl stir together sausage, hash browns and cheese. Pour into a lightly greased 13x9 inch baking dish. Whisk together eggs, milk, and remaining salt. Pour evenly over potato mixture. Bake 350 degrees for 35-40 minutes.

SMOTHERED FRIED RABBIT

My husband fondly remembers garden patrol in the spring when he was young. Granny always planted English peas, a favorite food of the rabbits. Her eyesight was failing so she called him to help with the rabbit patrol. He wore her head lamp and was trusted with her single shot .410 shotgun. As soon as dark came, he shined around the garden and bagged the critters eating the pea plants. The rabbits were brought back to the house, skinned, cleaned and prepared for breakfast. The next morning, the rabbits were smothered fried, served with grits and gravy, fried eggs, sautéed bananas and biscuits. Obviously, this wasn't a sporting event, but it sure saved the English peas and provided a unique breakfast as well as wonderful memories.

This tasty dish may be made with domestic or wild rabbits. We prefer it with the wild rabbits our son Trey brings home.

Serves 4

2½- 3 pound rabbit, cleaned
Salt and freshly ground
    black pepper, to taste)
1 cup all-purpose flour

1 tablespoon vegetable oil
½ cup unsalted butter
2 cups chicken stock

Wash rabbit and pat dry with paper towels. Trim silvery skin and loose fat from rabbit and cut into 6-8 pieces. Salt and pepper to taste. Heat a large cast-iron skillet over medium heat. Dust with flour. Add oil and butter to skillet. When oil is hot, add the rabbit, making sure not to crowd the pan.

Brown rabbit on all sides and remove from skillet. Remove all but 2 tablespoons of oil. Reduce heat to low. Add one and one half tablespoons of flour used to dust rabbit to skillet and stir until flour turns a nutty brown. Add chicken stock, bring to a slow boil and stir until smooth. Reduce heat and cook 3-5 minutes, adding additional stock if needed. Return rabbit, cover and continue to cook on low heat until rabbit is tender and gravy has thickened. Correct seasoning and serve with grits and biscuits. This recipe may also be used with tough squirrels.

Sautéed Bananas
4 Bananas peeled and sliced in half
2 tablespoons butter

1 teaspoon sugar
1 tablespoon lemon juice

Heat butter in skillet. Add bananas, cook until light brown, turn over. Sprinkle with sugar and lemon juice. Remove from skillet and serve hot.

HOG N' HOMINY

There is a paved road that begins close to the highest point in Florida, near Sweet Gum Head and crosses North Florida, going through those basketball dynasties of Campbellton and Malone and ending up in South Georgia. This road has been called Hog N' Hominy for as long as we can remember. Maybe it's because it winds through some of our best farming areas which produces many fine hogs and the corn and peanuts to feed them.

Serves 4-6

1 pound bulk pork sausage (recipe follows)
1 teaspoon marjoram, crumbled
1-15½ ounce can hominy, rinsed and drained
1 cup green onions, chopped
½ cup chicken stock
½ tablespoon parsley, minced
Salt and freshly ground black pepper, to taste

Form sausage into small patties. Place in large cast-iron skillet over medium heat and cook 2-3 minutes on each side until almost done. Pour off excess oil, reduce heat, add marjoram and stir. Add onions and cook until softened. Stir in hominy and add chicken stock. Cook for 10 minutes over low heat, scraping bottom of skillet and add additional chicken stock by the tablespoon if needed. Correct seasoning, sprinkle with parsley and serve.

PORK SAUSAGE

1 pound Boston butt with 30% fat content, cut into chunks
1¼ teaspoons salt
½ teaspoon red pepper flakes
1 teaspoon freshly ground black pepper
1 teaspoon powdered sage

Trim the meat of all gristle, chill thoroughly, and then cut into chunks. Grind chunks of the meat in a grinder on course grind then on fine grind, if desired. Place pork in a large bowl. Sprinkle seasonings evenly over meat and knead to distribute, be careful not to over work the mixture. Wrap in plastic wrap and refrigerate at least one hour or overnight. Just before serving shape into patties and pan fry a small teaspoonful, taste and correct seasoning if necessary. Fry patties in a cast-iron skillet, over medium heat until done, about 4 minutes per side.

Quincy meat market. Note thick fat content around hams, unlike todays leaner hogs, c 1940's.

SAWMILL GRAVY

The only large increase in population of North Florida that we know of occurred during the period when the virgin forests were clear cut. Thousands of families moved into North Florida to work in the sawmills and to harvest the millions of long leaf pine and cypress trees growing throughout the area. Many of the large sawmills were located at the mouth of the rivers where the logs were floated down to be processed into lumber. Trees were felled by crosscut saws and dragged by teams of oxen to the nearest stream which ultimately led to the sawmills. Sometimes the trees were branded to indicate which mill was to receive them.

Mill hands and loggers sometimes stayed in camps where the meals were prepared by the "camp cook." This dish was frequently served.

My sister Carolyn, always cooks this dish for our Christmas morning breakfast. It's served over Tawee's hot buttermilk biscuits.

Carolyn

Large 3,000 year old cypress tree in route to sawmill in Perry, c 1926.

Serves 4-6

**1 pound bulk pork sausage
1 cup onions, finely chopped
2 tablespoons all-purpose flour
Salt to taste
1 ½ cups milk or more
⅛ teaspoon nutmeg, freshly grated
¼ teaspoon cayenne pepper**

Heat a large cast-iron skillet over medium heat, add sausage and brown. Break up any large pieces. Add onions and cook until softened. Strain and pour off grease, set sausage aside, reserving 2 tablespoons of drippings to make roux. Return drippings to skillet. Reduce heat to low, add flour to drippings, stirring constantly for 2 minutes. Add milk and continue stirring; cook until mixture thickens. Add sausage and cayenne, adding additional milk if needed. Correct seasonings. Split biscuits, pour gravy on top and serve.

MULLET ROE

*I*n the late fall, local mullet are often full of yellow roe, which we consider a delicacy. The demand has caused over-fishing, which has greatly depleted our mullet supply.

We've been known to organize fish fries in the fall featuring mullet just to get the roe. The salted roe is enjoyed the next morning for breakfast.

Serves 4

4-6 teaspoons salt
8 thick slices of lean smoked bacon
8 tablespoons unsalted butter
4 small pairs of mullet roe
½ cup cornmeal
⅛ teaspoon salt
⅛ teaspoon freshly ground black pepper
2 tablespoons medium-dry sherry
¼ cup chopped parsley
2 lemons, cut in wedges

The day before serving, sprinkle salt on roe, place in a zip lock bag and refrigerate overnight. An hour before serving, rinse salt from roe and place roe on paper towels to drain. Heat a large cast-iron skillet, cook bacon until crisp, drain on paper towels. Add butter plus 1 tablespoon bacon drippings to another skillet and melt over medium heat. Add salt and pepper to cornmeal and coat roe, shaking off excess meal. Cook covered, for 3- 4 minutes, turn and cook, covered, 3 more minutes. The roe will sputter as it cooks. Uncover roe and add sherry, cook 2 minutes. Remove from heat, add parsley and stir. Place on heated plates with bacon and some pan juices. Garnish plates with lemon wedges.

SHRIMP PASTE

*I*f we catch a good mess of shrimp one night, we have this dish the next morning using the smallest shrimp. Serve a dollop on top of your old-fashioned speckled heart stone ground hominy grits for a wonderful taste treat.

Makes 1 cup

1 pound boiled shrimp, shelled and deveined
½ cup unsalted butter, softened
⅛ teaspoon nutmeg, freshly grated
1 tablespoon brandy or sherry
⅛ teaspoon cayenne
1 teaspoon lemon juice
½ teaspoon salt
⅛ teaspoon white pepper

Place all ingredients in a food processor and process until smooth. Put into container with tight fitting lid and refrigerate at least 4 hours before serving.

BISCUITS, BREAKFAST AND BRUNCH

BODACIOUS BRUNCH DISHES

The Florida Winter Chautauqua was a cultural event that was held annually at the turn of the century in DeFuniak Springs. People arrived on the L&N trains and stayed in large hotels and homes while attending lectures, classes and other cultural events.

The Chautauqua auditorium is located on Lake DeFuniak and still plays a part in the Chautauqua Festival that is held each April. The rear of the auditorium which could seat thousands of guests was destroyed by hurricane Eloise in the 1970's.

Chautauqua auditorium, DeFuniak Springs.

Eggs Chautauqua
Serves 4
Choron Sauce
1 teaspoon bacon drippings
4 thin slices Smithfield type ham or smoked ham
12 fresh asparagus, steamed
4 poached eggs
4-3 inch buttermilk biscuits

Prepare Choron Sauce (see page 89), set aside and keep warm. Heat a cast-iron skillet over medium-high heat. Add bacon drippings and ham, cook until brown on both sides. Remove ham to heated plate. Steam the asparagus and set in warm place. Poach the eggs and set aside, keeping them warm. Split the biscuits, butter lightly and toast. To assemble, place a half biscuit on heated plate, top with slice of ham, egg, asparagus and Choron Sauce. Use remaining half of biscuit to spread with your favorite preserve. Garnish the plate with fresh parsley and fruit in season. Serve immediately.

Eggs Nassau
Serves 4
1 recipe Nassau grits
8 poached eggs
Choron Sauce
12 boiled shrimp, shelled and deveined (reserve 4 whole shrimp)
Shrimp Paste

Cook one recipe of Nassau Grits. Substitute diced shrimp for ham and use shrimp stock for water. Spread in buttered glass dish a half inch thick. Place in refrigerator overnight. Cut into 4 inch rounds, dredge with flour, shake off excess and pan fry in butter until golden brown. Place two poached eggs on top of each cake and 1 tablespoon of shrimp paste(see page 73). Cover with Choron Sauce (see page 89). Place a whole shrimp on top, garnish with parsley and fresh fruit.

Eggs Lafitte
Serves 4

4 artichoke hearts
8 poached eggs
Crab Lafitte, below
Salt to taste
Pepper to taste
Hollandaise sauce, (see below)
Paprika
8 sausage patties, fried

Place two poached eggs on each artichoke heart. Cover with dollop of Crab Lafitte then cover with Hollandaise Sauce. Sprinkle with paprika, garnish with parsley and fruit. Serve with a couple of sausage patties.

Crab Lafitte
Serves 4

1 stick unsalted butter
2 green onions, minced
1 pound lump crab meat
½ teaspoon freshly ground black pepper
2 ounces sherry wine
Dash paprika

Sauté green onions until limp. Add crab meat and seasonings. Gently stir. Add the sherry and simmer until heated through. Sprinkle with paprika.

Hollandaise Sauce

Melt 2 sticks unsalted butter and put aside. Whisk 4 egg yolks, juice from one lemon, maybe more, a half teaspoon Worcestershire and 9 dashes Tabasco in the top of a double boiler over simmering water until mixture has a sheen, about 3 minutes. Gradually add the butter in a stream until the sauce thickens. Taste for seasoning and serve. If the sauce should separate, remove from heat, add 1 tablespoon water and whisk vigorously.

Béarnaise Sauce

In a small saucepan add 2 tablespoons dry white wine and 2 teaspoons crumbled, dried tarragon leaves. Reduce mixture to 1 teaspoon and add to prepared Hollandaise Sauce (above).

Creole Sauce
Makes 2 cups

Melt 2 tablespoons unsalted butter in a large skillet. Cut 1 cup each of onion and bell pepper into thin strips, and 2 stalks of celery cut into thin strips. Sauté vegetables and add 2 cloves garlic, thinly sliced and 1 bay leaf. Cook until transparent. Add 2 teaspoons paprika, 2 cups diced tomatoes, 1 cup tomato juice, 4 teaspoons Worcestershire, 4 teaspoons hot sauce. Stir and simmer until sauce reduces by a fourth. Combine one and a half tablespoons cornstarch in a half cup water, stir into sauce until sauce is glazed, about 2 minutes.

BISCUITS, BREAKFAST AND BRUNCH

BREAKFAST FRITTATA

Serves 4

1 ½ tablespoons unsalted butter
½ pound mushrooms, sliced
1 teaspoon lemon juice
2 teaspoons olive oil
2 new potatoes, cooked
¾-1 cup Marinara Sauce
6-8 eggs
Salt and freshly ground black pepper, to taste
6 slices smoked country bacon, cooked and crumbled
1 cup cooked zucchini
1 cup Monterey Jack cheese, grated

Preheat oven to broil. Heat a medium cast-iron skillet over medium heat, add 1 tablespoon butter and sauté mushrooms. Add lemon juice, cook until mushrooms release their juices, remove from skillet and set aside. Cut potatoes into fourths. In same skillet add 1 teaspoon olive oil over medium-low heat, cook potatoes until slightly brown, salt and pepper, remove from skillet and set aside. Add remaining teaspoon olive oil and remaining a half tablespoon of butter to a large cast-iron heated skillet. Beat the eggs with salt and pepper to taste and pour into skillet. Do not disturb eggs until they are slightly set around the edges. Carefully lift the edges to let the uncooked eggs flow underneath, pulling the eggs to the center of the skillet with a wooden spoon. When eggs are three-fourths cooked, begin scattering mushrooms, potatoes, Marinara Sauce (see page 229), bacon, zucchini and sprinkle with cheese. Remove from heat and place under broiler until cheese has melted. Serve at once.

TOAD-IN-THE-HOLE

This dish is what our grandmothers served to entice us to eat eggs when we were young, and it still works today. During his younger years, our nephew Kyle McDonald liked his egg yolk runny so he could play the dip egg game.

Remove the center of a slice of bread, leaving a hole about the size of a tennis ball. Heat an 8 inch non-stick skillet over medium-low heat. Butter both sides of remaining ring of bread. Place bread in skillet and lightly toast both sides. Add remaining butter in center of bread. Break egg into center. Cook until white is set and partially cooked, flip and cook until white is firm and yolk is runny. Serve at once.

Kyle McDonald, alias "The Dip Egg Kid", c 1965.

ODE TO THE OMELET

Perfect Omelet

Serves 1
3 eggs, room temperature
1 tablespoon unsalted butter
Salt and Freshly ground black pepper

Break eggs into a bowl, add salt and pepper. Whisk vigorously until eggs are well mixed. Heat omelet pan over medium-high heat. Add butter; tilt the pan so that the butter coats the bottom and sides of the pan. When the foam subsides and the butter begins to brown slightly pour in the beaten eggs. Wait for 4-5 seconds or until the eggs somewhat form in the bottom of the pan. Lift edge of formed eggs in several places and draw to center of pan to allow the uncooked eggs to run under the cooked eggs. When eggs are barely set add any of the warmed fillings below to the opposite side of the pans handle. Hold a plate in your left hand and fold omelet out of pan so that the side with no filling folds over to top the filling.

Fillings: Make sure fillings are warm before adding to omelet. Add 3-4 tablespoons of filling to each omelet.

Seafood Filling:

Sauté 2 tablespoons chopped green onions until limp in 1 tablespoon butter. Add 4 oysters, 4 shrimp, 2 ounces lump crabmeat, 2 mushrooms, sliced and 1 ounce dry white wine. Cook for about 1 minute, or until shrimp changes color, stir gently, being careful not to break up the crabmeat. Add 1 ounce cream, stir and remove from heat. Add to inside of omelet.

Asparagus Filling:

Cook 4 slices of bacon until crisp. Remove bacon to drain and add 4 thinly sliced green onions, and cook until limp. Add 10 asparagus stemmed and cut into bite size pieces, add salt and pepper and cook 2-3 minutes. Add to inside of omelet. Sprinkle with a third cup grated parmesan cheese and fold omelet.

Creole Filling:

Prepare a fourth cup of Creole Sauce (see page 75) and a fourth cup grated cheddar cheese and add to inside of omelet.

Pesto Filling:

Prepare 2 teaspoons pesto sauce (see page 296), add to the inside of omelet and fold. Sprinkle a fourth cup Fontina or Swiss cheese, grated on top of omelet. Garnish with parsley and 3 grape tomatoes, halved.

Florentine Filling:

Make one cup of white sauce (see page 24), stir in a fourth teaspoon Tabasco, a fourth teaspoon salt and a half cup cooked and chopped spinach. Add a third cup grated Parmesan cheese or Feta cheese and cook until mixture is hot. Add to inside of omelet and fold.

DADDY'S FIG PRESERVES

It was always a challenge for Daddy to stay one step ahead of the mocking birds. Up at daylight anyway, he would try to beat the birds to the choicest figs. As each year has passed, the fig tree has grown larger and a ladder has been necessary to reach the tallest limbs. Last year, Daddy resorted to climbing to the roof of an adjacent shed to pick the figs on the very top, which is quite a feat when you consider he was eighty-two years old.

Figs were introduced in St. Augustine in the 1500's by the Spanish. Fig trees are common in many Southern yards, and the fruit is usually canned as preserves or jams, but seldom eaten fresh. We enjoy fresh figs simply halved and served with thin slices of salty ham.

50 Brown Turkey Figs
1 cup sugar

Trim the stems from figs, wash and place in a heavy bottomed pot. Sprinkle figs with sugar, cover and let sit overnight. Remove lid and cook figs on medium heat until they begin to boil. Reduce heat to low and cook for 35-45 minutes or until they are reddish brown. Stir occasionally, being careful not to mash figs. Place figs in canning jars, adding enough syrup to cover figs. Wipe the rim and threads of jar with damp cloth, cover with lids and screw bands on tightly.

Aubrey McDonald, c 1955.

FREEZER JAM

Makes 5 one-half pints.

2 cups chopped fresh
   strawberries or peaches
4 cups sugar

1 package fruit pectin
¾ cup water

Measure sugar exactly and mix in a large bowl with fruit. Set aside for 10 minutes. Mix cold water and fruit pectin in a saucepan. Stir and heat to a full rolling boil for 1 minute. Stir pectin into fruit mixture and stir constantly for 3 minutes. Pour into freezing containers. Let sit for 24 hours on counter. Store in freezer. Remove from freezer the night before you plan to serve and place in refrigerator. Keep in refrigerator after opening.

CHICKASAW PLUM JAM

The Chickasaw plum trees grow wild throughout North Florida. Sometimes these plum orchards will have up to a hundred or more trees. It is the first tree to bloom in the spring. We like to drive around the woods and spot these orchards with their white blossoms, and return later in the summer to pick the delicious fruit, if someone hasn't beaten us there.

A teaspoon of almond extract may be added for additional flavor.

Makes 10-12 half pints.

5 pounds ripe
   chickasaw plums
½ cup water

1 box Sure-Jell
8 cups sugar

Place washed plums in 6-8 quart pot with a half cup water. Bring to a slow boil, reduce heat to simmer and cook 20-25 minutes or until skin is tender. Strain juice into large measuring cup and place pulp in a colander. When cool, mash pulp with hands to remove seeds. Discard the seeds. Add Sure-jell to fruit and bring to a full rolling boil over high heat, stirring constantly. Stir sugar into fruit mixture, bring to a full boil and boil 1 minute, stirring constantly. Skim off any foam with a metal spoon. Fill clean canning jars immediately to an eighth inch of tops. Wipe jar rims with damp cloth. Cover quickly with lids and screw bands on tightly.

MAYHAW JELLY

The month of May meant one thing to Granny. It was time to load all the grandchildren into her three-hole Buick and search for the elusive "mayhaw". Once the fruit-laden trees were located, the older kids would climb up the trunks and shake the limbs until their eyes wouldn't focus. Granny and the little kids would pick up the berries from the ground or ponds. Ticks and leaches were of little concern because we were on a mission - to fill the dish pans with enough berries to make enough jelly to last until next May.

Sure, it was a lot of work, but if you could taste one of Granny's hot, made-from-scratch biscuits, slathered with fresh churned butter and a big dab of Mayhaw Jelly, you would think it comparable to a religious experience.

Mayhaw trees grow in low wet areas throughout North Florida. Often, when the fruit is ripe, the trees are standing in water. Fortunately, the ripe fruit floats and is easily harvested after someone climbs the tree and shakes the fruit off. This fruit is treasured by many who use it to make jelly and butter. A gift of a jar of Mayhaw jelly is a true token of love.

Makes 4 pints

4 cups mayhaw juice
1-1¾ ounce package Sure-Jell
5½ cups sugar

Wash and place 6 quarts mayhaw berries in a heavy bottomed large 8 quart pot and just cover with water. Bring to a boil, reduce heat to low and cook until berries are soft, about 30 minutes. Use a large piece of doubled cheese cloth or a cloth bag to strain berries. Strain and extract as much juice as possible, twisting cheese cloth and squeezing to get every drop of concentrated juice. Use a potato masher to press all liquid from berries.

Cousin Tom Harcus posing behind Granny's three-hole Buick, c 1950's.

Heat mayhaw juice in a heavy bottomed pot. Add Sure-Jell to mayhaw juice and stir constantly. Bring to a full rolling boil over high heat. Add sugar quickly to juice mixture. Bring to a full rolling boil and boil for one minute, stirring constantly. Remove from heat and skim off any foam with a metal spoon. Fill jars immediately to ⅛ inch of tops. Wipe jar rims and threads with a damp cloth. Cover quickly with lids and screw bands on tightly.

SAND PEAR PRESERVES

*P*ear trees are extremely hardy and will survive many years with absolutely no care. Sometimes, a pear tree and the remnants of an old chimney are the only evidence of prior inhabitance. Pear preserves in the South are made with Keiffer pears or what we call "Sand Pears". They are hard and crisp like an apple and hold up better for preserving. If it has been a wet summer, adding water to the recipe may not be necessary.

1 gallon sand pears, peeled, cored and sliced thin	**3 cups sugar** **¼ cup water**

Place pears in a large heavy bottomed pot. Cover with sugar and add water. Cook over low heat until moisture is drawn from fruit. Increase heat to medium and bring to a boil. Taste and add more sugar if needed. Reduce heat to low and cook until the pears change color and syrup is slightly thickened. Fill jars immediately to an eighth inch of tops. Wipe jar rims and threads. Cover quickly with lids. Screw bands on tightly.

SCUPPERNONG JAM

*S*ir John Hopkins visited Fort Caroline, the French outpost at the mouth of the St. Johns River, in 1564. The English seafarer reported that the colonists had produced 20 hogsheads of wine from the native grapes. Scuppernongs are also called muscadines. They are thick-skinned grapes that are very fragrant and sweet, and either bronze or a deep purple.

1 gallon Scuppernongs	**3 cups sugar**

Wash scuppernongs and drain. Squeeze and separate the pulp from the skins into two heavy bottomed pots. Cook pulp, for 10-15 minutes over low heat, stirring occasionally. Place pulp in a sieve and stir with a wooden spoon to separate seeds from pulp. Discard seeds, combine pulp and juice with hulls. There should be enough liquid in bottom of pot to keep grapes from scorching, if not, add a fourth-a half cup of water. Cook over low heat for 20-30 minutes or until hulls are tender. Reduce heat if needed and stir occasionally. To each cupful, add three fourths cup of sugar and bring to a boil, stirring frequently, until juice becomes noticeably thicker, about 10-20 minutes. Fill canning jars immediately to an eighth inch of tops. Wipe jar rims and threads. Cover quickly with lids. Screw bands on tightly.

CORNCOB JELLY

Corncobs were used for many things by the early farmers. They could be handles for tools, corncob pipes and stoppers for jugs. Sometimes they could even be found in the outhouse when the Sears and Roebuck Catalogue ran out. Innovative parents would shape toys and dolls from the corncobs and shucks. Social events sometimes evolved around the shucking and shelling of the dried corn. We have heard it told that around Westville someone even came up with a beverage made from corn. But you didn't hear that from me cause I ain't one to gossip.

This recipe is even another use for the versatile corncob.

12 medium red corncobs, freshly picked and corn removed
2 quarts water
1¼ ounce package powdered pectin
3 cups sugar

Wash the corncobs and cut into 4 inch lengths. Put into large pot, add water and bring to a boil. Reduce heat and boil slowly for 40 minutes. Strain the juice. Measure 3 cups of juice into a large container. Add the pectin and bring to a boil. Add the sugar, bring to boil and boil 5 minutes. Skim and pour into canning jars, wipe rims with damp cloth, seal and screw bands on tightly.

Portable Moonshine Still, St Johns County, c 1920's.

Appetizers and Tailgate Food

The World's Original Alligator Farm established in 1893, c 1940's.

Apalachicola Oysters on
  the Half-Shell, 86
Oyster Dipping Sauce, 86
Oysters Andy Jackson, 87
Original Oysters Rockefeller, 87
Oysters Rock-A-Damn-Feller, 88
Oysters Wakulla, 89
Oysters Bienville, 90
Oyster Kabobs, 91
Black Tip Shark Kabobs, 91
Grilled Gator Tail, 92
Stuffed Artichokes, 92
Marinated Calico Scallops, 93
Parmesan Cheese Toast, 93
Bern's Steak Tartare, 94
Rabbit Liver Pate, 94
Garfish Balls, 95
Sauce Dijon, 95

Choctawhatchee Bay
  Smoked Mullet, 96
Smoked Mullet Dip, 96
Artichoke Dip, 96
Avocado Dip, 97
Bean Dip, 97
Spicy Cheese Dip, 98
Jewel's Tailgate Dip, 98
Crab Stuffed Mushrooms, 98
Bubba's Beer Cheese, 99
Fried Mozzarella Cheese, 99
Panhandle Pickled Shrimp, 99
Shrimp Remoulade in
  Avocado Shell, 100
Shrimp Toast, 100
Seared Scallops with
  Peanutty Sauce, 101
Tuna Ring with Almonds, 101
Campbell's Shrimp Ring, 102
7 Seas Shrimp Cocktail, 102

The Sand Fleas'
  Stuffed Shrimp, 103
Conch Fritters, 104
Key Lime Sauce, 104
Kapok Tree Corn Fritters, 105
Stone Crab Claws, 105
Stone Crab Mustard Sauce, 105
Our Favorite Sandwiches, 106-107
A Dozen Deviled Eggs, 108
Scottish Eggs, 108
A Peck of Pickled Peaches, 109
Ice-Box Pickles, 109
Green Tomato Pickles, 110
Bread and Butter Pickles, 110
Watermelon Rind Pickles, 111
Mango Chutney, 111
Datil Pepper Jelly, 112
Prickly Pear Jam, 112

APPETIZERS AND TAILGATE FOOD

Appetizers are served to calm hunger and whet the appetite. They can be served as hors d'oeuvres, first courses, or for outdoor meals and highlight some of Florida's best seasonal flavors. Appetizers are more common in restaurants and at catered parties than in home cooking. Our favorite appetizer has to be the Apalachicola oysters served raw on the half shell or baked in one of the oyster dishes featured in this section. Marinated or fried blue crab claws are also popular as first courses. Crab, shrimp and smoked mullet dips are often served at our table to calm the appetite until the main course arrives. Delicious Gulf shrimp are served boiled, grilled, barbecued or pickled, and are usually accompanied by a tangy dipping sauce. Unique dishes such as stone crab claws, grilled gator tail and garfish balls are interesting additions and are very tasty.

It doesn't take much of an excuse for the local folks to get together and have a party. Often, the events are centered around some sort of food in season. In the good ol' summer time we really take advantage of the warm weather and have many crab and shrimp boils down at the beaches and bays. These usually end with natures perfect dessert the watermelon.

In the autumn, peanut boils and oyster roasts are popular social events. They're typically held over an open fire which also helps take the chill off the crisp fall air. These roasts and boils are held in an open area and pick-up trucks are parked around the fire so the tailgates can be used for tables and seats. Tailgates also make a handy oyster bar when out hunting.

For decades, in November, many good folks from towns like Fargo, Hahira, Cairo, and Metter, Georgia meet up with some other good folks from towns like Two Egg, Sopchoppy, Steinhatchee and Spuds, Florida. The location would be the parking lots of the Gator Bowl in Jacksonville. The event is the annual Florida-Georgia football game or the "World's Largest Outdoor Cocktail Party" as it is also known. The topics of conversation would be the weather, the price of oranges and onions and oh yes, the integrity of the opposing football team might also be mentioned.

The main event is the game, but the mood is to eat, drink and party. Tailgates and card tables are laden with chips and dips, salads and vegetables, homemade pickles, buckets full of fried chicken, barbecue and maybe a beer or two.

The infamous "Time Out" game. The last Florida Georgia game played in the old Gator Bowl, c 1993.

After the game a winner is declared and bragging rights for a whole year begin. Then everyone sits in the parking lot finishing up the last of the chicken, potato salad and talking about "you just wait till next year."

APPETIZERS AND TAILGATE FOOD

Barbecues are popular year round, but especially in the fall and winter when wild game is available to cook over black jack oak coals. Apalachicola oysters are sometimes served on the half shell to the guests as they wait for the main course to cook. Next venison or wild boar sausages are grilled over coals until done, then sliced and served with Sauce Dijon. Marinated dove breast wrapped in smoked bacon and grilled medium rare are the next course, smoked ribs and shoulders from wild boars are the main courses served with side dishes of potato salad, slaw, baked beans and finished with a big ol' peach cobbler.

In the spring, the woods of North Florida are alive with the blooms of millions of dogwood trees, honeysuckle and mountain laurel bushes, and delicate wildflowers scattered along the country roads. This is one of our favorite times to get out of the house and enjoy the fresh air, as well as a picnic with food we enjoy: fried chicken, always, along with an assortment of sandwiches, deviled eggs, homemade pickles, and a couple of desserts. Soon we have another family memory, hopefully some great pictures for the family album, and a bouquet of wild flowers that fade all too soon.

North Florida picnic, c 1898.

APALACHICOLA OYSTERS ON THE HALF-SHELL

Our Apalachicola oysters are savored by connoisseurs everywhere as some of the tastiest oysters in the world. We prefer them raw or "on the half shell" as it is called by the local oyster bars.

If they are salty, and they usually are, we typically eat the first dozen or so with just a shot of lemon juice or hot sauce. Then we like to mix a lot of horseradish with a little cocktail sauce for variety and put a little dab on each oyster or a dash of Datil "Bottled Hell" Pepper Sauce to liven things up. Oyster Dipping Sauce is also delicious on raw oysters. No side dishes are served except saltine crackers. The usual drink of choice is ice cold champagne, (champagne of bottled beer that is) or a R. C. Cola. You can eat oysters all year round now, but we still prefer them in the "R" months when the weather is cool.

My husband likes to keep a few dozen iced down in the back of his truck when he is out hunting. He used to complain a lot about the price, which seemed to go up each year. Back in 1993, we visited our daughter, Cameron, who works in New York City. We took her to lunch and she ordered a half-dozen Apalachicola oysters. The check was $18.00, $3.00 each. I haven't heard my husband complain lately about the price of local oysters.

OYSTER DIPPING SAUCE

We got this basic recipe from Yano, the owner of several Japanese restaurants in Jacksonville. We have added a few new ingredients over the years.

- **1 cup rice vinegar**
- **2 teaspoons sugar**
- **2 tablespoons lemon juice**
- **1 teaspoon black pepper**
- **4 tablespoons tamari**
- **4 tablespoons mirin**
- **1 tablespoon chili garlic sauce**

Mix all ingredients and chill. Serve over raw oysters on the half shell.

If your oysters aren't salty enough simply sprinkle with salt 10 minutes before serving.

Harvesting oysters from the Apalachicola Bay, c 1940's.

OYSTERS ANDY JACKSON

When the interior of West Florida was settled in the 1820's Andy Jackson and his Tennessee Volunteers came through and captured the hostile Indians from Georgia who had been raiding and stealing the settlers livestock. His reward was being named the first Governor of Florida.

Serves 4

- 2 dozen large select oysters (shucked with deeper half of shell reserved)
- 1 recipe Crabmeat Lafitte
- 1 recipe Béarnaise Sauce
- Lemon juice
- Paprika

Place oysters in smoker and smoke until edges slightly curl. Remove to a baking sheet, sprinkle each oyster with a few drops of lemon juice, a dollop of Crabmeat Lafitte (see page 75), a dollop of Béarnaise Sauce (see page 75). Sprinkle with paprika and place under broiler until glazed.

THE ORIGINAL OYSTERS ROCKEFELLER

This appears to be the original recipe as created by Jules Alciatore at Antoines restaurant in New Orleans around 1900. Because it was such a rich dish it was named after John D. Rockefeller, the richest man alive at the time.

Serves 4

- 4 sprigs Italian parsley
- 4 scallions
- ½ cup celery leaves
- 6 fresh tarragon leaves
- 6 fresh chervil leaves
- ½ cup bread crumbs
- 1½ sticks unsalted butter
- Salt and pepper, to taste
- Tabasco, to taste
- 2 tablespoons Herbsaint
- Rock salt
- 24 oysters on half shell

Mince first five ingredients as finely as possible or put into food processor. Add bread crumbs and butter and work into smooth paste. Season with salt and pepper, Tabasco and Herbsaint. Place oysters on rock salt in baking pan, spoon equal amount of paste on each oyster. Broil 4-5 minutes until edges curl. Serve at once.

OYSTERS ROCK-A-DAMN-FELLER

Our friend Sally, who hails from Georgia, renamed this classic New Orleans dish one night after a "Champagne Dinner" at the now closed Green Turtle Restaurant in Southside Jacksonville. We can't remember why she renamed it but have called it by this name ever since.

The Green Turtle like the Steer Room, Green Derby, Stricklands, Le Chateau and many other great supper clubs have unfortunately faded away to be replaced by franchised food restaurants.

Since the original recipe was such a big secret, we had to create our own Rock-a-damn-feller from several New Orleans restaurant versions.

John D. Rockefeller at his winter home in Ormand Beach, c 1930s.

Serves 4

- 2 dozen large select oysters, shucked with 12 of the deeper shells and oyster liquid reserved
- Clam juice
- ½ cup green onions
- ½ cup celery
- ½ cup parsley
- 10 ounces spinach chopped
- ½ cup unsalted butter
- ⅓ cup all-purpose flour
- 10 anchovies, finely minced
- ¼ teaspoon cayenne pepper
- Salt to taste
- ¼ cup Pernod
- ½ tablespoon Lemon juice
- Rock salt

Preheat oven 400 degrees. Place rock salt to a depth of a half inch in four 8 inch pie pans. Place pans in oven to heat. If there is less than one and a half cups reserved oyster liquid, make up difference with clam juice. Drain and squeeze the spinach completely dry. Place onions, celery, parsley and spinach in food processor, pulse until finely minced. In a large saucepan, melt butter over medium-low heat. Add garlic, stir in flour and mix, using a whisk to keep any lumps from forming. Cook, stirring constantly for 3 minutes, do not allow flour to brown. Add oyster-clam liquor slowly, cooking and stirring constantly to keep mixture smooth. Stir in anchovies, cayenne pepper and spinach mixture. Reduce heat to low and cook, stirring occasionally, for 3-5 minutes. Remove from heat and stir in Pernod and lemon juice, taste for seasonings. Place oyster shells in heated rock salt, pressing to imbed. Place 2 oysters in each shell, sprinkle with salt if needed and spoon sauce over the oysters. Bake in middle of oven for 15 minutes or until sauce is bubbly, then slide them under a hot broiler to brown.

OYSTERS WAKULLA

*T*he late Ed Ball controlled the vast DuPont holdings based in Jacksonville, which once included a large chain of banks and over a million acres of timberland located mostly in North Florida. He is credited with buying and preserving the natural beauty of Wakulla Springs, which is now a state park located south of Tallahassee.

We named this original rich dish in honor of North Florida's own rich celebrity.

- 2 dozen large select oysters, shucked with deeper half of shell and liquid reserved
- ½ cup green onions, chopped fine
- 3 tablespoons unsalted butter
- ½ cup Smithfield ham, chopped fine
- 3 tablespoons Pernod
- 1 cup cooked mustard or turnips greens
- 1-1 ½ cups White sauce
- 6 tablespoons Parmesan cheese, freshly grated
- Salt and freshly ground black pepper, to taste
- Rock salt

Preheat oven 350 degrees. Spread rock salt to a depth of about a half inch in four 8 inch pie pans. Place in oven to heat for 10 minutes while you prepare oysters. In a heavy skillet, sauté green onions in butter over medium-low heat until softened. Add ham and cook for 1 minute. Remove as much liquid as possible from cooked mustard or turnips and chop. Stir in greens and Pernod and remove from heat. Combine 4 tablespoons Parmesan cheese with white sauce and add to spinach. Taste and add salt and pepper. Remove rock salt from oven and place deeper oyster shell in salt, pressing on shell to imbed in salt. Add 2 drained oysters to each shell. Cover each oyster with the spinach sauce. Sprinkle with remaining Parmesan cheese. Bake in middle of oven for 15 minutes, then slide them under a hot broiler to brown the tops, if desired.

Ed Ball. "Confusion to the enemy" was his favorite toast, c 1965.

OYSTERS BIENVILLE

*I*f you live in an area where oysters in the shell are hard to find, pick up some oyster shells the next time you visit an oyster bar, then wash and store them. The shells may be reused using oysters from the super market for these oyster appetizers.

When you combine salty Apalachicola oysters with some country smoked bacon and fresh gulf shrimp, you get a combination of flavors that is out of this world. Serve this dish often and at any special occasion.

Serves 6

- 3 dozen large select oysters, shucked with deeper half of shell and liquid reserved.
- 6 slices smoked bacon, cut into small pieces, drippings reserved
- 4 tablespoons unsalted butter
- ½ cup green onions, chopped
- 1 tablespoon garlic, minced
- 1 pound mushrooms, chopped fine
- ⅔ cup all-purpose flour
- 1 cup evaporated milk
- ½ cup sherry
- 1 cup reserved oyster liquid, add clam juice to make one cup
- 2 tablespoons lemon juice
- ¼ cup parsley, chopped
- 1½ pounds raw shrimp chopped fine
- Salt to taste
- ½ teaspoon cayenne pepper, or to taste
- 4 egg yolks, beaten
- ½ cup Parmesan cheese, freshly grated
- ½ cup French bread crumbs
- ½ teaspoon paprika
- Rock salt

Preheat oven 400 degrees. Spread rock salt to a depth of about a half inch in four 8 inch pie pans. Place pans in oven to heat for 10 minutes. Heat a large skillet over medium heat, cook bacon until crisp and set aside. Add butter to bacon drippings. Add green onions, garlic and mushrooms to skillet, cook 2 minutes. Sprinkle flour in and stir to keep smooth, cook 5 minutes. Gradually add milk, stirring constantly to keep lumps from forming, cook 3 minutes. Add sherry, oyster liquid, and lemon juice, continue stirring until blended and smooth. Add parsley and shrimp, cook 1 minute. Remove from heat and add bacon, salt, pepper and egg yolks, mixing thoroughly. Place shells in heated rock salt, pressing to imbed. Place 2 oysters in each shell, lightly salt if oysters aren't salty and top with sauce. Mix Parmesan cheese, bread crumbs and paprika together and sprinkle over oysters. Bake in middle of oven 15 minutes, or until heated thoroughly. Slide them under the broiler until tops are golden brown. Serve at once.

OYSTER KABOBS

*T*his is a marvelous way to cook oysters shish kabob style. A perfect appetizer for a seafood dinner finish with a lemon meringue pie.

Serves 6

10 slices smoked bacon
36 Apalachicola oysters, freshly shucked
½ cup all-purpose flour
Salt and freshly ground black pepper, to taste
2 eggs, beaten
2 cups cracker meal
Peanut oil for deep frying
2 teaspoons parsley, minced
Lemon wedges
6 wooden skewers, soaked in water

Cut bacon into one and one half inch pieces and cook over medium-low heat in a cast-iron skillet until edges are brown, but not crisp. Remove and drain on paper towels. Pat oysters dry with paper towels. Alternate on skewers with bacon. Dredge in flour seasoned with salt and pepper, dip in beaten eggs and roll in cracker meal. Heat oil to 350-375 degrees and fry oysters and bacon for 3 minutes or until lightly brown on both sides. Remove and drain on metal wire rack. Sprinkle with parsley and serve with lemon wedges.

BLACK TIP SHARK KABOBS

*O*ur neighbor Robert (Bert) Schur keeps us supplied with black tip shark he catches in the surf. He paddles a kayak out past the waves and drops the bait in the deep water. Then he quickly paddles back to shore.

Serves 6-8

3 shark steaks 1 inch thick
Mojo Sauce
Lime wedges
Wooden skewers, soaked in water

Cut steaks in bite size pieces, place in a large ziplock bag with Mojo sauce (see page 259) and marinate for 30 minutes. Thread on wooden skewers and grill over hot coals until done. Serve with lime wedges and Tartar Sauce (see page 207).

Bert the Shark killer, c 2000.

APPETIZERS AND TAILGATE FOOD

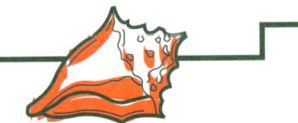

GRILLED GATOR TAIL

The wetlands of Florida provide a perfect habitat to a unique creature, the American alligator. Early wildlife attractions like the St. Augustine Alligator Farm, founded in 1893, discovered that the alligator would successfully breed and thrive in captivity. Their expertise has been shared amongst other pioneering farmers and today over thirty Florida farms raise alligators from egg to adult. Lucky for us several alligator farms sell the meat already cleaned, which is good news to anyone who has ever cleaned a gator before.

Serves 6

- 2 pounds young gator tail, sliced thin
- 1 cup dry white wine
- 2 cloves garlic, minced
- 2 tablespoons olive oil
- 1 teaspoon salt and black pepper, freshly ground
- 2 tablespoons lemon juice

Mix ingredients in glass container and marinate gator tail 2-3 hours. Grill gator tail over hot coals and serve immediately with lemon slices.

STUFFED ARTICHOKES

Serves 4

- 4 large artichokes
- 3 tablespoons olive oil
- 1½ cups onion, finely chopped
- 2 cloves garlic, minced
- ½ bell pepper, finely chopped
- 1½ cups bread crumbs
- Salt and freshly ground black pepper, to taste
- ½ cup chicken stock
- 1 cup grated Parmesan
- ½ pound shrimp, peeled, and cut into 3-4 pieces

Cut the stem off the artichoke so it will sit flat. Cut the top 1 inch off the artichoke and cut the sharp tips of the leaves down about a half inch. Rub the cut places with half of a lemon to keep it from discoloring. Steam the artichokes until tender, about 20 minutes. Remove from steamer and use a spoon to scoop out the fuzzy choke in the center, set aside. Heat the olive oil in a cast-iron skillet over medium heat. Add the onions and cook stirring for 2-3 minutes. Add the garlic and bell pepper and cook for 7-8 minutes. Stir the shrimp in and cook for 1 minute. Remove from heat. Add the bread crumbs and season with salt and pepper. Stuff the center of the artichoke with the bread crumb mixture and between the leaves, pushing the stuffing down toward the bottom. Sprinkle artichoke with additional olive oil and Parmesan cheese. Pour the chicken broth around them in a baking dish and place in a preheated 350 degree oven for 20 minutes. Serve with Vegetable Dipping Sauce.

APPETIZERS AND TAILGATE FOOD

MARINATED CALICO SCALLOPS

Scallops thrive in the bays around Panama City and Pensacola. They tend to congregate and hide in areas with grassy bottoms. The best way to catch them is using a snorkel, diving mask and small net sack. You have to be quick because they can propel themselves out of reach with a squirt of water. Only the tiny muscle which opens and closes the shell is edible, so it takes about a wash tub full of bay scallops to yield enough meat for a meal.

Our daughter, Cameron loves scallops no matter how they are served. This is an easy appetizer and always a hit with everyone. Summer is an ideal time for this cool, refreshing dish.

Serves 4

1 pound bay scallops
2 tablespoons fresh lime juice
½ tablespoon green onions, minced
1½ tablespoons lemon juice
1 teaspoon Dijon mustard,
6 tablespoons olive oil
Salt and freshly ground black pepper, to taste

1 teaspoon capers
4 Kalamata olives
1 tablespoon parsley, minced
2 medium summer tomatoes, cut into wedges
1 Florida avocado cut into 8 wedges
1 head of Boston lettuce

Slice scallops in half across the grain. Toss in a bowl with lime juice and onions, salt lightly, cover with plastic wrap and refrigerate at least one hour. In a bowl, whisk the lemon juice and mustard together, add the salt and pepper, and slowly add olive oil in a stream. Add capers, olives, parsley, tomatoes, and avocado to dressing and gently toss, set aside to marinate 15 minutes. Place lettuce on individual salad plates, arrange scallops, tomatoes and avocado slices on top. Whisk the marinade again and drizzle over all. Serve chilled with Parmesan cheese toast.

PARMESAN CHEESE TOAST

1 Loaf French bread
1 stick unsalted butter
2 cloves garlic, finely minced

¼ cup fresh dill
½ cup Parmesan cheese, freshly grated

Preheat oven 375 degrees. Place butter in a bowl, add garlic, dill, and Parmesan cheese, stir until creamy. Slice bread lengthwise, spread butter mixture on bread and cut into 1 inch thick slices. Bake 5-8 minutes or until golden. Serve immediately.

BERN'S STEAK TARTARE

Bern's Steak House, located in Tampa, is one of the premier steak houses in the nation. They age beef five to eight weeks, cut, trim and weigh to individual order and grill the meat over charcoal. They also roast and grind their own coffee daily, make their own ice cream, use pesticide-free greens and vegetables organically grown on their own farm.

This dish is for folks who like their beef really rare.

Serves 4-2 ounce servings

- 5 ½ ounce steak, as fresh, lean and red as possible
- 4 tablespoons shallots (finely chopped)
- 2 tablespoons green pepper (peeled and finely chopped)
- 2 tablespoons red wine mixture (80% red wine/20% cream sherry)
- ¼ teaspoon salt
- ⅛ teaspoon freshly ground black pepper
- 1 egg yolk
- 4 celery strips (for garnish)
- 4 onion slices (for garnish)
- Parsley (for garnish)
- 1 teaspoon fine herbs (Spice Island)

Hand-chop steak into small pieces, removing any strains of fat or gristle. Chop shallots and green pepper into steak so that steak is chopped a second time—or put into food processor 7 seconds. Add other ingredients except for garnish and blend well (do not purée). Garnish with celery strips, onion slices and parsley. Serve with toast.

RABBIT LIVER PATÉ

Serves 8

- ¾ pound rabbit livers
- ½ cup shallots, sliced thin,
- 1 clove garlic, sliced thin
- 2 bay leaves, crumbled
- ¼ teaspoon thyme, crumbled
- ¼ teaspoon allspice
- 3 tablespoons Calvados
- ¾ cup water
- 2 teaspoon Kosher salt
- ¾ cup unsalted butter cut into tablespoons
- ¼ cup heavy cream

In a small boiler combine the livers, shallots, garlic, bay leaves, thyme, allspice, 2 tablespoons of the calvados, water and 1 teaspoon salt. Bring to a boil, reduce heat and simmer for 5 minutes. Remove from heat and let stand 10 minutes. Drain, reserving the liquid. Remove the bay leaves and discard. Place the mixture in a food processor and puree. With the motor running add the butter a tablespoon at the time. Add the remaining salt, pepper to taste, the cream and remaining tablespoon of calvados. Blend well. Spoon into a three-fourths cup serving bowl and chill, covered for 2 hours.

GARFISH BALLS

Garfish are found in the rivers and lakes along the Gulf Coast. These prehistoric looking fish are considered predators and are often killed because of this. The gator gar can reach 10 feet in length and is one of the largest fresh water fish.

The fish are encased in an armor of diamond shaped, thick enamel scales. William Bartram, in his travels through Florida in 1774, noted the native Indians were utilizing the Gar scale as points for their arrows. These scales were once collected by local fisherman and sold to Sears, Roebuck and Company who made them into buttons. Today they are collected by Gartec (my sisters and me) and used in making Christmas ornaments, we sell down at the Emerald Coast.

Poinsettia ornament handmade with sand dollar and garfish scales, c 1999.

Serves 6

- 2 pounds garfish meat, ground
- 1 pound potatoes, boiled and mashed
- 1 large onion, finely chopped
- 1/3 cup fresh parsley, minced
- 1/3 cup celery, minced
- 1/3 cup green onions, minced
- 2 teaspoons garlic, minced
- Salt and freshly ground black pepper, to taste
- Tabasco to taste
- 1 cup Sauce Dijon
- 1 cup all-purpose flour
- Vegetable oil for deep fat frying

Cut garfish down the back and remove the meat using a spoon or fork. In a large bowl mix garfish, potatoes, onion, garlic, parsley, celery, green onions, salt, pepper and Tabasco thoroughly. Shape into one and one half inch balls, roll in flour. Deep fat fry until golden. Drain on metal wire rack and serve at once with Sauce Dijon.

SAUCE DIJON

- 2 tablespoons unsalted butter
- 2 tablespoons all-purpose flour
- 1 cup rich chicken stock
- 1 tablespoon lemon juice
- 2 tablespoons Dijon mustard
- Salt and freshly ground black pepper, to taste

Melt butter in saucepan over medium-low heat. Stir in flour until blended, stir constantly and cook 2 minutes. Add chicken stock and stir until well combined. Cook, stirring, until thickened. Add lemon juice, mustard, salt and pepper. Cool, stirring occasionally to prevent film from forming.

CHOCTAWHATCHEE BAY SMOKED MULLET

Rinse mullet and dry with paper towels. Slice mullet along backbone, leaving ¼ inch hinge along dorsal fin so that mullet can be opened like a book. Leave scales on. Douse flesh side of fish with Worcestershire, red pepper sauce and a shot of Tabasco. Salt and pepper generously. Use green hickory or hickory chips for smoke. Place flesh up in hot smoker. Smoke for 8-10 hours. Check after 4 hours to make sure mullet is cooking evenly, it should be watched closely. Fish cooks in its own oils, comes out brown, moist and deliciously smokey.

Trey with catch of the day, fresh mullet, c 1984.

SMOKED MULLET DIP

- 1 pound smoked fish, such as mullet, grouper, dolphin or 3-4 ounces smoked clams, chopped
- 8 ounces cream cheese
- 1 cup sour cream
- ⅓ cup green onions, chopped fine
- ¼ cup mayonnaise
- ½ teaspoon Tabasco sauce
- 1 teaspoon Worcestershire
- Lemon juice, to taste

Remove bones and skin from fish and flake if using mullet. Place cream cheese in food processor and pulse until mixture is creamy. Add sour cream, mayonnaise, Tabasco, Worcestershire, lemon juice and pulse to mix thoroughly. Remove to bowl and add mullet and green onions. If too thick, add more sour cream or whipping cream. Refrigerate 2-3 hours before serving. Sprinkle with chopped parsley and serve with saltine crackers.

ARTICHOKE DIP

Serves 10-12

- 1-14 ounce can artichoke hearts, drained and finely chopped
- 1 clove garlic, mashed
- ½ teaspoon salt
- 1 cup Hellmann's mayonnaise
- 1 cup Parmesan cheese, freshly grated
- ½ Datil pepper, minced
- 1 tablespoon parsley, minced
- Juice of half a lemon

Mix all ingredients together and place in a shallow baking dish, bake 350 degrees for 15 minutes. Serve with your favorite crackers and chips.

AVOCADO DIP
"Guacamole"

*R*ipe avocados have a buttery texture and a nutty flavor. An avocado is ripe when it yields all over to very gentle pressure. Makes 1 cup.

- 1 ripe avocado, peeled and pitted
- 1 teaspoon fresh lemon juice
- 1 tablespoon fresh lime juice
- ½ teaspoon salt, or to taste
- ⅛ teaspoon sugar
- ⅛ teaspoon cumin
- ½ teaspoon garlic, minced
- 2 tablespoons sour cream
- 2 tablespoons green onion, minced
- 2 teaspoons Jalapeño pepper, minced and seeded
- 2 tablespoons fresh cilantro, chopped
- 2 tablespoons plum tomatoes, chopped
- Tabasco to taste

Mash the avocado in a bowl using a fork, sprinkle with lime and lemon juice. Add the salt, sugar, cumin, garlic, green onion, Jalapeño pepper, cilantro, tomatoes, sour cream, and Tabasco, mix until blended. Press plastic wrap directly on the surface of the guacamole, removing any air bubbles and chill until ready to serve.

BEAN DIP
"Hummus"

Serves 4

- 1-16 ounce can garbanzo beans, drained
- 3 tablespoons tahini paste
- ¼-½ cup fresh lemon juice, or to taste
- ¼ cup onion, chopped
- ½ teaspoon garlic, chopped
- ⅛ teaspoon cumin
- ½ teaspoon salt
- Pinch of cayenne pepper
- 2 tablespoons olive oil
- 2-3 Jalapeño peppers, finely chopped
- 1 tablespoon parsley, finely minced

Tahini which is made from sesame seed, must be stirred well before using as the oil is usually separated. Place drained garbanzo, reserving a fourth cup of the liquid, sesame paste, lemon juice, onion, cumin, salt, cayenne and 1 tablespoon of the olive oil in a food processor and purée. If a thinner consistency is desired stir in reserved liquid from garbanzo beans, a tablespoon at the time. Stir in the Jalapeno pepper. Place in a small bowl, cover with remaining olive oil and sprinkle with parsley. Serve with wedges of Pita bread.

SPICY CHEESE DIP

2 pounds ground sausage
2 pounds processed cheese
5-6 jigs tabasco
1 can Ro-Tel diced tomatoes
1 can Ro-Tel extra hot tomatoes and chilies

Cook and breakup sausage in a large cast-iron skillet. Remove meat to paper towels to drain. Place all ingredients in a covered casserole dish. Microwave on high for 5 minutes or until cheese has melted. Stir to mix.

JEWEL'S TAILGATE DIP

Serves 12

11 ounces cream cheese
2 tablespoons milk
One 2½ ounce jar dried beef cut into bite-size pieces
1 small onion, grated
Black pepper, to taste
1 teaspoon fresh dill, chopped
1 tablespoon parsley, chopped
1 cup sour cream
1 teaspoon Beau Monde

Mix all ingredients together in a baking dish. Bake 350 degrees for 20 minutes. Serve with pumpernickel bread chunks.

CRAB STUFFED MUSHROOMS

Crabmeat has a delicious and delicate flavor. It is best enjoyed plain or with a light sauce. Unfortunately, the flavor of crab is sometimes overpowered by the other ingredients.

This appetizer lets the taste of crab come through and is always popular for a before the meal treat.

Makes (20-24) 2 inch mushroom caps

20-24 mushroom caps
1 ½ cups fresh crabmeat
2 tablespoons butter
4 tablespoons green onions, finely chopped
1 cup white sauce
Dash of Tabasco
½ teaspoon lemon juice
Salt and white pepper, to taste
2 tablespoons Parmesan cheese, freshly grated

Preheat oven to 350 degrees. Carefully look over crabmeat and remove any cartilage. Melt the butter over medium heat and cook the green onions until they are soft. Stir in the crabmeat and cook until heated through. Add the white sauce (see page 24), Tabasco, lemon juice, salt and pepper, mixing thoroughly. Butter a shallow baking dish large enough to hold the mushroom caps in one layer. Sprinkle the inside of the mushroom caps with salt, spoon in the crab mixture, mounding slightly. Arrange in buttered dish and sprinkle with cheese. Bake in upper third of oven for 10 minutes, place oven on broil and brown tops of mushrooms. Serve immediately.

BUBBA'S BEER CHEESE

10 ounces cheddar cheese, softened
8 ounces cream cheese, softened
1 teaspoon Worcestershire
5-6 jigs Tabasco
4 slices bacon, fried crisp
⅓ cup beer

In a small saucepan add all ingredients except bacon. Stir and cook on low heat 5 minutes or until cheeses have melted. Remove from heat and stir in crumbled bacon.

FRIED MOZZARELLA CHEESE

Serves 4

1 recipe of Marinara sauce
8 ounces whole-milk mozzarella
½ cup plain flour
2 eggs, beaten
2 cups bread crumbs
⅓ cup olive oil

Cut mozzarella into four equal slices. Place flour in a plate, eggs in another plate and bread crumbs in another plate. Flour cheese slices on all sides, shaking off the excess. Dip in the beaten eggs, letting excess drip off, then coat with bread crumbs. Put battered cheese on a rack to dry for 30 minutes. Place oil in heated skillet and cook until golden brown on one side, turn and brown the other side. Place heated Marinara Sauce (see page 229) on serving plate and place fried mozzarella on top. Serve immediately.

PANHANDLE PICKLED SHRIMP

We were very flattered when Sheila Lukins, the co-author of *The Silver Palate Cookbook*, asked for this recipe to include in her *USA Cookbook*.

Serves 20-25

5 pounds medium shrimp, cleaned and deveined
2 medium onions, peeled, cut into ¼ inch slices and separated into rings
4 lemons, cut crosswise into ⅛ inch thick slices
½ cup minced fresh parsley
6 small bay leaves
20 black peppercorns
1 teaspoon each dill seed and mustard seeds
½ teaspoon celery seeds
⅔ cup lemon juice
3 teaspoons salt
1 tablespoon sugar
1 cup olive oil
1 cup vegetable oil

Place all ingredients except shrimp, onions and parsley in a large pan. Bring to a boil and simmer 10 minutes. Add the shelled and deveined Shrimp and cook briefly, simmering for about a minute, or until they turn pink. Remove Shrimp with a slotted spoon; let liquid cool to warm. In a large wide-mouthed glass jar with screw top, layer the shrimp, onion rings and parsley; cover each layer with a little of the liquid. Cover and refrigerate 24-48 hours before serving. Shrimp should keep at least 2 weeks refrigerated.

SHRIMP REMOULADE IN AVOCADO SHELL

*R*emoulade is a traditional French sauce. This version is a Creole adaptation which has a reddish color and a zesty flavor. The combination of shrimp and avocado compliment the sauce, and it is always popular as an appetizer.

Avocados are sometimes called alligator pears in the local markets.

Serves 4

- 2 ripe avocados
- 1 pound boiled large shrimp, peeled and chilled
- 3 green onions
- 3 sprigs parsley,
- 2 ribs celery
- 2 tablespoons Creole mustard
- 4 tablespoons olive oil
- 1 tablespoon lemon juice
- ¾ teaspoon paprika
- Salt and freshly ground black pepper, to taste

Place green onions, parsley, celery, mustard, olive oil, lemon juice and paprika in food processor. Pulse until vegetables are finely minced and all ingredients are thoroughly mixed. Chill in a covered dish. Cut shrimp in 2-3 pieces, chill until ready to use. Cut avocados in half and remove seed.

Place shrimp in avocado halves, spoon remoulade sauce on top and serve.

SHRIMP TOAST

Makes 24

- ½ pound shrimp, minced
- 1 egg white
- 4 teaspoons cornstarch
- 1 teaspoon rice wine
- ¾ teaspoon salt
- 6 slices light bread, crust removed
- 1 teaspoon sesame seeds, toasted
- 1 ounce Smithfield ham, minced
- 2 dozen fresh cilantro leaves, minced
- Peanut oil

Combine shrimp, egg white, cornstarch, wine, salt and pepper. Stir until well combined, set aside. In a cast-iron skillet heat 1 inch of oil until 350 degrees. Cut bread into 24 triangles. Spread 1 teaspoon of shrimp mixture on each triangle. Sprinkle with sesame seeds, ham and cilantro. Press into bread. Deep fry until golden on both sides. Drain on paper towels and serve immediately.

SEARED SCALLOPS WITH PEANUTTY SAUCE

Serves 8

¼ cup creamy peanut butter
2 tablespoons chicken broth
2 tablespoons rice wine vinegar
1 tablespoon soy sauce
1 tablespoon vegetable oil
1 ½ teaspoons sugar
2 teaspoons ginger, finely minced
2 teaspoons chili sauce
1 clove garlic, finely minced
2 green onions, thinly sliced
1 tablespoon dry-roasted peanuts, chopped
4 tablespoon cilantro leaves
12 sea scallops
2 teaspoons sugar
½ teaspoon olive oil

Whisk together first 11 ingredients in a small bowl, an hour before serving, and set aside.

Pat scallops dry with paper towel. Heat a medium-large cast-iron skillet over medium-high heat. Sprinkle scallops with sugar on each side. Add oil to skillet and swirl to coat the bottom. Sear scallops on both sides until golden brown. Ladle sauce over scallops, sprinkle with cilantro and serve.

TUNA RING WITH ALMONDS

Serves 12

2 envelopes unflavored gelatin
½ cup cold water
1 cup boiling water
2 -8 ounce packages cream cheese, softened
2 tablespoons lemon juice
1 tablespoon curry powder
¾ teaspoon salt
¼ teaspoon garlic powder
½ cup green onions, finely chopped
1 roasted red bell pepper, diced
½ cup celery, finely diced
2 tablespoons parsley, minced
2-6 ounce cans Solid White Albacore tuna, drained
1 ¼ cups sliced almonds, lightly toasted

Sprinkle gelatin over a half cup cold water, stir and let stand 1 minute. Add 1 cup boiling water, and stir until gelatin dissolves. Add cream cheese, beat on low speed with electric mixer until blended. Add lemon juice, curry powder, salt and garlic powder, beating until blended. Stir onions, red bell pepper, celery, tuna and a half cup almonds into the cheese mixture. Stir into a 1 quart mold lined with plastic wrap. Chill 3 hours. Unmold onto serving dish. Press remaining almonds into mixture and serve with crackers.

APPETIZERS AND TAILGATE FOOD

CAMPBELL'S SHRIMP RING

As you have probably guessed, we are not big on recipes using canned soups. We are including this one because it's an old family favorite. The finished dish has a beautiful shrimp color and a welcome addition to any buffet style meal.

Campbell's Shrimp Ring may be made a couple of days in advance.

Serves 8-10

- 10¾ ounce can Campbell's tomato soup
- 2 tablespoons gelatin
- 3 - 3 ½ ounce packages cream cheese, softened,
- 1 cup mayonnaise
- ¾ cup green onions, chopped fine
- 1 teaspoon lemon juice
- ½ cup celery, chopped fine
- 1 tablespoon parsley, minced
- 1½ pounds boiled shrimp cut into 3-4 pieces
- Parsley, for garnish

Heat soup to boiling, remove from heat and add gelatin and cream cheese. Beat with mixer until creamy. Add mayonnaise, green onions, celery and shrimp. Mix thoroughly, place in mold and chill until set. To remove, run knife around top of mold to loosen, turn upside down on serving platter and place hot towels over bottom of mold. Garnish with parsley and serve with crackers.

7 SEAS SHRIMP COCKTAIL

For each cocktail place lettuce in bottom and sides of cocktail glasses, then place 6 or more jumbo boiled shrimp on edge of glasses. Spoon a large dollop of cocktail sauce into center of glass. Serve cold. Garnish with lemon slices.

Florida Department of Agriculture Cocktail Sauce

- ½ cup chili sauce
- ¼ cup horseradish
- 1 teaspoon Worcestershire
- 1 teaspoon onion, minced
- ½ teaspoon salt
- ⅛ teaspoon freshly ground black pepper
- 2 dashes hot pepper sauce
- 1 tablespoon vinegar
- 1 teaspoon celery seed
- 1 teaspoon celery salt
- 2 tablespoons sugar
- ½ teaspoon garlic salt

Mix and refrigerate so flavors blend.

THE SAND FLEAS' STUFFED SHRIMP

*T*he Sand Flea Restaurant formerly located on Okaloosa Island served this dish until the restaurant burned around 1990. Fortunately we were able to get the recipe to share with you. Shrimp may be broiled or deep-fried.

Serves 4-6

- 24 jumbo shrimp
- 12 smoked bacon strips, cut in half
- Crabmeat stuffing (below)
- 24 toothpicks, soaked in water
- 1 cup bread crumbs, seasoned with ¼ teaspoon Old Bay
- ½ cup all-purpose flour
- 1 egg, lightly beaten
- ¼ cup evaporated milk
- Vegetable oil for deep frying
- Lemon wedges
- 1 tablespoon parsley, minced

Crabmeat stuffing:

- 1 pound crabmeat
- 1 teaspoon Worcestershire
- 4 dashes Tabasco
- Salt and pepper, to taste
- 2 tablespoons Hellmann's mayonnaise
- 1 teaspoon Creole mustard
- 6 green onions, minced
- ½ bell pepper (red or green), minced
- 2 tablespoons butter
- 3 tablespoons lemon juice

Sauté onion and pepper in butter. Add remaining ingredients and mix well.

To broil:

Peel shrimp leaving the tail on, devein and split shrimp lengthwise forming a pocket. Place 1 tablespoon crabmeat stuffing in each pocket and wrap with bacon strip and secure with toothpick. Place shrimp in pan and drizzle with melted butter and dry sherry. Broil, turning to cook both sides. Cook until bacon is crisp.

To deep-fry:

Mix egg and evaporated milk in a large bowl. Roll shrimp in flour, shaking off the excess. Dip in egg wash and roll in bread crumbs. Refrigerate for one hour. Deep fry in 375 degree oil until golden brown. Drain on paper towels. Serve with lemon slices and sprinkle with parsley.

Shrimp boats, Apalachicola, c 1920's.

CONCH FRITTERS

Conch is the delicious mollusk we get from the islands and keys. It's rather tough so it's usually beaten or chopped fine. The food processor is ideal for this. Conch Fritters are a very popular appetizer in many Florida restaurants. Batter may be kept for the next day, if there is any left.

Serves 8

- 1 pound conch meat, chopped fine
- 2 eggs, beaten
- 4 cloves garlic
- 1 medium green pepper, seeded
- 1 Datil pepper, seeded, or 1 teaspoon cayenne pepper
- 1 medium white onion, peeled and quartered
- ¼ cup parsley
- 1 cup all-purpose flour
- 1 teaspoon salt
- 1 teaspoon black pepper, freshly ground
- 1 teaspoon baking powder
- 1 teaspoon thyme, crumbled
- ¼ cup whole milk
- Oil for deep frying
- Lemon or lime wedges for garnish

Place conch in food processor with metal blade. Pulse the meat until finely chopped. Place in a large bowl, add beaten eggs and stir. Add the garlic, green pepper, Datil pepper, onion and parsley to work bowl of processor, pulse until finely chopped. Drain the vegetables, in a sieve lined with a paper towel. Add vegetables to the conch and stir to combine. Stir the flour, salt, black pepper, baking powder and thyme together. Combine with conch and stir in milk, mix together to form a thick dough. Cover with plastic wrap and refrigerate until thoroughly chilled, at least 1 hour. Heat oil over medium heat, 350 degrees, drop by the teaspoonful into the hot oil and fry until golden brown. Drain on paper towels and serve immediately with Key Lime Sauce and lemon or lime wedges.

KEY LIME SAUCE

- ½ cup mayonnaise
- 1½ tablespoons whipping cream
- 1 teaspoon parsley, minced
- 2 teaspoons fresh Key lime juice

Combine all ingredients, cover and store in refrigerator until ready to serve.

KAPOK TREE CORN FRITTERS

*U*nfortunately the Kapok Tree Restaurant in Daytona is no longer open. However, they serve a similar fritter at the Dixie Crossroads in Titusville, as well as the best rock shrimp in Florida.

Serves 4-6

- 1 cup all-purpose flour, sifted
- 1 ½ teaspoons baking powder
- 1 tablespoon sugar
- 1 teaspoon salt
- 1 egg
- ¼ cup milk
- ½ cup whole kernel corn
- ½ cup confectioners sugar

Resift flour, baking powder, sugar and salt together. Add milk and corn, stir until well blended. Drop batter by tablespoonfuls into 350 degree oil and cook until brown. Drain on paper towels and sprinkle with confectioners sugar. Serve piping hot.

STONE CRAB CLAWS

*S*tone crabs are harvested in the Gulf of Mexico and along the Atlantic Coast. They live in little boroughs and are caught in traps. The claws are the only edible part, so when the crab is caught, one claw is removed and the crab is released to grow another. The claws are usually cooked as they are caught, so when you buy them at the market they are ready to eat. Serve with melted butter or Stone Crab Mustard Sauce.

Stone Crab

STONE CRAB SAUCE

Makes 1 cup

- 3 ½ teaspoons dry mustard
- 1 cup homemade mayonnaise
- 2 teaspoons Worcestershire sauce
- 1 teaspoon lemon juice
- ⅛ cup whipping cream
- ⅛ teaspoon salt
- ½ tablespoon parsley, minced

Combine mustard and mayonnaise and beat until completely mixed. Add remaining ingredients and beat until creamy.

APPETIZERS AND TAILGATE FOOD

OUR FAVORITE SANDWICHES

*I*n the old days, before the interstate highways and franchise restaurants, eating along the highways was uncertain at best. Eateries were few and far between. The safest bet was to take your next meal along with you. Wayside parks offered tables and benches for outdoor dining along the highways and beaches.

While the Earl of Sandwich might turn up his nose at some of these combinations, they have been enjoyed by our family for several generations.

Earl of Sandwich

PIMENTO CHEESE

Grate 16 ounces extra-sharp Cheddar cheese on coarse side of cheese grater. In medium sized bowl add the cheese, 7 ounce jar of sliced pimentos, drained, a half cup mayonnaise, 1 tablespoon lemon juice, Tabasco to taste and mix thoroughly. Can be used for sandwiches, as a dip, or to stuff celery ribs. Refrigerate if not using immediately. Will keep for 2 weeks refrigerated.

BACON, EGG'N OLIVE

In a medium bowl, mash 6 hard-boiled eggs using a fork. Add a fourth to a half cup mayonnaise, 4 slices crumbled, crisp bacon, a third cup Spanish green olives, sliced, salt and freshly ground black pepper to taste. Mix until yolks are creamy. Serve on rye or white bread.

TOMATO

Slather two slices of Bunny white bread with Hellmann's mayonnaise. Slice a vine ripe tomato and place on bread, sprinkle with salt and freshly ground black pepper. Take the phone off the hook and eat over the sink.

TUNA FISH

Drain liquid from one 6 ounce can of Bumble Bee tuna fish and place fish in a medium bowl. Add a half cup minced celery, 1 minced green onion, a half teaspoon lemon juice, 2 diced hard-boiled eggs, 2 tablespoons cubed pickles, 2-3 tablespoons mayonnaise, a half teaspoon ball park mustard and salt and freshly ground black pepper. Mix thoroughly and spread on bread of choice.

PARKWAY BAR-B-Q

The Parkway drive-in closed for good, then we had to learn how to make our own bar-b-cue sandwiches.
Open a can of Castleberry Bar-b-cue. Spread a couple spoonfuls on a hamburger bun with 5 dill pickle chips and grill until heated. Lynda, this one's for you. Goes great with an ice cold Dr. Pepper.

CAMEL RIDER

Cut a pita bread in half, spread Hellmann's mayonnaise inside pocket. Add sliced ham, cheese and lettuce and tomato or tabbouleh.

APPETIZERS AND TAILGATE FOOD

SISSIFIED CUCUMBER

Soften 4 ounces of cream cheese and mix with 2 tablespoons of homemade mayonnaise. Remove crust from slices of light bread and cut bread into squares, circles or triangles. Spread cream cheese on bread and place thinly sliced cucumber on top. Garnish with fresh dill. Always a hit at the poker games.

BANANA

The hardest part to making a banana sandwich is deciding which way to slice the banana. Some folks prefer to slice it lengthwise and others across the grain to make little rounds. Personally, if you put the correct amount of mayo (lots) on the bread, those little rounds keep sliding out, so we have opted for slicing lengthwise.

PINEAPPLE

Again, white bread and lots of mayo is the key here. Use three slices of canned pineapple and connect like a pretzel. No slipping and sliding—peeking and hiding.

SARDINE

Mash the contents of one can of sardines. Mix with a dollop of mayonnaise, juice of a half lemon, a jig of Tabasco, slice one hard boiled egg. Spread on white bread, top with a slice of onion.

FRIED BALONEY

You have got to peel off that red thing, then make four slits along the edge of the meat to keep it from curling when frying. It's hard to envision a baloney sandwich with Grey Poupon...Nah...use the French's, it's the only way.

PEANUT BUTTER 'N JELLY

In a saucer, mash the crunchy peanut butter in with the blackberry jelly until it is completely mixed. Then smear it all over the bread. You can add sliced bananas at this point, if you have any.

MEATLOAF

Slather sourdough bread with grainy mustard. Place a thick slice of meatloaf (see page 242) on bread. Add a leaf of lettuce and a slice of vine-ripe tomato.

B.E.L.T.

Fry up four pieces of smoked bacon in a skillet. In bacon drippings fry two eggs or one double-yolk egg, hard or soft. Slather two slices of Colonial light bread with Hellmann's mayonnaise. Place egg on one slice and bacon on the other, put two slices of vine-ripe tomato and a leaf of iceberg lettuce on top of the egg, salt and pepper. Put the bacon and bread on top of tomatoes.

CUBAN

Cut a 12 inch Cuban loaf of bread into 6 inch sections. Slice down the middle of each section. Spread top generously with regular mustard. Place dill pickle slices on bottom part of the sandwich. Add 4 thin slices of ham, 2 slices of roast pork and 2 slices of Swiss cheese. Put sandwich together and spread softened butter on the top. Grill smashing the sandwich flat. When golden brown and cheese has melted remove from grill and cut diagonally.

A DOZEN DEVILED EGGS

When there is a death in the South, it is customary for friends to take food to the home of the deceased. The food is for relatives, friends and neighbors who "sit-up" during the night. One item which seems to always appear is a big plate full of deviled eggs. Sometimes they are served on hand painted dishes which have individual spaces for each egg. You always know who sent the dishes because of the adhesive tape under the plate with the individual's name. This is not necessarily for credit of the deviled eggs but to insure that the plate is returned to its owner.

MAKES 12 DEVILED EGGS.

- 6 hard-boiled eggs, halved
- 1 tablespoon mayonnaise
- 2 tablespoon green olives, chopped
- 1 heaping tablespoon plain yogurt
- 2 tablespoons capers
- 1 tablespoon parsley, chopped
- 1 anchovy, minced very fine
- ½ teaspoon paprika

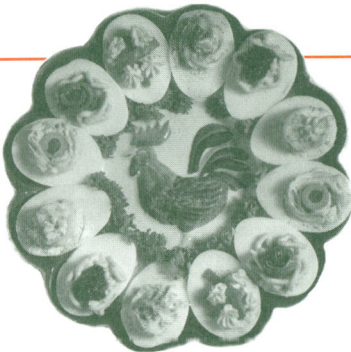

In a bowl mash the yolks and combine them with the olives, the capers, and the anchovy. Stir in the mayonnaise and the yogurt until the mixture is combined well and season the mixture with salt and freshly ground pepper. Divide the mixture among the egg whites and sprinkle the stuffed eggs with the parsley and paprika.

SCOTTISH EGGS

We first enjoyed this dish at the Scottish Games in Jacksonville. It's very simple to prepare and very tasty.

Serves 4

- 1¼ pounds bulk country sausage
- ½ cup all-purpose flour
- 1 teaspoon sage, crumbled
- 2 eggs, beaten lightly
- 1 cup fresh bread crumbs
- ¼ teaspoon cayenne
- Vegetable oil for deep-frying
- 4 hard-boiled eggs, peeled
- ½ teaspoon thyme, crumbled

In a large bowl combine the sausage, sage, thyme, and the cayenne, divide the mixture into 4 equal portions, and flatten each portion into a thin round. Enclose each hard-boiled egg completely in one of the sausage rounds. Dredge the sausage-coated eggs in the flour, shaking off the excess, dip them in the raw eggs, letting the excess drip off, and roll them gently in the bread crumbs, coating them well. In a deep fryer heat two and one half inches of the oil to 350 degrees, and in it fry the eggs, two at a time, turning them and transfer to paper towels to drain with a slotted spoon as they are done, for about 10 minutes.

A PECK OF PICKLED PEACHES

"A bushel and a peck and a hug around the neck."

This condiment is an old time favorite which has disappeared from many tables in recent years. Pickled peaches are excellent served with ham or cold turkey. Makes about 2 quarts

- 1 peck of small Florida peaches (about 25)
- A whole clove for each peach
- 4 cups sugar, depending on sweetness of peaches
- 1 cup water
- 4 three inch pieces cinnamon, broken
- 2 cups apple cider vinegar

To peel the peaches easily, blanch 3-4 at a time, in boiling water for 1-2 minutes, depending on their ripeness. The skins should peel off easily. Stick a clove in each peach and set aside. Bring to a boil the sugar, water, cinnamon and vinegar, stirring until the sugar dissolves. Add the peaches, reduce heat to low and simmer 8-10 minutes, or until peaches are tender. Place peaches in wide mouth canning jar, ladle syrup over the peaches with bits of cinnamon, completely covering them. Wipe the rims and threads of jars, cover with lids and screw bands on tightly. Set in a cool place 3-4 days before eating.

ICE-BOX PICKLES

When kept in a cold place these pickles will have a nice crunchy texture that goes great with barbecue and fried fish. They also make handy Christmas gifts when put into pint jars.

- ¾ gallon cucumbers, sliced
- ¼ gallon white onions, thinly sliced
- 4 cups sugar
- ⅓ cup salt
- 1 teaspoon celery seeds
- 1 teaspoon mustard seeds
- 3 cups white vinegar

Place sliced cucumbers and onions in a large container with a tight fitting lid. Place sugar, vinegar, salt, celery seeds, and mustard seeds in a saucepan over low heat. Cook until sugar has dissolved and liquid is clear. Pour over cucumbers and onions and let mixture cool. Cover and place in refrigerator overnight before using. Keep refrigerated.

GREEN TOMATO PICKLES

*T*he first time we tried to make these pickles we had a difficult time obtaining green tomatoes. The farmer we usually bought tomatoes from refused to sell us the green ones, even though we offered to pay him the same price as the ripe ones. We finally located some at the farmers' market, but had to buy a whole bushel. Well, we made enough Green Tomato Pickles to last us about ten years, even though we gave some to the neighbors and any relatives that dropped in. You can half this recipe if you are on the outs with the neighbors.

7 pounds green tomatoes, sliced ¼ inch thick
2 cups lime
2 gallons water
2 pints vinegar

5 pounds sugar
4 ounces pickling spice (to taste)
Few drops oil of cloves and cinnamon

Slice tomatoes into a large pot. Mix lime and water well and pour over tomatoes, making sure they are well covered. Let soak 24 hours, drain and rinse in cool water. Cover with cool water and let stand one hour. Do this three times, letting them sit for an hour each time. Drain. Mix vinegar and sugar in a large saucepan and bring to a boil. Pour over tomatoes and let stand 12 hours. Add pickling spice, oil of cloves and cinnamon and cook on low heat for 45 minutes to an hour. Put into sterilized jars, wipe rims with a damp cloth, seal and screw bands on tightly.

BREAD AND BUTTER PICKLES

Makes 7 pints

25 - 30 medium young cucumbers
8 medium size yellow onions
2 green bell peppers
½ cup salt

5 cups apple cider vinegar
2-4 tablespoons pickling spice
½ teaspoon powdered cloves
5 cups sugar

Wash and slice cucumbers and green peppers a fourth inch thick. Slice onions going from stem to root in a fourth inch slices. Pour salt over all. Cover and let stand three hours, then drain. Combine other ingredients in a large pot and bring to a boil. Add cucumbers, onions and bell peppers. Heat, but do not boil. Pickles are ready to can when they change color. Put in sterilized jars, wipe rims with a damp cloth, seal and screw bands on tightly.

WATERMELON RIND PICKLES

1 ripe watermelon
2 tablespoons slake lime
2 cups distilled vinegar
4 cups sugar
1 lemon sliced thin
1 tablespoon whole cloves
2 one inch pieces cinnamon

Use a sharp knife to cut off the green outer skin on the watermelon. Cut away any pink meat leaving only the white part. Cut the rind into chunks one to one and one half inches to make 8 cups. Soak for 12 hours in one half gallon of water with slake lime. Rinse well and let soak in clear water for 2 hours. Drain and set aside. Place 2 cups water, distilled vinegar, sugar, lemon, cloves, and cinnamon in a 8-10 quart pot. Bring to a boil over high heat and stir until sugar dissolves. Add the watermelon rind and, when the mixture returns to a boil, reduce heat to medium. Boil gently, uncovered, for about 45 minutes or until rind is tender and clear. Ladle into sterilized jars, cover with syrup, seal and store.

MANGO CHUTNEY

*M*ail order used to be our only source for fresh mangos. Now they are readily available in most farmers' markets and grocery stores. To get the best price, we buy them by the bushel at the farmers' market. There are many varieties available, including one variety that tastes like turpentine. Our favorite varieties are Kent, Haden, and Tommy Atkins. Serve this chutney with your curry dishes.

3-4 pounds green, hard mangos, peeled and diced
3-4 pounds ripe mangos, peeled and diced
1 ¼ quarts apple cider vinegar
2 pounds light brown sugar
1 tablespoon chili powder
1 teaspoon crushed red pepper
1 cup fresh lime juice
3 teaspoons ginger, grated
4 tablespoons salt
6 large onions, chopped
2 cloves garlic, finely chopped
1 tablespoon whole mustard seeds
1 tablespoon whole celery seeds
1 tablespoon ground cinnamon
1 tablespoon allspice
1 ½ teaspoon whole cloves
15 ounce box each yellow and dark raisins

In a large, heavy bottomed pot with lid, mix vinegar, sugar, chili powder, and crushed pepper. Bring mixture to a boil, stir and reduce heat. Simmer until sugar is dissolved. Add remaining ingredients, stir, and return to boil. Remove from heat, cover and let stand over night. Next day, stir to mix and simmer gently 4-5 hours, stirring often. Place in canning jars, wipe rims with damp cloth, seal, and screw bands on tightly.

DATIL PEPPER JELLY

*L*ocal legend in St. Augustine says that the Datil Pepper plant will grow only in the area around St. Johns County. We really don't know if that's true, but since a lot of peppers are grown in pots, we wonder. Wear rubber gloves when you remove the seeds from Datil peppers or your hands will burn for hours. Don't think this is not necessary because it is!

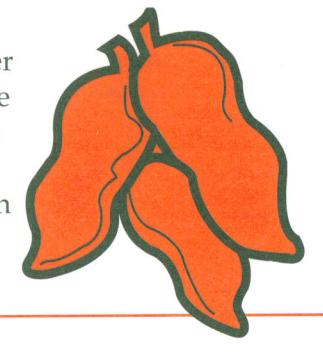

Makes 9 half pints

1 cup Datil peppers
1 cup green bell pepper
1 package Sure-Jell

3 cups white vinegar
7 cups sugar
Red food coloring

Remove stems and seeds from peppers. Place in a blender and chop fine. In a large pot, combine Sure-Jell and vinegar, bring to a boil and cook for 30 seconds. Add sugar and stir to dissolve. Bring to a boil and boil 1 minute. Add the amount of food coloring you desire, peppers, and boil 15 seconds. Remove from heat and stir, foam will disappear. Fill canning jars immediately to within an eighth inch of top. Wipe jar rims and threads with a damp cloth. Cover quickly with lids. Screw bands on tightly. Turn jars over and let rest 1 hour. Shake jars rapidly to distribute peppers. If peppers continue to rise, wait 30 minutes and shake again. Turn jars right side up and cool before storing.

PRICKLY PEAR JAM

*T*his jam has a beautiful color and is a popular appetizer when we are tailgating at the Florida Gator football games.

4 pounds of red ripe prickly pears
2 cups orange juice
1 teaspoon crushed red pepper

Water
3 cups sugar

Cut the thorns off the prickly pears, using tongs to hold them and scissors to cut off the thorns. Cut the prickly pears into chunks and place in a large heavy-bottom boiler with the orange juice and enough water to cover them. Cook until the pears are tender, then puree in a food processor. Measure 4 cups of fruit pulp into heavy-bottomed boiler. Stir in the pepper and sugar. Bring to a boil, stirring constantly. Reduce heat and simmer until jam falls off a metal spoon in a sheet. Pour into sterilized jars and seal. Serve with crackers and cream cheese.

Savory Soups, Gumbos and Chowders

Mrs. Catherine Evans Usina roasting oysters on North Beach in the early 1900's. Wealthy guest like the Flagers, Vanderbilts and Goulds frequented the beach. To the south, the Capo's served clam chowder, chicken pilau and all the fixings for a quarter.

Huguenot Onion Soup, 116
Beef and Barley Soup, 116
Summertime Vegetable Soup, 117
Wintertime Vegetable
   Beef Soup, 117
Crabby Mushroom Soup, 118
Oyster and Artichoke Soup, 119
Jimmy's Peanut Soup, 119
Cooter Soup, 120
Cold Zucchini Soup, 121
Creamy Broccoli Soup, 121
Rock Shrimp Bisque, 122
Cedar Key Clam Bisque, 122
Crab and Corn Bisque, 123
Tomato Bisque, 123

Navy Bean Soup, 124
Red Bean Soup, 124
Black Bean Soup, 125
Ham and Split Pea Soup, 125
Cuban Collard Green Soup, 126
Fernandina Shrimp Mull, 127
The Authentic Original way
   to make Oyster Gumbo, 128-129
Wood Duck Gumbo, 130
Filé Gumbo, 131
Creole Gumbo YaYa, 132
Gulf Coast Seafood Gumbo, 133
Grandpa's Gopher Gumbo, 134
Graveyard Gumbo, 135
Gumbo z' Herbs, 136

Okra Gumbo, 136
St. Augustine Minorcan
   Clam Chowder, 137
Welatka Bass Chowder, 138
Red Snapper Cheek Chowder, 139
Mama's Crab Goulash, 140
Boggy Bayou Mullet Stew, 141
Brunswick Squirrel Stew, 142
Suwannee Catfish Head Stew, 143
Apalachicola Oyster Stew, 144
North Florida Gazpacho, 144
Florida Bouillabaisse, 145
The Children's
   Beef Bourguignon, 146

SAVORY SOUPS, GUMBOS AND CHOWDERS

Soups were seldom served as a first course during our childhood. Instead, soup was a large pot of thick stew served as the whole meal. In the long days of summer, soup was made with fresh vegetables from the garden, flavored with a ham bone. Freshly picked vine-ripe tomatoes, butter beans, and sweet corn cut from the cob and of course okra thickened the soup and combined the wonderful flavors of the summer garden in one dish.

After deep sea fishing trips out of Destin, red snapper and grouper were enjoyed in thick creamy chowders. Trips to the bays and bayous yielded abundant crabs which were enjoyed in goulash and gumbos then mixed with fresh gulf shrimp. In the cool fall nights, we often had rich soups thickened with dried beans or okra.

Hunting trips in the fall yielded squirrels, ducks and turkeys which were enjoyed in in stews and gumbos. As winter appeared, the local Apalachicola oysters are plump and at their best. Delicate oyster stews were often served as a light supper.

It was later in life when we discovered the lighter soups featured as a first course, as well as, (can you believe it?) cold soups! These Gazpachos and cold vegetable soups were a welcome refresher, especially with our warm climate.

Soups like gazpacho, black bean, and collard green show the Spanish and Cuban influence in North Florida, where many cultures have joined to give our cuisine a unique flavor.

The Creoles on the Gulf Coast are given credit for our delicious gumbos.

There seem to be as many different versions of gumbos as there are cooks. They can be made with meat, fowl, fish, shell fish, sausage or any combination of the above, along with onions, bell pepper, celery and thickening agents like okra, roux or file powder (ground young sassafras leaves.)

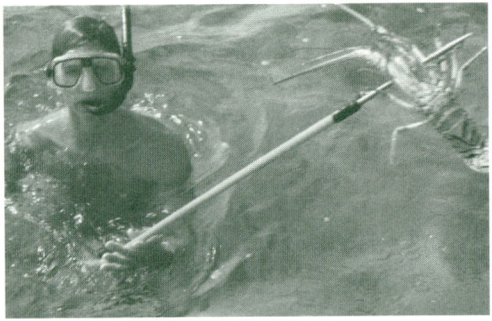

Trey speared a spiny lobster for supper. Bahamas, c 1999.

On the Atlantic Coast, seafood stews take on names like mulls, bisques and chowders. All are equally good when made with fresh local shrimp, oysters and other seafood. Lobster and conch are available from the islands and keys and are sometimes featured in the chowders.

Pokey the Backyard Gopher, c 1977.

SAVORY SOUPS, GUMBOS AND CHOWDERS

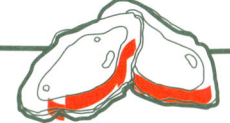

The Minorcan clam and conch chowders served around St. Augustine feature the unique local Datil peppers. These yellow-green, waxy-skinned peppers have a flavor unlike any other and are utilized by the natives of St. Augustine to flavor sauces, perlos, vegetable dishes and in their chowders. Local legend has it that these peppers were brought to Florida in the late 1700's by the Minorcan families who were brought over as indentured servants to work on a large plantation in New Smyrna. When the plantation failed, many of the Minorcans moved to St. Augustine where their culture and cuisine mixed with that of the Spanish, Italian, Greek and Native Americans.

Fresh water fish, frogs, crawfish and turtles are caught in the many interior lakes, rivers and creeks, and are featured in chowders, stews and soups throughout North Florida. The poor Gopher turtle has gotten a reprieve and is no longer featured as the main ingredient in the stews and gumbos enjoyed by many generations of Florida settlers. However, the swamp cabbage, which was stewed and eaten regularly by the settlers, is available in limited quantities and is still served in a few North Florida restaurants.

Lucky day out of Destin, top row shows 30 pound Groupers, the rest are Trigger and Snapper, c 1978.

HUGUENOT ONION SOUP

*T*he Huguenots settled on the St. Johns River at Ft. Caroline in 1564, just east of Cowford, now called Jacksonville. Jean Ribault and his troops settled the area once populated by the fishermen/farmers of the Timucua Indian tribe. They were later massacred by the Spanish forces.

Serves 6

- 12 cups St. Augustine Sweets, onions chopped fine
- 3 tablespoons olive oil
- 3 tablespoons butter
- 6 cups double strength beef stock
- Salt and freshly ground black pepper
- 1 tablespoon sugar
- 1 pound Gruyére cheese, grated
- 6 heaping tablespoons Parmesan cheese, freshly grated
- 6 slices white bread, toasted and trimmed to fit six earthen soup bowls

Preheat oven 375 degrees. Place onions, olive oil and butter into large boiler over low heat and cook until onions have softened. Add stock, sugar, salt and pepper to taste. Bring to a slow boil, reduce heat to low and simmer 30 minutes. Divide onions and broth into bowls that can be placed in the oven. Mix the two cheeses and set aside. Float toast on top of soup and sprinkle cheese over toast. Bake for 10 minutes. Place under broiler until cheese is lightly brown. Serve piping hot.

BEEF AND BARLEY SOUP

*T*his hearty soup is especially good on a cold winter night. Serve with Daddy's Crusty Cornbread (see page 41).

Serves 6

- 2 cups canned tomatoes
- ¾ pound boneless chuck, cut into 1 inch cubes
- 1½-2 teaspoons salt
- ¼ teaspoon pepper
- 1 cup celery tops, chopped
- 2 sprigs parsley
- ¼ cup regular barley
- 1 cup tomato juice
- 1 cup fresh green beans
- ½ cup rutabaga, chopped
- 1½ cups cabbage, coarsely chopped
- ½ cup carrots, sliced
- ½ cup celery, sliced
- ½ cup onions, thinly sliced

Drain tomatoes and add enough water to make 2 quarts. Place liquid in a large pot with chuck, salt, pepper, celery tops and parsley. Cover and cook slowly for 1 hour. Add the barley and cook 1 hour longer. Remove and discard celery and parsley. Cover and cook slowly for 1 hour. Add remaining ingredients, including reserved tomatoes. Bring to a boil, reduce heat and cook 45 minutes and serve.

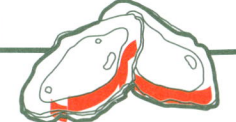

SUMMERTIME VEGETABLE SOUP

"Red Rover, Red Rover let Anna Jo come over."

Summertime was our favorite season as children. We could go barefoot, swim in the creek and camp out. The long days also meant we could stay outside longer and play our favorite games of Red Rover and Guinea, Guinea All-Squat. About twilight, we would throw rocks up in the sky and watch the bullbats follow them to the ground. Twilight was also when we were entertained by the skeeter hawks and lightnin' bugs. Later, we learned the rest of the world called them dragonflies and fireflies, but hell, we never much cared what the rest of the world did anyway.

Serves 8-10

- 4 quarts ham stock
- ½ pound smoked ham, diced
- 1 pint fresh field peas, shelled
- 1 pint fresh butter beans, shelled
- 2 dozen ears fresh corn, cut off cob
- 4-6 large vine ripe tomatoes, peeled, seeded and chopped
- 2 tablespoons bacon drippings
- 2 cups fresh okra, sliced
- Salt black pepper, to taste

In a large heavy bottomed pot, bring ham stock (see page 23), to a boil. Add ham, peas and butter beans. Return to a boil, reduce to simmer, cover and cook 45 minutes.

Add corn and tomatoes, cook 30 minutes more. Add bacon drippings to a cast-iron skillet over medium heat. When hot, add okra and cook until no longer slimy, stirring often. Add to soup and continue to cook 15 minutes. Season soup with salt and pepper to taste. May be frozen.

WINTERTIME VEGETABLE BEEF SOUP

Serves 6

- 3 pounds beef short ribs
- 2 ½ quarts water
- 2 bay leaves
- ½ teaspoon thyme
- 2 tablespoons olive oil
- 2 medium onions, chopped
- 2 cloves garlic, minced
- 3 ribs of celery, chopped
- 2 cups whole peeled plum tomatoes, chopped
- 1 pound okra, chopped
- 4 carrots, sliced ½ inch thick
- 2 Irish potatoes, cut in chunks
- ⅓ cup barley
- ⅓ cup parsley minced
- Salt and pepper, to taste

Place ribs and water in a large saucepan, add bay leaves, thyme, and bring to a boil over medium high heat. Reduce heat to low and simmer, covered, for 1 to one and a half hours or until tender. Heat olive oil in a large skillet and add the onions, cook, stirring for 2 minutes. Stir in the garlic and celery and cook 6-7 minutes, or until vegetables are translucent. Add onion mixture to the beef ribs. Add the tomatoes, okra, carrots, potatoes, barley and parsley. Continue to cook 25-30 minutes or until barley and vegetables are tender. Season with salt and pepper. Cook 2-3 minutes more and serve with a crusty loaf of bread.

CRABBY MUSHROOM SOUP

When owner/chef Bill Cissel opened R.P. Mc Murphy's as a sports bar, no one in Jacksonville Beach took it seriously as a place for good food. Sure, he had the best burgers in town, but soon locals discovered the delicious homemade soups and fresh fish served with unique toppings. Snapper, grouper, trigger, wahoo, and dolphin are featured in different sauces each day.

Crabby Mushroom, our all time favorite soup of his, is usually on the chalkboard at least once a week. When Bill gave us the recipe, he mentioned it was a very simple soup to make, but his recipe made 15 gallons at a time. Reducing it to a family-sized serving was a bit more difficult.

Serves 8-10

- ½ pound unsalted butter
- 2½ pounds fresh mushrooms, chopped
- 3 medium white onions, chopped fine
- ½ teaspoon granulated garlic
- ½ teaspoon granulated onion
- 1 tablespoon Worcestershire
- 1 tablespoon soy sauce,
- 1 teaspoon white pepper
- 1 cup all-purpose flour
- ¼ teaspoon nutmeg
- ½ cup sherry
- 4 chicken bouillon cubes dissolved in 1 cup of hot water
- 1 cup whipping cream
- 1 pound crabmeat, picked over
- ½ gallon whole milk
- 9 jigs Tabasco, or to taste
- ¼ teaspoon Cayenne pepper or to taste
- Salt and freshly ground black pepper to taste
- 1 bunch green onions, chopped

Melt butter in a large skillet over medium heat. Sauté mushrooms and onions until onions have softened. Add garlic, onion, Worcestershire, soy sauce and half of sherry. Stir in flour, a little at the time until smooth and mixture forms a paste, add nutmeg and cook about 3 minutes. Place in large soup pot and add bouillon mixture and remaining sherry, stirring constantly.

Reduce heat and simmer 3-5 minutes. Add whipping cream and crabmeat, stirring gently. Maintain heat, do not let mixture boil. Add milk, stir and simmer until desired consistency is reached. Add Tabasco, cayenne, salt and black pepper to taste. Stir in green onions, and serve.

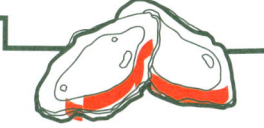

OYSTER AND ARTICHOKE SOUP

More than half the entire shellfish harvest of Florida comes from 180,000 acres of oyster beds in Apalachicola Bay which produces 300,000 bushels of oysters per year. The majority of these will turn up in the oyster bars around the country. Most oyster bars will shuck you a pint for this soup. This will insure the oysters will be at their freshest.

Serves 4

4 tablespoons unsalted butter
2 tablespoons all-purpose flour
½ cup green onions, chopped
¼ cup celery, chopped
1 teaspoon garlic minced
1 bay leaf, crumbled
⅛ teaspoon thyme, crumbled
   teaspoon cayenne pepper
1 pint oysters, cut into quarters, liquid reserved
1¾ cups chicken stock
14 ounce can artichoke hearts, drained and chopped
2 tablespoons parsley, minced
½ cup whipping cream, warmed
Salt and freshly ground black pepper, to taste
Dash nutmeg, freshly ground

In a heavy bottomed pot, melt butter over medium heat. Add flour and cook slowly, 2-3 minutes, to make a white roux. Stir constantly, do not brown. Add green onions, celery, garlic, bay leaf, thyme, cayenne, chicken stock and reserved oyster liquid. Cook over low heat 10 minutes, stirring frequently. Add oysters, artichoke hearts and parsley. Simmer 10 minutes, or until edges of oysters curl. Stir in cream and remove from heat. Correct the seasoning and add a dash of nutmeg. Serve at once.

JIMMY'S PEANUT SOUP

2 cups peanut butter
2 quarts milk
2 tablespoons flour
2 tablespoons onions, minced
Salt and pepper to taste
Salted peanuts, chopped

In a small bowl thin the peanut butter with two cups of the milk. Scald the remaining milk in a double boiler. Mix a small amount of milk with the flour until smooth. Whisk into the milk in the double boiler. Combine the peanut butter and milk mixture. Add onion, salt and pepper. Simmer for 20 minutes. Sprinkle each bowl with chopped nuts and serve.

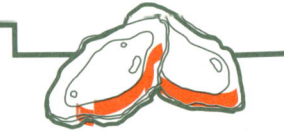

COOTER SOUP

Cooters, North Florida's soft shell turtle, are considered a delicacy by many gourmets. The local cooter, Pseudemy floridana, also known as the Suwannee Chicken, is considered the tastiest member of the cooter family. The lakes, rivers and ponds of North Florida still have a supply of cooters.

This delectable soup is best made with fresh soft shell turtle meat, if not available, use any turtle meat.

Serves 10-12

2 pounds turtle meat with bones
2 quarts water
½ large onion
1 bay leaf
1 cup unsalted butter
¾ cup all-purpose flour
1 cup celery, minced
1½ cups onion, finely chopped
1½ teaspoons garlic, minced
½ teaspoon thyme, crumbled
1 teaspoon oregano, crumbled

½ teaspoon salt and freshly ground black pepper
2 bay leaves
1½ cups tomato purée
1 tablespoon Worcestershire
1 quart rich beef stock
½ cup lemon juice
2 tablespoons parsley, minced
Dry sherry
1 lemon sliced

Place the turtle and water in a large pot and bring to a boil. Skim off the foam and add the onion and bay leaf and reduce heat to low. Partially cover and simmer for two hours or until turtle meat is tender. Transfer the meat to a platter, cool and debone. Cut meat into a half inch pieces and set aside. Strain the stock and reserve. In a large cast-iron skillet, melt butter over medium heat. Add flour and cook roux, stirring constantly, until it is a medium brown. Stir in celery, onions, garlic, and seasonings and remove from heat, stirring constantly until it cools. In a 5 quart saucepan, add turtle meat, tomato purée, Worcestershire and stocks. Simmer 30 minutes. Stir in roux, a tablespoon at a time, stirring constantly until soup thickens lightly and is smooth. Cook 30 minutes. Correct the seasoning, adding more salt and pepper if needed. Stir in the lemon juice and parsley. Put 1 tablespoon of sherry in each soup bowl before ladling in the soup, float a lemon slice on each and serve.

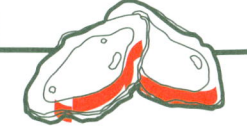

COLD ZUCCHINI SOUP

*C*old soups are appreciated in our warm climate, especially on one of those hot humid evenings. Cold soups are excellent for entertaining because they can be prepared and chilled in advance, while allowing the flavors to blend and develop.

Serves 6

3 large zucchini, sliced
1 green bell pepper, chopped
½ cup onion, chopped
3 cups chicken stock
1 cup sour cream

1 tablespoon parsley, chopped
1 ½ tablespoons fresh dill or more to taste
Salt and freshly ground black pepper, to taste

In a medium saucepan, place the zucchini, bell peppers, onion and stock. Bring to a boil, cover and simmer 15 minutes. With a large slotted spoon, remove zucchini, onion and bell pepper from stock and place in a food processor; purée until almost smooth. Add remaining stock, sour cream, parsley, dill and blend until smooth. Chill at least 4 hours.

CREAMY BROCCOLI SOUP

*T*his soup is for folks, like President Bush that don't like broccoli. The lemon juice and cream tones down the taste and is very satisfying.

Serves 6

3 cups fresh broccoli
2 cups chicken stock
½ cup butter
5 tablespoons plain flour

1 cup of milk
2 cups whipping cream
Salt and pepper to taste
5 tablespoons lemon juice

Break broccoli into florettes. Heat chicken broth in a medium pot. Add the broccoli and cook until just tender. Remove broccoli with a slotted spoon and place in a food processor. Pulse to chop into bite size pieces and return to pot with the leftover broth. Set aside. In a skillet melt the butter over medium-low heat, stir in the flour until smooth, cook 3 minutes, stirring constantly. Stir in the milk, whipping cream, salt and pepper to taste. When thickened, add to broccoli, stir and heat thoroughly. Add the lemon juice. Do not let it boil.

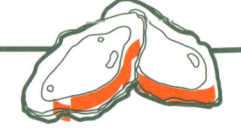

ROCK SHRIMP BISQUE

*R*ock shrimp have a texture and taste more like a lobster than a shrimp. It's not always available so we buy it when it does appear at the market.

Serves 6-8

- 1 pound rock shrimp
- ¼ cup brandy
- 1½ quarts shrimp stock
- 1 cup dry white wine
- ¼ cup unsalted butter
- ¾ cup all-purpose flour
- 1 cup whipping cream
- Salt and freshly ground black pepper, to taste
- 2 tablespoons dry sherry
- Freshly grated nutmeg

Peel shells from rock shrimp, devein and finely chop. Crush shells in a food processor and place in a large pan. Add brandy and ignite, shake pan until flames go out. Add shrimp stock (see page 23) and the wine. Bring to a boil and reduce heat to low, simmer 20 minutes. Strain through a fine sieve and set aside. In another pan, melt the butter and stir in the flour. Cook this roux until it turns golden. Stir in the shrimp stock, stirring constantly until thickened and smooth. Cook for 25 minutes, strain through a fine sieve. Stir in reserved rock shrimp and cook 1 minute. Add cream and cook until heated through. Salt and pepper to taste, stir in sherry, sprinkle with nutmeg and serve.

CEDAR KEY CLAM BISQUE

*A*quaculture is an important part of North Florida's economy. Clam farms around Cedar Key produce some of the tastiest clams available. Up North this bisque is known as New England clam chowder.

Serves 6 or more

- One 6 ounce bottle clam juice
- ½ cup celery, chopped
- ½ cup onion, chopped
- 1 clove garlic, minced
- 1 large potato, cut into small chunks
- 4 strips smoked bacon
- 1 pound fresh clams, chopped
- 1 quart of half and half
- 1 quart heavy cream
- Freshly grated nutmeg
- Sherry

Reduce clam juice to half. Fry bacon until crisp and remove from pan. Add the celery, onion and garlic, and sauté until tender. Boil potatoes in water until just done and drain. In a large pot, simmer clams and clam juice, add vegetables. Add half and half and cream slowly by the cup fulls. Cook until thickened, do not boil. Sprinkle with chopped bacon, top with freshly grated nutmeg and a dash of sherry.

CRAB AND CORN BISQUE

Serves 8

1 cup unsalted butter
1 cup all-purpose flour
4 cups shrimp stock
4 ears of fresh corn, cut from the cob
¼ teaspoon cayenne pepper,
1½ cups heavy cream

1 pound lump crab meat
Salt and freshly ground black pepper
Freshly grated nutmeg
Dry sherry, if desired
1 cup green onions finely chopped

Melt butter in a heavy-bottomed pot over low heat. When melted, stir in the flour. Stir constantly to remove all lumps, cook 3-5 minutes. Do not let mixture brown. Stir in the shrimp stock (see page 23) and bring to a boil, reduce heat to low and simmer 15-20 minutes. Stir occasionally. Add corn, stir, and cook 10 minutes. Add the cayenne and cream and heat through. Gently stir in the crab, salt and pepper . Remove from heat, taste for additional seasoning. Ladle into serving bowls and add a couple of gratings of nutmeg, sprinkle with sherry and green onions.

TOMATO BISQUE

Serves 6

10 plum tomatoes
5 tablespoons olive oil
2 cloves garlic, minced
½ teaspoon oregano, crumbled
2 teaspoons fresh basil, chopped
½ teaspoon black pepper
½ cup onion, minced

1 cup chicken broth
¼ cup red wine
½ cup cottage cheese
½ cup heavy cream
½ cup tomato paste
2 tablespoons Parmesan freshly grated

Preheat oven 475 degrees. Cut tomatoes in half lengthwise, brush with olive oil, sprinkle with herbs and pepper, roast until edges of tomatoes are charred, about 20 minutes. Place tomatoes in food processor and process until almost smooth. In a saucepan, cook onions in remaining olive oil until softened. Add the chicken broth and wine. Whisk in the cottage cheese, cream, tomato mixture and tomato paste. Stir in parmesan cheese and simmer until heated through. Add a dollop of pesto (see page 296) to each serving, if desired.

SAVORY SOUPS, GUMBOS AND CHOWDERS

NAVY BEAN SOUP

Serves 6-8

¼ pound smoked bacon,
  cut into half inch pieces
2 cups onion, chopped
2 large cloves garlic, minced
1 bay leaf
2 ribs celery, chopped
2 carrots, coarsely chopped
2 quarts chicken broth

2 cups navy beans, soaked
  in water overnight
½ teaspoon cumin
½ teaspoon thyme
⅛ teaspoon saffron
½ pound smoked ham, cubed
Salt and pepper, to taste
Créme Frâiche

Cook bacon in a heavy bottomed Dutch oven, over medium heat, until the fat is rendered. Add the onions and cook 2-3 minutes. Stir in the garlic, bay leaf, and celery and cook until vegetables are translucent about 10 minutes. Add the carrots, chicken broth, drained beans, cumin and thyme. Bring the soup to a simmer and cook until beans are tender, 30-35 minutes. Add the saffron and ham and simmer 10 minutes more. Mash a half of the beans on the edge of the pot to thicken. Taste for seasoning, remove bay leaf and serve with a dollop of Créme Frâiche (see page 125).

RED BEAN SOUP

1½ cups red beans
4 tablespoons butter
1 cup onion, finely chopped
1 clove garlic, minced,
1 cup celery, chopped
1½ cups smoked ham, minced
1 smoked ham bone

1 bay leaf
½ teaspoon thyme
Salt, if needed
½ teaspoon black pepper
  freshly ground
½ cup dry sherry
Créme Frâiche

Wash beans, cover with water and soak overnight. Drain beans the next day and set aside. In a medium skillet, melt the butter over medium heat. Add the onions and cook for 2-3 minutes. Stir in the garlic and celery and cook until transparent, about 7-8 minutes. In a large cast-iron Dutch oven, combine the beans, onion mixture, minced ham, ham bone, bay leaf, and thyme. Cover with 4 quarts of water and bring to a boil. Reduce the heat and simmer, partially covered, for one and a half hours, or until beans are tender. Mash most of the beans with a metal spoon on the sides of the Dutch oven to thicken. Add salt and pepper if needed. Add a tablespoon of sherry to each soup bowl and ladle soup into the bowls. Add a dollop of Créme Frâiche (see page125) and serve.

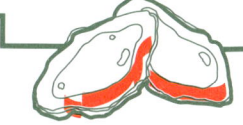

BLACK BEAN SOUP

Serves 10-12

- 2 cups black beans
- 2 cups onion, chopped
- ½ cup celery, chopped
- 1 teaspoon garlic, chopped
- 1 bay leaf
- 7 cups water
- 1 large ham hock
- 2 tablespoons butter
- 6-7 cups beef stock
- ⅓ cup sherry or Madeira
- Salt and freshly ground black pepper, to taste
- 2 lemons, sliced thin and dipped in minced parsley

Soak the beans in 10 cups of water overnight and drain well. In a heavy bottomed pot, melt the butter and cook the onions, celery, garlic and the bay leaf for 5 minutes or until onions are translucent. Add the ham hock, beans, beef stock and bring to a boil, reduce the heat and simmer for two and a half-three hours, uncovered, adding water if necessary to keep beans covered. Stir occasionally. Remove ham hock to cool. Transfer bean mixture in batches to blender and blend until roughly pureed. Remove any meat from ham hock and chop. Return meat and beans to pot, stir in the sherry, the salt and pepper. Thin soup with hot water if necessary. Ladle into soup bowls and garnish with lemon slices and a dollop of Crème Fraîche (below).

CRÈME FRAÎCHE

Place 1 cup heavy cream with 1 tablespoon buttermilk in a jar with a tight fitting lid and shake vigorously for 1 minute. Let stand at room temperature for 8 hours.

HAM AND SPLIT PEA SOUP

- 1½ cups dried split peas
- 2½ cups cold water
- 1 medium onion, chopped
- 1 smoked ham shank
- 1 teaspoon salt
- ¼ teaspoon pepper
- 7 cups water
- Créme Fraîche, see above

Soak dried peas in cold water overnight. Drain. Cut 1 tablespoon of fat off the ham shank and place in a heavy-bottomed pot over medium heat. Cook some of the fat out and add the onions and cook until transparent. Add the drained peas, ham shank, salt and pepper and the 7 cups of water. Bring to a slow boil, cover, reduce heat and simmer for 2 hours. Remove ham shank, cut meat into an eighth inch dice and return meat to soup. To make a thin white sauce: Melt 1 tablespoon butter in a saucepan, add 1 tablespoon of flour cook, stirring for 2 minutes. Add 2 cups of milk, stirring constantly and cook for 5 minutes. Combine with peas and simmer for 10 minutes. Serve with a dollop of Crème Fraîche (above).

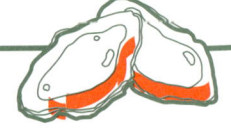

CUBAN COLLARD GREEN SOUP

Lucy, "You got a lot of splainin' to do."

No self-respecting Southerner can make it through the year without planting a collard patch. Just about every home, big or small, rich or poor has at least one row of collards planted somewhere in the yard. Cuban Collard Green Soup is a meal in itself served with Cuban bread.

Serves 6-8

- 1 cup dried Northern beans
- 2 quarts water
- 1 pound ham hocks, quartered
- ½ pound beef short ribs
- 1 bay leaf
- 1 teaspoon salt
- 2 Idaho potatoes, peeled and diced
- 10 ounce package frozen collards (thawed)
- ½ teaspoon sugar
- ½ tablespoon bacon drippings
- ¼ pound ham, diced
- 2 chorizo sausages, 4 inches long, cut in half lengthwise, sliced into ¼ inch pieces
- 1 medium onion, chopped
- ½ green bell pepper, chopped
- 1 teaspoon garlic, minced

Soak beans overnight in enough water to cover. Add water, ham hocks, short ribs, bay leaf and salt to a large soup pot. Bring to a boil, removing any foam with a large metal spoon. Lower heat and simmer one and a half hours. Replenish water if needed. Add drained beans and cook, covered, for 30 minutes or until tender. Add potatoes, collards and sugar. Place bacon drippings in a cast-iron skillet over medium heat and cook the sausage and ham 3 minutes, stirring occasionally. Reduce the heat to low, add the onion, bell pepper and garlic, and cook until softened, add to soup. Bring to a slow boil, reduce heat to low and simmer, covered, for 30-45 minutes or until potatoes and beans are tender. Remove bones and fat from soup. Thicken soup by mashing some of the beans and potatoes against the side of the pot and correct seasoning. Serve in large bowls with fresh Cuban bread.

A collard patch stripped bare, c 1890.

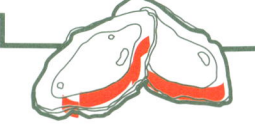

FERNANDINA SHRIMP MULL

The Amelia Island Shrimp Festival is held in Fernandina each April. Over 100,000 people attend and enjoy the local shrimp, crawfish, chowder and seafood dinners served by local nonprofit organizations in Nassau County.

Mulls are a popular dish in Coastal Florida and Georgia for parties and get-togethers, and sometimes served along with an oyster roast. Like most other regional dishes, everyone seems to have a different version.

Serves 16

- ½ cup bacon drippings
- 1 cup onion, finely chopped
- 1 cup bell pepper, finely chopped
- 4 cloves garlic, minced
- 4 bay leaves
- ½ cup sugar
- 2 tablespoons chili powder
- ¾ cup flour
- 1 cup shrimp stock
- 1-6 ounce can tomato paste
- 2 tablespoons Worcestershire
- 1 cup dry white wine
- 1 whole lemon, sliced
- ½ cup lemon juice
- 1 cup chili sauce
- 1 cup ketchup
- ¼-½ cup prepared mustard
- 5 pounds shrimp, peeled, deveined and cut in half
- Salt and Tabasco to taste
- ¼ cup butter
- 1 ½ cups green onion, chopped
- ¼-½ cup saltine crackers crumbled, (optional)

In a large pot, heat bacon drippings over medium-low heat. When hot, add onions and bell pepper, cook until softened, stir in the garlic and bay leaves. Add sugar and chili powder, cook until sugar has dissolved. Stir in flour and cook until a light brown, stirring constantly. Add shrimp stock (see page 23), tomato paste, Worcestershire, wine, lemon slices, lemon juice, chili sauce, ketchup, and a fourth cup of the mustard. Stir until well mixed, reduce heat to low and cook 30 minutes. Add shrimp, salt, Tabasco to taste and butter. Stir and return to a boil, remove from heat and stir in green onions. Taste for additional seasoning and add remaining mustard if needed. If mull is too thin, thicken with saltine crackers. Serve over rice.

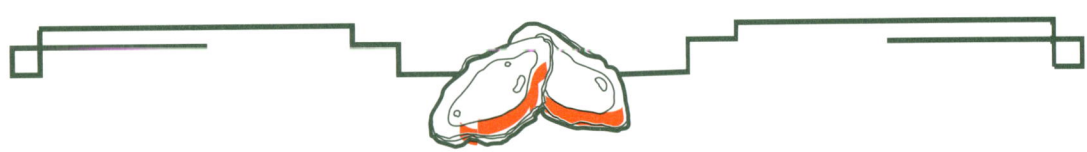

We found this Gumbo in *"A Dash of Sevillity"* printed by the Pensacola Heritage Foundation. It was credited to Manual Francisco Gonzalez VI.

THE AUTHENTIC ORIGINAL WAY TO MAKE OYSTER GUMBO

This is a fine Gumbo in the manner of Pensacola's old families. It is founded in antiquity, and handed down by word of mouth from one generation of family cooks to the next—hereditary and unique. The only other place it is prepared the same is in Mobile, and the Mobilians obtained their knowledge of this noble concoction by intermarriage with Pensacola families. The dish is more Spanish and Indian than French or Creole. Most Louisiana Gumbos are reddish, and the flavor obscured by vegetables and inappropriate herbs.

Things to have on hand for Oyster Gumbo—

1. One full quart of Tennessee sour-mash bourbon for the chef and helpers.
2. One elderly 7 pound rooster, cleaned and drawn, and with his liver, heart and gizzard minced. A rooster is better than a hen because he is not full of yellow fat. If a hen is used, the broth must be partly cooled several times for skimming. Cut up the rooster.
3. Sprinkle him with salt and finely ground Malabar white pepper.
4. Put yellow onion about the size of a small orange, cut fine, and 2 cloves of garlic in a bowl and leave handy.
5. One small purple Spanish onion, cut up, and 6 scallions with one and a half inches of the tops, and 2 more cloves of garlic. Put this in another bowl. To this bowl, add: 7 whole Java black peppercorns, 9 whole Jamaica allspice kernels, and minced giblets. Set this aside, not so handy.
6. Take remainder of the tops of three of the scallions and a baby's handful of fresh parsley and tie in cheesecloth with white kitchen thread. Leave near 2nd bowl.
7. One tightly packed quart of small to medium size local freshly opened oysters in their own liquor, cleaned of shell particles.
8. Have on work table: measuring cup of plain dry claret wine and a kitchen spoon of fresh finely powdered filé—pure sassafras leaves.

(No bay leaf or thyme.)

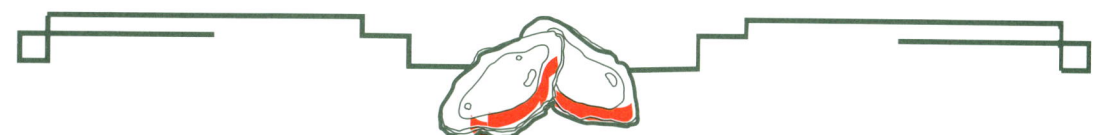

Have a deep cast iron pot (8 qt.) on the stove with a big kitchen spoon of cold bacon drippings and 1 minced strip of bacon in it. Have one kitchen spoon of plain wheat flour nearby. Meanwhile, have a kettle of water briskly boiling. Get iron pot hot. When the bacon is completely shriveled, start shaking in the flour gradually, stirring all the while. This is the beginning of the roux. We want a dark one, so be careful not to scorch while bringing to the color of strong coffee with cream. Do not stop stirring. When the "coffee with cream" color is reached, add the contents of the 1st bowl and continue stirring until onion is clear. Quickly dump in all pieces of rooster, and stir roux vigorously, trying to get each piece on the bottom of the pot for a while. This takes a strong arm. Continue until either (1) rooster pieces are brown, or (2) roux is all absorbed, or (3) you are afraid of scorching, or (4) your arms drop off.

With the other arm, pick up the boiling tea kettle, and more than cover the bird with this water. Keep stirring. If you have lost an arm by now, you need a friend. Dump contents of bowl that wasn't so handy, and a third cup of wine, in pot. Tie the cheesecloth sack to pot handle so that it dangles in liquid.

Add additional scalding water to as near the top as possible. Stir, then let the whole concoction boil hard for 30 seconds. Turn down to simmer, and cover pot tightly.

Now you and your friend can sit down and enjoy your drinks. Your work is almost done except for sniffing, watching, and an occasional stir. Let the iron pot simmer gently with the lid tightly closed until the rooster is tender. This should take about 2 hours.

One can tell from the aroma when the ingredients have wedded—and at this time you should taste the broth for salt only. Taste one of the raw oysters you will add later. They may be very salty. When rooster is tender, broth level in pot will have receded slightly, making room for oysters. Dump in the oysters with their liquor. Turn up flame and boil rapidly until oysters curl. Turn down flame and let sit still until there remains the barest simmer. Quench this simmer with $\frac{2}{3}$ cup of the claret. Now sift in slowly one heaping kitchen spoon of filé powder, stirring. Be careful that little balls of filé do not stick together, as it would be unpleasant to encounter later in pure form. The gumbo is ready. **Caution:** Never allow to boil after adding filé. Serve on white rice in deep bowls, with one nice piece of rooster for everyone. This is ample for 8. Have little dishes of hot, fresh peppers, such as torrido or birds-eye, along with salt shakers on the table.

WOOD DUCK GUMBO

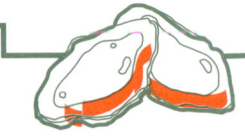

Wood ducks are the main duck around North Florida. Many of them refuse to migrate and stay here the year round. Ducks Unlimited groups often build wooden houses for them to nest, in areas where varmints might eat their eggs.

These ducks nest in hollow places in trees. They like to roost in shallow ponds and especially like beaver ponds. Wood ducks fly from the roost about daylight and spend the day in the creeks and rivers foraging for berries, and acorns. This diet gives their meat a distinct non-fishy taste which we prefer.

Wood Duck

Wood ducks are very alert and difficult to shoot. Our son loves to hunt them and sometimes he crawls on his belly through brush and briars in order to get a shot off as the ducks fly away. We've heard of hunters who surround a beaver pond about dark and shoot the ducks coming in to roost. But you didn't hear that from me, cause I ain't one to gossip.

This dark, rich gumbo is our favorite wild duck dish. If you use a domestic duck, remove as much fat as possible.

Serves 12-20

- 3 tablespoons salt
- 1 tablespoon cayenne pepper
- 1 tablespoon freshly ground black pepper
- 2 teaspoons white pepper
- 3-4 wild ducks, depends on size- wood ducks are wonderful
- 1 cup flour
- 1 cup vegetable oil,
- 3 cups dark brown roux
- 6 quarts chicken stock
- 2 large yellow onions, chopped
- 2 bell peppers, chopped
- 2 ribs celery, chopped
- 2 teaspoons thyme, crumbled
- 1 pound lean sausage, cut in ¼ inch slices
- 1 cup green onions, chopped
- 1 cup parsley, minced
- 2-3 cups okra, cut into ¼ inch slices sautéed in 2 tablespoons bacon drippings
- ½ cup additional green onions, chopped

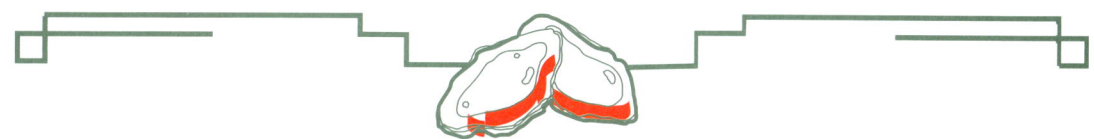

Mix the salt and dry peppers in a small bowl and set aside. Cut ducks into 4-6 pieces. Place duck pieces in a large bowl with a third of the salt and pepper mixture and rub into meat. Place flour and 2 teaspoons of salt and pepper mixture into large baking pan and mix well. Heat oil in a large cast-iron skillet over medium-high heat. Coat duck pieces with flour, reduce heat to medium if it is too hot. Add duck to oil when hot and cook until brown on all sides. Remove duck as it browns to paper towels to drain and cook remaining duck. When all pieces of duck have cooked, pour oil into a glass measuring cup. Add additional oil to measure 1 cup of oil and return to skillet. Use remaining seasoned flour, adding additional flour to measure one and a half cups.

Place skillet on medium-high heat and gradually add the flour, stirring constantly with a whisk until smooth. Continue to stir with a wooden spoon and cook the roux until it is a dark brown. Remove from heat and continue to stir until roux has cooled, set aside. Place stock in a large pot with onions, bell pepper, celery, the remaining salt and pepper mixture and thyme. Lay paper towels on top of roux to soak up excess oil. Bring stock to a boil, reduce heat to low and stir in 2 cups of the roux by the spoonfuls until incorporated. Add duck pieces and simmer, uncovered, for one and a half hours. Add sausage and continue to simmer 20 minutes.

Remove gumbo from heat and let sit for 15-20 minutes. Add remaining roux if gumbo needs thickening. Spoon off any fat from surface of gumbo. Bring gumbo to simmer and stir in 1 cup green onions, parsley, and okra. Cook 5 minutes to heat through, taste for additional seasonings and thicken with additional roux if needed. Ladle gumbo over rice and sprinkle with remaining green onions.

CAPÉ GUMBO

"Crawfish pie me-o-my filé gumbo."

½ pound ham, chopped
4 pound hen
2 tablespoons butter
½ teaspoon garlic, minced
2 large onions, chopped
1 teaspoon salt
2 teaspoon Creole seasonings
½ pod of Datil pepper, minced
1 quart oyster liquor and water
3 dozen oysters, liquid reserved
1 tablespoon filé (ground sassafras leaves)

Chop ham fine, cut hen into ten pieces. Place butter, hen and ham in a large pot, cover and fry until done. Add garlic, onions, salt, Creole seasoning (see page 181) and Datil pepper. Stir until brown. Add oyster liquor and water slowly. Bring to a boil and reduce heat to simmer. Cook until hen is tender, about two hours. Remove hen and debone. Return meat to pot, add oysters and cook until oysters just curl. Stir in filé and serve over white rice.

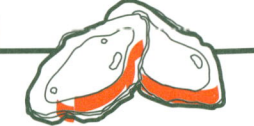

CREOLE GUMBO YA YA

Most people associate Creole cooking with New Orleans. But actually, many Creoles of French and Spanish heritage settled around Pensacola and Mobile as these cities were being built. They featured the local produce and seafood in their complex cooking and spiced up the local cuisine.

Ya, an African word for rice and gives this gumbo part of its name. So in Africa it would be called " Creole Gumbo Rice Rice." Filé powder is the young leaves of the sassafras tree dried, pulverized in a large mortar and pestle. Filé is added to gumbos just before serving to flavor and thicken.

This gumbo is rich and dark and has become one of our "comfort" foods.

Serves 6-8

- **A 2-3 pound chicken**
- **½ cup vegetable oil**
- **½ cup all-purpose flour**
- **1 pound smoked sausage, cut into ¼ inch slices**
- **1½ cups onion, chopped**
- **1 cup green bell pepper, chopped**
- **1 cup celery, chopped**
- **1 tablespoon bacon drippings**
- **1 teaspoon Tabasco**
- **Salt and freshly ground black pepper, to taste**
- **2 teaspoons filé powder**
- **5-6 cups cooked rice**

Wash chicken and place in Dutch oven with 10 cups of water. Bring liquid to a boil, skimming the froth. Reduce heat to simmer, cover and cook the chicken for 45 minutes-1 hour. Remove chicken to cool and reduce chicken stock to 6-7 cups. Heat a small cast-iron skillet until smoking over medium-high heat. Add oil and flour, stirring constantly, until roux is a dark brown, remove from heat and stir until cooled. In a large pot, cook sausage, onion, bell pepper and celery in bacon drippings over medium heat, about 10 minutes. Add reduced stock and bring to a boil. Reduce heat and simmer the mixture for 10 minutes. Remove a half cup of stock and set aside. Lay paper towels on top of roux to soak up excess oil. Stir roux into stock, stirring constantly until thoroughly mixed and simmer 20 minutes.

Add skinned and boned chicken, Tabasco and salt and pepper to taste. In a small bowl, dissolve filé powder in a half cup cool stock, add to gumbo and simmer for 10 minutes, do not let boil. Remove excess oil from top of gumbo with paper towels and serve over rice.

GULF COAST SEAFOOD GUMBO

Good seafood gumbo should be thick with lots of ingredients and rich with flavor. This gumbo is probably the most popular of all gumbos served in many of the seafood restaurants along the Gulf Coast. You may use any type of seafood desired.

Serves 8

- 3 cups onions, chopped
- 2 cups green bell peppers, chopped
- 2 cups celery, chopped
- 28 ounce can plum tomatoes, seeded and chopped
- 1 cup canned tomato purée
- 1½ teaspoons thyme, crumbled
- 4½ teaspoons garlic, minced
- 2 bay leaves
- ½ teaspoon cayenne pepper
- 1 teaspoon salt
- 1 teaspoon black pepper, freshly ground
- 1½ pounds okra, cut into ½ inch pieces
- 6 cups fish stock
- 1 pound grouper filets, cut in cubes
- 1 dozen small crabs, cleaned
- 2 pounds shrimp, shelled and deveined
- 1 pound scallops

In a large pot, cook onions, peppers, celery, tomatoes and tomato purée over moderate heat, stirring occasionally, for 10 minutes. Reduce heat to simmer and stir in thyme, garlic, bay leaves, cayenne, salt and pepper. Simmer mixture for 10 minutes. Add okra and cook mixture for 5 minutes, or until okra is tender and no longer slimy. Add fish stock (see page 22), grouper and bring to a boil. Reduce heat and simmer for 20 minutes. Discard bay leaves. Break crabs in half and add to gumbo, cook about 5 minutes, add shrimp and scallops cook until shrimp turn pink. Remove from heat, cover and let sit 5 minutes. Serve over cooked rice.

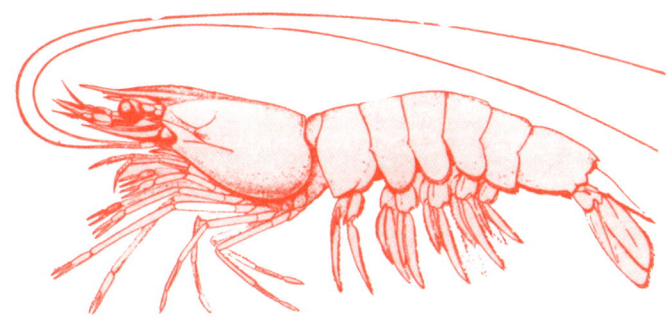

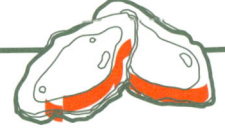

GRANDPA'S GOPHER GUMBO

Gophers, *Gopherus polyphemus* are land tortoises which used to be fairly common throughout North Florida. They were eaten when there wasn't much other meat available. During the Great Depression, gopher was referred to locally as "Hoover Steak."

Gophers reside underground in "gopher holes," usually along with other critters such as skunks and rattlesnakes. Grandpa harvested them by using a long grapevine with a hook. This would be "jugged" into the hole until the hook made contact with the gopher shell. The gopher was then pulled to the surface and kept in a pen until there were enough for a stew or gumbo.

Today the gophers are endangered, so we recommend that you substitute turtle meat for the poor ol' gopher.

Great Grandparents Mary Tallulah and Frank Jorden Baker standing in cotton patch in Ponce de Leon, c 1930's.

Serves 6
Meat from one gopher
Salt and freshly ground black pepper, to taste
4 slices thick sliced smoked bacon
2 cups onions, chopped fine
1 bell pepper, chopped
1½ teaspoons thyme, crumbled
1 clove garlic, minced
28 ounce can crushed tomatoes
2 Irish potatoes, diced
1 Datil pepper, seeded minced
4 hard-boiled egg yolks, mashed
4 tablespoons scuppernong wine

Cut meat into 2 inch pieces and place in 5 quart pot. Cover with water and bring to a boil, cover, reduce heat and cook until meat is tender, about one and a half hours. Add salt and pepper and reduce liquid to 2 cups.

Fry bacon until crisp, remove bacon and lower the heat. Add onions and bell pepper to bacon drippings. Stir and cook for 1 minute or until onions have softened, add thyme and garlic. Add tomatoes and cook 10 minutes, add to gopher, cover and cook 2 hours. Stir in potatoes and Datil pepper and cook 20 minutes, thicken broth with egg yolks. Add wine, correct seasonings and serve.

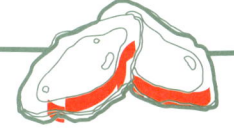

GRAVE YARD GUMBO

*T*his is our little secret way to use up the leftover Thanksgiving turkey, which used to last for days. Sometimes we smoke an extra turkey to ensure there are enough leftovers for our hearty, traditional gumbo.

We enjoy this gumbo freshly made, then freeze the rest to enjoy later at our annual clean-up at the church cemetery.

Serves 12

- 1 leftover smoked turkey carcass and bones, meat reserved (about 5 cups)
- 3 quarts chicken stock
- Water
- 3 ribs celery, chopped
- 3 cups yellow onion, chopped
- 1 large bell pepper, chopped
- 2 ½ cups dark-brown roux
- 2 Datil peppers, seeded and chopped (optional)
- 1½ tablespoons salt, or to taste
- 2 teaspoons thyme, crumbled
- 1½ teaspoons cayenne pepper
- 2 teaspoons white pepper
- 1½ pounds smoked pork sausage, sliced ½ inch thick, sautéed to remove fat
- 2 cups green onions, chopped
- 1 cup parsley, chopped

Place chopped turkey carcass and bones in a large stock pot. Add chicken stock and water to cover carcass by an inch. Bring to a boil, reduce heat, cover and simmer one and a half-two hours. Make roux (see page 24), in advance and set aside for 30 minutes, pour off excess oil. Lay paper towels on top of roux to soak up remainder of excess oil. Remove turkey carcass and bones and discard. Add celery, onions and bell peppers to stock. Gradually stir in roux to thicken. Add Datil pepper, thyme, salt, cayenne and white pepper. Simmer for 1 hour. If gumbo is too thick, add additional stock. Chop the reserved turkey meat into bite-size pieces, add sausage and turkey to gumbo and cook 15-20 minutes more. Remove from heat, stir in green onions and parsley. Serve in large bowls over rice.

Mae McKinnon and Stuart Knox Gillis's headstone in Walton County Presbyterian Cemetery, in the Euchee Valley.

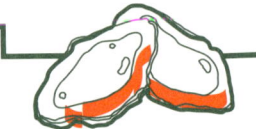

GUMBO Z' HERBS

*T*his is a very old gumbo that is not thick like most gumbos and popular with the Creoles of the Gulf Coast. Years ago, in early Pensacola, peddlers sold bouquets of various greens that were needed for this gumbo. You can substitute just about any greens available. It's rarely found in restaurants anymore so you'll have to make it yourself to enjoy it.

Serves 10-12

- 1 pound mustard greens
- 1 pound spinach
- 1 pound turnip greens
- 1 cup parsley
- 1 large yellow onion
- ½ gallon water
- 2 pounds lean Boston butt pork, cut into 1 inch pieces
- 1 pound smoked ham, cut into 1 inch pieces
- ½ pound smoked bacon, diced
- 1 cup red onion, chopped
- 1 teaspoon thyme, crumbled
- 1 bay leaf
- 1 teaspoon red pepper flakes
- ½ teaspoon marjoram, crumbled
- Additional water
- Salt and freshly ground black pepper, to taste

Wash the greens thoroughly, trim the center ribs, use only tender leaves. Bring greens, parsley and yellow onion to boil, reduce heat and cook until tender, about 30 minutes. Strain, reserving water greens were cooked in, cool, chop very fine and set aside. In a cast-iron Dutch oven, cook bacon until crisp and set aside. Add pork to bacon drippings and brown, stir only after meat is brown, add ham and brown meat on all sides. Cover and simmer 30 minutes, stir occasionally, to avoid burning. Add red onion, thyme, bay leaf, red pepper flakes, marjoram and stir, cooking until onion has softened and mixture is a rich brown. Add reserved water greens have been cooked in along with enough water to measure 2 quarts. Add greens and bring to a boil, reduce heat to low and simmer one-one and a half hours or until meat is tender and falling apart. Season with salt and pepper, crumble bacon and stir into gumbo. Serve with hot rice.

OKRA GUMBO

Serves 4

- 2 tablespoons bacon drippings
- 1 cup onions, chopped
- 1 cup bell pepper, chopped
- 1 cup tomatoes, chopped
- 1 cup okra, sliced
- 1 cup chicken broth
- ½ teaspoon oregano
- ½-1 teaspoon Creole seasonings

Heat bacon drippings in a heavy-bottom pot, stir in onions and pepper cooking until soft. Add all remaining ingredients. Cook over medium-low heat until thick, stirring often.

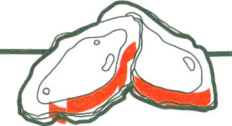

ST. AUGUSTINE MINORCAN CLAM CHOWDER

Datil peppers are enjoyed by St. Augustine locals in sauces, perlos, vegetable dishes and in their Minorcan Clam Chowder. This chowder is served in most of St. Augustine's seafood restaurants and the quality of the chowder is usually an indication of the meal to follow. The flavor of this chowder improves if made the day before serving.

A chowder cook-off is held each November at the Conch House, a well-known St. Augustine watering hole which serves a pretty mean chowder itself.

Serves 6-8

- ⅛ pound salt pork or smoked bacon, chopped fine
- 2 large St. Augustine Sweet onions, chopped
- 1 bell pepper, chopped
- 16 ounces fresh clams, chopped fine, juice reserved
- 1-2 Datil peppers, minced
- 3 cups canned plum tomatoes, drained, seeded and chopped
- ½ cup tomato purée
- ½ tablespoon thyme, crumbled
- ½ tablespoon salt
- ¼ teaspoon cayenne
- ½ teaspoon freshly ground black pepper
- 1-2 bay leaves, crushed
- 2 - 8 ounce bottles clam juice
- 3 cups fish stock
- 2 cups new potatoes, diced

Sauté pork in large pot over medium-low heat until fat is rendered. Remove pork and set aside. Add onions, bell pepper and cook until softened. Add clams, reserved clam juice, Datil peppers, tomatoes, tomato purée, seasonings, clam juice, fish stock (see page 22) and reserved pork.

Bring to a boil. Reduce heat and simmer one hour. Add potatoes and cook 30-45 minutes more. Add additional stock or clam juice if too thick. Remove bay leaves and serve piping hot.

WELATKA BASS CHOWDER

The St. Johns River is one of the few rivers in the world that flows north. It begins in central Florida and enters the Atlantic Ocean at Mayport, east of Jacksonville. It has been called Welatka, the Riviere de Mai and the Rio de San Juan depending on which country claimed it at the time. Many large bass are caught annually in the St. Johns River and its tributaries. This is an old camp type recipe utilizing the once abundant fresh water bass.

Welatka is a small community located on the St. Johns River across from the Oklawaha River. The old Spanish rice fields are about one mile north of Welatka.

Serves 12-15

- 6 pounds wide-mouthed bass, or any firm fleshed fish
- 1 pound smoked thick sliced bacon, cut in ¼ inch pieces
- 1 pound onions, peeled and sliced thin
- 2 pounds new potatoes, unpeeled and sliced thin
- 4-8 ounces saltine crackers, crumbled
- 1 large clove garlic, minced
- ½ cup unsalted butter, cut into ½ inch pieces
- 1 teaspoon thyme, crumbled
- Salt and freshly ground black pepper, to taste
- Water to cover
- 1 quart Half and Half, heated
- ¼ cup parsley, minced

Wash and filet fish, cut into large pieces. Place a fourth of the bacon in bottom of large cast-iron Dutch oven. Cover with a fourth of the fish filets, a fourth of the onions, garlic, potatoes, crackers, butter, thyme, salt and pepper. Repeat layering until ingredients are used. Add boiling water to almost cover stew. Cover with tight fitting lid and cook 30 minutes. Remove cover and cook 15-30 minutes until most of the water has evaporated. Stir gently 2-3 times while cooking, making sure to stir the bottom. When most of the water has evaporated, add the Half and Half. Add parsley, gently stir, and serve.

Chad Manning with his big bad Bass, c 1994.

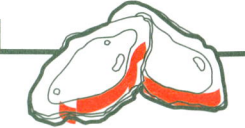

RED SNAPPER CHEEK CHOWDER

Snapper "cheeks" and throats are the richest and most delicately flavored parts of the fish and may be purchased separately at some seafood markets. The small triangular pieces of flesh taken from the ventral side of the head are the throats; the cheeks are taken farther back from the head. Both can be enjoyed for chowder and can also be fried.

Serves 12

- 3 medium Irish potatoes, diced
- 3 pounds red snapper throats and cheeks
- ¾ cup bacon, diced
- 3 medium onions, chopped
- 1 clove garlic, minced
- 28 ounce can plum tomatoes, chopped
- 1 green bell pepper, minced
- 1 cup celery, chopped
- 6 ounce can tomato paste
- ½ teaspoon thyme, crumbled
- 1 Datil pepper, minced
- Salt and freshly ground black pepper, to taste
- 1 teaspoon Worcestershire
- 1 cup fish stock, if needed
- 2 tablespoons parsley, chopped

Barely cover potatoes with water and cook until just tender. Strain and reserve water, set potatoes aside. Place fish in same pot, cover with water and bring to a boil. Reduce heat and cook until fish is tender. Strain and reserve water. Remove bones and skin of fish and break into small pieces.

Fry bacon in a large cast-iron skillet and remove from pan. Add onions to bacon drippings and sauté until softened, add garlic and stir until partially cooked. Add plum tomatoes, the bell pepper and celery, cook until tender.

Stir in tomato paste and thyme. Place potato water, snapper water, tomato mixture and Datil pepper in a large pot. Bring to a slow boil, reduce heat and simmer for 30 minutes. Continue to cook if necessary to strengthen. Add potatoes, snapper, salt and pepper, Worcestershire and simmer 20 minutes. Add fish stock if chowder needs thinning, and correct seasoning. Stir in bacon and parsley, and serve the chowder with buttered slices of warm crusty French bread.

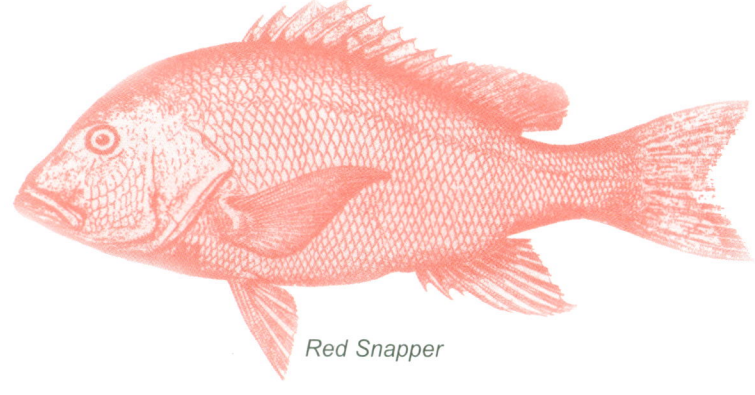

Red Snapper

MAMA'S CRAB GOULASH

When we first told our family and friends we were putting a book together on North Florida food, the first question was, "Are you including your Mama's Crab Goulash?" Of course, we couldn't leave this one out.

No one in our family can remember how this stew got the name "goulash." It's an old family favorite and was probably developed to utilize leftover crabs, fish and shrimp.

Serves 8

- 3 ribs celery, chopped
- 4 small white onions, chopped
- 1 bell pepper, chopped
- ¼ cup bacon drippings
- ⅓ cup all-purpose flour
- 28 ounce can plum tomatoes, seeded, chopped and juice reserved
- 2 teaspoons salt, or to taste
- ¼ teaspoon cayenne pepper
- 1 teaspoon black pepper, freshly ground
- 6 ounce can tomato paste
- 2 tablespoons Old Bay seafood seasoning, or to taste
- 6 cups shrimp stock
- 4 cups water
- 1 ½ dozen crabs, cleaned and broken in half
- 1 pound snapper cheeks, cooked and flaked
- 2 pounds medium shrimp, shelled, deveined and cut into 2-3 pieces

Sauté celery, onions and pepper in bacon drippings until onions have softened. Add flour slowly and stir constantly for 5 minutes; set roux aside.

In a large pot, add tomatoes, juice, tomato paste, salt, peppers, seafood seasoning, shrimp stock (see page 23) and water. Bring to a slow boil, reduce heat, cover and simmer 45 minutes. Stir in roux, a tablespoon at the time. Increase heat to high and add crabs. Cook 5 minute stirring occasionally. Reduce heat to medium low and add fish and shrimp. Cook about 2 minutes or until shrimp turn pink. If goulash is too thick, add more stock. Correct seasonings and serve over rice.

Mary Lucille Manning, c 1946.

BOGGY BAYOU MULLET STEW

"MULLET FOR THE GULLET" This is the theme of the Boggy Bayou Mullet Festival held each October in Niceville. Fried and smoked mullet plates are served by the Boggy Bayou Boys Hunting Club, Fort Walton Beach River Rats, The Choctawhatchee Fisherman's Association and Venter's United Methodist Church. These plates are served with grits, coleslaw, baked beans, potato salad and topped with hot hush puppies. About 10-12 tons of mullet are enjoyed each year at this festival.

Food booths, run by area restaurants, offer other delicious mullet dishes as well as bacon-wrapped stuffed shrimp, amberjack sandwiches, fried crab claws and seafood gumbos.

We like mullet served any style as long as it is fresh. This stew is an old recipe utilizing the local mullet.

Serves 6

28 ounce can tomatoes,
2 pounds mullet filets, skinned
1½ cups celery, chopped
1 cup onion, chopped
1 clove garlic, minced
¼ cup unsalted butter
1 teaspoon thyme, crumbled
1 cup tomato sauce

2-3 cups fish stock
3 cups new potatoes, peeled and diced
1 teaspoon sugar
2 teaspoons salt
1 teaspoon freshly ground black pepper
Dash of Tabasco, or to taste

Place paper towel in strainer and gently pour juice from canned tomatoes. It will take a while to drain, but you want only the clear juice. Cut fish into 1 inch pieces and set aside. In a large pot, cook celery and onion in butter until softened over medium heat. Stir in garlic and thyme, and cook for 1 minute. Add tomatoes, tomato juice, tomato sauce, and fish stock (see page 22). Bring to a boil, reduce heat to simmer and cook 15 minutes. Add fish, potatoes, sugar, salt, pepper, Tabasco and thyme. Cover, simmer 10 minutes or until fish flakes easily and serve.

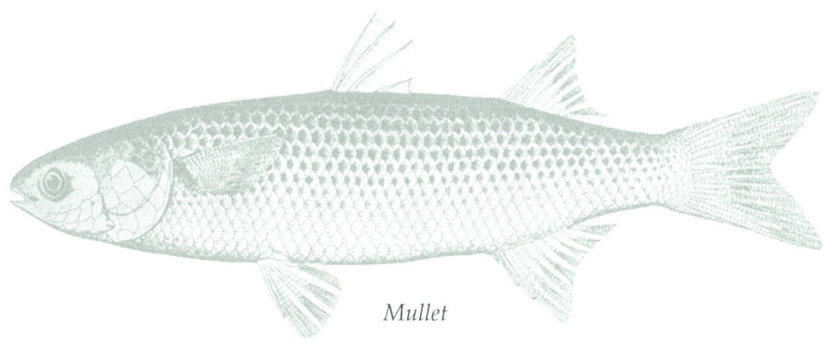

Mullet

SAVORY SOUPS, GUMBOS AND CHOWDERS

BRUNSWICK SQUIRREL STEW

*S*quirrels are one of the easiest game animals for a young hunter to bag. Our son, an excellent hunter, has kept us well supplied over the years with squirrel meat. This stew is traditionally served as a side dish with barbecue.

Serves 8-10

- 1-2 squirrels
- 3 pound chicken
- 1 pound smoked ham hocks, cut in half
- 1 large onion, chopped
- 28 ounce can plum tomatoes, drained, seeded and chopped
- 2 cups green lima beans, fresh or frozen
- 3 cups potatoes, peeled and cubed
- 1 teaspoon thyme, crumbled
- 1 teaspoon sugar
- ½ teaspoon red pepper flakes
- Salt and freshly ground black pepper, to taste
- 3 cups fresh corn, cut off cob
- ½ pound tender okra, ends trimmed and cut into ½ inch pieces
- ¼ cup unsalted butter
- ¼ cup parsley, chopped

Cut squirrel into six pieces and chicken into eight pieces. Place squirrel, chicken, ham hock, onion and thyme in a large pot. Pour in enough cold water to cover ingredients by an inch. Bring almost to a boil, skim off any foam rising to the top, reduce heat to simmer and cook for one and a half hours. Remove ham hocks, chicken and squirrel, and set aside to cool. Add tomatoes, lima beans, potatoes, sugar, red pepper flakes and black pepper. Cover and simmer for 30 minutes. Discard skin and bones from ham, chicken and squirrel and return meat to pot. Carefully skim fat from stew. Add corn and okra, and salt to taste. Cook 10-15 minutes more, leaving pot uncovered. Stir in butter and parsley. Add chicken stock to thin stew if needed, stir and correct seasoning. Serve stew hot in large bowls.

Stewing stew, c 1930's.

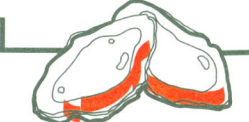

SUWANNEE CATFISH HEAD STEW

There are several varieties of catfish in our Florida waters, but the channel catfish is the one favored for eating. Catfish are bottom feeders and sometimes take on a muddy taste when grown in small fish ponds. We prefer the ones caught in spring fed creeks and rivers, usually caught with set hooks or trot lines. Set hooks are baited, weighted hooks attached to a small sapling and then stuck in the creek bank. Trot lines are weighted lines with hooks every few feet that are baited and strung across the water. With both methods, you leave them for a while and come back later to see what you've caught. Some folks make traps of chicken wire baited with cantaloupe and cat food, but you didn't hear that from me cause I ain't one to gossip.

Catfish are usually fried like mullet but are also good in this stew. They are skinned with pliers, hence the phrase "skinning the cat".

Serves 4

- 6 slices lean, smoked bacon
- 1½ cups onion, finely chopped
- 28 ounce can plum tomatoes, seeded and chopped
- 3 cups potatoes, peeled and cut in 1 inch cubes
- 1 pound catfish heads, eyes removed
- 1 tablespoon Worcestershire
- 1 teaspoon sugar
- 1 teaspoon thyme, crumbled
- 2 teaspoons salt
- Freshly ground black pepper, to taste
- 2 pounds catfish filets, cut into 1½ inch cubes
- 1 cup water
- ½ teaspoon Tabasco

In cast-iron Dutch oven, fry the bacon until crisp. Transfer to paper towels to drain. Add the onions to the bacon drippings, cook over medium-low heat until onions have softened, about 5 minutes. Line sieve with paper towel and strain tomato juice. Add tomatoes, strained tomato juice, potatoes, catfish heads, Worcestershire, Tabasco, sugar, thyme, salt, pepper and bring to a boil. Reduce heat to low, cover and simmer 30 minutes. Remove catfish heads and discard. Add catfish fillets and water if needed, cover and continue to simmer for 10 minutes, or until fish is cooked. Crumble bacon, sprinkle on top of stew, correct seasonings and serve.

Early Ferry " Way down upon the Suwannee river", c 1907.

SAVORY SOUPS, GUMBOS AND CHOWDERS

APALACHICOLA OYSTER STEW

Apalachicola holds a Florida Seafood Festival each November. King Retsyo ("oyster" spelled backwards), the once exiled King of the River's deltas and shellfish nurseries, presides over activities along with the reigning Florida Seafood Queen. Events include the solemn and colorful Blessing of the Fleet, oyster eating, an oyster shucking contest and the Blue Crab Race.

Serves 4

- ½ cup plus 1 tablespoon butter
- ¼ teaspoon Tabasco
- ½ teaspoon paprika
- ½ teaspoon celery salt
- 1 teaspoon salt
- 1 pint oysters, liquid reserved
- ½ cup whipping cream
- ½ cup milk
- 1 teaspoon paprika
- 1 teaspoon parsley, minced

In a heavy 2-3 quart saucepan, melt a half cup butter over moderate heat, being careful not to let it burn. Add Tabasco, paprika, celery salt and salt. Add oysters, oyster liquid and bring to a boil over high heat. Reduce heat to low, add cream and milk. Stir gently and cook 2-3 minutes or until oysters are plump. Taste for seasoning, divide among four heated soup bowls, placing pat of butter on each. Sprinkle with paprika and parsley. Serve hot with oyster crackers.

NORTH FLORIDA GAZPACHO

Gazpacho is one of the light cold soups we enjoy in the warm months. It is actually very simple to prepare. It's a contribution from Spanish pioneers, although the tomato has only been eaten in Florida for about the last 100 years.

Serves 8

- 28 ounce can peeled tomatoes
- 28 ounce can crushed tomatoes
- 1 cup tomato juice
- 1 red or green bell pepper, chopped
- 2 cucumbers, peeled, seeded, and chopped
- 1 cup celery, finely chopped
- 1 clove garlic, minced
- ¼ cup olive oil
- 1 tablespoon red wine vinegar
- ¼ cup olive oil
- 1 tablespoon lemon juice
- ½ teaspoon Tabasco
- 2 teaspoons fresh thyme, minced
- 2 teaspoons fresh cilantro, minced
- 2 teaspoons fresh parsley, minced
- 2 teaspoons ground cumin
- ½ teaspoon sugar
- Salt and freshly ground black pepper, to taste
- 2 green onions, chopped

Dice plum tomatoes and place in a large bowl. Place paper towel in sieve and pour reserved tomato juice in. Let the juice strain, it will take about 10 minutes. Add can of crushed tomatoes to bowl. Add rest of ingredients to tomatoes in large bowl. Add strained tomato juice and mix thoroughly. Cover with plastic wrap and chill for 3-4 hours. Correct seasoning and serve with green onions.

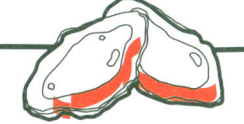

FLORIDA BOUILLABAISSE

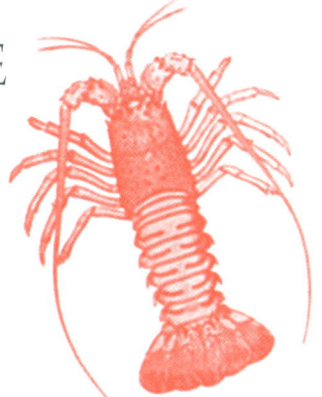

Bouillabaisse was traditionally made as a fisherman's stew to use up the fresh fish they were unable to sell at the market. This version is dressy enough to serve at an elegant dinner party. Don't skimp on the saffron, which gives this dish its delicate flavor.

Serves 8-10

- 2 cups onion, sliced thin
- 1 cup leeks, sliced thin
- ¾ cup olive oil
- 8 cups water
- 2 cups dry white wine
- 2 pounds fish heads and carcasses
- 4 cloves garlic, mashed
- 28 ounce can crushed Italian plum tomatoes
- ½ teaspoon dried fennel, crushed
- 1 teaspoon garlic, chopped fine
- 3 inch piece orange peel, no white pith
- 1 teaspoon dried thyme, crushed
- 2 sprigs parsley
- 1 bay leaf
- ¼ teaspoon saffron threads
- Salt and freshly ground black pepper, to taste

SEAFOOD:

- 2 - 1 pound Florida lobsters, or 2 pounds Blue Crabs, cleaned, cut up and claws cracked
- 1½ pounds firm fleshed fish (snapper, trigger, grouper) filets cut into 2 inch pieces
- 2 pounds mussels, in shells
- 2 pounds clams, in shell
- ½ pound scallops
- 8 stone crab claws, cracked
- Fresh parsley, minced

TO PREPARE SEAFOOD:

Bring soup stock to a rapid boil, add lobster or crabs, and fish. Cook 5 minutes, add mussels and clams and cook another 5 minutes. Add scallops and stone crab claws, cook 1 minute; do not overcook. Taste for seasoning and serve with fresh French or Cuban bread.

SOUP STOCK:

In a 6 quart stock pot, cook onions and leeks in oil over low heat, stirring frequently, for 5 minutes or until softened. Add water, wine, fish heads and carcasses, garlic, tomatoes, herbs and seasonings and cook, uncovered, over moderate heat 45 minutes. Strain stock into a large pot, pressing juices out of ingredients. Correct the seasonings and strength. Add bottled clam juice or fish stock to strengthen if needed.

THE CHILDREN'S "BEEF BOURGUIGNON WITH PASTA"

When our children were young, they were often not interested in eating the dinners we were making. We served them this 4-food-groups-in-one dish, then ate our own dinner later. In fact, we served this dish to our children so often they threatened to call the child abuse authorities and leave home. They begged us to never serve it again, and we haven't. But we saved the recipe, ha!

Cameron and Trey, this one's for you. Also for Elizabeth, Amelia and Ruby.

Serves 2 (ungrateful) children 3 meals.

- 1 pound lean ground beef
- ½ tablespoon bacon drippings
- 1 cup onion, chopped fine
- 16 ounce can tomatoes
- Salt to taste
- 4 cups cooked elbow macaroni
- 1-9 ounce package frozen English peas, thawed
- ½ teaspoon sugar

Brown ground beef in large cast-iron skillet. Remove and set aside. Add bacon drippings to skillet over medium-low heat. Add onions and brown. Return beef to skillet with onions and add tomatoes. Salt to taste. Stir in macaroni and peas. Correct seasoning and serve.

Trey enjoying a bowl of Beef Bourguignon, c 1980.

25 years later Trey's niece Amelia enjoying a bowl of Beef Bourguignon, c 2004.

Simply Scrumptious Salads

Harvesting potatoes in Hastings

Our Favorite Vinaigrette
  Salad, 150
Vinaigrette Dressings, 151
Our Favorite Salad with
  Creamy Dressing, 152
Creamy Dressings, 153
Bern's Caesar Salad, 154
The Derby Salad, 155
Derby Cheese Spread, 155
Fresh Spinach Salad, 156
Marinated Tomato Salad, 156

Pappas Greek Salad, 157
Heart of Palm Salad, 158
Spanish Salad, 159
Tamari Salad, 160
Ann's Conch Salad, 161
Gulf Coast Shrimp Salad, 161
Tuna and Northern
  Bean Salad, 162
Cracked Crab Salad, 163
West Indies Salad, 163

Crab Boats, 164
Wilted Lettuce with Bacon, 164
Old Florida Chicken Salad, 165
Whiteway Tabbouleh, 166
Spuds New Potato Salad, 167
Pensacola Gaspache Salad, 168
Fried Okra Salad, 168
College Inns' Macaroni Salad, 169
Fresh Salsa, 169
1905 Perfection Salad, 170

A Spanish proverb tells us that four persons are necessary to make a good salad dressing: "A spendthrift for oil, a miser for vinegar, a barrister for salt and a madman to stir it up." This shows at once that there should be more oil than vinegar, the salt must be added showing good judgment and the tossing should be fast and continual until all ingredients are thoroughly mixed.

Our mild North Florida climate enables us to reap the freshest ingredients to make a great salad the year round, from the first tender lettuces and onions in the spring garden to the cabbage and mustard greens harvested in the winter. Salads have come a long way from the iceberg wedge and bottled dressing of yesteryear to the interesting combinations of different lettuces and vegetables along with a variety of cheeses, mustards, flavored vinegars and numerous oils we have today. Topping the salad with freshly ground black pepper can be the difference between good and great.

North Florida has many unique salads that are featured in restaurants and homes. From Pensacola, the Gaspache salad is a favorite that has been handed down through many generations of families of Spanish descent. It contains hardtack, a sea biscuit from days of old and reflects Pensacola's importance as a sailing port. Many ships docked there to export cotton, lumber and rosin from the virgin pines that once dominated the landscape of North Florida. Pensacola was also a leading port in the processing and shipping of red snapper and at one time provided 80% of the world's supply.

The cracker kitchens from the interior of North Florida have given us the tasty heart of palm salad made with the bud or "heart" of the Sabal Palmetto Palm. The heart of palm can be served simply with a vinaigrette or with the dressing featured in this chapter.

Many of North Florida's first resort hotels like the Keystone in Fernandina had their own gardens for vegetables, salad greens and herbs. Watercress was gathered from nearby streams. Milk cows, chickens and ducks were kept for fresh milk, butter and yard eggs.

The fertile farms around St. Johns County are the top producers of cabbage and potatoes in the state. We utilize these vegetables to make our tangy slaws and potato salads enjoyed at fish frys, barbecues and at most any outside event.

From the groves along the Indian River comes the juicy Naval oranges, grapefruit and satsumas we enjoy in our fruit salads and ambrosia during the winter holidays.

SIMPLY SCRUMPTIOUS SALADS

Salads along the Atlantic Coast sometimes include toasted croutons made from Pita bread, a contribution from our Middle Eastern friends who also introduced us to the Tabbouleh salad, which features chopped parsley and burghul wheat.

The Tamari salad is popular in some of the St. Augustine restaurants, the dressing combines tamari sauce, yeast and garlic.

The European custom of serving salad as the last course has never caught on in North Florida. Salads are usually served before or during the meal. Shrimp or crabmeat are sometimes added to the salads and are served as the main course for a lunch or light supper.

The tomato, which is a very important ingredient in some salads, is a relatively new addition. Prior to the 1900's, tomatoes were considered poisonous and were grown only for ornamental value. Fortunately, the Italians discovered the merits of fresh and cooked tomatoes and sent them back to the New World. Today, our salads may include the luscious "love apple," as well as the many other delicious seasonal ingredients.

Today's supermarket tomatoes are nice to look at but have very little taste. Tomatoes should be almost ripe when picked. We prefer the older heritage varieties, the seeds are available from several mail order sources: Manaluci, Brandywine, and Beefsteak are our favorite varieties.

We like to plant basil, rosemary, tarragon, thyme, bay, sage, oregano, parsley, mint, and chives. Other herbs and spices are bought in small quantities and stored in a dark cabinet. Peppercorns and nutmeg are ground fresh as needed for cooking and at the table. We usually use fresh garlic instead of garlic powder or garlic salt.

Our favorite salad varies on which ingredients are available. A large handful of greens is usually enough for one person. A variety of greens are included along with chopped green onions with fresh herbs, parsley, thyme, oregano or basil. Vine-ripe tomatoes when available and Feta cheese, or a blue cheese or a goat cheese. This is topped with our homemade dressing, usually six tablespoons of extra-virgin olive oil, one clove of garlic, finely minced and one to one and one-half tablespoons of a flavored vinegar or lemon juice. Of course salt and lots of freshly ground black pepper. Toss on grilled chicken or shrimp and it becomes a meal in itself.

OUR FAVORITE VINAIGRETTE SALAD

We start our salad by selecting whatever greens are the freshest at the market. For a perfect salad, wash 2-3 different salad greens, dry thoroughly using a salad spinner, if possible and tear into bite size pieces. A large handful of greens is usually enough for one person. Store the remaining lettuce for your next salad. Spinach will not keep, it should be used the same day it is washed. If making a salad for a dinner party we often clean the lettuce and tear into bite-size pieces, place greens in large plastic bag and refrigerate until serving. If the salad is going to be small we cover the lettuce with paper towels, wrap in a clean dish towel and refrigerate for at least an hour to crisp before serving. Prepare salad additions (vine-ripe or plum tomatoes, garlic, green onions, mushrooms, cheese, cucumbers, celery, herb's, etc.) and place in a large wooden bowl, add lettuce and toss with minimum amount of dressing. Taste and correct amount of dressing needed. Serve in chilled salad dishes and top with freshly ground black pepper.

The dressing for this salad is a basic vinaigrette. A quality olive oil, lemon or lime juice or flavored vinegar, garlic, salt and pepper, are all the ingredients necessary for a great salad dressing. A Dijon style mustard with or without seeds may also be added and any herb or cheese may be used. This is a very versatile salad which can be changed with what's on hand.

Serves 4

- 1 clove garlic, finely minced
- 6 tablespoons virgin olive oil
- 1½ cups tomatoes, cubed
- 3 green onions, chopped
- ⅓ cup parsley, minced
- ¾ teaspoon thyme or oregano or basil, crumbled
- ½ teaspoon salt
- 1½-2 tablespoons lemon juice
- 4 ounces feta or goat cheese, crumbled
- Freshly ground black pepper
- 4-6 handfuls of Spring green mix salad greens

Place garlic in olive oil 2 hours before serving. Place tomatoes, onion, parsley and oil with garlic in a large salad bowl. Sprinkle with herb of choice and salt. Toss and let mixture marinate 30 minutes. Add salad greens and toss thoroughly. Sprinkle with lemon juice, cheese of choice, and black pepper. Toss thoroughly and serve.

SIMPLY SCRUMPTIOUS SALADS

BALSAMIC VINAIGRETTE

½ cup extra-virgin olive oil
⅛ cup balsamic vinegar
½ teaspoon salt
1 teaspoon freshly ground black pepper

Place all ingredients in a food processor and process for 10 seconds.

HONEY MUSTARD VINAIGRETTE

2 tablespoons red wine vinegar
2 teaspoons Dijon mustard
1 tablespoon Tupelo honey
½ cup extra virgin olive oil
½ teaspoon salt
½ teaspoon freshly ground black pepper

Place all ingredients in a food processor and process for 10 seconds.

ORIENTAL VINAIGRETTE

½ cup tamari
¼ cup sesame oil
6 tablespoons rice vinegar
2 tablespoons sugar
2 tablespoons rice wine
¼ teaspoon salt
¼ teaspoon black pepper, freshly ground

Place all ingredients in a food processor and process 10 seconds.

Tamari is a less salty version of soy sauce. It can be found in oriental markets.

CREOLE VINAIGRETTE

1 egg
3 tablespoons Creole mustard
1 teaspoon salt
1 teaspoon black pepper, freshly ground
1 teaspoon Tabasco sauce
3 tablespoons Worcestershire
1 teaspoon garlic, minced
4 tablespoons Parmesan cheese, grated
2 teaspoons horseradish
⅓ cup apple cider vinegar
1 cup extra virgin olive oil

Combine all ingredients in large mixing bowl, except olive oil. Whip vigorously until thoroughly mixed. Pour olive oil in slowly, while whisking.

KEVIN'S COWBOY VINAIGRETTE

1 pint red wine vinegar
3 pints olive oil
2 tablespoons of salt
2 tablespoons pepper (White)
1 tablespoon Basil
1 tablespoon Oregano
1 tablespoon Thyme
½ cup sugar
1 tablespoon Garlic

Place all ingredients in a food processor and process until very smooth. Transfer to a jar, cover and let stand 1 hour before serving.

BASIL VINAIGRETTE

1 cup fresh basil leaves
¾ cup extra virgin olive oil
2½ tablespoons balsamic vinegar
¼ teaspoon salt

Place all ingredients in a food processor and process 10 seconds.

OUR FAVORITE SALAD WITH CREAMY DRESSINGS

Salads during our childhood consisted of a wedge of iceberg lettuce topped with a commercial orange French dressing. Today we still like iceberg lettuce along with vine-ripe tomatoes, a slice of red onion, thinly sliced cucumbers, grated carrots, strips of red bell pepper, Kosher salt and freshly ground black pepper, with Creamy Blue Cheese Dressing served on the side. This recipe doesn't call for much cheese so buy the best quality you can find.

Creamy Blue Cheese Dressing

There were only two types of cheese available when we were young: good on everything Velveeta and the sharper Hoop cheese which was typically eaten by the grown-ups on saltine crackers. No one ever considered putting cheese in a salad. Of course they served pimento n' cheese and grilled cheese sandwiches down at the drug store, but we usually went for a root beer float on the rare times we had a spare dime and a nickel.

Make this dressing 24 hours before serving and refrigerate to give the flavors a chance to develop. We prefer serving the dressing on the side.

8 ounces sour cream
¾ cup homemade mayonnaise
¼ cup lemon juice

3 green onions, minced
4 ounces Blue cheese or Roquefort, crumbled

In a large bowl, mix sour cream, mayonnaise, lemon juice, and onions. Thin with whipping cream if needed. Stir in cheese. Place in air tight container and refrigerate. Will keep in refrigerator 2 weeks. Makes 2 cups

Homemade Mayonnaise

1 egg
1 tablespoon lemon juice
½ teaspoon salt

¼ teaspoon white pepper
1½ cups vegetable oil

To make mayonnaise, use the metal blade of your food processor. Add egg, lemon juice, salt, white pepper and process 2-3 seconds. Leave the machine running and gradually add vegetable oil through the feed tube. The mayonnaise should thicken within seconds. Taste for additional salt and refrigerate. Makes one and three-fourth cups. Any fresh minced herb or combination of herbs maybe added to the mayonnaise.

SIMPLY SCRUMPTIOUS SALADS

Thousand Island Dressing
Makes 2 cups

- 1 cup Hellmann's mayonnaise
- ⅓ cup Heinz chili sauce
- 1 teaspoon yellow onion, finely diced
- 1 tablespoon parsley, chopped
- 1 tablespoon pimento, finely diced
- ½ teaspoon lemon juice
- 1 tablespoon honey
- 1 teaspoon capers
- 1 hard-boiled egg, finely chopped

In a small bowl, combine all ingredients and blend well. Store in refrigerator.

Creamy French Dressing
Makes 6 cups

- 1 cup vegetable oil
- ¼ cup fresh lemon juice
- 1½ cups ketchup
- ½ cup sugar
- ¼ cup onion, grated
- ¼ cup fresh horseradish, grated
- ¼ cup Worcestershire
- ½ cup apple-cider vinegar
- ½ teaspoon celery seeds
- ½ teaspoon salt
- Freshly ground black pepper, to taste

Combine all ingredients and mix well. Refrigerate until ready to use.

Note: If using prepared horseradish adjust the quantity accordingly.

Ranch Dressing
Makes 1½ cups

- ¾ cup sour cream
- ¼ cup buttermilk
- ¼ cup Hellmann's mayonnaise
- 3 tablespoons fresh lemon juice
- ½ teaspoon salt
- Freshly ground black pepper, to taste
- 3 tablespoons parsley, chopped
- 3 tablespoons green onions, chopped

Combine all ingredients well. Refrigerate until ready to use.

Louie Dressing

Louie Louie was a popular song in the 60's with words no one could understand, (sound familiar kids?) there were several versions of the lyrics going around. None could we could print here though. This is a refreshing dressing for seafood that also became popular in the 60's.

- ½ cup mayonnaise
- ⅛ cup whipping cream
- ¼ cup chili sauce
- 1 tablespoon Worcestershire
- 1 tablespoon lemon juice
- ⅛ teaspoon cayenne pepper
- ½ teaspoon salt
- 1 tablespoon green onion, minced
- Seafood of choice

Combine all ingredients for dressing in a large bowl except seafood. Whisk until thoroughly mixed. Mix with seafood. Cover bowl with plastic wrap and refrigerate for at least one hour before serving.

BERN'S CAESAR SALAD

One of the best Caesar Salads we have enjoyed was at Bern's Steak House in Tampa. The salad was prepared at our table with the very freshest ingredients. Bern is our kind of restaurateur. He insists on freshness and quality in every phase of the menu. Not only does he grow his own vegetables and herb's, but the fish you order is swimming in a large tank in the kitchen. He ages his own steaks and has one of the largest wine cellars in the world. As you can tell, it is one of our favorite restaurants.

Serves 4

- 1 clove fresh garlic (peeled)
- 6 large anchovies (chopped)
- ⅔ cup Bern's Caesar Oil (Recipe to follow)
- 4 tablespoons lemon juice (2 lemons)
- Freshly ground black pepper
- 2-3 coddled eggs (boiled 1 minute)
- 1 cup freshly grated Parmesan cheese (or blend of Parmesan and Romano)
- 1 large head of Romaine lettuce torn in salad size pieces (enough for 4 servings)
- 1 cup Bern's Garlic Croutons (recipe to follow)

Rub large wooden salad bowl with garlic clove. In the wooden bowl, mix together anchovies, Caesar oil, lemon juice, pepper and egg until well blended. Add Romaine pieces. Toss to coat every piece. Add three-fourths of the cheese, reserving remaining cheese to sprinkle on salad. Toss again. To serve, place in individual chilled salad bowls and sprinkle with croutons and cheese.

BERN'S CAESAR OIL:

- 1 cup fine quality olive oil
- ½ ounce garlic (peeled, 1-2 cloves)
- Oil from 2 ounce tin of anchovies
- ½ anchovy

Purée all ingredients. Remember to use only two-thirds of this for salad recipe, (yield: 1 cup).

BERN'S GARLIC CROUTONS:

- 4 slices tight knit bread (allow to air dry).
- 2-4 garlic cloves (peeled)
- Spike seasoning (available at health food stores)

Put a small "dab" of Spike seasoning in a dish, then dip the peeled garlic in the seasoning and rub the bread (both sides) with the seasoned garlic. Cut in small cubes and toast lightly. (Yield: 1 cup)

THE DERBY SALAD

The Green Derby, located in Riverside, in Jacksonville, was one of those restaurants we fondly remember. The owner, Joe Adeeb would greet you at the door and treat you like family. Behind him was a large cooler filled with aged steaks he was serving that evening. After he seated you the waitress would bring the pumpernickel toast and a crock of complimentary cheese spread and took our cocktail orders. It was our daughter, Cameron's favorite restaurant because the waitress would bring her a Shirley Temple along with our cocktails. The waitress would then roll the salad cart to our table and prepare the most delicious salad from scratch. You could choose from the various ingredients to create the best salad ever and top it with crunchy pita croutons. The steaks arrived, sizzling and cooked to perfection. Then the waitress would fluff your baked potato by pounding it on the cart, and stir in the butter, sour cream and chives while the potato was still hot. Ah, those were the days...

We thought this salad was gone for good, when the Green Derby closed in the 1970's. But a long time friend and local raconteur, the late Paul Broome, came across the recipe and gave it to us to share with you.

Serves 4

- 1 large head Iceberg lettuce, cut in ½ inch squares
- 1 cup parsley, chopped
- ½ cup scallions, chopped
- 1 Syrian (Pita) bread cut into one inch squares and toasted
- 8 tablespoons Olive oil in which pieces of garlic marinate
- 3 tomatoes, quartered
- 4 tablespoons wine vinegar
- Salt and pepper, to taste
- ⅛ teaspoon accent
- ½ teaspoon oregano, crumbled
- ½ cup Parmesan cheese, freshly grated

Measure into a large wooden salad bowl: olive oil, wine vinegar. Add salt, pepper, accent, and oregano. Add tomatoes and chop into dressing. Add lettuce (in squares), parsley and scallions. Add toasted croutons. Toss lightly and place in bowls. Sprinkle with Parmesan cheese. Salad must be served immediately.

GREEN DERBY CHEESE SPREAD

Soften 8 ounces cheddar cheese grated, to room temperature. Mix with 3 tablespoons port, one eighth teaspoon garlic powder and chill. Serve with Pumpernickel toast.

SIMPLY SCRUMPTIOUS SALADS

FRESH SPINACH SALAD

"I yam what I yam."

Our family always ate greens by the truck load. We enjoyed turnip greens, mustard greens, and even the lowly collard green. To us, spinach was that stuff that Popeye the sailor man squirted out of the can and consumed when he had to save Olive Oyl, or when Bruno needed an attitude adjustment. It was later in life when we discovered fresh spinach. We've been trying to make up for it ever since. We enjoy fresh spinach often in salads and also sautéed with garlic and olive oil.

Serves 4

- 4 slices smoked bacon, cooked and crumbled
- 2 garlic cloves, crushed
- ½ cup olive oil
- 1 slice pita bread, for croutons
- 1 tablespoon balsamic vinegar
- Salt and freshly ground black pepper, to taste
- 6 cups fresh spinach, washed and stemmed
- ¼ cup red onion, thinly sliced
- ½ cup Feta cheese, crumbled
- 8 Calamata olives
- 4 canned artichokes, cut into fourths
- 1 tablespoon small capers

Preheat oven to 350 degrees. In a small bowl, combine garlic and one half cup olive oil. Brush both sides of pita bread with garlic-oil mixture, cut into cubes, scatter on baking sheet and bake 5-7 minutes, or until crisp. Set aside to cool. Add vinegar, salt and pepper to remaining oil mixture. In a salad bowl, toss spinach, onion, cheese, olives, artichokes and capers. Add vinaigrette and toss again. Sprinkle with bacon, pita croutons and serve immediately.

MARINATED TOMATO SALAD

Serves 4

- 3 vine ripe tomatoes, sliced
- ½ pound mushrooms, sliced
- 2 ounces mozzarella cheese, sliced
- 10 fresh basil leaves, julienne
- 1 clove garlic, minced
- Salt and freshly ground black pepper, to taste
- 4 tablespoons olive oil
- 1 tablespoon lemon juice

Our brother, Charles Lee McDonald with his 4 pound home grown tomatoes, c 2000.

In deep platter, add tomatoes, mushrooms, mozzarella and basil leaves. In small bowl, mix garlic, salt, pepper, olive oil and lemon juice. When thoroughly combined, pour over tomato mixture. Cover with plastic wrap and marinate 1 hour before serving. Spoon dressing over tomatoes and mushrooms 2-3 times while marinating.

PAPPAS GREEK SALAD

The Greeks have been active in the restaurant business, contributing to our cuisine, as well as fishing, shrimping and sponge diving along our coastal cities for many, many years. Several of our larger cities like Jacksonville, St. Augustine and Pensacola have annual Greek Festivals celebrating the Greek culture and featuring delicious Greek foods.

This salad has a treat of potatoes hidden under the lettuce. It's always on the table when we have a crab boil.

Serves 4

- 4-6 large new potatoes
- 4 green onions, chopped
- ¼ cup parsley, minced
- 3 tablespoons vinegar
- 3-4 tablespoons mayonnaise

Cover potatoes with water and cook for 25-30 minutes, or until tender. Drain, peel potatoes while hot and dice into bowl. Add onions, parsley, vinegar and mayonnaise. Stir until mixture is almost consistency of stiff mashed potatoes. Cool, cover and refrigerate.

- 1 head Romaine lettuce
- 1 large head Iceberg lettuce, shredded
- 2 tomatoes, cut into wedges
- 1 peeled cucumber, seeded and cut into thin strips 1 inch long
- 1 avocado, peeled and cut into wedges
- 1 green bell pepper, cut into thin strips 1 inch long
- 1 red bell pepper, cut into thin strips 1 inch long
- 8 slices canned beets
- 8 shrimp, cooked, peeled and chilled
- 8 anchovy filets (optional)
- 12 Greek olives
- 12 salonika peppers
- 4 whole green onions
- 8 ounces feta cheese, crumbled
- ¾ cup olive oil
- ¼ cup white distilled vinegar
- 1 teaspoon dried oregano, crumbled
- Salt and freshly ground black pepper, to taste

Line individual salad bowls with Romaine lettuce leaves. Mound potato salad in center of each bowl. Cover with shredded lettuce. Add tomatoes around base of salad. Arrange cucumber, avocado, bell pepper, beets, shrimp, anchovies, olives, peppers, green onions, and feta over shredded lettuce. In a glass jar, mix vinegar, olive oil, oregano, salt and pepper by shaking vigorously, drizzle over salads and serve.

HEART OF PALM SALAD

*F*lorida's state tree, the *"Sabal Palmetto"* is also known as the cabbage palm. In times past, palm logs were used for fortification, dock pilings or sometimes log cabin walls. Baskets, mats and hats were made from the leaves. The fiber from the base of young leaves was used in the manufacture of whisk brooms.

Seminole Indians built hurricane-proof dwellings roofed with cabbage palm fronds and were probably the first to discover the nutty sweet taste of the heart. Heart of palm is eaten raw or boiled and is still enjoyed by those fortunate enough to live close to a palm thicket.

Since removing the heart means certain death to the tree, we encourage limiting your supply to trees being cleared for construction or agricultural purposes. Fresh heart of palm is difficult to find for most folks, so use the canned hearts from Brazil.

Serves 4

- 3 cups heart of palm, chopped
- 2 cups fresh, chopped, or one 14 ounce can artichoke hearts, sliced
- 4 anchovies
- 1 cup celery, minced
- ½ cup parsley, minced
- ¾ cup green onions, minced
- Salt and pepper, to taste
- 2 vine ripe tomatoes, cut into wedges
- 3 cups lettuce
- 2 hard-boiled eggs sliced
- 1 recipe anchovy vinaigrette (recipe below)

In a bowl mix celery, parsley, green onions, salt and pepper. Divide into four equal parts. Place lettuce on four salad plates. Arrange heart of palm and artichokes in center. Place tomatoes and eggs on the side, top with anchovies and spoon anchovy vinaigrette over all.

ANCHOVY VINAIGRETTE

- ½ cup parsley
- 1 clove garlic
- 2 tablespoons red wine vinegar
- ½ cup olive oil
- 6 anchovy fillets
- Salt and pepper to taste
- 1 tablespoon capers

Process parsley and garlic in food processor until minced. Add remaining ingredients and process 30 seconds.

Princess Sonja Martin displaying recently harvested palm heart, c 1994.

SPANISH SALAD

Spanish salad makes an exceptional first course. Serve with a large pitcher of Sangria and follow with a dish of Arroz con Pollo (Chicken and Rice). Don't forget the flan for dessert.

Serves 4-6

- 1 large head Iceberg lettuce
- 2 garlic cloves
- 2 green onions, chopped
- ½ bell pepper, chopped
- 2 ribs celery, chopped
- ¼ pound Swiss cheese, cut into thin strips
- ¼ pound ham, cut into thin strips
- 8 green Spanish olives
- 1 small cucumber, seeded and cut into 1 inch strips
- Salt and freshly ground black pepper, to taste
- 8 Greek olives
- 2 teaspoon parsley, minced
- 2 teaspoons oregano, crumbled
- ½ cup Spanish olive oil
- 1 tablespoon red-wine vinegar
- Juice of 1 lemon or lime
- 1 large tomato, cubed
- ½ cup Parmesan cheese, freshly grated
- 4-6 anchovy filets (optional)

Tear lettuce and place in plastic bag, and refrigerate. Press garlic and put in a jar, cover with olive oil and set aside 1 hour. Rub wooden salad bowl with 1 tablespoon garlic-oil mixture. Place green onion, bell pepper, celery, cheese, ham, and olives in wooden bowl. Salt and pepper to taste, sprinkle with oregano and toss. Add torn lettuce to salad bowl, drizzle remainder of olive oil over salad, toss to coat thoroughly and add the vinegar. Squeeze lemon/lime juice over all, add tomato and sprinkle with Parmesan cheese. Mix thoroughly and serve at once. Top salad with anchovies if desired.

WHITE SANGRIA

Carlos White (Chautauqua Muscadine) wine with fruit.

Serves 4-6

Pour 1 bottle white wine, one quarter cup brandy and one quarter cup sugar into a large pitcher. Add one half lime, sliced, one half lemon, sliced, one half orange, sliced one half apple, sliced and stir until sugar dissolves, add more sugar if desired. Cover and refrigerate until chilled. Just before serving add 6 ounces of club soda and stir to mix.

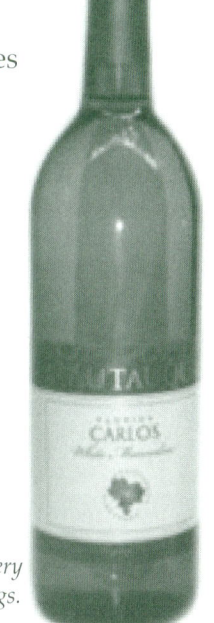

Chautauqua winery DeFuniak Springs.

TAMARI SALAD

This is an unusual and delicious salad popular in several restaurants around St. Augustine. The dressing is a combination of tamari, yeast and garlic and gives the salad a perky flavor. Active dry yeast seems have a more yeasty flavor than rapid rise yeast. Alfalfa sprouts are easily grown and add flavor and texture to fresh salads.

Serves 4

- 1 packet of yeast
- 2 tablespoons warm water
- 2 teaspoons sugar
- ½ cup vegetable oil
- 1 teaspoon sesame oil
- ⅓ cup sesame paste
- 1½-2 tablespoons lemon juice
- 2 tablespoons tamari or soy sauce
- 1 clove garlic, crushed
- Dash of cayenne pepper
- 1 head Romaine lettuce, torn into bite-size pieces
- 1 large carrot, finely grated
- 1 cup alfalfa sprouts
- 8 tomato wedges
- 4 tablespoons sunflower seeds, toasted

Place yeast in a small bowl with warm water, add sugar and set aside. Add vegetable oil, sesame oil, sesame paste, garlic, lemon juice, tamari, cayenne and yeast mixture to blender and mix thoroughly. Chill until ready to serve. In 4 individual salad bowls, equally divide the Romaine. Divide carrot into fourths and place in each bowl. Sprinkle a fourth cup of alfalfa sprouts on each salad. Place 2 tomato wedges in each bowl. Pour salad dressing over each salad. Sprinkle each salad with 1 tablespoon sunflower seeds and serve. Keep any leftover dressing in refrigerator with loose fitting lid.

SOIL-LESS ALFALFA SPROUTS

- 1 wide mouth jar
- 6x6 inch piece of cheese cloth
- Rubber band
- 1 ½ tablespoons alfalfa seeds

Place seeds in jar, add enough water to cover them, cover jar with cheese cloth and place rubber band around top of the jar, pulling cloth tight. Soak seeds overnight. Drain soaking water through cloth. Rinse seeds well without removing cloth. Turn jar upside down in dish drainer and place in dark, warm place. Rinse seed 2 times each day. Gently shake jar to distribute seeds around walls of jar. Sprouts should be 1-2 inches long after 4-5 days. Place in sun for a couple of hours to develop bright green color. Refrigerate.

ANN'S CONCH SALAD

*C*onch are easy to catch but difficult to clean. Hit the shell base, with a welding hammer and slice muscle with a knife. To release the meat pull out the hole on the opposite end.

Serves 4

1 pound conch
6 limes
1 cucumber, peeled, seeded and chopped
½ cup red onion, chopped
1 cup olive oil
½ cup cilantro, chopped
2 teaspoons fresh oregano, chopped
1 teaspoon sugar
½ teaspoon salt
Freshly ground black pepper

Chop conch into one eights pinch pieces, cover with lime juice. Marinate 2-4 hours. Drain conch. Place conch in a large bowl and add remaining ingredients. Refrigerate for at least 1 hour.

GULF COAST SHRIMP SALAD

*S*ometimes we take our abundant fresh shrimp in North Florida for granted. Guests from out of state can't seem to get enough and some will eat shrimp for every meal. Shrimp may be prepared in hundreds of ways and served for almost any course in a meal. This salad is one of our favorites for the noon meal; it is also excellent for a light supper.

Serves 4

4 ribs celery, minced
1 pound large shrimp, boiled cut into 2-3 pieces
Juice of ½ lemon or to taste
½ cup Homemade Mayonnaise
1 tablespoon chili sauce
¼ cup fresh dill, chopped (optional)
Salt and freshly ground black pepper, to taste
Shredded lettuce
2 tomatoes, cut in wedges
1 cucumber, sliced
1 avocado, sliced
1 tablespoon fresh parsley, minced

In a bowl, add celery, shrimp and lemon juice and toss to coat. Mix mayonnaise, chili sauce, parsley and dill in a small bowl. Add to shrimp with salt and pepper to taste, and toss until thoroughly mixed. Cover with plastic wrap and refrigerate for 1-2 hours before serving. Serve on shredded lettuce, garnish with tomatoes, cucumber, avocado and sprinkle with parsley.

TUNA AND NORTHERN BEAN SALAD

O.K. what are Northern beans doing in a Southern cookbook, you say? Because it's about Northern Florida, don't you know. This is one of our favorite salads and we couldn't leave it out just because it has Northern beans. If you happen to have fresh tuna, use it, if not, canned is fine. This salad should marinate for several hours before serving. It is great for a summer Sunday supper. Serve with freshly baked Sunflower Bread.

Serves 6

1 cup dried Great Northern white beans

3 cups chicken stock

Bring stock to a boil, add beans, cover, turn heat off and let sit for 1 hour. Return beans to a boil, reduce heat and cook on low heat one and a half hours or until tender, add water if needed. Do not overcook beans. Drain and refrigerate at least one hour.

4 tablespoons lemon juice
2 teaspoon Dijon mustard
Salt and freshly ground black pepper, to taste
2/3 cup olive oil
3 cups cooked Northern beans
4 green onions, sliced thin
4 ribs celery, sliced thin
5 cups shredded Romaine lettuce

2 vine ripe tomatoes, cut into wedges
2 hard-boiled eggs, quartered
1 tablespoon small capers
3 tablespoons fresh dill, chopped
2 - 7 ounce cans water packed tuna, drained and flaked with fork

In a large bowl, whisk together lemon juice, mustard, salt and pepper. Add oil in a stream, whisking until mixed. Add beans, green onions, celery, capers, parsley, dill and tuna. Toss mixture lightly, cover with plastic wrap and refrigerate one hour. Arrange Romaine on a large platter, mound tuna salad on top. Garnish with tomato wedges, eggs and Bread and Butter Pickles, and serve.

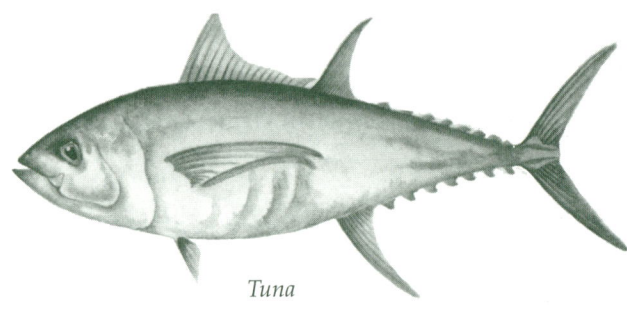

Tuna

CRACKED CRAB SALAD

You're really going to love this one. When we have a crab boil we always cook more crabs than we can eat because we have to have this salad the next day.

Serves 4

- ½ cup olive oil
- 2-3 tablespoons lime juice
- 1¼ teaspoons salt
- ¾ teaspoon black pepper, freshly ground
- ¼ teaspoon dry mustard
- ¼ teaspoon thyme, crumbled
- ¼ teaspoon basil, crumbled
- 2 tablespoons fresh parsley, minced
- ½ cup green onions, chopped
- ⅛ teaspoon sugar
- 4-6 large boiled blue crabs, with claws cracked
- 1 large head Romaine lettuce

Put all ingredients except crab and lettuce in small bowl and mix well. Remove red, hard shell of boiled crabs, the triangular covering on the underside or "apron", pull off the fibrous "dead man" matter, and cut off the legs. Use a sharp knife to break or crack the bodies in half, then break each half into thirds. Place crabs in large shallow dish, with tight fitting cover, pour dressing over all and toss, refrigerate for at least 4 hours. Stir crab several times while refrigerated. Wash, dry and tear lettuce into bite-sized pieces. Place in large bowl, add crab mixture and toss. Taste, correct the seasonings and serve.

WEST INDIES SALAD

This salad originated over in Mobile, Alabama.

Serves 6-8

- 2 pounds crab meat
- 2 small onions, minced
- Couple of dashes of salt
- Freshly ground black pepper
- 6 tablespoons olive oil
- 4 tablespoons lemon juice
- ½ cup white vinegar
- Couple of dashes of Worcestershire
- Scant half cup of ice water

Spread a layer of crab meat into a bowl and cover with a thin layer of onions, salt and pepper. Repeat until all the crab meat and onions are used. In another bowl pour the oil, lemon juice, vinegar and Worcestershire. Whisk together and pour over crab meat mixture. Pour ice water along with some crushed ice over the entire surface until all is used. Add more ice water if needed to cover surface. Place bowl in refrigerator overnight. Seal in quart jar. Serve in small bowls as an appetizer. Garnish with tomato wedges.

CRAB BOATS

This delectable salad is served in the avocado shells and makes a very impressive salad course.

Serves 6

- 3 ripe avocado
- 2 pounds lump crab meat, picked over
- ½ cup celery, finely chopped
- ¼ cup fresh lemon juice
- ¼ cup white wine vinegar
- ½ cup cilantro, chopped
- 2 teaspoons fresh oregano, chopped
- 1 teaspoon sugar
- ½ teaspoon salt
- Freshly ground black pepper

Half, pit and remove the avocado with a spoon and cut into 1 inch pieces, save the avocado shells. In a large bowl combine the avocado, crab meat, and celery. Whisk together in a small bowl the lemon juice, vinegar, olive oil, shallots and cayenne, pour dressing over avocado mix and gently stir. Mound salad in avocado shells on plates lined with lettuce leaves, garnish with tomato and lemon wedges.

WILTED LETTUCE WITH BACON

This is an old Southern classic. Serve with the first lettuce that gets by the rabbits in the spring garden. The lettuce should be completely dry before tossing with hot bacon drippings or the oil will spatter.

We often serve this as a side dish with barbecue ribs and Granny's Green Rice.

Serves 6

- 1 small purple onion, sliced thin
- 1 large head leafy lettuce
- 1 large head curly endive, or red leaf lettuce
- 6 slices smoked bacon
- Bacon drippings
- ⅓ cup apple cider vinegar
- 2 tablespoons sugar
- ½ cup Blue , Roquefort or Gorgonzola cheese, crumbled
- Salt and freshly ground black pepper, to taste

Cut onion into very thin slices and place in bowl of ice water, set aside. Tear lettuce into bite-size pieces and place in large wooden bowl. Mix vinegar and sugar together, stir to dissolve, and set aside. Cook bacon until crisp, remove, drain on paper towels, cool and crumble. Pour bacon drippings into measuring cup, adding more if necessary to make two thirds cup. Return bacon drippings to pan and heat until hot but not smoking. Drain onions and pat dry with paper towels. Drizzle bacon drippings over salad and toss. Add vinegar-sugar mixture, cheese, and toss. Salt and pepper salad, toss and add onions and crumbled bacon. Correct seasoning and serve immediately.

OLD FLORIDA CHICKEN SALAD

In the old days when we had chicken salad sometimes the yard bird would be tough. Granny would often run it through a meat grinder, so it was easy on the gums.

This salad is ideal for a summer meal. The avocado and its rich, buttery texture is a perfect addition.

Serves 8-10

- 2 - 3½ pound chickens
- 2 onions, cut in half
- ½ cup apple cider vinegar
- 1 rib celery, cut into fourths
- 1 bay leaf
- ½ teaspoon thyme, crumbled
- 2 teaspoons salt
- 2 avocados, peeled, seeded and cut into wedges
- 1 tablespoon lemon juice
- 1 cup celery, minced
- ⅔ cup green onions, minced
- ½ pound bacon, cut into ½ inch pieces
- 1 ½ cups roasted pecans, chopped
- Salt and freshly ground black pepper, to taste
- ½ cup Homemade Mayonnaise
- 2 vine-ripe tomatoes, cut into wedges

In a large pot, combine chickens, onions, vinegar, celery, parsley, bay leaf, thyme and salt. Add enough water to barely cover chickens. Bring liquid to a boil, skimming and removing foam. Reduce heat to low, cover and cook 1 hour, or until chicken is tender. Transfer chickens to a platter, reserving stock. When chicken has cooled, remove skin and bones, keeping meat in large chunks. Transfer chicken to a large bowl, cover with plastic wrap and chill. Before serving, cut meat into bite-sized pieces, place in a large bowl and set aside. In a small bowl, gently toss avocado with lemon juice. Cook bacon until crisp, drain on paper towels and crumble when cool.

Add celery, green onions, drained avocado, bacon, roasted pecans (see page 62), salt and pepper to chicken. Mix one quarter cup of reserved chicken stock, with mayonnaise, mix and pour over chicken and toss gently. Line a larger platter with Bibb lettuce and mound with chicken salad. Garnish with vine-ripe tomato wedges.

WHITEWAY TABBOULEH

The Whiteway Deli has been a Jacksonville landmark for over 85 years. It's operated today by brother and sister team, Sammy and Ann Salem. Walk past all the food products displayed along the aisle and make your way to the back where Ann and her helpers are busily preparing the yummy foods. Give them your order, grab a drink and chips and take a seat. Our favorite is a combination rider with tabbouleh, meat and cheese served in pita bread. While no longer $1.50 a dozen, the sandwiches are reasonably priced. When you are ready to leave just tell Sammy, at the cash register, what you had and he will ring it up with a smile. Years ago Sammy gave our son Trey a nickname of "The Honeybun Kid", for obvious reasons.

Tabbouleh is a refreshing, healthy salad featured in many sandwich shops in Northeast Florida. This salad also appears at many tailgate parties and luncheons along with another Middle East favorite, Hummus, a simple dip made with puréed chick-peas (garbanzo beans), garlic and sesame paste.

The cracked wheat (burghul) used in Tabbouleh has a nutty flavor, and a chewy texture that soaks up flavors. If you are using tabbouleh in a sandwich this method will keep the sandwich from becoming too soggy.

Serves 4-6

- ½ cup burghul (cracked wheat)
- ½ cup green onions, finely chopped
- 1 cup vine-ripe tomatoes, finely chopped
- ¾ cups cucumber, peeled, seeded and finely chopped (optional)
- 4 cups parsley, finely chopped
- 2 tablespoons fresh mint, finely chopped
- ½ cup extra-virgin olive oil
- ½ cup lemon juice
- ¾ teaspoon salt

Whiteway Deli, c 1927.

Place burghul in bowl and wash with warm water. Drain, wrap in kitchen towel and squeeze completely dry. Do not let burghul soak in water. Place in large bowl with onions, tomatoes, cucumber, parsley, mint, olive oil, lemon juice, salt and toss thoroughly. The burghul will soak the juices from the salad making it tender and more flavorful. Taste for seasoning, cover with plastic wrap, chill at least 2 hours and serve.

SPUDS NEW POTATO SALAD

Spuds is a small community located smack dab in the middle of the potato producing area of St. Johns County, located between St. Augustine and Hastings. Supposedly, the name Spud is the acronym for The Society for Prevention of Unwholesome Diets, a group in colonial Virginia who promoted potatoes as a wholesome necessity for a nutritional diet. Most of the potatoes grown around Spuds are marketed as potato chips, but many are also used for baking and salads.

New potatoes, sometimes called red bliss, are harvested in the spring. We like to pick out the smallest potatoes, about the size of a jaw breaker for English peas with a light cream sauce and chopped salty ham. The larger potatoes are ideal for this salad.

Genevieve

My sister, Genny, who keeps the best herb garden ever, prefers this salad over the old-fashioned potato salad and serves it often.

Serves 8-10

- 4 pounds medium red potatoes
- 1½ cups mayonnaise
- 1½ cups sour cream
- 1½ teaspoons horseradish
- 1 teaspoon salt
- ½ cup celery, minced
- 1 teaspoon lemon juice
- 1 cup fresh parsley, chopped
- ½ cup fresh basil, chopped
- 3-4 green onions, chopped
- 4 slices bacon, cooked and crumbled
- 1 Jalapeno finely chopped
- Additional salt, if needed

Cover unpeeled potatoes with water in a large saucepan. Add salt and bring to a boil. Reduce heat, cover and cook potatoes for 30 minutes or until tender when pierced with a fork. Drain potatoes and slice them into one quarter inch slices while still warm. In a large mixing bowl, stir mayonnaise, sour cream, horseradish, salt, celery and lemon juice. Add the potatoes toss gently. Cover and chill. Before serving sprinkle with basil, green onions, bacon and Jalapeno.

Harvesting Potatoes in Spuds, c 1947.

PENSACOLA GASPACHE SALAD

Gaspache salads are a Pensacola specialty, handed down through many generations of Spanish families. It calls for hardtack, which is a rock hard bread (sea biscuit) that has to be soaked in water. We sometimes substitute stale pita bread and soak it for a shorter period of time. This salad should be served very cold. It keeps several days, refrigerated and improves with age.

Serves 6-8

- 2 hardtack, soaked in water
- 2 large tomatoes, sliced thin
- 1 bell pepper, sliced in thin strips
- 2 cucumbers, peeled and sliced thin
- 1 sweet Vidalia onion, sliced thin
- 1-1½ cups mayonnaise
- ⅓ cup claret wine
- Salt and freshly ground black pepper, to taste

Soak hardtack in water until soft, about one hour. Press and squeeze water out of bread until dry, set aside. In a large deep bowl, layer a third of crumbled hardtack. Sprinkle with a third of the wine and cover with one fourth the mayonnaise. Layer half the tomatoes overlapping, add salt and pepper. Next, layer half the bell pepper, onions, and cucumbers, salt and pepper and layer with one fourth of the mayonnaise. Continue to layer, ending with layer of hardtack, wine and mayonnaise.

FRIED OKRA SALAD

- 1 pound small fresh okra
- 2 cups buttermilk
- 1 pound bacon, cut into ½ inch pieces
- 1 cup cornmeal
- 1 cup all-purpose flour
- ¾ teaspoon black pepper, divided
- 1¼ teaspoons salt, divided
- 1¼ cup olive oil
- 3 tablespoon red wine vinegar
- 1½ tablespoons Dijon mustard
- 3 tablespoons Tupelo honey
- 1 pound Bibb lettuce
- 6 vine ripe tomatoes, quartered

Stir okra and buttermilk together, let stand 20 minutes. Thoroughly drain okra in a colander. Cook bacon in a large cast-iron skillet until crisp and drain on paper towels. Place cornmeal, flour, half the black pepper and one teaspoon salt in a large ziplock bag. Shake to mix thoroughly. Add 1 cup oil to skillet that you have fried bacon in over medium-high heat. Fry okra until golden brown on all sides. Remove to paper towels to drain. Whisk together in a medium bowl remaining salt, and pepper, vinegar, mustard and honey. Drizzle in remaining oil, whisking constantly. Tear lettuce in individual salad bowls, add tomatoes and fried okra. Drizzle salad dressing on top of salad and serve.

COLLEGE INNS' MACARONI SALAD

Cafeteria food in the South, at one time, meant highly seasoned vegetables, hot breads and eye appealing salads and desserts.

The now closed College Inn Cafeteria, formally located across from the University of Florida campus always served this version of macaroni salad with chunks of Cheddar cheese, which gave color and character to an otherwise drab dish. Our version is similar to the one served there.

Living large in the red ragtop. Gainesville, c 1966.

Serves 6-8

- 8 ounces elbow macaroni
- 1 cup Mayonnaise
- 2 tablespoons buttermilk
- 1 tablespoon lemon juice
- ¾ teaspoon salt
- 1 pound ham cubed
- Black pepper, freshly ground
- 1 cup sharp Cheddar cheese cubed
- 1 cup celery, diced
- 2 tablespoons parsley, minced
- ½ cup green onions, chopped
- ½ cup red bell pepper, chopped

Cook macaroni in a large pot of boiling, salted water until al dente. Drain well and let cool slightly. Mix the mayonnaise, milk, lemon juice, salt and pepper, and ham in a large bowl. Toss the macaroni with half the dressing, cover with plastic wrap and chill for several hours. Add the cheese, celery, parsley, green onions, red bell pepper and the remaining dressing to the macaroni.

Stir gently and blend well. Season with additional salt and pepper if desired. Serve immediately or cover and chill until needed.

FRESH SALSA

- 9 ounces frozen corn niblets
- 2 fresh plum tomatoes, diced
- ½ small cucumber, diced
- ¼ cup green onion, diced
- 1 garlic clove, crushed
- 2 tablespoons red bell pepper, chopped
- 1 Datil pepper, seeded and minced
- 2 tablespoons cilantro, minced
- ½ teaspoon ground cumin
- 1½ tablespoons olive oil
- 1 tablespoon lime juice
- Salt to taste

In a medium bowl place all ingredients. Cover with plastic wrap and refrigerate 4 hours. Remove from refrigerator an hour before serving.

1905 PERFECTION SALAD

For years we had been looking for an old wood burning stove to put in our pond house at Eucheeanna. One day my nephew Keaton Mc Donald called and said he had found one. It was rusty and dirty but we bought it anyway.

Keaton sandblasted it and painted it black, then it looked brand new. It was manufactured by Martin Foundry in Florence, Alabama. It has "Perfection" stamped across the front. After Keaton installed it he said, "Be careful Aunt Jo, I don't want to come back and you have "Perfection" branded on your butt!"

This salad is the mother of the endless parade of congealed salads popular in the 50's and 60's.

½ envelope Knox's Gelatin
½ cup cold water
½ cup vinegar
Juice of 1 lemon
1 pint boiling water
½ cup sugar
1 teaspoon salt
2 cups celery, cut in small pieces
1 cup avocado, mashed
1¼ cups tomato juice
3½ ounces diced pimentos

Soak gelatin in cold water two minutes, add vinegar, lemon juice, boiling water, sugar and salt. Strain, and when beginning to set add remaining ingredients. Ladle into a mold and chill. Serve on lettuce leaves with mayonnaise.

There are two major types of avocadoes in the supermarkets. The California (Haas) and the larger one from Florida. Use either type in this recipe. To keep avocadoes, artichokes, apples, pears and bananas from darkening sprinkle with lemon juice and toss.

Avocadoes are ripe when the skin gives to pressure. If they ripen too much use them to make Guacamole (see page 97).

Keaton and son Kelton McDonald standing on our Perfection wood-burning stove at the pond house at Eucheeanna, c 2004.

Seafood, Fishes and Pond Critters

300 pound grouper, caught in Pensacola around the turn of the century.

Fried Apalachicola Oysters, 174
Datil Cocktail Sauce, 174
Panny-ma City Pan Roast, 175
Grilled Shrimp with Herbs, 176
Basil Mayonnaise, 176
St. Augustine Famous
   Fried Shrimp, 177
O'Steen's Shrimp Sauce, 177
Grecian Shrimp, 178
Amelia Island Shrimp Gravy, 179
Fernandina Boiled Shrimp, 180
Shrimp Creole, 181
Shrimp Curry, 181
Basil Shrimp, 182
Smothered Rock Shrimp, 183
Sopping Barbecue Shrimp, 184
A Crawfish Dish, 185
Mama's Deviled Crab, 186
Minorcan Deviled Crab, 187
Fried Blue Crabs n'
   Hushpuppy Stuffing, 188
Fried Soft-Shell Crabs, 189
Boiled Blue Crabs
   with Pita Toast, 190
Panhandle Seafood Boil, 191
Apalachicola Seafood
   Casserole, 192
Seafood Newburg, 192
Florida Lobster with
   Crabmeat Stuffing, 193
Florida Lobster Thermador, 193
Ingram's Fish Fry, 194
Tuna Steaks with Rosemary
   Butter, 195
Mayport Galvanized Kingfish, 196
Speckled Trout Amandine, 197
Gulf Grouper Victor, 197
Blackened Redfish with
   Mango Salsa, 198
Pecan Crusted Catfish, 198
Red Snapper Vera Cruz, 199
Snapper Anastasia with
   Mango Curry, 200
Scamp with Wine Sauce, 201
Trigger Fish with Shrimp
   Centre Street, 201
Cobia with Dill Sauce, 203
Grilled Dolphin with
   Creole Seasonings, 204
Black Creek Flounder, 205
Grecian Style Grilled
   Pompano, 206
Salmon Croquettes with
   Tartar Sauce, 207
Cross Creek Cooter, 208
Oklawaha Frog legs
   with Curry Sauce, 209
Fried Gator Tail, 210

After enjoying the first spring picnics in the local woods, we'd plan our first excursion to the bayous near the Choctawhatchee bay. The picnic food was pretty much the same, but the highlight of the trip was catching the first crabs of the season.

We crabbed from the bridges using a wire trap with sides that folded down so the crabs could crawl in for the fish head bait. If this got too boring, we would tie chicken necks to a strong cord and dangle it in the shallow water, trying to catch the crabs with a net before they dropped off. This would usually yield a small mess of crabs for a meal, but seldom enough for leftovers for a gumbo and deviled crab. Dip net crabbing in the Choctawhatchee Bay is probably a lost art these days. Almost all the Blue Crabs available today are caught by commercial crabbers using wire traps marked by white floats. Earlier commercial crabbers used a hair rope 100 feet long which they baited with salted bull noses and secured on each end by two inner tubes. The crabs were captured at night with a crab net while munching on bait.

Catching crabs Apalachicola, c 1948.

Our serious crabbing came in the summer after the water warmed up. The crabbers converged, nets in hand, on the shallow bay edges. Close behind, begrudging short-legged children (yours truly), too slow to chase the critters, pulled several #3 wash tubs along to collect the crabs. The crabbers spread out in a line, from shallow to waist deep water. The convoy of dippers would begin wading in unison, picking up the crabs and putting them in the tubs.

Some crabs fell right out of the nets, while others had to be untangled from the net and other crabs. It seemed like an eternity to the poor tub pullers but really, after only a mile or two, the wash tubs would become "crawling out full" and it was time to stop. The tub-pullers could finally go swimming and play while some of the grown-ups brought the cars around and loaded the precious cargo to be iced and taken home. There were sore backs, arms and legs but that was a minor concern, cause everyone was thinking of the feast to come.

North Florida's humid summer months are the perfect time to go flounder gigging in the creeks, bays and waterways. Be sure to take plenty of bug spray for the dog flies and no-see-ums. Flounder lie on the bottom of the brackish waters of North Florida. The easiest way to harvest them is to use a gig, but they can also be caught using a hook and line.

Flounder giggers in the old days used fat lighter knots for illumination. This was a little dangerous because the hot pine tar could drip on your hands.

Today we use a sealed beam headlight mounted on a long pole and rigged to a car battery. Use the gigs to pole along until you spot a flounder.

SEAFOOD, FISHES AND POND CRITTERS

Quickly jab the gig and flip the flounder into the boat. You might be able to pick up some crabs as a bonus. Flounder gigging is a fun way to spend a summer night, just take an extra battery and don't gig a stingray.

If you are ever fortunate enough to take a leisurely drive along the St. Johns River between Orangedale and Spuds, you will notice a string of platforms along the rivers edge in Tacoi near Picolata. These platforms are used in the summer and fall by fishermen and shrimpers.

Shrimp spawn in the Gulf of Mexico and Atlantic Ocean and swim up the many rivers, creeks and marshes to mature. Once grown, they begin to return to the salt water to spawn. This is when the amateur shrimper gets a chance to harvest shrimp before they reach professional shrimp boats and show up at the markets at $10 per pound.

Each shrimper has their favorite spot. It might be from a dock or boat or even wading out in shallow water. After the spot is selected, the shrimper places the bait. Each one has their formula for bait, but it is usually something like cat food mixed with mud, prepared the day before and dried in the sun. Bait is scattered in the water at the secret spot and a few hours later, a cast net is thrown over that area. It usually takes about one six pack of beer and a can of bug spray to fill a 5 gallon bucket with shrimp.

In the winter months we enjoy oyster picking in the creeks. Make sure you aren't on leased land. Most of the oysters on the Gulf Coast are in waters 6-10 feet deep. These have to be harvested with oyster tongs, which resemble extra long post hole diggers with two iron-tooth yard rakes on the end to collect oysters. Many are "singles," ideal for serving on the half shell.

On the Atlantic Coast, oysters are found in marshes and creeks and are totally exposed at low tide. Check with county officials to make sure the water does not contain harmful bacteria. At low tide wade up the creeks wearing rubber boots. The oysters are in clusters and are sometimes attached to rocks and other objects.

Use a ball peen hammer to break up the clusters, keeping only the large live oysters. Scatter the rest of the shells back along the creek so they will provide homes for next years oysters. Oyster clusters or "coon" oysters, as they often called, are best roasted over an open fire and served with melted butter and ice cold beer.

Charles Manning and Johnny West with a mess of Reedy Creek Bream, c 1958.

Although catching fresh fish and seafood is often a big effort, we think it's well worth it. If you can't catch your own, find a seafood market you can trust and buy what's fresh and in season.

SEAFOOD, FISHES AND POND CRITTERS

FRIED APALACHICOLA OYSTERS

*T*his is probably the most popular way of cooking our Apalachicola oysters. If you tend to be on the wimpy side, reduce the amount of Datil "Bottled Hell" pepper sauce the first time you try this.

Serves 4

- 1 ½ pints Apalachicola oysters, freshly shucked
- Peanut oil for frying
- 2 cups cornmeal, medium grind
- 2 teaspoons salt
- Freshly ground black pepper, to taste
- Lemon wedges

Drain oysters in a colander. Heat oil in a deep fryer to 375 degrees. Combine cornmeal, salt and pepper in a 9 x 13 inch pan and mix thoroughly. Place 10-12 oysters in meal and coat, lay on sheet of wax paper, continue until all oysters are coated. Drop 8-12 oysters in deep fryer, making sure not to crowd, fry 2-3 minutes or until golden, be careful not to overcook or they will become tough and rubbery. Remove with slotted spoon and drain on metal wire rack or brown paper bags for a minute. Keep warm in a 200 degree oven on wire racks set on platter until all oysters are cooked. Serve on heated plates with lemon wedges and lots of Datil Cocktail Sauce.

Shucking and Jiving, Apalachicola, c 1920.

DATIL COCKTAIL SAUCE

- 1 cup mayonnaise
- ½ cup Datil "Bottled Hell" pepper sauce
- 1 teaspoon lemon juice
- 2 teaspoons horseradish, freshly grated
- 2 tablespoons dill pickles, chopped

Mix all ingredients together and serve.

PANNY-MA CITY PAN ROAST

"Don't have a condo in Panny-ma City"

Ask anyone in the Deep South where their favorite beach is and you probably are going to hear "Panny-Ma City." This beautiful beach is packed all summer with fun loving vacationers that come down to "The Redneck Riviera" to get a belly full of seafood, sun and sand.

Several restaurants around "Panny-Ma City" feature seafood with a Greek and Italian flavor. This dish is a great sample of this style of cooking.

This is a super duper way to serve baked oysters. The herbs and spices compliment the oysters' delicate flavor.

Serves 4

2 pints oysters, liquid reserved
10 green onions, chopped
½ cup unsalted butter
1 teaspoon oregano, crumbled
¼ teaspoon cayenne pepper
½ teaspoon thyme, crumbled
1 teaspoon garlic, minced fine
1 cup dry French bread crumbs
Salt and freshly ground black pepper, to taste
2-4 tablespoons Parmesan cheese, freshly grated

Preheat oven 350 degrees. Drain oysters, reserving liquid. Sauté onions in butter for 2 minutes; add seasonings and oysters. When edges of oysters begin to curl, add reserved liquid. Remove from heat and fold in bread crumbs. Place in a shallow buttered casserole dish. Sprinkle with Parmesan cheese, bake for 15-20 minutes and serve.

NOTE : Oysters should be freshly shucked if possible. Never wash an oyster. Drain and reserve the liquid or liquor as it is sometimes called. Strain the liquor through a paper towel or cheese cloth to remove bits of shell and add the liquor to whatever dish being prepared.

Harvesting oysters in Apalachicola Bay, c 1930.

GRILLED SHRIMP WITH HERBS

Shrimp start to deteriorate as soon as they are caught, so get them on ice immediately. Most shrimpers remove the heads after a day or so because the heads deteriorate first.

When shrimp were first marketed in North Florida, they sold for 5 cents a pound or 3 pounds for a dime. Nowadays, shrimp are one of the most expensive seafoods at the market, so we like to savor each bite. This dish is a great way to do that.

This is our very, very, very favorite way to cook large-jumbo shrimp and we serve them with Vegetables on the Grill (see page 311) and Basil Mayonnaise (below) for dipping.

Serves 6

- 6-10 inch wooden skewers, possibly more
- ¾ cup olive oil
- ½ teaspoon grated lemon rind
- 2 tablespoons lemon juice
- 1 tablespoon parsley, minced
- 2 garlic cloves, crushed
- 1 teaspoon salt
- ½ teaspoon basil, crumbled
- ½ teaspoon thyme, crumbled
- 2 teaspoons oregano, crumbled
- ½ teaspoon freshly ground black pepper
- 2 pounds extra-large shrimp in shells

Soak skewers in water 30 minutes. In a 9 x 13 inch shallow glass dish, combine oil, lemon rind, lemon juice, parsley, garlic, basil, oregano, salt and pepper. Use scissors to slit shrimp on the top side, removing the vein. Add them to marinade, turning every 30 minutes for 2 hours. Thread shrimp on skewers, securing both ends of shrimp. Cook over hot coals for 2-3 minutes on each side, until just pink making sure not to overcook.

BASIL MAYONNAISE

Makes 2½ cups

- 2 cups fresh basil leaves
- 1 tablespoon parsley, minced
- 1 garlic clove
- ⅛ teaspoon salt
- Freshly ground black pepper to taste
- 1 teaspoon Dijon-style mustard
- 1 teaspoon lemon juice
- 1 cup mayonnaise

Add basil, parsley, garlic, salt and pepper to food processor. Process until basil and garlic are finely chopped. Add mustard, lemon juice and mayonnaise. Process until well combined. Place in container with tight fitting lid and refrigerate until ready to serve.

ST. AUGUSTINE'S FAMOUS FRIED SHRIMP

Just about all the seafood restaurants around St. Augustine serve a version of fried shrimp and most are very good. However if you ask the locals where they like to go for fried shrimp you are most likely going to hear O'Steen's. This small, very clean, shrimp haven is tucked along a major thoroughfare but you would never notice it if it wasn't for the line of customers sitting patiently along the front. Service here like the shrimp is the best in town.

Several other restaurants in town have hired former O'Steen assistant cooks and serve a similar fried shrimp, but there is really no secret ingredient. Just quality shrimp freshly peeled, battered and deep fried in fresh oil.

Serves 4

36 extra-large shrimp
2 eggs
¼ cup water
1 cup cracker meal

¼ cup all-purpose flour
1 teaspoon salt
½ teaspoon cayenne pepper
Peanut oil

Peel and devein shrimp, leaving the tails intact. Slice lengthwise from top or bottom to fan out the shrimp. Mix the eggs with the water. Combine cracker meal, flour, salt and pepper. Pour oil to a depth of 2 inches in a large skillet and heat to 350 degrees. Dip shrimp, one at the time, in egg mixture, drain excess, then in coat evenly with cracker mixture. Cook in batches so the shrimp are not crowded. Cook about 2-3 minutes until golden brown, do not overcook. Drain on metal wire racks and serve with O'Steen's Shrimp Sauce.

O'STEEN'S SHRIMP SAUCE

Makes 2 cups
1 cup mayonnaise
¾ cup ketchup
3 tablespoons Worcestershire
3 tablespoons horseradish
1½ tablespoons Louisiana Hot Sauce

Mix thoroughly, chill and serve cold with fried shrimp and French fries.

Shrimp boats, c 1950.

GRECIAN SHRIMP

*T*his dish features that wonderful Feta cheese made from sheep's milk. Feta cheese is popular in Grecian and Middle Eastern cooking.

Our forefathers tended herds of sheep when they settled in Walton County, but they were primarily grown for the wool. There is no evidence cheese was made from the sheep milk.

Serves 4

- 2 medium onions, sliced thin
- ½ cup olive oil
- 4 cloves garlic, minced
- 7-8 fresh plum tomatoes or canned plum tomatoes, chopped
- 2 small bay leaves
- 2 teaspoons oregano, crumbled
- 1 teaspoon basil, crumbled
- ½ cup parsley, minced
- 1½ teaspoons fresh dill, minced
- 1 teaspoon Tabasco
- Salt and freshly ground black pepper, to taste
- 1½ pounds shrimp, shelled and deveined
- ½ pound Feta cheese, crumbled
- 16 Greek olives, pitted and halved
- 1 lemon
- Fresh parsley, minced, for garnish
- ¼ cup Ouzo, optional

Preheat oven 475 degrees. In a cast-iron skillet, cook onions over medium heat in olive oil until softened. Add garlic, tomatoes, bay leaves, oregano, basil, parsley, dill, Tabasco, salt and pepper. Reduce heat, cook and stir occasionally for 10-15 minutes. Cut shrimp in half. Spread tomatoes and juice in a shallow baking dish. Arrange shrimp on top of tomatoes. Sprinkle with Feta cheese and arrange olive halves on top. Squeeze lemon juice and Ouzo over all. Bake for 10 minutes. Garnish with freshly minced parsley and serve at once.

> The cleaning method is the same for raw (green) or cooked shrimp, but it is simpler to do it raw. The vein (usually black) located along the upper curve is commonly referred to as the "sand vein." Most people prefer to remove it to prevent any sand or "grit" in the cooked shrimp. The vein which is located on the under curve is part of the circulatory system and need not be removed.

SEAFOOD, FISHES AND POND CRITTERS

AMELIA ISLAND SHRIMP GRAVY

My friend George T. Davis, who graciously gave me the photographs of the Palace Bar and the Keystone Hotel is a delightful, young-spirited man who lives in Fernandina. He recently took me on a reminiscing tour of Fernandina on Amelia Island, a major seaport and the birthplace of modern shrimping. We went to "Old Town" where Fernandina was originally located. You can feel the history and enjoy the beauty of the area where sea captains built their homes. Several of these homes are still standing. Old Town has a view like no other in Florida. From the bluff, where wild chives grow you can view Tyger Island. The Intracoastal Waterway makes a winding path through Amelia Island, where moss covered oak trees are bent and gnarled by the northeastern winds.

In talking with some of the local cooks around Amelia Island, I questioned if there was a history behind Shrimp Gravy, and the simple answer was, "I guess they used what was on hand and that was bacon drippings and shrimp."

Serves 6

- 2-3 slices smoked bacon, cut in ¼ inch pieces
- ½ cup onions, minced
- ½ cup green bell pepper, minced
- 1 clove garlic, minced
- 1½ pounds raw shrimp, shelled and deveined
- 1 cup shrimp stock
- ½ teaspoon soy sauce
- Salt and freshly ground black pepper, to taste
- Dash Worcestershire sauce
- Pinch crushed red pepper
- 4-6 cups cooked rice or grits
- 1 tablespoon fresh parsley, minced

In cast-iron skillet, cook bacon over medium heat until crisp. Remove with slotted spoon to drain on paper towel. Pour off half of bacon drippings. In remaining drippings, cook onion and bell pepper until almost softened. Add garlic and shrimp to vegetables and cook, stirring, until shrimp turn pink, about 2-3 minutes. Remove vegetables and shrimp to a warm place. Add shrimp stock (see page 23) and soy sauce to skillet, bring to a boil, reduce heat to simmer and cook 2 minutes. Season to taste, add the Worcestershire and red pepper. Return bacon, vegetables and shrimp to skillet to reheat briefly. Serve over rice or grits and garnish with parsley.

FERNANDINA BOILED SHRIMP

The Palace Bar in Fernandina Beach, which was built in 1878, claims to be the oldest bar in Florida. It is an interesting place to visit, have a cold beer and sample their famous boiled shrimp. Spices are mixed in with the shrimp and give a nice appearance and taste.

Even though shrimp cooked by this method are generally referred to as "boiled shrimp," shrimp or any other seafood should not be boiled. The liquid in which the shrimp is cooked should only simmer, never boil after adding shrimp.

Serves 4

- 3 quarts water or flat beer
- 1 lemon, sliced
- 4 pounds heads-on large fresh shrimp
- 3 ounce box of Zatarain's or Yogi Crab and Shrimp boil
- ½-¾ cup salt

Place lemon, salt and seasoning into a large pot with water or beer, cover and boil for 30 minutes. Add shrimp and simmer shrimp until they just turn pink, about 2-3 minutes. Do not let shrimp return to boil, cooking time will vary according to size of shrimp. Remove from heat, drain and serve warm or cold, letting each person peel their own.

This is how the Palace Bar looked in 1906 before prohibition. The towels hanging on the bar were of the elite customers from nearby Cumberland Island. The towels were used to dry their mustaches before they bought their stogies located to they left of the bar. Above the cigar counter hung a gas-fired lighter. It's said that the Carnegies like to fire up a greenback from the gas lighter and then ignite their stogies with the flaming bill.

SHRIMP CREOLE
This is the first spicy dish we can remember trying.

Serves 4-6
- 3 tablespoons unsalted butter
- 3 tablespoons flour
- 2 medium onions chopped
- 2 medium bell pepper, chopped
- 2 cloves garlic, finely minced
- 2-16 ounce cans of diced tomatoes
- 2 teaspoon fresh lemon juice
- 2-3 teaspoons Creole seasoning (see below)
- 2 bay leaves
- 2 teaspoons Worcestershire
- 2 pounds medium shrimp meat, cleaned and deveined
- 2 teaspoons parsley, chopped
- 4 green onions, chopped

Melt the butter in a large cast-iron skillet over medium heat. Whisk in the flour, stirring constantly until mixture is a peanut butter color roux. Stir in the onions, bell pepper, garlic. Cook stirring until onions are transparent, about 8 minutes. Add tomatoes and their liquid, lemon juice, Creole seasoning and bay leaves. Stir and bring to a boil, cover, reduce heat to low and cook for 45 minutes. Remove cover if sauce needs thickening. Stir in the Worcestershire and shrimp and cook 5 minutes more or until shrimp just turn pink. Remove the bay leaves and stir in the parsley and green onions. Serve over hot rice.

CREOLE SEASONING
- 4 tablespoons salt
- 3 tablespoons garlic powder
- 2 tablespoons black pepper
- 2 teaspoons dried basil, crumbled
- 3 teaspoons cayenne pepper
- 3 tablespoons paprika
- 3 teaspoons cumin
- 3 teaspoons onion powder

Place all ingredients in a pint jar with tight fitting lid and shake vigorously until evenly distributed.

SHRIMP CURRY

Serves 6
- 3 tablespoons unsalted butter
- 2 medium onions, finely chopped
- ½ teaspoon Habanera, minced
- ½ teaspoon cinnamon
- ½ teaspoon tumeric
- ½ teaspoon cumin
- ½ teaspoon chili powder
- 3 tablespoons cilantro, minced
- ½ teaspoon salt
- 1 ¾ cups shrimp stock
- 2 pounds shrimp, shelled, and deveined

Heat butter in a large skillet over medium-low heat, add the onions, garlic and habanera and cook for 2 minutes, stirring. Add the cinnamon, tumeric, cumin, chili powder, half the cilantro and salt. Cook 1-2 minutes longer. Add the shrimp stock (see page 23) and bring to a boil, reduce heat and simmer 3 minutes. Add the shrimp and cook until shrimp turn pink, about 2 minutes. Serve shrimp over rice and sprinkle with remaining cilantro.

BASIL SHRIMP PASTA

Basil is one of the most delicious herbs of all and one of the easiest to grow. When we have an abundant supply of fresh basil to harvest, this dish is a must, right after Pesto and Basil Mayonnaise.

Keep basil fresh by placing stem down in a glass of water or cover with olive oil and then use both oil and leaves in cooking.

Serves 4

- ½ cup loosely packed parsley
- 3 large cloves garlic, peeled
- 28 ounce can Italian plum tomatoes, drained, seeded, juice reserved,
- ⅓ cup plus 1 tablespoon olive oil
- 1 teaspoon dried oregano, crumbled,
- Salt and freshly ground black pepper, to taste
- 2 cups tightly packed fresh basil leaves
- ½ pound thin spaghetti
- 1 pound medium shrimp shelled and deveined
- ¼ cup Parmesan cheese freshly grated

Process the parsley with the metal blade of a food processor, until minced; remove from processor and set aside. Drop 2 garlic cloves through the feed tube with motor running and process about until minced. Add tomatoes to processor and coarsely chop. Place paper towel in sieve and strain tomato juice. Heat 2 tablespoons olive oil in a large skillet and add tomato-garlic mixture, strained tomato juice, 2 tablespoons of the parsley, oregano, salt and pepper, stirring often until tomato liquid has almost evaporated. Finely chop basil (6-8 pulses) in processor. With motor running, add 2 tablespoons olive oil through the feed tube. Cut shrimp in half lengthwise and cut remaining garlic in half. Heat remaining olive oil in a large skillet, add garlic halves and lightly brown, remove and discard garlic. Cook shrimp in the oil, tossing until they just turn pink, about 2 minutes. Reduce heat, stir in tomato mixture and basil-oil. Mix thoroughly and turn heat off. Cook spaghetti until tender and drain. Add pasta to shrimp, tossing to coat pasta with sauce. Sprinkle with remaining parsley and freshly grated Parmesan and serve at once on heated plates.

SMOTHERED ROCK SHRIMP

*T*his uniquely delicious creature has a texture like that of a lobster, while the flavor is between the lobster and shrimp. Remember, it takes only seconds for them to cook, otherwise you are going to end up with a texture like rubber. If unavailable substitute shrimp or crawfish tails.

Rock shrimp yield half their weight after being cleaned.

Serves 8

- 1 cup unsalted butter
- ½ cup all-purpose flour,
- 2 cups onion, chopped
- ⅔ cup green bell pepper, chopped
- ⅔ cup celery, chopped
- ½ tablespoons garlic, minced
- 1 teaspoons salt
- 1 teaspoons freshly ground black pepper
- ½ teaspoon cayenne
- 1 teaspoon thyme, crumbled
- ½ teaspoon sugar
- 3 cups fish stock
- 1 cup green onions chopped
- 2 pounds raw rock shrimp meat, or shrimp peeled and deveined, or crawfish tails
- 1 teaspoon lemon juice
- ½ teaspoon grated lemon rind
- ¼ cup parsley, chopped
- 6 cups cooked rice

Melt one half cup butter over low heat in a large cast-iron skillet. Gradually add the flour, turn heat to medium-low and stir constantly with a whisk until smooth. Use a wooden spoon and continue to stir constantly until roux is a reddish brown, about 6-7 minutes.

Add onions, bell pepper, celery and garlic, reduce heat to low and cook, stirring occasionally, for 10 minutes.

Add half the seasoning and stir. Add fish stock (see page 22), 1 cup at a time and stir until smooth. Stir in lemon juice, lemon rind and sugar. Simmer, about 10 minutes, stir occasionally. Melt remaining butter in a large skillet over medium-low heat, add the green onions and cook until softened. Add shrimp, and remaining seasonings and cook, stirring, for 20 seconds. Add gravy, stir and cook 20 seconds. Taste for additional seasonings, add the parsley and serve at once with hot cooked rice.

> To clean rock shrimp, hold the tail section in one hand with the legs down towards the palm of the hand. Using kitchen shears, insert one blade of the scissors in the sand vein opening and cut through the shell along the outer curve to the end of the tail. Pull the sides of the shell apart and remove the meat. Wash thoroughly in cold water to remove all the sand vein.

SOPPING BARBECUE SHRIMP

We once spent over two hours in the bar of a famous New Orleans restaurant waiting to try its renown barbecue shrimp. What a surprise—it wasn't barbecue at all. It was just another version of our sopping shrimp.

The shrimp heads contain fat which adds flavor to the sauce. If the heads offend your guests, remove them before serving. Baking will separate the shrimp meat from the shell, making the shrimp extra flavorful and easy to peel. A good French bread is essential to sop up the delicious sauce.

The black pepper is a very important ingredient in this dish. If you aren't grinding your own, at least open a fresh can of medium-course ground black pepper.

Serves 4

- ½ cup unsalted butter
- 2 teaspoons garlic, minced
- 1 cup celery, minced
- 2 bay leaves
- 2 teaspoons rosemary, crumbled
- ½ teaspoon basil, crumbled
- ½ teaspoon oregano, crumbled
- 1-1½ teaspoon salt
- ¼ teaspoon cayenne pepper
- 1½ tablespoon freshly ground black pepper
- 2 pounds large-jumbo shrimp with heads, eyes pinched off
- ½ cup shrimp stock or clam juice
- ½ cup beer
- 1 lemon, sliced thin

Melt butter in a 12 inch cast-iron skillet, sauté celery, garlic, and add all seasonings. Simmer on low heat for 10 minutes. Remove from heat and let mixture stand for 30 minutes. Add shrimp and cook over medium heat, stirring, until shrimp turn pink. Add stock, beer, and lemon, cook 2 minutes longer. Bake in skillet for 10 minutes in 450 degree oven (optional). Serve in a deep plate with salad, new potatoes and lots of French or Cuban bread. Wet towels are appreciated at the end of this meal.

> Shrimp are usually sold according to size or grade based on number of headless shrimp per pound. This is indicated by the names jumbo, large, medium and small, with jumbo indicating 15 or less shrimp per pound, and small 60 or more per pound. Fresh shrimp are firm in texture and have a mild odor.

A CRAWFISH DISH

You get a line and I'll get a pole.
We'll go fishing at the crawfish hole.

Years ago, we made spending money by picking and selling blackberries, tung nuts and even pine cones. In the summer when three of us kids got together we sometimes would slip down to Blue Creek and catch crawfish and take them down to the ice house to sell for a penny a piece. The fishermen from Alabama bought them for bass bait in the river.

How many kids does it take to catch crawfish? Three, two to pull the net and one to hold the bucket. On a good day we would catch forty or fifty which gave each of us money for a pack of cheese crackers and a Nehi soda water or maybe a pack of peanuts that we would pour into our R.C.'s and shake until it fizzed. If there was any change left, we usually bought a Three Musketeer candy bar and split it three ways. Damn, those were the good ol' days.

Nowadays, farmers are growing crawfish in ponds like catfish so they are more abundant and reasonably priced, (twelve pennies each). We enjoy crawfish boiled like crabs and shrimp but also enjoy the tails in other dishes like this one served over rice or pasta.

Serves 4

- 1 cup celery, minced
- 1 cup onions, minced
- ½ cup bell peppers, minced
- ¾ cup unsalted butter
- 1 teaspoon garlic, minced
- ½ teaspoon thyme, crumbled
- 5 teaspoons Creole Seasonings
- ¼ cup flour
- ½ cup water
- 1 cup fish stock
- 1½ cups whipping cream
- ¼ teaspoon Tabasco
- ½ cup smoked ham, chopped
- ½ cup green onions, chopped
- 1 pound cooked crawfish tails
- 1 tablespoon parsley, minced

Melt 1 stick of butter in a large cast-iron skillet over medium-low heat. Add the celery, onions and bell pepper and cook until softened. Reduce heat to low and simmer for 45 minutes, stirring occasionally. Stir in the garlic, thyme, 3 teaspoons of the Creole Seasonings (see page 181), and cook 3 minutes. Gradually stir in the flour and cook, stirring constantly for 5 minutes or until mixture is a medium brown. Add the water, fish stock (see page 22), whipping cream, and Tabasco. Bring to a slow boil, reduce heat to low, stir occasionally and cook 30 minutes. In another cast-iron skillet melt the remaining butter over medium-low heat. Add the ham and green onions and cook until onions have softened. Stir in remaining Creole Seasonings and crawfish tails, and cook until crawfish are heated through. Combine crawfish with the cream mixture, correct seasoning, sprinkle with parsley and serve on heated plates. Serve over rice or pasta.

MAMA'S DEVILED CRAB

Mama was always the last to get up from the table after a crab boil. She and any volunteers would pick the leftover crabs until there was enough crabmeat for her deviled crabs the next day.

She always ordered deviled crab in any seafood restaurant that served it, mainly to compare it with hers. She judged them by the percentage of crabmeat to the filling, and was pleased when the crabmeat was at least half. This is her deviled crab recipe. We haven't changed a thing.

Serves 4

- 2 cups fresh blue crabmeat
- 1/3 cup green bell pepper, minced
- 1/3 cup celery, minced
- 1/3 cup white onion, minced
- 1/2 cup unsalted butter
- 1 1/2 cups saltine crackers, broken into coarse crumbs
- 1/4 cup Pet evaporated milk
- 2 tablespoons parsley, minced
- 1 teaspoon dry mustard
- 1/4 cup mayonnaise
- Salt to taste
- 1/8-1/4 teaspoon cayenne pepper
- Lemon wedges

Preheat oven 350 degrees. Pick over crabmeat and remove any shell. Sauté bell pepper, celery and onions in butter until softened. Add mixture to a large bowl with cracker crumbs, milk, parsley, mustard, mayonnaise, salt and pepper, mix thoroughly. Add crabmeat and toss together with a fork.

Spoon into crab shells or make into crab patties, 2 inches in diameter and bake 20-25 minutes. Broil for 3 minutes or until golden brown, place on heated plates, garnish with lemon wedges and serve at once.

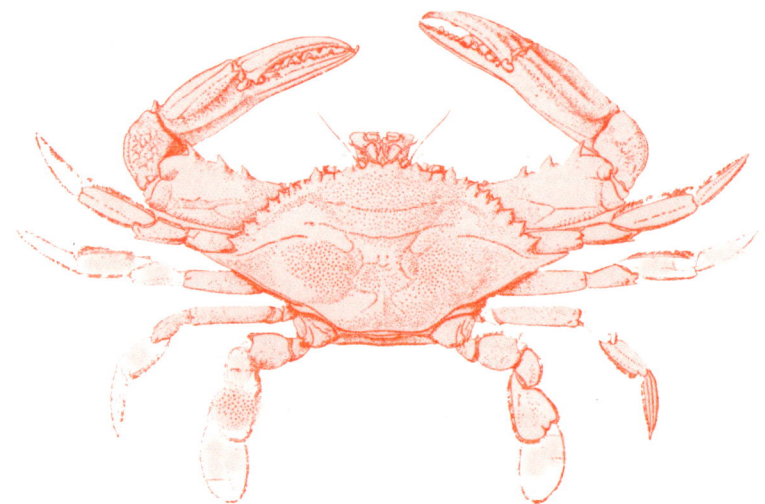

MINORCAN DEVILED CRAB

*T*he Datil peppers in this dish give a new meaning to the term "deviled." One version of Datil Pepper sauce, available in a small neighborhood grocery store between Jacksonville and St. Augustine, is called Granny Pappy's "Hell Ain't No Hotter." Actually, the Datil pepper is enjoyed more for its flavor than hotness, but believe me, it can bring tears to the eyes of many unsuspecting pepper lovers who are accustomed to eating Jalapeños whole.

Serves 4

- 1 pound fresh blue crab claw meat
- ⅓ cup St. Augustine Sweet onion, minced
- ⅓ cup celery, minced
- ⅓ cup bell pepper, minced
- ½ cup unsalted butter
- 5 slices white bread, toasted and crumbled
- 1-2 Datil peppers, seeded and chopped fine
- Salt and pepper to taste
- Peanut Oil for frying
- Lemon wedges
- 1 tablespoon parsley, minced

Makes 8 patties

Pick over claw meat and remove any shells. Sauté onion, celery and bell pepper in butter until softened. Add to a large bowl with bread crumbs, Datil pepper, salt and pepper, mix thoroughly. Gently stir in crab claw meat. Make into 12 patties two and a half inches in diameter. Heat oil to 400 degrees and deep fry patties in batches, for 3-4 minutes, or until golden brown. Drain on a wire rack in a warm oven until all are fried. Arrange on heated plates, sprinkle with parsley, garnish with lemon wedges and serve immediately.

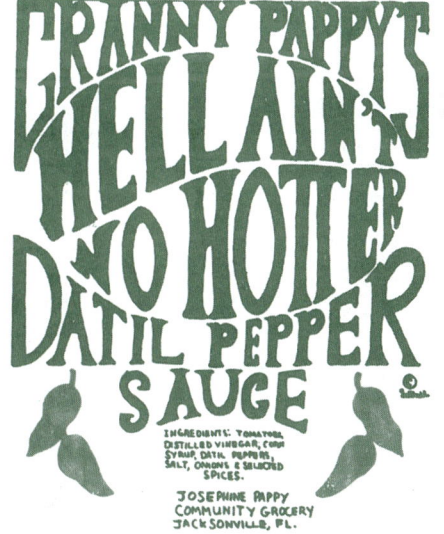

FRIED BLUE CRABS N' HUSH PUPPY STUFFING

*F*ried blue crabs have a sweeter taste than boiled blue crabs. Both are delicious. The fried crabs have to be cleaned before cooking, so allow time for this. Place the crabs in your sink and cover with ice water. This sedates them so you can handle them safely while cleaning.

This method of preparing blue crabs is popular in the homes of North Florida, but we have never seen it offered in restaurants.

Serves 4-6

12 blue crabs, cleaned
1 egg
1 cup milk
2 teaspoons milk
½ teaspoon cayenne pepper

2 cups all-purpose flour
Peanut oil for deep frying
Hush puppy mix
Parsley for garnish
Lemon wedges for garnish

Beat egg and add it to the milk. Heat oil (at least 3 inches) to 350-360 degrees in a large deep fryer. Fill cavity of crab with hush puppy mix (see page 42). Mix salt, cayenne pepper and flour together in 9x13 inch pan. Dip crab pieces in egg-milk mixture, roll in seasoned flour, and shake off excess. Fry crabs in a single layer in a basket that will fit inside the fryer, and cook until golden brown. Drain on metal wire rack, set in warm oven, until all are fried. Place crabs on heated platter with parsley and lemon wedges and serve at once.

To clean crabs cover with ice for several hours to sedate. The first thing to do is to cut the damn claws off with tin snips or a pair of scissors. With crab upside down, grasp the legs on one side firmly with one hand, and with the other hand lift the flap (apron), pull back and down to remove the top shell. Turn the crab right side up, remove the gills and wash out the intestines and spongy material with a vegetable brush. Cut the legs off close to the body. Now the crabs are ready to fry or be used in a gumbo.

Joel Bulan and Bill Redding frying hushpuppies at a Fall fish fry, c 2004.

DEEP FRIED SOFT-SHELL BLUE CRABS

*Y*ears ago, we were very fortunate when we picked up 2 or 3 soft-shell blue crabs on a crabbing trip. These were cooked, eaten and savored immediately upon returning to the kitchen. Today, commercial crabbers separate the molting crabs from the carnivorous hard shell crabs to provide a stable supply of soft-shell crabs for the market. Soft-shell blue crabs are one of Florida's true delicacies and bring top dollar at seafood markets. The cleaned crab, shell, body, legs and all may be eaten when cooked. We enjoy this dish served with Choron Sauce (see below).

Serves 4

- 8 soft-shell blue crabs
- 2 cups buttermilk
- 1½ cups self-rising flour
- ½ teaspoon cayenne pepper
- 1 teaspoon paprika
- ½ teaspoon garlic powder
- ½ teaspoon thyme, crumbled
- ¼ teaspoon oregano, crumbled
- Peanut oil for deep frying
- 1 tablespoon parsley, minced
- Lemon wedges for garnish

Clean crabs just before cooking by removing the gills (dead men fingers) located just beneath the top of the shell. Cut off the mouth and eyes, remove the sand bag from underneath points on each side, and remove the apron on the bottom. Soak crabs in butter-milk 10-15 minutes, remove and drain well. Mix seasonings with flour in a large zip lock bag. Add enough oil to completely submerge crabs and heat to 350-360 degrees, test temperature with deep-frying thermometer. Flour crabs just before frying and make sure to shake off the excess. Fry 2-3 crabs at a time, let the legs fry first, by holding the body with tongs, just above the oil, until the legs fold, then immerse the crab body in oil, shell side down for about 5 minutes or until golden brown. Remove and drain on metal wire rack, set in warm oven while you fry the remainder. Serve on heated platter, sprinkle crabs with parsley and garnish with lemon wedges. Gild the lily and serve with Choron Sauce.

CHORON SAUCE

To make Choron Sauce, reduce over medium heat 2 cups peeled and chopped tomatoes to half its original quantity, or until very little liquid remains. Add to one half cup of Béarnaise Sauce (see page 75) and mix together.

BOILED BLUE CRABS WITH PITA TOAST

We like to serve Boiled Blue Crabs with Pita Toast and Pappas Greek Salad. Crab boils are one of our favorite summertime parties. They usually last for hours because everyone is picking their own crabs. You must serve a Greek Salad (see page 157) along with the crabs (so the guests don't starve while picking out the crabmeat) and Pita Toast (see below).

Serves 4-6-8
- 6 quarts water
- 2-4 dozen live blue crabs
- 2-3 ounce boxes crab boil in a bag
- ⅓ cup Creole Seasonings
- 4 ounces concentrated liquid crab boil
- 2 cups salt
- 2 lemons, sliced
- Lemon wedges, for garnish

Fill a large 10-12 quart stock pot with 6 quarts of water. Add all ingredients, including Creole Seasonings (see page 181), except crabs, and bring to a boil, reduce heat and simmer 30 minutes. Return liquid to a rapid boil and add enough live crabs to come to top of pot and cover. Return to the boiling point, reduce heat and simmer crabs 5 minutes. Drained crabs and transfer to a large platter. Add remainder of crabs and cook as before. Clean crabs by holding the crab upside down, grasp the legs on one side with one hand, and with the other hand lift the flap (apron), pull back and down to remove the red top shell. Turn the crab right side up, and remove the gills and wash out the middle with a vegetable brush, place on towel to drain then place on platter. Garnish platter with lemon wedges and claws that fell off during cooking. Serve crabs hot, warm or cold.

PITA TOAST

- 6 tablespoons unsalted butter, softened
- 1½ tablespoons parsley minced
- 2 green onions, minced
- 1 tablespoon lemon juice
- 1 garlic clove, pressed
- Salt to taste
- 2 Pita bread

Cream the butter and add remaining ingredients, stir to combine. Cover with plastic wrap and let the mixture stand at room temperature for at least an hour. Preheat oven 450 degrees. Cut pita bread into small triangles, about 8 pieces per loaf. Separate each slice so that you have 32 pieces in all. Spread butter mixture on each piece. Arrange slices on large baking sheet in one layer. Bake in the top third of oven for 5 minutes, or until lightly toasted. Serve immediately.

PANHANDLE SEAFOOD BOIL

We have many beautiful days in North Florida to enjoy the outdoors and we certainly take advantage of it, whether on the beach, at a lake or even in the back yard. A fish fry and seafood boils are a great way to enjoy wonderful food and spend time with family and friends. Chilled watermelon is perfect after this meal. Serve generous slices and see how far you can spit the seeds.

Per Person:

2 small new potatoes
1 onion, 2 inches in diameter
1-3 inch piece of smoked sausage
½ ear corn, shucked
2 large blue crabs
6 large shrimp, with heads
Lemon wedges

Seasoning:

4-3 ounce packages crab boil
2-4 ounce bottle liquid crab boil
⅔ cup Creole Seasonings
Salt to taste (1½-3 cups)
4 lemons, halved
Datil "Bottled Hell"

Fill a 8-10 gallon pot with 6 gallons of water, add seasonings including Creole Seasonings (see page 181) and lemon halves, cover and bring to a rapid boil. Reduce heat and simmer 30 minutes. Bring back to boil and add potatoes, onions and sausage, cook 15 minutes. Add the corn and bring back to a rapid boil. Add the crabs; this will bring down the heat. Simmer and cook until crabs are bright red, about 5 minutes. Add shrimp to pot, cook until shrimp turn pink, about 2-3 minutes.

Drain and place on center of table that you have covered with many, many layers of news paper. Serve with lemon wedges, Datil "Bottled Hell" Pepper Sauce, or Datil Cocktail Sauce. Add shrimp to pot, cook until shrimp turn pink, about 2-3 minutes. Drain and place on center of table that you have covered with many, many layers of news paper. Serve with lemon wedges.

Gathering watermelons, c 1890.

APALACHICOLA SEAFOOD CASSEROLE

Serves 10-12

2 pounds shrimp, boiled
1 pound crawfish tails
1 pound crabmeat
1 pound scallops

Sauce:

4 tablespoon butter
⅓ cup flour
2 cups milk
1 cup light cream
½ pound cheddar cheese, diced
½ cup Sherry wine
1 teaspoon salt
⅛ teaspoon freshly ground pepper
⅛ teaspoon dried thyme, crumbled
½ cup saltine cracker, crumbled

Melt butter in a one and a half quart sauce pan. Add flour, remove from heat and mix thoroughly. Add milk and cream stirring constantly to mix. Return to heat until thickened, add cheese, sherry and seasonings. Place seafood in a 2 quart casserole, cover with sauce, sprinkle with crackers and bake in 350 degree oven for 20 minutes or until heated through.

SEAFOOD NEWBURG

Serves 6

1 pound sea scallops
1 pound shrimp, boiled
1 pound crabmeat
1 pound boiled lobster meat, diced
¼ cup unsalted butter
6 tablespoons Medium-dry sherry
1½ cups heavy cream
¼ teaspoon freshly grated nutmeg
4 large egg yolks, slightly beaten
2 tablespoons parsley, minced
1 teaspoon paprika

Cook scallops in butter over medium heat for 2 minutes on each side, add shrimp and lobster, add 5 tablespoons sherry, stir and cook 1 minute. Remove seafood. Add the cream to the skillet and reduce cream slightly. Stir in the remaining sherry, nutmeg, and egg yolks. Whisk and cook for 2 minutes more. Stir in the shrimp, crabmeat, and lobster meat and heat through. Sprinkle with parsley and paprika and serve.

FLORIDA LOBSTER WITH CRABMEAT STUFFING

The Florida lobster, also known as "spiny" lobster, is a beautifully colored and tasty crustacean found in the Gulf of Mexico and the Atlantic Ocean. Florida lobster is distinguished from the Northern variety by the absence of the claws and the presence of two long antenna protruding from the head. Highly regarded for the sweet flavor and firm texture, the Florida lobster is a culinary delight.

Serves 4

4-1 pound Florida lobsters
Crabmeat Stuffing
¼ cup melted butter
2 limes, cut into wedges
1 tablespoon parsley, minced

Preheat oven 400 degrees. Lay lobster on its back. With a sharp knife cut lobster in half lengthwise. Remove stomach and intestine vein. Rinse and clean body cavity thoroughly. Place crabmeat stuffing (see page 103) in body cavity and spread over surface of the tail meat. Drizzle with a fourth cup of melted butter. Place on baking pan and bake 10-12 minutes. Then broil 3 minutes until lightly browned. Sprinkle with parsley and serve immediately with lime wedges.

FLORIDA LOBSTER THERMADOR

Serves 6

3 pounds boiled lobster, diced
4 tablespoons butter
8 ounces of mushrooms, sliced
4 tablespoons flour
1 teaspoon dry mustard
1 teaspoon salt
⅛ teaspoon cayenne
⅛ teaspoon nutmeg
½ cup milk
1 cup heavy cream
2 egg yolks, slightly beaten
1 tablespoon fresh lemon juice
3 tablespoons sherry
½ cup bread crumbs
2 tablespoons Parmesan cheese, grated
2 tablespoons melted butter

Preheat oven 400 degrees. Melt 4 tablespoons of butter in saucepan and add mushrooms. Cook until they turn brown and blend in the flour, mustard, salt, cayenne, and nutmeg. Gradually add milk and cream. Cook over medium heat, stirring constantly, until mixture thickens. Stir small amount of mixture into egg yolks then add to sauce. Remove from heat and stir in the lemon juice, sherry and lobster. Place in buttered casserole dish and sprinkle with bread crumbs, cheese and 2 tablespoons melted butter. Bake about 15 minutes, or until nicely brown and serve.

INGRAM'S FISH FRY

The Red Horse Sucker is a bottom feeding fish similar to the catfish. Each Spring, around the full moon in March, the suckers travel from the rivers, up the creeks, of North Florida to spawn.

We suspect the Euchee Indians were gigging suckers in Bruce Creek long before they taught our Scottish ancestors how to gig them. The suckers stay in the deep " sucker holes" in the creek during the daytime and only travel at night. The Euchees would make torches out of fat lighter. At night they would light the torches and gig the fish as they swam up the creek, only taking enough for a meal and allowing the rest to continue up the creek to spawn. Today descendants of the Scottish settlers still wade up Bruce Creek in search of the Red Horse Suckers. The only difference is today they use Coleman lanterns instead of the fat lighter torches.

Our youngest brother, Ingram, thinks fresh oil is the secret to a good fish fry. It must be hot enough to light a kitchen match when thrown into the oil. He cooks over gas burners, this keeps the heat and grease out of the kitchen.

The Red Horse Suckers have a unique sweet taste that not too many folks have enjoyed. Because of the fine bones the fish must be scored every one quarter of an inch. If you can't find Red Horse Suckers substitute fresh catfish or mullet filets.

Serves 8

- 4 pounds of Red Horse Sucker filets, scored every ¼ inch, may substitute catfish or mullet,
- 1 pound bag of Fink's medium stone-ground cornmeal
- Salt and pepper to taste
- 1 gallon peanut oil

Place oil in a large cast-iron pot to come within four inches of the top. Heat oil to 360 degrees preferably outside over gas burners. Salt and pepper fish to taste and place in bag with cornmeal. Shake the filets until coated, shake off the excess cornmeal and cook the filets in oil until golden brown. Place the filets on brown paper bags to drain. Spread the hushpuppy mix (see page 42) about one quarter inch thick on a wooden paddle. With a butter knife slice off one half inch puppies and drop into the hot oil turning each one until brown on all sides, serve with sliced onions and dill pickles. Don't forget the Guava jelly for the hushpuppies.

Ingram, frying fish for the gang, c 1997.

SEAFOOD, FISHES AND POND CRITTERS

TUNA STEAKS WITH ROSEMARY BUTTER

Most of the fresh tuna caught off the Florida Coast usually winds up in Japan where it is eaten raw as Sushi. Occasionally, it appears in local fish markets. When it does, this is our favorite way to prepare it. Cook it like you would a beef steak, rare to medium-rare.

Serves 4

- 4 tuna steaks, cut 1-1½ inches thick, Blood line removed
- 1 ½ teaspoons dried rosemary, crumbled
- 1 tablespoon olive oil
- 12 sprigs fresh rosemary
- ½ teaspoon salt and freshly ground black pepper

At least 4-6 hours before grilling, rub tuna steaks with oil and place in glass dish that will hold steaks in one layer. Coat dried rosemary on each side of tuna. Crush rosemary sprigs and sprinkle over tuna. Cover with plastic wrap and refrigerate. Remove from refrigerator 30 minutes before grilling. Sprinkle steaks with salt and pepper, and grill over hot coals for 3-4 minutes on each side for medium rare. Place the crushed rosemary on grill as you are grilling. Place on heated plates and serve with tablespoon of Rosemary Butter.

ROSEMARY BUTTER

- ¼ cup unsalted butter, softened
- 2 teaspoons parsley, minced
- 2 teaspoon fresh rosemary, minced
- 1 small garlic clove, pressed
- ½ tablespoon lemon juice
- ¼ teaspoon salt
- ¼ teaspoon black pepper freshly ground

In a small bowl cream butter with parsley, rosemary, garlic, lemon juice, salt and pepper. Cover with plastic wrap and let stand 2 hours before serving.

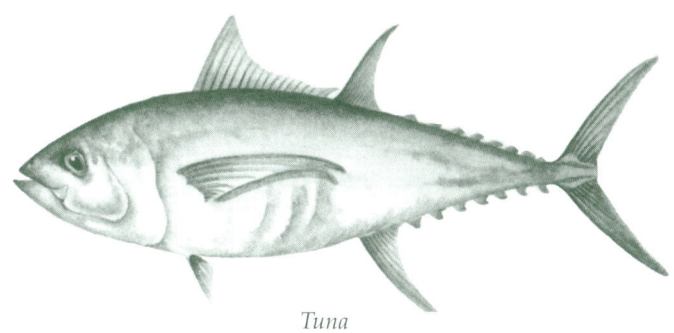

Tuna

MAYPORT GALVANIZED KINGFISH

The Annual Kingfish Tournament is held each July in Jacksonville Beach at Mayport. A thousand boats compete each year for almost a half a million in cash and prizes. King mackerel is not one of our favorite fish for eating, but when you invest a lot of money in a boat and motors, fees, license, gas, bait, tackle and ice, it's not too hard to eat the fish.

This marinade process is called galvanizing by some of the local fish experts.

Serves 4

- 4 tablespoons lime juice
- 4 tablespoons soy sauce
- 2 tablespoons olive oil
- ½ teaspoon oregano, crumbled
- ¼ teaspoon freshly ground black pepper
- 1 clove garlic, crushed
- 1 tablespoon parsley, minced
- 2 pounds king mackerel filets or steaks
- Lime wedges

In a 9 x 13 inch shallow glass dish, combine lime juice, soy sauce, olive oil, oregano, pepper, garlic, and parsley. Add the fish and marinate 15 minutes, turn and marinate 15 minutes more. Cook over hot coals 4-5 minutes, turn and baste with marinating sauce, cook 4-5 minutes more or until fish flakes when tested with a fork. Serve on heated plates with lime wedges.

Skinning a filet is easier to do when filet is not scaled. Lay the filet, skin side down, on cutting board. Hold the tail end of the filet with the fingers of one hand. With a sharp knife at an angle, make a cut about a half inch from the fingers through the flesh to the skin, being careful not to cut through the skin. Lay the knife blade against the skin and push the knife forward along the skin while holding the free end of the skin firmly with the fingers.

Kingfish

SEAFOOD, FISHES AND POND CRITTERS

SPECKLED TROUT AMANDINE

Serves 4

- 2 pounds of trout filets
- ¼ cup flour
- 2 tablespoons melted butter
- 1 teaspoon salt
- ½ teaspoon paprika
- ¼ teaspoon pepper
- ½ cup sliced almonds
- 2 tablespoons melted butter
- 2 tablespoon lemon juice
- 1 tablespoon parsley, chopped

Preheat the broiler. Mix flour, salt, pepper and paprika in a ziplock bag. Shake fillets in the mixture and place in a well greased baking pan, skin side down. Spread melted butter equally over fillets. Broil on top rack until done, about 8-10 minutes. Sauté almonds in butter until golden brown. Add lemon juice and parsley. Pour sauce over the fillets, serve immediately.

GULF GROUPER VICTOR

Grouper can grow to be very large, sometimes over 300 pounds. If you catch even a 30-35 pounder in the Gulf, you have a man-sized job getting that rascal out of the water and into the boat. If you catch one of the really big ones, you might as well cut the line. Grouper is probably the preferred fish in North Florida for chowders and stews.

Serves 4

- 2 pounds grouper filets
- ½ stick unsalted butter
- ½ cup mayonnaise
- 2 tablespoons lemon juice
- ½ cap almond extract
- 1 clove garlic, pressed
- Salt and pepper, to taste
- ½ cup slivered almonds
- ⅓ cup white wine
- ½ teaspoon Paprika

Preheat oven 375 degrees. Mix butter, mayonnaise, lemon juice, almond extract, garlic, to form a paste, salt and pepper grouper, cover fish with paste, sprinkle with slivered almonds and place in baking dish. Pour wine around the fish and bake 20 minutes. Remove to heated plate and serve.

You win Andy, Double Brested, Bahamas, c 2003.

BLACKED REDFISH WITH MANGO SALSA

*R*edfish were one of the least expensive fish on the market, before Paul Prudhome developed his Blackened Redfish in New Orleans. That fact soon changed in fact the dish became so popular that it almost drove the Gulf Redfish to extinction.

Serves 4

4 redfish fillets, 6 ounces each
½ tablespoon olive oil
½ teaspoon salt
2 tablespoons blackened seasoning
2 large ripe mango, peeled and diced into small chunks
½ cup purple onion, chopped fine
4 tablespoons fresh cilantro, chopped
2 tablespoons fresh mint, chopped
6 tablespoons Florida orange juice
2 jalapeno, seeded and minced
1 teaspoon salt

Heat a large cast-iron skillet over medium-high heat.. Sprinkle redfish evenly with olive oil, salt and blackened seasoning. Place redfish in skillet and cook 2 minutes on each side or to desired degree of doneness. Gently stir all other ingredients together and spoon over fillets.

PECAN CRUSTED CATFISH

Serves 4

4-6 ounce catfish fillets
Olive oil
¾ cup flour
1 ½ cups pecans
1 teaspoon Creole Seasonings
2 eggs, beaten
Lemon wedges

Place one half cup of the flour in a food processor, add the pecans and Creole Seasoning (see page 181). Pulse to combine and chop pecans. Set aside in a shallow dish. Place remaining one quarter cup flour in another shallow dish. Beat eggs until frothy in another shallow dish. Dust fish in flour, shaking off excess. Dip fish in beaten eggs, letting excess drip off. Place in third dish of pecan mixture and coat both sides, pressing mixture into fish. Heat a large cast-iron skillet over medium heat. Add olive oil and when hot add and cook fish about 4 minutes on each side. Serve with lemon wedges.

Garrett caught a keeper, c 2004.

RED SNAPPER VERA CRUZ

*T*his is a great dish for a dinner party. Bring it to the table in the baking dish right from the oven—the whole fish garnished with parsley and lemon slices is an impressive sight. The sauce can be cooked in advance, giving extra time to spend with guests.

Red Snapper

Serves 4-6

- 1 - 4 pound whole red snapper
- 1 teaspoon salt
- 2 cloves garlic, crushed
- ¼ cup fresh lime juice
- 2 tablespoons olive oil
- 28 ounce can plum tomatoes, seeded, chopped and juice reserved
- 10-12 Spanish green olives, sliced in half
- 1 red bell pepper, cut in 1 inch cubes
- 1 cup onion, sliced very thin
- 2 Datil peppers, seeded and minced
- ½ teaspoon oregano, crumbled
- ½ teaspoon thyme, crumbled
- 2 bay leaves
- 1 tablespoon small capers
- 2 tablespoons unsalted butter
- Parsley sprigs for garnish
- 1 lemon, sliced

Preheat oven 400 degrees. Make three deep vertical slashes, going almost to bone, on one side of fish and place in a large shallow glass dish. Make a paste with salt and garlic and rub over fish. Sprinkle with lime juice, cover with plastic wrap and marinate for an hour. Heat 2 tablespoons of oil in a 12 inch cast-iron skillet over medium heat and sauté onion until softened, about 3 minutes. Place reserved tomato juice in sieve with paper towel and strain. Add tomatoes, reserved tomato juice, olives, red bell pepper, Datil pepper, oregano, thyme and bay leaves. Simmer sauce, uncovered, 5 minutes.

Stir in capers and cook 5 minutes more. Remove sauce to a bowl and keep warm. Discard marinade, butter large baking dish, and set fish in dish. Cover with foil and bake 35 minutes. Pour sauce over fish and bake 15-20 minutes more, uncovered, or until fish flakes easily. Sprinkle with parsley and lemon slices, and serve with rice.

Palm Valley Chef Michael Kelly preparing Red Snapper Vera Cruz with 12 pound snapper.

SNAPPER ANASTASIA WITH MANGO CURRY

Our favorite fish is the tasty hog snapper. Unfortunately, it's not available in the fish markets. We only enjoy it after a trip to the islands with Charles and Ann, where we snorkel over the reefs and rocks trying to spot hog snapper, grouper or maybe a lobster. When the fish is spotted, we quickly swim down and try to spear it before it swims into one of the holes in the reef. It's a lot of work but the exceptional flavor and firm texture of fresh hog snapper makes it all worth while.

Serves 4

- 4 snapper filets, skinned 2 pounds
- 2 bananas, cut in half and sliced lengthwise
- 1 large ripe mango
- 1 teaspoon curry powder, or to taste
- Salt and white pepper, to taste
- ½ cup flour
- 1 tablespoon olive oil
- 5-6 tablespoons unsalted butter
- Juice of ½ lemon
- ¼-⅓ cup sherry
- ¼ cup fresh parsley, minced
- Juice of ½ lemon, or to taste

Sprinkle curry on fish and bananas and set aside. Peel and slice the mango and set aside. Salt and pepper filets, lightly flour fish and bananas, shaking off excess. Heat a large cast-iron skillet over medium-high heat. Add oil and 1 tablespoon butter. When butter has melted, add bananas, flat side down. Sauté until golden brown, turn, sprinkle with lemon and sherry and continue to sauté. Transfer to warmed plate. Add filets to skillet and sauté, adding 1 tablespoon butter if needed. Turn and sprinkle with half the lemon juice and sherry, adding additional tablespoon of butter if needed. Cook until golden brown. Transfer to warmed dinner plates. Add remaining 2 tablespoons of butter, mango slices, bananas, parsley, remaining lemon juice and sherry until heated through, swirl to mix and pour over filets. Serve at once on heated plates.

Trey holding Grouper and Hog Snapper the gang speared in the islands, c 2002.

SCAMP WITH WINE SAUCE

*"Tiny bubbles in the wine,
make me happy, make me feel fine."*

Scamp is a member of the grouper family, smaller and more tender than bigger grouper. It's found in most seafood markets and restaurants along the Gulf Coast.

Serves 4

Six 8 ounce scamp fillets
Salt and black pepper, to taste
Paprika, to taste
3 sticks unsalted butter
Juice of 3 lemons

¼ cup water
1 pint lump crabmeat
½ cup white wine
⅛ cup parsley, minced

Sprinkle both sides of fillets with salt, pepper and paprika. Melt 2 sticks of the butter in a large skillet. Slightly brown the butter, add the fillets and cook for 2 minutes over medium heat. Add the lemon juice, turn the fillets over, and add the water. Cover the fish and cook for about 8 minutes. Remove cover and cook an additional 2-3 minutes more until the fish is done. Transfer fillets to a heated platter, stir the sauce remaining in the skillet. In another skillet melt remaining stick of butter over medium heat, add crabmeat and wine, gently stir to keep from breaking up the crabmeat and heat through. Serve the scamp topped with the crabmeat, spoon sauce over all and sprinkle with parsley.

SEAFOOD WINE SAUCE:

Combine 1 cup dry white wine and a fourth cup of shallots finely chopped in small saucepan over medium heat. Reduce all wine completely over medium heat. Add 2 tablespoons whipping cream and turn heat very low. Add a half stick unsalted butter and salt to mixture, one tablespoon of butter at a time, stirring and shaking the pan constantly. Butter should not totally liquefy, but become a creamy mixture.

Remove pan from heat periodically to cool. Serve over any type of seafood.

San Sebastian winery located in St. Augustine.

TRIGGER FISH WITH SHRIMP CENTRE STREET

*"Shrimp boats are a-coming, their sails are in sight.
Shrimp boats are a-coming we're dancing tonight."*

The shrimpers around Fernandina, where modern commercial shrimping originated in 1913, claim their shrimp are the best in the world because of a low iodine content. While they are quite good, the shrimp from the Gulf of Mexico are good also. Use either type in this tangy recipe.

Centre Street divides the business district of Fernandina in half and ends at the docks where the first commercial shrimp boats docked to unload their catch.

Serves 4

- 2 tablespoons unsalted butter
- 4 tablespoon green onions
- 1 teaspoon garlic, minced
- 1 tablespoon lemon juice
- ½ cup dry white wine
- ½ cup whipping cream
- 1 tablespoon Dijon mustard
- 1 pound medium-large shrimp shelled and deveined
- 4 trigger filets, skinned ⅓-½ pound each
- ½ tablespoon olive oil
- Salt to taste
- 1 tablespoon parsley, minced

Heat a large pan over medium-high heat and melt butter. Add the green onions and garlic, cook, stirring, for a moment. Add the lemon juice and white wine, reduce slightly. Stir in the whipping cream and bring to a boil. Add the mustard, stir and add the shrimp. Cook 2 minutes or until shrimp turn pink. Remove shrimp with a slotted spoon and keep warm. Continue stirring sauce until it thickens. Correct seasoning, adding salt if needed, keep in a warm place. Rub filets with olive oil and salt to taste. Grill over hot coals until done, depending on heat of coals. Reheat sauce and shrimp. Place fish on heated plates, divide sauce and shrimp equally, garnish with parsley and serve.

Shrimp boat out of Fernandina, c 1963.

SEAFOOD, FISHES AND POND CRITTERS

COBIA WITH DILL SAUCE

Cobia is a large fish we sometimes catch while trolling offshore. It has a large rounded head and resembles a catfish. Cobia like to hang around the shade of a manta ray, so if you come across a manta ray, chances are a large cobia might be nearby.

Serves 4

4 cobia steaks or 1⅓-2 pounds cobia filet
1 tablespoon olive oil
Salt to taste

Dry fish with paper towels, brush lightly with olive oil on each side and salt to taste. Grill over hot coals, about 3-4 minutes on each side. Fish should flake easily when tested with a fork. Remove and serve at room temperature or slightly chilled with Dill Sauce.

Bubba done caught hisself a 50 pound cobia. Too bad we were in the Kingfish Tournament, Man!, c 1989.

DILL SAUCE

1 cup sour cream
2 tablespoons mayonnaise
2 tablespoons lemon juice
½ teaspoon Dijon mustard

2 tablespoons whipping cream
¼ cup fresh dill, minced
Salt and freshly ground black pepper, to taste

In a glass bowl, combine sour cream, mayonnaise, lemon juice, mustard and whipping cream. Stir in the dill, salt and pepper to taste, and refrigerate for at least an hour before serving.

GRILLED DOLPHIN WITH CREOLE SEASONINGS

Mahi, Mahi it's so nice they named it twice.

No, this is not Flipper but the beautiful fish we catch off shore. Some of the swanky restaurants call it mahi-mahi.

Dolphins travel in schools, so if you catch one, quickly stop the boat and throw out every line you have before the school swims by. The large bull dolphins can grow to be over 50 pounds.

Serves 4

1 ½-2 pounds dolphin filets, skinned
1 tablespoon olive oil
Lemon wedges
Fresh parsley, minced
4-6 teaspoons Creole Seasoning

Dry filets with paper towels and brush lightly with olive oil on each side. Sprinkle each side with Creole Seasonings (see page 181). Place filet on very hot grill. Cook 3-4 minutes on each side, making sure not to over cook. Place on plates that have been heated in a 200 degree oven, garnish with lemon wedges and sprinkle with fresh minced parsley.

It is not necessary to completely dress the fish in order to filet it. Scale the fish, unless the fish is to be skinned. With a sharp knife, cut through the flesh along the backbone from the tail to just behind the head. Then cut down to the backbone just behind the collarbone. Turn the knife flat and slide along the rib bones to the tail, cutting the flesh away from the backbone. Turn the fish over and repeat the operation.

Nice Catch Charles! c 1992.

BLACK CREEK STUFFED FLOUNDER

*Y*ears ago, we enjoyed flounder gigging in the Choctawhatchee Bay. We had only one outboard motor and usually rented several boats from the Black Creek Lodge. Charles mounted the motor on the lead boat and pulled the other boats like a choo-choo train. This worked great until one night we were caught in a storm and almost drown before we could get back to the lodge. Did we tell you that you could buy flounder at the fish market?

Serves 4

½ cup celery, chopped
½ cup green onions, chopped
1 clove garlic, minced
½ cup unsalted butter, melted
1 cup soft bread crumbs
1 egg, beaten
1 cup boiled shrimp
1 cup crabmeat
2 tablespoons parsley, chopped
Salt, black pepper, freshly ground, and cayenne, to taste
3-4 dashes of Tabasco
2 tablespoons lemon juice
4 small flounder for individual servings
1 tablespoon parsley, minced
Sherry (optional)

Cook celery, onion and garlic in 4 tablespoons of the butter over low heat until softened, and remove from heat. Add bread crumbs, egg, shrimp, crabmeat, 2 tablespoons parsley, salt, black pepper, cayenne, thyme, and Tabasco, and mix well. Split thicker side of the flounders lengthwise and crosswise, and loosen meat from bone to form a pocket for stuffing. Salt fish lightly and stuff pocket with bread mixture. Mix 4 tablespoons remaining melted butter with lemon juice. Place fish in buttered pan and brush with lemon butter. Broil 3-4 inches from heat until fish flakes easily with a fork, about 3-5 minutes. Baste with remaining lemon butter and pan juices during baking. Sprinkle with sherry and parsley, and serve on heated plates.

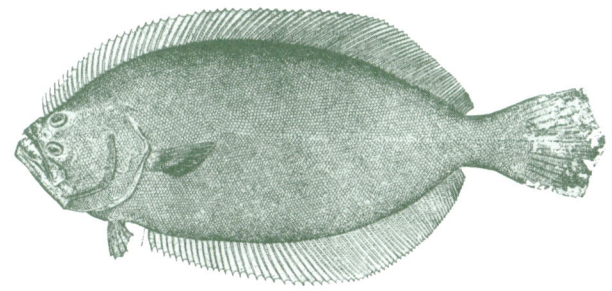

Flounder

GRECIAN STYLE GRILLED POMPANO

Pompano is one of the most popular fish we have in North Florida. It's certainly one of the most expensive. Pompano are sometimes caught in the surf with a rod and reel or in a seine net.

Pompano is excellent served grilled with a light sauce, especially if lump crabmeat and shrimp are included in the sauce. This cooking method is popular at restaurants from the Panhandle down to Tarpon Springs.

Serves 4

1 ½ pounds pompano filets

½ tablespoon olive oil

Sauce:

1 cup unsalted butter,
3 tablespoons olive oil
½ cup lemon juice
½ cup lump crabmeat
½ cup boiled shrimp, chopped

4 tablespoons green onions chopped
4 tablespoons parsley, minced
Lemon slices
Greek olives

Brush nonstick pan lightly with olive oil. Wash filets with cool water and dry fish with paper towels. Brush each side lightly with remaining olive oil.

Broil 3-4 inches from heat for 3-4 minutes making sure fish is firm but not overcooked.

Remove from broiler and set aside. Place butter, olive oil, and lemon juice in a small saucepan over low heat. Add crabmeat and shrimp to heat through. Place fish on heated plates, pour sauce over the fish and garnish with green onions, parsley, lemon slices and Greek olives.

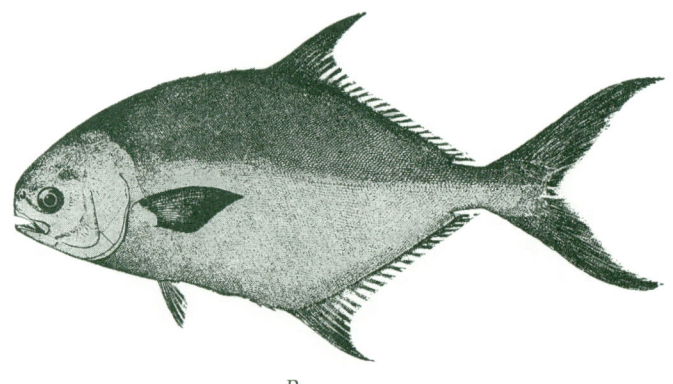

Pompano

SALMON CROQUETTES

Holmes County Crab Cakes

Salted mullet was about the only semi-fresh seafood available in the grocery stores back when were young. The mullet was sliced down the back, salted and shipped in five gallon lard cans. The bony filets looked pretty rough and we don't remember too many folks that bought them.

Of course, sardines were always available, but these were usually eaten on fishing and hunting trips. Canned tuna and salmon were the other seafoods. The tuna showed up in tuna fish salad, but the salmon was always featured in salmon croquettes. This is one of our old favorites. These croquettes can be made with any cooked fish.

Serves 4-6

14¾ ounce can pink salmon
1 egg, slightly beaten
1 cup onion, minced
¼ teaspoon thyme
¼ teaspoon salt and freshly ground black pepper
1 tablespoon minced dill
¼ cup parsley, minced
2 tablespoons lemon juice
½ cup medium cornmeal
1 cup peanut oil
Lime wedges

Drain salmon and remove bones and skin. Add remaining ingredients, mixing thoroughly. Tear a sheet of wax paper 12-14 inches long. Equally divide salmon mixture into 12 servings and make into patties. Heat a 12 inch cast-iron skillet over medium-high heat and add oil. Add salmon croquettes and fry on both sides until golden brown. Drain on metal wire rack. Serve on heated plates with Tartar Sauce and lime wedges.

TARTAR SAUCE

1½ cups mayonnaise
¼ cup fresh parsley, minced
1 tablespoon Vidalia onion, minced
1 tablespoon dill pickle juice
⅓ cup dill pickle, minced
1-1½ tablespoon lemon juice
2 teaspoons minced dill

Place all ingredients in bowl and thoroughly mix. Refrigerate until ready to use.

CROSS CREEK COOTER

Marjorie Kinnan Rawlings mentions in *Cross Creek Cookery* five types of turtles available in North Florida. They are the protected sea turtle (prized for its eggs, which can number up to 200), the hard-shell inland turtle, the alligator cooter, the soft-shell cooter and the gopher land tortoise, which is also now protected. Turtles have both white and dark meat, but the alligator turtle has the whitest and sweetest meat of all.

Several restaurants have operated in the Cross Creek area over the years and most have featured the local fried cooter and frog legs.

Serves 4

- 2 pounds turtle meat
- 1 cup self-rising flour
- ½ teaspoon freshly ground black pepper
- 2 cups evaporated milk
- ½ teaspoon cayenne
- Peanut oil
- Lemon wedges

Wash meat and pat dry with paper towels. Combine flour, black pepper and cayenne in a large ziplock bag. Place meat in bowl and cover with evaporated milk, drain. Dredge in seasoned flour. Deep fry turtle in peanut oil over medium-high heat, 350 degrees, until golden brown, making sure to not crowd the pan. Drain on metal wire rack, keep in warm oven until all pieces of turtle are fried. Serve immediately on heated plates with lemon wedges.

Marjorie Kinnan Rawlings home in Cross Creek, c 1970's.

OKLAWAHA FROG LEGS WITH CURRY SAUCE
"Ribbit, Ribbit"

Bull frogs are usually harvested at night from a boat or air boat. Their eyes glow when a light is flashed across the water. You have to be quick with a gig to get enough of the critters for a meal. Gator eyes also glow, but are orange, so give them plenty of room. Only the back legs of the bull frog are eaten.

Serves 4

- 8 bull frog legs or 24 smaller frog legs
- 8 tablespoons butter
- ¾ cup all-purpose flour
- ¼ teaspoon freshly ground black pepper
- 1½ teaspoons salt
- ¼ cup cornstarch
- ½ teaspoon cayenne pepper
- 2 tablespoons parsley, minced
- 2 lemons, cut in wedges
- Curry Sauce

Wash and pat frog legs dry with paper towels. In a large skillet, melt butter over medium heat. Mix flour and cornstarch together. Salt and pepper and lightly dust frog legs with flour mixture. Sauté until golden brown on both sides. Remove and drain on metal wire rack. Keep in warm oven until all have been cooked. Sprinkle with parsley and serve on heated plates with lemon wedges and Curry Sauce.

CURRY SAUCE
Makes 1 cup
- ½ cup sour cream
- ¼ cup mayonnaise
- 1½ tablespoons lemon juice
- 1½ tablespoons green onion, chopped
- 1 small clove garlic, pressed
- 2 teaspoons cilantro, minced
- ½ tablespoon curry powder
- ¼ teaspoon Dijon-style mustard
- ¼ teaspoon paprika
- Salt and white pepper to taste
- Dash of Tabasco

Combine all ingredients mixing thoroughly and serve.

Hildegard loading Rosin, c 1900"s.

FRIED GATOR TAIL

We always looked forward to camping trips down at Sandy Creek. We pitched our army surplus pup tent under the train trestle. A big campfire was a must as soon as dark came. The first night sounds were of the whip-poor-will and the hoot owl, and then the bull frogs with their deep bass voices piped in.

Sometimes the sounds of an ol' gator could be heard in the distance. This usually necessitated chunking another log on the fire. Everything was fine until the freight train came roaring through about 3:30 A.M. and our faithful watchdog Rascal hightailed it to the house.

Years ago, alligators were hunted so hard for their hides that they were placed on the endangered species list. Fortunately, they have made a big comeback and are being harvested again on a limited basis. Some resorts even have to hire hunters to keep the lakes safe for their guests.

By the way, you should never order "Alligator" tail. It's "Gator" tail. If anyone tells you it tastes like chicken, hit them with your alligator purse.

Serves 4

- 2 pounds alligator tail meat
- Juice of 2 lemons
- 2 tablespoons soy sauce
- ½ teaspoon thyme, crumbled
- 1 teaspoon salt and black pepper, freshly ground
- ½ teaspoon garlic powder
- 1 cup flour
- 2 eggs, beaten
- ⅓ cup vegetable oil
- 2 tablespoons unsalted butter

Slice gator tail a half inch thick. Pound meat until an even thickness between sheets of plastic wrap. Place steaks in a glass dish and sprinkle with lemon juice and soy sauce. Cover with plastic wrap and allow steaks to marinate 4 hours. Place thyme, salt, pepper, garlic powder and flour in a large zip lock bag and shake to distribute the seasonings. Pat steaks dry with paper towels. Heat a large cast-iron skillet over medium-high heat. Place steaks in bag and coat with flour mixture, dip in egg wash, letting eggs drip off and flour once more. Add oil and butter to skillet and when foam subsides, sauté steaks quickly on each side. Drain on wire racks, place on platter and keep warm. Do not over cook. Serve immediately on heated plates with lemon wedges.

Large gator caught near Deland, c 1910's.

Yard Birds and Other Fowl

Feeding yardbirds on early North Florida farm, c 1910.

Granny's Hen and Dressing
　with Giblet Gravy, 214
Cranberry Sauce, 215
Granny's Chicken and
　Dumplings, 216
Ultimate Roasted Chicken, 217
Boarding House Chicken, 218
Creole Chicken on
　Homemade Pasta, 219
Spanish Chicken and Rice, 220
Mama's Chicken 'n Rice, 221

Deviled Chicken, 221
Coq Au Vin, 222
Chicken Valdosta, 223
Lemon Chicken, 224
Chicken Marabella, 224
Filipino Adobo, 225
Chicken Portabella, 225
Chicken Hunters Style, 226
Baked Game Hens with
　Walnut Stuffing, 226

Chicken Moutarde, 227
Chicken Piccata, 227
Gypsy Chicken
　with Marinara, 228-229
Turkey Tetrazinni, 230
Turkey Molé Olé, 231
Guinea with the Light
　Brown Flair, 232

YARDBIRDS AND OTHER FOWL

When the first chickens reached the docks in St. Augustine, they might have been met by the Florida Turkey, who had been around North Florida for several centuries. Now this turkey wasn't anything like the one that comes from the market today. It was lean and mean and used to foraging for miles in the forest scrub and swamp for bugs and such. It didn't fly much, usually just to roost in trees, but could take off like a bumble bee if it detected danger with it's keen eye sight. Those thighs and legs were toughened and could outrun a racehorse for a short distance. Actually, it was more of a quick trot than a run.

The recently domesticated chicken was similar in build and still able to fly, which came in handy when it was encountered by the sly ol' possum and fox, which liked chicken as much as the preacher. Years ago, chicken was eaten only on special occasions; usually on Sunday, when the preacher came to dinner.

Today chickens are raised in large houses and go from the egg to the market in less than eight weeks. While this makes chicken one of the most economical meats available it does nothing for the taste.

Ruby Williams shelling butterbeans, c 1970's.

So far, the guinea and game birds have escaped any meddling and remains the same bird as it was when it reached this area. Guineas are great watch birds and cluck loudly when somebody arrives. They roost in trees like game birds and can escape the varmints. Game chickens and guineas are difficult to catch for the dinner pot and some folks have resorted to shotguns out of frustration. But you didn't hear that from me, cause I ain't one to gossip.

Granny loved birds of all types and always had a yard full of turkeys, guineas, .geese, chickens of all types and even a parrot. No, she didn't eat the parrot, she got it to keep "Schlitz," the monkey, company.

"I was built for beauty, not speed." That was Granny's favorite reply when grandchildren complained that it was taking too long to make the banana pudding, or maybe it was an egg custard with fresh pears or possibly turning the left over biscuits into a delectable bread pudding.

I guess that today, Granny would be labeled a "Foodie," what with her wood burning oven, organic garden and free range chickens and guineas. Of course, she would reply that this was "the old timey way," which she contended was the "best way."

Granny thought nothing of driving miles out to the country just to get fresh churned butter and clabber for Grandaddy. She would seek the neighbor or friend who had the freshest "roastneers" or peas and butter beans, and would sometimes stay up past midnight preparing them for dinner (the noon meal) the next day. Peas, butter beans, corn and tomatoes were daily summer fare along with whatever meat caught her eye at the local food store.

Spending a winters night at Granny's meant cold bedrooms and soft beds layered with handmade quilts. Our alarm clock was the old radio on top of the refrigerator blaring gospel music from WOOF in Dothan, Alabama. When the rooster crowed, it would be a mad scramble from the bed to the fireplace. Clothes had been strategically placed the night before near the fire to be warmed. This was a small price to pay for the "old timey" breakfast to come!

Ruby Williams, blowing out a lot of candles on the chocolate cake. She was born April 1900. Married Charlie Williams July 1915, and went to her place in heaven June 1977.

The aroma of country smoked bacon and sausage frying in a cast-iron skillet would fill the house. There were also fresh yard eggs, grits and of course, Granny's biscuits with Mayhaw jelly. She always made a few small biscuits in the middle of the pan for her grandbabies. For Granny, chicken and dumplings was more than just a meal; it was an event. It began with the selection of the hen that laid the least number of eggs for the egg basket. The neck would be wrung, the head chopped off and the feathers plucked. The carcass would be singed over brown paper bags, and cleaned, saving the liver, gizzard, heart and the precious egg sac.

The hen would be boiled which would yield the delectable broth that was mixed with flour and made into those "melt in your mouth" dumplings.

Flour went everywhere when the rolling pin was in action. This usually brought on the sneezing and nose rubbing which everyone knew meant company was coming. Once the word was out granny was making chicken and dumplings company *was* coming. Somehow there was always enough to go around.

When the dumplings were done, the old hen was skinned, boned and the meat put through a meat grinder to become the ultimate chicken salad. Most recipes call for the chicken meat to be returned to the dumplings, but this was not Granny's "old timey way."

Everyone would have a large serving of the dumplings and chicken salad but the little yellow eggs from the sac were reserved for her grandbabies, along with a piece of gizzard or liver.

Granny has long gone to her place in Heaven, and we are fortunate that Aunt Carolyn saved most of her favorite recipes. If you have a favorite relative or friend who cooks special dishes for you, please record those recipes for the future, and let that person know today how much you enjoy them.

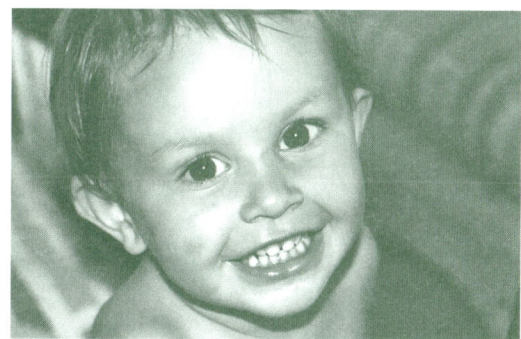

Granny's namesake great, great, granddaughter Ruby Wright, age 2.

GRANNY'S HEN AND DRESSING WITH GIBLET GRAVY

Granny always had a yard full of chickens. Rhode Island Reds, Dominikers, and the feisty little Bannys. These breeds are becoming endangered today.

The egg bread should be made the day before making the dressing.

EGG BREAD:
- 4 eggs
- 1 quart buttermilk
- 2 heaping teaspoons baking powder
- 2 teaspoons salt
- 1 tablespoon sugar
- 6 cups fine cornmeal

Preheat oven 350 degrees. In a large bowl, beat eggs and add buttermilk, baking powder, salt and sugar. Mix in cornmeal and make a stiff batter. Pour into greased 12 inch cast-iron skillet. Bake 45 minutes to an hour or until golden brown.

TO PREPARE HEN:
- One 4-5 pound hen
- Water

Wash hen under cool water and place in a large pot, save giblets and neck for Giblet Gravy. Cover with water by two inches and bring to a boil. Reduce heat to low and cover with lid. Cook one and half- two hours or until tender. Remove hen and set aside to cool. When cool, remove skin and bones and discard, set meat aside. Reduce stock to 5-6 cups and use to mix in dressing. Prepare Dressing and Giblet Gravy.

NOTE:
It's more economical to purchase a whole chicken. Cut into desired pieces and freeze neck, bones, and giblets for making a Giblet Gravy later.

Ruby Burdashaw Williams, c 1915.

YARDBIRDS AND OTHER FOWL

DRESSING:
1 cake Granny's egg bread, crumbled
5-6 cups rich chicken stock
2-4 tablespoons chicken fat or butter
4 stalks celery, chopped
1½ cups onion, chopped
4 hard-boiled eggs, chopped
Salt and lots of freshly ground black pepper, to taste

Preheat oven 350 degrees. Place egg bread and 5 cups of chicken stock in a large bowl, and mix. Sauté celery and onions in chicken fat or butter until softened. Add eggs, celery, onions, salt and pepper, to bread mixture and mix thoroughly. Add remaining stock if needed, batter should be thin. Stir in reserved hen meat. Correct seasoning, pour into buttered 9 x 13 inch baking dish. Bake 45 minutes-1 hour, or until firm and golden.

GIBLET GRAVY:
4 cups chicken or hen stock
4 -6 chicken necks
½ pound chicken gizzards
⅛ pound chicken livers
3 eggs, hard-boiled
¼ cup all-purpose flour
Salt and freshly ground black pepper, to taste

    Wash giblets, place necks and gizzards in pot with chicken stock, and bring to a boil. Reduce heat to simmer, cover and cook 30 minutes. Remove necks and gizzards and cool. Add livers to chicken stock and cook 5 minutes, or until cooked through, set aside to cool. Cut gristle from gizzards and chop meat, remove skin and scrap meat from neck with a fork, dice livers and place all in a small pot. Dice eggs and add to giblets. Strain stock and add water to make 4 cups. Place three-fourths cup of stock and flour in glass jar with tight fitting lid and shake vigorously to combine. Add remaining three and one quarter cups of stock to giblets. Cook stock and mixture of eggs and meat over low heat until heated. Stir in flour mixture and cook until thickened. Salt and pepper to taste and serve.

GRANNY'S CRANBERRY SAUCE
    Cut the top and bottom lids of a can of Ocean Spray cranberry sauce with a can opener. Slide the sauce out onto your prettiest serving dish, remove lids, place a butter knife on the dish so everyone can get as much as they want.

GRANNY'S CHICKEN AND DUMPLINGS

"Built for Beauty not for speed."

Serves 6

3-3½ pound hen
Salt and freshly ground back
  pepper, to taste

Wash chicken thoroughly and place in large pot with salt and pepper. Add enough water to cover chicken. Bring to a boil, cover, reduce heat and simmer until hen is tender, about 90 minutes. Remove chicken and let it cool, reserving stock. Skin, bone and cut into bite-sized pieces.

DUMPLINGS:
2½ cups all-purpose flour
¾ teaspoon salt
1 cup reserved cooled
  chicken stock

Place two and a fourth cups of flour and salt in a bowl and stir to distribute salt. Make a well in center of flour, add stock and mix to form ball. Lightly flour dough with remaining flour, using the remainder to dust work area, divide dough in half and roll on floured area, as if making a pie crust. Roll very thin, cut into 1 inch strips and let then stand 15-20 minutes, roll remaining dough, cut into strips and let them stand. Taste broth for seasoning and strength and reduce or add additional broth if needed. Bring broth to a boil. Let some flour cling to each piece of dumpling. Gather the dumplings, draping them over your fingers and drop into broth, one at a time. As each layer is added, sprinkle with black pepper. Stir gently and add remaining dumplings. Cover and cook on simmer for 20 minutes. The flour on the dumplings should thicken the broth. Add the meat and reheat or use in chicken salad. Taste for salt and pepper and serve with Moccasin Branch Cold Slaw.

THE ULTIMATE ROASTED CHICKEN

*S*ometimes the simplest recipes are the best. When we have a fresh chicken, it's a toss up between this recipe and Deviled Chicken. Both are excellent.

The yard birds hatched the settings in the early spring. Around June these young birds were enjoyed pan fried. As they grew older we also enjoyed them roasted with fresh herbs.

Serves 4

- 2 carrots
- 4 cloves garlic
- 1-3 pound chicken
- 2 ribs celery, cut in 2 inch pieces
- 1 onion, quartered
- 1 teaspoon basil, crumbled
- 1 teaspoon rosemary, crumbled
- 1 teaspoon oregano, crumbled
- 2 teaspoons salt
- ½ teaspoon cayenne
- ½ teaspoon black pepper, freshly ground
- ½ teaspoon onion powder
- ½ teaspoon garlic powder
- 1 tablespoon oil or butter
- 1 cup dry white wine

Preheat oven 450 degrees. Peel and cut each carrot into 4 pieces. Blanch carrots and garlic in boiling salted water for 5 minutes. Remove and set aside. Wash chicken under cool water and pat dry with paper towels. Remove excess fat. Loosen skin from breast, thighs and legs, being careful not to tear skin. Put herbs and spices in a mortar and mix until fine. Sprinkle seasoning mix, pushing it with your fingers to distribute between skin and meat. Rub skin with oil, sprinkle cavity and skin with seasoning. Tie legs together and place in a large cast-iron skillet with carrots, garlic, celery, and onion. Reduce heat to 350 degrees and bake for 1 hour. Test by piercing inner thigh; juices should run clear when cooked. Remove chicken to a heated platter. If vegetables are not quite done, return them to oven for a few minutes. Remove vegetables to heated platter and degrease skillet, reserving juices. Add wine to skillet and reduce by half. Add reserved juices, scrape up any browned bits and add meat juices that accumulated in platter. Taste for seasoning. Cut chicken into serving pieces, pour sauce over all and serve.

BOARDING HOUSE FRIED CHICKEN

*Y*ears ago, boarding houses were known as reasonably priced places for people to live and eat. Many times these establishments were run by women who were recognized as great cooks.

Hopkins Boarding House in Pensacola has been serving home-style vegetables and fried chicken for over 45 years. Some days they serve over 200 chickens. There's a special table we try to sit at each time we are there. It's large and round, seating 8 people, with a lazy susan in the center. It holds dishes of all the food prepared that day. A simple spin of the lazy susan presents you with the dish you were desiring—unless the folks on the other side of the table spin it as you are reaching for a piece of chicken and you wind up with a handful of potato salad.

When cutting up a chicken, make sure to cut it so there is a pulley bone or wishbone. This can provide after-dinner entertainment. Choose two competitors. The bone goes under the table and each person pulls until the bone breaks. The one who gets the shorter bone gets a wish. Or is it the longer one? Oh, well...

Serves 4

3-3 ½ pound chicken, cut into 11 pieces
2 cups buttermilk
Vegetable oil

1½ teaspoons freshly ground black pepper
1 cup self-rising flour

Wash chicken with cool water and pat dry with paper towels. Place in bowl and cover with buttermilk. Heat a large cast-iron skillet on medium-high heat and add one and one half inches of oil. While oil is heating, place pepper and flour in a large ziplock bag. Add drained chicken, coat with flour and shake off any excess. Use a frying thermometer to check temperature of oil. When oil reaches 350 degrees, add only as many chicken pieces, skin side down, as will fit without touching. Overcrowding will lower the temperature of the oil and make your fried chicken greasy. Fry chicken about 8 minutes, turn and continue to fry. Check temperature and always stay near the frying pan; it needs constant attention. Rotate chicken and turn again to get it an evenly rich brown. As chicken is cooked, transfer to a metal wire rack to drain and place in a warm oven. Season and flour remaining chicken and fry. Chicken takes about 25 minutes to cook.

CREOLE CHICKEN ON HOMEMADE PASTA

W e remember when chicken was a special dish and served on Sundays. Pioneers like Henry Kober's processing plants, located in Walton County, automated chicken production and soon the old yardbird became an everyday meal.

This spicy dish is extra good with fresh homemade pasta.

Serves 6-8

- ½ recipe fresh homemade pasta
- 2 pounds chicken thighs, skinned, boned
- ¾ cup unsalted butter
- 1 cup onion, finely chopped
- 2 ribs celery, minced
- 3 teaspoons garlic, minced
- 3 ½ cups chicken stock
- 2 teaspoons Worcestershire
- ½ teaspoon Tabasco
- 8 teaspoons Creole Seasoning
- ½ pound mushrooms, sliced
- 2-15 ounce cans tomato sauce
- 2 tablespoons sugar
- 2 cups green onions, chopped
- 2 tablespoons parsley, minced
- Parmesan cheese, freshly grated

Prepare one half recipe for fresh homemade pasta (see page 294) and cut on the thinnest cutter of pasta machine. Place pasta in 13x9 inch pan, cover with plastic wrap and freeze. Cut chicken into one half inch cubes and sprinkle with 4 teaspoons of the Creole seasoning (see page 181), set aside. In a large cast-iron skillet sauté onions and celery in one half cup of butter over medium-low heat until onions are brown and caramelized but not burned. Add remaining Creole Seasoning, minced garlic, chicken stock, Worcestershire and Tabasco. Cook 10 minutes on low heat. Stir in mushrooms

Elizabeth Wright cranking out pasta just like a pro, c 2005.

and tomato sauce, and bring to a boil. Reduce heat to low and add sugar, and 1 cup of green onions, cook uncovered for 20 minutes. In another large cast-iron skillet melt one half cup of butter over medium heat. Add remaining green onions and parsley and sauté about 3 minutes. Add seasoned chicken, but don't stir until chicken is brown on one side, about 3 minutes. Stir and cook 3-4 minutes longer or until chicken is a medium brown. Add tomato sauce mixture to chicken and cook over low heat 10-15 minutes. Taste and correct seasoning. Cook homemade pasta in boiling water until "al dente" and drain. Spoon generous helping of sauce over pasta and sprinkle with freshly grated Parmesan cheese.

SPANISH CHICKEN AND RICE
"Arroz con Pollo"

Chicken n' Rice was served often when we were growing up. It was usually made with the bony pieces of the chicken such as the neck, back, saddle, and wings as well as the gizzard. Some folks call it perlo. The Spanish call it Arroz con Pollo, but we still call it chicken n' rice.

Serves 4

- 2½ pound chicken, cut up, reserving neck, wings, and backbone for stock
- Salt and freshly ground black pepper, to taste
- 1 tablespoon olive oil
- 1 cup onion, chopped
- 1¼ cups green bell pepper, chopped
- 2 chorizo sausages, cut into ¼ inch rounds
- 1 teaspoon garlic, minced
- ¼-½ teaspoon saffron threads
- ¼ teaspoon cumin
- 1 cup canned plum tomatoes, seeded and cubed
- ½ cup dry white wine
- 1 cup rice
- 1 bay leaf, crumbled
- 2 parsley sprigs
- 1 teaspoon lemon juice
- ¼ teaspoon red pepper flakes
- 1 cup chicken stock
- Garnish: 3 cooked artichokes hearts, quartered
- ⅓ cup frozen English peas, thawed
- 1 tablespoon pimento strips

Wash and pat chicken dry with paper towels. Season with salt and pepper. Heat a large cast-iron skillet over medium heat. When hot, add the oil and brown chicken on all sides, about 4 minutes on each side. Remove chicken and drain oil leaving sediment and 1-2 tablespoons of oil. Return chicken to skillet. Scatter onions, bell pepper and sausage around chicken. Cook 1 minute, stir in garlic, saffron and cumin and cook for 3 minutes. Stir in tomatoes and wine. Add rice, bay leaf and parsley. Sprinkle with lemon juice and pepper flakes. Pour stock over all, making sure rice is covered with broth, taste for additional seasonings. Cover and simmer for 20 minutes or until rice has absorbed all liquid. Garnish with artichokes, peas and pimento, return cover, and turn heat off. Let chicken sit undisturbed for 2-3 minutes before serving.

Saffron threads are the dried stamen of the crocus blossoms. It takes 75,000 of the blossoms to make 1 pound of saffron. The golden orange stigmas provides the yellow glow. They are used to both color and flavor many dishes.

MAMA'S CHICKEN N' RICE

*T*his is an old family dish. It was served many times as we grew up.

10-12 bony chicken pieces (back, saddle, neck, wings and giblets)
Salt to taste
2 tablespoons unsalted butter

1 small onion
1 celery rib
5 cups water
1½ cups Uncle Ben's Long Grain Rice

Heat butter in Dutch oven. Salt chicken and cook until golden, about 5 minutes. Add onion and celery, cover and cook 20 minutes. Add water and cook 35 minutes. Remove onion and celery. Stir in rice, bring to a boil and cover. Reduce heat to low and cook until rice is done, about 20 minutes.

DEVILED CHICKEN

*T*he combination of Deviled Chicken and linguine with Basil Pesto Sauce is one of our all time favorites. It is simple to prepare, very tasty, and best with a bird that has never seen a freezer. We have this often when fresh basil is available for the pesto.

Serves 4

1 fresh 2½-3 pound chicken
1 tablespoon olive oil
Salt to taste
Lemon wedges

2 teaspoons red pepper flakes, more if you prefer
½ cup dry white wine

Preheat oven on broil. Split chicken in half and remove backbone from each half. Wash and pat dry with paper towels. Brush a large cast-iron skillet with oil. Use remaining oil to rub chicken on both sides. Salt each chicken half and sprinkle with pepper flakes. Place chicken in skillet and broil, skin side down, on second rack of oven for 15 minutes. Turn skin side up and broil 10-12 minutes more. To be sure the chicken is cooked, pierce thickest part of thigh, juices should run clear. Remove chicken from oven and transfer to heated plates. Drain all but 2 tablespoons of oil from skillet, place on medium heat, add wine and scrape up the browned bits with a wooden spoon. Reduce by half, correct seasoning and pour sauce over chicken. Serve with lemon wedges, linguine, Basil Pesto Sauce and salad.

COQ AU VIN

(Rooster in Wine)

"We will kill the old red rooster when she comes."

There are not many mountains in North Florida to come around, but we used to sing this song, at the top of our voice, on school trips. Right after "99 bottles of beer on the wall."

This dish was created long ago to use up tough old roosters, but it works well with young birds, too. Years ago, rooster (cock) fighting was an accepted pastime. The owner of the winning bird kept the losing bird as the trophy, maybe for this dish.

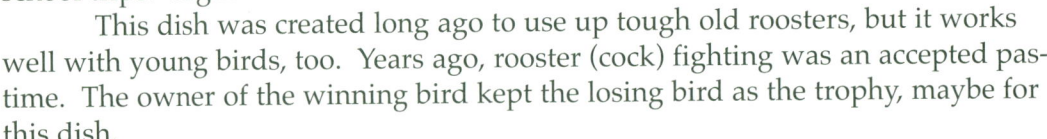

Serves 4

- ⅓ pound thick sliced bacon, cut into ½ inch pieces
- 1 - 3½ pound chicken, cut into 8 pieces
- 1 ¼ cups onion, chopped
- 3 tablespoons all-purpose flour
- ⅓ cup medium shallots, minced
- 2 teaspoons garlic, minced
- ½ teaspoon thyme, crumbled
- 2 cups dry red wine
- 1½ cups beef stock
- 2 teaspoons tomato paste
- 1 bay leaf
- ½ rib celery
- Salt and freshly ground black pepper, to taste
- 20 small white boiling onions, peeled
- ½ pound mushrooms, quartered
- Chopped parsley for garnish

Add bacon to a small saucepan and cover with water. Bring to a boil, drain, and pat dry with paper towels, set aside. Cook white onions in a saucepan of boiling water until tender, about 5 minutes; drain, peel and set aside. In a large cast-iron skillet, cook bacon over medium heat until crisp on outside but soft inside, about 3-5 minutes. Remove pan from heat, remove bacon with slotted spoon and drain on paper towels. Wash and pat dry with paper towels. Heat bacon drippings over medium-high heat. Add chicken in a single layer and cook 4-5 minutes or until brown, turn and brown on the other side. Remove chicken and all but 2 tablespoons of grease and sediment. Add chopped onion, reduce heat to medium and cook until onions begin to brown, about 3 minutes. Sprinkle with flour and stir to mix flour with oil. Continue to stir and cook until flour is lightly browned, about 3 minutes. Stir in shallots, garlic and thyme and cook 1 minute. Add chicken, wine, stock, tomato paste, bay leaf, celery, salt and pepper. Reduce heat to low, cover and cook for 30 minutes. Discard bay leaf and celery. Skim any fat from sauce and reduce until slightly thickened. Add small onions, mushrooms, and bacon to chicken. Cover and cook for 15 minutes. Garnish with parsley and serve with rice.

CHICKEN VALDOSTA

No, this dish didn't come from Valdosta, Georgia. It's our own version of the Italian dish "Veal alla Valdostana." Chicken Valdosta has become a frequent dish at our table and besides, it's easier to pronounce.

Serves 4

- 4 chicken breasts, boned, skinned, sliced thin lengthwise to make 8 slices
- 6 ounces (2 inches x 3 inches) thinly sliced Smithfield type country ham
- 1 tablespoon olive oil
- 2 tablespoons unsalted butter
- Salt and white pepper, to taste
- ⅓ cup flour
- ¼ stick unsalted butter
- ⅓ cup shallots or green onions, minced
- ½ pound mushrooms, sliced
- ⅔ cup chicken stock
- ½ cup Sweet Marsala wine
- 10 ounces fresh spinach, wilted
- 4-6 ounces Fontina or Fontinella cheese, sliced ¼ inch thick

Wash chicken under cool water and pat dry with paper towels. Pound chicken breasts between sheets of plastic wrap until thin. Heat a large cast-iron skillet over medium-high heat. Trim fat from slices of ham, add to skillet and fry until fat is rendered, remove fat pieces from skillet. Add ham and cook briefly on each side, or until lightly brown, set a side. Lightly salt and pepper chicken, dredge in flour and shake off any excess. Add olive oil and butter to skillet. When butter melts, add chicken and sauté on both sides until golden brown, adding addition butter if necessary. Remove chicken to a heated plate.

Add a fourth stick of butter to skillet. When melted, add shallots and sauté 1 minute, stirring; add mushrooms and cook another minute, stirring constantly. Add chicken stock and reduce by half, add wine, and reduce heat to low. Return chicken to pan and top with ham, spinach and cheese. Cover and cook until cheese has melted and sauce has thickened. Correct seasoning and serve in skillet. Serve with Cornmeal Coush.

CORNMEAL COUSH

Serves 6-8

- 5 cups chicken stock
- 1 ½ cups coarse-ground yellow cornmeal
- 2 tablespoons unsalted butter
- ½ cup Parmesan cheese, grated
- Salt to taste

Bring chicken stock to a boil in a large heavy saucepan. Slowly stir in cornmeal with a wooden spoon, stirring continuously until mixture thickens. Remove from heat when you can see the bottom of the pan as you stir, about 2 minutes. Immediately stir in the butter and cheese, correct seasoning and serve.

LEMON CHICKEN

Serves 4-6

- 2½-3 pound chicken
- 1 cup fresh lemon juice (9-10 lemons)
- ½ cup olive oil
- ½ tablespoon red-wine vinegar
- 1 teaspoons garlic, minced
- ¼ teaspoon dried oregano, crumbled
- Salt and pepper, to taste
- 2 tablespoons parsley, chopped

Preheat broiler. Cut chicken in half. Broil chicken halves in a large cast-iron skillet, skin side down for 15 minutes. Turn chicken over and broil 10 minutes more. Place lemon juice, olive oil, red-wine vinegar, garlic, oregano and salt and pepper in a glass bowl and whisk until well blended, set aside. Remove chicken from pan and pour the grease from the skillet. Cut chicken into serving pieces, cutting the breast into two pieces. Return chicken pieces to skillet. Whisk lemon sauce and pour over the chicken, tossing to coat. Return chicken to broiler, and broil 2 minutes, turn each piece and broil another minute. Remove chicken pieces from skillet and place on a platter that has a two inch lip. Place skillet with lemon sauce over high heat, boil for two minutes. Pour sauce over chicken, sprinkle with parsley and serve with crusty bread.

CHICKEN MARABELLA

Serves 8-10

- One 12-ounce package pitted, dried Prunes
- One 3.5 ounce jar capers
- One 5 ounce jar oregano
- 6 bay leaves
- 1 garlic bulb, minced
- 1 cup pimento stuffed olives
- ½ cup red wine vinegar
- ½ cup olive oil
- 1 tablespoon coarse sea salt
- 2 teaspoons black pepper, freshly ground
- 8 pounds of mixed chicken pieces
- 1 cup brown sugar
- 1 cup dry white wine
- ¼ cup parsley, minced

Combine first 10 ingredients in in an extra-large ziplock bag. Remove excess fat from chicken. Add chicken pieces, turning to coat, set in a very large pan and refrigerate overnight. Turn the bag several times while marinating. Arrange chicken in a single layer in two 13 x 9 inch baking pans. Pour marinade evenly over chicken, and sprinkle evenly with brown sugar. Pour wine around chicken and bake at 350 degrees for 1 hour, basting frequently. Remove chicken, prunes and olives to a serving platter and drizzle with pan juices. Sprinkle with parsley and serve.

FILIPINO ADOBO

Serves 4-6

8 chicken legs and thighs
1 ½ cups white vinegar
3 large cloves garlic, crushed
2 bay leaves
1 cup water
½ tablespoon peppercorns, crushed
¾ cup soy sauce
3 tablespoons vegetable oil
8 cups cooked rice

Combine chicken, vinegar, garlic, bay leaves, peppercorns, and 1 cup of water in a large pot. Bring to a boil, reduce heat, cover and simmer 20 minutes. Transfer chicken to a plate. Boil liquid until reduced to 1 cup. Cool, remove bay leaves and skim fat. Fry chicken in oil for 5 minutes. Place on platter and pour sauce over all. Serve over rice.

CHICKEN PORTABELLA

Serves 8

1 ¼ teaspoons salt
1 teaspoon paprika
¼ teaspoon cayenne
¼ teaspoon white pepper
½ teaspoon onion powder
½ teaspoon garlic powder
½ teaspoon basil
¼ teaspoon thyme
¼ teaspoon black pepper
8 chicken breast, boned with skin on
4 tablespoons unsalted butter
2 cups diced tasso or ham
4 cups portabella mushrooms, sliced ¼ inch thick
1 cup green onions, chopped
1 recipe Béarnaise Sauce

Preheat oven 350 degrees

Thoroughly mix seasonings. Sprinkle chicken on both sides generously with the mix, patting it in. Preheat a large cast-iron skillet for 2 minutes over high heat. Place chicken breast skin side down in the skillet and place chunks of butter on top. Bake uncovered on the floor of the oven for 35 minutes. Turn meat over and continue baking 10 minutes or until golden brown on both sides. Remove chicken and set aside. Pour drippings into glass measuring cup and reserve. In the skillet used to cook the chicken, cook the tasso (if you are using ham, you will need to add an additional a half teaspoon garlic powder, one half teaspoon cayenne, and one half teaspoon black pepper) over high heat until well browned, 3-4 minutes, stirring occasionally. Add about half of the reserved drippings, stir in the mushrooms and sauté for 1 minute. Add remaining drippings if pan is dry, stirring constantly. Stir in the onions and cook another minute. Place chicken breast on serving plate and sprinkle with mushroom mixture and spoon a generous amount of Béarnaise Sauce (see page 75) over all. Serve with Steamed New Potatoes.

CHICKEN HUNTER'S STYLE

Serves 4-6

1-3 pound fryer
1 teaspoons salt
3 tablespoons olive oil
1 tablespoon parsley, minced
1½ celery stalks, chopped
1 clove garlic, minced
2 bay leaves
1 cup dry white wine
4 tablespoons chicken stock
Freshly ground black pepper

Cut the chicken into ten pieces and salt. Brown chicken in olive oil over medium-high heat for ten minutes. Add parsley, celery and garlic and continue to cook until chicken is well browned on all sides. Add bay leaves and wine and cook until wine is almost evaporated. Add the broth and scrape the bottom of the skillet with a wooden spoon. Add additional salt and pepper to taste. Simmer 10 minutes until chicken is tender and sauce has darkened. Serve with an Italian bread.

BAKED GAME HENS WITH WALNUT STUFFING

Serves 4

4 game hens
Walnut stuffing (recipe follows)
Salt and pepper, to taste
4 tablespoons butter
½ cup chicken stock
¼ cup dry white wine
1½ teaspoons all-purpose flour
2 tablespoons medium-dry sherry

Preheat oven 450 degrees

Wash the hens thoroughly and dry with paper towels. Fill cavities with stuffing and truss. Season with salt and pepper and rub with butter. Place hens in baking pan and place in the oven for 10 minutes. Lower temperature to 350 degrees and continue to roast for 30-40 minutes, or until juices run clear. Remove to a platter, add stock and wine to pan juices, scrap bottom of the pan with a wooden spoon, sprinkle with flour and whisk until sauce is smooth and thickened. Stir in sherry, cook 1 minute and pour over hens.

WALNUT STUFFING

Melt 4 tablespoons unsalted butter in a large skillet over medium heat. Add one half cup minced Smithfield ham, one and one half tablespoons minced parsley, one half teaspoon thyme and sage and one and one half cups bread crumbs. Mix well and add 1 egg and one half cup chopped walnuts. Add enough chicken broth to make a moist dressing.

CHICKEN MOUTARDE

*T*here was only one type of mustard in rural North Florida when we were young—the bright yellow type now referred to as "ball park mustard." We loved it then and still do. Some dishes seem to taste richer and tangier with one of the imported mustards, such as Dijon. Actually, a lot of the Dijon type mustards are made from seeds grown in Canada and processed in the good ol' U.S.A.

Serves 4

- 4 chicken breasts, skinned, boned and sliced lengthwise to make 8 thin slices
- Salt and freshly ground black pepper, to taste
- ½ cup all-purpose flour
- 2-3 tablespoons olive oil
- 2-3 tablespoons unsalted butter
- ¼ pound Smithfield type ham, minced
- 8 mushrooms, quartered
- 3 canned artichoke hearts, quartered
- 2 tablespoons brandy
- ½ cup dry white wine
- ¾ cup whipping cream
- 2 tablespoons capers, drained
- 6 Greek olives, cut in half and pitted
- 2 tablespoons Dijon mustard
- 1 tablespoon parsley, minced

Wash and pat chicken dry with paper towels. Salt and pepper chicken, dredge in flour, shake off any excess. Heat a large cast-iron skillet over medium-high heat. When hot, add half the oil and butter, cook chicken breasts on each side until golden brown, adding additional oil if needed.

Transfer chicken to a heated plate. Add remaining butter, ham, mushrooms, artichoke hearts. Lower heat to medium, and cook, stirring, for 3 minutes.

Add brandy and wine, reducing to 3 tablespoons. Add cream and reduce until sauce thickens. Return chicken and accumulated juices, add capers, olives, and mustard. Correct seasonings, sprinkle with parsley and serve on heated plates.

CHICKEN PICCATA

Serves 6

- 4 chicken breasts, skinned, boned and sliced lengthwise to make 8 thin slices
- Salt to taste
- ½ cup flour
- 1 tablespoon olive oil
- 2 tablespoons butter
- ¾ cup dry white wine
- Juice of ½ large lemon
- 1 lemon sliced
- 2 tablespoons capers, drained
- 1-2 tablespoon parsley, chopped

Salt chicken slices and dust with flour. Add olive oil and butter over medium-high heat. Add the chicken slices, and cook until light brown. When both sides are done, pour in the wine, and let bubble. Add the lemon juice, sliced lemon, capers and spoon sauce over chicken. Sprinkle with parsley and serve.

GYPSY CHICKEN

After he sold the cafe on Malaga Street, owner/chef Ned Pollack relocated to Anastasia Island and opened the Gypsy Cab Co. restaurant where he is widely known for his exciting "urban cuisine." Ned uses fresh local fish, seafood and meats seasoned with herbs, spices and sauces accompanied by vegetables in season and delicious pasta.

The menu is printed on a chalk board and changes frequently. Gypsy chicken, a signature dish, can usually be ordered even if it's not on the chalk board.

Serves 4

- 4 whole chicken breast, attached, boned and skinless
- 1 tablespoon garlic
- 1 teaspoon fennel
- ¼ cup fresh basil
- ¼ cup fresh parsley
- ½ cup unsalted butter
- ½ lemon
- 1 tablespoon capers
- ½ teaspoon crushed red peppers
- 2 tablespoons Marinara Sauce (recipe follows)
- Salt and freshly ground black pepper to taste
- 8 tablespoons Swiss cheese, grated
- ½ cup all-purpose flour
- 2 eggs, beaten
- 2 cups homemade dry bread crumbs

Place garlic and fennel in food processor and process until finely minced. Add basil, parsley, butter, lemon juice, capers, crushed red peppers and process until well mixed. Add Tomato (Marinara) Sauce, salt and pepper, pulse to mix and set aside. Wash chicken under cool water and pat dry with paper towels. Remove loose skin and fat from chicken and discard. Pull chicken filets out and serve at another meal. Place whole breast between plastic wrap and flatten slightly. Place two tablespoons of Swiss cheese and tomato mixture on one side of each breast. Fold remaining breast over and press edges of together. Heat a large heavy bottomed skillet over medium heat. Lightly salt and pepper breast, dust with flour, dip in beaten eggs and roll in bread crumbs. Place chicken in refrigerator 30 minutes to chill. Preheat oven 350 degrees. Add enough vegetable oil to just coat bottom of skillet. When hot add the chicken breast and sauté until lightly brown on one side. Turn breast over, place in 350 degree oven and continue to cook until well browned on both sides, about 15-20 minutes. While chicken is cooking, prepare sauce and set aside in a warm place.

SAUCE:

Prepare the sauce in advance and keep in a warm place. It is difficult to give the exact measurements Ned uses since his is made in large quantities but these measurements work for me. Perhaps the best way to judge is by visiting the restaurant and ordering the Gypsy Chicken. Then determine if the sauce should have more sweetness or more citrus flavor to your liking. This dish is great for a dinner party since the chicken can be prepped in advance leaving only the breading and cooking to be done just before serving.

½ cup sweet sherry
½ cup orange juice
2 tablespoons shallots
1 teaspoon garlic
2 cups demi-glace
1 teaspoon tarragon, crumbled

2 tablespoons white sauce
½ pound mushrooms, sliced one fourth inch thick and sautéed in butter

Reduce sherry, orange juice, shallots and garlic by one-fourth. Add demi-glace (see page 23) and reduce by one-fourth. Stir in the white sauce (see page 24), tarragon and mushrooms. Salt and pepper to taste and cook until slightly thickened.

MARINARA SAUCE

2 tablespoons olive oil
⅓ cup green onions, minced
1 teaspoon thyme, crumbled
½ tablespoon garlic, minced
1 tablespoon parsley, minced

28 ounce can peeled plum tomatoes, seeded, chopped and juice reserved
1 cup dry red wine or chicken broth

Heat olive oil in 8-10 inch skillet. Add green onions and sauté over medium-low heat. Cook onions until softened but not brown; add thyme, garlic, and parsley and cook stirring for 1 minute. Stir in tomatoes and wine, reduce heat to simmer. Strain juice through paper towel placed in sieve and add to tomato sauce. Salt and pepper to taste. Cook sauce 20 minutes, or until most of the liquid has cooked out..

When chicken is done. Place on heated plates and spoon sauce on top of each. Garnish with minced parsley and serve.

TURKEY TETRAZINNI

Serves 4

- 1 leftover turkey carcass, cut-up
- 1½ cups turkey shredded
- ½ pound mushrooms, sliced thin
- 5 tablespoons unsalted butter
- ½ pound linguine, cooked
- 2 tablespoons flour
- 1 cup heavy cream
- 3 tablespoons medium-dry sherry
- Freshly grated nutmeg, to taste
- ½ cup Parmesan cheese, freshly grated
- 1 tablespoon parsley. minced

Place turkey carcass in a large pot and cover with water by 2 inches, bring water to a boil, reduce heat and simmer the turkey for 20 minutes. Let the turkey cool in the broth. Remove the meat and set aside. Reduced the broth by half. Strain the broth and discard the bones and skin. Boil the broth until reduced by 2 cups. While the broth is reducing sauté the mushrooms in 2 tablespoons of the butter. Stirring until softened and set aside. Bring a large pot of salted water to a boil, add the linguine, cook until just done and drain. Preheat oven to 350 degrees. Melt remaining 3 tablespoons of butter over low heat, when melted stir in the flour, and cook, stirring for 3 minutes. Whisk in the broth, cream, and the sherry. Bring mixture to a boil, whisking and simmer for 5 minutes. Season the broth with nutmeg, salt and freshly ground black pepper. In a large bowl add the sauce, mushrooms, the shredded turkey and linguine. Combine the mixture well and pour into a buttered two and a half quart baking dish. Sprinkle with Parmesan cheese and bake for 25 minutes, or until heated through. Sprinkle with parsley and serve.

Early hunter with a fine North Florida wild turkey, c 1900's.

TURKEY MOLÉ OLÉ

Turkeys are thought to be dumb birds by many, supposedly because they will open their beaks during a rain and drown. We don't know about that but the Florida Wild Turkey is one of the smartest and craftiest game hunted. So next time someone calls you a turkey, they might be paying you a compliment.

This dish can also be made using chicken. The flavor improves if refrigerated overnight.

Serves 4

- 2 fresh Jalapeño peppers
- ½ teaspoon coriander seeds
- 2 cloves garlic, peeled
- 1 tablespoon sesame seeds
- ½ teaspoon aniseed
- Pinch cinnamon
- Pinch ground cloves
- ¼ teaspoon salt, more if necessary
- ¼ teaspoon black pepper, freshly ground
- 2 teaspoons cilantro, minced
- 1-2 tablespoons peanut oil
- ½ cup canned plum tomatoes
- ½ cup onion, chopped
- 1 teaspoon sugar
- 4 turkey thighs (3 pounds), deboned, with fat removed
- 2 cups chicken stock
- 3 tablespoons smooth peanut butter
- ¼ cup dry red wine
- 1 tablespoon cornstarch, dissolved
- 1 ounce unsweetened chocolate, grated
- 1 avocado, cut into 10 slices
- Cilantro sprigs

Cut Jalapeños in half lengthwise, discard membrane and reserve seeds. In a large cast-iron skillet over medium heat, toast seeds from peppers with coriander seeds and garlic, stirring for 3 minutes. Add sesame seeds and aniseed, and continue cooking 2 minutes. Peel garlic, crush with a knife and put into a mortar with toasted spices, cinnamon, cloves, salt, pepper, cilantro and grind to a paste. In same skillet, add 2 teaspoons oil and fry peppers over medium heat until they begin to brown on all sides, about 2-3 minutes. Leave oil in pan, place peppers in a small dish and cover with water. Cook onion over low heat in pepper oil 8-10 minutes until they begin to brown, add garlic-spice paste. Drain water from peppers, chop and add to mixture. Add tomatoes and cook over medium-low heat until almost all moisture evaporates, about 5 minutes. Remove mixture from pan and set aside. Washed and dry turkey pieces with paper towels. Heat a large cast-iron skillet over medium-high heat, add enough oil to coat bottom of pan, cook turkey in a single layer and brown well on both sides. You may need to cook in 2 batches. Pour off all fat, add tomato mixture, stock, and peanut butter, stir to mix. Cover and simmer 30 minutes. Degrease by tearing paper towels into strips and laying them gently on top of chicken. Repeat until all grease is removed. Add wine mixture, chocolate and stir until slightly thickened, about 2-3 minutes. Correct seasoning, thinning with stock if necessary. Serve or transfer to a glass casserole and refrigerate overnight. Reheat next day and serve with avocado slices and cilantro sprigs.

GUINEA WITH THE LIGHT BROWN FLAIR

With apologies to Stephen Foster.

Guineas are not native to this continent, but were brought from Africa years ago and have thrived. These noisy birds are great watch birds, and needs to give the armadillo a lesson in road crossing. We have never seen a guinea road kill. These birds tend to be on the tough, dry side and should be basted many times during baking.

Serves 4

- 2½-3 pound guinea hen
- 1 tablespoon olive oil
- Salt and freshly ground black pepper, to taste
- ½ cup Smithfield type ham
- 1 cup onions, chopped fine
- 2 tablespoons unsalted butter
- 1 cup mushrooms, sliced
- ½ tablespoons all-purpose flour
- ¾ cup dry white wine
- 1½ cups chicken stock
- 1½ teaspoons rosemary, crumbled
- Fresh rosemary sprigs

Wash guinea with cool water and pat dry with paper towels. Split the guinea down the back and press firmly so it will lay flat. Sprinkle with salt and pepper. Heat a large cast-iron skillet over medium-low heat, add the olive oil and brown guinea on both sides. Remove guinea and set aside.

Add ham to skillet and cook until almost crisp, add the onions, stir and cook until onions are brown but not burned. Add 1 tablespoon of the butter to the skillet with the rosemary, stir for 30 seconds, add the mushrooms and cook until they release their juices. Stir in the flour, cook 1 minute, stirring constantly. Add wine and reduce liquid by half. Add stock and bring to a boil. Return guinea to skillet, spoon sauce over all and cover. Reduce heat to low and cook 90-120 minutes, or until tender. Baste frequently, 7-8 times so guinea will not dry out. Remove guinea to heated plates and reduce sauce if it needs thickening. Spoon sauce over guinea and garnish plates with fresh rosemary sprigs before serving.

Wild Game Cracker Cattle and Piney Woods Rooters

The goatman logged over 100,000 miles on the backroads.
You could smell him coming 30 minutes before he got to town, c 1941.

Bruce Creek Venison Stew, 237
Trophy Buck Chili, 238
Jail House Chili, 239
Grilled Venison Backstrap, 240
Venison Chops, 241
Chicken-Fried Venison
  with Gravy, 242
Venison Loaf, 242
Liver a L' Orange, 243
Wild Boar Stew, 243
Marsh Hens with Gravy, 244

Grilled Doves with
  Smoked Bacon, 245
Plantation Quail, 246
Southern Fried Quail, 247
Quail Stuffed with Figs, 247
Rabbit n' Rice, 248
Rabbit Dijon, 248
Tupelo Teal, 249
Seahorse Stables
  Squirrel Gravy, 250
Florida Wild Turkey, 251

Steak Salteado, 252
Mother's Roast Beef
  with Gravy, 253
Veal Camille, 254
Veal "Saltimbocca", 255
Scottish Rib Roast, 255
T-Bone Steak al a Carte, 256
Lamb Shanks, 257
Dixie Ham, 258
Cuban Pork Roast, 259
Possum and Taters, 260

Fall is the season most associated with wild game. Hunting season begins in September with much anticipated dove hunts. In the mid-1900's, when corn and peanuts were widely planted in North Florida, hogs were turned into the fields to root out the last nuts and grains. These fields made ideal feeding plots for doves. Many memorable dove hunts were held, which easily yielded the limit to the average hunter. Doves are still migrating through the state, but in fewer numbers. They don't hang around very long because of fewer farms, and today, the limit is not easily reached. Some hunters have resorted to adding additional feed to the fields to keep the doves from flying south, but you didn't hear that from me cause I ain't one to gossip.

A successful dove hunt, c 1940's.

A few early duck hunts are available each fall for avid duck hunters. Unfortunately, the local wild duck hunting has declined in recent years. The wood duck is about the only duck that is hunted with any success. Groups like Ducks Unlimited are making strides to increase the breeding grounds up North and we encourage you to join and participate. Hopefully, wild ducks will make a comeback like the whitetail deer.

Around Thanksgiving deer season begins and the good ol' boys get to go after that trophy buck. Today North Florida has a large population of whitetail deer. This was not always the case. Less than 30 years ago, the deer population had almost been wiped out by disease and fire hunting. Fortunately, strong wildlife laws and conservation practices have brought the deer back to its original numbers.

There are two popular methods of hunting deer. Some folks prefer using dogs to chase the deer from the swamps and thickets, and some prefer still hunting without dogs. We like both methods although hunting with dogs lends itself to more entertainment and camaraderie, especially if using CB radios, which is probably the best thing that has happened for the deer. Some hunters like to sit in their trucks and jaw back and forth on the C.B. radios and will let the deer slip right by them. But of course you didn't hear that from me cause I ain't one to gossip.

After deer season is closed around February many hunters concentrate on the small game like the bobwhite quail. Before 1949, North Florida had open range laws which allowed cattle and hogs free access to any land that was not fenced. Large tracts were burned each year to allow new grass to grow. This also gave cattle and hogs grazing land, kept the palmettos and briars under control, and gave bird hunters ideal quail hunting grounds. Since the passing of the state fence law, quail hunting has declined in much of North Florida, however plantations around Tallahassee still practice controlled burning and offer excellent quail hunting.

WILD GAME, CRACKER CATTLE, AND PINEY WOODS ROOTERS

Wild (feral) hogs come in a variety of colors.

North Florida has a good population of small game such as squirrels, rabbits, snipes, coons, possums and armadillos. These are relatively easy to harvest, especially with a good dog, and most are quite delicious, although we must confess there are a few on this list we haven't tried. For those of you who aren't familiar with snipes, they are tasty little birds that stay around wet areas. The only way to catch them is on a very dark night with a paper bag, you must be very quiet.................

Wild turkeys in North Florida.

In the spring when the woods are colorful with native dogwoods, honeysuckle, mountain laurel and wildflowers, the ol' tom turkey begins to search for the hens and this is the season to hunt the tom, the most difficult game bird to harvest.

Dedicated hunters in camouflage, with hands and faces smeared with black and green paint stalk the crafty bird. Each hunter has a particular calling device. These may be made of wood, slate and even snuff cans. The hunter must be totally hidden and be able to make a sound very similar to the hen turkey, which calls the strutting tom close enough for a shot. The reward for all this is a very tasty bird and maybe even a trophy beard to hang on the gun case.

Summer is when we like to thin the herds of wild hogs. Florida has no season for hogs on private land. Hernando de Soto is credited with bringing swine to Florida. These old Piney Woods Rooters, as they are now known, were well suited to Florida's climate and terrain and soon populated most of the scrub woods and swamps. These hogs lived on nuts and roots, and would eat anything that didn't eat them first. Early farmers would round up the little pigs and cut and mark them for later harvest. When the hogs were the proper size, they would be caught, usually with hog dogs or trapped in pens. Then fattened on whatever food available, butchered, and hung in the smoke house in the form of hams, middling (bacon) and sausage. The lard was rendered and used for cooking and making lye soap. So the old piney woods rooter became a welcome addition to the early settlers' food supply and also a new game animal for North Florida hunters.

Although bison (buffalo) roamed the prairies of Florida several centuries ago the first domestic cattle in North Florida were brought to St. Augustine by the Spanish setters in the mid-1500's. These Florida cattle grazed in the surrounding ranches around St. Augustine and as far north as Fort Diego, which is now Ponte Vedra and south down to Paines Prairie.

These early ranches were mostly wooded acres with poor grazing, so it took many acres to feed those old Spanish cattle. The breed was well suited to this climate and survived and multiplied in spite of the harsh conditions (including panthers, black bears and Indians that regularly raided the ranches). The breed survived and today is listed as Cracker Cattle (also referred to as Piney Woods or Southern Woods Cattle). A herd can be seen at the Florida Department of Agriculture Lab in Tallahassee.

Ingram's oldest son Kyle and grandson Garrett each bagged a nice buck opening day, c 2004.

Cracker cattle located in the Agricultural Museum in Tallahassee.

We know there are some folks that are against the hunting of wild game. We respect their views and hope they respect ours. Hunting in our family is an old tradition passed from fathers to sons, and sometimes daughters (our daughter preferred ballet.) The basic rule followed was safety first. Each hunter was taught to be a safe hunter before ever firing that first shotgun. We only kill what we can eat and we eat what we kill.

Hunting dogs help in locating and retriving game and make great pets as well.

Hunting and preparing game dishes is an excellent way for families to spend time together. It also teaches children responsibility, pride of accomplishment, and safety. We also feel that game, properly dressed and prepared, offers unique flavors not found in domestic animals and fowl.

When properly managed, game will reproduce to offset harvesting by hunters. Game numbers are controlled more by food availability than any other factor. We strongly recommend to anyone interested in wildlife and the outdoors to join or participate in the organizations like Ducks and Quail Unlimited, as well as local groups that promote wildlife conservation.

BRUCE CREEK VENISON STEW

*T*he venison stews we enjoyed down at the Mosley Place on Bruce Creek were made with whatever ingredients that were available. Charles would cook up the venison along with some potatoes, onions, flour, salt and black pepper, while we made a run to the Handy Pak for the beverages and a loaf of light bread to sop up the delicious gravy.

In recent years we have added a few new ingredients, but we still call it Bruce Creek Venison Stew for old times sake.

Serves 6-8

- 3 pounds venison, gristle removed and cut into 2 inch cubes
- Salt and freshly ground black pepper, to taste
- 2 tablespoons unsalted butter
- 1 medium-large onion, chopped
- ½ cup smoked country ham, minced
- 1 large clove garlic, minced
- 2 bay leaves
- 1 teaspoon dried thyme, crumbled
- 1½ tablespoons flour
- 2 cups water
- 4 cups beef consommé
- ½ pound fresh mushrooms, quartered
- 3 carrots, peeled and cut in 2 inch pieces
- 12 new potatoes, cut in half
- Grated rind of 1 lemon
- 2 tablespoons parsley, minced

Pat venison dry with paper towels, season with salt and pepper. Heat a very large cast-iron skillet over medium-high heat, add butter and lightly brown venison on all sides. Add onions and cook until softened and lightly brown, stirring occasionally. Reduce heat to low and add ham, garlic, bay leaves and thyme, stir and cook 2 minutes. Add additional tablespoon of butter, if needed and flour. Stir and cook for 2 minutes. Add water and bring to a boil, stirring constantly. Add consommé, return to boil, cover and reduce heat to low. Simmer stew 2 hours or until meat is tender. Add mushrooms, carrots, potatoes and lemon rind, and cook 30 minutes more or until vegetables are tender. If thicker stew is preferred, remove carrots and potatoes and reduce liquid. Return vegetables to reheat, sprinkle with parsley and serve on heated plates.

Trey bagged this 7 point buck in his secret 7 point deer stand, located somewhere near Bruce Creek, c 2001.

TROPHY BUCK CHILI

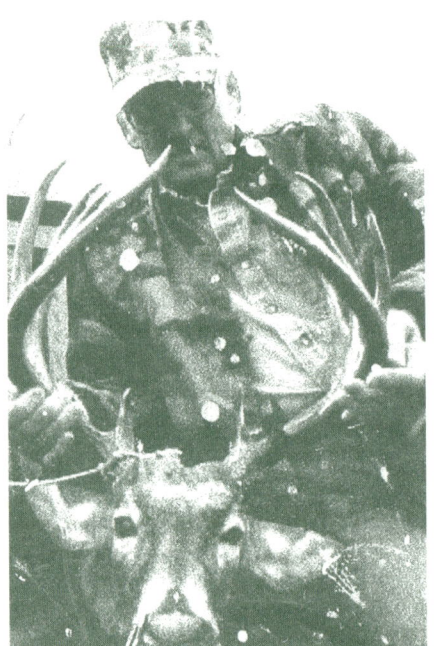

*E*very deer hunter wants to bag that trophy buck. You know, the big one, the one that was seen last year but managed to slip away. This dish has become a tradition in our home on Super Bowl Sunday. Since the flavor improves with time, we make it on Saturday and enjoy the chili on Sunday during the game. If you are short a trophy buck like we usually are, substitute any lean venison or beef.

Longtime friend and neighbor Delbert Spence showing off his 19 point North Florida trophy buck. Delbert claims he shot it on his side of the fence-oh well, c 2004.

Serves 6

- 6 fresh Jalapeño peppers
- 1 cup water
- 3 pounds lean venison, cut into ¼ inch pieces
- 4 tablespoons rendered beef fat
- 4 garlic cloves, minced
- 1½ tablespoons cumin
- 2 cups crushed canned tomatoes
- 1 tablespoon cocoa powder
- ½ teaspoon crushed red pepper
- ½ teaspoon dried oregano, crumbled
- 1 bay leaf
- 3 cups water
- Salt to taste
- Tabasco to taste, optional
- 4 cups onions, chopped

` Ask your butcher to grind a half pound of beef fat to make the rendered fat. Place beef fat in a small cast-iron skillet over medium heat. Cook until fat liquifies, cool and strain. Heat a small cast-iron skillet over medium heat. Add peppers and 1 teaspoon of beef fat. Toast the peppers, turning until all sides are toasted. Remove peppers to dish and cool. Stem and seed peppers, and remove the membrane. Place peppers in a small pan with 1 cup of water. Bring water to a boil, reduce heat and simmer 5 minutes. Purée pepper mixture in a food processor. Trim venison of fat and gristle, and pat venison dry with paper towels. In a large cast-iron skillet cook half the meat, in 2 tablespoons beef fat over medium-high heat until brown. Transfer meat to a bowl and brown remaining meat and transfer.

Add 2 tablespoons of beef fat to skillet with onions and garlic, cook over medium heat until onions have softened. Reduce heat to low, add cumin to onions, cook and stir for 1 minute. Add venison, chili purée, tomatoes, cocoa, red pepper, bay leaf, oregano and stir well. Add enough water to barely cover meat, bring to a boil, reduce heat to simmer and cook 2 hours. Add more water to keep meat barely covered, stirring occasionally. Add salt to taste, and add one and one half teaspoons red pepper flakes if chili needs more punch. Simmer chili 1 hour more or until meat is very tender and liquid is reduced to desired consistency. The chili will improve in flavor if cooled, covered and chilled over night. Add Tabasco if desired. Serve chili with grated extra-sharp Cheddar cheese, sour cream, minced green onions, minced Jalapeño peppers, Guacamole and tostadas.

JAIL HOUSE CHILI

Serves 10

- 5 pounds shoulder venison or beef, cut into 2 inch pieces
- Creole Seasonings
- ½ pound beef suet
- 6 cloves garlic, minced
- Salt to taste
- 2 tablespoons hot chili powder
- 2 tablespoons mild chili powder
- Beef broth
- 1 lime
- 2 teaspoons oregano
- 1 tablespoon cumin seeds, toasted and ground
- Dried peppers, to taste
- Masa Harina

Sprinkle and rub meat with Creole seasoning (see page 181), let set 3 hours. Place in smoker and let cook 15 minutes, turn and cook 15 more minutes. Remove, let cool and cut into bite size pieces and salt lightly. Fry out suet in a large cast-iron Dutch oven. Stir in garlic and cook 30 seconds. Add meat, meat juices and beef broth to cover. Add lime juice and rest of seasonings including Creole Seasoning. Cook for three hours. Add Masa Harina, a tablespoon at a time, until desired thickness. Serve with beans, guacamole, cheddar cheese and sliced jalapeno peppers.

Two cell jail in Ponce de Leon, built in the 1920's.

GRILLED VENISON BACKSTRAP

Venison has a reputation of being tough and gamey tasting. This is only true when the deer is very old, not properly dressed or over cooked. Many venison recipes call for days of marinating in all sorts of concoctions, but we prefer a simple grilling with a garlic-butter basting sauce.

Backstrap to a deer is the same cut as New York strip in beef.

Serves 4

- 6 venison backstrap steaks, cut ½ inch thick, or any venison steaks
- ½ cup unsalted butter
- 4-6 large cloves garlic, thinly sliced
- Salt and freshly ground black pepper, to taste

Let steaks come to room temperature while you prepare garlic butter. Melt butter in a small saucepan over low heat, add garlic to butter and cook until softened, but not brown. Mash the garlic against the side of the pan with a wooden spoon and let stand for at least 30 minutes. Trim the steak of all silvery skin, fat and gristle. Pat steaks dry with paper towels and brush one side lightly with garlic butter. Place steaks, buttered side down, on hot grill, cook 2-3 minutes on each side, basting with garlic butter. Season with salt and pepper before last basting. Do not over cook. Serve on heated plates with Marchand De Vin Sauce (recipe follows), Wild Rice and Wild Pecans.

MARCHAND DE VIN SAUCE
"The sauce of the wine merchant"

- 6 ounces mushrooms, sliced
- 6 tablespoons unsalted butter
- 1 cup green onions, minced
- 1 ½ cups Chautauqua red wine
- 1½ cup beef stock (p.23)
- 1 tablespoon lemon juice
- ¼ teaspoon black pepper
- ½ teaspoon salt
- 1 tablespoon cognac

Sauté mushrooms in butter. Add green onions, cook five minutes, add all other ingredients and cook 10-15 minutes.

Chautauqua winery DeFuniak Springs.

VENISON CHOPS JACK DANIEL'S SAUCE

*V*enison chops are our favorite cut of the deer. It is the backstrap, cut into small T-bone steaks with the bone in. When only one or two deer are killed, the Bruce Creek Hunting Club divides the venison and each hunter only gets 2-3 chops, so we save the chops until we have enough for this dish.

Jack Daniel's is considered a "sipping whiskey" by most of the club members, but we call it "cooking spirits" and also enjoy it in this sauce.

Serves 4

- 8 Venison Chops, ¾ inch thick
- Salt and freshly ground black pepper, to taste
- ½ tablespoon olive oil
- 5 tablespoons unsalted butter
- ⅓ cup green onions, minced
- ½ cup plus 5 tablespoons Jack Daniel's Tennessee Whiskey
- 1 tablespoon cornstarch
- 2 cups beef stock
- 1 tablespoon Dijon mustard
- Juice of half a lemon
- 2 tablespoons parsley, chopped
- 1½ tablespoons green peppercorns, lightly crushed

Remove chops from refrigerator an hour before cooking. Trim the chops of all fat, skin and gristle. Pat the meat dry with paper towels. Heat a cast-iron skillet over medium-high heat. Add one and half tablespoon olive oil and 1 tablespoon of the butter to skillet. Sear well on the first side, turn over the meat, salt and pepper, sear on second side and season, cook about one to one and one half minutes per side. Remove chops and keep warm. Reduce heat to low and sauté green onions in 2 tablespoons of the butter until softened. Add the stock, 1 tablespoon of the peppercorns and one half cup of the bourbon, reduce by half. Mix the cornstarch and mustard with remaining 5 tablespoons of bourbon and stir into stock with accumulated juices from chops and remaining peppercorns, lemon and parsley. Arrange two chops on each plate and top with sauce.

Bring on the Jack Daniel's, c 1999.

CHICKEN-FRIED VENISON WITH GRAVY

Serves 4

2 pounds venison steaks
2 cups buttermilk
1 cup self-rising flour
Freshly ground black pepper
¼ teaspoon cayenne pepper
2 cups water or beef stock
1 cup peanut oil

Place the venison in a large bowl and cover with buttermilk. Combine the flour, black pepper and cayenne in a large ziplock plastic bag. Seal and shake the bag to distribute peppers. Heat a large cast-iron skillet over medium-low heat. Place a few pieces of venison in the ziplock and shake to coat with flour. Shake off any excess flour and add to oil when it is hot, don't crowd the pan. Transfer meat to a wire rack, placed in a warm place until all meat is cooked. Pour off the oil remaining in the skillet, leaving 4 tablespoons with sediment in the skillet. Whisk in a fourth cup of the remaining seasoned flour into the oil. Cook, stirring constantly, for 2-3 minutes, being careful not to burn. Gradually whisk in 2 cups of water or beef stock. Cook 5-8 minutes, stirring constantly until gravy has reach desired thickness. Taste for additional salt and pepper and serve over rice.

VENISON LOAF

Serves 8

4 large eggs
2 teaspoons salt
Freshly ground black pepper, to taste
½ teaspoon Louisiana Hot Sauce
1 tablespoon Worcestershire
½ teaspoon dried rosemary, crumbled
2 pounds ground venison
2 pounds ground pork
½ pound ground pork fat
1 cup fresh bread crumbs
1 cup onion, finely chopped
½ cup celery, finely chopped
1 small bell pepper, chopped
3 cloves garlic, minced
½ cup parsley, minced
6 slices smoked bacon, cut in half
15 ounce can tomato sauce
1 cup Parmesan cheese, grated

Preheat oven 350 degrees. Mix all ingredients (except bacon) in a large bowl. Form into a large loaf, drape bacon over loaf and place in a 13x9 inch pan and bake 1 hour. Remove from oven and pour tomato sauce over top. Return loaf to oven and bake an additional 20 minutes. Cool 10 minutes before slicing.

LIVER A L' ORANGE

Bruce Creek Hunting Club rules gives the liver and head to the hunter who kills the deer. The rest of the deer is divided equally "amongst" the hunters. This dish may be prepared with young deer or calf liver.

Serves 4

- 8 slices smoked bacon
- 1 medium onion, sliced
- 4 slices deer or calf liver
- Salt and freshly ground black pepper, to taste
- ⅔ cup fresh orange juice
- 2 teaspoons cornstarch
- 3 oranges, peeled and sectioned
- 1 teaspoon orange zest

Cook bacon in a large cast-iron skillet until crisp and drain on paper towels. Remove bacon drippings, reserving 2 tablespoons. Add onion to skillet over medium- high heat and sauté in reserved bacon drippings until softened. Pat liver dry with paper towels, salt and pepper, add to skillet with onions and brown meat on both sides. Add orange juice to pan, cover and simmer 8-10 minutes. Remove liver to heated plates. Blend cornstarch with 1 tablespoon cold water and add to skillet. Stir and cook until mixture thickens. Add orange sections and orange zest, stir gently and heat through.

Spoon sauce over meat, top with crisp bacon and serve.

WILD BOAR STEW

Serves 6-8

- 1½ pounds pork shoulder, cut into 1 inch cubes
- 1 onion, roughly chopped
- 2 cloves garlic, chopped
- 2 quarts chicken stock
- ½ pound cheddar cheese, grated
- 4 jalapeno peppers
- Salt, to taste
- 1½ cups whole hominy
- 2 tablespoons oregano, crumbled
- 1 teaspoon thyme, crumbled
- 3 limes, cut into wedges
- 2 red onions, finely chopped

Place pork, onion and garlic in a large Dutch oven and add chicken stock. Bring liquid to a boil, skim off foam, reduce heat, cover and simmer for 1 hour. In the meantime remove and discard seeds from jalapenos, cut into strips and soak in warm water for 1 hour. Drain peppers and place in blender and puree. Stir in pureed jalapenos, oregano, thyme, plus salt to taste, and continue simmering for 1 hour. Stir in hominy, add cheese and onions, bring to a boil, lower heat and simmer for 15 minutes. Garnish with lime wedges.

MARSH HENS WITH GRAVY

Marsh hens thrive in the marshes along the Atlantic Coast. The best hunting is during a high tide the day before or after a full moon. The birds are in the marsh grass and can stay hidden with low tides. When spooked, the birds will fly up and out of the grass, this is the best time to get off a shot. Most marsh hen hunters have an old shotgun they use for this hunting since the salt water causes guns to rust.

Serves 4

- 8 marsh hens
- 1 teaspoon salt
- 1 teaspoon black pepper, freshly ground
- ½ teaspoon onion powder
- ½ teaspoon garlic powder
- ¼ teaspoon cayenne pepper
- ½ teaspoon paprika
- 1 cup all-purpose flour
- Vegetable oil
- 2 cups onions, chopped
- 2 ½-3 cups chicken stock

Cut marsh hens in half, wash under cool water, and pat dry with paper towels. Combine the salt, black pepper, onion and garlic powder, cayenne and paprika. Rub 2 teaspoons of mixture into the marsh hens. Add remaining seasonings to the flour and mix well. Heat a large cast-iron skillet over medium heat. When skillet is hot add vegetable oil, dredge 3 marsh hens in flour, shaking off excess. Fry hens on both sides until golden brown and drain on wire racks. Cook remaining hens. Drain oil, reserving 2 tablespoons with sediment. Add onions to skillet and cook until lightly brown. Sprinkle with two and a half tablespoons flour reserved from dredging and stir, cooking until flour browns, about 2 minutes. Add 2 cups chicken stock and stir until smooth. Return marsh hens to skillet. Cover and bake for 1 hour, basting with gravy 2-3 times while baking.

If gravy becomes too thick, add remaining stock. Correct seasoning and serve with rice.

Marsh Hen

GRILLED DOVES WITH SMOKED BACON

Roscoe P. Cocoatrain was his name—total destruction was his game. What was the cutest Chocolate Lab puppy you can imagine quickly turned into a very large dog that chewed everything in sight, including shoes, socks and all the wooden baseboards he could reach.

It was a memorable day we took him to his first and last dove shoot. Roscoe retrieved his first dove like a champion except he ate the entire bird within 3 seconds. This wasn't enough—he then proceeded to prance around the field and eat the other hunters doves. As you can imagine that was the last time we were invited.

We once read of a Japanese Kobe beef cow that was fed beer and massaged daily to make it the most expensive meat known to man. Well, have we got news for them. My husband contends that the dove is, by far, the most expensive meat known to man, because each ounce of dove usually cost over $5 in license fees, shells, gas, etc. Our son is a better shot, he only spends $4.75.

Roscoe P. Cocoatrain

Serves 4

8 dove breasts with bone
4 slices smoked bacon
4 metal skewers, 6 inches long

1 Bottle Newman's Own Italian Dressing

Wash doves with cool water and pat dry with paper towels. Cut bacon slices in half and wrap around each dove. Skewer 2 doves on each metal skewer, making sure to secure bacon ends with skewer. In a large ziplock bag marinate Dove for 1 hour in Italian dressing keep refrigerated. Grill doves over hot coals 2-3 minutes on each side for medium rare. Cooking time will depend on temperature of grill. Serve on heated plates with Dirty Rice and Skillet Red Cabbage.

PLANTATION QUAIL

The Bobwhite quail is considered the ultimate game bird by many. Quail are found in coveys of 10-30 birds. The most successful method of hunting uses a good bird dog to locate the quail. Even with a good dog, it's not easy. The birds usually all fly at once, making the choice difficult for the experienced hunter, and startling the inexperienced hunter who might just be used to shooting them on the ground. Of course, you didn't hear that from me, cause I ain't one to gossip.

Serves 2

4-3½ ounce quail
1 head red leaf lettuce, washed and dried thoroughly
2 plum tomatoes or 2 canned plum tomatoes seeded, and diced
¼ cup fresh basil, chopped
4 fresh sprigs thyme, crushed
1 teaspoon rosemary, chopped
2 tablespoons fresh parsley, chopped
1 clove garlic, minced
½ cup olive oil
3 tablespoons red-wine vinegar
Salt to taste
¼ teaspoon white pepper
1 red bell pepper, cut in 2" strips

Wash quail in cool water and pat dry with paper towels. Split quail down the back and lay flat. In a large glass dish, mix tomato, basil, thyme, parsley, garlic, oil, vinegar, salt and pepper. Add quail and marinate 30 minutes. Remove quail from marinade and reserve marinade. Grill quail over hot coals, basting often, for 2 minutes on each side. Remove quail to a heated plate. Heat a large skillet over medium heat and add reserved marinade. Add lettuce, stir until wilted and place on a heated platter. Place quail on top of lettuce, pour sauce over all and serve with Old-Fashioned Cornmeal Coush.

*Old style hunting wagon at Welaunee Plantation north of Tallahassee.
This wagon was used to transport wealthy quail hunters to the fields.
c 1929.*

SOUTHERN FRIED QUAIL

*D*efinitely the preferred Southern way of cooking, these tasty birds are cooked and simmered until they melt in your mouth. We used to have this dish only during hunting season, but now quail is available in super markets or directly from game farms. Doves may also be prepared in this manner.

Serves 4

- 6 quail
- Salt and freshly ground black pepper, to taste
- ¾ cup all-purpose flour
- 2 tablespoons bacon drippings
- ½ cup unsalted butter
- 1-1⅓ cups chicken stock
- Whipping cream (optional)

Split quail in half, wash under cool water and pat dry with paper towels. Heat cast-iron skillet with tight fitting lid over medium-high heat. When skillet is hot add bacon drippings and butter. Season quail with salt and pepper and dredge in flour. When butter melts, add quail and fry until golden brown on both sides. Remove quail and pour off most of the oil, leaving about 2 tablespoons with sediment. Return quail to pan and add stock. Cover and simmer 30 minutes. If gravy becomes too thick, add more stock or whipping cream. Correct seasonings and serve on heated plates over grits or rice.

QUAIL STUFFED WITH FIGS

Serves 8

- 24 Brown Turkey Figs
- ¼ pound Smithfield Ham, pounded thin, cut into 16 strips
- Salt and freshly ground black pepper
- 16 partially boned quail
- ¼ cup olive oil
- ½ cup dry white wine
- 2 tablespoons cold unsalted butter
- 1 tablespoon parsley, chopped

Preheat oven 475 degrees

Wrap 16 of the figs with ham. Sprinkle wrapped figs and quail with salt and pepper. Stuff each quail with a wrapped fig. Heat 2 tablespoons of olive oil in a large skillet. Add half the quail and brown all over. Transfer to a shallow roasting pan. Repeat with remaining quail adding additional olive oil if needed. Roast quail on top rack of oven for 5 minutes. Add remaining figs to pan and cook 5 minutes more. Transfer quail and figs to serving platter. Set roasting pan over 2 burners on medium heat. Add wine, scrapping bottom of pan, add any accumulated juices from quail , simmer briefly. Remove pan from burners and whisk 1 tablespoon butter into sauce, one at a time. Drizzle sauce and parsley over quail and serve.

RABBIT N' RICE

Serves 4

- 2½ - 3 pound rabbit, cut into 6-8 pieces
- 2 tablespoons flour
- 3 tablespoons olive oil
- 3 cloves garlic, minced
- 4 ounces Smithfield ham, diced
- 2 teaspoons rosemary, crumbled
- 1½ tablespoons flour
- ½ cup dry vermouth
- 1½ cups chicken stock
- 1 large roasted red bell pepper
- Salt black pepper, to taste
- Fresh rosemary sprigs
- 3-4 cups cooked white rice

Remove loose fat and membrane from rabbit. Wash rabbit with cool water and pat dry with paper towels. Heat a large cast-iron skillet over medium-low heat and add oil. Dust rabbit with flour, shaking off excess. When oil is hot, add rabbit and brown on all sides. Remove skillet from heat and transfer rabbit to a warm plate. Add garlic, ham and rosemary to skillet, return skillet to medium-low heat and cook, stirring, for 1 minute. Add flour and cook, stirring, for another minute. Add vermouth, 1 cup of the stock and bring to a boil; reduce slightly. Return rabbit to skillet, cover and cook on low heat 45 minutes. Baste rabbit 3-4 times while cooking. Add roasted red bell pepper (see page 254) and continue to cook for 20 minutes. Add additional one half cup of stock if needed or uncover and reduce liquid if needed, baste 2-3 times. Correct seasoning if needed. Garnish heated plates with fresh rosemary sprigs and serve with white rice.

RABBIT DIJON

Someone once told us a wok was what you throw at a wabbit. While you can cook this silly wabbit in a wok, we prefer our cast-iron skillet.

Serves 4

- 1- 2 pound rabbit (cut into 8 pieces)
- 2 tablespoons unsalted butter
- ½ cup shallots, minced
- ½ teaspoon thyme
- 1 cup dry white wine
- 1 tablespoon Dijon mustard
- 3 cups chicken broth
- 1 tablespoon parsley, chopped
- 1 bay leaf

Wash rabbit and pat dry with paper towels. Heat a cast-iron skillet over medium heat, add butter and sauté rabbit until brown on both sides, about 15 minutes. Add shallots between rabbit pieces and cook 1 minute more, stirring. Add thyme and the bay leaf to the skillet. Mix mustard, wine, and broth together and pour over rabbit. Bring to a boil, cover and reduce heat to simmer for one and a half-two hours. Baste rabbit every 15 minutes and turn half way through cooking. Add additional broth or water if needed. Taste and season with salt and pepper if needed. Discard Bay leaf and sprinkle with parsley and serve over rice.

TUPELO TEAL

Duck hunters have to be the most dedicated hunters of all. Some drive great distances to get to the old hunting grounds. Then get out of the sack at 4:00 A.M., put on all the hunting paraphernalia, paddle an old canoe or boat complete with an old smelly dog in ice cold water, and proceed to scatter decoys from hell to creation. Then the poor devils sit out in the freezing cold all morning and hope to get the limit, which might be just two birds. Oh well, someone has got to do it, and we're glad they do, cause we shore do like the taste of wild duck.

Serves 4

- 4 teal ducks, or 2 large ducks
- ¼ cup unsalted butter, melted
- 1 teaspoon black pepper, freshly ground
- Salt to taste
- 2 teaspoons thyme crumbled
- ¼ cup unsalted butter, melted
- ¼ cup bacon drippings
- 1 cup tupelo honey
- ¼ teaspoon dry mustard
- 4 teaspoons lemon juice
- 2 teaspoons orange zest
- 6 tablespoons Florida orange juice
- 1 large apple, unpeeled cut into wedges
- 2 Florida navel oranges, unpeeled, cut into ½ inch slices
- ⅓ cup tawny Port
- 1 tablespoon cornstarch
- 1 tablespoon parsley, minced

Preheat oven 450 degrees. Combine pepper, salt, and thyme and rub half of the mixture inside the ducks. In a small saucepan combine butter, bacon drippings, honey, mustard, juices and orange zest, and heat over low heat. Remove from heat and when mixture is cool, rub about 2 tablespoons of mixture inside each duck. Equally divide apple and orange slices, and place in cavity of ducks. Truss and rub remaining seasoning mixture over outside of ducks. Place ducks on a rack in a roasting pan and cover with remaining honey mixture. Cover loosely with foil and bake for 15 minutes, baste, reduce heat to 350 degrees. Bake for 45 minutes basting with drippings several times. Uncover and bake until brown (10 minutes), continue basting with drippings. Place ducks on heated plates and keep in a warm oven. Add cornstarch to port and stir into drippings to thicken. Sprinkle with parsley and serve sauce on the side.

SEAHORSE STABLES SQUIRREL GRAVY

For several years the seahorse stables on Amelia Island hosted a dinner featuring delicacies which were "shot, caught, grown and home-cooked." We were fortunate to be invited to some of these get togethers and often wondered if it also included run-over.

These feasts featured venison, armadillo, wild pigs, various duck, squirrel, dove, and quail dishes, oyster dressing, garden vegetables and swamp cabbage, plus a multitude of homemade desserts.

The entertainment was by a local "Country Grass Band" and our gracious hostess Barbara Zuber made sure everyone had a chance to learn how to "buck dance." The party wound up about midnight with a hayride on the beautiful moonlit beach.

Squirrels have a diet of mostly acorns and also hickory and pine nuts. This nutty diet gives the squirrel meat a nice flavor and it is one of our favorite game animals. Squirrels have two large chunks of meat under the jaw, which give them the power to crack a hickory nut, which is quite a feat. Some folks cook the squirrel with the heads to get the extra meat and also enjoy the squirrel brains with grits.

Serves 4

- 4 squirrels, cut up
- Salt and freshly ground black pepper, to taste
- ½ teaspoon cayenne
- 1 cup all-purpose flour
- 4 tablespoons vegetable oil
- 4 tablespoons unsalted butter
- 1½ cups onions, finely chopped
- ¼ pound smoked bacon, cut into ¼ inch pieces
- 2 teaspoons garlic, minced
- 2 cups chicken stock
- 2 cups sour cream
- 2 tablespoons parsley, minced

Wash squirrel under cold water and pat dry with paper towels. Sprinkle with salt and peppers. Heat a large cast-iron skillet over low heat. Place flour in a large ziplock bag and drop the squirrel pieces into it, a few at the time. Shake bag to coat with flour, remove meat and shake off the excess flour. Set aside on wax paper until all pieces are coated. Add the oil and butter to the skillet, increase heat to medium. When foam subsides, add the squirrel, making sure not to crowd the pan, cover the skillet and reduce the heat to low. Cook 30 minutes.

Remove squirrel to a heated platter. Pour off all but a tablespoon of fat with sediment in skillet. Add onion and ham, and cook, 3-4 minutes, stirring. Add the garlic and cook, stirring for 1 minute. Pour in the chicken stock and bring to a boil. Cook rapidly until it is reduced by half, turn the heat down. Whisk in the sour cream slowly. Simmer only long enough to heat the gravy through. Return the squirrel to the skillet and taste for seasoning. Sprinkle with parsley and serve over white rice.

FLORIDA WILD TURKEY

Florida has two of the four types of wild turkey that grow in North America. North Florida has the Eastern variety and South Florida has the Oceola variety.

Florida wild turkeys are smart and crafty and not too easy to bag. This is the way we like to cook it when we luck up and bag one.

Turkey call.

Serves 8

1 wild turkey breast
1 teaspoon salt and pepper
¾ cup self-rising flour
¼ cup cornmeal

Additional salt and pepper
  to taste
Peanut oil

These clowns killed a wild tom turkey? Give me a break, c 1989.

Remove the breast from turkey with a sharp knife and cut into a half inch steaks. Salt and pepper both sides. Stack into a pile and let sit until salt has dissolved. Place three-fourths cup self-rising flour and a fourth cup cornmeal in a ziplock bag. Add the turkey, shaking excess flour mixture off. Fry in a large cast-iron skillet with sizzling peanut oil. After all turkey is cooked, pour off all but 2 tablespoons of the oil. Stir in 2-3 tablespoons flour, cook stirring 2 minutes. Add 1 pint of water and stir vigorously until gravy is smooth. Add salt and pepper to taste, continue to cook for 1-3 minutes. Serve gravy over rice or biscuits if desired.

STEAK SALTEADO

This is an uptown version of beef stew popular in many Spanish and Cuban restaurants. Chorizo is a spicy Spanish sausage made with pork bits, paprika, garlic, herb's and spices, and then smoked.

Serves 8

- 2 cups vegetable oil,
- 2 Russet potatoes, peeled and cubed
- ¼ cup olive oil
- 1 pound Delmonico steak, cut in ½ inch x ½ inch cubes
- 1 ¼ cups chopped St. Augustine sweet onions
- ½ cup green pepper, chopped
- 2 cloves garlic, minced
- 2 Spanish sausages-Chorizo cut in ¼ inch slices
- ½ pound mushrooms, quartered
- 1-1¼ teaspoons salt, or to taste
- ¼ cup demi-glace
- ½ cup dry red wine
- 2 tablespoons parsley, chopped
- ½ cup frozen English peas, thawed

Trim all fat and gristle from steak and pat dry with paper towels. Heat vegetable oil to 350 degrees and fry potatoes until golden brown. Remove and drain on paper towels.

Keep in a warm place. Heat a large cast-iron skillet over medium-high heat, when skillet is hot add 1-2 tablespoons olive oil. Lightly salt steak, add to skillet and sear meat on all sides. Do not stir meat until it has seared. Remove to a heated platter. Reduce heat and add remaining oil to skillet if needed. Sauté onions, bell pepper and cook 1 minute, add garlic and cook until mixture has softened. Add chorizo, mushrooms and salt, stir and cook until mushrooms have released their juices. Return meat and any accumulated juices to skillet.

Increase heat, add demi-glace (see page 23) and reduce by one fourth. Stir in the wine and reduce slightly, taste and correct seasoning. Sprinkle with parsley and peas, and stir. Serve at once with potatoes on the side and Spanish Yellow Rice.

RED SANGRIA

- ½ lemon, cut ¼ inch slices
- ½ orange, cut in ¼ inch slices
- ½ apple, cut into thin slices
- ⅓ cup sugar
- 1 bottle San Sebastian vinters red wine
- ¼ cup brandy
- 6 ounces chilled club soda

Combine the lemon, orange, apple and sugar in a large pitcher. Pour in the wine and brandy and stir until sugar is dissolved. Refrigerate for one hour or more. Add the soda, stir and serve.

San Sebastian winery located in St. Augustine.

MOTHER'S ROAST BEEF WITH GRAVY

*"Doodle bug, doodle bug,
your house is on fire."*

Sweet days of youth. Lazy summer afternoons spent under the porch trying to coax a doodle bug to come out of its crater home by repeating the chant over and over while twirling a twig at the bottom of the little crater. The sounds of a dirt dauber busily building a new wing to its condominium under the porch. The aroma of food cooking, drifting down from the kitchen window was sometimes a hint of things to come. Mother used garlic sparingly, so the smell of garlic usually meant one of my favorite dishes, roast beef with gravy, would soon be on the table. You can be sure I quickly lost interest in doodle bugs and dirt daubers, and began working my way towards the table with my hands and face now sparkling clean.

Serves 8

- 4 ½-5 pound rump roast
- 1 teaspoon freshly ground black pepper
- 4 small cloves garlic, peeled (optional)
- 1 tablespoon salt
- 1-2 tablespoons vegetable oil
- 4 tablespoons all-purpose flour
- 4-5 cups water or beef stock

With a sharp knife, make 4 evenly spaced holes in roast, stuff with garlic, making sure garlic is not exposed. The roast will brown nicer if it does not come directly from the refrigerator, pat dry with paper towels. Rub the roast with salt and pepper. Heat a heavy bottomed pot over medium heat and add oil to lightly coat bottom of pot. Brown the roast on all sides, giving it an even, dark, rich brown coloring. The secret of course, is the proper browning. Remember, the roast should be a mahogany color before turning. Cover and reduce heat to low. Cook 3 hours or just until meat is tender and is close to falling apart. Remove roast and transfer to a platter. Stir flour and 2 cups of the water together until smooth. Stir into pan drippings, cook over low heat, stirring to keep smooth until gravy forms. Add the remaining water, one half cup at the time until desired consistency is reached. Correct seasoning and serve gravy over roast with lots of mashed potatoes. Leftover roast is great the next day for sandwiches with Horseradish Sauce (see below).

HOMEMADE HORSERADISH SAUCE

Mix 2 cups sour cream, 6 tablespoons freshly grated horseradish, one half teaspoon salt, 2 tablespoons minced fresh parsley and store in glass jar in refrigerator.

VEAL CAMILLE

Our daughter was born the same year hurricane Camille hit the Gulf Coast. We have been asked in later years if she was named for the hurricane or vice versa.

Veal Camille is an elegant dish. The brandy and demi-glace gives it a rich and exceptional taste. If you're squeamish about veal substitute chicken breast.

Cameron Camille Manning and Aubrey McDonald, c 1986.

Serves 4

- 8 slices veal, or chicken pounded thin
- Salt and freshly ground black pepper, to taste
- ½ cup all-purpose flour
- 1 tablespoon vegetable oil
- 2 tablespoons unsalted butter
- ⅓ cup demi-glace
- 1 cup whipping cream
- 1 large roasted red bell pepper, (see below)
- ¼ pound mushrooms, sliced thin and sautéed in 2 tablespoons unsalted butter
- 1 tablespoon parsley, minced

Dry meat with paper towels, season with salt and pepper, dredge in flour and shake off any excess. Heat a large cast-iron skillet over medium-high heat and add oil and butter. When melted, add meat, making sure not to crowd pan. Transfer pieces to a warm plate as they brown. Add cognac, ignite and shake skillet until flames go out. Liquid should be reduced by half. Add demi-glace (see page 23), cream, red bell pepper and sautéed mushrooms. Reduce sauce until slightly thickened and correct seasoning. Return meat and heat through. Serve on heated plates and sprinkle with parsley.

ROASTED RED BELL PEPPER

Place bell peppers on foil lined baking pan. Broil until skin is blistered and charred, turn peppers and continue to cook until all sides are charred. Place in a small brown paper bag and twist top. Leave pepper in bag until cool, about 10 minutes. This will loosen the skin and it can easily be peeled off. Seed and tear into strips.

VEAL SALTIMBOCCA

"Jump in your mouth"

Serves 4

1¼ pounds veal scallops or chicken breast, boned and skinned
¼ pound Smithfield ham, sliced thin
Fresh sage leaves
Toothpicks
½ tablespoon olive oil
3 tablespoons unsalted butter
Freshly ground pepper, if desired
½ cup dry white wine

If using the chicken, remove the tenderloin. Slice the veal or chicken breast in half horizontally. Pound the meat between sheets of plastic wrap until they are between a fourth-an eighth inch thick. Place ham between sheets of plastic wrap and pound until they are an eighth inch thick. Cover the meat with sage leaves. Place ham on top of sage and skewer with toothpicks so that they will lay flat. Heat a large cast-iron skillet over medium heat. Add olive oil to pan and swirl to coat the bottom. Add 1 tablespoon of butter and when foam subsides add the meat slices, ham side down. Cook until meat turns white around the edges, about 1-2 minutes, turn the pieces over and cook 2 minutes more. Remove the meat to a warm platter and add the wine to the skillet. Reduce liquid by half and swirl in remaining butter by shaking the pan. Pour sauce over meat and serve at once.

SCOTTISH RIB ROAST WITH YORKSHIRE PUDDING

One Rib Roast

Preheat oven to 450 degrees. Cook standing rib roast, in an open skillet 15 minutes. Reduce temperature to 350 degrees and continue to roast 15 minutes to the pound.

Yorkshire Pudding:
1 cup flour
⅛ teaspoon salt
⅛ teaspoon baking powder
1 cup milk
2 eggs
4 tablespoons roast drippings

Sift flour, salt and baking powder together, add milk and stir until smooth paste. Add eggs and beat with mixer until well mixed. Preheat oven to 375 degrees. Add drippings and stir again. Pour into flat greased pan and bake 25 minutes until done. Serve with juices from roast.

T-BONE STEAK AL A CARTE WITH MACHO GRAVY

One of our favorite meals is when we cook out down on Bruce Creek. We usually invite a few other couples to share the good times. We start the day with breakfast at Mamie's (the best grits and eggs in town). Then it's down the street to the Thriftway where Bill cuts us some of his T-bone steaks one inch thick while we select the salad greens and the "Ideho" potatoes. Then it's back to the Big House where we prepare the salad and cook up a batch of Macho Gravy. Then we head out to the Old McDonald farm in Euchee Valley.

We build a big fire of oak and hickory then we pick wildflowers and native berries in season, while the fire burns down to coals. Then we chunk the potatoes, covered in foil into the coals. When the potatoes are almost done we throw the T-bone steaks on the grill, and warm up the Macho Gravy. The potatoes are slathered with butter, sour cream and chives. The steaks are cooked medium rare and covered with Macho Gravy served with a Derby Salad and beverage of choice. Boys, it don't get no better than this.

One T-bone or Porterhouse steak 1 inch thick, per person

Allow steak to come to room temperature. Pat dry with paper towels. Cook steaks over hot hardwood coals until desired doneness. Serve immediately with Macho Gravy. Make gravy ahead and store in refrigerator, if desired.

Macho Gravy:

- 1 cup beef stock
- 2 tablespoons soy sauce
- 1 tablespoon Worcestershire
- 2 tablespoons all-purpose flour
- 4 ounces mushrooms, sliced
- 2 tablespoons butter
- 4-5 jigs Tabasco sauce

Mix beef stock, soy sauce, Worcestershire, Tabasco sauce and flour in glass jar with tight fitting lid. Shake vigorously until well combined. Cook mushrooms in butter until they give up their juices. Add stock mixture and stir until mixture thickens to gravy consistency.

Cookout on Bruce Creek, c 2000.

LAMB SHANKS WITH PINTO BEANS

*O*ur forefathers brought sheep with them from Scotland. They marked each sheep on its ear and turned them loose to fend for themselves. Mutton was usually eaten but occasionally young lamb was eaten on special occasions.

Serves 6

- 2 cups dried pinto beans, soaked overnight and drained
- 3 large onions
- 3 whole cloves
- 1 bay leaf
- 11 cloves garlic
- 1 tablespoon salt
- 4 tablespoons unsalted butter
- 6 tablespoon olive oil
- 6 meaty lamb shanks, studded with slivers of garlic rubbed with crumbled rosemary and salt, to taste
- ¼ teaspoon rosemary, crumbled
- 1¼ cups beef stock
- 1¼ cups dry red wine
- 6 slices lean bacon
- ½ cup dry bread crumbs

In a heavy bottomed pot combine the beans with water to cover by 1 inch and add 1 of the onions, stuck with the whole cloves, the bay leaf, 8 of the garlic cloves and the salt. Boil the mixture for 5 minutes and simmer it, covered, for 25-30 minutes, or until the beans are just tender. In a large cast-iron skillet heat 3 tablespoons of the butter and 3 tablespoons of the oil over moderately high heat, until the foam subsides, add the lamb shanks. Add the rosemary, stock, and wine and bring to a boil, cover, and reduce heat to simmer for 1 hour. In another skillet cook the remaining 2 onions, sliced thin, in the remaining 3 tablespoons oil over moderate heat until they are lightly brown, cover and cook until softened, season with salt and pepper. Drain the beans, reserving the cooking liquid, put half of the beans in an 8 quart casserole, and top them with the onions and the remaining 3 cloves of garlic, chopped fine. Transfer the shanks with a slotted spoon to the casserole, top them with the remaining beans and pour the lamb braising liquid over the mixture. (If there is not enough liquid to cover the beans, add some of the reserved bean liquid.) Top the mixture with the bacon and cook it uncovered in the middle of a preheated 350 degree oven for 1 hour. Sprinkle the top with a half cup dry bread crumbs, dot with the remaining tablespoon butter, cut into bits and bake uncovered for 20-25 minutes.

DIXIE HAM

*"Oh I wish I was in the land of cotton,
old times there are not forgotten,
Look away, look away,
look away, Dixie Land."*

Uncle Bill Lundy of Laurel Hill was Florida's last surviving Confederate soldier. When shown a jet fighter down at Eglin Air Force Base he showed great interest in the flying machine, " That would have helped us whup them yankees."

Someone once defined eternity as two people and a ham. This definition can quickly be found untrue because no leftover can outshine ham in its many uses. It can be kept up to three weeks if properly stored—ready and waiting to be sliced, chopped, diced, minced or ground. It can be used right down to (and including) the bone for your favorite dried bean dishes.

Have your butcher cut the hock end of ham off and save to season vegetables. Preheat oven 325 degrees Place ham in large cast-iron skillet and cover with foil. Bake 20 minutes to the pound for one half ham or 25 minutes per pound for a whole ham. Uncover last hour of baking and glaze if desired or remove and save the juice to season vegetables and rice but remember to adjust the amount of salt and discard most of the fat.

Glaze:
¼ **cup brown sugar**
1½ **teaspoons Dijon mustard**
2 **tablespoons fruit syrup,
    orange juice or brandy**

About an hour before ham is fully baked, remove skin and cut diagonal lines in ham to make diamond shapes. Spread glaze on using a paint brush. Return to oven, basting several times for 45 minutes-1 hour. Raise heat to 425 degrees the last 10-15 minutes of baking. Make sure to slice ham thin.

*Uncle Bill Lundy, age 107, c 1955.
And yes, those are "brogans" boys and girls.*

CUBAN PORK ROAST

Serves 8-10

- 4 pound Boston Butt pork roast
- 2 cloves garlic, crushed
- ½ teaspoon salt
- ¼ teaspoon pepper, freshly ground
- ½ teaspoon oregano
- ½ teaspoon cumin
- 1 tablespoon olive oil
- ½ cup Seville (sour) Orange juice

Note: Sour orange juice may be made with one half sweet orange and one half lime or lemon juice.

Preheat oven 450 degrees. Combine garlic, salt, pepper, oregano, cumin and olive oil in a mortar and mash into a smooth paste. Pat roast dry with paper towels. Remove excess fat from roast and pierce with a 60-penny nail, in about a dozen places. Rub roast well with paste and place in a large ziplock bag. Add remaining paste, Seville orange juice, and refrigerate overnight, turning meat several times. Allow roast to come almost to room temperature before cooking.

Place roast in cast-iron skillet, in lower third of oven, bake 10 minutes. Reduce heat to 325 degrees. Cook roast 30-35 minutes to the pound. Check halfway through cooking to see if roast is browning too quickly. If so, put a tent of aluminum foil over roast. Remove cover last 30 minutes of cooking.

Use an instant meat thermometer to check for doneness, internal temperature should register 160 degrees. Remove skillet from oven and transfer roast to a heated platter. Cover loosely with foil and let roast sit in a warm place at least 15 minutes before carving. Add accumulated juices from platter to sauce. Serve with Mojo Criollo Sauce on the side.

CUBAN MOJO CRIOLLO SAUCE

Mojo is pronounced (Moho), Cuban slang for soul, so maybe this is another soul food dish for the deep South.

Crush 4 cloves garlic and 4 tablespoons minced onion with 1 teaspoon salt. Pour a half cup olive oil in pan and heat. Add garlic mixture and a fourth cup lime juice. Simmer 5 minutes.

POSSUM AND TATERS

Granny kept a large barrel for possums out back and offered a reward to any of the local kids who brought her live possums. She would put them in the barrel and feed them for several weeks to "clean them out" and then roast them on special occasions.

The Possum Festival has been held annually over in Wausau for the last 35 years. Events include the Possum King and Queen Contest, "Possum Trot" (5,000 Meter Footrace), Coon Dog Treeing, Cornpone Baking, Possum Auction, Hog Calling and Rooster Crowing Contest.

Serves 6-8

- 1 half grown possum, cleaned
- 1 cup salt
- 2 teaspoons salt,
- 3 pods of red pepper
- 1 large onion
- 8 black peppercorns
- 8 slices smoked bacon
- 6 medium sweet potatoes peeled and sliced ½ inch thick

Place the possum in large pot with 1 cup salt and cold water to cover and let stand overnight. Remove possum from salt water, rinse and cut into serving pieces. Place possum in large pot with water to cover and cook for 1 hour. Skim and remove fat continually. Remove possum, drain and discard water. Place possum in another pot and barely cover with water, add 2 teaspoons salt, red peppers, onion and peppercorns. Bring to a boil, reduce heat to simmer and cook 30 minutes or until skin can be pierced with a fork easily. Preheat oven 375 degrees. Remove meat and place in a roasting pan, skin side up. Reduce possum broth to 2 cups. Cover meat with bacon strips.

Pour broth over possum and bake 30 minutes, basting every 10 minutes. Place potatoes around meat and continue to bake for another 30 minutes or until potatoes are done and meat is tender. Serve on heated plates with A Mess of Greens and Daddy's Crusty Pone Corn Bread.

The greatful citizens of Wausau erected this monument of the lowly opossum whose meat and fur helped them make it through the great depression, c 2004.

Finger Lickin' Deep South Barbecue

Early pit barbecue, c 1920's.

Dry Rubs, 265
  Carolina, 265
  Florida, 265
  Creole, 265
  For Fish, 265
  For Pork Ribs
Marinades, 266
  Poultry, 266
  Venison, 266
  Oriental, 266
Sauces, 267-269
  Bubba's All Southern, 267
  Carolina Clear, 267

Carolina Red, 267
Florida Sweet Rib, 268
Georgia Red, 268
North Florida Mustard, 268
Florida Citrus, 268
Texas, 269
Oriental, 269
Minorcan, 269
Quick, 269
Instructions for Pig and
  Oyster Roast, 272-275
Barbecue Essentials, 271
Bubba's Black Beans, 276

Grilled Corn, 276
Plantation Fried Corn, 278
Minorcan Perlo, 277
Rosin Potatoes, 277
Calico Beans, 278
Moccasin Branch Coleslaw, 279
Wayne's Wilted Slaw, 279
Beer Can Yardbird, 280
Popcorn Chicken, 280
Backyard Barbecue Party, 281
Best Rum Cake Ever, 282

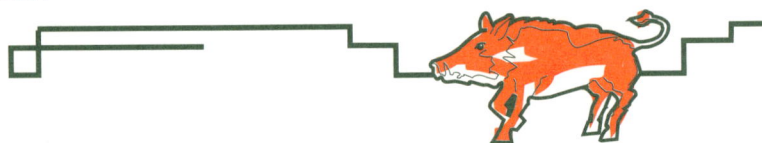

The word barbecue has a provocative history. Research suggests that it was derived from the Spanish word barbacoa, used by Spanish explorers to describe the Indians' cooking methods. They also recorded that Indians cooked on wooden skewers over open fires. This simple method of cooking game and fish by Native Americans has been taken to new levels by ingenious barbecue cooks throughout the South. In no other type of cooking are regional impacts more apparent than in Southern barbecue.

The Carolinas are divided between a clear vinegar sauce and a spicy red sauce. Georgia, Alabama, Texas and South Florida prefer a tomato based sauce, but North Florida goes for an orange-mustard sauce.

Pork, beef and chicken are the prime barbecue meats. Other regional meats like goat, mutton, gator and turkey can also be found on menus in many southern barbecue restaurants.

The recent trend of franchised barbecue restaurants has drastically lowered the quality of barbecue. The old-style owner-operated restaurants typically serve better quality barbecue. Some hints for finding a good barbecue restaurants are, look for a wood pile of local hard woods and names like Red's, Bubba's or Junior's, which show pride of ownership. Check the parking lot for local tags with a good mixture of Cadillacs and pick-ups. Smell it out—smoke should be coming from the cooking area. Original sauces and regional side dishes often indicate quality of barbecue.

Pork is the preferred barbecue meat in the South and ribs are the favorite cut. There are three types of pork ribs: spare ribs, back ribs and country style. All are good barbecued.

If you have a smoker-type grill, all that is needed is a good dry rub. Cook over coals with hickory chips until done and add barbecue sauce of choice the last 10 minutes.

Slice into individual ribs and serve extra sauce on the side. Pork ribs are extra good with a sweet sauce.

Another favorite pork cut is the pork loin. Both the loin and tenderloin are great barbecued. We typically grill the tenderloin simply with fresh herbs, olive oil, salt and pepper. Pork cooked this way should remain pink in the middle. We like to serve it with fresh summer vegetables and corn bread. The pork loin is best cooked over coals of oak and fruit woods, then sliced and served with a tomato-based sauce of your choice.

Lee Ingram pulling pork, c 2001.

When cooking pork for a crowd, the front shoulders, or Boston butts as they are called around here, are the most economical cut of pork. Cook up as many as needed and cut or pick the meat from the bones. Have at least one clear, one tomato and one mustard type barbecue sauce on the table so each guest may select the type and amount of sauce. Also have bread and buns for sandwiches. Coleslaw, calico beans and bread and butter pickles are excellent side dishes.

Jon Marc, Joel, Tom, and Keaton, Ready, Set, Go!, c 2001.

Beef steaks are best when cooked directly over wood coals. A very hot grill is necessary to sear the steaks to retain the juices. The meat should be at room temperature before grilling and dried thoroughly with paper towels.

Beef brisket is the meat of choice in Texas. Use a dry rub and smoker grill for authentic Texas brisket. This is typically served with a tomato based sauce.

We find that the flavor of a ham can be improved by cooking in a smoker at 225 degrees for 3-4 hours. Serve hot from cooker. Pork should be cooked until internal temperature reaches 160 degrees. Inexpensive cuts of pork such as jowls, necks and ham hocks can be smoked along with ham and used later to season vegetables, soups and gumbos. Sweet potato halves are also excellent smoked this way.

Chicken is another economical meat for barbecue. We prefer it cooked in an enclosed smoker, but it is also good cooked directly over coals. In the smoker, use a dry rub and wrap in aluminum foil the last hour to prevent it from becoming too dark and dried out. It is good with either a tomato or mustard sauce. Turkeys cooked in water smokers seem to be the juiciest, but we also cook them in the smoker grill.

Cutting up the pig, c 2001.

Fish and shrimp are good smoked or grilled over wood coals. Smoke oily fish like mullet and mackerel. Trigger, grouper, snapper and scamp are great grilled over coals with a few herbs like thyme and rosemary sprinkled over them. Serve with a light sauce to complement the fish.

Any season is the perfect time for a barbecue. There is nothing better than sitting around a wood fire with good friends enjoying the aroma of barbecue cooking, swapping lies and enjoying freshly prepared regional food

Scraping the hair off the guest of honor, c 2001.

METHODS OF COOKING:

DIRECT-HEAT .....In this method, meat is placed directly over the fire so the fat and juices drip over the coals and steam up to flavor the meat. This type of cooking is recommended for whole hogs, large cuts of pork and beef steaks. Gas grills have become more convenient, but the flavor from wood coals is far superior. Gas grills are okay for occasional use when time is short, but shame on you if you use it on the weekends. Direct heat grills can be elaborate cookers costing hundreds of dollars or just a simple one made from a few brickbats and racks from an old stove or refrigerator.

INDIRECT SMOKING.....In this type of cooking the fire is adjacent to the grill and the heat and smoke exit through the vent at the opposite end. This method is recommended for pork, ribs, chicken, turkey and briskets. We have invested in a heavy duty metal smoker grill and use it regularly. But just as effective smokers can be made from old refrigerators, plywood or 55-gallon metal drums. It's the end result (the taste of the meat) that's important.

WET SMOKING.....Used in closed grills with a pan of water inside. We prefer this for moist cooking, recommended for fish, poultry and thin cuts of meat.

FUELS:
    Any nut or fruit wood is ideal for barbecuing. A lot of folks use charcoal because of convenience. Charcoal can be used to get the coals hot, then hardwood can be added for flavor. Non-soaked briquettes are preferred since the lighter fluid seems to give an artificial flavor to the food.
    Use a coffee can with holes punched along the bottom, or chimney from Walmart, to get the fire started. Place wadded-up newspaper in the bottom of the can and pile charcoal on top. Light the newspaper, and in no time the coals will be ready to spread. Add additional charcoal and hardwood, depending on the volume of food to be cooked. We prefer Black Jack Oak that is slightly green, then add green hickory towards the end of cooking.

ESSENTIAL TOOLS:
    Heavy duty long-handled tongs to move meat on grill.
    Restaurant spatula- 6-8 inches long to flip burgers and fish.
    Long-handled fork to move grill and stir coals.
    Metal skewers with square rods so food will stay in place.
    Large cutting board and several sharp knives.

FINGER LICKIN' DEEP SOUTH BARBECUE

SEASONINGS:

Every serious barbecue chef has their favorite rub, marinade and sauce. We are including a few of our favorites, but we encourage you to experiment. Who knows, you too can be a legend in your own back yard.

Dry Rubs.....This is simply a mixture of spices rubbed into meat prior to cooking. Dry rubs are easy to make and add flavor to the food without altering the texture. We use them on fish and seafood as well as some pork and poultry. Mix ingredients and rub on meat one hour prior to cooking.

Carolina Dry Rub
½ cup salt
½ cup sugar
½ cup brown sugar
½ cup cumin
½ cup chili powder
½ cup black pepper
¼ cup cayenne pepper
1 cup paprika

Florida Dry Rub
½ cup brown sugar
½ cup black pepper
½ cup paprika
2 teaspoons grated orange rind
¼ cup chili powder
¼ cup dry mustard
2 teaspoons cayenne pepper

Creole Dry Rub
4 tablespoons salt
3 tablespoons garlic powder
2 tablespoons black pepper
2 teaspoons basil, crumbled
3 teaspoons cayenne pepper
3 tablespoons paprika
3 teaspoons cumin
3 teaspoons onion powder

Dry Rub For Fish
⅓ cup salt
⅓ cup paprika
3 tablespoons granulated onion
⅓ cup cayenne
¼ cup black pepper
¼ cup granulated garlic
3 tablespoons thyme, crumbled

Dry Rub For Pork Ribs
3 tablespoons paprika
2 teaspoons seasoned salt
2 teaspoons black pepper
1 teaspoon cayenne
1 teaspoon oregano
1 teaspoon dry mustard
1 teaspoon chili powder

MARINADES.....Barbecue experts disagree on whether a marinade actually tenderizes the meat. But all agree that it adds flavor and moisture, especially when it is used to baste the meat during cooking. Be careful with the length of time you marinate because the texture of some foods can be altered by swimming too long in the marinade

---

Poultry (4 breasts)... Marinate 30 minutes
3 tablespoons soy sauce
2 tablespoons lime juice
2 tablespoons olive oil
½ teaspoon thyme, crumbled
½ teaspoon parsley, minced
½ teaspoon black pepper

Venison (3-4 pounds)... Marinate 2-3 hours
2 cups dry red wine
¼ cup red wine vinegar
1 onion, sliced
3 cloves garlic, minced
2 bay leaves, crushed
½ teaspoon Accent

Oriental (3 pounds poultry, beef or pork)... Marinate 3-5 hours
5 cloves garlic, crushed
½ cup soy sauce
½ cup French dressing
1 bay leaf, crushed
2 lemons, sliced thin
2 tablespoons brown sugar
2 tablespoons ginger, grated
½ cup ketchup

Barbecue smoker grill.

FINGER LICKIN' DEEP SOUTH BARBECUE

BARBECUE SAUCES.....Every serious barbecue chef has his or her own original sauce. The ingredients can vary and can include just about everything in the kitchen except the sink which can be used to mix it.

Serious chefs are always looking for new ingredients to make their sauce unique. Most include some type of pepper for hotness and other ingredients from beer to cough syrup. These sauces are typically based with tomato, mustard or vinegar and other secret ingredients are added for unique flavors.

Bubba's All Southern: No tomato in this one, so it will not burn on grill.

- 3 tablespoons butter
- 1 medium onion, chopped
- 2 medium cloves garlic, crushed
- 2 tablespoons dry mustard
- ½ cup cider vinegar
- 2 tablespoons sugar
- 1 tablespoon Worcestershire
- 1 tablespoon Tabasco
- 12 ounces beer
- 1 lemon, sliced thin
- 1 tablespoon black pepper
- 1 tablespoon chili powder
- 1 tablespoon paprika
- ½ teaspoon cayenne pepper

Simmer onion and garlic in butter until softened. Add mustard, vinegar and sugar. Cook on medium heat for 10 minutes. Add remaining ingredients and simmer 10 additional minutes. Use immediately and refrigerate any leftover sauce.

Carolina Clear Sauce:

- 1 cup white vinegar
- 1 cup cider vinegar
- 1 tablespoon crushed red pepper flakes
- 1 tablespoon Tabasco
- 1 tablespoon salt
- 1 ½ tablespoons black pepper
- 1 tablespoon sugar

Heat in saucepan for 10 minutes. Use immediately for basting and sauce.

Carolina Red Sauce:

- ¾ cup tomato purée
- ½ cup apple cider vinegar
- ¼ cup Worcestershire
- 4 tablespoons apple juice
- 2 tablespoons brown sugar
- 2 tablespoons dry mustard
- 1 teaspoon chili powder
- 1 teaspoon Tabasco
- ½ teaspoon cayenne
- ½ teaspoon ground celery seeds
- 1 teaspoon salt
- ½ teaspoon black pepper

Combine in stainless steel pan and bring to a boil. Simmer for 5 minutes. Use immediately and refrigerate leftovers. Will keep for weeks.

Florida Sweet Rib Sauce:

¼ cup peanut oil
¾ cup onion, chopped
3 cloves garlic, minced
¾ cup Tupelo honey
1 cup ketchup
1 cup red wine vinegar
¼ cup Worcestershire
2 tablespoons dry mustard
2 teaspoons salt
1 teaspoon oregano, crumbled
1 teaspoon thyme, crumbled
1 teaspoon black pepper
1 lemon, sliced

Heat oil over medium-low heat, add onion and garlic. Sauté until softened. Add remaining ingredients, bring to a boil, reduce heat and simmer 5 minutes. Baste ribs during last half of cooking and serve remaining sauce on side.

Georgia Red Sauce:

4 tablespoons butter
1 Vidalia onion, minced
2 cloves garlic, minced
¼ cup Worcestershire
¼ cup brown sugar
2 tablespoons dry mustard
¾ cup ketchup
1 lemon, sliced thin
⅓ cup peanut oil
½ cup apple cider vinegar

Melt butter over medium-low heat and cook onion and garlic until softened. Add remaining ingredients and bring to a boil. Reduce heat and simmer 20 minutes, uncovered. Use immediately or store in the refrigerator.

North Florida Mustard Sauce:

1 pound butter
3 tablespoons black pepper
3 tablespoons cayenne pepper
2 lemons, sliced thin
12 ounces prepared mustard
1 ½ pints apple cider vinegar
3 tablespoons salt
6 tablespoons sugar

Melt butter and add remaining ingredients. Bring to a boil, reduce heat and simmer 10 minutes. Refrigerate until ready to use.

Florida Citrus Sauce:

½ cup orange juice
½ cup ketchup
¼ cup soy sauce
6 tablespoons orange blossom honey
1 tablespoon black pepper
1 tablespoon Worcestershire
2 tablespoons mustard
2 tablespoons orange rind, grated

Combine all ingredients and simmer 15 minutes. Use for marinade and basting sauce for pork or chicken.

FINGER LICKIN' DEEP SOUTH BARBECUE

Texas Sauce:

4 slices bacon
1 medium onion, sliced
½ green bell pepper, diced
½ red bell pepper, diced
3 tomatoes, seeded and chopped
2 cloves garlic, minced

12 ounces apple cider vinegar
1 cup honey
18 ounces chili sauce
3 ounces tomato paste
¾ cup brown sugar
2 tablespoons chili powder

Cook bacon until crisp, drain on paper towels and set aside. Add onions, peppers, tomatoes and garlic and cook until softened. Add vinegar and reduce by half. Add remaining ingredients and bring to a boil. Reduce heat and simmer 1 hour. Add crumbled bacon and use to baste or on meat.

Oriental Sauce:

2 cups onions, chopped
2 cloves garlic, minced
½ cup butter
1 ½ cup tomato purée

1 cup light brown sugar
¾ cup soy sauce
¾ rice wine vinegar
3 tablespoons chili with garlic

Cook onions and garlic in butter until softened. Add remaining ingredients and cook 30 minutes, stir occasionally.

Minorcan Sauce:

1 onion, sliced salt
1 cup celery, diced
3 tablespoons butter
1 cup Datil "Bottled Hell" pepper sauce
2 tablespoons yellow mustard

2 tablespoons vinegar
1 teaspoon
½ can light beer (you know what to do with the rest)
2 tablespoons lemon juice
2 tablespoons brown sugar

Place butter in pan over low heat. Sauté onion and celery until light brown and softened. Add remaining ingredients, bring to a boil, reduce heat and simmer 30 minutes.

Quick Sauce:

1 bottle Bono's Barbecue Sauce
½ bottle of your favorite beer
1 lemon, thinly sliced

Heat all ingredients and serve.

THE WORLD-FAMOUS PIG AND OYSTER ROAST

Serves 100 Lucky Gourmands

For more than twenty years, my husband and his business partner hosted a big pig and oyster roast for clients and friends. This was usually in early December, before the other parties were held. The roasts were always successful, and just like the county fair, they got bigger and better each year.

These parties began modestly with a few close friends. They quickly grew and over 100 lucky gourmands enjoyed our last pig and oyster roast. The parties combine the Southern traditions of oyster roasts and whole hog pit barbecue, along with North Florida side dishes of Calico Beans, Wilted Slaw, Heart of Palm Salad and Minorcan Clam Chowder. Desserts were brought by willing guests.

After much pleading, I was able to get my husband to write down the directions and recipes. It soon became obvious that we had lots of barbecue information and recipes, so we decided to devote a whole chapter to Deep South Barbecue. We hope you will try some of the recipes because they are easy to prepare and mighty good eating, too.

Portable backyard pit used in Pig and Oyster Roast, c 1978.
"patent pending"

FINGER LICKIN' DEEP SOUTH BARBECUE

ESSENTIALS:

For The Grill:
1 cord black jack oak wood, split
2 gallons Minorcan Clam Chowder
1 apple
10-15 pieces green hickory
250 pounds of hog, cut into hams, shoulders, and middling, usually 2-3 pigs-one whole with head on for show
6 yard birds (lunch for cooks)
10 pounds gator tail

Secret Basting Sauce:
1 new mop
1 large pot for basting sauce
1 part oil (1 gallon)
2 parts vinegar (2 gallons)
4 parts water (domestic)
½ part brown sugar (2 boxes)
Cayenne pepper to taste
Salt to taste during last hour of cooking

For The Bar:
300 pounds hard ice
2 kegs of beer
8 liters white and red wine
40 liters soft drinks
6 bottles cocktail sauce
2 bottles horseradish
2 bottles Louisiana hot sauce
2 bottles Datil (Bottled Hell) Pepper sauce
6 bushels Apalachicola oysters
10 lemons and limes
10 oyster knives
10 work gloves
4 pints Smoked Mullet Dip (p.96)
6 boxes saltine crackers
1 pound butter, melted
200 disposable drink cups

For The Table :
3 gallons Calico Beans
3 gallons coleslaw
1 gallon barbecue sauce
8 loaves French bread
3 fresh pineapples, sliced
Miscellaneous bowls and platters for various foods

For the little boy who lives down the lane:
10 rolls paper towels
200 heavy-duty paper plates
6 large garbage cans
3 dozen heavy-duty garbage bags
300 heavy duty napkins
150 disposable coffee cups, forks, knives and spoons
125 name tags
Outside lights (as needed)

FINGER LICKIN' DEEP SOUTH BARBECUE

INSTRUCTIONS FOR PIG AND OYSTER ROAST

Over the years many guests told us they had always dreamed of having a pig roast, but didn't know what to do. Well Bubba, just read this next section and go do it!

Start by mailing invitations, with R.S.V.P., 2-3 weeks before the party date. You should start preparations about 2 weeks before the party. The most important thing is to locate a source for whole dressed hogs. This might be harder than you think. Find a butcher that will sell you several smaller pigs, about 75-80 pounds dressed, because they will take less time to cook. Allow about 2 and one half pounds whole hog per guest. It is usually better to get several small hogs rather than one large one. Leave the heads on for show. If you don't have a cooler that will hold these hogs, make sure you can pick them up very early the day of the party. Also order oysters and gator tail at this time. After you have resolved the source of pork, now concentrate on the grill.

You will need a grill 6'x4'. This can be fabricated from 2" galvanized pipe and covered with chain link fencing or heavy duty chicken wire. Make sure to secure the fence to the pipe with heavy wire. You will also need about 100 brick bats and about 50 concrete blocks (cinder blocks if you don't eat grits). Cut about 1 cord of good oak wood like blackjack or scrub oak. This can be slightly green. Also have some green hickory, pecan or any fruit wood for flavor and a little fat lighter to get the fire started.

My business partner and I have always shared the chefs job but since it's so much fun we always let a few friends help with the cooking. In later years we have included Charley, one of our truck drivers, to help in the cooking.

Two or three days before the party, select a flat area away from any trees or buildings for the pit. Dig the pit 6 feet long, 4 feet wide and 2 feet deep. Line the bottom of thepit with the brick bats and stack the concrete blocks on three sides of the pit, leaving one end open to add wood to the fire. Place the grill on the blocks and make sure it fits, adjust blocks if necessary.

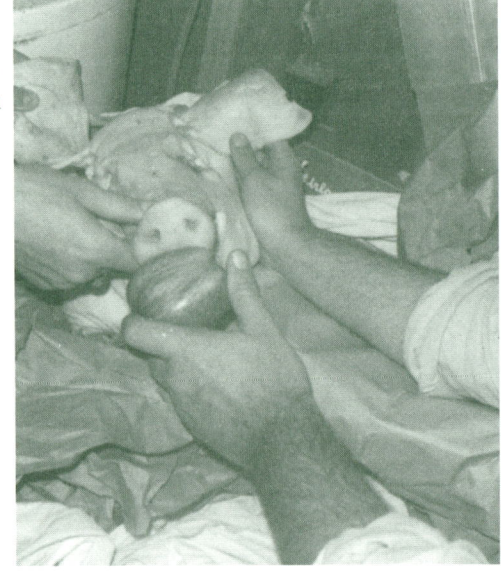

Seeing if the apple fits, c 1975.

The day before the party everything should be ready. Check the list and make sure you have the ingredients to make the various side dishes as well as the barbecue sauces.

The night before, stack some of the wood in the pit for the next morning. Place the fat lighter on the bottom and stack the oak about 2 layers high, cover with a tarpaulin. Now lay back, have a cocktail and admire your handy work. Set the alarm for 4:30 A.M. and go to bed. After the alarm goes off put it on snooze at least twice or until your wife kicks you out of the bed. Immediately call each friend that is helping and ask their wife if they have left yet. Be sure to mention to the wife that the husband asked you to call so the husband will catch hell and not you.

Go outside, remove the tarp and light the pine. Then go back to bed if your wife will let you.

As soon as the help arrives, serve them some coffee and put them to work. Have one wash and ice the oysters, one rig up the garden hose with spray nozzle, and one ice the beer keg.

One of my favorite cooking outfits is a pair of old overalls so I can keep my oyster knife in the side pocket, army boots, camo shirt and my favorite go-to-hell hat. Since standing around a wood fire all day will flavor these garments, don't plan on wearing them again anytime soon.

By now, the wood should have burned down to coals. Spread the coals evenly over the bottom of the pit and place the meat on the grill. Slice the hams and shoulders 3-4 times to the bone for heat distribution and put them on the hottest part of the grill. Put the middlings on the rest of the grill. Now prepare the secret basting sauce. Swear each helper to secrecy. Place the basting sauce in a metal pot on the grill and baste the pork with a new mop. Now is a good time to call the neighbors and beg them to not call the fire department.

It's hard to find decent help these days, c 1979.

After 30-40 minutes, turn each piece over and baste again with secret basting sauce. Dip the yard birds in the basting sauce and chunk them on the grill now. Add wood, 1-2 pieces at a time, as needed to maintain constant heat.

As fat begins to drip on coals, it will be necessary to spray with the garden hose to keep the flames down. This hose is also handy to keep the help from dozing off throughout the day.

Check the oysters from time to time for saltiness. Oh yes, tap the keg of beer to make sure it's not flat. There will be plenty of volunteers for this. Continue to turn the meat and baste every 30 minutes. Since the help didn't get any breakfast, they will probably want an early lunch. Now is the time to bring out the loaf of light bread for the chicken sandwiches. Take the yard birds from the grill after 3 hours, cut each one into four pieces, place each fourth on a piece of light bread, generously salt and pepper. Splash with hot sauce and barbecue sauce, top with another slice of bread and serve to the help with a large glass of ice cold beer. Serve some raw oysters for dessert. What could possibly be better than this? Oops! Time to get the hose out.

After the pork has cooked 8-9 hours, the help will need to go home, shower and get ready for the party. No need to mention the call that woke the wives at 4:30, they will find out soon enough.

Continue to add hickory wood and finish cooking the hogs if necessary. About 10 hours of constant heat should cook all the pork, cut into the thicker pieces and check for doneness. Continue cooking if necessary. Continue basting pork to keep moist. Pork is done when the internal temperature reaches 160 degrees.

As guests begin to arrive, give them a name tag, in Pig Latin "get it?", a drink and invite them to join you at the pit for a sample of pork. Slice them a couple of ribs or a piece of loin as an appetizer. Be sure to keep control of the knife at all times or large volumes of pork will disappear. Now, while you are accepting all the praise and compliments, it's time to push the pork to the rear of the grill and put the gator tail on to cook. This only takes a few minutes to cook. Pass it around for appetizers. At this point, you might mention to the ladies this was the meanest gator you've ever killed with a pocket knife.

Family and friends at the pig n' oyster roast, c 1979.

FINGER LICKIN' DEEP SOUTH BARBECUE

By the time the gator tail has disappeared, some of the help should have returned. Hand them a good strong drink and let them begin roasting the oysters. They should line the front of the grill with raw oysters in the shell and cover them with wet croaker (burlap) sacks. As the oysters pop open, pass around with melted butter and cocktail sauce. Also offer raw oysters on the half shell with the sauces.

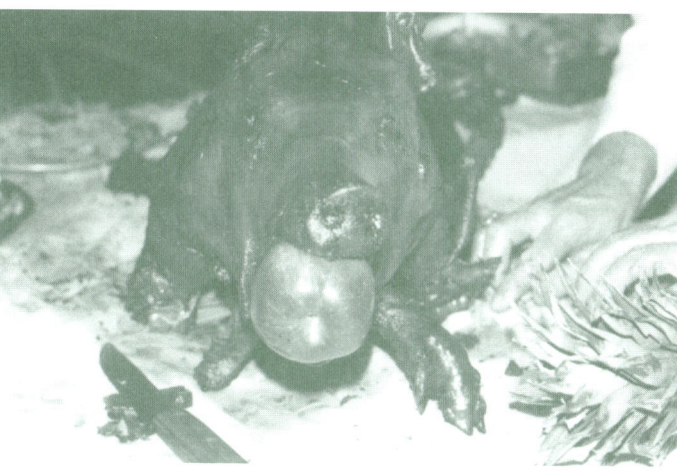

Don't forget the apple, c 1976.

It's best to place dips and chips next to the bar areas, which should be located away from pit to keep guests circulating. If Minorcan Clam Chowder is served, keep warm on the grill and serve in disposable coffee cups.

When it's time to eat, set up carving tables with plenty of light. Ask 3-4 willing guests to help with the carving. Have them slice and pull the meat from the skin and bones and place on platters. Cover some with barbecue sauce and leave some without. Place pig head on platter and stick an apple in its mouth. Let the help or whichever guests that have had the most to drink (it may take two) carry the pig head around to show it off.

Arrange the pork on serving table along with the pig head and North Florida side dishes, fresh pineapple and chowder, if any is left. Place the desserts and coffee on a separate table and let the guests serve themselves.

As the last plate is filled you will begin to notice an eerie silence-no one will be talking. Just sounds of ribs being stripped of meat and oohs and aahs-it's always rewarding when first-time guests tell you that they have never experienced anything like this before.

As everyone begins to leave, offer the ham bones and hocks to be taken home for seasoning beans and vegetables. Also make sure each helper is placed in his respective vehicle with his wife; you don't want any surprises in the morning, the yard will be enough.

Folks, this party is an evolution of over twenty years of trial and error. Pray for clear weather, but have a tarp or tent ready just in case.

Bon Appetite!

BARBECUE SIDE DISHES

While coleslaw and French fries have become universal side dishes in most franchise barbecue joints, the older barbecue emporiums still offer regional favorites. In South Carolina, hash made from the hog liver is sometimes served. In Georgia, a lot of barbecue is served with a dish of Brunswick stew. Serve one or more of the following side dishes for authentic North Florida barbecue.

BUBBA'S BLACK BEANS

Black beans and rice are standard fare in Spanish and Cuban restaurants. Bubba's version has become a popular side dish at our outdoor barbecues and reunions. Serve over rice or alone.

Serves 6-8

- 12 ounces of black beans
- 1 large onion, minced
- 3 cloves garlic, minced
- ½ cup olive oil
- 1 teaspoon cumin
- 1 teaspoon chili powder
- 1-2 Datil pepper, minced
- 2-3 bay leaves
- 6 pack of Stroh's beer
- 2 cups soak water
- 2 tablespoons red-wine vinegar
- Salt and pepper to taste
- 3 green onions, chopped
- 1 teaspoon sugar

Wash beans and pick out any culls. Cover with fresh water by 2-3 inches. Soak beans overnight, drain and reserve 2 cups soak water. In a large heavy bottomed pot sauté onions and garlic in olive oil until softened. Add cumin, chili powder, Datil peppers, sugar and bay leaves. Add soak water and one beer, cooks can drink the rest. Save bottles for Bottled Hell. Add beans and cook over low heat until beans are soft, about 3 hours. If more liquid is needed add more beer. Stir in vinegar, salt and pepper and simmer 10 minutes. Serve with green onions sprinkled over the top of beans.

GRILLED CORN WITH HERB BUTTER

12 ears of corn, husk pulled back and silk removed. Soak in water for 10 minutes and cook over a hot grill about 20 minutes. Serve with herb butter.

Herb Butter: Cream one stick of softened butter, 2 tablespoons fresh herbs (your choice of thyme, basil, dill or rosemary). Prepare one day in advance, place in container with tight fitting lid and refrigerate.

FINGER LICKIN' DEEP SOUTH BARBECUE

MINORCAN PERLO

*P*erlos are often found at reunions and barbecues. This version features smoked chicken and gives the perlo a unique smoky flavor.

Serves 25-30 People as a side dish.

- 2 - 2 ½-3 pound smoked chickens
- 8 cups chicken stock
- 2 cups bell pepper, chopped
- 4 cups onion, chopped
- 1 carrot, chopped
- 2 cloves garlic, minced
- 6 celery ribs, chopped
- 1 pound smoked bacon
- 4 cups rice
- Salt and freshly ground black pepper, to taste
- 2 Datil peppers, seeded and minced
- 2 bay leaves
- 2 teaspoons thyme, crumbled

Skin, bone and shred chicken, set aside. Simmer vegetables in chicken stock 30 minutes. Fry bacon in large kettle over low heat until crisp, remove with a slotted spoon and set aside. Drain bacon drippings, reserving 4 tablespoons. Add the rice, stirring constantly to coat each grain with drippings. Add stock, chicken, salt and pepper, Datil peppers, bay leaves and thyme. Cover and cook 25-30 minutes or until all stock is absorbed by the rice. Remove bay leaves, sprinkle with bacon and serve.

ROSIN POTATOES

This method of cooking potatoes probably originated in the turpentine camps, prominent in North Florida years ago.

Save the rosin in the wash pot for future use. Heat rosin in cast-iron wash pot until boiling. Add baking potatoes and cook until potatoes float to top. Remove potatoes with tongs and place on butcher paper cut 1 'x 1', fold paper over and twist ends tight. Cool, leave paper on, cut each potato in half lengthwise, and serve. Sweet potatoes may also be prepared using this method.

Tapping rosin from a Florida yellow pine, c 1930.

75 years later, Catface almost healed over. Miller Homestead, Holmes County, c 2004.

PLANTATION FRIED CORN

A great side dish for barbecues and fried or smoked mullet. Plantation fried corn is still served in the older barbecue emporiums around Jacksonville.

Serves 6
6 ears of fresh corn
Enough vegetable oil for deep fat frying

Remove husks and silk from corn. Break ears of corn in half. In a large pot, heat oil to 350 degrees. Test temperature with thermometer. Carefully drop half of the corn in hot grease and fry until kernels are brown. Remove and drain on metal wire racks or brown paper bags. Fry remaining corn and serve immediately.

CALICO BEANS

This dish is good enough to stand alone. Serve with a good bread and cold beer and it makes a very tasty supper.

Serves about 30 as a side dish.

- 8 cups dried pinto beans
- ½ pound smoked bacon
- 4 cups onion, chopped
- 4 large cloves garlic, minced
- 1½ cups tomato barbecue sauce
- ⅓ cup prepared mustard
- ¼ cup chili powder
- 4 tablespoons salt
- 2 Datil peppers, minced, or
- 3 teaspoons Tabasco
- 2 cups barbecue pork or chicken, chopped
- 1½ cups cane syrup

Wash beans and soak overnight or place in very large pot with 6 quarts water. Bring to a boil, uncovered, and cook 2 minutes. Remove from heat, cover and let sit 1 hour. Drain and cover with water by one inch. Bring to a boil, reduce heat and simmer one half hour or more until tender. In a large cast-iron pot, cook bacon until crisp, drain on paper towels and set aside. Add onions and garlic to bacon dripping and cook until softened. Add beans, barbecue sauce, mustard, cane syrup, chili powder, salt, Datil peppers and barbecue pork or chicken. Cook in 300 degree smoker grill or oven for 30 minutes. Crumble bacon, sprinkle on top of beans and cook 15 minutes more. Serve from the pot.

MOCCASIN BRANCH COLESLAW

Moccasin Branch is a small community located in the cabbage producing area of St. Johns County. It was founded many years ago by Minorcan families whose descendants live there today.

Freshly picked cabbage makes the best slaws.

Serves 20

- 3 cups mayonnaise
- 1 cup white vinegar
- 2 tablespoons evaporated milk
- ⅔ cup sugar
- 1 tablespoon celery seeds
- Salt and freshly ground black pepper, to taste
- 2 medium heads of cabbage, grated (about 4 pounds)
- 2 carrots, grated

Mix mayonnaise, vinegar, milk, sugar, celery seeds, salt and pepper in a large bowl. Add cabbage and carrots and toss thoroughly. Cover with plastic wrap and refrigerate 4 hours before serving.

WAYNE'S WILTED SLAW

This slaw has to be made in advance, so it's great for plan ahead parties. It's a lot better if it is made several days ahead of time. No mayonnaise is used, so it's ideal for picnics and outdoor parties.

Serves 8

- 1 medium-large cabbage, thinly shredded
- 1 bell pepper, slivered
- 1 medium onion, slivered
- 1 cup sugar
- ½ cup white vinegar
- ¾ cup vegetable oil
- 1 teaspoon celery seeds
- 1 teaspoon mustard seeds
- 1 teaspoon salt, or to taste

Combine cabbage, bell pepper and onions in a large bowl and toss. Sprinkle sugar over raw vegetables, do not stir. Bring vinegar, oil, celery seeds, mustard seeds and salt to a boil, and pour mixture over vegetables, cover and refrigerate overnight.

BEER CAN YARDBIRD

We don't know who gets credit for this method of cooking yardbirds, but we suspect it was some rednecks, sitting around the fire, drinking beer.

Serves 20

12 ounce can of beer
3 ½-4 pound yardbird
2 tablespoons Florida Dry Rub
2 teaspoons vegetable oil

Pop the top of beer can and drink one-half. Using a church key make two additional holes in the top of the can. Remove the giblets from the yardbird, rinse and rub with oil. Distribute the rub (see page 265) inside and outside of yardbird. Place woodchips on grill, place yardbird over beer can. Pull legs forward for support, and place on grill. Cover and cook until done one-one and a half hours. Internal temperature should be 180 degrees, cover with foil after 45 minutes of cooking.

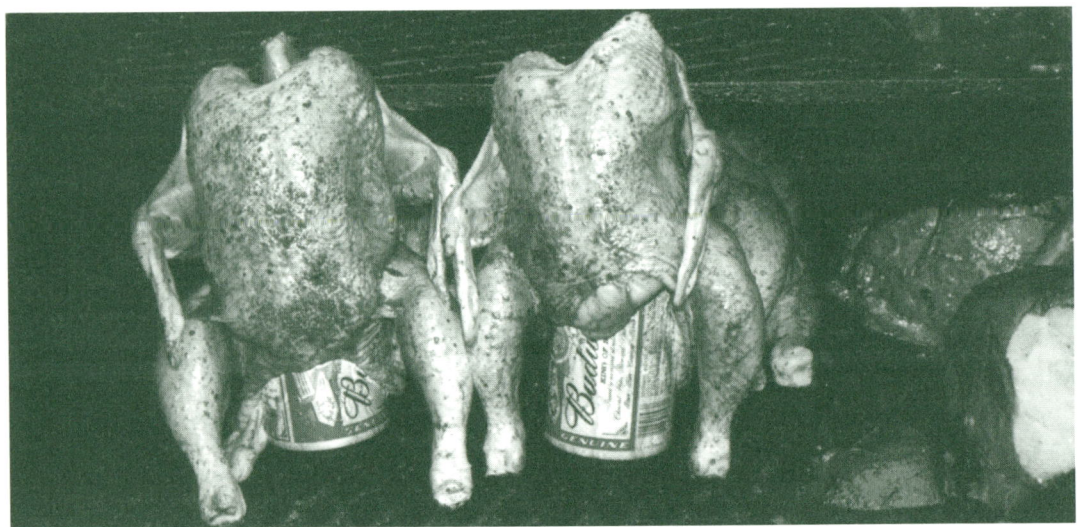

Do you come here often? c 2002.

POPCORN CHICKEN

Wash a two and a half-three pound chicken, and pat dry with paper towels. Remove giblets and place giblets in freezer for future use. Pour 1 jar of Newman's Own Popcorn (the profits go to a good cause), into the cavity of the chicken. Truss the chicken with a needle and thread. Tie the legs together with butchers string and place in a 350 degree oven.

When the oven door pops open and the preachers nose comes flying across the kitchen, the chicken will be done.

FINGER LICKIN' DEEP SOUTH BARBECUE

BACKYARD BARBECUE PARTY

*T*his is one of our favorite ways to entertain and enjoy time with our friends. Side dishes can be made in advance and the cooking can be part of the entertainment. Barbecue is always best straight from the grill.

Serves 10-12

- 2 Boston butts (about 5 pounds each)
- ½-1 cup of your favorite rub
- 4 cups your favorite barbecue sauce
- Several cases champagne (Miller bottled beer)
- ½ gallon coleslaw
- 1 quart bread and butter pickles
- 2 dozen burger buns or 2 loaves light bread
- Dessert of choice

Make rub and sauce ahead of time. Invite 10-12 close friends to party. Ask a few to help cook.

Rub pork butts with dry rub and ice down beer 2-3 hours prior to cooking. Start oak fire in smoker type cooker—try to maintain about 180-200 degrees. Place butts on grill and slow cook for about 4-5 hours or until internal temperature reaches 160 degrees. This will require new wood every 30 minutes and several champagnes. Use green hickory wood the last hour for flavor.

After butts are done and tender, remove from smoker and cut or shred meat. Serve with sauce on the side and slaw and pickles. Barbecue sandwiches can be made if desired. Give everyone a bottle of champagne, put a little George and Tammy on the tape player and kick back and enjoy. As the feller on T.V. says, "Boys, it don't get any better than this." That is, unless you start with a couple dozen Apalachicola oysters on the half shell and finish with a bowl of Granny's Banana Pudding or a serving of the Best Rum Cake Ever. (recipe follows)

"This barbecuing is hot, tiring work, pass me another beer, please." c 1979.

FINGER LICKIN' DEEP SOUTH BARBECUE

BEST RUM CAKE EVER

1 or 2 quarts of rum
1 cup butter
1 teaspoon sugar
2 large eggs
1 cup dried fruit

Baking powder
1 teaspoon soda
Lemon juice
Nuts

    Before you start, sample rum to check for quality (good, isn't it?) Now go ahead .....select a large mixing bowl, measuring cup, etc. Check the rum again, it must be just right. To be sure the rum is of the highest quality, pour one level cup into a glass and drink it as fast as you can. Repeat.

    With an electric mixer, beat one cup of butter in a large fluffy bowl. Add one teaspoon of thugar and beat again. Meanwhile, try another cup of rum. Open second bottle if necessary. Add 2 large leggs, 2 cups fried druit and beat until high. If druit gets stuck in beater just pry it louce with a drewscriver. Sample rum again, checking for tonscistincy.

    Next sift two cups of pepper or salt (it really doesn't matter which) sample rum again. Sift one half pint of lemon juice. Fold in chipped butter and strained nuts. Add 1 bubblespoon of brown thugar, or what ever color you can find. Wix mell. Grease oven and turn cake pan to 350 gedrees. Now pour the whole mess in coven and ake. Check the rum again and go to bed

No Drunks or Wild Parties...damn, they took away all the fun. Tourist cottages, Pensacola Beach, c 1940.

Perlos, Rice Dishes and Pasta

Former slaves and descendants Kingsley Plantation, Fort George Island. The remains of the slave quarters are still standing today, c 1875.

Seafood Perlo, 285
O'Steen's Shrimp Perlo, 286
Smoked Sausage Perlo, 287
Panther Creek Rod and
  Gun Club Perlo, 288
Savannah Rice Perlo, 288
Palm Valley Pig Perlo, 289
Yardbird Perlo, 289
Dirty Rice, 290
Cameron's Nutty Rice, 290
Wild Rice with Wild Pecans, 291

Wild Rice Casserole, 291
Savannah Red Rice, 292
Granny's Green Rice, 292
Thanksgiving Brown Rice, 293
Spanish Yellow Rice, 293
Fresh Homemade Pasta, 294
Potato Pasta with Creamy
  Tomato Sauce, 295
Basil and Pinenut Sauce, 296
Pasta Ho-Style, 296
Pasta with Smoked Bacon, 297

Pasta with Cream Sauce, 297
Spaghetti n' Meatballs, 298
Spaghetti Fisherman's Style, 298
Spaghetti, Olive Oil, Garlic, 298
Linguine with Clam Sauce, 299
Morrison's Macaroni
  and Cheese, 299
Lasagne for a Crowd, 300
Mayport Seafood Lasagne, 301
Philippine Pancit, 302

PERLOS, RICE DISHES AND PASTA

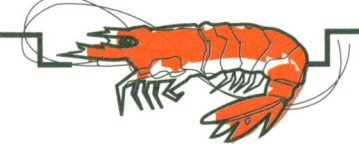

The low country plantations around Charleston, South Carolina and coastal Georgia grew the first rice in the new country. A few plantations in North Florida, near Fort George, also grew limited quantities. This grain was a welcome addition to the sparse table of early settlers and broke the monotony of grits three times a day.

Rice was sometimes mixed with local seafood or game and called perlos by grateful settlers. Almost any type of meat, game or seafood can be used in a perlo. Tasty perlos can be made from ingredients such as roosters, coots, rabbits, gizzards, pork backbone, gopher, vegetables and eggs can be substituted for meats.

Around St. Augustine the natives call it "perlo" pronounced "pur-lo", but we have seen it spelled Pilau-Pilaf-Perloo-Purlo. It can be served as an entree or a side dish and are very popular at indoor and outdoor social gatherings. The Minorcans in Northeast Florida added the fiery hot capsicum, Datil pepper and thyme to perlos, which spiced them up. Tomatoes were added to some perlos after it was discovered that the poison label was a myth.

On the Gulf Coast, rice was added to extend flavorful gumbos and stews. Rice, mixed with seafood and pork, took on the name Jambalaya. The cookbook Southern Recipes, published in 1913, listed the following recipe for "Jumbalaya."

"Cut one ten-cent veal steak, raw, one ten-cent piece of ham raw, and ten cents' worth of shrimp, one and a half dozen oysters, chicken scraps also added, in small uniform pieces, casting aside all skin and bones. Fry veal, ham and shrimp brown in hot lard, then add by degrees one scant cup of boiling water; now add the oysters, pepper and salt, season slightly and lastly, after stew has cooked thoroughly, sprinkle in one cup full of rice with the hand. Cook well, and stir as little as possible after putting in the rice, boil about twenty minutes."

Rice production on the Atlantic Coast declined during the 19th century after the Civil War and a few devastating hurricanes flooded the fields with salt water. Some of the old abandoned rice fields are now used for crawfish farming. This tasty mudbug is a welcome addition to our table and is usually served in a sauce over rice or pasta.

There wasn't much pasta available when we were growing up in rural North Florida. Elbow macaroni and dried spaghetti were about the only pastas we remember eating. Later "I"-talian restaurants appeared and we learned about lasagne, "pizza pie" and that wonderful pasta, fettuccine. Fettuccine Alfredo featured wonderful tender, fresh pasta, similar to Granny's dumplings, but with a different texture and taste. Served with a cream sauce, it was ambrosia to us. We soon discovered these tender pasta strips could be made at home. Rolling the dough thin took a lot of brute force, and we finally located and purchased a pasta machine. Soon we were turning out fettuccine as good as the "I"-talian restaurants, along with tender spaghetti, ravioli and lasagne noodles. Fresh pasta tastes nothing like the dried noodles we grew up eating. We can't imagine how we ever got along without our pasta machine.

We still enjoy dried pasta when we haven't time to make fresh. Dried linguine and spaghetti often turn up at our table with pesto, homemade tomato sauce and smoked bacon and olive oil.

SEAFOOD PERLO

We hope each of you are fortunate enough to have a neighbor like Jefferson Davis Williamson, a true Southern gentleman, who moved to Florida from Meridian, Mississippi. Mr. Williamson (he said, "Just call me J.D.") and his wife, he called her Mama, were always willing to help anyone in need.

Mr. Williamson loved Apalachicola oysters almost as much as his bourbon (Mama limited him to one drink about Bull Bat time(twilight.) My husband enjoyed taking a few dozen oysters down to his house and would shuck them while J.D. told stories of the old days.

Their daughter, Millie, also a good friend, gave us this recipe several years ago and we have enjoyed it many times. It combines ham and rice with fresh shrimp and oysters to create the ultimate Seafood Perlo, or Jambalaya, if you're from Mississippi.

Serves 6

- 1 tablespoon bacon drippings
- 2 medium onions, chopped
- ½ pound smoked sausage, sliced ¼ inch thick
- 1 tablespoon all-purpose flour
- ½ pound country ham, cut into small cubes,
- 3 medium tomatoes, peeled, seeded and chopped
- 1 cup long-grain rice
- 1 large clove garlic, minced
- 2 cups shrimp or chicken stock
- 1 ½ inch piece dried red pepper or ¼ teaspoon cayenne
- ½ teaspoon thyme, crumbled
- ½ cup bell pepper, diced
- 4 tablespoons parsley, minced
- 1 ½-2 pounds raw shrimp shelled and deveined
- 1 pint large oysters, drained
- 1 pound bay scallops

In a large heavy-bottomed pot with a tight fitting lid, melt the bacon drippings over medium-low heat. Add the onions and sausage, sauté until onions have softened. Stir in the flour and cook three minutes, stirring constantly. Add the ham and tomatoes, simmer 10 minutes.

Stir in the rice, garlic, stock, red pepper, thyme, bell pepper and 3 tablespoons parsley. Cover and simmer 20 minutes, do not stir.

Add shrimp, cook 1 minute, add oysters, and scallops and cook 2-3 minutes or until edges of oysters curl. Lightly sprinkle shrimp and oysters with salt if needed. Sprinkle with remaining tablespoon parsley and serve on heated plates.

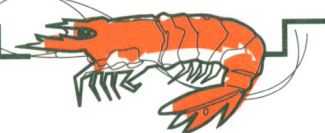

O'STEEN'S SHRIMP PERLO

The locals in St. Augustine know that if you want some of the best fried shrimp you've ever tasted, you go to O'Steen's and be there early—because the lunch line starts forming about 10:30. If you arrive later don't despair, the service is prompt and courteous, and the line moves quickly.

The locals also know if you go for lunch, owner/chef Lonnie Pomar offers a couple of specials in addition to his famous fried seafood. These specials vary each day and might be fried mullet and grits, boiled local shrimp, seafood casserole or one of his delicious perlos served with fresh vegetables, hot biscuits and corn bread. Lonnie prefers East Coast shrimp in his perlos because he feels these shrimp are sweeter and hold up better in cooking.

Serves 4-6

- ¼ pound white bacon or salt pork, cubed
- 2 large onions, chopped
- 1 bell pepper, chopped
- 2-10 ounce cans tomatoes, chopped
- 1 heaping tablespoon tomato paste
- 1 tablespoon marjoram, crumbled
- 1 tablespoon Italian seasoning, crumbled
- 1 tablespoon granulated garlic
- 1 tablespoon gravy-bouquet
- Salt and freshly ground black pepper, to taste
- 1-2 Datil Peppers, minced
- 2½ cups shrimp stock or water
- 1 tablespoon thyme, crumbled
- 2 pounds shrimp, peeled and deveined
- 1 cup rice
- Additional water if needed

Cook bacon in cast-iron Dutch oven until bacon bits are crisp, but not burned. Add onions and bell pepper and cook until tender. Add tomatoes, tomato paste, thyme, marjoram, Italian seasonings, garlic, gravy, salt and pepper, and Datil pepper. Cook base down for 2 hours on low heat, being careful not to burn. Add water to base and bring to a boil. Add shrimp and return to boil. Stir in rice, cover and cook 30-45 minutes or until most of the liquid has evaporated. Add additional water if dish is getting too dried out, do not stir. Crack lid if there is too much liquid. Perlo should be just right, not too dry but not too wet.

SMOKED SAUSAGE PERLO

On a recent hunting trip to South Carolina we were fortunate to sample some sausage perlo Carolina style. This was made using venison sausage as well as country sausage. It was cooked in a large cast-iron Dutch oven over an open fire. After questioning the cook about the unique taste, he admitted he intentionally "burned" the sausage in a cast-iron frying pan before adding it to the perlo. When asked if he made shrimp perlo, he replied he makes shrimp Creole when he has fresh shrimp.

This is the way sausage perlo is made around St. Johns County.

Serves 6

- 1 pound smoked link sausage, cut into ¼ inch slices
- 1 cup onion, chopped
- ½ cup bell pepper, chopped
- 1 large clove garlic, minced
- 1 Datil pepper, seeded and minced
- 1 teaspoon thyme, crumbled
- ½ teaspoon sugar
- 1 cup plum tomatoes, seeded, chopped and juice reserved
- 2 cups chicken stock
- 1 cup long-grain rice
- ¼ cup parsley, minced
- Salt and freshly ground black pepper, to taste

Brown sausage over medium heat in a large cast-iron skillet. Remove sausage with a slotted spoon and set aside. Add onions, bell pepper and garlic; sauté until softened and onions are slightly brown. Place coffee filter or paper towel in a sieve and strain tomato juice. Add Datil pepper, thyme, tomatoes, strained tomato juice, sugar and chicken stock to skillet.

Stir and bring mixture to a boil. Add rice and sausage, stir to mix, reduce heat, season with salt and black pepper, if necessary, cover and cook 20-25 minutes or until all liquid has evaporated. Remove from heat and set lid ajar for 5 minutes before serving. Sprinkle with parsley and serve.

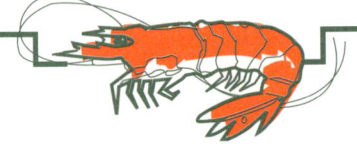

PANTHER CREEK ROD AND GUN CLUB PERLO

Since turkey season falls in the Spring we substitute a tame turkey breast when we have this perlo in the Fall. This is one of the favorite meals at hunting camp when the hunters come into camp after a long day of hunting.

Serves 20

- 2 wood ducks
- 1 wild turkey breast
- 2 wild rabbits
- 2 cups onions, chopped
- 2 cups celery, chopped
- 1 cup bell pepper, chopped
- ½ cup bacon drippings
- ½ cup Datil pepper vinegar
- ½ tablespoon salt
- 2 boxes Uncle Ben's Wild Rice mix
- Chicken stock

Simmer ducks, turkey and rabbit in large cast-iron kettle with water to barely cover. Remove meat from bones when cooked and cool. Reduce stock by half. Sauté vegetables in one half cup bacon drippings. Pour stock into measuring cup and add chicken broth if needed to measure four and one half cups. When rice is done add the game, vegetables with bacon drippings, vinegar, and salt. Mix well with a large fork. Serve with additional Datil pepper vinegar.

SAVANNAH RICE PERLO

Serves 6-8

- 1 pound hot link sausage, cut in ¼ inches slices, and each round cut in half,
- 1½ cups onion, chopped
- 4 cloves garlic, minced
- 1 cup celery, chopped
- ½ stick butter
- 1 package Uncle Ben's Wild Rice Mix
- ½ tablespoon Worcestershire
- 1¾ cups chicken stock
- 10 ounce can Ro-tel tomatoes with chilies
- 3 pounds shrimp, shelled deveined and chopped
- 2 tablespoons parsley, minced

In a large cast-iron skillet fry sausage and remove to a paper towel to drain. Pour grease off, add butter and sauté onion, garlic and celery until transparent. Add the rice and stir until grains are coated with butter. Add the sausage meat, stir with a fork. Stir in Worcestershire, stock, and tomatoes. Bring to a boil, reduce heat, cover and cook about 20 minutes. Add the shrimp, cover and cook another 5 minutes. Sprinkle with parsley and serve.

PALM VALLEY PIG PERLO

*P*alm Valley is a small community located along the Intracoastal Waterway in Northern St. Johns County. It is known for the wild Pineywoods Rooters, that thrive in the palm thickets and swamps, as well as being the hometown of the late Ernest Mickler of *White Trash Cooking* fame.

Serves 8

- 2 pounds lean pork, cubed
- 1 pound smoked bacon, crumbled
- 2 cups onions, chopped fine
- ¾ cup bell pepper, chopped
- 2-3 Datil peppers, minced
- 2 cups long-grain rice
- 16 ounces crushed tomatoes
- 1 teaspoon sugar
- Salt and black pepper, to taste
- 2 tablespoons parsley, minced

Place pork in a large pot with water to cover by 1 inch. Bring to a boil, cover and cook until tender, about an hour. In a large cast-iron skillet, cook bacon until crisp, remove with a slotted spoon and set aside. Add onions and bell pepper to skillet and cook until softened. Place a coffee filter or paper towel in a sieve and strain tomato juice. Add onions and bell pepper to pork.

Stir Datil pepper, rice, tomatoes, strained tomato juice, sugar, and salt and pepper into pork mixture. Cover and cook until all liquid is absorbed. Taste for seasoning, sprinkle with crumbled bacon and parsley and serve.

YARD BIRD PERLO

*S*ome versions of this popular dish call for tomatoes as in the pork and shrimp perlos. Our version, popular around St. Augustine, has no tomatoes but uses a wild rice mix with the flavors of thyme and Datil peppers.

Serves 4

- 1 clove garlic, minced
- 2 cups onion, chopped
- 1 cup bell pepper, chopped
- 3 ribs celery, chopped
- 2 ½-3 pound yard bird cut into 8 pieces
- 2 cups chicken stock
- salt and pepper to taste
- 1 teaspoon thyme, crumbled
- 1-2 Datil peppers, minced
- 6 ounce package Uncle Ben's Long-Grain and Wild Rice
- ¼ cup parsley, chopped

In a large 4 quart pot, add garlic, onions, bell peppers, celery, chicken, stock and water. Bring to a boil, cover, reduce heat to simmer and cook 45 minutes-1 hour. Remove chicken from pot and set aside to cool. Skin and bone chicken, cut meat into bite size pieces. Reduce stock to two and one half cups, add chicken pieces, salt, pepper, thyme, Datil pepper and rice. Bring to a boil, reduce heat to low, cover and cook 25 minutes or until all liquid is absorbed. Sprinkle with parsley and serve on heated plates.

DIRTY RICE

Many of our chicken dishes do not use giblets, so we freeze the giblets until we have enough to prepare this dish. This rice dish is excellent with Grilled Venison Backstrap. The name comes from the "dirty" appearance the finely-chopped giblets add to the rice.

Serves 6

- 1 pound chicken gizzards
- ¼ cup bacon drippings
- 1 ½ tablespoons garlic, minced
- 2 cups onion, chopped
- ⅓ cup celery, chopped
- 1 bell pepper, chopped
- ⅓ cup fresh parsley, minced
- 2 tablespoons flour
- ¼ pound chicken livers
- ¼ teaspoon thyme
- 1½ teaspoons salt
- 1 teaspoon freshly ground black pepper
- ¼ teaspoon cayenne pepper
- 1 teaspoon Worcestershire
- 2 tablespoons chicken stock
- 3 cups cooked long-grain rice
- 2 green onions, chopped

Remove meat from gizzards and discard the gristle; mince meat. Heat a large cast-iron skillet over medium-high heat and add bacon drippings. Add gizzards and cook until meat begins to brown. Add garlic, onion, celery, pepper, half of the parsley and flour, stir, reduce heat and cook for 10 minutes or until vegetables have softened. Stir occasionally, scraping the bottom of the pan. Chop chicken livers and add to skillet along with thyme, salt, black pepper, cayenne and Worcestershire. Stir until livers are cooked.

Add stock and cook for 2 minutes, stirring, and remove from heat. Fluff rice with a fork and add to meat. Toss until completely mixed, sprinkle with remaining parsley and green onions, and serve.

CAMERON'S NUTTY RICE

Serves 6

- 2 cups Japanese short grain rice (sticky rice)
- 2 cups water
- 3 tablespoons butter
- ¼ cup pinenuts or almonds
- ⅓ cup green onions, chopped
- 2 tablespoons parsley, minced

In a large pot wash rice 4-5 times, rubbing the grains until the water is clear. Drain all water. Add 2 cups water to rice. Cover and bring to a boil. Reduce heat immediately to lowest setting. Cook 7 minutes. Do not remove lid. Remove from heat and allow rice to sit 5 minutes. Heat 1 tablespoon butter in a small skillet over medium heat. When melted add nuts and stir constantly until golden. Remove to small bowl. In same skillet heat 2 tablespoons butter, add the green onions and sauté until limp. Add to same bowl along with parsley. Use a large kitchen fork to stir in the nuts, green onions and parsley. Serve at once.

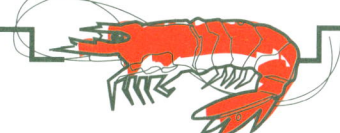

WILD RICE WITH WILD PECANS

*P*ecan trees unlike the chinquapin and hickory are not native to North Florida, but were introduced from Texas. While the hybrid pecans are larger and easier to shell, we prefer the taste of the wild or seedling pecan. Several of the large hybrid pecans such as the Mahan and Stewart varieties were developed at a nursery in Monticello.

Serves 6

- 1 cup uncooked wild rice
- 3 ¼ cups chicken stock
- 4 tablespoons unsalted butter
- 1 cup onion, chopped
- 1 cup wild pecans, coarsely chopped (may substitute hybrid)
- 1 clove garlic, finely minced
- 2 ribs celery, chopped
- 3 tablespoons parsley, minced
- Salt to taste
- ½ teaspoon freshly ground black pepper

Preheat oven 350 degrees. Wash rice well in cold water, drain completely and place in a medium sized saucepan. Add chicken stock, bring to a boil, cover and simmer 40-50 minutes or until rice is tender and most of the grains have split. Drain any excess liquid. Melt 2 tablespoons of the butter in a large skillet over medium heat. Add onions, garlic and celery, and cook until softened, remove to bowl. Cook pecans in remaining butter until pecans are toasted. In a large bowl combine cooked rice, onion mixture, pecans, parsley, salt and pepper. Toss well and correct seasonings. Place in a buttered one and one half quart casserole, bake 30 minutes and serve.

WILD RICE CASSEROLE

Serves 6

- 1 box Uncle Ben's Wild rice mix
- 6 green onions, thinly sliced
- ¼ cup all-purpose flour
- 1 ½ cups chicken broth
- 3 cups smoked chicken, chopped
- 1½ cups half and half
- ½ pound mushrooms, sliced
- 1 tablespoon parsley, minced
- 1 teaspoon salt
- ½ teaspoon freshly ground black pepper
- ½ cup sliced almonds

Cook rice according to directions on package, set aside. Melt butter in a cast-iron Dutch oven over medium heat. Sauté onions until translucent. Stir in flour and cook 1 minute. Add chicken broth and stir constantly until thicken. Use a large fork to stir in rice, smoked chicken, half and half, mushrooms, parsley, salt and pepper. Place in lightly greased 11x7 inch baking dish. Sprinkle with almonds. Bake 350 degrees for 15-20 minutes.

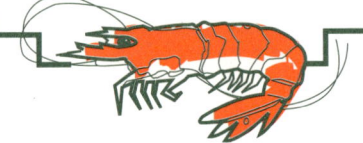

SAVANNAH RED RICE

Savannah, Georgia is one of our favorite cities to visit. It has many great restaurants serving coastal dishes with that low country flavor. Savannah claims this dish but it's popular from Charleston, South Carolina down to St. Augustine. Red rice is a delicious mixture of rice, tomatoes, peppers and bacon.

How are Savannahians like the ancient Chinese? Goes an old saying, "Because they eat rice and worship their ancestors."

Serves 6-8

- 5 slices smoked bacon
- ¾ cup onions, chopped
- ½ cup bell pepper, chopped
- 1 Datil pepper, seeded and chopped fine
- 2 cups crushed plum tomatoes
- 1 teaspoon sugar
- 1 teaspoon thyme, crumbled
- 1 ½ cups long-grain rice
- 2 cups chicken stock
- Salt and freshly ground black pepper, to taste

In a large cast-iron skillet, sauté bacon until crisp and drain on paper towels. Remove all but 2 tablespoons of the bacon drippings. Reduce heat and add onions, bell pepper and Datil pepper to skillet and cook until onions are softened. Stir in tomatoes, sugar, thyme, rice, stock, salt and pepper.

Mix thoroughly, increase heat and bring mixture to a full boil. Cover and reduce heat to simmer. Cook 15-20 minutes, stir with a fork and cook 10-15 minutes more or until rice has absorbed all liquid. Crumble bacon, sprinkle over rice and serve.

GRANNY'S GREEN RICE

Serves 6

- ½ cup unsalted butter
- 1 cup onion, chopped fine
- 2 ribs celery, chopped fine
- ½ cup bell pepper, chopped fine
- 1 cup green onions, chopped
- 1 large clove garlic, minced
- ½ teaspoon basil, crumbled
- ½ pound mushrooms, sliced
- 1 cup chicken stock reduced to ¼ cup
- 2½-3 cups cooked rice
- 1 cup extra-sharp Cheddar cheese, grated
- Salt and cayenne pepper, to taste
- ½ cup parsley, minced

Preheat oven 350 degrees. Heat butter over medium heat in a large skillet. Add onion, celery, bell pepper, green onion, garlic, basil, and mushrooms, and cook, stirring, until onions are softened. Remove from heat and add chicken stock, rice and cheese. Use a fork to mix. Add salt and pepper to taste, parsley, toss thoroughly and place in a buttered casserole. Heat in oven for 10-15 minutes and serve.

THANKSGIVING BROWN RICE

This is a tradition at every Thanksgiving dinner.

Serves 6

- ½ cup unsalted butter
- 1 medium onion, chopped
- 1 cup brown rice, washed
- 2-10½ ounces cans beef consommé or rich stock
- ½ pound fresh mushrooms, sliced and sautéed in 2 tablespoons butter
- 1 teaspoon salt
- 1 tablespoon parsley, minced

Preheat oven 350 degrees. Sauté onions in butter until softened. Place in a 9 x 13 inch glass baking dish. Wash rice, add to baking dish and stir. Add beef stock, sautéed mushrooms with juice and salt. Stir to dissolve salt and distribute mushrooms. Bake for 35-40 minutes. Garnish with parsley and serve.

SPANISH YELLOW RICE

Yellow rice gets its wonderful, vibrant color and distinctive taste from saffron threads, made from the dried stamens of the crocus flower. Saffron is expensive stuff, but this recipe only requires a few threads.

Serves 6

- 2 tablespoons olive oil
- 1 cup onion, finely chopped
- 1 clove garlic, minced
- 1 bell pepper, finely chopped
- 2 fresh tomatoes, chopped
- 3 cups chicken stock, heated
- 1 teaspoon salt
- ¼ teaspoon freshly ground black pepper
- ½ teaspoon cumin
- ⅛-¼ teaspoon saffron, crumbled
- 1½ cups long-grain rice

Heat olive oil in a large pot over medium-low heat. Cook onions, garlic and bell pepper until softened, but not brown. Add tomatoes stir and cook 1 minute. Stir in stock, salt, pepper, cumin, and saffron, and bring to a boil. Stir in the rice. Cover the pot, reduce heat to low and cook 20-25 minutes or until all liquid has been absorbed, stirring occasionally with a fork. Remove from heat, fluff rice with a fork and serve.

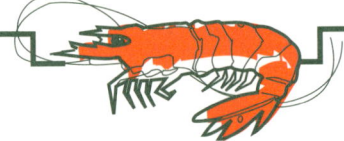

FRESH HOMEMADE PASTA

*A*t one time we made fresh pasta the "old-fashioned" way by mixing eggs and flour by hand and rolling it out like pie dough. Now we use the food processor and pasta machine and believe it tastes just as good.

Pasta should be cooked until just tender, or as an Italian restaurant owner once told us, "until it is cooked al dente, meaning to the bite, just tender enough to please." Fresh pasta will cook faster than dried.

For many years my nieces visited us in the summer. One of their favorite events was when we made Fettuccine Alfredo. They helped with the homemade pasta. Flour went everywhere, just like when granny made dumplings. Our nieces are now grown up and have nieces of their own. We hope they are keeping the tradition alive.

Serves 8

3½ cups all-purpose flour
¼ teaspoon salt
4 eggs
1 tablespoon extra virgin olive oil
¼ cup water

Place flour, salt. eggs and olive oil in a food processor with metal blade. Pulse 3-4 times, turn machine on and add water through feed tube. Process until dough forms a ball, about 20 seconds. Transfer dough to a lightly floured surface and knead until dough is smooth, about 1 minute. Divide dough into 6 equal portions, lightly flour and flatten into a 1 inch thick rectangle. Adjust the rollers of pasta machine to widest setting, #8, of hand cranked pasta machine. Pass dough through once, fold dough into thirds, and pass it through again, and again. Reset machine to #6 and pass dough through unfolded 3 times. Lightly flour dough as needed and pass through # 3 or #2 depending on desired thickness. Allow pasta to dry 10-15 minutes, cut the pasta in half crosswise before passing through appropriate cutter.

Drop pasta into 4 quarts of lightly salted boiling water. Bring water back to a full boil and gently stir. Cooking time varies with different types and thickness of pasta, about 30 seconds to 1 minute or until just tender. Drain well and add to sauce or pour cold water over until completely cool. To keep cooked pasta from sticking together, add 1-2 tablespoons vegetable oil, depending on amount of pasta, and toss with your fingers, set aside until ready to sauce and reheat.

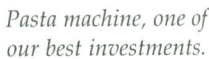

Pasta machine, one of our best investments.

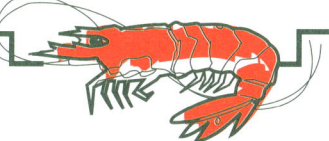

POTATO PASTA WITH CREAMY TOMATO SAUCE

"Gnocchi"

These potato dumplings are often served with freshly grated Parmesan cheese, nutmeg, fresh sage and melted butter. We prefer it served with a Creamy Tomato Sauce. Denting the pasta with the tines of a fork creates a surface that the sauce will cling to.

Invite the whole family to help. We usually make potato pasta first thing in the morning, cover with plastic wrap and place in the freezer until dinner time.

Serves 4

- 1½ pounds Idaho baking potatoes, about 3 potatoes
- ½ teaspoon salt
- 1 egg yolk, slightly beaten
- 7-8 ounces all-purpose flour

Cook scrubbed potatoes in water to cover until tender, about 30-45 minutes. Drain, peel and quarter potatoes while still hot, then put through a ricer or food mill into a large mixing bowl. Use a wooden spoon to stir in egg yolk mixed with salt, adding a half cup of flour at the time. Transfer dough to a lightly floured surface and knead for 3-4 minutes, adding more flour to keep dough from sticking. When dough is smooth, divide into 6 equal pieces. Roll each piece into a 16-18 inch cylindrical shape, "snake", about a half inch in diameter. Cut dough into one half-three-fourths inch pieces. Press each piece of dough with your thumb, on the back of a lightly floured fork, rolling dough off end of tines to curl. Place in a single layer on a lightly floured cookie sheet. Repeat with remaining dough, flouring the fork often. Let the gnocchi dry about 2 hours or it can be frozen on a cookie sheet and transferred to plastic bag for later use. Do not thaw dumplings if frozen before cooking.

To cook dumplings, gradually drop into a large pot of boiling, salted water and cook until they float to the surface - about 1 minute. Remove the ones that surface immediately with a slotted spoon, drain and place in a heated bowl. Have sauces previously prepared, add dumplings and reheat briefly, stirring gently. Serve with Creamy Tomato Sauce and topped with freshly grated Parmesan cheese and freshly grated nutmeg.

CREAMY TOMATO SAUCE

In a small saucepan combine one and one fourth cups whipping cream and 2 ounces cream cheese and bring to a simmer. Stir in three-fourths-one cup Marinara Sauce (see page 229) and heat through. Cook over low heat until slightly thickened, stirring occasionally, about 10 minutes. Serve sauce over potato pasta and sprinkle with one fourth cup freshly grated Parmesan cheese.

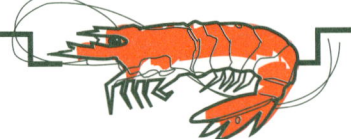

BASIL AND PINE NUT SAUCE
"Pesto"

This sauce was originally made with a mortar and pestle, hence the name. Some purists still insist on this method. However we make it in the food processor and enjoy it just as much.

Serves 6

- 1-2 cloves of garlic, or more
- 2 cups fresh basil leaves
- ½ cup pine nuts or walnuts
- ¼ cup olive oil (extra virgin)
- ½ teaspoon lemon juice
- ½ cup Parmesan cheese, freshly grated
- ½ stick unsalted butter
- Salt and pepper, to taste
- 1 pound dried linguine

In bowl of food processor add garlic, basil and pine nuts. Process 15 seconds. Scrape down sides of bowl and add oil, lemon juice, cheese and butter. Process 15 seconds. Scrape down sides of bowl and process until creamy. Salt and pepper mixture to taste. Process again until well mixed. Place in container with tight fitting lid and refrigerate. Will keep for weeks in refrigerator, remove 30 minutes before serving to soften. Serve over linguine.

PASTA HO-STYLE
"Puttanesca"

This tasty dish was made popular in Italy by the ladies of the evening because it was easy and quick to prepare between customers.

Serves 2

- 4 cloves garlic, minced
- ½ teaspoon red pepper flakes
- ¼ cup extra virgin olive oil
- ⅓ cup parsley, minced
- 4 canned plum tomatoes, chopped
- ⅓ cup juice from tomatoes
- 4 anchovies filets, minced
- 6 nicoise olives, seeded and chopped
- 2 teaspoon capers
- ½ pound cooked spaghetti
- 2 tablespoons Parmesan cheese, freshly grated

Cook garlic and pepper in oil over low heat for 20 seconds. Stir in parsley, tomatoes and tomato juice, and cook 1 minute. Add anchovies, olives, and capers and cook 2 minutes. Serve over spaghetti and sprinkle with cheese.

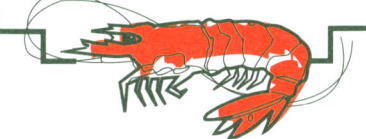

PASTA WITH SMOKED BACON
"Carbonara"

Serves 4

- ¼ pound lean salt pork or thick-sliced smoked country bacon
- 3 tablespoons olive oil
- ½ tablespoon freshly ground, black pepper
- 2 large eggs
- 2-3 tablespoons Parmesan cheese, freshly grated
- 1 pound thin spaghetti
- 1 tablespoon fresh parsley finely chopped

Cut bacon crosswise into a fourth inch strips, and cook over medium-low heat in a small cast-iron skillet with olive oil and half the black pepper until slightly brown; remove from heat.

Add eggs to a large platter and beat until foamy, add remaining freshly ground black pepper. Cook pasta in a large pot of salted water and stir with a wooden spoon making sure strands do not stick together. Cook until pasta is tender, drain, reserving 2 tablespoons of water. Reheat bacon and oil. Toss pasta with eggs using two forks. Add bacon and oil and toss, mixing everything together thoroughly. The heat from pasta, bacon and oil will cook the eggs. Sprinkle pasta with cheese and parsley, toss and add reserved water by the tablespoon until mixture is creamy, all water may not be needed. Serve at once.

PASTA WITH CREAM SAUCE
"Fettuccine Alfredo"

*T*his dish can be made with dried pasta, but fresh pasta makes it so much better. Fettuccine means ribbons in Italian.

Serves 4

- 6 quarts water
- 6 teaspoons salt,
- ½ recipe of fresh homemade pasta, cut for fettuccine
- 4 tablespoons unsalted butter
- ¾-1 cup whipping cream, warmed
- ¾-1 cup Parmesan cheese freshly grated
- Black pepper, freshly ground

Add butter to a large platter and place in a warm, 200 degree oven. Bring water to a boil, add salt and fettuccine. Cook fettuccine, about 3-5 minutes or until pasta is tender. Heat cream, set aside and keep warm. Drain pasta thoroughly, place on platter with the butter, and toss. Add warmed cream and two-thirds of the cheese. Toss gently until sauce is well distributed. Sprinkle with remaining cheese and serve. Add freshly ground black pepper if desired.

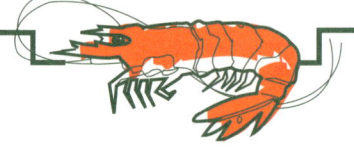

SPAGHETTI N' MEATBALLS

*T*he kids love this dish. It's an evolution of many recipes for meatballs.

Serves 12

- 1 pound ground beef
- ½ pound ground pork
- 1 cup Parmesan cheese, freshly grated
- 1 cup milk
- 1 egg
- 1 cup soft bread crumbs
- ½ cup parsley, chopped
- 2 cloves garlic, minced
- ¼ teaspoon pepper
- ½ teaspoon oregano, crumbled
- ¼ cup unsalted butter
- ¼ cup olive oil

Combine all ingredients except for butter and oil. Shape into meatballs and brown in butter and olive oil. As meatballs are cooked place in hot Marinara Sauce (see page 229). When all meatballs are cooked, cover, reduce heat to low and cook an additional 10 minutes.

SPAGHETTI FISHERMAN'S STYLE

- 3 tablespoons olive oil
- 4 garlic cloves, minced
- 2 red pepper pods, seeded and chopped
- 3 cups ripe, peeled plum tomatoes
- 3 anchovy filets, minced
- ¼ coarsely chopped parsley
- 1 pound spaghetti

Heat the olive oil in a large frying pan over medium heat. Add the garlic and all other ingredients, except parsley. Cook the mixture for 5-6 minutes, stirring frequently. Stir in the parsley and continue cooking for another 5 minutes.

Cook spaghetti until tender, drain and add to the sauce, toss and serve.

SPAGHETTI WITH OLIVE OIL AND GARLIC

- 6 large cloves garlic, sliced thin
- ¼ cup olive oil
- 2 tablespoons parsley, minced
- ½ pound spaghetti

Sauté garlic in the olive oil in a large skillet over medium heat. When the garlic is golden remove from heat. Stir in parsley, add cooked and drained spaghetti. Turn and mix, so that all the pasta is covered with oil, garlic and parsley. Serve immediately.

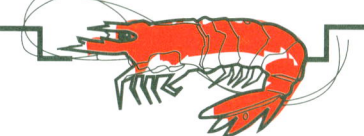

LINGUINE WITH CLAM SAUCE

Serves 4

- 2 pounds fresh Mahogany clams
- 4 tablespoons olive oil
- 2 cloves garlic, sliced thin
- 2 cups peeled plum tomatoes, chopped
- 2 tablespoons parsley, minced

Sauté clams in a skillet with 1 tablespoon olive oil over high heat until open. Remove meat from shells reserving 6 clams with meat in shells. Filter clam juice and oil through a coffee filter and set aside. Chop clams coarsely. Brown the garlic lightly in remaining olive oil, add the clams and sauté quickly. Add tomatoes and the strained clam juice and cook until sauce thickens slightly, about 15 minutes. Sprinkle parsley in sauce and serve over linguine.

MORRISON'S MACARONI & CHEESE

"No waitin' on da main flo."

Years ago in downtown Jacksonville, about noontime these chants, "No waitin' on da main flo" and "sho't line in da carriage room," could usually be heard outside the Morrison's Cafeteria. The head waiter shouted the chants to entice potential customers to be lured inside to try the luscious desserts (always the first item on the serving line), salads, seafood, meats, well-seasoned Southern vegetables, and the always popular mac n' cheese.

The cooks of African heritage presented all the Southern favorites in what seemed like one quarter mile long serving line. All the customer had to do was slide their tray along and pick up whatever caught their fancy. Then waiters hovering at the end balanced all this food on a tray and carried it to your table without spilling even a drop of water from the glass that the check was wrapped around.

Serves 6

- 2½ cups elbow macaroni
- ¼ cup unsalted butter
- ¼ cup all-purpose flour
- 2¼ cups milk, warmed
- 1 teaspoon salt
- ½ teaspoon freshly ground black pepper
- 2 eggs
- 2 cups grated extra-sharp Cheddar cheese

Preheat oven 400 degrees. Cook macaroni according to package directions and drain. Heat butter in a small saucepan over medium-low heat. Stir in flour and cook 1 minute. Use a whisk and add milk, stirring constantly, until sauce thickens. Add salt and pepper. Beat eggs slightly and add small amount of sauce to eggs, then add remaining egg mixture to sauce. Set aside one third cup grated cheese for top. Add one third macaroni to a buttered 2 quart casserole, alternating layers of macaroni and cheese. Pour sauce over all and add reserved cheese. Bake 25 - 30 minutes and serve.

LASAGNE FOR A CROWD

If you don't count French Fries, Italian food is probably the favorite ethnic food in North Florida. We have many great "I"-talian restaurants in North Florida that introduced us to "pasta," "Parmesan" and "Pizza Pie."

Mom and Dad's Italian restaurant located on U.S. 90 between DeFuniak Springs and Mossy Head, was one of the first to introduce "Pizza Pie" to North Florida. When it opened in 1949, the only cheese available locally was Cheddar or "Hoop" cheese as it was called. They used this yellow cheese on pizza and other dishes, which gave them a unique flavor and orange color. It is still served that way today. You have to ask for "white cheese" if you want Mozzarella.

Serves 12-14

TOMATO MEAT SAUCE:
- 2 slices thick-sliced smoked bacon
- 2 cups onion, chopped
- ½ cup carrots, chopped
- ½ cup celery, chopped
- 1 tablespoon garlic, minced
- 2 tablespoons olive oil
- 2 teaspoons oregano, crumbled
- ½ teaspoon thyme
- 1 pound lean ground beef
- ½ pound ground veal
- ½ pound ground pork
- 2 cups dry red wine
- 1 tablespoon salt
- 2 cups beef stock
- 2 - 28 ounce cans crushed plum tomatoes
- 12 ounce can tomato paste
- 1 cup water
- 1 tablespoon sugar
- Additional salt and freshly ground black pepper, to taste

Place bacon, onions, carrots, celery, and garlic in a food processor and pulse until mixture is almost a paste. Heat a large iron skillet over medium-low heat, add olive oil and sauté mixture until softened. Add oregano, thyme, beef, veal, and pork; brown thoroughly, breaking up lumps. Add wine, increase heat and boil briskly until most of the liquid has evaporated, stirring occasionally. Add salt, beef stock, crushed tomatoes, tomato paste, water and sugar. Reduce heat, partially cover and simmer for one and one half-two hours.

Correct seasoning and cool to room temperature, place in container with cover and refrigerate. Lift off any accumulated fat and discard before using.

PASTA:

1 recipe fresh homemade pasta, left in long sheets, then cut with a sharp knife in 6-8 inch lengths. Bring 6 quarts water to a boil, add 6 teaspoons salt. Cook lasagne noodles, a few at a time, for 30 seconds. Use a slotted spoon to remove noodles and place in a large bowl of cool water. When pasta is cool enough to handle, spread them out on a kitchen towel. Repeat process until all noodles are cooked.

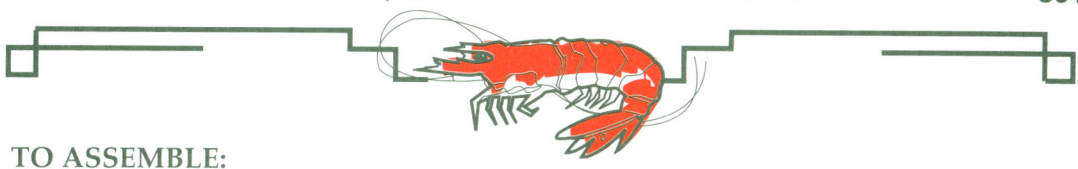

TO ASSEMBLE:

- 2 cups Parmesan cheese, freshly grated
- 1½ pounds whole milk mozzarella, grated
- 2 pounds ricotta cheese
- ½ cup fresh minced parsley
- 1½ teaspoons salt

Mix ricotta cheese with parsley, salt and 1 cup of the Parmesan cheese. Spread a thin layer of meat sauce in bottom of 18x12x3 inch casserole. Add a layer of pasta, spread with a thin layer of ricotta and sprinkle lightly with Parmesan and mozzarella. Repeat layering with pasta, ricotta, Parmesan and mozzarella until casserole is filled. The last layering should be pasta, 2 cups tomato meat sauce, mozzarella cheese and Parmesan cheese. Cover with plastic wrap and allow lasagna to stand at least 4 hours, or refrigerated over night. Bake uncovered in a preheated 350 degree oven for 30-40 minutes or until sauce is bubbling hot. If lasagne has been refrigerated it should be covered with foil and baked longer until heated through. Cool 10 minutes before cutting so that lasagne will hold together. Serve lasagne with remaining meat sauce on the side.

MAYPORT SEAFOOD LASAGNE

Serves 8

- 4 tablespoons unsalted butter
- ½ cup green onions, minced
- 1 pound shelled raw shrimp
- 2 pounds sea scallops, cut into fourths
- Salt and freshly ground black pepper, to taste
- 1 pound lump crabmeat
- 2 tablespoons dry sherry
- 4 cups White Sauce
- ¼ teaspoon nutmeg, freshly grated
- 9 homemade lasagne strips, cooked
- 2 tablespoons capers
- 14 ounce can artichoke hearts, drained
- 1½ cups Parmesan cheese, grated

Mayport Lighthouse

Melt 2 tablespoons of the butter in a large skillet over medium heat, add one-fourth cup green onions. Cook for about 30 seconds and add the shrimp and scallops and cook 2 minutes. Sprinkle with salt and pepper. Remove shrimp and scallops to a bowl, in the same skillet, add remaining 2 tablespoons butter. When butter has melted add remaining one-fourth cup of green onions. Cook for 30 seconds and add the crab, sprinkle with sherry, heat through and add to bowl with shrimp. Gently mix seafood. Butter a 9x12 inch casserole dish. Stir nutmeg into white sauce (see page 24). Spread a thin layer of sauce, about one-fourth inch deep, on the bottom of the pan. Lay 3 lasagne strips over the sauce. Cover with half the seafood. Sprinkle with the capers. Use a sharp knife to slice the artichoke hearts into fourths. Lay artichokes over the seafood. Cover with thin layer of white sauce. Lay three more lasagne strips on top, cover with seafood mixture. Spoon more sauce over the seafood, top with 3 lasagne strips, ending with sauce. Sprinkle with cheese and bake in preheated 350 degrees for 20-30 minutes.

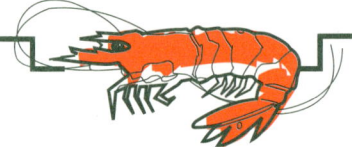

PHILIPPINE PANCIT

O ur Filipino friends Dotty and Ellen Bulan make a great team. He loves to catch seafood and they both like to cook it. Dotty is a master of the cast net and sometimes brings us fresh shrimp he catches down at Guana River which are excellent in this dish.

- ¼ pound bikon noodles
- ¼ pound long rice noodles
- 2 tablespoons vegetable oil
- 1 medium onion, chopped
- 2 garlic cloves, minced
- 1 cup smoked ham, cut in ¼ inch strips
- 1 cup shrimp, cut in half
- Salt to taste
- ½ teaspoon black pepper freshly ground
- 1 teaspoon paprika
- 2 cups water
- 2 carrots, cut in thin ¼ inch diagonal strips
- 2-3 stalks celery, cut in ¼ inch diagonal strips
- ½ pound green snap beans cut in ¼ inch diagonal strips
- 2 tablespoons fish sauce
- 2 tablespoons butter
- 2 green onions, chopped

Soak Bikon noodles for 5 minutes in water to cover, drain and set aside. Soak rice noodles in water to cover for 10 minutes, drain and set aside. Heat wok over medium heat, add oil and sauté onion and garlic until onions have softened. Add ham, shrimp, salt, pepper, paprika, and 1 cup water. Add carrots, celery, and beans, and simmer until vegetables are just cooked but still crunchy. Remove vegetables and meat to warm plate. Pour remaining cup of water into wok. Add Bikon and rice noodles, stir and cook until all water has evaporated. Add 2-3 tablespoons fish sauce and return vegetables and meat. Stir in 2 tablespoons butter, sprinkle with green onions and serve.

Dotty Bulan casting for shrimp, c 1994.

Southern Garden Vegetables and Swamp Cabbage

Keystone Hotel, Fernandina, built in 1905 with a large garden behind the hotel that supplied the restaurant with fresh vegetables. A natural spring helped to irrigate the garden. Wild watercress still grows along the banks of the spring.

Fried Eggplant with
  Kudzu Sauce, 306
Sautéed Carrots, 306
Crookneck Squash Casserole, 307
Tom's Roasted Asparagus, 307
Stuffed Chayote, 308
Skillet Okra, 308
Butter Beans w/ Gravy, 309
Battered Onion Rings, 310
Baked St. Augustine Sweets, 310
Vegetables on the Grill, 311
Cauliflower Au Gratin, 311
Potatoes Anna, 312
Brabant Potatoes, 312
Twice Baked Potatoes, 313
Oven Roasted Potatoes, 313
New Potatoes, Cream Gravy, 314
New Potatoes, English Peas, 314
Potatoes En Papillote, 315
Hellenthal's German Potatoes, 315
Orange Sweet Potatoes, 316
Sweet Potato Soufflé, 316
Creole Stuffed Eggplant, 317
Creamed Spinach, 317
Turnip Root Potato Purée, 318
Sautéed Spinach with Garlic, 318
String Beans w/ New Potatoes, 319
Fresh English Peas, 319
Florida Cracker Hashbrown
  Casserole, 320
Fried Zucchini, 320
Rutabaga and Wild Watercress, 321
Skillet Red Cabbage, 321
Zucchini with Spinach, 322
Matchstick Vegetables, 322
Sautéed Broccoli, 322
Spinach Timbales, 323
Smothered Cucumbers, 323
Cucumber Yogurt, 323
Skillet Squash 'N St. Augustine
  Sweets, 324
Broccoli Soufflé, 324
Buttermilk Fried Okra, 325
Swamp Cabbage Deluxe, 325
Gunn's Swamp Cabbage, 326

Gartec (McDonald) Girls--Genny, Ruby, Tawee, Elizabeth, Carolyn and Anna Jo.

*I didn't have any grits,
so I substituted rice.
I didn't have saffron,
so I used another spice.*

*I was out of tomato sauce.
I used tomato paste.
A whole can, not a half can,
I don't believe in waste.*

*My sister gave me the recipe,
Said you couldn't beat it.
There must be something wrong with her,
I couldn't even eat it!*

                    Anonymous

When winter leaves seasonal Florida the camellias begin to fade, their beauty is replaced with the brilliant multi-colored azaleas, dogwoods, redbud and the vivid purple magnolias, signifying that spring has arrived. Spring is when the first long- anticipated vegetables are ready in the garden: English peas, new potatoes, salad greens, and the first green onions are ready to be enjoyed in salads and side dishes, and later topped off with a big bowl full of fresh strawberries and cream.

As the weather warms up, the azaleas fade and are replaced with colorful oleanders, crept myrtle and daylillies, accompanied by the fragrance of jasmine and the majestic magnolia trees. Graceful palms, banana trees and flowering fruit trees frame many homes. The summer garden is now overflowing with fresh vegetables. If you don't have a garden now is the time to find the "real thing".

True Southerners hold food and especially vegetables close to their hearts. The summer months are bountiful with fresh vegetables, but to find the real thing, you must locate a farmer's market, u-pick-'em, or roadside produce stand.

Backroad rural areas are often the place to find these "real thing" markets, and also provide an opportunity to chat with the farmer who grew the produce. Usually, they can help you pick out ripe, delicious fruits and vegetables and tell you about them.

Homegrown tomatoes at our cabin in Eucheeanna, c 2004.

SOUTHERN GARDEN VEGETABLES AND SWAMP CABBAGE

To enjoy fruits and vegetables at their wholesome best use freshly picked when possible and wash just before cooking. If you weren't raised by a good Southern cook (and paid attention) it may take some trial and error to get the texture and flavor just right, but the finished result makes it all worthwhile.

Daddy's garden, c 1979.

Plates are never large enough to hold all the summer vegetables. At one sitting, we may have fresh corn cut from the cob, peas and butter beans cooked with ham hocks with okra pods added at the last minute, or fried okra, squash sautéed in bacon drippings with onions, sliced fresh red tomatoes, pickled cucumbers with green onions, pear relish, Datil "Bottled Hell" pepper sauce and lots of hot crusty pone corn bread and butter. Third helpings are not uncommon. No room for meat, but we have that too!

In cool October, as trees take on the fall colors, look for greens of all kinds like mustard, turnips, kale, collards and the root vegetables, rutabaga, turnip roots and sweet potatoes. Root vegetables sometimes have a bland or bitter taste and are not real popular, especially with children. But when seasoned with smoked meat and a sweetener the flavor becomes enhanced and delicious.

Winter brings the dormant season for the shrubs and trees to rest for the spring growth. The sasanquas and japonicas bend this rule and give color to an otherwise drab landscape. This is when we enjoy the last of the fall greens and collards which are now tender after the first frost, as well as when we enjoy the swamp cabbage served in stews.

Swamp cabbage, or "heart of palm," is something you might have to really look for—it's a unique product available along the Atlantic and Gulf Coast. Usually served stewed with tomatoes and sometimes cream, it can also be eaten raw in salads.

Authentic Southern cooking requires bacon drippings, and it is far better if it comes from smoked bacon. It distinctively flavors vegetables, breads and rice dishes. Its sweet smoky flavor cannot be duplicated with any other seasoning. Of course, doctors tell us bacon drippings aren't good for us if we use it too often, but we know some local folks who lived to be over 100 and used bacon drippings every day. I guess if they had substituted yogurt and wheat germ, they might have made 110.

FRIED EGGPLANT WITH KUDZU SAUCE

Kudzu is a dirty word in the deep South. This vine that was originally planted for erosion control has run mayhem in many areas and has been known to cover entire buildings in a matter of days. Most Southerners aren't aware of its culinary and medicinal qualities. The roots, which can grow to over 400 pounds, are promoted in Japan as a food additive that aids in the cure of everything from anemia to hangovers.

A Chipley farmer, Mr. C. E. Pleas, spent over 40 years of his life promoting the virtues of kudzu as animal fodder. After Pleas' death in 1954, a bronze marker was erected on U.S. 90 in Chipley proclaiming that "Kudzu was developed here." Workers at the adjacent Agricultural Center claim that "people driving down from Georgia and Alabama see the marker and stop just so they can come in and cuss us." Someday this marker might be the only thing in West Florida not covered with kudzu.

You can make your own Kudzu powder but believe me it's far easier to buy it at an Oriental market. If you can't find kudzu powder substitute cornstarch, but it won't cure a hangover.

Serves 6

3 tablespoons vegetable oil
3 eggplant, cut in 1 inch slices
½ cup plus 2 tablespoons water
1 teaspoon kudzu powder
1 tablespoon miso (soybean) cream

Sauté eggplant in oil until brown on both sides. Combine kudzu powder with one half cup of water. Remove eggplant to a warm platter, add kudzu mixture to pan and bring to a boil. Reduce heat and simmer until sauce is transparent. Mix miso cream and remaining 2 tablespoons of water and add to pan, stir and cook 30 seconds. Pour sauce over eggplant and serve.

SAUTÉED CARROTS

Serves 4

6 large Carrots
2 tablespoons unsalted butter
1 tablespoon sugar

Wash and peel carrots with a vegetable peeler. Shred carrots on the largest side of grater. Heat butter in a large skillet. When melted add carrots and toss with a large fork. Sprinkle with sugar and toss again, Cook 5 minutes and serve.

CROOKNECK SQUASH CASSEROLE

There are many different versions of this dish throughout the South. Delicately flavored crookneck squash are very versatile and are successfully served fried, sautéed with onions, in salads and in casseroles such as this one.

Serves 6-8

- 6 cups crookneck squash, sliced
- 1 large St. Augustine sweet onion, chopped
- 1 egg, lightly beaten
- 5 tablespoons unsalted butter, melted
- ½ cup mayonnaise
- 1 teaspoon sugar
- 1 red bell pepper, chopped
- 1½ cups Ritz cracker crumbs
- Salt and freshly ground black pepper, to taste
- ½ teaspoon thyme, crumbled
- ½ teaspoon oregano, crumbled
- 1½ cups extra-sharp Cheddar cheese, grated

Preheat oven 350 degrees. Place squash and onions in saucepan with a half cup water, bring to a boil, cover and reduce heat to low. Cook until squash are just tender, about 10 minutes. Drain, reserve liquid and place in large bowl. Add egg, 4 tablespoons butter, mayonnaise, sugar, half of cheese, red bell pepper, half of cracker crumbs, salt, pepper, thyme and oregano. If mixture seems too dry, add reserved vegetable broth by the tablespoon until moist. Mix well and place in buttered one and one half quart casserole. Combine remaining cheese, cracker crumbs and tablespoon of butter. Spread on top of casserole, bake 20-25 minutes and serve.

TOM'S ROASTED ASPARAGUS

Serves 4

- 24-32 spears pencil thin asparagus
- ½ tablespoon olive oil
- Shaved parmesan cheese
- Salt and freshly ground black pepper

Snap woody ends off asparagus and place in a large bowl. Add olive oil, salt and pepper to taste. Toss to coat asparagus. Place on cookie sheet in a single layer and broil for 5-8 minutes. Arrange on heated platter and top with shaved parmesan cheese. Serve at once.

SOUTHERN GARDEN VEGETABLES AND SWAMP CABBAGE

STUFFED CHAYOTE

*F*resh Chayote would sometimes appear on our doorstep from an anonymous neighbor. Of course, everyone in the neighborhood knew that Jefferson Davis Williamson had the largest chayote vine in town.

One year the vine grew to the top of his pecan tree and the squirrels had a feast too, much to J.D.'s disgust.

Serves 4

- 2 medium chayote
- ½ cup green onions, chopped
- 4 tablespoons unsalted butter,
- 4 inch piece of lean smoked sausage (casing removed and chopped)
- 2 teaspoons Creole Seasonings
- 1¼ cups soft bread crumbs
- Salt to taste
- ½ pound boiled shrimp
- 2 teaspoons parsley, chopped
- ¼ cup Parmesan cheese, freshly grated

Cover chayote with water and simmer covered until fork tender, about 40 minutes. Cool, peel and cut each in half lengthwise. Remove the seed and carefully spoon out the center, leaving a one quarter inch shell. Place shells upside down on paper towels to drain. Coarsely chop the pulp and set aside. Heat a skillet over medium heat, add 2 tablespoons of the butter and sauté the green onion until softened. Add the reserved chopped chayote with 1 teaspoon of the Creole Seasonings (see page181), cook 2-3 minutes or until most of the liquid from chayote evaporates, remove to a mixing bowl.

In same skillet cook sausage until fat is rendered and meat is a little crisp, remove to same bowl. Preheat oven 375 degrees. Add 1 cup of the bread crumbs to bowl with remaining seasonings, parsley and shrimp, and mix thoroughly. Spoon stuffing into chayote shells, mounding the tops. Mix the remaining bread crumbs and cheese, sprinkle over chayotes, dribble with 2 tablespoons remaining butter and bake for 20 minutes or until heated through. Place on heated plates and serve with Béarnaise Sauce (see page 75).

SKILLET OKRA

Serves 6

- 2 pounds small tender okra
- Salt to taste
- 1-2 teaspoon bacon drippings

Wash okra and cut into one half inch pieces. Heat a large cast-iron skillet over medium heat for 3-5 minutes. Add bacon drippings and okra. Stir and season with salt. Cook, occasionally stirring for 15-20 minutes. Taste for seasoning and serve.

SPECKLED BUTTER BEANS WITH GRAVY

*"Just a bowl of butter beans,
Pass the corn bread won't you please,
I don't want no collard greens,
just another bowl of butter beans."
To the tune of "Just A Closer Walk With Thee."*

Butter beans grow on low bushes and are back breaking to pick. My husband reflects on having to pick a bushel hamper full each day before he could go swimming down at the creek. He says he probably complained a lot about picking and shelling, but definitely not about eating them.

Shelling butter beans "As the World Turns," even Sam, the sausage dog, is hooked on the soaps, c 1962.

Serves 6
½ **pound smoked bacon**
½ **cup all-purpose flour**
1 **medium onion, chopped**
4 **cups fresh speckled butter beans, shelled**
Salt and freshly ground black pepper, to taste
¼ **teaspoon cayenne pepper**
½ **teaspoon sugar**
2½ **cups beef stock**

Heat a cast-iron skillet over medium-low heat, fry the bacon until crisp and drain on paper towels. Sprinkle flour in bacon drippings and whisk until smooth. Stir constantly until roux is a peanut butter color. Add onions, lower heat and cook until onions have softened. Remove from heat and stir until cooled. Add stock to a large saucepan and bring to a boil. Add butter beans, salt, pepper, cayenne, sugar. Stir in roux, a tablespoon at a time. Reduce heat to simmer, cover and cook about 30 minutes. Stir often, cooking until gravy has thickened and beans are tender. Crumble bacon and stir into beans. Correct seasoning and serve.

Our neighbor, Linda gave Butterbean her name for obvious reasons, c 2004.

CHAMPAGNE BATTERED ONION RINGS

*T*hese fried onion rings are crisp and delicious every time. Onion rings are inexpensive to make and we don't understand why some restaurants charge such a high price. Probably the same reason some triple the prices on their wine list. Serve hot with steaks or fried seafood.

Serves 4

- 1 cup all-purpose flour
- 1 cup champagne (Miller High Life beer)
- 1 teaspoon salt
- ¼ cup parsley, finely minced
- 2 large St. Augustine Sweet onions, cut into ¼ inch slices
- Vegetable oil for deep frying

In a large bowl, beat together flour, beer, salt and parsley until smooth. Cover with plastic wrap and let stand 3 hours at room temperature.

Separate the onion slices into rings (save smaller rings for another use). Cover with ice water and refrigerate for 2 hours. Drain onions and pat dry with paper towels. Dip rings in batter, coat well and let excess drip off. Fry, a few at the time, at 375 degrees for 1-2 minutes or until golden brown, make sure not to crowd the pan. Place on metal wire racks to drain, keep them warm in a 200 degree oven until all are fried. Place on heated platter and serve immediately.

BAKED ST. AUGUSTINE SWEETS

Serves 4

- 4 large St. Augustine Sweet onions
- ½ cup butter, softened
- 1 cup sour cream
- 1 teaspoon brown sugar
- 1 tablespoon lemon juice
- 2 teaspoons parsley, minced

Preheat oven 350 degrees. Place unpeeled onions in a foil lined 9x13 pan. Bake for 45 minutes. Remove skin from onions and place in casserole. Mix together the butter, sour cream, brown sugar and lemon juice. Pour over onions and return to oven for 10-15 minutes. Sprinkle with parsley and serve.

Possibly the beginning of the St. Augustine Sweet...

VEGETABLES ON THE GRILL

Backyard barbecuing became popular in the late 1950's, it was popular for burgers, weenies, chicken and an occasional sirloin steak. It never occurred to any of us to try anything else, especially vegetables.

Today we grill almost any type meat, fowl or seafood and especially like the flavor grilling adds to marinated vegetables.

Serves 4

- 2 garlic cloves, crushed
- 1 teaspoon salt
- 1½ teaspoons rosemary, crumbled
- Black pepper, freshly ground
- ½ cup olive oil
- 1 medium eggplant, sliced, 1¼ inches lengthwise
- 2 red bell peppers cut in half and seeded
- 12 medium-large mushrooms
- 4 zucchini, sliced 1¼ inches lengthwise

In a 9x13 inch glass dish, combine garlic, salt, rosemary, black pepper and olive oil and mix well. Cut zucchini and eggplant the same thickness and add to dish. Add red bell pepper and mushrooms, toss vegetables to coat with oil and seasonings. Marinate 1 hour, turning frequently. Soak 6 inch wooden skewers in shallow bowl of water for 30 minutes to keep them from burning. Thread mushrooms on skewers. Grill the red bell pepper over hot coals until skin is charred, place in marinade dish. Add eggplant, zucchini and mushrooms and cook until tender, about 5 minutes. Serve with Basil Mayonnaise (see page 176).

CAULIFLOWER AU GRATIN

Serves 6

- 1 cauliflower, cut into florettes
- 3 tablespoons butter
- 3 tablespoons all- purpose flower
- 1½ cups milk
- ⅔ cup cheddar cheese, shredded
- 1 tablespoon pimento, diced
- 1 teaspoon salt
- ¼ teaspoon celery salt
- ¼ teaspoon black pepper, freshly ground

Arrange cauliflower in a steamer basket, cover and steam for 10 minutes, or until crisp tender. Place in a lightly greased 2 quart casserole dish. Melt butter in a heavy saucepan over medium-low heat. Whisk in flour, whisking until smooth. Cook whisking constantly for 1 minute. Gradually whisk in milk, whisking constantly until thickened. Add the cheese, pimentos salt, celery salt and pepper. Whisk until smooth, pour over cauliflower. Bake 350 degrees for 25 minutes and serve.

POTATOES ANNA

Not your classic Anna with onions and bread crumbs. Mine is just a simple dish of potatoes, cream and butter, and one of our favorites. This is a classic potato dish when properly prepared, there is nothing finer. The potatoes absorb the cream as they cook. It is always a temptation to add more potatoes and fill the dish, don't. This dish goes well with steaks.

Serves 4

1½ pounds new potatoes
1-1½ cups whipping cream
3 tablespoons butter
Salt to taste

All through school I was known as Annie Jo. When we applied for a marriage license my birth certificate revealed my name was actually Anna Jo, which I've gone by ever since. Of course at class reunions everybody still calls me Annie Jo. Two bits - Four bits.

Preheat oven 300 degrees. Peel potatoes and slice as thin as possible, no thicker than a penny. Place in a large bowl of cold water. Butter a 9x13 baking dish liberally. Drain potatoes and pat dry with paper towels. Heat cream and remaining butter until warm, and butter has melted. Spread half of potatoes in baking dish. Pour half the cream over the potatoes and sprinkle with salt. Arrange remaining potatoes, salt, and pour remaining cream over them. Butter one side of aluminum foil and place over potatoes. Set a cast-iron skillet on top of the foil. Bake 45 minutes, remove skillet and foil and continue to bake 30 minutes, or until cream has thickened and potatoes have absorbed most of the cream. If top browns, break the crust and spoon some of the cream over the potatoes. Grated Gruyére or Swiss cheese may be added the last 3-5 minutes and broiled until lightly brown. Serve at once.

BRABANT POTATOES

Serves 4

2 pounds red potatoes,
**   washed and halved**
1 bay leaf
Chicken stock

Salt and Freshly ground
**   black pepper, to taste**
2 tablespoons parsley, minced
1 stick unsalted butter

Place potatoes and bay leaf in a medium pot and cover with chicken stock by 1 inch. Bring to a boil over high heat, reduce heat to low, cover and simmer 10-12 minutes. Drain when are barely tender and discard the bay leaf. Melt butter in a large cast-iron skillet, over medium-high heat. Add the potatoes, salt and pepper to taste, and toss until potatoes are brown and crisp on all sides. Sprinkle with parsley and serve at once.

TWICE BAKED POTATOES

We like our baked potatoes rubbed with bacon drippings and lightly salted before placing in the oven, baked, then topped with sour cream and chives. When we make twice-baked potatoes, we leave off the salt.

Serves 6-12

- 6 baking potatoes, washed and patted dry
- 2 tablespoons bacon drippings
- ½ teaspoon salt
- 8 slices country smoked bacon cut into ½ inch pieces
- ½ cup fresh dill, chopped
- ½ cup sour cream
- 2 large eggs, beaten
- Salt and freshly ground black pepper, to taste
- 1⅓ cups onion, chopped

Preheat oven 400 degrees.

Rub potatoes with bacon drippings, lightly salt skins and bake for one hour. Fry bacon until crisp, remove to drain on paper towels. Add onions to skillet and sauté until golden. Transfer with a slotted spoon to a large bowl, reserving drippings. Slice potatoes in half and scoop out the potato with a fork, leaving a one quarter inch shell. Place potato pulp in large bowl with onions. Add bacon, sour cream, bacon drippings, dill, eggs, salt and pepper. Mix with a fork until potatoes are fluffy. Mound into potato shells, reheat for 10 minutes and serve.

> Note: Potatoes will bake quicker and more even if a 60-penny nail is inserted lengthwise, so the nail protrudes on each side. The nail makes the potato flaky.

OVEN ROASTED POTATOES

Serves 4

- 6 cups of new potatoes, quartered
- 6 cloves garlic, minced
- 1 medium onion, sliced
- ½ cup unsalted butter
- Salt and freshly ground black pepper
- 1 tablespoon parsley, minced

Preheat oven 350 degrees. Place potatoes, garlic, onion, butter, salt and pepper in a large cast-iron skillet. Bake for 10 minutes and stir. Continue to bake 40 minutes, stirring occasionally until potatoes are brown. Check for doneness, sprinkle with parsley and serve.

NEW POTATOES WITH CREAM GRAVY

New potatoes have a thin red skin. When they are first dug, the skin is easily removed by scraping with a paring knife. I know, because it was my job as a child to sit on the back steps and scrape enough potatoes to feed a family of ten. The job wasn't bad. It was the quantity of potatoes and the stained brown fingers that lasted for days that I disliked. Eating this dish made me feel a little better, but not much.

Serves 4

- 10-12 new potatoes, peeled (about 1½ pounds)
- ¼ cup unsalted butter
- 1½ cups onion, chopped
- 1 cup water
- ½ cup chicken stock
- ¼ cup whipping cream
- Salt and freshly ground black pepper, to taste
- 1 tablespoon all-purpose flour

Peel potatoes and slice them one-fourth inch thick. Place butter and onions in saucepan over low heat and cook until onions have softened, do not let brown. Add potatoes and water. Bring to a boil, cover and reduce heat to low. Cook 8-10 minutes or until potatoes are just tender. Place flour and stock in a jar with tight fitting lid, shake vigorously until combined. Add to potatoes and gently stir. Add cream, salt and pepper, continue to cook uncovered on very low heat for 20 minutes, stirring occasionally until sauce has thickened. Correct seasoning and serve.

NEW POTATOES AND ENGLISH PEAS

New potatoes and English peas come from the garden at the same time and are great cooked together.

Serves 6-8

- 1½ pounds new potatoes
- 2 cups fresh, shelled sweet English Peas
- ¾ cup whipping cream
- 3 tablespoons fresh dill, chopped
- 2 tablespoon butter
- 1 teaspoon salt

Cook potatoes in boiling water to cover in a large pot, about 15 minutes. Add peas; cover and cook 5 minutes more or until potatoes are tender. Drain. Stir in whipping cream, dill, butter and salt. Serve immediately.

POTATOES EN PAPILLOTE

This dish is spectacular served straight to the table. The fragrance of the various herbs is released as the parchment is opened.

Serves 4

- ⅓ cup parsley, chopped
- 1 teaspoon dried thyme, crumbled or, 10 sprigs of fresh, cut in 1 inch pieces
- 1 teaspoon dried oregano, crumbled or, 10 sprigs of fresh, cut in 1 inch pieces
- ½ teaspoon dried rosemary, or 1 teaspoon fresh, chopped
- 8 cloves garlic
- 10 medium mushrooms, sliced
- 2 tablespoons olive oil
- 1 teaspoon salt
- 1 teaspoon black pepper freshly ground
- 4-16x12 inch sheets of Parchment paper
- 1½ pounds unpeeled new potatoes, cut into fourths

Preheat oven 400 degrees. Combine all ingredients in a large bowl, mix thoroughly. Fold and crease each piece of parchment paper in the center. Divide herbs, potatoes and mushrooms equally between the four sheets. Fold the parchment in half, enclosing the ingredients. Seal the packets by folding and crimping the edges to create a semicircular shape. Place on a large baking sheet and bake 20-25 minutes. Serve immediately.

HELLENTHAL'S GERMAN POTATOES

*H*ellenthals' restaurant on the westside (the best side) of Jacksonville was one of our favorite places for T-bone steak and mushroom gravy. Alas, it too faded away years ago.

- 5 potatoes
- 1 small diced onion
- ⅔ cup white vinegar
- 1 teaspoon salt
- 5 slices of bacon
- 2 egg yolks, beaten
- ⅔ cup beef boullion

Peel and slice potatoes. Cook 15 minutes, drain.. Fry bacon and drain. Lay potatoes in shallow dish, crumble bacon over potatoes. Sauté onions in bacon drippings, drain and sprinkle over potatoes and bacon. Combine remaining ingredients in saucepan, heat well and pour over potatoes. Gently toss...gently.

SOUTHERN GARDEN VEGETABLES AND SWAMP CABBAGE

ORANGE SWEET POTATOES

The water table in Florida is close to the surface, and root cellars are not practical. Sweet potatoes, grown throughout the South, are dug in the fall and banked (covered with pine straw and soil) to sweeten. Later they are uncovered and eaten as a vegetable or prepared as a dessert.

Banking sweet potatoes, DeFuniak Springs farm, c 1988.

1¼ pounds baked sweet potatoes, (Georgia Red variety)
⅓ cup brown sugar
Grated zest of 1 orange
⅓ cup fresh orange juice
2 tablespoons Grand Marnier
¼ cup butter, melted
1 teaspoon vanilla

Preheat oven 350 degrees. Peel and slice cooled sweet potatoes a half inch thick and layer in a buttered 8x8 inch glass dish. Mix remaining ingredients in a small bowl and pour sweet over potatoes. Bake 20 minutes or until heated through and serve.

SWEET POTATO SOUFFLE'

This isn't a true soufflé, but what the hell! That's what everybody calls it.

5 cups hot sweet potatoes, mashed
½ cup salted butter, softened
5 eggs
1 teaspoon vanilla
1 cup sugar
½ teaspoon allspice
½ teaspoon cinnamon
1 can condensed milk

Preheat oven 350 degrees. Mix sweet potatoes and butter. Beat eggs, vanilla, sugar, allspice, cinnamon and milk together. Stir mixture into potatoes and mix well. Pour into a buttered 9x13 inch baking dish and bake for 30 minutes. Add topping.

SOUFFLÉ TOPPING:
¼ cup salted butter
1½ cups chopped pecans
1½ cups brown sugar

Reduce temperature in oven to 325 degrees. Mix all ingredients together and sprinkle over the top of the sweet potatoes. Return to oven and bake for 20 minutes.

CREOLE STUFFED EGGPLANT

Serves 4

1 large eggplant, stem removed
1 teaspoon salt
Freshly ground black pepper
2 tablespoons vegetable oil
¼ cup onion, chopped
¼ cup bell pepper, chopped
1 tablespoon celery, chopped
1 garlic clove, chopped
¼ cup chicken livers, coarsely cut-up
7½ ounces fresh lump crab meat
⅓ cup dry bread crumbs
1 tablespoon butter

Cut eggplant in half lengthwise, place in a large saucepan with 1 inch boiling water, cover, and steam for 12-15 minutes, or until tender. Drain, remove skin when cool enough to handle, and chop the flesh coarsely. Transfer eggplant to a large mixing bowl, mash with a fork, stir in the salt and pepper to taste, and set aside. Heat oil in a large skillet, add onion, pepper, celery and garlic, cover and cook over low heat for 10 minutes. Uncover and cook for 10 minutes, stirring. Preheat oven to 375 degrees. Remove skillet from heat and stir in the crabmeat, add mixture to the eggplant and stir until well blended. Spoon mixture into a 1-quart shallow baking dish, sprinkle with bread crumbs and dot with butter. Bake uncovered for 20 minutes.

CREAMED SPINACH

This recipe is excellent poured over oysters on the half shell then broiled until bubbly.

Serves 6

3 pounds spinach
12 tablespoons butter
9 tablespoons flour
¾ cup milk
8 slices smoked bacon, chopped
3 shallots, chopped
¾ cup heavy cream
Salt and freshly ground black pepper, to taste
Freshly ground nutmeg
1 teaspoon Pernod, optional

Blanch spinach, drain, squeeze out excess water, chop and set aside. Melt 8 tablespoons butter in saucepan, add flour and whisk for 2 minutes. Gradually add milk, stir until smooth and thick, remove and set aside. Fry bacon in a cast-iron skillet until brown, add shallots and cook 3 minutes. Stir in spinach and flour-milk paste. Add cream and remaining butter. Season with salt, pepper nutmeg and Pernod cook until thickened.

RHETT'S TURNIP ROOT AND POTATO PURÉE

"As God is my witness, I'll never go hungary again."

If Scarlet had tried this dish maybe she wouldn't have complained so much about eating turnip roots. Most Southerners are fond of turnip greens but some dislike the roots which sometimes may be bitter.

The addition of sour cream and potatoes smooth out the flavor of the turnip roots and makes this a delightful dish.

Serves 6

- 3 pounds potatoes
- ¾ pound purple-topped turnip roots
- ½ cup sour cream
- 6 tablespoons unsalted butter, softened
- ¼ cup green onions, minced
- Salt and freshly ground black pepper, to taste
- ¼ teaspoon Hungarian paprika

Additional:
- ½ cup sour cream
- 1 tablespoon green onions, minced

Place potatoes in a large saucepan and cover with water. Bring to boil, cover and reduce heat to simmer. Cook potatoes 25-30 minutes or until tender. Transfer to a bowl and set aside. In same saucepan, place turnip roots and cover with water. Bring to a boil, cover and reduce heat to simmer. Cook turnips 25-30 minutes or until tender. Preheat oven 350 degrees. Peel potatoes and turnips and purée, using a ricer or food mill, into a large bowl - don't try using a food processor or mixture will become pasty. Mix in sour cream, butter, green onions, salt, pepper and paprika. Transfer mixture to a buttered 1 quart baking dish. Make a well in center of mixture, leaving a 1 inch rim. Bake for 15 minutes. In a small bowl, combine sour cream and green onions. Spread in well and bake an additional 10 minutes and serve.

SAUTÉED SPINACH WITH GARLIC

Serves 4

- 4-6 large cloves of garlic, sliced thin
- 1-2 tablespoons olive oil
- 1-10 ounce bag of spinach
- Salt to taste

Heat a large skillet over medium heat. Sauté garlic until lightly brown, stirring frequently. Add spinach, using tongs to stir and turn spinach. Add salt and remove spinach from heat as soon as it begins to wilt. Serve at once.

STRING BEANS WITH NEW POTATOES AND HAM HOCK

*T*he older varieties of beans had a gen-u-wine string along the edge that had to be removed before cooking. In today's beans the strings are more tender and the beans are easily snapped. We usually add new potatoes, with the red skin left on, since they get to the market about the same time.

Serves 4-6

2 pounds green pole beans
1 pound smoked ham hocks, cut in fourths
½ teaspoon sugar
2 pounds new potatoes
1½ quarts water
Salt to taste

Snap ends off green beans, remove strings and snap into 1 inch pieces. Bring water and ham hocks to a boil, cover and reduce heat to simmer. Cook for 1 hour. Add green beans, sugar and potatoes and cook 30-45 minutes. Remove ham hocks from pot, cool, shred meat and return to beans. Add salt if needed. Flavor improves if cooked and allowed to sit. Reheat when ready to serve.

FRESH ENGLISH PEAS

*T*he best deterrent to rabbits in the pea patch is a .410 shotgun. If this is not your style, sometimes aluminum pie pans attached to the plants will help save the English peas from the rabbits.

Fresh English peas from the spring garden are nothing like canned or frozen peas. When buying fresh English peas test for freshness by rubbing two stiff and crisp pods together, they will squeak if fresh.

Serves 4-6

4 cups fresh English peas
2 tablespoons bacon drippings, or butter
Salt to taste
½ teaspoon sugar
2 teaspoons cornmeal

Place peas in a large saucepan and cover with a half inch of water. Bring to a boil, cover and reduce heat to low. Cook 25-30 minutes, or until peas are tender. Add bacon drippings, salt, and sugar. Cook 2-3 minutes, sprinkle cornmeal over peas and stir. Taste, correct seasoning and serve.

FLORIDA CRACKER HASHBROWN CASSEROLE

Some of Florida's early settlers were cowhands who tended large herds of Spanish cattle. These cowhands used long whips to control the cows. The cow hunters became known as crackers because of the sound their whips made. The cows became known as cracker cows. Later Floridians living in rural areas were called Florida Crackers. Their homes, typically wooden dog trots with tin roofs, are called cracker houses.

Serves 10

26 ounces of russet potatoes, grated or one 26 ounce package frozen hashbrown potatoes, thawed
2 cups Colby cheese, shredded
½ cup onion, minced
1 cup milk

12 saltine crackers, crumbled
½ cup beef broth
2 tablespoons butter, melted
Dash garlic powder
1 teaspoon salt
¼ teaspoon black pepper

Preheat oven 425 degrees. Toss hashbrowns and onions in a large bowl. Combine milk, broth, half the butter, salt and pepper in another bowl, mix well and pour over hashbrowns and crackers. Heat remaining butter in a large skillet. Spoon in mixture and cook until cheese has melted, about 8 minutes. Put skillet in oven and bake 45-50 minutes or until dark brown.

FRIED ZUCCHINI

Serves 10

1 packet of yeast
1¼ cups warm water
½ teaspoon salt
1 cup Parmesan cheese, freshly grated

1½ cups all-purpose flour
4-5 zucchini
Vegetable oil for deep frying
2 lemons, cut into wedges

Dissolve the yeast in the warm water, stir to make sure it all melts. Add the salt and slowly stir, sprinkle in the flour, stir with a whisk or fork until batter is smooth. Let rise in a warm place for 1 hour or until it has doubled in bulk. Slice zucchini in quarter inch strips removing pulp. Mix the grated cheese into the batter. Lightly coat zucchini with additional flour shaking off the excess. Dip into batter, letting excess drip off and fry in hot vegetable oil until golden brown. Drain on paper towels and serve immediately with lots of lemon wedges.

RUTABAGA AND WILD WATERCRESS

Wild watercress can be found along some of the fresh water streams in North Florida. It is excellent in salads, ham sandwiches or mixed with rutabagas.

Serves 4

- 1 pound rutabaga
- 1 cup watercress leaves, firmly packed
- 2 tablespoons unsalted butter
- ½ teaspoon sugar
- Salt and freshly ground black pepper, to taste
- ⅛ teaspoon nutmeg, freshly grated
- ¼ cup whipping cream

Preheat oven 350 degrees. Peel rutabaga and cut into chunks. Place in a vegetable steamer with 1 inch water and steam for 30 minutes or until tender. Remove and place in food processor with steel blade. Add watercress to small pan of boiling water and blanch until wilted. Drain in a sieve, refresh under running water and squeeze dry. Add to processor with butter, sugar, cream, salt, pepper and nutmeg. Process until blended and smooth. Check for additional seasoning. Remove to buttered baking dish, bake for 10 minutes to reheat and serve with any wild game and Dirty Rice (see page 290).

SKILLET RED CABBAGE

This dish goes great with wild game and adds a lot of color to the plate.

Serves 6

- 1 medium head red cabbage, thinly sliced
- 1 cup onion, thinly sliced
- 4 tablespoons butter
- 3 tablespoons apple cider vinegar
- Salt and freshly ground black pepper
- 2 slices of crumbled bacon
- 1 tablespoon parsley, chopped

Grading cabbages, Elkton, c 1950's.

Prepare cabbage and onions, set aside. Melt butter over medium-low heat in a large cast-iron skillet. Cook onions until translucent. Add cabbage and toss, cook 3-4 minutes stirring occasionally. Add vinegar and salt and pepper to taste. Sprinkle with bacon, parsley and serve.

ZUCCHINI WITH SPINACH

Serves 4

3 medium zucchini
Salt to taste
3 green onions, chopped
1 tablespoon butter
½ tablespoon olive oil
1 cup cooked, chopped spinach, squeezed dry
Freshly ground black pepper

Cut ends off zucchini. Grate zucchini and place in a strainer. Sprinkle with salt and toss and let drain 15 minutes. Heat butter and olive oil in skillet. When butter has melted add the green onions. Cook stirring until limp, squeeze the juices out of zucchini and add to the skillet. Toss with a fork, cook 1-2 minutes and add the spinach continuing to toss for 1-2 minutes. Taste for seasoning adding additional salt if needed and pepper to taste.

MATCH-STICK VEGETABLES

Serves 4

3 zucchini
3 yellow squash
3 carrots
1 medium onion
1 tablespoon olive oil
1 tablespoon unsalted butter
2 teaspoons Creole Seasoning

Cut ends off zucchini and yellow squash. Peel skin with some of the white into a fourth-a half inch thick slices. Stack and cut into match-stick size pieces. Peel carrots with a vegetable peeler, stack and slice length-wise and cut into match-stick size pieces. Peel onion and cut in half, slice thin. Heat oil and butter over medium heat, when butter melts add the onions and sauté until slightly limp. Stir in the zucchini, squash and carrots. Cook 3-4 minutes and sprinkle with Creole Seasoning (see page 181) mix stirring to distribute. Serve at once.

SAUTÉED BROCCOLI

Serves 4

2 pounds broccoli
Salt to taste
1 tablespoon olive oil
3 green onions, chopped
2 cloves garlic, chopped

Wash broccoli and cut off florets. Steam broccoli for 10-15 minutes or until barely tender. Drain thoroughly and salt lightly. Heat olive oil in a large skillet over medium heat, add green onions and garlic and sauté until onions are limp. Add broccoli and cook 3 minutes, stirring occasionally. Serve immediately.

SPINACH TIMBALES

Serves 2

- 2 tablespoons unsalted butter
- 3 tablespoons plain flour
- 1-10 ounce package frozen chopped spinach, thawed
- ¼ cup sour cream
- ⅛ teaspoon nutmeg, freshly grated
- Salt and pepper, to taste
- 2 egg yolks, lightly beaten
- Butter for molds

Heat skillet over medium-low heat, add butter, when melted sprinkle in flour, whisking constantly. Cook for 3 minutes. Squeeze liquid out of spinach and stir into roux. Add sour cream and salt, pepper and nutmeg, stirring until incorporated. Transfer to a bowl and let cool. Stir in egg yolks, and divide mixture between two buttered 4 ounce timbale molds. Set molds in a small baking pan and pour enough water hot water into the pan to reach halfway up the sides. Cover the pan with foil and bake in a preheated 325 degree oven for 20 minutes. Remove molds from pan and let it set 5 minutes. Run a thin knife around edge of molds and invert onto serving plates.

SMOTHERED CUCUMBERS

Serves 4

- 6 cucumbers
- 1 tablespoon salt
- ¼ cup butter plus 1 tablespoon
- Freshly ground black pepper, to taste
- 1 teaspoon fresh dill, snipped

Peel, halve lengthwise and seed cucumbers. Cut into a half inch slices and place in a bowl. Sprinkle with salt and let sit 30 minutes. Drain cucumbers in a colander and pat dry with paper towels. In a saucepan melt the one-fourth cup of butter over low heat. Add the cucumbers and cover with a buttered round of wax paper and a lid. Cook 10 minutes, or until they are translucent but still crisp. Add remaining tablespoon of butter, sprinkle with pepper and dill and serve at once.

CUCUMBER YOGURT

Serves 4

- 2 cups plain yogurt
- 1 clove garlic, minced
- Salt and pepper, to taste
- Juice of ½ lemon
- 1 large cucumber, peeled, seeded and finely chopped

Place yogurt in a bowl and add the remaining ingredients. Chill in the refrigerator until ready to serve.

SOUTHERN GARDEN VEGETABLES AND SWAMP CABBAGE

SKILLET SQUASH 'N ST. AUGUSTINE SWEETS

St. Augustine Sweet onions are much sweeter than Spanish, white or red onions, and have as much natural sugar as you'd find in an orange.

These onions are grown in the cabbage and potato areas around St. Augustine. Many onion lovers claim they are comparable to the Vidalia and the good news is they get to the market weeks earlier.

Serves 4-6

- 2 pounds yellow crookneck squash, sliced ¼ inch thick
- 2 cups St. Augustine Sweet onions, sliced ¼ inch thick
- 4 tablespoons smoked bacon drippings
- Salt and freshly ground black pepper, to taste

Wash and dry squash, remove ends and slice. Heat a 12 inch cast-iron skillet over medium heat. Add bacon drippings and onions; sauté until onions are light brown. Stir in squash, cover and cook 10 minutes. Stir occasionally, remove cover and season with salt and pepper. Cook uncovered until tender, about 5-6 minutes. Correct seasoning and serve.

BROCCOLI SOUFFLÉ

If you have never tried making a soufflé, try this one. It's easy and delicious. It is especially good with simple meats such as roasted chicken or fried pork chops.

Serves 4-6

- 1½ cups cooked broccoli
- 1 cup white sauce, made with whipping cream
- 3 egg yolks
- Unsalted butter
- 6 ounces extra-sharp Cheddar cheese, grated
- Salt and freshly ground pepper, to taste
- 3 egg whites, beaten stiff

Preheat oven 350 degrees. Place broccoli in food processor and pulse until finely minced. Add broccoli to a large bowl with white sauce (see page 24), egg yolks, cheese, and salt and pepper to taste. Fold in egg whites. Place in a buttered one and one half quart glass baking dish. Bake 30-35 minutes and serve immediately.

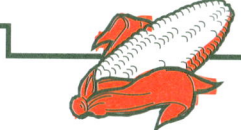

BUTTERMILK FRIED OKRA

*O*nce you begin to nibble and snitch the first batch after it cooks, which our children, my husband and I always do, you can't stop. Everyone plays innocent and wants to know what happened to all the okra by the time we get to the table. Green or slightly ripened, cubed tomatoes and squash can also be fried this way.

Serves 4

1½ pounds okra
1 cup buttermilk
2 cups cornmeal

2 teaspoons salt, or to taste
Peanut oil for deep frying

Wash and cut okra into a half inch slices. Thirty minutes before cooking place the okra in a bowl, add buttermilk and stir to coat. In a large zip-lock bag, mix cornmeal and salt. While oil is heating to 350 degrees, place okra in colander and drain. Place okra in bag with cornmeal and shake until all wet spots are covered with meal. Drop half the okra into hot oil, fry, stir occasionally with a slotted spoon until golden brown and crisp, about 8-10 minutes. Drain on brown paper bags and cook remaining okra. Serve immediately.

SWAMP CABBAGE DELUXE

*T*his cracker dish was sometimes "gussied-up" and served at dinner parties. Marjorie Kinnan Rawlings talked about adding "Dora's" (her Jersey milk cow) cream to make it a finer dish and served it for company.

Serves 4

¼ pound smoked bacon
4 cups fresh heart of palm, sliced thin
½ cup water

Salt to taste
½ cup whipping cream
1-2 tablespoons unsalted butter

Place bacon in large cast-skillet and cook over medium-low heat until crisp. Remove and drain on paper towels. Drain all but 2 tablespoons of bacon drippings. Add cabbage and stir. Add water, cover and cook 10 minutes. Remove cover, stir and test cabbage for tenderness. Bring to a boil and reduce until most of the liquid has evaporated. Reduce heat and stir in cream and butter. Heat through, correct seasoning and place in serving bowl. Crumble bacon, sprinkle over cabbage and serve.

RAYMOND GUNN'S SWAMP CABBAGE STEW

*T*he first time we enjoyed this dish was at a family gathering. It was brought by a niece's boy friend. When we asked for the recipe, his Mother sent us the following:

"This recipe is from the kitchen of Raymond Gunn (my Father). Best eaten with fish and hush puppies. Good with venison too. Some of the best times I can remember with my Dad was when we went fishing and had a cook out. He always cooked the swamp cabbage and no one could cook it as good as he did. I always watched everything he put in it, because I knew one day I wanted to be able to make it as good as he did. I was about 25 when my Dad was killed, so I was glad that I had learned how to make it.

I hope you enjoy it as much as my family has enjoyed it."

Peggy Browning

Serves 4-6

2-3 swamp cabbage
4-5 pieces bacon
Enough water to cover cabbage
1 teaspoon sugar

Salt and freshly ground black pepper, to taste
16 ounce can tomatoes

Cut and wash cabbage. Brown bacon in a large saucepan over medium-low heat. Put in cabbage and water. Add sugar, salt, and pepper. Cook about 5 minutes on high heat. Add tomatoes, and reduce heat to medium-low, cook 25-30 minutes or until tender.

Note: Raymond Gunn was from Perry where the cooking of fried mullet has been taken to a form of art. However the local custom of serving Guava jelly with the hush puppies hasn't caught on in the rest of North Florida.

Desserts and Sweet Thangs

Tea party, c 1880.

The Chocolate Cake, 330
Robert E. Lee Cake, 331
The King's Favorite Cake, 332
The Queen's Lemon
  Cheese Cake, 333
Lafayette Grill Cake, 334
Johnny's Feud Cake, 335
Jimmy's Sponge Cake, 335
Prize Winning Peanut Cake, 336
Peach Upside Down Cake, 337
Strawberry Short Cake, 338
Almond Cakes, 339
Fig Preserve Cake, 339
White Fruit Cake, 340
Key Lime Cheesecake, 341
Amaretto Cheesecake, 341
Black Forrest Cheesecake, 342
Peanut Butter Pie, 342
Watkins Coconut Pie, 343
Buttermilk Pie, 344
Blackberry Pie, 344
Black Bottom Pie, 345
Southern Pecan Pie, 346

Mocha Pecan Pie, 346
Pecan Sweet Potato Pie, 346
Sweetie Pie, 347
Sweet Potato Pie, 348
Pinto Bean Pie, 348
Spanish Bakery Sweet
  Potato Turnovers, 349
Granny Smith's Apple Pie, 349
Fresh Pumpkin Pie, 350
Strawberry Pie, 350
Mandarin Orange Pie, 351
Florida Key Lime Pie, 352
Jeff Davis Pie, 352
Scuppernong Pie, 353
Cherry-O-Pie, 353
Bartlett Pear Pie, 354
Lemon Meringue Pie, 354
Tawee's Chocolate Pie, 355
Chocolate Ice Box Pie, 355
Sisters Fabulous Fudge, 356
Molten Lava Cakes, 356
Fudgy Brownies, 357
Fresh Fruit Tart, 358

Apple Torte, 359
Libby Love's Pie Berry, 360
Terre's Dewberry Cobbler, 361
Lazy Day Fruit Cobbler, 362
Miss Lilly's Whiskey Cakes, 363
Apricot Scones, 363
Creamy Rice Pudding, 364
Butterscotch Pudding, 364
Granny's Banana Pudding, 365
Bread Pudding, 366
Old-Timey Charlotte, 366
Tupelo Panna Cotta, 367
Silky Smooth Flan, 367
Hospitality Pineapple Fluff, 368
Lemon Squares, 368
Pecan Pralines, 369
Hickory Nut Cakes, 369
Secret Oatmeal Cookies, 370
Grayton Sand Tarts, 370
Dessert Crepes, 371
Vanilla Ice Cream, 372
Fruit Sorbets, 373
Scottish Trifle, 374

DESSERTS AND SWEET THANGS

One of our first seasonal sweets to arrive in the spring are luscious strawberries. We enjoy them as we are picking and then later with shortcake and chantilly cream.

Dewberries signal the first of summer when barefoot weather is official. Blackberries and blueberries are ripe soon after and are enjoyed in all sorts of desserts. Juicy peaches are next, followed by cantaloupes, watermelon, and honeydews, and later pears and scuppernongs. Falls bountiful harvest includes sweet potatoes, persimmons and pumpkins for our traditional pies as well as an assortment of luscious pears to enjoy in puddings, pies and cakes. Winter is the time to sit around the fireplace and shell the peanuts and pecans harvested in the fall. These popular nuts will later appear in a variety of cakes, candies and the infamous sinful Southern pecan pie.

Many fond memories come from the numerous church socials, dinners on the ground and family reunions we enjoyed during our childhood, where the main attraction was food. Each family brought their special dishes and it looked like a roll call of the most choice Southern delicacies. The food was spread out on very long tables to be shared with everyone. There were the usual meats and vegetables, but the highlight of the affair was the dessert table.

It seemed each cook had a specialty that would appear each time we congregated. One lady would be known for her egg custards, another for her sinful chocolate cake, and the list went, thankfully, on and on.

If you had small, thin slices of cake or small spoonfuls of puddings, it was permitted to try several desserts at one time. We always made a point to brag on each of our favorite desserts because they were really delicious and we hoped they would reappear at the next dinner on the ground. Of course in those days, we didn't worry about fat or calories.

The biggest problems in those days in keeping desserts (besides relatives) were the ants and house flies. Insects have always been a major concern to North Florida cooks as evidenced in Marjorie Kinnan Rawlings story of "Antses in Tim's Breakfast."

Window screens and pie safes were the first line of defense from the house flies but some would always slip in and appear just when the food was placed on the table. After the meal, dishes were washed and clean dinner plates were returned to the table and turned upside down. Leftover food was covered with a tablecloth until the next meal. Then the flies were chased with a fly flap (swatter) until justice was done. But those tactics didn't stop the pesky little ants as they marched single file towards the desserts. "Head them off at the pass and build a moat" was accomplished by placing a jar lid under each leg of the dining table and filling with liquid. This usually stopped the invasion, at least until the liquid evaporated.

Another method was to soak a string in some kerosene and tie this around each table leg. Of course, the smell of kerosene didn't do much to enhance the flavor of the next meal.

Our favorite dessert we serve nowadays is our many-layered choco-

late cake. It began as a seven layer cake years ago and then the number of layers began to grow. Last Christmas, we were enjoying a get-together with my husband's family when our Aunt Carolyn walked in and presented him with a seventeen layer chocolate cake. Nobody has topped that one.

We now celebrate holidays at the big house on Circle Drive. One of the reasons we all like it is because of all the nooks and crannies that can serve as hiding places. Since we often have 40-50 relatives and friends at each gathering, desserts disappear in the blink of an eye. Several of my sisters have taken to hiding chunks of cake, whole pies, dozens of cookies or several pieces of fudge. Since each sister knows all the hiding places, it's a real challenge to stay ahead.

We have many fond memories of growing up in a small town. The security we all took for granted has given me an appreciation of the simplicity and peace we all seek today. We were blessed. Being raised in the hustle and bustle, of a large family of ten, could have been a nightmare. But our household was run with such grace that instead our childhood was full of positive attitudes, personal responsibility, respect and dignity. It didn't matter what you wanted to be. Just be the best you could.

One of my fondest memories was Wendolcoski"s, a small neighborhood grocery store three blocks from our house where they sold all the treats a small child could imagine, candy, ice cream, cookies and soft drinks. Mrs. Wendolcoski was always positioned behind the long glass counter where she sold penny candy. It didn't matter if you had two pennies or a whole dime she would get the small brown paper bag and walk up and down as you pointed and told her, "One of these, two of those and one of those. Sometimes there would be a new candy, nice Mrs. Wendolcoski would always let you change your mind and try the new one.

One day after we completed our chores Daddy gave me two dimes to purchase 4 boxes of Cracker Jacks to share with my siblings. I remember making sure the money was deep into my pocket so I wouldn't loose it. About half way there I reached in the pocket to make sure it was still there—-no money. I cried all the way to my grandparents' house which just happened to be on the way to the store. Granddaddy was standing on the porch and I told him my tale of woe. He reached into his pocket and handed me two more dimes to calm me. When I got to the store, I put the Cracker Jacks by the cash register and reached in my pocket for the the dimes to pay Mrs.Wendolcoski and found 4 dimes. Oh Lordy! It looks like we will be sharing 8 boxes of Cracker Jacks!

THE CHOCOLATE CAKE

*I*f I ever make it to heaven, this cake will be there waiting. The cake part has a buttermilky tang which is perfectly matched by smooth chocolate icing. It's infamous in our family always requested, and the first dessert to be snapped up.

If you're feeling like you need to show off a little, try making very thin layers—you'll end up with a beautifully layered cake with narrow, flavorful stripes. Six or seven layers are a minimum, but we've made it up to eighteen layers a few glorious times.

The first time you make this cake, keep a few toothpicks handy, just in case.

1 cup buttermilk, room temperature
½ teaspoon soda
1 cup unsalted butter
2 cups sugar

4 eggs, room temperature
1 teaspoon vanilla
¼ teaspoon salt
3 cups all-purpose flour

Preheat oven to 350 degrees. Cut rounds of wax paper to fit bottom of 8 inch cake pans. Butter sides and bottom of pans before putting wax paper in. Add soda to buttermilk in medium bowl, stir to dissolve soda and set aside. In a large bowl, cream butter and sugar until fluffy. Add eggs, one at a time and beat after each addition, blend in vanilla and salt. Add the flour in batches, alternating with buttermilk and ending with flour. Spoon a half to three-fourths cup of batter into prepared cake pans, using a half cup of batter if you want thinner layers, smoothing batter to edges of pan. Bake 10-12 minutes or until cake pulls away slightly from edge of pan.

Chocolate Icing

½ cup unsalted butter
½ cup cocoa
2 cups sugar

5 ounce can evaporated milk
1 teaspoon vanilla
Dash salt

In a heavy bottomed boiler, melt butter over very low heat, not allowing butter to brown. Add cocoa and sugar, and mix. Stir in milk, bring to a boil over medium heat. Cook, stirring, for three minutes. Remove from heat and add vanilla and salt. As cake layers are baked, remove from oven and pans. Ice between each layer with 4-5 tablespoons of icing, let icing drizzle down sides.

ROBERT E. LEE CAKE

Better than the "Better Than Sex Cake"

There is a shortcut version of this cake making the rounds in the South called "Better Than Sex Cake." It calls for yellow cake mix, instant pudding, crushed pineapple and such. Now we aren't saying our cake is better than sex mind you. But it is better than kissing your sister.

Cake:

- Two 9 inch cake pans, buttered and floured
- 8 eggs, separated, at room temperature
- 2 teaspoons grated lemon zest
- 2 tablespoon lemon juice
- 2 cups flour
- ½ teaspoon salt
- 2 cups sugar

Preheat oven 325 degrees. Beat egg yolks until they are very light and lemon colored. Slowly add the sugar while continuing to beat until the yolks are quite thick and tripled in volume. Beat in the lemon zest and juice. Sift the flour and salt together. Sprinkle the flour over the egg yolks and fold lightly until smooth. Beat the egg whites until stiff and fold in. Divide the batter between the cake pans. Bake for 25-30 minutes, or until the layers are golden brown and slightly pulled away from the sides. Remove to a rack and cool 10 minutes before turning out. Refrigerate overnight.

Filling:

- 1 orange and 2 lemons, zested
- 4 egg yolks
- ¾ cup sugar
- Juice of 1 orange and 2 lemons
- Pinch salt
- 6 tablespoons butter

Beat the egg yolks with the sugar, lemon zest and juice, and salt. Place over simmering water and stir constantly until thickened. Remove from heat and beat in the butter a tablespoon at the time. Refrigerate until cool.

Frosting:

- 1½ cups heavy cream
- 6 tablespoons powdered sugar
- 1 tablespoon orange flower water
- 1 cup fresh coconut

Add the heavy cream, powdered sugar, and orange flower water to a large mixing bowl. Beat with an electric mixer until peaks form. Beat in coconut. Slice cake layers so that you have four layers. Spread filling between layers. Ice with frosting. Keep the cake refrigerated.

DESSERTS AND SWEET THANGS

THE KING'S FAVORITE CAKE
"Laudy Miss Claudy"

The name pound cake originated from the ingredients: a pound each of flour, butter, sugar and eggs. Everyone has a favorite pound cake recipe and several versions always appear at our gatherings. Unfortunately, sometimes these cakes can be very dry and bland. Our version is one of the most moist we have found and we like to take it to any gathering because of the bragging rights.

We aren't sure this was actually the King's Favorite Pound Cake, but if he shows up at the Tastee Freeze we'll ask him.

- 1 cup unsalted butter, room temperature
- 3 cups sugar
- 7 eggs, room temperature
- 3 cups all-purpose flour, sifted twice
- 1 cup whipping cream
- 2 teaspoons vanilla extract

Butter and lightly flour a tube pan, shaking out the excess flour. Cream butter and sugar with an electric mixer until creamy and light, about 5 minutes. Add eggs, one at the time, beating well after each addition. Mix in half the flour, whipping cream then remaining flour. Beat 5 full minutes and add the vanilla mixing thoroughly. Pour batter into buttered and floured tube pan. Set in cold oven and turn heat to 350 degrees. Bake 60-70 minutes, or until a sharp knife inserted in center comes out clean. Remove cake from oven and cool in pan 5 minutes before turning out.

The King

STRAWBERRY TOPPING
- 2 pints strawberries, hulled and quartered
- ½ cup sugar
- ¼ cup orange juice

Place strawberries in a bowl, sprinkle with sugar and pour orange juice over all. Stir gently and let the mixture sit at room temperature for 30 minutes. Spoon over freshly baked cake and place a large dollop of Chantilly Sauce (see page 337) on top.

DESSERTS AND SWEET THANGS

THE QUEEN'S LEMON CHEESE CAKE

This cake has no cheese. It has been popular in the South for as long as we can remember. This version has thick layers, so we cut them in half horizontally and cover them with the delicious lemony icing.

This sister is very special to everyone in the family. She's gracious with a depth of understanding that translates into peace for others.

Queen Elizabeth

¾ cup Crisco
¾ cup unsalted butter, softened
3 cups sugar
4½ cups all-purpose flour
6 teaspoons baking powder
1½ teaspoons salt

1 cup milk
1 cup water
1 teaspoon almond extract
2 teaspoons vanilla extract
9 egg whites, room temperature, beaten stiff

Preheat oven 350 degrees. Sift flour and measure. Add baking powder, salt and sift three more times. Cream Crisco, butter and sugar until light and fluffy. Mix milk and water together. Add flour mixture alternately with milk mixture. Stir in almond and vanilla extracts. Fold in egg whites. Pour into 3 greased and floured 9 inch cake pans. Bake 30-35 minutes or until toothpick inserted in center of cake comes out clean. Cool cake and slice each layer in half horizontally to make six layers.

Icing

2¼ cups sugar
9 tablespoons cornstarch
¾ teaspoon salt

3¾ cups water
¾ cup lemon juice
13 egg yolks, beaten lightly

In top of a double boiler, combine sugar, cornstarch, and salt. Slowly add water and lemon juice to sugar mixture, stir constantly until mixture thickens and boils. Blend 1 cup of hot mixture into beaten egg yolks, then add to remaining mixture in boiler. Cook 1 minute, stirring constantly. Cool and spread between layers, top and sides.

LAFAYETTE GRILL CAKE

This cake supposedly originated at the Lafayette Grill, once located in the same building as the Seminole Club in downtown Jacksonville. My husband always asks for this cake on his birthday, he says it helps make growing old a little easier to take.

CAKE:
- 4 ounces unsweetened baking chocolate
- ½ cup unsalted butter
- 1 cup boiling water
- ½ cup sour cream
- 1½ teaspoons soda
- 2 cups sugar
- ¼ teaspoon salt
- 2 eggs
- 2 cups all-purpose flour

Preheat oven 350 degrees. Melt chocolate and butter in a small saucepan over low heat. When melted, pour into a large mixing bowl. Add boiling water, sour cream, soda, sugar and salt. Blend in flour and eggs, one at a time. Pour batter in 2 - 8 inch cake pans, buttered and lined with wax paper. Bake 25-30 minutes, remove from pans and cool to room temperature. Wrap cake layers in wax paper and refrigerate four hours or until chilled.

CHOCOLATE FILLING:
- 2 ounces unsweetened baking chocolate
- 1½ cups warm milk
- 1 cup sugar
- ⅓ cup all-purpose flour
- 2 egg yolks
- 2 tablespoons unsalted butter
- 1 teaspoon vanilla

Melt chocolate and milk in top of double boiler. Mix sugar and flour together and whisk into milk mixture until thickened, about 15 minutes. Beat egg yolks, pour some of custard into yolks and mix. Add yolks to boiler and mix with a wooden spoon. Cook custard until very thick. Remove from heat and add butter and vanilla. Pour custard into glass dish and place plastic wrap directly on top to keep film from forming. Refrigerate and chill four hours.

ICING:
- 1½ cups whipping cream
- 6 tablespoons powdered sugar
- ⅛ teaspoon Cream of Tartar

Place cream, sugar, and cream of tartar in chilled bowl. Beat with egg beater until firm peaks form.

TO ASSEMBLE CAKE:
Remove cake and custard from refrigerator. Slice each cake layer horizontally so that you will have 4 layers. Place chilled chocolate filling between each layer. Ice top and sides of cake with whipped cream. Cover with cake dome and refrigerate.

JOHNNY'S FEUD CAKE

*T*his delicious cake was made popular at the Seven Seas Restaurant in Panama City in the early 50's. When Johnny Patronis and his brother Jimmy, left the Seven Seas to take over Captain Anderson's Restaurant on Grand Lagoon they brought the cake recipe with them and thus continued the tradition.

Like many of our recipes, it seems to be a variation of a European dish, probably an almond cake of Italian origin. We particularly like it because it utilizes the residual pecan pieces and dust we have after chopping pecans for other dishes. If pecan meal is not available locally, make it in the food processor.

3 cups pecan meal
6 eggs, separated
1½ cups sugar
2½ tablespoons all-purpose flour
1 teaspoon baking powder

1½ pints whipping cream
1 teaspoon vanilla
⅓ cup powdered sugar
½ cup roasted pecans, finely chopped

Preheat oven 350 degrees. Butter two 9-inch cake pans. Cut wax paper to fit the bottom of each. Beat egg yolks until fluffy. Gradually add sugar, beating constantly. Add flour, baking powder and ground pecans. Beat egg whites until stiff and fold into batter. Pour batter into prepared cake pans and bake 25-30 minutes. Remove to racks to cool, then remove cake from the pans. Whip cream with vanilla and sugar. Ice between cake layers, top and sides. Sprinkle top with roasted pecans (see page 62), chopped. Keep cake covered with cake dome in the refrigerator.

JIMMY'S SPONGE CAKE

"Living on sponge cake, watchin' the sun bake"

6 jumbo or large eggs (room temperature)
1 cup sugar

1 cup sifted flour
1 teaspoon vanilla extract
Pinch of salt

Preheat oven to 350 degrees. Beat eggs, sugar, vanilla and salt in a large bowl on high speed until thick, about 5 minutes. Fold in flour until completely blended. Spoon into 2- 8 inch buttered wax paper lined cake pans and bake about 20 minutes. Cool 10 minutes in pans, then invert onto wire racks to cool completely. Remove wax paper and refrigerate until chilled.

PRIZE WINNING PEANUT CAKE

If I knowed you was a coming I'd a baked a cake.

As the boll weevil devastated cotton crops throughout the Southern states, farmers increasingly turned to peanuts as a cash crop. Today, Northwest Florida produces more than half of all peanuts grown in the state.

This old family recipe was created by our Granny and won a prize years ago at a Peanut Festival in Dothan, Alabama. But Granny didn't win it—a cousin had copied the recipe and submitted it for the prize.

---

1 cup unsalted butter
2 cups sugar
3 cups all-purpose flour
4 eggs
1 teaspoon baking powder
½ teaspoon salt
1 teaspoon vanilla
1 cup buttermilk

Preheat oven 350 degrees. Butter four 8 inch cake pans and cut wax paper to fit the bottom. Cream butter and sugar, add eggs, one at a time, beating after each addition. Add half the flour, baking powder, salt, vanilla and buttermilk. Add remaining flour and mix thoroughly. Bake 25-30 minutes. Cool before layering with icing.

We don't know who made the peanut more famous, George Washington Carver or Jimmy Carter. Early farmers called them ground nuts and goober peas.

Peanuts are harvested in the late summer so we get to enjoy the combination of boiled peanuts and scuppernongs as Dog Days of summer fade and cool fall arrives.

Peanut Cake Icing

---

2 pounds peanuts, shelled (4 cups)
2 cups sugar
1 cup evaporated milk
½ teaspoon salt

Parch peanuts in 300 degree oven about 20 minutes, turning frequently to avoid scorching. Cool nuts, remove skins and place in food processor. Process until finely ground. In medium sized boiler with heavy bottom, combine milk and sugar over medium heat and let mixture come to a boil, and boil 5 minutes. Reduce heat to low, add parched ground peanuts and salt. Cook until mixture has thickened and is the right consistency to be spread. Remove from heat and spread between cake layers, icing top and sides.

PEACH UPSIDE DOWN CAKE

In 1539, Hernando de Soto found peach trees growing around Indian villages. With the settlement of St. Augustine in 1565, the new colonists planted peach orchards. Persian and Spanish strains were favored.

Years ago, just about every home around rural North Florida had a peach tree planted somewhere close to the house. We're not sure whether they were planted for the fruit or the switches which were always so handy and kept many a wayward child on a straight and narrow path.

Older peach varieties had a lot of problems with bugs and diseases. Several new varieties have been developed for our climate and are grown commercially in some North Florida counties. They ripen early and bring top dollar at the market.

- 2½ cups fresh peach slices
- 1 cup unsalted butter
- 1 cup brown sugar
- 2 tablespoons light corn syrup
- 14 pecan halves
- ½ cup pecans, chopped
- 1 cup white sugar
- 2 cups all-purpose flour
- 1 teaspoon grated lemon rind
- 1½ teaspoon ground ginger
- ½ teaspoon nutmeg, freshly ground
- 1 teaspoon baking soda
- ¾ teaspoon salt
- ½ cup molasses
- ½ cup boiling water
- 2 eggs

Melt one half cup of butter in a 10 inch cast-iron skillet. Add brown sugar and corn syrup, stir over medium heat until blended, remove from heat and allow to cool. Arrange peach slices on top and dot with pecan halves. Sprinkle with chopped pecans. Cream a half cup of butter with 1 cup of white sugar until fluffy. Sift flour, ginger, nutmeg, soda, and salt together. In a separate bowl, mix molasses and boiling water. Add eggs, one at the time to the creamed butter and sugar. Stir in the grated lemon rind, add the dry ingredients alternating with the molasses mixture. Spread evenly over the peaches and bake for 1 hour and twenty-thirty minutes. Cool a little. Loosen sides with a spatula and turn out onto platter. Serve hot or cold with Chantilly cream.

CHANTILLY CREAM SAUCE

Makes about 2 cups

Add 1 cup heavy cream, 1 teaspoon vanilla, and 2 teaspoons Grand Marnier to chilled bowl and beat at medium high speed for 1 minute. Add a third cup sugar and continue to beat until soft peaks form - about 3 minutes. Add an eighth teaspoon cream of tartar and continue to beat until peaks form.

STRAWBERRY SHORTCAKE

*T*here is a strawberry u-pick-em patch located north of DeFuniak Springs called "The Berry Patch" they charge by the pound for the berries you pick. My husband, brother-in-law, Jan and brother Ingram hurry up there as soon as they open in the spring. When they brought their buckets in to be weighed, their lips and tongues were as red as a foxes behind at blackberry time. The owner told them that if they came back again he was going to weigh them before and after they picked and charge accordingly.

Makes 20-24 shortcakes

- 4 cups all-purpose flour
- ½ cup sugar plus 1½ tablespoons
- 5 teaspoons baking powder
- 2 teaspoons salt
- ¾ cup unsalted butter (chilled and cut into bits)
- 1 teaspoon lemon zest
- ½ cup whipping cream
- 1 cup half and half
- 1½ tablespoons melted butter
- 1 tablespoon Créme de Cassis
- 2 pints strawberries
- Chantilly Sauce

Preheat oven 350 degrees. In a large bowl, sift the flour, a half cup of the sugar, baking powder and salt together. Cut butter in with a pastry blender until mixture resembles meal. Add grated lemon rind, cream, half and half and mix until a soft dough forms. Place on a lightly floured work surface and knead for a minute. Roll out dough to thickness of three-fourths inch. Use a 3 inch cookie cutter and cut 20 circles. Gather remaining dough, roll and cut 4 more circles. Place on cookie sheet lined with parchment paper. Brush tops with melted butter and sprinkle with remaining sugar. Bake in the center of the oven 15 minutes or until lightly browned and cooked through, transfer to a rack and cool. Slice half the strawberries, reserving most attractive ones, and sprinkle with Cream de Cassis. Cut the cooled shortcakes in half and spread bottoms with some of the Chantilly Sauce (see page 337), berries and juice. Gently place shortcake tops over. Spoon Chantilly Sauce over and garnish with remaining whole berries and juice.

Elizabeth Gray Wright, picking strawberries in the Berry Patch, c 2001.

ALMOND CAKES

Makes 30

⅔ cup plus 30 whole
   blanched almonds
½ cup plus 1 tablespoon sugar
2 eggs, separated
½ teaspoon vanilla

2 drops almond extract
1 tablespoon orange flavor water
1 tablespoon Amaretto
¼ cup flour
Butter

Place almonds and 1 tablespoon sugar in a food processor and grind until a fine powder. In a bowl combine the ground almonds with the remaining sugar, egg yolks, vanilla, almond extract, orange flavor water, and amaretto. Stir with a rubber spatula until homogenous and soft. Divide into 30 pieces and roll into balls; roll lightly in flour. Place on a buttered cookie sheet, press lightly on each to make indention, and brush lightly with beaten egg white. Press an almond on each indention. Leave, uncovered at room temperature, for 2 hours. Preheat oven to 440 degrees. Bake 5-7 minutes, until done.

FIG PRESERVE CAKE

The late Ann Manning Barnes of Ponce deLeon was one of the best Southern cooks we have had the pleasure of knowing. Her Smothered Fried Quail would melt in your mouth. When we asked in 1994 if she had any recipes we could include in *Seasonal Florida* she replied, she only cooked country food and had nothing fancy enough for a cookbook.

Recently we were thumbing through *New Leaves From An Old Town* published by the Collard Festival folks around Ponce deLeon, we stumbled on Aunt Ann's recipe for the Fig Preserve Cake. Fancy enough for our cookbook.

3 eggs
2 cups sugar
1 cup Crisco oil
1 cup fig preserves
2 cups all-purpose flour

1 cup buttermilk
2 cups pecans, chopped
1 teaspoon each: salt, soda,
   cloves, cinnamon, vanilla

On high speed, beat eggs, and slowly add sugar. Beat until fluffy. Sift flour and all the dry ingredients. Add to egg mixture alternating with the buttermilk. Add the vanilla, pecans and figs. Mix well. Bake 350 degrees for 50 minutes.

Sauce
1½ cups sugar
1 stick salted butter

½ teaspoon soda
½ cup buttermilk
1 tablespoon Karo syrup

Add all ingredients to a one and one half quart heavy-bottom pot. Bring to a boil, stirring constantly. Reduce heat and cook for 3 full minutes. Slowly pour over cake.

WHITE FRUIT CAKE

My husband contends there is only one fruit cake in the world , and at Christmas it gets passed from family, to family to family... The fruit cakes of my Mothers era were dark and spicy, chock full of fruits and nuts, laced with rum and whiskey and covered with those red and green citrons. Definitely an acquired taste.

Then in 1898 a new cake was created by Emma Lane of Clayton, Alabama. It was quickly adopted by most of the cake ladies at the church and the Lane cake reined for many years, although the recipe called for a cup of whiskey.

Later the Japanese fruit cake appeared on the scene. A slight improvement but still not our cup of tea. We have always wondered if this cake actually came from Japan.

Last Christmas we were at the Big House preparing our traditional Christmas breakfast, my sister Carolyn (she's the one if it comes up it comes out) had cooked a big batch of Sawmill Gravy. My sister Tawee (she's the one with the direction) had made two skillets of her perfect biscuits and was strutting around the kitchen like a Banty rooster. Genevieve (she's the true flapper, the one who wears the hats) brought some fresh herb's from her garden. Elizabeth (she's the gentle one) had cooked a big pot of stone-ground grits and was scrambling the double yolk eggs Ingram (he never met a stranger) had dropped off earlier. Then the phone rings and it was my sister Ruby (she's the one who does everything perfectly) she said she was bringing a fruit cake up to the Big House, and we all said, "Don't bother". What a surprise! This "white fruit cake" was a real treat and quickly disappeared. This recipe is a variation of the white fruit cake popular in the Tampa area and now is a Christmas tradition at the Big House.

Makes one 9x5 inch loaf
3½ cups pecans, chopped
8 ounces candied pineapple
8 ounces candied red cherries
4 ounces candied green cherries
4 ounces dates, chopped
¾ cup all-purpose flour, sifted
¾ cup sugar
½ teaspoon baking powder
½ teaspoon salt
3 eggs, slightly beaten
1 teaspoon vanilla

Preheat oven to 300 degrees. Line 9x5 inch loaf pan with buttered waxed paper. Stir together nuts and fruit in large bowl; set aside. Combine dry ingredients. Sprinkle over nut mixture; toss lightly until nuts and fruit are well coated. Blend in eggs and vanilla. Spread into prepared pan. Bake 1 hour and 20 minutes, cover pan with foil the last 30 minutes. Cool completely before removing from pan. Store in air tight container in refrigerator.

KEY LIME CHEESECAKE

Filling:
2½ pounds cream cheese, room temperature
1¾ cups sugar
3 tablespoons all-purpose flour
2 teaspoons grated lime zest
¼ teaspoon vanilla
5 eggs plus 2 egg yolks
½ cup sour cream

Preheat oven 500 degrees.
 In a large bowl cream the cream cheese with an electric mixer on medium speed. Add the sugar, a little at the time, flour, lime zest, and vanilla, and beat well. Add eggs and egg yolks, one at the time, beating lightly after each addition. Add the sour cream and beat lightly. Pour the cheese cake mixture over the Graham cracker crust (p.44), bake for 10 minutes at 500 degrees, reduce heat to 200 degrees, and continue baking for one hour. Cover cake with foil if it begins to brown too much. Refrigerate cheese cake overnight.

Key Lime Topping:
Makes 1½ cups
4 egg yolks
¾ cup sugar
2 teaspoons lime zest
⅓ cup Key lime juice
Pinch of salt
6 tablespoons butter

 Beat egg yolks with the sugar add the salt, lime juice and zest. Place over simmering water and cook stirring constantly until thickened. Remove from heat and stir in the butter, a tablespoon at the time. Remove and strain through a sieve.
Chill for 2 hours and spread over top of cheese cake and refrigerate overnight.

AMARETTO CHEESECAKE

Serves 10-12
2½ cups sliced almonds, toasted
1¼ cups sugar
¼ cup melted butter plus additional for coating pan
4 (8 ounce) packages cream cheese, softened
3 eggs
¼ cup Amaretto

 Butter springform 9 inch pan. Process almonds in a food processor until ground, add ¼ cup sugar and butter and process until blended. Press into the bottom and 1 inch up the sides of pan. Bake 400 degrees for 10 minutes, remove from oven, cool on a wire rack. Reduce oven temperature to 275 degrees. When cool, line the outside of pan with heavy foil. Beat cream cheese and remaining sugar at medium-high speed for 10 minutes. Add eggs. Add amaretto and beat until blended. Spoon into crust, smooth top. Place in a shallow roasting pan and put in oven. Add 1 inch of very hot water to the roasting pan to create a water bath. Bake 275 degrees for 70-75 minutes, or until center appears set when shaken. Remove from oven, cool in pan on a wire rack for 30-45 minutes. Remove foil, cover and chill over night. Remove springform ring and serve.

BLACK FORREST CHEESECAKE

Serves 16

- 1 recipe Cookie Crumb (graham cracker) Crust
- One 21 ounce can cherry pie filling
- 5 packages (8 ounces each) Cream cheese, softened
- 1 cup of sugar
- 1 tablespoon vanilla
- 2 tablespoon Kirsch
- 1 package (8 squares) semi-sweet baking chocolate, melted, slightly cooled
- 1 cup sour cream
- 3 eggs

Preheat oven 325 degrees. Beat cream cheese, sugar, vanilla and kirsch with a mixer on medium speed until well blended. Add melted chocolate and sour cream; mix well. Add the eggs, 1 at the time, mixing on low speed until well blended. Pour half the cream mixture over the crust (see page 44), top with cherry pie filling. Cover with remaining cream cheese batter. Bake 45-50 minutes, or until center is almost set. Cool completely on wire rack. Refrigerate overnight.

PEANUT BUTTER PIE
"Peanut...Peanut Butter"

- 1 - 9 inch pie shell, baked
- 1 cup powdered sugar
- ½ cup plus 2 tablespoons of creamy peanut butter
- 3 egg yolks, beaten, reserve whites for meringue
- ⅔ cup sugar
- ⅛ teaspoon salt
- ¼ cup cornstarch
- 2 cups scalded milk
- ½ teaspoon vanilla

Blend powdered sugar and peanut butter until crumbly; set aside. In top of double boiler, mix egg yolks, sugar, salt and cornstarch. Whisk in milk and set boiler over simmering water. Cook until mixture is thick, about 12 minutes. Stir in peanut butter and vanilla. Remove from heat and stir until cooled to room temperature. Cover bottom of pie shell (see page 44) with two thirds powdered sugar and peanut butter mixture. Pour custard on top. Make meringue with reserved egg whites. Spread meringue over custard, making sure to spread meringue (see page 45) to edges of crust. Sprinkle remaining powdered sugar and peanut butter mixture over meringue. Bake in 350 degree oven until golden brown. Cool to room temperature and refrigerate.

FRESH PEANUT BUTTER:
Place 2 cups parched salted nuts and 1-2 tablespoons peanut oil in food processor or blender. Process until desired consistency. Taste for saltiness, adding more if needed.

WATKINS COCONUT CREAM PIE

*T*he "Watkins Man" was very important to the cooks in rural North Florida. Grandaddy's brother Uncle Monroe had the route in our neck of the woods. He drove a Model-A Ford sedan with shelves tacked inside and along the running boards to hold his products. A big chicken coop was tied to the back to keep the yard birds he sometimes took in trade for the Watkins flavorings, spices, toilet articles and insecticides he peddled from door-to-door. On Saturdays when everybody came to town to buy groceries, he would park his Model-A Ford across from the grocery store, then sell out of his car.

The recipes he gave out with the flavorings required the Watkins brand of various ingredients, some were very good, the coconut pie was one of our favorites. Our recipe is similar except we have included coconut milk for a more intense coconut flavor.

If your "Watkins Person" hasn't stopped by lately, use any brand of flavoring.

---

9 inch baked pie shell
2¼ cups coconut milk
⅓ cup all-purpose flour
¼ teaspoon salt
⅔ cup sugar

3 egg yolks, whites reserved for meringue
1 tablespoon unsalted butter
1 teaspoon Watkins vanilla
½ cups coconut

Scald 2 cups coconut milk until warm and set aside. In top of double boiler, add flour, salt, sugar and mix. Whisk in remaining a fourth cup milk. When smooth, whisk in remaining scalded coconut milk. Cook 15 minutes over hot water, stirring with a wooden spoon. Add a half cup mixture to egg yolks, beat and add to mixture in double boiler. Stir constantly and cook another 3 minutes. Remove from heat, add butter, vanilla and 1 cup coconut. Pour into baked pie shell (see page 44). Cover with meringue (see page 45), making sure meringue touches edges of crust and sprinkle meringue with remaining coconut. Bake in 350 degree oven until golden brown. Cool and serve or refrigerate.

Tawee teaching Amelia and Elizabeth pie making 101, c 2004.

BUTTERMILK PIE

*T*his is an old classic and very delicious dessert. Years ago, this recipe was a good way to use up buttermilk, a by-product of fresh churned butter. If you're short a milk cow, you can use buttermilk from the dairy store.

Prebake the pie shell until lightly brown, about 8-10 minutes to prevent a soggy crust.

Serves 6

- 1 unbaked 9" pie shell
- ½ cup unsalted butter, softened
- 1 cup sugar
- 3 large egg yolks
- 3 tablespoons all-purpose flour
- 2 tablespoons lemon juice
- 1 teaspoon lemon rind, grated
- 1 teaspoon vanilla
- 1 cup buttermilk
- ½ teaspoon nutmeg, freshly grated
- 1 tablespoon powdered sugar

Preheat oven 350 degrees. Cream butter and sugar with an electric mixer until light in color. Add egg yolks one at a time, beating well after each addition. Beat in flour, lemon juice, lemon rind, vanilla, buttermilk and nutmeg. Pour mixture into pie shell (see page 44) and bake in lower third of oven for 25 minutes. Reduce heat to 325 degrees and bake an additional 20-25 minutes or until it is set. Sprinkle sifted powdered sugar over the top. Cool to room temperature and serve.

BLACKBERRY PIE

Serves 6

- 1½ cups fresh blackberries
- 1¼ cups sugar, divided
- One 9" pie crust
- 3 tablespoons cornstarch
- 1¼ cups water
- ½ teaspoon vanilla
- 1 (3oz.) package raspberry gelatin
- Chantilly Cream Sauce

Gently toss berries with a fourth cup sugar in a large bowl, cover and refrigerate 8 hours. Drain and reserve liquid. Prick bottom and sides of pie crust (see page 44) with a fork and bake 425 degrees for 12-15 minutes or until lightly brown. Stir together cornstarch and remaining cup of sugar, add enough water to reserved juice to measure one and one fourth cups, and vanilla. Cook over medium heat, whisking constantly, until mixture thickens. Stir raspberry gelatin into the warm cornstarch mixture. Spoon blackberries into piecrust. Pour glaze evenly over berries, pressing down gently with a spoon coating all berries. Chill 2-3 hours. Serve with Chantilly Cream (see page 337).

DESSERTS AND SWEET THANGS

BLACKBOTTOM PIE

Marjorie K. Rawlings said in *Cross Creek Cookery* that this was her favorite pie. She wanted to be propped up in her dying bed and fed Black bottom Pie. Me too!

Filling:
1¾ cup milk
1 tablespoon cornstarch
4 tablespoons cold water
1 tablespoon gelatin
½ cup sugar
4 egg yolks
Pinch of salt

Chocolate layer:
2 squares melted chocolate
1 teaspoon vanilla

Rum-flavored layer:
4 egg whites
⅛ teaspoon cream of tartar
½ cup sugar
1 tablespoon rum

Topping:
2 tablespoons confectioners' sugar
1 tablespoon Grand Marnier
1 cup heavy cream
Grated chocolate

Soak the gelatin in the cold water. Scald the milk, add a half cup of sugar mixed with the cornstarch, pinch of salt, then beaten egg yolks. Cook in double boiler, stirring constantly, until custard thickens and will coat the back of a spoon. Stir in the dissolved gelatin. Divide the custard in half. To one-half add the melted chocolate and the vanilla. Turn while hot into cooled crust, dipping out carefully so as not to disturb crust. Let remaining half of custard cool. Beat the egg whites and cream of tartar, adding one-half cup of sugar slowly. Blend with the cooled custard. Add rum and stir. Spread carefully over the chocolate layer. Place in refrigerator to chill thoroughly, about 4 hours. When ready to serve, whip the heavy cream stiff, add in confectioners' sugar and Grand Marnier. Pile over top of the pie. Sprinkle with grated chocolate and serve.

Wood burning stove, located in the Marjorie Kinnan Rawlings House in Cross Creek, c 1975.

SOUTHERN PECAN PIE

Southern cookbooks have many versions of this delectable pie. We read one cookbook that had over ten pecan pie recipes. Pecan pie is one thing most Southerners can never get enough of. It's very rich, so have a small slice of pie with a cold glass of milk or a cup of freshly brewed coffee. This pie is always a favorite at our family gatherings.

Pecan trees unlike the chinquapin and hickory are not native to North Florida, but were introduced from Texas. While the hybrid pecans are larger and easier to shell, we prefer the taste of the wild or seedling pecan. Several of the large hybrid pecans such as the Mahan and Stewart varieties were developed at a nursery in Monticello.

1-9 inch unbaked pie crust
1 cup packed light brown sugar
2 tablespoons all-purpose flour
½ teaspoon salt
4 eggs, lightly beaten

¼ cup unsalted butter, melted
1 cup light corn syrup
1 teaspoon vanilla
2 tablespoons bourbon
2 cups pecans, chopped

Preheat oven 400 degrees. Mix all ingredients with a whisk except pecans and stir well. Add pecans and stir to coat pecans with syrup. Pour into pie shell, reduce heat to 325 degrees, and bake in center of oven for 40-45 minutes. Remove from oven and cool to room temperature. Serve with Chantilly Sauce, if desired.

PECAN PIE VARIATIONS:

MOCHA PECAN PIE
¼ cup Kahlua
16 ounces semi-sweet chocolate
9 inch unbaked pie crust

Cook as above. Combine and add to pecan pie mix before adding pecan pieces. Top with whipped cream with one and one half tablespoons of Kahlua added.

PECAN SWEET POTATO PIES
Makes 2 pies, give one to your neighbor.
2 -9 inch unbaked pie crust

Add a half recipe sweet potato mix (see page 348) before pouring in a half recipe of pecan mix into pie crust. Cook as above. Top with Chantilly Cream Sauce(see page 337).

SWEETIE PIE
In the '55 chevy
"Rambling Rose, Rambling Rose"

Sunday afternoons were special times after we reached "sparking" age. Our sweetie pies would pick us up in freshly washed cars with fender skirts and spinner hubcaps. We could ride around all afternoon on a "dollars worth of regular." If it wasn't a first date it was all right to sit close, especially at the Parkway drive-in restaurant, if any friends were there. Sometimes we would order a lemonade with two straws that was served on a metal tray that hung on the car window.

Occasionally boys from nearby towns visited the drive-in. Hey, that one in the '55 chevy convertible is kind of cute—wonder who he is—hmmm.

Unfortunately, those days are gone and the closest we get to a drive-in nowadays is to drop off the laundry. But we are reminded of those Sunday afternoons when we have this pie.

- 1½ cups sugar
- 1 teaspoon vanilla
- ½ cup butter, softened
- 1 tablespoon cornmeal
- 3 eggs
- ¼ teaspoon salt
- 1 whole thin-skinned lemon, seeded
- 9 inch partially baked pie shell

Preheat oven 350 degrees. Place sugar, butter, eggs, lemon, vanilla, cornmeal and salt into food processor or blender. Process until lemon is finely chopped. Pour into partially baked pie shell (see page 44) and bake 30 minutes, or until firm. Serve at room temperature.

"Sweetie Pie", Parkway Drive-in
DeFuniak Springs, c 1962.

SWEET POTATO PIE

The late Dub Bishop, c 1972.

Our brother-in-law, Dub Bishop, who hails from the Bridge Creek community, northeast of Argyle, likes to tell of the old days when he walked five miles to school each day. It was up hill both ways. Some days he took a baked sweet potato to school for lunch. He kept it in his back pocket and sometimes the older boys pushed him down and mashed it. This is a dish where you can use the mashed sweet potatoes.

1-9 inch unbaked pie shell
3 cups mashed sweet potatoes
½ cup evaporated milk
½ cup unsalted butter
2 eggs, beaten
2 teaspoons grated orange rind
Pinch of salt
1 teaspoon nutmeg, freshly grated
1 teaspoon vanilla
1 cup sugar

Preheat oven to 325 degrees. Place sweet potatoes in large bowl. Combine with remaining ingredients and stir until smooth. Pour into unbaked pie shell (see page 44) and smooth the top. Bake on lowest rack of oven for 10 minutes, reduce heat to 300 degrees and bake 1 hour more or until knife inserted in center of pie comes out clean. Serve at room temperature with Chantilly Sauce (see page 337).

PINTO BEAN PIE

Last spring our neighbor Lois Hillard, who had celebrated her ninety-fifth birthday showed up at the back door, grinning like a Chesshire cat and holding this pie. She said, "Bet you can't tell me what kind of pie this is." We all took a bite and agreed it was delicious but no one could guess the secret ingredient. "Pinto Beans" Lois said, with a chuckle.

Makes 2-9 inch pies, give one to your neighbor.

Bake 325 degrees.

2-9 inch pie shells
1 cup Pinto beans, washed, drained and mashed
2 sticks margarine, melted
2 cups sugar
1 cup coconut
1 cup pecans, chopped
2 tablespoons vanilla
1 teaspoon vanilla
Dash salt

Mix together all ingredients and pour into pie shells (see page 44). Bake approximately one hour.

SPANISH BAKERY SWEET POTATO TURNOVERS

*Y*ears ago when visiting St. Augustine we made a point to stop at the Spanish Bakery on St. George Street for these delicious sweet potato turnovers.

Then one day we stopped by and there were no turnovers. The cook said, "We ain't making them no mo." Well we panicked and begged for the recipe. She went into the kitchen and returned with the following recipe. When we asked how many this made she replied, "A whole lot."

1 gallon sweet potatoes
1 pint flour
2 pints plus 1 cup sugar
¼ cup lemon extract
Some nutmeg
Pie Crust dough

Make with basic pie crust dough (see page 44), cut into 6 inch circles. Place sweet potato mixture on half of the circle and fold opposite side over, crimp the edges with a fork to seal. Bake 350 degrees for 15-20 minutes or until brown.

GRANNY SMITH'S APPLE PIE

Preheat oven 425 degrees

2 recipes pie dough
¾ cup plus 2½ tablespoons sugar
3 tablespoons all-purpose flour
¾ teaspoon cinnamon
¼ teaspoon freshly grated nutmeg
¾ teaspoons freshly grated lemon zest
2½ pounds Granny Smith apples (about 6)
1 teaspoon fresh lemon juice
3 tablespoons cold unsalted butter, cut into bits
1 tablespoon cream
Aged cheddar cheese, grated
¼ teaspoon salt

Roll out one of the pie crust (see page 44) an eighth inch thick and place in a 9 inch glass pie plate, leaving a half inch over hang. Return to refrigerator to chill. In a large bowl combine the sugar, flour, cinnamon, nutmeg, salt and zest. Peel, quarter and core the apples, slice them thin and add to the sugar mixture tossing them to coat. Mound the apple mixture in the pie shell, sprinkle with lemon juice and dot with butter. Roll out the other piece of dough, a little larger than the pie plate and drape over the apples. Trim the top crust and press the two crust together using the tines of a fork to seal. Cut 5-7 steam vents in the top crust. Brush with cream and bake the pie in the lower third of the oven for 15 minutes. Reduce heat to 375 degrees and continue to bake 40-45 minutes or until filling is bubbling and crust is golden. Transfer to a rack, cover with grated cheese and let cool.

FRESH PUMPKIN PIE

When the Spanish explorers traveled through North Florida they encountered several Indian tribes including the Apalachee and Euchee tribes. These tribes were hunters/farmers and cultivated pumpkins along with their corn, beans and squash. Pumpkins were very important in their diet and were included in soups, stews, and were also made into bread.

This pie is a time-honored Thanksgiving favorite, we have it often in the fall, especially a few days after Halloween when pumpkins are so cheap. The flavor of fresh pumpkin is a whole lot better than canned.

9 inch pie shell, baked for 8 minutes
½ cups fresh pumpkin
1 cup evaporated milk
3 large eggs
1 cup light brown sugar
1 teaspoon ground cinnamon
½ teaspoon ground ginger
¼ teaspoon ground cloves
¼ teaspoon nutmeg, freshly grated
¼ cup brandy

Preheat oven 325 degrees. To cook pumpkin, wash, cut in half and remove seeds and strings. Place cut side up on a cookie sheet and bake one hour (or longer according to size) until tender. Remove from oven and cool. Scrape or cut pulp from shell and put through a ricer. Increase oven temperature to 375 degrees. Place pumpkin in a large bowl, add milk and eggs and stir with a whisk until smooth. Add sugar, spices and brandy; mix well and set aside.

Prepare the pie crust (see page 44), cut the over hanging dough flush with edge of the pie plate. Pour the filling into pie shell and with a sharp knife make a half inch cuts at three-fourths intervals all the way around the edge of the shell. Turn every other section in toward the center of the shell to form a decorative edge.

Bake in middle of oven for 1 hour, place on lowest shelf and continue to bake 10 minutes or until the filling is set, but the center still shakes slightly.

Serve at room temperature with Chantilly Sauce (see page 337).

STRAWBERRY PIE

Makes one 9 inch pie
1 cup sugar
1 cup water
3 tablespoons cornstarch
¼ cup strawberry gelatin
4 cups fresh strawberries, halved
1 baked 9 inch pie crust
1 recipe Chantilly Sauce

Bring sugar, water and cornstarch to a boil over medium heat, stirring constantly, until thickened. Stir in strawberry gelatin until dissolved. Remove from heat and refrigerate for 2 hours. Arrange strawberries in baked pie crust (see page 44), and pour gelatin mixture over strawberries. Cover and chill 4 hours. Serve with Chantilly Sauce (see page 337) if desired.

MANDARIN ORANGE PIE

Mandarin, located south of Jacksonville, is the location of some of North Florida's first commercial orange groves as well as the winter home of Harriet Beecher Stowe. Adventurous souls wanting to travel south of Jacksonville in the late 19th century could catch a steamer and in two days and nights make the 198 mile journey to Central Florida. There was keen competition between the steamboat lines. One had an arrangement with Harriet Beecher Stowe. Approaching her Mandarin home, the captain would sound the whistle, whereupon she would rush to a desk set up on the terrace and appear to be writing a sequel to Uncle Tom's Cabin.

The Mandarin orange is also known as the satsuma.

9 inch baked pie shell
¾ cup sugar
½ cup all-purpose flour
¼ teaspoon salt
1¼ cups water

2 egg yolks
½ cup fresh orange juice
1 tablespoon orange zest
2 tablespoons fresh lemon juice
Candied orange peel

Preheat oven 350 degrees. Combine sugar, flour and salt in the top of a double boiler over high heat. Stir in the water, keeping mixture smooth and free of lumps. Cook and stir 5 minutes, or until slightly thickened. Add egg yolks, cook 5 minutes longer, stirring constantly. Remove from heat, add orange and lemon juice and 1 tablespoon of zest. Continue to cook 2-3 minutes if needed. Place in pie shell (see page 44), cover with meringue, making sure meringue goes to edge of crust. Bake 10-15 minutes, or until lightly brown. Cool to room temperature and chill 4 hours before serving. Serve individual slices with a little candied orange on the plate.

CANDIED ORANGE PEEL:

Cut one orange peel into thin strips, cover with water, bring to a boil, reduce heat to low, cook 10 minutes and drain. Make simple syrup with a third cup sugar and a third cup water, stir over low heat until sugar has dissolved, add orange strips and boil until all syrup is absorbed. Place on rack to dry.

FLORIDA KEY LIME PIE

Since this pie became so popular, Florida's Key Lime trees can't keep up with the demand, so most of the Key Limes are imported from South America and Mexico. Lemons are sometimes used in this Key West original.

Graham cracker crust
4 egg yolks, beaten
14 ounce can condensed milk
½ cup key lime juice
2 teaspoons grated lime zest.
¾ cup whipping cream
⅓ cup powdered sugar
Lime slices for garnish

Combine egg yolks and condensed milk in a mixing bowl, and mix well. Add lime juice and grated zest. Mix until blended. Pour into the crust (see page 44) and bake for 10 minutes, or until the center is firm. Refrigerate until thoroughly chilled. Whip cream with powdered sugar and spread over the pie. Garnish with fresh lime slices and return to refrigerator until ready to serve.

JEFF DAVIS PIE

"Save your Confederate money boys, the South's gonna rise again."

2 cups sugar
1 tablespoon all-purpose flour
1 cup heavy cream
1 cup butter
6 eggs, beaten
1 teaspoon vanilla
½ cup pecans, chopped
1 unbaked 9 inch pie shell

Combine sugar, flour, and cream with the butter and beat until light and frothy. Add beaten eggs, vanilla and pecans. Pour into unbaked pie shell (see page 44). Bake 400 degrees for 10 minutes reduce heat to 350 degrees and bake 30 minutes. Spread pie with meringue(see page 45) and bake 350 degrees until meringue is lightly brown.

SCUPPERNONG PIE

Scuppernongs are a type of muscadine grape native to the South. You usually eat them whole and spit out the seeds and skin. The grapes can made into jam, jelly, desserts and wine. Several wineries have sprung up in North Florida featuring these local grapes. The Chautauqua and Alaqua wineries are located in Walton County. The San Sebastion winery is located in St. John's county.

Around the end of every August, Grandmother Ingram's huge scuppernong arbor was opened to all the grandchildren who had been diligent in shelling peas and butter beans for her throughout the summer. We didn't mind that you had to step carefully to avoid the chicken droppings. I guess the chickens had their allotted time in that screened off area to eat all the fallen grapes. She had those wonderful sweet tasting, big bronze grapes and they were enticement enough to make one forget pea shelling and dodging chicken droppings.

Serve with a scoop of Rich Vanilla Homemade Ice Cream (see page 372).

4 cups scuppernongs
Water
1 cup sugar, more if needed
2 tablespoons cornstarch
3 tablespoons butter
2 recipes of pie crusts

Separate pulp from hulls by pressing grape between thumb and forefinger and place in separate pots. Cover hulls with water, about a half inch above hulls. Bring to a boil, reduce heat and simmer for 20-30 minutes or until tender and all but one to one and a half cups of water has evaporated. Cook pulp over low heat for 10-15 minutes, stirring occasionally to separate seed from pulp. Pour pulp into a strainer over a bowl, stir with wooden spoon to remove pulp. Mix sugar and cornstarch together to avoid lumping and add to hulls, mixing thoroughly. Add pulp and butter and stir well. Taste for sweetness, adding additional sugar if needed. Scuppernongs can be very tart. Pour into pie shell (see page 44), roll and cut second crust into half inch strips. Weave strips, moisten ends and crimp with the tines of a fork. Bake for 10 minutes at 400 degrees, lower heat to 350 degrees and bake 20-25 minutes more. Cool to room temperature and serve.

CHERRY-O PIE

"Can you bake a cherry pie, charming Billy?"

8 ounces cream cheese, softened
14 ounce can condensed milk
1/3 cup fresh lemon juice
1 teaspoon vanilla
21 ounce can cherry pie filling
1 graham cracker pie crust

Cream the cream cheese, condensed milk, lemon juice and vanilla until smooth. Pour into graham cracker pie shell (see page 44). Indent 6 inch center section of cheese mixture and spread with cherry pie filling. Chill pie until cheese mixture is firm and serve.

BARTLETT PEAR PIE

Bartlett pears are too soft for our relish and preserves, but are perfect for this pie.

Serves 8-10

- 10 Bartlett pears
- 2 tablespoons lemon juice
- 1⅓ cups milk
- ⅔ cup whipping cream
- ¼ teaspoon nutmeg, freshly grated
- ⅔ cup all-purpose flour
- 4 large eggs
- 2 teaspoons vanilla
- 2 tablespoons butter, softened
- 2 tablespoons powdered sugar
- 1 cup sugar

Preheat oven 350 degrees. Peel, quarter, core and toss pears with lemon juice. Butter a shallow two and one half-three quart casserole. Arrange pears in the bottom. Use a food processor to blend milk, cream, two thirds cup sugar, nutmeg, flour, eggs and vanilla. Scrape down sides of bowl and pulse 30 seconds. Pour batter over pears and sprinkle with remaining sugar. Dot with butter and bake in upper third of oven for 45-50 minutes or until top is golden brown and pudding is set. Sprinkle with powdered sugar and serve while warm.

OLD-TIMEY LEMON MERINGUE PIE

*I*f we had to choose one perfect dessert that goes well with all our fried meats, fish dishes, spicy barbecue, Island dishes, and the wonderful seafood we enjoy, it would have to be a Lemon Meringue Pie. There is nothing comparable to the sweet, tangy, lemony taste of this old-timey dessert to finish a great meal. If you want a very lemony flavor add more zest.

- 8 inch baked pie shell
- ¾ cup sugar
- 3 tablespoons arrowroot
- Pinch of salt,
- 1¼ cups water
- 3 egg yolks, whites reserved
- 3 tablespoons unsalted butter
- ¼ cup fresh lemon juice
- 1 teaspoon lemon zest

Whisk together the sugar, arrowroot, salt and water in the top of a double boiler. Place over simmering water and stir constantly until mixture is thick and smooth, about 5 minutes. In a small bowl combine the egg yolks and lemon juice. Whisk one half cup of the hot syrup mixture into the egg yolks. Whisk mixture into the syrup. Cook 2-3 minutes, stirring constantly. Remove from heat and add butter and zest. Pour into baked 8 inch shell (see page 44), and cover with meringue, making sure meringue touches edge of crust. Bake at 350 degrees for 10-15 minutes or until golden brown. Cool and serve or refrigerate.

TAWEE'S FAVORITE CHOCOLATE PIE

Tawee

This is basically my old chocolate pie recipe. Recently my youngest sister, Tawee, substituted self-rising flour since we were out of plain and now claims that it's her recipe. Oh well, another culinary achievement at the big house.

My sister Tawee is youngest of eight children. The "baby" won't admit she was "spoiled rotten" but we have learned to live with it.

9 inch baked pie shell
1¾ cups sugar,
⅓ cup cocoa
½ cup self-rising flour
Dash of salt
2 cups whole milk

1 cup evaporated milk
5 large egg yolks, slightly beaten whites reserved
2 tablespoons unsalted butter
1½ teaspoons vanilla

In top of double boiler mix sugar, cocoa, flour, salt and a fourth cup milk until smooth. Place over simmering water and whisk in whole and evaporated milk. Stir continuously with wooden spoon until thickened, whisk if lumps begin to form. Whisk in egg yolks and beat. Cook 3 minutes more, stirring constantly. Remove from heat and stir in butter and vanilla, continue stirring until cooled to room temperature. Pour into baked pie shell (see page 44), smoothing top. Cover with meringue (see page 45), making sure meringue touches crust. Bake in 350 degree oven until meringue is golden brown. Cool and serve or refrigerate.

CHOCOLATE ICE BOX PIE

2 dozen ladyfingers
8 ounces semi-sweet chocolate
4 tablespoons boiling water

1 can condensed milk
1½ teaspoons vanilla

In a heavy bottomed pan melt chocolate, add condensed milk and cook until very thick, remove from heat. Add 4 tablespoons water and vanilla. Separate ladyfingers and line a loaf pan. Cover with chocolate mixture. Then add another layer of ladyfingers. Continue layers using remainder of chocolate mixture and ladyfingers, ending with ladyfingers. Cover with wax paper and refrigerate overnight. To serve-turnout onto serving plate and serve with a dollop of Chantilly Sauce (see page 337).

LADYFINGERS: Make one recipe Jimmy's Sponge Cake (see page 335). Place batter in pastry bag. Squeeze batter the size of a ladies finger on parchment paper, bake at 350 degrees for 8-10 minutes or until brown.

THE SISTERS' FABULOUS FUDGE

My youngest sister Tawee continues to persuade my older sister Ruby to make this fabulous fudge for her when she comes home. Ruby usually makes two batches at a time because Tawee has been known to eat an entire batch at one sitting or as she puts it, "until I have all I want."

Serves one (Tawee)
4 cups sugar
6 tablespoons cocoa
4 tablespoons lightly salted butter
2-5 ounce cans evaporated milk
⅛ teaspoon salt
2½ tablespoons vanilla
1½ cups pecans, chopped
2 heaping tablespoons creamy peanut butter

In a heavy-bottomed boiler, mix sugar, cocoa and melted butter. Add half of the milk and stir until blended. Add remaining milk and salt and cook on medium-high heat until soft ball stage registers on candy thermometer. Remove from heat, add vanilla do not stir. Keep thermometer in boiler, do not stir, until 150 degrees is reached on candy thermometer. Add pecans and peanut butter, only stir 4-5 times. Pour into buttered 8x10 pan. Cut fudge when it has set but is still warm.

MOLTEN LAVA CAKES

Serves 6
4 tablespoons unsalted butter, plus more for muffin tins
⅓ cup sugar, plus more for muffin tins
3 large eggs
⅓ cup all-purpose flour
¼ teaspoon salt
½ teaspoon almond flavoring
8 ounces bittersweet chocolate, melted
½ cup Raspberry Sauce
Fresh raspberries
½ cup sliced almonds, toasted
Confectioners' sugar

Preheat oven 400 degrees.
Butter six cups of muffin tin. Sprinkle with sugar and tap out excess. Set aside. Cream butter and sugar with an electric mixer for 3 minutes. Add eggs, one at a time, beating after each addition. With mixer on low speed, beat in flour and salt until just combined. Fold in almond flavoring and chocolate. Pour batter evenly into muffin tins and bake for 10-12 minutes, or until sides of cake are set. Let the cakes cool 2 minutes in tins. Place cakes on individual serving plates. Place small amount of Raspberry Sauce (see page 371) around plate, sprinkle with raspberries and almonds and dust with confectioners' sugar.

THE ULTIMATE FUDGY BROWNIES WITH CHOCOLATE ICING

The sister's searched for many years for the perfect brownie and decided this recipe was the best. These brownies are dense, chewy and very chocolatey.....perfect for a chocolate fix.

Wrap the brownies individually in plastic wrap and freeze. Eat them while partially frozen and the texture will be totally different, almost like fudge.

Makes 24 brownies
- 1 cup unsalted butter
- 6 ounces unsweetened chocolate, coarsely chopped
- 2 cups sugar
- 4 eggs
- 2 teaspoons vanilla
- 1 cup all-purpose flour
- ½ teaspoon salt
- ⅓ cup semi-sweet chocolate morsels
- 1½ cups walnuts or pecans, chopped

Preheat oven 325 degrees. Lightly butter a 9x13 inch glass baking dish. Over medium heat, melt butter in a double boiler until partially melted. Add chocolate and stir with a wooden spoon until both are completely melted. Remove from heat and stir in sugar. Beat in eggs, one at a time, with wooden spoon. Stir until fully incorporated and mixture is shiny. Stir in vanilla, flour, salt, chocolate morsels and stir until just combined.. Spread into glass baking dish. Sprinkle nuts over the top and gently press into brownies. Bake 30 minutes, cool and spread with Chocolate Icing if desired.

CHOCOLATE ICING

Makes 1 ½ cups
- 10 ounces semi-sweet chocolate morsels
- ½ cup whipping cream, warmed
- ¼ teaspoon salt
- ½ cup powdered sugar
- 1 cup chopped pecans (optional)
- 2 tablespoons unsalted butter

Melt chocolate in top of double boiler, stirring until smooth. Remove from heat and stir in cream, butter, salt and sugar. Spread over top of brownies and sprinkle with nuts, cool before cutting.

FRESH FRUIT TART

*F*resh and ripe fruit are essential for a successful fruit tart. Use any combination of fruit in season. Luscious strawberries sliced in half, blackberries, blueberries, raspberries, or peeled and sliced peaches, bananas, mangoes, and kiwis.

CUSTARD:
4 large egg yolks
⅓ cup sugar
1 teaspoon vanilla extract
1 teaspoon almond extract
1 tablespoon all-purpose flour
2 tablespoons cornstarch
Pinch of salt
1 cup milk, warmed
1 cup whipping cream, warmed
1 tablespoon unsalted butter
1 - 12 inch baked pie tart shell

Beat egg yolks in top of double boiler, gradually add sugar and whisk until mixture is pale yellow. Whisk in vanilla and almond extracts, flour, cornstarch and pinch of salt. Gradually whisk in milk and whipping cream. Cook until mixture has thickened. Remove from heat and stir until cooled to room temperature. Place plastic wrap directly on custard to prevent skin from forming and refrigerate.

GLAZE:
1 cup apricot jam
3 tablespoons cognac

Remove pulp of jam by placing it in a sieve and press it through with a wooden spoon. Place jam and cognac in a small saucepan over low heat. Stir until jam liquifies. Remove from heat and cool slightly. Spread over fruit while still warm with a pastry brush or back of a spoon.

TO ASSEMBLE: Spread custard in cooked pie shell (see page 44), decoratively add fruit and glaze with apricot mixture. If glaze becomes too thick, reheat. We prefer this tart chilled before serving.

Cameron's blueberry, mango, and kiwi fruit tart.

APPLE TORTE

*F*lorida's climate is better suited to citrus than apples. However, recent introductions from Israel have been very successful. The Anna, Ein Shener and Golden Dorset varieties thrive in North Florida and are being planted as a u-pick-'em fruit in some areas.

This is our favorite apple dessert. The cream cheese and sweet crust makes this an unexpected and memorable dessert.

Preheat oven 450 degrees.

CRUST:
- ½ cup unsalted salted butter, room temperature
- ⅓ cup sugar
- ½ teaspoon vanilla
- Pinch of salt
- 1 cup all-purpose flour

Lightly butter bottom and sides of 9 inch spring form pan. Cream butter and sugar. Add vanilla and salt, and blend in flour. Spread in bottom of pan, going up sides by 2 inches to form a crust.

FILLING:
- 8 ounce package cream cheese, softened
- ¼ cup sugar
- 1 egg
- ½ teaspoon vanilla extract
- ½ teaspoon almond extract

Cream the cream cheese and sugar with an electric mixer. Add egg, vanilla and almond extract. Pour filling into pastry shell.

TOPPING:
- ½ cup sugar
- ½ teaspoon cinnamon
- 4 cups Mc Intosh apples, peeled, cored and sliced thin
- 2 teaspoons lemon juice
- ½ cup sliced almonds
- 1 tablespoon unsalted butter

Combine sugar and cinnamon in large bowl. Toss apples in lemon juice then toss with sugar mixture. Cover cream cheese with apples. Melt butter in small skillet, add almonds and toss to coat. Sprinkle top of pie with almonds. Bake for 10 minutes in middle of oven. Reduce heat to 400 degrees and bake an additional 25 minutes. Cool to room temperature and serve.

LIBBY LOVE'S PIE BERRY

"Ol' Stew Ball was a race horse, and I wish he were mine. He never drank water, he always drank wine."

There are many ways to prepare cobblers. Our niece, Libby Love, re-named Mother's cobbler at a very young age. Now everyone in the family knows what "Pie Berry" is, a dumpling cobbler that can be made with any type of fresh fruit. Blueberries are our favorite, but when they aren't in season, blackberries, apples, pears and peaches also make us happy. The amount of water and sugar needed will vary according to the fruit and its sweetness.

The Andrews Sisters. Tammy, Kim, Libby Love and Stew Ball, c 1972.

Serves 6-8

6-8 cups fresh fruit
Pie crust (delete sugar)
2-3 cups sugar
2 tablespoons unsalted butter
Water

Prepare fruit and set aside. Roll pie dough (see page 44) thin and cut into 1 inch strips. Lightly butter a 9 inch, 3 inch deep round metal pie pan. Add enough fruit to cover the bottom of the pan. Sprinkle with a fourth to a half cup sugar. Lay strips of pie dough over fruit, sprinkle with sugar and repeat 3-4 times until all dough is used, ending with dough on top layer. Cut butter into pats and place on top of dough, sprinkle lightly with sugar. Add about a cup of water, according to type of fruit used. Apples, pears and peaches may require more.

Niece Libby Love and the Wolford boys. Lee, Douglas and Clay.

Tilt pan slightly and you should be able to see water. Cook on top of stove on medium-low heat. When pie begins to bubble, reduce heat to low and cook 25-30 minutes. Dip a spoon along side of pan and taste for sweetness. More sugar may be added immersed in teaspoon along sides of pan, if needed. Place in 350 degree oven for 30 minutes or until top is golden brown. If pie has too much liquid, place on low heat and cook until liquid has reduced. Serve warm with Rich Vanilla Homemade Ice Cream (see page 372).

TERRE'S DEWBERRY COBBLER

"Delta Dawn, what's them flowers you got on? Could it be a faded rose from days gone by."

Niece Terre Bulan and local naysayer and ner-do-well. Sack race Thanksgiving, c 1990.

Stifle yourself Edith! And get off my sore toe!

Oh no! The Wolford Boys. Now we will never win.

Dewberries are much like blackberries except they grow on low viney bushes and appear early in the spring. We usually eat these in pies and make jelly from blackberries which are more abundant.

As soon as the Dewberries are ripe in the spring, we team up with our niece Terre and head to our "secret" Dewberry patch down in the valley. We eat our fill and then pick enough for her cobbler, if it hasn't gotten too dark.

Makes two 9 x 13 cobblers

- 4 quarts dewberries, or blackberries fresh or frozen
- 2 cups sugar
- Juice of 2 lemons
- 2 cups sugar

- 2 cups all-purpose flour
- 2 teaspoons baking powder
- ½ teaspoon salt
- 2 cups milk
- 1 cup unsalted butter

Preheat oven 300 degrees. Place fruit, 2 cups sugar and lemon juice in a heavy bottomed pot. Cook over medium heat until sugar melts and mixture comes to a boil; set aside. Melt a half cup butter in each 9 x13 inch baking dish and set aside. Place 2 cups sugar, flour, baking powder and salt in a mixing bowl. Whisk in milk until batter is smooth. Pour equally into baking dishes with butter. Ladle fruit and juice equally over batter. Bake 1 hour and 15 minutes or until most of the juice is absorbed and has thickened. Remove from oven, serve hot with Rich Homemade Vanilla ice cream (see page 372).

MARY LIZZIE'S LAZY DAY FRUIT COBBLER

*G*ranny was a great cook, but she also loved to be outside. She enjoyed working in her vegetable and flower gardens, and was always experimenting with new varieties of fruit trees and shrubs.

While she was working in the garden in the fall, she usually had her .410 shotgun handy for rattlesnakes or any squirrels, rabbits, doves and quail that came for a snack in the garden.

In the summer after the garden work was finished, you could always find her in the old cypress boat down at the fish pond. When I stayed with her in the summer, this pie became our way to enjoy the fresh summer berries and fruits. We picked the fruit early in the morning when the dew was still on. Granny baked the pie while we were eating breakfast so it would be cooled in time for dinner, our noon meal.

½ cup butter
2 cups sugar
1 cup all-purpose flour,
1 teaspoon baking powder

2 cups milk
1 teaspoon vanilla
2 cups fruit (any fruit in season- peaches pears, blackberries, etc.)

Preheat oven 325 degrees. Melt butter in 9 x13 inch glass dish. Mix sugar, flour, baking powder, milk, and vanilla. Beat until well mixed. Pour into butter, do not mix. Pour or spoon fruit over batter, do not stir. It will fold together as it bakes. Bake 45 minutes or until light brown. Cool to room temperature and serve with Rich Vanilla Homemade Ice Cream (see page 372) or Chantilly Sauce (see page 337).

Mary Elizabeth Manning, Ponce de Leon, vegetable garden, c 1940.

MISS LILLIE'S WHISKEY CAKES
Little Brown Jug Don't I Love Thee

These cookies originally came from a genteel old lady from Mississippi, who served them with tea on her best china. She gave the recipe to Linda, my next door neighbor, who shared it with me. I count myself fortunate each time I bake them.

1 pound butter, room temperature
1 pound sugar (2 cups)
1 egg
1 pound self-rising flour (4 cups)
1 tablespoon sour mash bourbon
1 tablespoon lemon juice
1 tablespoon vanilla

Preheat oven 350 degrees. Cream butter until fluffy. Add sugar and continue to beat for 1 minute. Stir in egg, flour, whiskey, lemon juice and vanilla. Place cookie dough on wax paper and roll into a log. Chill until firm, slice one quarter inch thick. Use parchment paper as a liner for your cookie sheets, your cookies will bake much nicer. Bake 10-12 minutes.

APRICOT SCONES

Makes 16 scones

2 cups all-purpose flour
¼ cup sugar
1 tablespoon baking powder
¼ teaspoon salt
⅓ cup cold unsalted butter
½ cup dried apricots, chopped
½ cup pecans, chopped
1 teaspoon orange peel, grated
1 cup plus 2 tablespoons whipping cream, divided

Preheat oven 375 degrees. Combine the dry ingredients in a bowl. Cut in the butter until the mixture resembles fine crumbs. Add apricots, pecans, and grated orange rind. With a fork rapidly stir in 1 cup whipping cream just until moistened. Turn onto a floured surface and knead 5-6 times. Divide in half and shape each half into a ball. Flatten each ball into a 6 inch circle and cut each circle into 8 wedges. Place 1 inch apart on an ungreased baking sheet. Brush with remaining cream. Bake for 13-15 minutes and serve with Devonshire Cream and Apricot jam.

DEVONSHIRE CREAM

In a small bowl beat 3 ounces of cream cheese until creamy, add one half teaspoon vanilla, 1 tablespoon confectioners' sugar and beat until fluffy. Gradually add one quarter-one third cup heavy cream, add enough to achieve a spreading consistency. Cover and chill for at least 2 hours.

CREAMY RICE PUDDING

*T*his dessert is good enough to serve the preacher for Sunday dinner. Bottled rose water adds a distinct bouquet to rice pudding and can be found in specialty shops.

2 quarts whole milk	½ cup slivered blanched almonds
1 cup long-grain rice	½ cup pistachio nuts, chopped
2 cups sugar	(optional)
8 tablespoons butter	¼-½ cup rose water (optional)
¼ teaspoon salt	Mint leaves for garnish

In a heavy bottomed saucepan, bring milk to a boil over high heat. Stirring constantly, pour in rice. Reduce heat to lowest possible setting and simmer uncovered 30 minutes, stirring frequently. Stir in the sugar, butter, salt and almonds and continue stirring over low heat until the sugar has dissolved. Cook 30 minutes or until the mixture is thick enough to hold its shape in a spoon. Stir in the rose water and place in a serving bowl or individual bowls. Sprinkle the top with the chopped pistachio nuts. Refrigerate for at least 2 hours, or until the pudding is thoroughly chilled and firm. Garnish with mint leaves and serve.

BUTTERSCOTCH PUDDING

1 cup light brown sugar	5 egg yolks, lightly beaten
¼ cup cornstarch	¼ cup butter, sliced
¼ teaspoon salt	2 teaspoons vanilla
4 cups half-and half	

In a medium saucepan combine brown sugar, cornstarch and salt. Whisk in the half-and-half. Whisk constantly and cook over medium heat until mixture is thickened and bubbly. Remove from heat. Gradually whisk 1 cup of hot mixture into egg yolks. Add egg yolk mixture to mixture in pan, whisk constantly and cook for 2 more minutes. Remove from heat and whisk in butter and vanilla. Pour pudding into a large bowl. Cover surface of pudding with plastic wrap. Chill 4-5 hours. Remove plastic wrap and stir. Spoon into dessert dishes and serve.

GRANNY'S BANANA PUDDING

When you talk about comfort food, this has to be at the top of the list. My husband says it hasn't tasted the same since they stopped selling the bananas on the stalk. He might have something there, since the bananas need to be fully ripe for this recipe. Yeah, you can make this with instant pudding and Kool Whip, but it's not nearly as good.

Serves 10-12, unless Dub shows up.

1¾ cups sugar
½ cup self-rising flour
2 whole eggs
3 eggs, separated
12 ounces evaporated milk
12 ounces water

2 tablespoons unsalted butter
1 tablespoon vanilla extract
5-6 ripe bananas
Vanilla wafers
½ cup powdered sugar
⅛ teaspoon cream of tartar

In a medium size boiler, combine sugar, flour and 2 whole eggs, one at a time and beating after each. Add the egg yolks, saving the whites for the meringue. Beat until well mixed, slowly stir in the milk and 12 ounces of water (rinse out the can). Cook slowly over low heat until pudding consistency. Remove from heat and add butter and vanilla. Stir pudding until it cools completely or place plastic wrap directly over pudding and refrigerate until cool. To make meringue, beat egg whites until stiff, add cream of tartar and sugar slowly. Lightly butter a baking dish, place a third of pudding in bottom of dish. Slice bananas a fourth inch thick, place a third over pudding. Cover bananas with single layer of vanilla wafers, and repeat layering. Spread with meringue and brown under broiler. Cool to room temperature and serve.

We think someone is jealous, but a bowl of Granny's banana pudding will resolve that problem, c 1975.

BREAD PUDDING

"Had a piece of pie, Had a piece of puddin'
And gave it all away To see Sally Goodin'."

Granny sometimes made bread pudding with left over biscuits (when there were any) and added lemon flavoring. Today, we use a lighter bread such as French, Cuban or loaf white bread. To make this a special dessert, serve with 2 tablespoons Lemon or Whiskey Sauce in bottom of individual dishes before adding bread pudding and top with Chantilly Sauce.

1 cup sugar
½ cup unsalted butter, softened
3 eggs
1 cup whipping cream
1 cup milk

2 teaspoons vanilla
Pinch of salt
5 cups stale biscuits, white bread or French bread with crust, crumbled

In a large bowl cream together the sugar and butter. Add the eggs and beat on high until well blended. Beat in the cream, milk, vanilla and salt. Add the crumbled bread to bowl and toss. Let the mixture stand for 45 minutes. Pat the bread down occasionally. Stir gently and pour into a buttered 9x13 pan. Place in a 350 degree oven, cover with aluminum foil and bake 30 minutes. Remove foil and bake 15 minutes more, or until set. Serve with Lemon Sauce (see page 371), or Whiskey Sauce (see below) and top with Chantilly Sauce (see page 337).

WHISKEY SAUCE

½ cup unsalted butter
¼ cup whipping cream
1 cup sugar

1 egg
Pinch of salt
½ cup bourbon

Melt butter in top of a double boiler and add cream. Add sugar, egg and salt that have been beaten together. Cook 3 minutes, stirring constantly until sugar dissolves. Remove from heat and let cool completely before adding bourbon. Serve with warm bread pudding.

OLD TIMEY CHARLOTTE

2 envelopes Knox gelatin
¼ cup cold water
1¾ cups milk
1½ cups sugar

1 pint whipping cream, whipped
4 egg whites, whipped to form stiff peaks
¼ cup white wine

Dissolve gelatin in water. Heat the milk and sugar and add the gelatin. Put aside to cool. When it begins to jell around the edges, gradually stir in the cream. Gently stir in the wine. Place in the refrigerator and chill for 2 hours, or until set.

TUPELO PANNA COTTA

Makes 8-6 inch custard cups

2 envelopes unflavored gelatin
½ cup cold water
4 cups heavy cream
1 tablespoon Tupelo honey

½ cup sugar
2 teaspoon vanilla
1 pint fresh strawberries

Lightly butter ramekins and place on a baking pan. Sprinkle gelatin over a fourth cup of the water. Let stand until softened, about 10 minutes. In a heavy-bottomed sauce pan add the remaining water, cream, honey, sugar and vanilla. Heat mixture over medium heat until hot but not boiling. Remove from heat and stir in the gelatin until completely dissolved.   Pour mixture into custard cups, cool, cover and chill overnight. Run a knife around edges of cups to loosen. Invert onto the center of dessert plate and garnish with strawberries.

SILKY SMOOTH FLAN

Serves 6

1½ cups sugar
4 eggs
Dash of salt

2 cups whipping cream
2 ounces vanilla

Preheat oven 170 degrees. In a small cast-iron skillet, melt a half cup sugar over low heat. Stir until sugar turns to a liquid and becomes a caramel color, 3-4 minutes. Pour into a 6 cup, round, glass dish with handles, tilt to let caramel run up sides by a half inch. In a large mixing bowl, beat eggs with a whisk. Add 1 cup of sugar, salt, whipping cream and vanilla. Whisk until mixed well. Pour through a sieve into pan with caramel. Place flan dish in a 9x13 inch pan. Set in center of oven and fill larger pan with enough hot water to come half way up sides of flan dish. Bake four and a half hours or until knife inserted in center comes out clean. Remove flan from oven and water bath. Cool to room temperature, cover with plastic wrap and refrigerate at least 4 hours before serving. Refrigerating overnight will improve flavor. To serve, run sharp knife around rim of flan. Place platter over top of flan, invert and pour any remaining syrup over the flan.

HOSPITALITY PINEAPPLE FLUFF

*T*he pineapple is a symbol of hospitality and you'll find it carved above the door in many Southern plantations. It is also featured on bedposts on some of the antique beds in those mansions. Hmmm.

The pineapple does not continue to ripen once it is picked, so look for those that have a delightful aroma.

1½ cups fresh pineapple cut into chunks
2 cups whipping cream
½ cup powdered sugar, more if needed

Finely chop pineapple in food processor. Remove to glass bowl, cover with plastic wrap and refrigerate until chilled. Place cream and sugar in food processor. Process until whipped, add pineapple and additional sugar if needed. Pulse 3-4 times to blend. Serve in chilled wine glasses and garnish with fresh mint. Serve immediately.

LEMON SQUARES

Makes 16 squares
1 cup plus 2 tablespoons all-purpose flour
¼ cup confectioners' sugar plus additional for sprinkling over the top
2 large eggs
¾ cup granulated sugar
3 tablespoons fresh lemon juice
½ teaspoon double-acting baking powder
½ cup cold unsalted butter cut into bits

Preheat oven 350 degrees. In a bowl blend together 1 cup of the flour, the butter and a fourth cup of confectioners' sugar until it resembles meal. Pat the mixture into the bottom of an 8 inch square baking pan. Bake 12-15 minutes or until pale golden. In another bowl with an electric mixer beat the eggs until they are thick and pale, beat in the granulated sugar and lemon juice, and beat the mixture for 8 minutes. Sift in the remaining 2 tablespoons of flour and the baking powder, stir the mixture until well combined, pour it over the baked crust. Bake in the middle of the oven for 20 minutes. Remove from oven and sift the top with additional confectioners' sugar. Let cool in the pan before cutting into squares.

PECAN PRALINES

*T*here are two secrets to making perfect, creamy-textured pralines: evaporated milk and a heavy-bottomed pot. It is important to work quickly since the mixture stiffens in the pot in a very short time. Pralines are a classic Southern candy and truly worth the effort.

¾ cup unsalted butter
1 cup sugar
1 cup light brown sugar, firmly packed
½ cup whipping cream

1 cup pecans, chopped
2 cups pecan halves
2 tablespoons vanilla
2 tablespoons sour mash bourbon
1 cup evaporated milk

Melt butter over medium-high heat in a very heavy bottomed pot. Add granulated sugar, brown sugar and cream. Turn heat to high and cook for 1 minute, stirring constantly. With a whisk, add evaporated milk and chopped pecans. Cook 4 more minutes, whisking constantly. Reduce heat to medium and cook 5 more minutes, whisking constantly. Add pecan halves, vanilla, and bourbon stirring constantly with a wooden spoon. Cook for 15 minutes or until candy thermometer reads 240 degrees. The mixture will begin to pull away from the sides of pan as you stir. Lower heat if pralines are cooking too fast. Remove candy from heat and drop by heaping tablespoons onto wax paper.

HICKORY NUT CAKES

"Taught to the tune of a Hickory stick."

Makes 5 dozen

2⅓ cups all-purpose flour
2 teaspoons baking powder
1 teaspoon salt
1 cup unsalted butter
¾ cup light brown sugar

½ cup light corn syrup
2 eggs
1 teaspoon vanilla extract
1 cup coarsely chopped hickory nuts
¼ cup milk

Combine flour, baking powder and salt. Cream butter and add sugar gradually and cream until light and fluffy. Add the corn syrup and blend thoroughly. Add eggs, one at the time, beating well after each addition. Stir in vanilla and hickory nuts. Add dry ingredients alternating with milk. Drop by teaspoonfuls onto greased baking sheet. Bake 375 degrees for 12-15 minutes.

RUBY'S SECRET OATMEAL COOKIES

*T*he secret is not in the recipe, but in the location where the cookies are hidden. When our family gets together, there are lots of us. So, when someone brings a great dessert, you can count on some of it being hidden in some nook or cranny for later enjoyment.

I know just about all the hiding places, so I still get my fair—or maybe unfair—share.

Ruby

Makes 5 dozen cookies

1½ cups all-purpose flour
½ teaspoon salt
1 teaspoon baking powder
1 teaspoon baking soda
2 cups light brown sugar
1 cup unsalted butter, room temperature
2 eggs
1 teaspoon vanilla
3 cups Old-Fashion Quaker Oats
2 cups pecans, coarsely chopped
½-1 cup semi-sweet chocolate morsels
1 cup powdered sugar

Sift flour, salt, baking powder and soda into a medium bowl, set aside. In a large bowl, cream sugar, butter, eggs and vanilla. Add flour mixture and stir well. Stir in oats, pecans and chocolate morsels. Cover with plastic wrap and chill until firm. Preheat oven to 350 degrees. Roll dough into 1 inch balls and coat with powdered sugar. Place on cookie sheet and press with bottom of glass until slightly flattened. Bake 8-10 minutes, making sure not to over bake.

GRAYTON SAND TARTS

When we were young, Grayton Beach was where we enjoyed the beautiful Gulf of Mexico. We had many wonderful beach parties on those sugar white sands. It has been called the most beautiful beach in the world by many and we wholeheartedly agree.

1 egg white
1 cup butter
1 cup sugar
1 egg yolk
2 teaspoons vanilla
2 cups all-purpose flour
1 cup pecans, chopped fine

Preheat oven 275 degrees. Beat egg white until soft peaks form. In another bowl, cream butter and sugar. Add egg yolk, vanilla, flour, nuts and mix thoroughly. Spread in a buttered 10x15 jelly roll pan. Brush with egg white and bake for 45 minutes. Remove from oven, cool for 2-3 minutes, no longer and cut into 1 inch x 2 inch cookies.

DESSERT CREPES

½ cup all-purpose flour
¼ teaspoon salt,
3 eggs

1 cup milk
4 tablespoons unsalted butter melted

Place the flour, salt, eggs, milk and butter in a food processor, and process for 1 minute. Let batter stand at room temperature for 30 minutes. Pour 3-4 tablespoons of batter into a lightly greased, heated, 8 inch crepe pan. Tilt the pan so that the batter clings to and quickly covers the bottom. Cook the crepe until it turns a light brown. Flip with a spatula and cook the other side. Slide onto a plate. Regrease the pan and continue to cook more. Crepes can be stacked on top of one another.

Raspberry Sauce

2 cups fresh raspberries
¼ cup sugar
1 tablespoon lemon juice
2 tablespoons cognac

Purée raspberries in food processor, about 30 seconds. Add the remaining ingredients and process until sugar is dissolved. Strain the purée and discard the seeds. Refrigerate until ready to serve. Makes 1 cup.

Lemon Sauce

2 tablespoons lemon juice
½ cup water
¼ cup sugar
2 teaspoons cornstarch
1 teaspoon vanilla
2 tablespoons unsalted butter
½ teaspoon grated lemon rind
Dash salt

Place lemon juice, water, sugar and cornstarch in a double boiler. Cook until thickened, stirring constantly. Remove from heat and stir in vanilla, butter, lemon rind and salt. Makes three-fourths cup.

Orange Sauce (Suzette)

8 tablespoons unsalted butter
½ cup sugar
Juice of one orange
3 ounces of brandy
3 ounces Grand Marnier

Put butter and sugar in a skillet, cook over moderate heat stirring constantly until sugar is caramelized. Stir in orange juice a little at the time, stirring constantly. When all the juice has been added and the sauce is smooth, add brandy and Grand Marnier and ignite. Spoon the flaming sauce over the crepes.

Blackberry Sauce

2 cups fresh Blackberries
¼ cup sugar
1 tablespoon lemon juice
2 tablespoons cognac

Purée Blackberries in food processor, for about 30 seconds. Add the remaining ingredients and process until sugar is dissolved. Strain the purée and discard the seeds. Refrigerate until ready to serve. Makes one cup.

RICH HOMEMADE VANILLA ICE CREAM

Real vanilla beans give a rich taste that you just can't get at the ice cream parlor. In the summer, we love to put any type of fresh fruit over the ice cream and sprinkle it with Creme de Cassis, a French liqueur made from black currants. It's also great with Hot Fudge Sauce (below).

Makes 2 quarts

1 quart milk
2½ cups sugar
2 vanilla beans or

2 tablespoons vanilla extract
6 egg yolks, beaten
2 cups whipping cream

If using vanilla beans, chop in half pieces and place in food processor with 1 cup sugar. Pulse until beans are pulverized and set aside. Heat milk in a heavy saucepan-do not let boil. Stir in sugar and vanilla beans until sugar is dissolved. Remove from heat and let cool slightly. Stir in egg yolks. If not using vanilla beans, stir in vanilla extract and cream. Strain through fine sieve and cool to room temperature. Refrigerate until chilled. Place in ice cream freezer and freeze following manufacturer's directions.

Amaretto Pecan Ice Cream
This is a wonderful combination. We wonder why Howard Johnson never tried it. Amaretto has an almond vanilla flavor and it's one of our favorite liqueurs from Italy. A perfect match with pecans. Add 12 tablespoons Amaretto to Vanilla Ice Cream mix.. Cool, cover with plastic wrap and chill. Pour chilled mixture into freezer and freeze according to directions. Add 2 cups roasted, chopped pecans the last 5 minutes of freezing. Makes 2 quarts.

Fresh Peach Ice Cream
Peel and pit 16 medium peaches, add to bowl of food processor with 2 tablespoons lemon juice. Pulse in food processor until peaches are in small chunks. Stir in 12 tablespoons Peach Amaretto and chill. Place chilled mixture in ice cream freezer and freeze according to instructions. Makes 2 quarts.

HOT FUDGE SAUCE

Melt 3 squares of unsweet chocolate and a fourth cup butter in double boiler over medium-low heat, stirring constantly. When melted, blend in 1 cup XXXX sugar and stir with a wooden spoon until dissolved. Add 3 tablespoons of cream or milk and stir rapidly until mixture is smooth. Add remaining cream, 1 teaspoon vanilla, 2 tablespoons Grand Marnier, one- eighth teaspoon salt and stir to blend smooth. Makes one and one half cups.

FRUIT SORBETS

Fruit Sorbet

Pour two-two and a half cups fruit purée and 1 cup of simple syrup and a fourth cup lemon juice into container and stir. Place in refrigerator to chill. Pour into bowl of ice cream freezer and freeze, about 20 minutes.

Mango Sorbet

Mix two-two and a half cups mango purée with I cup simple syrup and one-fourth cup lemon juice into container, stir and cover. Place in refrigerator to chill. Freeze in ice cream freezer, about 20 minutes.

Raspberry Sorbet

Strain two and a half to three cups raspberry purée to remove seeds before mixing. Stir with 1 cup simple syrup and a fourth cup lemon juice, cover and place in refrigerator to chill. Freeze in ice cream freezer, about 20 minutes.

Strawberry Sorbet

Mix 3 cups strawberry purée with 1 cup simple syrup and a fourth cup lemon juice, cover and place in refrigerator to chill. Freeze in ice cream freezer, about 20 minutes.

Watermelon Sorbet

Remove seeds and rind from watermelon. Purée water melon. Add three and a half cups watermelon purée to 1 cup simple syrup and a fourth cup lemon juice, cover and place in refrigerator to chill. Freeze in ice cream freezer, about 20 minutes.

Pear Sorbet

Purée 12 peeled and cored pears and add to 1 cup simple syrup and a fourth cup lemon juice, stir , cover and chill in refrigerator. Freeze in ice cream freezer, about 20 minutes.

Satsuma Sorbet

Add 4 cups satsuma juice and zest of 2 satsuma to 1 cup simple syrup and a fourth cup lemon juice. Stir, cover and chill in refrigerator. Freeze in ice cream freezer, about 20 minutes.

Blackberry Sorbet

Strain two and a half to three cups blackberry purée to remove seeds before mixing with 1 cup simple syrup and a fourth cup lemon juice. Stir, cover and chill in refrigerator. Freeze in ice cream freezer, about 20 minutes.

SIMPLE SYRUP

Place 4 cups sugar and 4 cups water in a saucepan and simmer until sugar is dissolved. Cool to room temperature, refrigerate covered.

DESSERTS AND SWEET THANGS

SCOTTISH TRIFLE

"Did you ever see a Lassie go this way and that"

*T*his is our favorite dessert when strawberries and peaches are at their best.

Serves 10-12

- 2 recipes Custard Sauce (4 cups)
- Sponge Cake
- 6 ripe peaches peeled and pitted
- 1½ cups water
- ½ cup sugar
- 1 teaspoon vanilla
- ½ cup Peach Amaretto liqueur
- ⅓ cup sliced almonds, toasted and cooled
- 1 pint strawberries, sliced ¼ inch thick
- 1 cup Chantilly Sauce
- 2 sprigs fresh mint leaves, for garnish

Make the Custard Sauce (see page 397) and bake sponge cake (see page 335). Slice each Sponge Cake in half horizontally; there will be 4 layers. Blanch peaches in boiling water for 20 seconds. Rinse under cold water, drain and peel. Bring one and a half cups of water, sugar and vanilla to a boil. Cook until sugar dissolves. Add peaches, cover and simmer for 4 minutes. Remove peaches with a slotted spoon. Reserve a half cup of the poaching liquid. Place 4 of the peaches in the refrigerator, pit and chop the remaining peaches and add to the half cup of poaching liquid syrup. Simmer peaches until syrup reduces and thickens, about 6 minutes. Transfer to a dish, cover and refrigerate. Assemble the trifle in a two and a half quart straight-edge glass serving bowl in the following order: Place a half cup of the custard in the bottom of the bowl. Add a layer of the cake, brush with peach amaretto, arrange a third of the peach slices over cake layer and a third of the strawberries, arrange some of the slices against the side of the bowl so they will show. Lightly cover with custard. Repeat the steps but reserve 10 slices of the strawberries and peaches for garnish. Spread the remaining Custard Sauce. Chill overnight. Cover with Chantilly Sauce (see page 337), garnish with the almonds, reserved peach slices, strawberry slices, and mint leaves. Serve this dessert on special occasions.

Butch and Sundance.

Family and Friends

Tom Wright with our granddaughters Amelia Tallulah, Elizabeth Gray and Ruby Violet Wright, c 2002.

Leek and Potato Soup, 378
Leg of Lamb, 379
Scottish Scones, 379
Shepherd's Pie, 380
Tallulah's Chicken Pie, 381
Snips and Snails, 382
Mimosa Salad, 382
Rack of Lamb, 383
Decadent Chocolate Pie, 383
Cameron's Favorite Salad, 384
Mashed Red New Potatoes, 384
Steak Dianne, 385
Banana Betty, 385
Antipasto, 386
Risotto Milanese, 386
Osso Bucco, 387
Broccoli Rabe 387
Stuffed Veal Chops, 388
Polenta, 389
Italian Wedding Cake, 389
Veal King Ferdinand, 390
Soup du Jour, 390
Red Beans and Rice, 391
Cajun Cornbread, 391
Jo's Pub Burgers, 392
Stuffed Peppers, 393
The Ultimate Mac n' Cheese, 393
Cracked Conch, 394
Pigeon Peas and Rice, 394
Bahamian Salt Fish, 395
Jamaican Jerk Goat, 395
Szechwan Stir Fry, 396
Middle Eastern Meatloaf, 397
Tuscon Style Pasta, 397
Southern Fried Chicken, 399
Mama's White Cake, 399
Sloppy Jo, 400
Granny's Biscuit Pudding, 401
   Custard Sauce, 401
Pork Red Gravy, 402
Mama's Pear Salad, 402
She Crab Soup, 403
Bloody Mary, 403
Charlie's Pear Wine, 404
Ingram's Camp Stew, 405
Jo's Camp Stew, 405
Ingram's Camp Cornbread, 405
Joyce's Coconut Cake, 406
Old-Timey Egg Custard, 407
Pound Cake, 407
Mother's Carrot Cake, 408
Mother's German
   Chocolate Cake, 409
Mother's Lane Cake, 409

FAMILY AND FRIENDS

Book signing at the Big House, c 1994.

When we first published *Seasonal Florida* in 1994 we were overwhelmed. We suddenly realized there were 5,000 books to be sold and had not a clue as how to do it. On weekends my husband and I would drive around and knock on doors at bookstores and gift shops. We were selling books but at a much slower pace than we had hoped. But then all of a sudden orders were coming in from family and friends. The books were flying out the door. Sisters, brothers, nieces, nephews and friends from all over Florida were out selling our book to their friends and families and before we knew it the first edition had sold out in less than a year. We were getting requests for book signings at many of the book stores. The word had spread and orders were coming in from practically every state and several foreign countries.

Many wrote and thanked us for a recipe that they had remembered enjoying in childhood. Some sent their version of an old family favorite.

Now into our fourth printing we have an opportunity like Garth's "Friends in Low Places" to add a new chapter to include some of the recipes we left out in the first editions. Hopefully this chapter on Family and Friends will put an end to the fussing, but I doubt it.

While researching some of our family recipes we stumbled on to some family history and decided to research the McDonald side of my family. After a lot of digging we discovered that my great, great, grandfather, Lauchlin McDonald, had immigrated from the Isle of Skye, Scotland to North Carolina in 1795. Then in the 1820's the McDonalds and about fifty other Scottish families relocated to Northwest Florida and settled in and around the Euchee Valley in Walton County.

Pond house and dock at Eucheeanna former kitchen to the original house, c 2004.

This was about twenty years before Florida became a state. We found in Tallahassee a copy of the 1828 deed documenting Lauchlin's purchase of 80 acres north of Bruce Creek for $100.00. He soon built a large double pen split-log house with a hall running through it and reared twelve children on that farm. Four of his sons served in the Confederate Army during the War of the Yankee Oppression, unfortunately only one returned, my great grandfather Norman McDonald.

Norman and his three brothers had left behind another brother, Archibald to look after the farm and their four "old maid" sisters. Archie joined the home guard and everything was fine until the last days of the war when a Yankee raiding party came from Pensacola. General Asbouth took the Giles Bowers home as his headquarters and his troops pitched their tents in the open pasture between the Bower's house and Eucheeanna. The Yankee soldiers then rounded up the home guard of the valley and put them in the jailhouse at Eucheeanna.

The troops then scoured the country side and took all the food they could find. The general sent a raiding party out to the McDonald farm to capture Archibald. But the sisters had been warned and had hidden Archie under the house in a hole made when clay had been dug out to build the chimney.. The Yankee soldiers began to round up the livestock but the yardbirds were too wild to be caught, so they shot them with their rifles. A wounded rooster ran under the house and flopped around near where Archie was hiding. A soldier crawled under the house and yelled "I've got you now!" Archie thought he was caught but the soldier had caught the rooster.

Archie's sister said "when Archie crawled out from under the house, two days later, his hair was as white as the sand on the beach".

Archie McDonald, c 1910.

After the War, Archie and his sisters sold the farm and moved to Eucheeanna, the county seat of Walton County at that time.

Fortunately my husband and I recently had the opportunity to buy back the same farm for our children, grandchildren and hopefully on and on. We plan on rebuilding the log cabin in the same location as the original one and stocking the pastures with a few Florida cracker cattle and Gulf Coast native sheep. Also stock the ponds with Bass, Bream and Channel catfish.

Marshall Dillon and Miss Kitty, c 1980.

We also plan to plant some peach, plum, mayhaw, pear, persimmon, black walnut, chinquapin, pecan and chestnut trees. And later build a small scuppernong arbor for future generations and perhaps plant a small herb and vegetable garden near the kitchen.

Bruce Creek still has plenty of fish and the creek swamp is full of deer, turkeys, squirrels, rabbits and wood ducks. Blackberries, blueberries and wild grapes are abundant as they were when Lochlin and his family settled there in 1828.

We think you can go back.

THE FOODS OF SCOTLAND

Soon after we discovered my great, great grandfather Lochlin McDonald had immigrated from the Isle of Skye, Scotland we planned a trip there. We wanted to see the land they left behind and visit any relatives still there. We learned the Head of Clan Donald was Lord Godfrey Macdonald and he had converted his hunting lodge "Kinloch" into an Inn. So we made reservations and stayed at Kinloch while visiting in Skye. The accommodations were wonderful and the food was scrumpdillyicious. A typical Scottish breakfast at Kinloch began with freshly squeezed orange juice, wonderful hot coffee, yogurt and heather honey, a large bowl of porridge (oatmeal), with thick cream and Damascus sugar. Next came free range chicken eggs, cooked to order, back bacon, sausage, black and white puddings and kippers (smoked fish), broiled tomatoes, great homemade bread and scones, orange marmalade and more hot coffee. Sorry, no grits to be found. After eating a breakfast like that, it made us want to run out and shear a sheep.

Lord Godfrey's wife Lady Claire MacDonald is an authority on Scottish food and has written fourteen cookery books. She graciously gave us permission to share the following recipes from her books with you.

Leek and Potato Soup

This soup is similar to Scotland's famous Cock-a-leekie soup, but without the cock and prunes. Claire says this Leek and Potato soup is at the top of her list for favorite soups because of the numerous ways to make it. Cold and velvety-smooth in hot summer evenings, with snipped chives stirred through (Vichyssoise), or hot and smooth on chilly evenings.

Serves 6

- 1 oz butter plus 2 tablespoons sunflower oil
- 1 onion, skinned and chopped
- 1 stick of celery, washed and trimmed and very finely sliced
- 4 leeks-more if they are small washed and trimmed, sliced diagonally (because it looks nicer) into thin strips
- 4 medium potatoes, peeled and diced neatly
- 1 teaspoon medium-strength curry powder
- 2 pints good chicken or vegetable stock
- Salt and freshly ground black pepper
- 1-2 tablespoons chopped parsley

Melt the butter and heat the oil in a saucepan and add the chopped onion. Cook for 2-3 minutes, till the onion is soft and transparent, then stir in the celery and leeks and cook for a further few minutes. Add the diced potatoes and stir in the curry powder. Cook all together for a minute or two, then pour in the stock. Simmer very gently for 25 minutes. Cool, liquidize half the soup, return it to the saucepan with the remainder of the soup and stir all together well. Taste, and season with salt and pepper. Sprinkle with parsley and serve.

Leg of Lamb

The Isle of Skye is one of the most beautiful places we have ever visited. It is surrounded by picturesque seashores and has gorgeous mountains with streams and lakes at every turn. It's hard to find any countryside there that is not dotted with sheep, sheep and more sheep. Some are solid white and some have black faces. In the spring each ewe has one or two lambs at her side. Because of their diet of heather and wild grasses Scotland's lamb is considered, by many, to be the best in the world.

Uncle Floyd McDonald, c 1940 with lambs descended from sheep brought from Scotland in the 1800's.

To roast lamb:

Trim off excess fat and rub the leg all over with softened butter, then stick a sharp knife into it in frequent places and stick slivers of garlic in the cuts. Season the leg with salt and plenty of black pepper, and scatter rosemary over it. Pour about one pint of red wine over the lamb in its roasting tin and roast it for 20 minutes per pound weight in a very hot oven initially - for the first 45 minutes of cooking at 425 degrees, then reduce the heat a bit, to 400 degrees, for the rest of the cooking time. Allow about 20 minutes after the cooking time is up for the lamb to sit in a very low-temperature oven before carving, if you are serving it hot-this allows the juices to settle and makes carving much easier, of course this isn't necessary if you are serving the lamb at room temperature.

Scottish Scones

Makes 20-25
1½ pound self-rising flour
1 rounded teaspoon salt
2 rounded teaspoons sugar (optional)
2 rounded teaspoons baking powder
2 eggs
2 tablespoons sunflower oil
About ¾ pint of milk

Stir the dry ingredients together into a mixing bowl. Beat together the eggs and oil in a measuring jug and make up to 1 pint with milk. Stir the egg, oil, and milk mixture into the dry ingredients. Knead (it will be fairly sticky), then pat the mixture out on a floured surface until it is about 1 inch thick. Cut scones out with a two and a half inch cutter. Bake in a hot oven, 425 degrees, for 10-15 minutes. These are best made and eaten the same day, but they freeze well. You can add some grated cheese to the basic recipe - to this quantity add 4 tablespoons of grated cheese. Warm buttery cheese scones are delicious and go surprisingly well with jam, particularly strawberry, raspberry or blackberry.

THE MEAT PIES

When our Scottish ancestors came to Walton County, in the 1820's they brought with them cattle and sheep. They also brought with them the art of making high quality whiskey but that is another story. My Grandfather Charlie McDonald and great Uncle Charlie Garrett kept large flocks of sheep. They would burn the woods before each Spring to encourage the grasses to sprout early. The sheep were allowed free access to all the land that was not fenced, which was pretty much all of the county. Each sheep had it's owners mark. Great Uncle Charlie Garrett registered his mark at the Walton County Courthouse. It was a crop split and under bit in the right ear. Crop and under crop and over bit in the left ear. The flocks were rounded up in the Spring, the new lambs were marked and the older sheep sheared, then the wool was sold as a cash crop.

After we bought the old McDonald farm in Walton County I asked my husband what could we do with it. He replied he wanted to stock it with a few sheep as did my great great grandparents. When I asked what on earth for? He replied, when folks asked him what he did for a living he could tell them he was a shepherd!

His version of the old standby Shepherd's Pie is a little different but it's really very good.

Shepherds Pie

Serves 4

- 1 onion, chopped
- 1 tablespoon bacon drippings
- 1 pound roasted lamb, beef or venison, cut into bite size pieces
- 1 teaspoon thyme, crumbled
- 1 recipe of Macho Gravy
- 4 hard-boiled eggs, sliced
- 1 cup carrots, sliced
- 1 cup English peas
- Salt and pepper to taste
- 3 cups garlic mashed potatoes

Cook onions in a large cast-iron skillet in bacon drippings until translucent. Add roast, thyme and Macho Gravy (see page 356). Stir and cook 10 minutes on low heat. Place the roast mixture in a 9x12 inch pan. Next add eggs, carrots and peas, salt and pepper to taste. Cover with Garlic Mashed Potatoes (see page 36) and bake in 400 degree oven for 20 minutes.

I eat my peas with honey,
I've done it all my life,
It makes them taste funny,
But it keeps them on the knife.

Sally, Trey's Australian Shepherd.

My husbands great grandma Tallulah Baker was known all over North Florida and South Alabama for her chicken pie. At any gathering for the community or church dinners on the ground, she would bring the chicken pie and always got lots of compliments. When someone in the community passed away she would be there with her chicken pie. You could always count on it at family reunions. Kinfolk would come from all over just to get a helping of that chicken pie. We wish we could give you the recipe for grandma Baker's chicken pie but grandma took it to her grave. Please don't be a Grandma Baker. Write your recipes down and share them with family and friends.

Grandma Baker always grew a huge vegetable garden and sold the surplus in town. In 1926 she bought a brand new Model T Ford roadster at the Ponce de Leon Motor Co. for $477.80. One of the conditions of buying the car was that the salesman, John Creel, who later owned the Ford dealership in DeFuniak Springs, would teach her how to drive, which he did. In this car she carried her surplus vegetables and eggs to town and sold them to help make the $27.65 per month car payment.

After talking with her two surviving grandchildren, who are in their eighties, we think our recipe is very much like hers. We think Grandma Baker would whole-heartedly approve. Especially if you wring the neck, pluck, clean, singe over brown paper bags and cook the chicken as she always did. As Grandpa Baker would say, "You're gonna love this pie or grits ain't groceries."

Grandma Baker's Model T Ford, c 1962.

Tallulah's Chicken Pie

1 Fat hen
Water
8 hard-boiled eggs

1 stick butter
2 cups milk

Makes two pies.

Boil a fat hen in water to barely cover until very tender. Cool in broth. Remove skin and bones and discard, cut meat in pieces. Divide the chicken and broth into fourths and place one-fourth in the bottom of two casseroles. Barely cover with the broth and season to taste. Add two sliced hard-boiled eggs, a fourth stick butter (cut into small pieces) and a half cup milk to each casserole. Place cris-crossed strips of pastry (see page 44, delete sugar) over the top. Repeat procedure with remaining chicken, more hard-boiled eggs, broth, milk and butter. Cover with pastry strips and bake at 350 degrees, for about an hour or until crust is brown and filling is bubbling. YUM YUM, give me some!

FAMILY AND FRIENDS

THE BIRTHDAY SUPPERS

TREY'S BIRTHDAY SUPPER

Snips and Snails
Mimosa Salad
Rack of Lamb
Spinach Timbales
Potatoes Anna
Decadent Chocolate Pie

Snips and Snails

Serves 4
½ cup butter, softened
2 tablespoons shallots, very finely minced
10 cloves of garlic, pressed or very finely minced
1-1¼ teaspoons salt
⅛ teaspoon white pepper
⅓ cup parsley, finely minced
4½ ounce can snails (escargot)
Dry vermouth

Preheat oven 450 degrees. Rinse snails with cold water, drain and pat dry with paper towels. Cream butter, shallots, garlic, salt, pepper and parsley. Let mixture set at room temperature 2 hours. Place 1 teaspoon of butter mixture in individual snail containers or shallow scallop shells. Add the snails and the remaining butter. Sprinkle with dry vermouth. Bake 10 minutes in center of oven.
Serve with thinly sliced French bread that has been toasted.

Mimosa Salad and Mimosa Dressing

Serves 4
½ teaspoon salt
Freshly ground black pepper, to taste
1 medium shallot, chopped fine
5 tablespoons extra virgin olive oil
1 tablespoon fresh thyme, chopped
2 tablespoons Italian red wine vinegar

Place all ingredients in a glass jar with a tight fitting lid. Shake vigorously and let sit 15 minutes.

1 hard boiled egg, sieved
1 tablespoon parsley, chopped
1 head of bibb lettuce
¼ pound arugula
1 cup grape tomatoes, quartered

Combine the sieved egg with the chopped parsley, this mixture is called the "mimosa" and set aside. Wash bibb, remove outer leaves and dry. Tear in bite size pieces into large bowl, add arugula and lightly toss with dressing. Arrange on individual salad plates with tomatoes on top. Sprinkle mimosa over each salad and serve.

Rack of Lamb

Serves 4
Two 1 to 1¼ pounds racks of lamb, Frenched, and cracked
1 tablespoon olive oil
Salt and pepper to taste
2 teaspoons dried rosemary, crumbled

Trim racks of fat so that only a thin layer of fat remains. Rub the lamb with olive oil and sprinkle with salt, pepper and rosemary, coating all sides. Let the lamb rest at room temperature for one hour. Preheat oven to 500 degrees. Arrange the lamb fat side up in a small roasting pan. Roast for 10 minutes. Reduce heat to 400 degrees and roast for another 10 minutes for medium-rare meat. Start with Snips and Snails. Let the roast stand 10 minutes before cutting into chops. Arrange on plates and serve with Potatoes Anna and Spinach Timbals.

Decadent Chocolate Pie

Crust:
One recipe pie crust rolled to fit an 11 inch tart pan. Fill shell with weights and bake 12-15 minutes until brown.

Serves 12
Filling:
2 cups semisweet chocolate chips
1 ½ teaspoons vanilla
⅛ teaspoon salt
1 ½ cups whipping cream, scalded
6 egg yolks
Chilled raspberry sauce

Add chocolate chips, vanilla and salt to the bowl of a food processor and process until chips are pulverized. Add scalded cream and process until all chocolate has melted. Add egg yolks and process 10 seconds. Pour mixture into tart shell and freeze overnight.

Crème Anglaise:
7 egg yolks
½ cup sugar
1 cup milk
¾ cup heavy cream
1 teaspoon vanilla extract

Beat egg yolks and sugar in the top of a double boiler until pale yellow. Gradually add the milk and cream, stirring constantly. Cook over simmering water until mixture will coat the back of a wooden spoon, about nine minutes. Refrigerate overnight.

To assemble place 2-3 tablespoons Crème Anglaise on dessert plate and tilt until bottom of plate is covered. Remove pie from freezer and place a slice of pie on top of sauce. Make 5-7 small circles with Raspberry Sauce (see page 375) around outer edge of Creme Anglaise. Drag a toothpick, beginning in center of raspberry circles, and connect circles to make heart shapes and serve.

THE BIRTHDAY SUPPERS

CAMERON'S BIRTHDAY SUPPER

Marinated Calico Scallops
Camerons' Favorite Salad
Mashed Red New Potatoes
Steak Dianne
Banana Betty
The Chocolate Cake

Cameron's Favorite Salad

1 bag premixed tender whole leaf baby lettuces
1 fennel bulb
¼ pound blue cheese
½ cup roasted walnuts
⅓ cup extra virgin olive oil
Juice of half a lemon
Salt and freshly ground black pepper

Divide lettuces equally in salad plates. Wash and quarter fennel bulb. Slice fennel bulb thinly with a mandoline or potato peeler. Arrange on top of salad Crumble cheese and roasted walnuts and sprinkle over each salad. Drizzle with olive oil and lemon juice, salt and pepper to taste.

Mashed Red New Potatoes

2 pounds small red new potatoes
Salt and freshly ground black pepper, to taste
¼ cup butter
½ cup whipping cream

Partially peel potatoes and cut into chunks. Place in boiler, barely cover with water, add salt, cover and bring to a boil. Reduce heat to simmer and cook about 20 minutes or until tender. Drain off water and leave in pan. Add butter and use a fork to mash leaving some lumps. Stir in whipping cream and pepper, taste for additional salt and serve.

Steak Dianne

Serves 4

- 4 Delmonico (rib-eye) steaks,
- 2 tablespoons green peppercorns, crushed
- 2 tablespoons soy sauce
- 1 tablespoon Worcestershire
- ½ tablespoon olive oil
- 4 tablespoons unsalted butter
- ¼ cup green onions, chopped
- ¼ cup parsley, chopped
- 1 tablespoon cornstarch
- 1 tablespoon Dijon mustard
- 1½ cups beef broth
- ½ lemon
- ¼ cup Madeira wine

Trim the fat from the steaks. Crush peppercorns between sheets of plastic wrap with meat pounder. Press the peppercorns into both sides of the meat , pound steaks between sheets of plastic wrap until a half inch thick. Sprinkle the steaks with soy sauce and Worcestershire. Heat a cast-iron skillet over medium-high heat, add the oil, when hot add one tablespoon of the butter. When foam subsides add the steaks and sear one and one half- two minutes on each side. Mix the cornstarch, mustard and broth together and set aside. Reduce heat to medium and continue to cook steaks 1-2 minutes on each side. Remove steaks to a heated platter and pour the fat from the pan. Add remaining three tablespoons butter, add green onions and parsley and cook for a moment. Stir in the broth mixture and cook until slightly thickened. Add the lemon juice and Madeira. Add any juices from platter. Stir and reduce sauce if needed, add the steaks to the skillet and spoon the sauce over them. Place steaks on individual plates with mashed potatoes and pour additional sauce over the steaks.

Banana Betty

- 1 recipe gingersnap piecrust
- 1 recipe custard
- 1 tablespoon dark rum
- 5-6 ripe bananas sliced
- Juice of half a lemon
- 1 recipe Chantilly Sauce
- 3 tablespoons crushed ginger snaps

Prepare custard (see page 397), adding rum and stirring well until cool. Sprinkle bananas with lemon juice, lightly toss and drain. Pour half of cooled custard into piecrust (see page 44), add bananas and cover with remaining custard. Cover with plastic wrap and cool 30 minutes. Cover with Chantilly Sauce (see page 337) and sprinkle with crumbs.

THE BIRTHDAY SUPPERS

JUNIOR'S BIRTHDAY SUPPER

Antipasto
Fried Zucchini
Osso Bucco
Risotto Milanese
Broccoli Rabe
Lafayette Grill Cake

Antipasto

Cantaloupe slices wrapped with proscuitto
One half roasted red bell pepper, julienne
Anchovies wrapped around capers
One half vine ripe tomato, sliced
Slices Buffalo mozzarella
Fresh basil leaves, torn

Salami cut into chunks
Mushroom's sautéed in butter Sprinkled with lemon juice
Greek olives
Marinated artichoke hearts, quartered
Lemon
Extra virgin olive oil

Arrange above on a large platter. Drizzle with extra virgin olive oil and lemon juice. Lightly salt and add freshly ground black pepper.

Risotto Milanese

Serves 6-8
8 tablespoons unsalted butter
1 cup onion, minced
1 tablespoon beef marrow, chopped
Salt to taste

5 cups chicken stock
¼ teaspoon saffron threads
6-8 tablespoons grated Parmesan cheese
2 cups Arboria rice

Place saffron in a fourth cup of hot chicken broth to let flavors develop. In a wide mouth large pot, melt the butter over medium heat until melted. Add the onions and stir in the beef marrow, breaking it up until it melts. Cook and stir until onions are translucent.

Add the rice and stir to coat with the butter. Add just enough broth to cover the top of the rice. Stir constantly. As the broth is absorbed add more broth, about a half cup at the time until all broth is used. Stir in the saffron mixture until evenly colored. Stir in Parmesan cheese and serve at once.

Osso Bucco

Serves 6-8
4 tablespoons unsalted butter
1½ cups onion, finely chopped
½ cup carrots, finely chopped
½ cup celery, chopped
1 teaspoon garlic, finely chopped
6-7 pounds veal shanks (8 pieces, cut 2 inches thick)
Salt and pepper to taste
All-purpose flour
¼ cup olive oil
1 cup dry white wine
¾ cup chicken stock
½ teaspoon dried thyme, crumbled
½ teaspoon dried basil, crumbled
3 cups plum tomatoes chopped
6 parsley sprigs
2 bay leaves

Heat a large cast-iron skillet over medium heat. Melt the butter in the skillet, when foam subsides add the onions, carrots, celery and garlic. Cook, stirring occasionally, for 10 minutes or until onions are translucent. Remove from heat and spread in the bottom of a large, shallow casserole with a tight fitting lid. Tie butchers string around the circumference of the veal, season with salt and pepper. Dredge in the flour, coating all edges, shake off the excess flour. Heat a large cast-iron skillet over medium heat. Add half the olive oil and brown the veal on all sides. Cook veal in two batches adding more olive oil if needed. Remove veal to casserole as it browns and place on top of vegetables. Heat oven to 350 degrees. Discard most of the oil from skillet leaving the sediments. Add the wine and reduce by half. Scrape any brown bits clinging to the pan. Stir in the broth, thyme, basil, tomatoes, parsley and bay leaves, pour it over the veal. The liquid should come half way up the veal. Add additional broth if needed, cover and cook in the lower third of the oven for 1 hour and 30 minutes (longer if shanks are very thick). Baste the veal 2-3 times while cooking. Serve with Risotto Milanese and finish with Lafayette Grill Cake (see page 334).

Broccoli Rabe

Serves 8
2½ pounds broccoli rabe
⅓ cup olive oil
2 large cloves garlic, sliced thin
Salt, to taste
Freshly ground black pepper, to taste
Lemon wedges

Wash broccoli rabe and remove thick stems. Bring a large pot of lightly salted water to a boil. Add broccoli rabe and cook until just wilted. Drain and set aside. Heat a large skillet over medium-low heat, add olive oil and sliced garlic. Cook until garlic just begins to brown. Add the broccoli rabe, and toss until heated through. Taste for additional salt and add pepper. Serve with lemon wedges.

THE BIRTHDAY SUPPERS

JO'S BIRTHDAY SUPPER

Oysters Wakulla
Stuffed Veal Chops
Sautéed Spinach
Polenta
Italian Wedding Cake

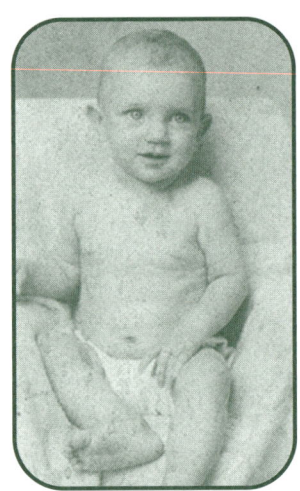

Stuffed Veal Chop

Serves 4

- 4 ounces Fontina cheese
- 4 small, thin slices Smithfield ham
- 4 veal chops, 10-12 oz. each,
- Sprinkles of salt, pepper and flour
- 2 eggs, beaten
- Salt and pepper
- 1 cup bread crumbs
- ⅓ cup olive oil
- 1 tablespoon chopped shallots
- 1 teaspoon chopped garlic
- 2 tablespoons unsalted butter
- ½ pound mushrooms, sliced
- 1 cup dry white wine
- ¼ cup demi-glace
- 1 cup whipping cream
- 4 sprigs rosemary

Preheat oven 450 degrees.

Cut the Fontina into 4 slices. Cut a slit in the side of each veal chop. Insert the ham and cheese into the slits deep enough so it can't come out. Dust the chops with salt, pepper and flour. Pass each chop through egg wash to get it good and wet. Then dredge in bread crumbs to coat thoroughly. Set chops on a rack to dry for 30 minutes. In a large skillet heat oil over medium-high heat. Brown the veal chops two at a time, until crusty brown on both sides. Remove chops and add two remaining chops, cook until brown. Then put skillet with all chops into oven and bake for 12-15 minutes, until top is dry and brown and cheese is beginning to flow from pockets. After baking remove chops and set aside. Pour off oil from skillet and sauté shallots and garlic in butter until translucent. Add mushrooms and stir, cooking 30 seconds. Add the wine and let it come to a boil, cook 1 minute. Add the demi-glace (see page 23) and cream and reduce by half. Pour over veal, garnish with rosemary and serve.

Polenta

Serves 6
2 ½ cups chicken stock
¾ cup polenta
½ cup Parmesan cheese, grated
Salt to taste
Marinated Tomatoes

Bring chicken stock to a boil. Using a whisk slowly pour in the polenta, whisking until smooth. Change to a wooden spoon, stirring constantly until thick. You should be able to see the bottom of the pot when you stir. Remove from heat and stir in Parmesan cheese and salt to taste. place two Marinated Tomatoes (see page 156) on each serving. Serve immediately.

Italian Wedding Cake

1 cup unsalted butter, room temperature
2 cups sugar
5 eggs, room temperature
2 cups all-purpose flour
1 teaspoon baking soda
1 cup buttermilk
1 cup flaked coconut
1 cup roasted walnuts, chopped
1 teaspoon vanilla
Dash salt

Preheat oven 350 degrees. Butter and flour three 9 inch cake pans. Cream sugar and butter with an electric mixer for 5 minutes. Beat in eggs, one at a time. Sift dry ingredients. Add to butter mixture a little at the time. Mix in buttermilk, coconut, walnuts, vanilla and salt. Spread into prepared pans and bake 25-30 minutes or until tooth pick comes out clean. Invert onto racks and let cool.

Icing:
8 ounces cream cheese, room temperature
½ cup butter, melted
1 pound powdered sugar
1 cup roasted walnuts, chopped
Dash of salt
25 whole roasted walnuts

Beat cream cheese and butter until well mixed. Add the sugar and continue to mix. Add 1 cup walnuts and salt. Spread icing between cake layers and over the top and sides of cake. Arrange whole walnuts on top of icing and refrigerate until icing is set.

THE FOOD OF NEW ORLEANS

One of our favorite restaurants in New Orleans was the Andrew Jackson where we enjoyed Soup Du Jour and Veal King Ferdinand. Once back home we tried to re-create the dish, but it wasn't the same. On our next trip to New Orleans we were looking forward to having it again, but alas, the Andrew Jackson had closed. Man!

We had resigned ourselves to the loss, but then one day a friend who lived in New Orleans sent us an old New Orleans cookbook, low and behold there it was, the recipe for Veal King Ferdinand. Try it, we think you will agree it's definitely a keeper.

Veal King Ferdinand

Serves 4
8 medallions of veal
2 eggs
Salt and pepper, to taste
1 cup flour
1 cup bread crumbs
½ pound picked crab meat
2 green onions, chopped
2 ounces sherry wine
⅓ cup butter
1 tablespoon olive oil
40 green, thin steamed asparagus spears
1 recipe Béarnaise Sauce

Make a Béarnaise Sauce (see page 75) and keep over warm water, stir occasionally. Beat eggs well for egg wash. Pound veal between sheets of plastic wrap to get an even thickness. Salt and pepper veal. Pass veal through flour, egg wash, and bread crumbs—in that order. Melt half of the butter and olive oil in a cast-iron skillet. Brown veal on both sides until golden. Set veal aside and melt remaining butter in skillet. Sauté green onions until tender. Add crab meat and gently blend until warm. Add sherry and simmer. To serve, place two slices of veal on each plate. Place one-fourth of crabmeat in center of veal. Place asparagus on crabmeat and spoon Béarnaise Sauce over all.

Ferdinand, "The Bull of the Woods", Kyle McDonald's Ranch, c 2000.

Soup Du Jour

4 ripe Haas avocados or 2 Florida avocados, peeled, seeded and sliced
6 jigs of Tabasco
Juice of 1 lemon
3 green onions, chopped
1½ cups heavy cream
1½ cups sour cream
½ pound lump crabmeat
Salt to taste

Place all the ingredients excluding crabmeat into a blender and blend until smooth. Chill completely. Place soup in individual bowls divide crabmeat equally and serve cold. Serves 6-8

Red Beans and Rice

My old red beans recipe had evolved over the years from several recipes we had been given by family and friends. Last year we were visiting our friends Randy and Lillian Torrey, who now live in Blue Mountain Beach, and began discussing red beans. Lillian who lived in New Orleans for over thirty years said she had some Camellia red beans, but didn't have a ham bone. Well I said we had a ham bone but no beans. So we had a spur-of-the-moment supper the next night. Just Caesar salad, red beans, rice, cornbread and a bottle of Beaujolais. What a feast.

Lillian graciously gave us her recipe which we think is the best version we have ever enjoyed. She says she cooks all types of dried beans this way.

Serves 6
1 medium onion, chopped,
3 cloves garlic, minced
1 to ¾ inch piece of fatback slab, cut into ½ inch pieces
1 pound package red beans (preferably Camellia brand)
1 smoked ham bone broken in half
2 - 8 inch links of andouille or country sausage sliced ¼ inch thick
Minced green onion, to taste
Tabasco, to taste

Camellia

In a large cast-iron pot add fat back and cook on a low heat until some of the fat is released, add onions and garlic and cook for a minute. Add the beans, ham bone and water to cover by 2 inches. Cook two hours on med-low heat with lid off. Stir every now and then and add sausage. Add additional water if needed. Cook three more hours with lid on, stir occasionally. Serve over long grain rice with minced green onions and Tabasco to taste.

Cajun Cornbread

Serves 6
1½ cups cornmeal
4 tablespoons flour
½ teaspoon salt
1 teaspoon baking soda
1 cup cream corn
2 eggs
¼ cup vegetable oil
1 cup buttermilk
1 cup onion, chopped
½ pound sharp cheddar cheese, grated
½ cup Jalapeno minced

Preheat oven 400 degrees.
Mix all ingredients well except cheese and peppers, pour half the mixture into greased cast-iron skillet. Sprinkle with cheese and peppers. Spread remaining batter on top and bake 30-35 minutes.

THE SMALL TOWN CAFES

If you want low-fat food, eat at the hospital.

If you ask anyone in North Walton County who has the best burger, you are gonna hear "Tastee Freeze". While technically this cafe hasn't been a Tastee Freeze for many years, the locals still say, "Let's go to the Tastee Freeze for a pub burger."

The pub burger is a meal in itself. A generous half pound freshly ground beef patty, grilled to perfection, with all the condiments you desire. Add a large Co-Cola and the cost is $3.95. You can add crushed cherries to the Coke for a nickel.

The old Tastee Freeze is now Ed's restaurant.

Now the pub burger only comes well-done and the cheese is pure American so I guess our version of the Pub Burger is gussied up a bit. You might as well splurge and get an order of tatertots.

Jo's Pub Burger

Serves 4
- 8 slices of smoked bacon,
- 2 pounds ground chuck
- Kosher salt
- 4 teaspoons soy sauce
- 4 teaspoons Worcestershire
- 4 teaspoons lemon juice
- ½ cup Spanish onion (coarsely chopped)
- 8 tablespoons grated sharp cheddar cheese
- 4 Kaiser rolls
- 4 pats butter
- 4 leaves iceberg lettuce
- 4 slices vine-ripe tomatoes
- Freshly ground black pepper
- Hellmann's mayonnaise
- Dijon mustard
- Dill pickles, sliced thin

Fry bacon in a large cast-iron skillet. Drain bacon on paper towels and set skillet aside. Shape meat into four 4-inch round patties, and set aside. Pour bacon drippings into a jar and save for later use, leave just enough bacon drippings to coat the bottom of the skillet. Heat skillet on medium-high heat. Spread 1 tablespoon Kosher salt around skillet and sear the 4 patties for about 1 minute. Flip each patty and sprinkle each one with soy sauce, Worcestershire and lemon juice. Add onion chucks in voids between patties. Reduce heat to medium-low and cook another 2 minutes on each side. Sprinkle cheese on each patty, cover skillet and steam until cheese melts. Remove patties and onions to a warm plate. They will be medium-rare. Cut rolls in half and smear each side with butter. Place cut side down in skillet and grill until brown. Smear the top of the roll with mayonnaise and the bottom with mustard. Place patties on bottom, add onions, pickles and bacon as desired. Place lettuce and tomato on top of onions add a generous grind of black pepper. Place the top of the bun over all. Now folks you ain't gonna get this baby into your mouth until you mash it down a little bit. Serve with tatertots and a cherry coke.

Blue Plate Special

Just about every small town in the South has at least one cafe that features a blue plate special each day. A choice of one meat and 2-3 side dishes. It usually comes with all the sweet tea you can drink and a cute little dessert served in a dish you couldn't fit a egg into.

Mamie's, best grits and eggs in town.

Stuffed Peppers

Serves 6
6 medium green or red bell peppers
1 pound ground chuck
½ cup onion, minced
16 ounce can whole peeled plum tomatoes, drained and chopped
½ cup drained tomato juice
½ cup long-grained rice
Freshly ground black pepper
½ teaspoon salt
1 teaspoon Worcestershire
¼ cup parsley, minced
5 ounces sharp cheddar cheese, grated

Cut a half inch off the tops of the bell peppers, carefully remove the seeds and membranes and discard. Plunge trimmed peppers into boiling water and parboil 3 minutes. Remove to colander and drain. When cool enough to handle turn peppers upside down on paper towels to drain. In a large skillet lightly brown ground chuck and onion over medium heat until onions are transparent. Drain off the fat and add the tomatoes, tomato juice, rice, pepper, salt, Worcestershire and parsley, bring to a simmer and cover. Cook about 15 minutes or until rice is tender. Sprinkle in most of the cheese, saving some for the top.

Preheat oven 350 degrees. Stuff peppers with ground beef mixture and set in a 13x9 inch pan. Sprinkle with remaining cheese and bake 20 minutes or until melted.

The Ultimate Mac-n' cheese

Serves 6
2 cups uncooked penne macaroni
2 tablespoons butter
½ teaspoon black pepper, freshly ground
½ teaspoon salt
4 ounces sharp cheddar cheese, grated
2 eggs
½ cup Hellmann's mayonnaise
Pinch of nutmeg, freshly grated
1½ cups evaporated milk
4 ounces sharp cheddar cheese, cut in ½ inch cubes
½ cup buttered bread crumbs

Preheat oven 350 degrees.
Cook macaroni according to box instructions until tender, not overdone. Drain in a colander. Place pasta in a large bowl and toss with butter, salt and pepper, and grated cheese. Pour into a buttered 9x12 inch baking dish. In a two cup glass measuring cup, beat the eggs, mayonnaise, nutmeg and enough evaporated milk to measure two cups, pour liquids over the pasta. Sprinkle top with the cubed cheese, sprinkle with bread crumbs and bake in a 350 degree oven for twenty-thirty minutes.

THE ISLAND FOOD

"Jimmy cracked conch and I don't care de masters gone away." Mon

We look forward each summer to trips to the islands with my husband's brother Charles and his wife Ann. We snorkel over the reefs and spear snapper and grouper and sometimes pick up a few crawfish (lobster) for supper each night. We also might pick up a few conch to enjoy in a salad, fritters or cracked conch.

After a hard day of gigging and collecting, Charles would beach his boat the "Fry Pan" on a secluded island and we would clean the fish, lobster and conch. As the sun set over the tranquil water we would enjoy a cocktail and Charles would make the toast, "Wonder what the PO folks are doing?"

Cracked Conch

Slice four conch into one quarter inch slices and pound (crack) or as a native Bahamian cook once told us, "I bruise them a bit," with a metal tenderizer on each side. Beat them to hell and back or until tender.

Place 2 cups self-rising flour in a 9x11 inch pan. Pour 2 cups buttermilk in a wide mouth bowl. Add all of the conch, drain and flour only the pieces that will fit into skillet, shaking off excess flour. Fry in peanut oil until golden brown. Garnish with lime wedges, and serve with Pigeon Peas and Rice (see below), Potato Salad and Salsa.

Fry Pan, c 1995.

Pigeon Peas and Rice

Serves 6

- 2 slices thick sliced smoked bacon
- 1 tablespoon olive oil
- 1 garlic clove, minced
- 3 tablespoons onion, chopped
- 3 tablespoons green bell pepper, chopped
- 15.5 ounce can pigeon peas
- 2 tablespoons tomato paste
- ½-¾ cup fresh tomatoes, chopped
- 1 Datil or Habañero pepper, finely diced
- 1 teaspoon salt
- ½ teaspoon thyme
- 6 cups cooked white rice

Over medium-low heat cook the bacon in the olive oil until crisp, drain on paper towels. Add the garlic, onion and bell pepper to the oil and cook until onions are transparent, about 20 minutes. Add remaining ingredients, including the liquid of the peas, bring to a boil, cover and reduce heat to low. Cook 20 minutes, stir and serve over white rice.

Bahamian Salt Fish

Years ago before refrigeration the only way to keep fish was to salt them down. Schools of mullet were caught in nets in the bay and gulf, cleaned and cut down the middle and covered with salt. The fish would be sold at general stores in all the small towns in North Florida and South Alabama. The fish would keep for several months and could be soaked overnight and cooked the next day.

This is a tasty dish featuring salt fish. Since salt mullet is hard to find these days we substitute salt cod which is available in most supermarkets.

Serves 4
- 1 pound salt fish
- ⅓ cup golden raisins
- ⅓ cup unsalted roasted pine nuts
- 1 teaspoon oregano, crumbled
- Black pepper, freshly ground
- 4 tablespoons olive oil
- 2 cloves garlic, thinly sliced
- 35 ounce can whole peeled plum tomatoes
- 1½ teaspoons capers, drained
- ½ cup Greek and Spanish olives
- ¼ teaspoon cayenne pepper
- Pinch of sugar

Rinse fish thoroughly in cold water. Place in a shallow dish and cover with water and plastic wrap, soak overnight. Change the water at least three times. Cover raisins with warm water and let stand. Drain the fish and rinse, pat dry with paper towels. Cut into 8 equal pieces, about 2 inches square. Place in an oiled baking dish. Sprinkle with a half teaspoon oregano, pepper and drizzle with 2 tablespoons olive oil. Heat remaining 2 tablespoons oil in a large skillet over low heat. When hot add the garlic and cook until softened but not brown. Crush the tomatoes in your hand and add along with the juice. Bring to a boil, reduce heat to low and simmer 5 minutes. Place rack of oven on top shelf, preheat oven 450 degree. Drain raisins and pat dry with paper towel, stir into tomatoes along with nuts, capers, olives, remaining oregano, cayenne pepper and sugar. Simmer sauce 10 minutes. Pour sauce over fish and bake on top shelve of oven for 8 minutes. Reduce heat to 375 degrees. Spoon fish with tomato sauce and continue to bake 15 minutes longer. Serve immediately.

Jamaican Jerk Goat

For each pound of goat, sliced into thick strips, prepare the following marinade.

- 2 tablespoon black pepper, freshly ground
- 1 tablespoon allspice seeds, ground
- ½ cup onion, finely minced
- 2 tablespoons thyme
- Datil or Scotch Bonnet pepper, finely minced, to taste

Blend all ingredients in food processor. Rub mixture well into goat meat and marinate in refrigerator for 3 hours. Grill over charcoal until done. This marinade works on pork, beef, and poultry.

THE ETHNIC FOODS

Szechwan Stir-fry

Our first encounter with Oriental food was at the New Canton restaurant on Julia Street in Jacksonville, it's still open today, forty years later. We ordered their signature dish,, Lobster Cantonese. Lobster meat was 50 cents extra so we splurged. The kitchen help kept looking out of the kitchen to see who the big spenders were. Szechwan Stir-fry is especially good served with Filopino Siopao.

Serves 6

Marinade for chicken, shrimp and scallops :

1½ tablespoon cornstarch	1 pound skinless, boneless
3 tablespoons rice vinegar	chicken thighs, cut into
3 tablespoons water	bite size pieces
3½ tablespoons soy sauce	½ pound shrimp
1½ teaspoon dark sesame seed oil	½ pound scallops

Combine all, but the meat and seafood, in a large bowl, stir to mix. Marinate chicken for 20 minutes, remove chicken to a colander to drain. Add shrimp and scallops to marinade for 10 minutes. Drain the shrimp and scallops.

Broth mixture: Combine in a small bowl and set aside.

2 tablespoons sugar	2½ tablespoons rice wine
1½ tablespoons cornstarch	2½ teaspoon worcestershire
1 cup chicken broth	1½ teaspoons dark sesame seed oil
3½ tablespoons soy sauce	

Place in another small bowl a half cup roasted cashews, chopped and set aside.

½ cup green onions, sliced thin	1-2 tablespoons Sriracha Chili Sauce
2½ tablespoons garlic, minced	1½ pounds Spinach
2 tablespoons ginger, minced	½ cup Cashews, chopped

In a large skillet sauté 1 teaspoon minced garlic, and a half teaspoon minced ginger root in 1 teaspoon vegetable oil for 30 seconds, add spinach. Add salt to taste. Use tongs to toss spinach. As soon as the spinach wilts, place on a plate and set aside.

Heat a wok over high heat. Add 2 tablespoons peanut oil to wok, use a large spoon and spread oil on the sides of the wok. When oil is hot add the chicken, making sure to place some of the chicken up on edges of the wok. Let the chicken lightly brown before stirring. Stir-fry until chicken separates and changes color. Remove to a platter. Add shrimp and cook stirring for 1 minute, add the scallops to the shrimp and continue to cook for another minute. Remove shrimp/scallops to platter with chicken. Add 1 tablespoon peanut oil to wok if needed. Add remaining green onions, ginger and garlic and stir for 30 seconds. Add chili sauce and stir-fry another 30 seconds. Stir in the broth mixture, cook until thickened. Return chicken, shrimp and scallops to wok and heat through. Drain any liquid that has accumulated from spinach. Arrange spinach around edge of platter, place stir-fry in the center, sprinkle with cashews, serve with Japanese sticky rice.

Middle-Eastern Meatloaf

Meatloaf is definitely the newlyweds friend. When we first married my menus were very simple. We had spaghetti with meat sauce on Monday, hamburger steaks on Tuesday. pork chops wednesday, fried chicken on Thursday and meatloaf on Friday. Meatloaf sandwiches for lunch on the week-end. I would try different meatloaf recipes, but they all tasted pretty much the same. Then one day at a Middle-Eastern restaurant in Jacksonville we ordered this version. Wow! It was exceptional, so we badgered the owner for the recipe and have been enjoying it ever since.

Serves 6

½ pound finely ground beef
½ pound finely ground lamb
1 small onion, chopped
1 egg
½ cup cracker crumbs
1½ teaspoons salt
¼ teaspoon cinnamon
¼ teaspoon allspice
1-8 ounce can tomato sauce
2½-3 cups water, approximately
2 medium potatoes, slice ½ inch
½ teaspoon black pepper

Thoroughly mix all ingredients except tomato sauce, potatoes and water. Form into a loaf about 1 inch thick. Place in the bottom of a 9x12 inch pan. Peel and slice potatoes a half inch thick and place over the meat. Mix the tomato sauce with the water and pour over the potatoes (so that the potatoes are barely covered). Bake in a 400 degree oven for 35-40 minutes, or until potatoes are tender. Serve with Tabbouleh, Hummus, Cucumber Yogurt and pita bread.

Tuscan Style Pasta

One recipe Marinara sauce
1 teaspoon tomato paste
½ pound sweet Italian sausage
1 large fennel bulb, halved, cored and sliced crosswise
¼ cup fennel fronds, chopped and set aside
2 cups broccoli florets
1 pound penne
1-19 ounce can Cannellini beans, rinsed
2 tablespoons parsley, chopped
20 basil leaves, torn
½ cup Parmesan cheese, grated

Stir tomato paste into the Marinara sauce (see page 228). In a medium saucepan of water, simmer the sausage over medium heat for 8 minutes, or until cook through. Drain and cut into a fourth inch rounds and add to the tomato sauce. Cook the fennel slices and broccoli in a large pot of salted boiling water until just tender, about 5-8 minutes. Remove with a slotted spoon to drain. Cook penne in the same pot until just tender. Drain and place in a very large bowl. Add tomato sauce with sausage, fennel, fennel fronds, broccoli, Cannellini beans, parsley, basil and half of the Parmesan cheese. Toss thoroughly, sprinkle with remaining cheese and serve.

THE BIG WEDDING

Right before Cameron and Tom's wedding his parents, grandparents and other relatives came down from up North a few days early to help with the preparation. We decided to show our Southern hospitality and invited all of them over to the big house for supper. When asked what dishes they would like us to prepare we got a unanimous "Southern Fried Chicken."

We scoured around the countryside searching for fresh vegetables. We had brought a large box of Mr. Worley's Manalucie tomatoes from Jacksonville. We got several bushels of white acre peas and speckled butterbeans from Mr. Alford's vegetable stand and spent the afternoon on the porch swing shelling them. My husband located some Silver Queen corn north of Ponce De Leon, and Tom's cousins shucked the corn and cut it off the cob. The cucumbers, squash and okra came from Mr. C.J. Laird's picnic table stand and my sisters brought the banana pudding, chocolate cake and several pies for dessert.

My brother Ingram raises chickens commercially on his farm. He stops by the big house each morning for coffee. He only stays a few minutes, then he jumps up and says "I gotta go to the chicken house!" then he gets into his pick-up and heads to the Thriftway Supermarket for coffee with his friends Bill and J.W. Adkinson.

We generally get our chickens at the Thriftway Supermarket. But since we were feeding such a crowd, Ingram and my husband went out to the Henko processing plant and picked up a whole box of freshly dressed fryers. They fried the chicken giblets first outside over gas burners and passed them around for appetizers, while they fried the rest of the chicken. We cooked up the vegetables and several batches of Daddy's Pone Cornbread. The table wine of choice was several gallons of sweet tea with sliced lemon. With the help of our family and our new Yankee friends we created another memorable meal.

Southern Fried Chicken
"Talk About Good"

Serves 4
1 fresh fryer
1½ cups self-rising flour
1½ cups buttermilk
1 inch Peanut oil
4 tablespoons bacon drippings
Salt and Black pepper to taste

Cut chicken into legs, thighs, pulley bone and breast. Divide breast into 4 equal pieces. Put chicken in a bowl with buttermilk. Place flour, salt and pepper in a large zip-lock bag, shake to mix. Place chicken in flour mixture, shake to coat, shake off excess. In a large cast-iron Dutch oven pour in oil and bacon dripping. Heat oil and bacon drippings over medium-high heat. Fry chicken 10 minutes on one side, turn and cook additional 10 minutes. Drain chicken on wire racks.

Mama's White Cake

About a year after we published *Seasonal Florida* we had a phone call from an inspired potential cookbook writer, Nancy Duty, who is originally from Fernandina Beach. We asked her over and gave her as much advice and encouragement as possible but really didn't know if she would follow it through. About a year later Nancy called and wanted to bring her book by. It is a lovely book entitled *Recipes of Mother's and Others*, a collection of recipes of her family and friends. Mama's White Cake is a recipe her grandmother passed down to her mother, who taught Nancy how to bake the cake.

1⅔ cups sugar
2 sticks butter
3 cups sifted cake flour
¼-½ teaspoon salt
1 teaspoon vanilla
¼ teaspoon almond
4 egg whites and ⅓ cup sugar
3 teaspoons baking powder

Grease cake two 9 inch cake pans with Crisco. Line with wax paper and lightly flour, shaking off excess. Cream sugar and butter. Sift cake flour and shake down a little in the cup. Add flour, baking powder and salt first and last alternating with water. Add vanilla and almond. Beat egg whites, gradually add a third cup sugar, until almost stiff but still moist. Fold whites in cake batter last. Bake at 325 degrees for approximately 35-40 minutes.

Seafoam Icing

1⅛ cups sugar
3 tablespoons water
3 egg whites
¾ cup white Karo corn Syrup
¼ teaspoon cream of tartar
1 teaspoon vanilla
Sprinkling salt

Cook in double boiler over boiling water, beat with a mixer and stir from the bottom often or the egg will cook and not blend well. When icing forms peak and is fairly thick, ice the cake, Do not over beat. It should be firm, but light and fluffy.

THE FISHING TRIPS

The fishing trip to Becton Pond began when granddaddy made funnels out of screen wire and put them in the mouth of quart mason jars. We put bread inside and placed the jars in a shallow part of the creek to catch minnows for bait.

Granddaddy would then pound a stob (Gaelic for wooden stake) into the ground and rub it with a brick bat to snore up some earthworms, which we put into an old coffee can. Granny would pack our lunch while we loaded the bait, cane fishing poles, and the old paddle into the three hole buick for the trip to Becton Pond.

When we arrived at the pond everything was loaded into the old wooden boat which granddaddy would scull through the Cypress trees with the paddle in his right hand. With his left hand he would cast his bait into the tiniest hole between the lily pads. As soon as he caught the first fish, he would stop the boat while we all got to "wet our bait." Soon we would have a mess of red-breast bream, shell crackers, warmouth , bluegills and maybe a bass or two for another memorable meal.

Our grandparents typically carried sardines and Vienna sausage when they went fishing at Becton Pond or the Choctawhatchee River but today we prefer these Sloppy Jos washed down with an ice cold Royal Crown cola.

Our Sloppy Jo is a bit tastier than the one served in school lunch rooms throughout the South. We found this version at a bait and tackle store in Orange Park. We had stopped to buy some crickets and Catalpa worms and noticed folks lined up buying these sandwiches. So, we got in line and bought a sack full for lunch. But they didn't make it to lunch, they were gone by mid-morning.

Charlie Williams and son Jack. at Becton pond, Washington County, c 1940's.

Sloppy Jo's

Serves 4
1 pound stew meat
¾ cup chopped onion
½ cup chopped green pepper
½ cup chopped celery
1 carrot, grated
1 #2 can tomatoes
6 ounces tomato puree
¾ teaspoon salt
½ teaspoon black pepper
Dill pickles (optional)
4 submarine rolls

Brown beef in a large skillet, remove fat and gristle, if any. Stir in carrots, onion, green pepper, celery and sauté until cooked. Add tomatoes and tomato puree. Stir and season with salt and pepper. Simmer for a half an hour. Serve in submarine rolls with Dill pickles.

FAMILY AND FRIENDS

One of our fondest childhood memories was the times we stayed with our grandparents. We awoke each morning to a wonderful breakfast of smoked meats, country fried eggs, grits and gravy and granny's homemade biscuits. Granny cooked her biscuits in a large cast-iron skillet. She always made small biscuits in the middle for the grand kids. We were happy when there were 4-5 biscuits leftover because the next day Granny would make her biscuit pudding with custard sauce.

Granny's Biscuit Pudding

Serves 6
4-5 baked day old biscuits
2 cups milk
1 cup sugar
4-5 eggs, beaten
1 tablespoon vanilla
1 teaspoon lemon extract

Crumble biscuits in bowl. Cover with milk (really saturate) then mash the biscuits good and add sugar. Add eggs, vanilla and lemon extracts. Pour into a buttered dish and bake in a 350 degree oven until firm. Serve with Custard Sauce.

Junior with his new best friend fishing in Granny's cement pond, Bonifay, c 1950.

When Junior was born in July 1944 his Dad was in combat in Normandy, France. It was December 1945 (18 months later) when his Dad first saw his oldest son.

Mr. and Mrs. Charlie Williams showing off a fine collection of Bream and Shellcrackers, c 1950's.

Custard Sauce

2 cups half and half
6 large egg yolks
2/3 cup sugar
1/2 teaspoon vanilla

Bring half and half to a boil. Whisk egg yolks and sugar for 1 minute. Add a half cup of the half and half to the egg mixture and mix. Whisk the cream-egg yolk mixture into remaining cream and cook over low heat, stirring constantly, until thick enough to coat the back of a spoon. Stir in the vanilla, place plastic wrap directly on pudding to keep a skin from forming and cool for 2 hours.

Granddaddy loved bananas and he would sneak in and dip them in the sugar bowl which made Granny mad as a wet-setting hen, but that didn't faze him one little bit.

THE LOW-COUNTRY FOODS

As children we always looked forward to the trips to Pensacola to visit with Mama's high school best friend Mildred Martin, Mama called her Polly. She and Mama were cheerleaders for the Bonifay Blue Devil's a few years back. Mildred and her husband Bernard Tillman lived on a bayou near the navy base. When visiting we could catch fish and blue crabs off their dock and water ski in the bayou. If we were lucky Bernard would cook-up a batch of his mother's spaghetti and pork red gravy, which was quiet a bit different from the spaghetti sauce we grew up with at home. Bernard's Mama was from Charleston, South Carolina, one of our favorite food cities. We love Charleston's She crab soup and low country cuisine.

As for the Alka Seltzer, Bernard says, "You can have them now or have them later."

Charleston Pork Red Gravy

Serves 10

3 - 24 ounce cans tomatoes
12 ounce can tomato sauce
12 ounce can tomato paste
6 Alka Seltzer tablets
4 pounds pork shoulder "Boston Butt", trimmed of fat and cut into bite size pieces
3 large onions, chopped
3 cloves garlic, minced
3 tablespoons bacon drippings
1 bell pepper, chopped
3 celery stalks, chopped
8 ounce can mushrooms, drained
Salt and pepper to taste

In a large pot combine tomatoes, tomato sauce and tomato paste. Add Alka Seltzer tablets and let sit 15 minutes. Then add pork. Sauté onions and garlic in bacon drippings and then add to pot. Cook on low heat for 30 minutes, then add bell pepper, celery and mushrooms and cook another 30 minutes. Salt and pepper to taste. Serve over pasta of choice.

Mama's Pear Salad

Mama dearly loved her pear salad. In the late summer she would round up her friends to help prepare the salad pears, which they dyed various colors.

For each salad place 2 salad pear halves on a leaf of iceberg lettuce. In the center of each pear put a dollop of Hellmann's mayonnaise and sprinkle with shredded cheddar cheese. Place cherry on top.

Polly and Mama, cheerleaders at Holmes County High School, c 1940.

She Crab Soup

Charleston, South Carolina is one of our favorite food cities in the South. For many years, we traveled to Charleston in February for the Southeastern Wildlife Expedition. We stayed at one of the bed and breakfast inns and indulged at great restaurants featuring low country cuisine as well as the seafood shacks on Shem Creek.

We enjoyed the wildlife art, displays and shows but the highlight was the food booths. Many of the local restaurants featured their specialties. Bloody Marys, baked oyster dishes, stuffed shrimp, gumbo, benne biscuits and this signature She Crab Soup.

Serves 4-6

¼ cup unsalted butter
½ cup onions, minced
3 tablespoons all-purpose flour,
2 cups whole milk
2 cups heavy cream
1 teaspoon white pepper
2 teaspoons salt

2 tablespoons Worcestershire
2 tablespoons cornstarch
1 pint fresh lump crabmeat
   picked over carefully
½ cup crab roe and fat
Dry sherry to taste
Freshly ground nutmeg

In the top of a double boiler, melt the butter over low direct heat, add the onions, and cook until soft. Gradually add the flour and stir until mixture thickens. Place the pan over the bottom of the double boiler half filled with boiling water and slowly add one and a half cups of the milk, stirring constantly. When milk is hot, add the cream, nutmeg, pepper, salt and Worcestershire and cook 5 minutes. Dissolve the cornstarch in the remaining milk, remove pan from hot water, and stir in the cornstarch mixture. Return pan to the top of the double boiler and cook the mixture until hot. about 5 minutes longer. When ready to serve, add the crabmeat and roe, heat the soup thoroughly over boiling water and lace with sherry. Sprinkle each bowl with freshly ground nutmeg and serve.

Low Country Bloody Mary

Serves 6

1 quart tomato juice
1 cup vodka
1 tablespoon lime juice
1 tablespoon Worcestershire

1 teaspoon salt
¼ teaspoon Tabasco
1 bottle clam juice
6 celery sticks and 6 pickled okra

Combine all ingredients in a 2 quart pitcher. Stir well and refrigerate until chilled. Garnish each glass with a celery stalk and a pickled okra.

THE FAMILY GATHERINGS

We have two pear trees at the Big House and even though we give pears to our family and friends, make pear pies, cakes, jam, preserves, relish and salad pears we still have pears galore.

My double first cousin Lee Ingram, (he's the one who can dance the horns off a billy goat), picks up the surplus pears and feeds them to the wild hogs he catches. He keeps hog dogs and catches wild hogs in the valley. He fattens the hogs up in a pen and then has a hog killing and bar-b-cue on the Saturday after Thanksgiving. The men-folk clean and butcher the hogs early and Lee cooks the hogs over Oak and Hickory coals while we cook up a batch of Bertie's Bar-b-cue Sauce. Family and friends bring the side dishes and desserts leftover from the Thanksgiving feast. Kyle brought the keg of beer in the back of his pick-up and Lee's wife Carrie brought a jug of pear wine. The pear wine was the hit of the party. Sorry Lee there won't be any more surplus pears. Trey and Keaton showed up with a bushel of Apalachicola oysters and a good time was had by all.

Lee Ingram with his wild hog, c 2000.

Charlie's Pear Wine

When our ancestors arrived in Walton County in the 1820's, they brought with them their Gaelic Bible, sheep, cows, a fiddle and the knowledge of making high quality whiskey. This knowledge was passed from father to son and they took pride in their home brew. My Grandfather Charlie McDonald and his brother Johnny were said to have made some of the best whiskey and wine in the valley. They wouldn't sell the whiskey and wine, but used it for medicinal purposes, and if you believe that, let me tell you about their catch and release program for gopher turtles.

Dice sand pears include some peel, stew slowly in limited water until tender. Strain through cheese cloth and add two and a half to three pounds sugar per gallon. Put into narrow mouth glass, stone or wooden containers. Leave open for several days till fermentation is well started. Cork leaving a vent for gasses (a rubber tube with end immersed in water) store in cool, dark place. Completely cork when fermentation ceases, 2-3 weeks.

Grandfather Charlie McDonald on his Hog, c 1940.

Ingram's Camp Stew

For many years our youngest brother, Ingram would go on trail rides with his friends and camp out overnight in Sealy's pasture, where they would prepare Camp Stew for supper. The next day he would return home, and brag about how good the camp stew was but he couldn't share the "secret" recipe with his sisters. We would pitch hissy fits but Ingram still wouldn't spill the beans.

So last year my sisters and I planned a surprise 60th birthday party for Ingram and invited his old friends to cook the camp stew and guess what? All it contained, was a can of corned beef, a can of tomatoes, onions, and potatoes, what a rip off! But, I've got to admit with a little Tabasco sauce and hot cornbread it was pretty damn good.

Hi-yo Silver away!

Ingram's oldest grandchild, Karley Marie on her first horse--now she's winning awards barrel racing on her real horse Beaudroux, c 1995.

Jo's Camp Stew

Serves 8-10

5 pounds stew venison, stew beef or lamb cut into 1½-2 inch cubes
Salt and pepper to taste
Bacon drippings
2 cups onions, chopped
2 large cloves garlic, minced
1 tablespoon tomato paste
3 tablespoon flour
4 cups water
4-14 ounce cans beef consommé
1 pound mushrooms, sliced
6 carrots, cut in 3" pieces
24 new potatoes, cut in half
1 cup grits, uncooked

Season meat with salt and pepper. Heat a large cast-iron Dutch oven and when hot add the bacon drippings and half the meat. Cook in two batches until brown on all sides. Remove the meat. Add more bacon drippings if necessary, then add the onions and garlic and cook until softened. Stir in the flour and cook stirring for a couple of minutes. Return the meat to the Dutch oven, add the tomato paste, water and consommé, stir, and let it come to a boil. Reduce heat and simmer 2-4 hours or until meat is tender. Add the mushrooms, carrots and potatoes and cook another half an hour. Stir in the grits and cook 10 minutes more. Serve with hot cornbread and ice cold beer.

Ingram's Camp Cornbread

One large package Aunt Jemima's cornbread mix, follow the directions.

THE DINNERS ON THE GROUND

"Shall we gather at the river, the beautiful, the beautiful river."

Around the time the McDonalds, McLeods, and McKinnons were settling in the Euchee Valley, other Scottish families, including the Andersons, were settling to the north of the valley along Sandy Creek, at the Pleasant Grove Community. A descendant of these families, Lance Anderson, with the help of some family and friends, put a collection of family recipes together a few years ago in a book *A Mess O' Greens*. In it he describes this church supper so vividly you think you were there walking along the food line.

Lord Help Us! It's Joyce's Coconut Cake

Actually, Joyce only calls this four-layer beauty "a Coconut Cake," the rest of the title was added one Sunday night at Pleasant Grove Baptist Church. A once-in-a-while dieter was able to fend off temptation as she struggled along past tables which were loaded with true "as good as it gets." Then she saw the coconut cake in all its glory. She said the words like a prayer but temptation had its way with her.

1 cup butter
2 cups sugar
4 egg yolks
3 cups White Lilly self-rising flour

1 cup milk
1 teaspoon vanilla
1½ cup chopped nuts

Cream butter and sugar; add egg yolks, one at a time, beating well after each addition. Sift flour, add alternately with milk. Add vanilla and nuts. Divide into four greased and well floured cake pans. Bake at 350 degrees until done:

Icing for Coconut Cake:

2 cups of sugar
½ cup Karo syrup (white)
¼ teaspoon cream of tarter
½ cup water

2 egg whites
½ teaspoon vanilla
Shredded coconut

Combine sugar, syrup, cream of tarter, and water. Boil until it spins a long thread. Beat egg whites while syrup is cooking. Pour over egg whites slowly; spread between layers and sprinkle with coconut.

Note that Joyce says "sprinkle"--to get and idea of what she means, her coconut cake looks like a super thick white shag carpet.

Joyce Davis Nolin

Old-Timey Egg Custard

*"Amazing grace how sweet the sound, that saved a wretch like me.
I once was lost, but now I'm found, was blind, but now I see."*

Church dinners on the ground usually included three or more egg custards — our favorite pie when we were young. Granny would sometimes add fresh pears or apples to this old-timey recipe for variety.

4 eggs
1 cup sugar
2 tablespoons all-purpose flour
1 cup evaporated milk
¼ cup water
1 tablespoon vanilla

1 tablespoon butter, melted
¼ teaspoon salt
One 9 inch pie shell
Additional melted butter
   for painting crust

Preheat oven to 425 degrees. Prebake pie shell (see page 44) until lightly brown, 10-12 minutes to prevent a soggy crust. Remove from oven and paint with melted butter. Beat eggs well, add sugar and beat until a light lemon color. Add flour, evaporated milk, water, vanilla, butter and salt. Pour custard into shell, reduce heat to 350 degrees and bake 30 minutes or until firm. Serve at room temperature.

Lois Hillard's Pound Cake

"Eating good in the neighborhood."

Soon after we bought the Big House on Circle Drive, my sisters and I began to clean it out, it had been vacant for over ten years. The first day we were cleaning there was a knock on the back door. We opened the door and there was Lois Hillard our neighbor from across the street holding a pound cake, hot from the oven. We immediately took a break and enjoyed the hot pound cake with butter and freshly made coffee. Over the years Lois has brought us numerous cakes, pies, candy, cookies and muffins.

2 sticks oleo, room temperature
1 stick butter flavored Crisco
3 cups sugar
5 large eggs, room temperature
3 cups all-purpose flour

1 teaspoon baking powder
¼ teaspoon salt
2 teaspoons vanilla
1 teaspoon lemon extract
1 cup milk, room temperature

Take the oleo, eggs, and milk out the night before baking. Cream the oleo, Crisco and sugar for a long time, at least 5 minutes or until it is very creamy. Add the eggs, one at the time and beat. Sift the flour then measure. Add the baking powder and salt to the measured 3 cups of flour and sift again. Alternate the flour mixture and milk until all is combined. Stir in the vanilla and lemon extract. Pour into a buttered and floured tube pan and bake in the center of a 300 degree oven for 1 hour-1 hour and 15 minutes or until a toothpick comes out clean. Cool and remove from pan.

FAMILY AND FRIENDS

MOTHER'S COOKING

My cakes don't taste like Mother's,
    I've never touched her bread—
But Grandma's plainest cooking
    Excelled her best, she said.

And Grandma said her mother
    Could put great chefs to shame.
Great-grandma was a genius,
    She said, with fowl and game.

I treated my foods praise lightly,
    My family's flattering zest—
For somehow, "Mother's cooking"
    Has always tasted best.
            Marjorie Kinnan Rawlings
            c1928

Leola Ingram McDonald, c 1932.

Mother's Carrot Cake

To make one 9 inch 3 layer cake:

- 2 cups plain flour
- 2 cups sugar
- 1 teaspoon salt
- 2 teaspoons soda
- 2 teaspoons cinnamon
- 1½ cups vegetable oil
- 4 eggs
- 3 cups carrots, grated

Preheat oven 350 degrees:

Sift dry ingredients together, add oil, eggs and carrots and mix well. Pour batter into cake pans, dividing it equally. Bake in middle of oven for 35 minutes. Remove from oven and cool in pans 10 minutes. Remove from pans and cool to room temperature.

Icing:

- 8 ounces cream cheese, softened
- 1 stick salty butter, softened
- 1 box xxxx confectionery sugar
- 2 teaspoons vanilla
- 1½ cups pecans, chopped

Beat cream cheese, butter and sugar together until well mixed. Stir in the pecans thoroughly. Spread and smooth icing over each cake layer and sides.

Mother's German Chocolate Cake

- 1 package Baker's German Sweet Chocolate
- ½ cup boiling water
- 1 cup butter
- 2 cups sugar
- 4 egg yolks, unbeaten
- 1½ teaspoons vanilla
- 2½ cups cake flour
- 1 teaspoon baking soda
- ¼ teaspoon salt
- 1 cup buttermilk
- 4 egg whites, stiffly beaten

Melt chocolate in a half cup boiling water. Cool. Cream butter and sugar until light and fluffy. Add egg yolks, one at a time, beating after each. Add vanilla and melted chocolate and mix until blended. Sift flour with soda and salt. Add sifted dry ingredients alternately with buttermilk, beat after each addition until batter is smooth. Fold in stiffly beaten egg whites. Pour half of batter into three, greased and floured, 8 inch round layer pans, lined on bottom with wax paper. Bake at 350 degrees for about 15 minutes. Remove cake from pans onto rack to cool. Bake remaining batter in relined cake pans.

Coconut Pecan Filling and Frosting
- 2 cups evaporated milk
- 2 cups sugar
- 4 egg yolks, slightly beaten
- 1 cup butter
- 2 teaspoons vanilla
- 2⅔ cups Baker's Flake Coconut
- 1½ cups chopped pecans

Combine milk, sugar, egg yolks, butter and vanilla in a saucepan. Cook over medium heat, stirring constantly, until mixture thickens, about 12 minutes. Remove from heat. Add coconut and pecans. Stir until cool, and spread over layers.

Mother's Lane Cake

Batter:
- 8 egg whites
- 1½ cups butter, softened
- 2 cups sugar
- 3½ cups plain flour
- 3 teaspoons baking powder
- 1 cup milk
- 1 teaspoon vanilla

Preheat oven 400 degrees. Beat egg whites until stiff, set aside. Cream sugar, butter and vanilla together for 5 minutes. Sift flour and baking powder together and add alternately together with milk to creamed mixture. Grease and flour 6 cake pans. Spread one and one third cups of batter in each pan. Bake 16 to 18 minutes, until cake tops are barely brown.

Filling:
- 2 pounds pecans
- 1 large box of coconut (7 oz.)
- 2 pounds of raisins
- 1 cup butter
- 2 cups sugar
- 8 egg yolks
- 4½ cups milk

Grind pecans, coconut and raisins. Cook with butter, sugar and egg yolks. Cook 15-20 minutes, stirring constantly. Add additional milk, if needed, to thin.

The General Store

The general store in our hometown was an interesting place. The screen door advertised "Colonial is good bread." The owner, who lived in an apartment above the store, sold just about everything from gasoline and hardware to groceries and meat. The drink box was right by the front door. You could buy a Co Cola, Nehi or RC cola for a nickel, if you had brought an empty bottle. Bananas hung on a stalk above the counter. You could select the ones that caught your fancy. The owner was also the butcher. He butchered the beef and pork and ground the hamburger meat as needed. The salt mullet was always in a lard can in front of the meat case.

The owner pumped the gasoline which was 32.9 cents a gallon. We could ride around all Sunday afternoon on a dollars worth of regular. Gas wars were common and sometimes brought gasoline below 25 cents a gallon.

The fruit was seasonal. In the winter it was oranges, grapefruit and tomatoes from South Florida, in the fall we got apples from the Carolinas. In the spring strawberries from Plant City. Summer brought peaches from Georgia, locally grown peas, butterbeans, corn, squash, okra, cucumbers and tomatoes.

Just about all the customers had a charge account. We would sometimes stop by the store on the way home from school and charge a nickels worth of "baloney", which was about four slices. Then when we got home we could make fried baloney sandwiches, with light bread, mustard, and pickles and have a snack up in the tree fort hidden in the top of the Magnolia tree. Colonial is good bread.

Watercolor by Dothan, Alabama artist Keith Newby

Bed and Breakfast Inns and Boutique Hotels

Hotel DeFuniak
This building once housed a masonic lodge and drugstore. Today it's home of a Boutique Hotel, fine dining restaurant and ice cream parlor, c 2004.

Addison House, 409
Alexander Homestead, 415
Allison House, 414
Amelia Island Williams House, 409
Archibald House, 412
At Journey's End, 415
Agustin, 415
Bailey House, 409
Bayfront Marin House, 415
Bayfront Westcott, 417
Beachfront Bed and Breakfast, 417
Bryant House, 410
Carriage Way, 416
Casablanca Inn on the Bay, 416
Casa de la Paz, 416
Casa de Solona, 416
Casa de Suenos, 416
Casa Monica, 416
Castle Garden, 416
Cedar House Inn, 416
Cedar Key, 410
Fairbanks House, 410
Centennial House, 417
Elizabeth Pointe Lodge, 409
Chalet Suzanne Country Inn, 413
Clark House, 413
Club Continental, 414
Combs House, 410
Five Oaks, 414
Gibson Inn, 410
Governors Inn, 411
Greyfield Inn, 411
Herlong Mansion, 413
Homeplace, 418
Hotel DeFuniak, 411
House on Cherry Street, 412
Hoyt House, 410
Inn on Charlotte, 417
Island Hotel, 410
Josephine's, 415
Kenwood Inn, 417
Lakeside Inn, 414
Magnolia Plantation, 412
Old Powder House Inn, 419
McFarlin Inn, 414
Old City House Inn, 419
Old Mansion Inn, 419
Palmer Place, 413
Peace and Plenty, 419
Penny Farthing Inn, 419
Riverview, 414
St. Francis Inn, 418
Secret Garden, 419
Sequi Inn, 419
Seven Sisters Inn, 414
Southern Wind, 418
St. George Inn, 418
Sweet Water Branch, 412
Victorian House, 418
Wakulla Springs Lodge, 418
Westcott House, 416
Willows, 412
1735 House, 410
44 Spanish Street Inn, 419

Seasonal Florida has many historic bed and breakfast establishments that offer gracious southern hospitality. Genuine Innkeepers make these off-beat historic lodgings a comfortable and memorable experience. Guest are greeted with a warm welcome and a chance to experience a trip back in time to the simple life of yesterday. Bed and breakfast Inns have something special to offer and give that little something different. A chance to sit in a rocking chair and prop your feet up on the porch railing, enjoy and relive the past.

Innkeepers are usually eager to share the locations of the areas best restaurants, whether it's gourmet or down-home eating. They also know what distinguishes their surrounding area and the special attractions to visit during your stay.

Some of these picturesque inns are located on sites with beautiful waterfront views on the Atlantic Ocean, Gulf of Mexico, scenic rivers and lakes. Some are in secluded rural areas while many are downtown within historic districts in Fernandina and St. Augustine. These inns offer a welcome home base for sight-seeing and shopping.

Most inns offer a morning meal which can range from muffins and juice to a full blown southern breakfast of smoked meats, eggs, grits and gravy, fruits in season, hot biscuits with homemade preserves and jelly. Some even offer evening dining as well and may pack a picnic lunch on request.

Greyfield Inn, Cumberland Island.

Many of *Seasonal Florida's* bed and breakfast inns are in historic buildings, where the architecture and antiques all have stories. Most are restored with air-conditioning and furnished with period antiques from claw-footed tubs in the private baths to the four poster feather bed. While we haven't found a bed where George Washington slept, Hey! Jefferson Davis, Calvin Coolidge and Sidney Cats ain't half bad.

Elizabeth Pointe Lodge

AMELIA ISLAND (FERNANDINA)
Addison House, Ash Street, 904-277-1604
Nine rooms in the historic District. Continental breakfast.

Ash Street Bed and Breakfast, 102 s. 7th Street, 904-277-4941
Two historic homes, 10 guest rooms with private baths, one spa suite. Full breakfast served on front porch. Homemade cookies and lemonade.

Amelia Island Williams House, 103 South 9th Street, 904-277-2328
Oldest bed and breakfast on Amelia Island. Antebellum mansion built in 1856 and visited by Jefferson Davis, 240 feet of veranda's, large suites with fireplaces and private baths. Museum quality antiques are located throughout.

Bailey House, 28 South 7th Street, 904-261-5390
Circa 1895 Queen Ann Victorian style located in Historic District. Wide staircase with stained glass windows. Four guest rooms with private baths.

Elizabeth Pointe Lodge, 98 S. Fletcher Ave., 904-277-4851
Oceanfront splendor-1890's Nantucket shingle style exterior-offers bed & breakfast operational courses, 10 rooms with private baths. Cozy oceanfront library.

ELIZABETH POINTE LODGE ORANGE BREAD
Makes eight 9x5 inch loaves

- 4 cups soft butter
- 10 cups granulated sugar
- 16 large eggs
- 12 cups sifted unbleached flour
- 8 teaspoons baking powder
- 2 teaspoons salt
- 2 cups orange juice
- 2 cups milk
- 2 tablespoons orange zest

Preheat oven to 325 degrees

Using soft butter, grease the inside of 8 bread pans (9x5x3 inch). Line the boom of each pan with wax paper and set aside. Cream butter and sugar together in large bowl, set aside. Whip eggs in a small bowl until airy and add to the creamed mixture, stir and set aside. Sift together flour, baking powder and salt. Blend with a wooden spoon until well mixed, set aside. Pour into a medium bowl the orange juice and milk, set aside. Add one-fourth of the liquid measure to the creamed mixture and blend. Add to the creamed mixture one-fourth of the dry ingredients and blend. Continue to add one-fourth portions of liquid and dry until all of is blended together and creamy. Add orange zest and stir well. Pour batter into the pan three-fourths full and set in a preheated oven. Bake approximately 45 minutes then test for doneness. Cool on a cooling rack on its side for approximately 45 minutes then remove from the pans.

AMELIA ISLAND (CON'T)
Fairbanks House, 904-277-0500
Italianate Villa built in 1885. Located in the heart of the Historical District of Fernandina. Ten rooms, suites, or cottages and private baths.

Hoyt House, 804 Atlantic Avenue, 904-277-4300
Built by a successful banker in 1905. Located in the downtown Historical District. Full gourmet breakfast. All rooms with private bath.

1735 House, 584 S. Fletcher St., 800-872-8531
Charming oceanfront Inn, has one and two bedroom suites all with ocean views. Doctor built this house for leisure in the 1920's.

APALACHICOLA
Bryant House Bed and Breakfast, 101 SW 1st Street,
Antique filled Victorian home Serving a German breakfast.

Coombs House, Number 80 6th Street, 850-653-9199
Elegant three-story Victorian mansion features high ceilings, nine fireplaces and antique furniture. All rooms have private baths. Continental breakfast. Located in the heart of Historical District.

Gibson Inn, 100 Market Street, 850-653-2191
Restored four story hotel with lots of porches, rockers and fans. Thirty-one rooms with baths (some with original claw-footed tubs). Interesting bar and restaurant.

CEDAR KEY
Cedar Key Bed and Breakfast, Corner of 3rd and F Street, 352-543-9000
Victorian home built in 1880 of native yellow pine. Located in one of the oldest seaports in Florida. All rooms have high ceilings, paddle fans, access porches and have private baths. Homemade breakfast.

Island Hotel, 2nd and B Streets, 352-543-5111
A pre-Civil War building with Jamaican style architecture. Rustic and authentic, with much of the original structure. Gourmet seafood dining room, serving local Cedar Key specialties. Cozy lounge bar with murals painted 50 years ago.

BED AND BREAKFAST INNS

CUMBERLAND ISLAND
Greyfield Inn, 904-261-6408

Located across the St. Mary's River in Georgia, Cumberland Island is accessible only by boat or small plane. The office for Greyfield is in Fernandina so we are including it with the others. The R.W. Ferguson ferries guest to the secluded haven from the docks of Fernandina Beach. The Greyfield Inn has nine rooms, one with private bath. One cottage has two rooms with private bath. The 1902 mansion has many of he original furnishings. Three scrumptious meals a day are included.

GREYFIELD INN FRIED SOFTSHELL CRAB WITH PARSLEY BUERRE BLANC

- 1 soft shell blue crab (per person), cleaned
- ½ cup flour
- 1 teaspoon cayenne pepper
- ¼ teaspoon fresh ground black pepper

Combine flour and two peppers. Rinse and dry crabs. Lightly dust with flour mix. Fry in hot oil (preferably deep fryer) approximately one minute. Set aside on paper towels to drain.

Sauce:
- 1 cup white wine
- 1 finely diced shallot
- 2 tablespoons apple cider vinegar
- Juice of 4 lemons
- ½ cup butter
- ¼ cup chopped parsley
- Salt to taste

In saucepan, combine wine and shallots; reduce by three-fourths. Add vinegar and one-half lemon juice. Bring liquids to a boil. Add butter by the tablespoons lightly whisking between additions. Add parsley and salt to taste. Drizzle remaining lemon juice over crabs and serve with sauce.

DEFUNIAK SPRINGS
Hotel DeFuniak, 400 E. Nelson Ave. at 8th Street, 850-892-4383

Built in 1920, newly restored and not to be missed. Hotel DeFuniak is the only deluxe small hotel with an exceptional dining room in the inland panhandle.

GAINESVILLE
Magnolia Plantation, 309 S.E. Seventh Street, 352-375-6653

1885 Victorian with antiques, mahogany staircase and pine floors. Ten fireplaces, five bed chambers with private baths. Claw footed tubs and ceiling fans. Landscape gardens. Full breakfast.

Sweet Water Branch, 625 East University Avenue, 352-373-6760

1885 Victorian home, hardwood floors, and antique furnishings. Located adjacent to Gainesville downtown in the Historic District. Six bed chambers, four with private baths with claw footed tubs. Full breakfast.

JACKSONVILLE
House on Cherry Street, 1844 Cherry Street, 904-384-1999

Historic Riverside, antiques, decoys, Oriental rugs, antique coverlets on canopied beds, and ceiling fans. Street ends at the St. Johns River.

Archibald House, 125 W. 2nd St., 904-634-1389

Built in 1903, former judge's home located in the historic Springfield area. Two rooms and suites with private baths. Adjacent carriage house with sleeping loft.

Willows, 1849 Willow Branch Terr., 904-387-9152

Lovely Riverside home built in the 1920's by lumber baron. Three rooms with bath swimming pool.

MICANOPY
Herlong Mansion, 402 NE Cholokka Blvd. 352-466-3322

Classic Revival imitation of a Southern Colonial design three story brick structure built over an 1840 two story home. There are four suites, six bedrooms and one cottage with private baths. Full breakfast.

INNKEEPER'S ICEBOX CAKE

12 ounces vanilla wafers
6 ounces fresh coconut
8 ounces dates, chopped
1½ cups golden raisins

16 ounce jar of cherries, drained and coarsely chopped
1 quart pecans, coarsely chopped
1¾ cups condensed milk

Place vanilla wafers in a food processor with metal blade in place. Process until finely chopped. Put in a large bowl and add the coconut, dates, raisins, cherries, and pecans. Mix thoroughly and pour one and one half cups condensed milk over mixture. Mix until moist and mixture holds together. Add remaining milk if needed. Press into a buttered loaf pan, cover with plastic wrap and refrigerate for several days. Unmold, place on platter, slice and serve.

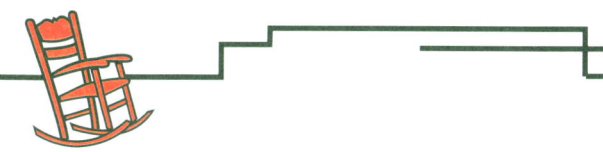

LAKE WALES
Chalet Suzanne Country Inn, 402 NE Cholokka Blvd., 800-466-3322
Historic Country Inn and gourmet restaurant that has been selected repeatedly as one of the top 10 Best Inns in the USA. Thirty room inn, established in 1931.

CHALET SUZANNE BROILED GRAPEFRUIT

Serves 2
- 1 Florida grapefruit, room temperature
- 3 tablespoons butter
- 14 tablespoons cinnamon-sugar mixture
- 1 teaspoon sugar or Tupelo honey

Slice grapefruit in half and cut membrane around the center of fruit. Cut around each section half, close to membrane, so that the fruit is completely loosened from its shell. Fill the center of each half with one half the butter. Sprinkle half teaspoon sugar over each half, then sprinkle each with half cinnamon-sugar mixture. Place grapefruit on a shallow baking pan and broil just long enough to brown tops and heat until bubbling hot. Remove from oven and serve.

MONTICELLO
Clarke House, 580 West Washington Street, 850-997-1348
Victorian architecture built in 1890. Wide heart pine hardwood floors. Two bedrooms with a shared bath. English breakfast that is an extravaganza.

Palmer Place, 625 West Mill, 850-997-5519
One of the oldest homes in North Florida, construction began in 1829 and was completed in 1836. Palmer Place has 7,500 square feet and sits on ten acres of land. Five bedrooms with private baths, central heat and air.

MOUNT DORA
Lakeside Inn, 100 North Alexander Street, 352-383-4101
11The Lakeside Inn is a classic showplace of period architecture and craftsmanship. The main colonial manor is accented by English Tudor Gables and terrace wings which were dedicated in 1931 by their distinguished guest, President Calvin Coolidge.

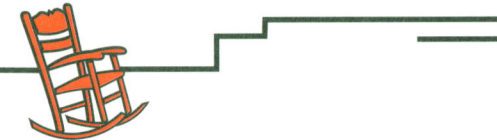

NEW SMYRNA BEACH
Riverview, 103 Flagler Ave., 1-800-945-7416
Restored hotel on the picturesque Indian River. Eighteen rooms with views, overlooking adjacent marina. Has restaurant and quaint gift shop.

Seven Sisters Inn, 820 South Fort King Street, 352—867-1170
Built in 1888, Queen Ann Style-Victorian. Full gourmet breakfast. Voted one of 12 Best Inns in country by Country Inns.

ORANGE PARK
Club Continental, 2143 Astor St., 1-800-877-8070
Former home of Palmolive Soap king, built on the St. Johns River. Five large rooms with private baths.

PALMETTO
Five Oaks Bed and Breakfast, 1102 Riverside Drive, 1-800-658-4167
Classic Florida home with an old Spanish tiled roof and magnificent wrap-around porch on the Manatee River. Graceful oak staircase, spacious rooms with private baths.

QUINCY
Allison House, 215 North Madison St., 850-875-2511
The house itself is one of the oldest in North Florida and was constructed in 1843 by A.K. Allison who was the governor of Florida. Furnished with antiques from the British Isles. Quincy was once the shade tobacco capital of the world.

McFarlin House Inn, 305 E. Kings St., 850-875-2526
Beautifully restored Queen-Anne Victorian located in the heart of the Historic District. Nine guest rooms, includes full breakfast. Magnificent hand-burled curly pine staircase.

SEASIDE
Josephine's, 850-231-4224
Located at Seaside on the Gulf of Mexico. Josephine's is a recreation of an 1840's antebellum mansion with six twenty-two foot columns framing the porch. It has seven bedrooms and two master suites. The rooms are furnished with period antiques and four poster beds. Seven of the rooms have wood-burning fireplaces.

CRIOLLA'S CURRIED OYSTERS

Makes four entree servings or eight appetizer servings.

1 cup all-purpose flour
1 tablespoon curry powder
¾ teaspoon salt
1 to 1¼ pounds shucked oysters, drained
2 tablespoons salad oil
1 tablespoon lemon juice
1 tablespoon fresh cilantro, coarsely chopped

Combine flour, curry powder and salt in a plastic bag. Add several oysters to the bag and shake to coat evenly with breading mix. Lift out oysters and set aside. Repeat with remaining oysters. Set a 10-12 inch frying pan over medium heat and add oil, when it is very hot but not smoking, add oysters in a single layer (you may need to cook oysters in two batches) and cook, turning oysters once, until golden on both sides, about two minutes per side. Transfer oysters to a plate and pour off oil that remains in pan. Return oysters to pan and toss gently with lemon juice and cilantro. Divide oysters among plates.

ST. AUGUSTINE
Alexander Homestead, 14 Seville St., 904-826-4147
A restored Victorian home which has 4 chambers with private baths, one with Jacuzzi. The twelve room inn was renovated in 1993. Serves a full country breakfast.

At Journey's End, 89 Cedar Street, 904-829-0076, 888-806-2351
1800's Victorian style home offers an international flair in newly designed and decorated theme rooms, Safari, Egypt, China and Victorian bedrooms with private baths. Full breakfast is served.

Agustin Inn, 29 Cuna Street, 904-823-9559
Located in heart of Historic District. Eight guest rooms, full breakfast.

Bayfront Marin House, 142 Avenida Menendez, 904-824-1502
Recently renovated, furnished with period antiques

ST. AUGUSTINE (CON'T)

Bayfront Westcott House, 146 Avenida Menendez St., 904-824-4301
Built for Dr. John Westcott in the late 1880's, Westcott's house is a fine example of vernacular architecture of St. Augustine's history. Each guest room is furnished with American and European antiques, with king size beds and private baths.

Beachfront Bed and Breakfast, 904-461-8727
Elegant and romantic, all rooms and suites have private baths. Five miles from St. Augustine.

Carriage Way Bed and Breakfast, 70 Cuna St., 904-829-2467
Classic Victorian home built in 1883, and restored 100 years later. Located in the heart of the Historic District. The Carriage Way has nine bed chambers decorated with period antiques and reproductions.

Casablanca Inn on the Bay, 24 Avenida Menendez, 904-829-0928,1-800-826-2626
One of Florida's first residence hotels. Elegant suites with panoramic bayviews. Private entrances and baths. The 12 room inn was renovated in 1993.

Casa de la Paz, 22 Avenida Menendez, 904-829-2915
A Mediterranean Revival style located on St. Augustine's historic waterfront. The six guest rooms feature tiled baths, queen size beds and hardwood floors.

Casa de Solano, 21 Aviles St., 904-824-3555, 1-888-796-0980
Built in 1763 for Spanish officer Don Manuel Solano. Five-room bed and breakfast located in the heart of the historic district.

Casa de Suenos Bed and Breakfast, 20 Cordova St., 904-824-0804
Beautiful turn of the century Mediterranean Inn. Five exquisite rooms including two suites. All rooms have private bath with showers, three with Jacuzzi tubs.

Casa Monica Hotel, 95 Cordova St., 800-648-1888
Majestic Landmark, built in 1888, restored in 1999. Heart of Historic St. Augustine. AAA four diamond restaurant.

Castle Garden, 15 Shenandoah St., 904-829-3839
Castle Garden is a newly renovated 1860's Moorish Revival Inn with hardwood floors, located in Historic District. Six rooms with private baths, two with Jacuzzi. Coquina exterior remains virtually untouched. Full country breakfast.

Cedar House Inn, 79 Cedar St., 904-829-0079, 1-800-233-2746
Restored 1893 Victorian Bed and Breakfast in the heart of Historical St. Augustine. Four bedrooms, heart of pine floors and 10 foot high ceilings.

ST. AUGUSTINE (CON'T)

Centennial House, 26 Cordova St., 800-611-2880
Nationally registered "certified historic structure" Fully restored eight room inn, private baths, oversized Jacuzzi and fireplaces.

Inn on Charlotte, 52 Charlotte St., 800-355-5508
Built in 1918 and restored in 2003 with large porches. Seven guest rooms, single or double Jacuzzi, King or queen beds, all have private baths.

Kenwood Inn, 38 Marine St., 904-824-2116
Built as a private home in 1865, became a lodging in 1866. Three stories with wrap-around porches, 14 rooms with private baths.

La Fiesta Oceanfront Inn and Suites, 1-800-852-6390
A fireplace and jacuzzi are two features of these six new townhouse suites. Two oceanfront balconies.

OLD CITY HOUSE FRIED GRITS WITH LOW COUNTRY BACON GRAVY

Serves 6-8
1 cup hominy grits
3½ cups fish stock
½ cup heavy cream
1 cup cheddar cheese, grated
¾ pound shrimp (diced)
1 cup thin sliced scallions

Bring fish stock to a boil, add grits and return to boil then simmer for one hour stirring frequently. Add cream, shrimp, salt and pepper to taste and cook 3-5 more minutes. Remove from heat, add cheddar cheese and scallions mixing thoroughly. Pour into greased 2 quart loaf pan and chill. After thoroughly cooling, slice into one quarter inch pieces and dredge in flour. Pan fry in butter over medium-high heat until golden brown on each side. Top with Low Country Bacon Gravy.

Low Country Bacon Gravy
1 pound smoked bacon
⅓ cup yellow onions, diced
2 cups chicken stock
1½ cups heavy cream
3 tablespoons flour
2 tablespoons Creole spice

Cook bacon until crisp, add onions and cook 3 more minutes. Stir in flour and cook 3 more minutes. Add chicken stock and cream slowly over high heat and cook until boiling. Reduce heat and add Creole spice. (Can be thinned out with heavy cream if necessary). Pour over fried grits and garnish with one grilled shrimp.

ST. AUGUSTINE (CON'T)

Old City House, 115 Cordova St., 904-826-0113
Located in a restored 19th century building. The 1870's building originally served as a stable, was renovated in 1896 and became a winter cottage rented to Northerners. Gourmet restaurant serves the freshest of what ever is available. Five rooms with queen sized beds and private baths.

Old Mansion Inn, 14 Joiner St., 904-824-1975
Three story mansion constructed in 1872 by a spinster from North Carolina. All accommodations have a kitchenette, shower/bathroom. Breakfast is in the typical English style.

Old Powder House Inn, 38 Cordova St., 904-824-4149
Built in 1899 on the site of the structure which stored gun powder for nearby Fort Castillo de San Marcos. Nine rooms with elaborate woodwork and private baths. Located in the Historic District. Full gourmet breakfast.

Peace and Plenty Inn, 87 Cedar Street, 904-829-8209, 877-468-3651
Built in 1890's, located in the Historic District. Five luxury suites with king/queen beds, jacuzzi and shower baths. Private walled garden with fountains. Gourmet breakfast.

Penny Farthing Inn, 83 Cedar St., 904-824-2100, 800-395-1890
Located in the heart of the ancient city. Built in 1897, restored in 1990. Seven rooms, porches, private baths. One suite with private porch.

Pirate Haus Inn and Hostel, 904-808-1999
European style lodging in the heart of St. Augustine.

Saragossa Inn, 34 Saragossa Street, 904-808-7384, 877-808-7384
Six guest rooms with private baths. Full gourmet breakfast served.

Secret Garden Inn, 56 ½ Charlotte t., 904-829-3678
In the center of the Historic District. Three suites, private entrances, baths and kitchenettes.

Sequi Inn, 47 San Marco Ave., 904-825-2811
Built in 1914. Located on the edge of the Historic District. Spacious bedrooms with private baths.

ST. AUGUSTINE (CON'T)

Southern Wind, 18 Cordova St., 904-825-3623

Built in 1919 by Henry Flagler's physician. Each bedroom is furnished with antiques reminiscent of the Flagler era. Four rooms and three suites, private baths.

St. Francis Inn, 279 St. George St., 800-824-6062

Originally built by Senor Gaspar Garcia in 1791, is constructed of native coquina limestone. All rooms and suites have private baths, some with fireplaces, kitchenettes, whirlpool baths. Full breakfast in the Inn's dining room, in your room, on a balcony, or in the courtyard.

St. George Inn, 2-6 St. George Street, 904-827-5740

Twenty-two rooms with Old World charm and modern conveniences.

Victorian House, 11 Cadiz St., 904-824-5214

Restored 1897 Victorian wood frame with heart pine floors, canopy beds, stenciled walls and period antiques. Located in the Historic District. Eight rooms, (all have private baths/or showers).

44 Spanish Street Inn, 44 Spanish Street, 904-826-0650, 800-521-0722

Old Florida-style apartment house built in the 1920's. Converted into a bed and breakfast in 2003. In the heart of the Historic District. Eight guest rooms with queen beds, full breakfast.

STUART

Homeplace, 501 Akron Ave., 407-220-9148

The "Homeplace," Stuart's premier bed and breakfast inn, built in 1913 and restored in 1989. Wicker front porch and turn-of-the-century parlor, lush patio, pool and heated spa. Breakfast features "Old Florida" recipes and fruit picked from the yard.

TALLAHASSEE

Governors Inn, 209 W. Adams St., 800-342-7717

Forty room hotel located in Historic District. Has bar and meals may be ordered in room.

WAKULLA SPRINGS

Wakulla Springs Lodge, 1 Springs Drive, 850-224-5950

Located on picturesque Wakulla Springs, Twenty-seven guest rooms with private marble bathrooms. Adjacent restaurant features Florida cuisine.

Seasonal Menus

If we had to pick the one most important factor in good Southern cooking it would be without a doubt freshness. There is no substitute. The taste in most produce and seafood begins to decline as soon as it is picked or harvested. The sugar in fresh corn begins to turn to starch the minute it is picked. Fish and seafood deteriorate soon after they are caught, and the list goes on.

Even in North Florida our fruits and vegetables are seasonal. Oysters and wild game are best harvested in the fall and winter. Crabs, most vegetables and fruits are more abundant during the spring and summer. We have adjusted our menus to take advantage of the freshness and low prices of foods by eating these seasonal foods at their peak.

We have also discovered that some dishes just plain taste better when served with another dish, and some entrees just beg for a certain dessert. Deviled chicken would be a totally different dish if not served with linguine and pesto sauce. Fried mullet without coleslaw and hush puppies, or a seafood perlo without a Caesar salad is like a day without sunshine.

Included are some of our favorite menu combinations using the North Florida recipes from this book. Hopefully you will be trying some of them with fresh fruit, vegetables or herbs you have grown or at least picked from a u-pick-'em farm near you. We have included a list of u-pick-'em farms and farmer's markets to help in that area.

North Florida has many food related festivals celebrating everything from collards to possums. We encourage you to visit some of these festivals and enjoy the many regional foods available. Many feature local crafts as well as unique food.

After this book is completed, we will continue to add to our web site: seasonalfloridacookbook.com. This web site will feature articles on local foods, North Florida restaurants, festivals and new recipes. Hopefully we will be able to supply you through the mail with those hard to find items like Datil peppers, stone-ground grits and cornmeal, tupelo honey, mayhaw jelly, barbecue sauces, etc.

If you would like more information please look for us on the web: seasonalfloridacookbook.com.

Bon Appétit!

Jo Manning
Yardbird Productions

seasonalfloridacookbook.com

Breakfast and Brunch Menus

Country Fried Steak Tomato Gravy
Speckled Heart Grits
Country Fried Yard Eggs
Daddy's Hoecake
Mayhaw Jelly

Wild Blueberry Muffins
Pesto Omelet
Fruit in Season

Mullet Roe with Smoked Bacon
Country Fried Yard Eggs
Cheddar Cheese and Datil Pepper Grits
Sautéed Bananas
Orange Fig Muffins

Broiled Grapefruit
Libby's Heavenly Hots
Cane Syrup
Smoked Link Sausage

Fried Country Ham
Speckled Heart Grits
Shrimp Paste
Poached Eggs
Rise and Shine Biscuits
Scuppernong Jam

Fresh Squeezed Florida Orange Juice
Eggs Chautauqua with Choron Sauce
Smoked Bacon
Fried Vine-ripe Tomatoes
Fruit in Season
Chickasaw Plum Jam

Smothered Fried Rabbit
Country Fried Yard Eggs
Old-Fashioned Speckled Heart Grits
Mother's Buttermilk Biscuits
Corncob Jelly

Ham and Red-Eye Gravy
Nassau Grits
Country Fried Yard Eggs
Biscuits
Sand Pear Preserves

Corned Beef Hash
Poached Eggs
English Muffins
Marmalade

Fresh Strawberries and Sour Cream
Whole Grain Griddle Cakes
Cane Syrup, Tupelo Honey
Thick Sliced Smoked Bacon

Fresh Fruit in Season
Omelet Florentine
Smoked Bacon
Orange Fig Muffins

Broiled Grapefruit with Tupelo Honey
Breakfast Frittata
Granny's Banana Bread

Hog and Hominy
Country Fried Yard Eggs
Fried Green Tomatoes
Sweet Potato Biscuits
Fig Preserves

NORTH FLORIDA SEASONAL MENUS

Spring and Summer Menus

Anchovy Vinaigrette Salad
Sopping Barbecue Shrimp
Steamed New Potatoes
Cuban or French Bread
Hospitality Pineapple Fluff

Granny's Chicken and Dumplings
Fresh Field Peas and Butterbeans
Buttermilk Fried Okra
Daddy's Crusty Pone Cornbread
Sliced Tomatoes
Marinated Cucumbers
Datil "Bottled Hell" Pepper Sauce
Pickled Peaches
Granny's Banana Pudding

Gulf Coast Shrimp Salad
Mama's Crab Goulash
White Rice
Cuban or French Bread
Silky Smooth Flan

Spanish Gazpacho
Scamp with Wine Sauce
Steamed Asparagus
Potatoes en Papilote
Pear Pudding

Marinated Tomatoes
Deviled Chicken
Linguine with Basil and Pinenuts
The King's Favorite Pound Cake
Fresh Florida Strawberries
and Chantilly Sauce

Marinated Calico Scallops
Tamari Salad
Black Creek Stuffed Flounder
Potatoes Anna
Johnny's Feud Cake

Grilled Shrimp with Herbs
Steamed New Potatoes
Vegetables on the Grill
Cuban or French Bread
Mango Sorbet

Pork Tenderloin Grilled with Rosemary
Speckled Butterbeans with Gravy
Stewed Okra and tomatoes
Roast Neers
Fried Sweet Potatoes
Skillet Cornbread
Prize Winning Peanut Cake

Barbecue Ribs
Mustard Sauce
Swamp cabbage Stew
Spuds New Potato Salad
Rise and Shine Biscuits
Fresh Peach Ice Cream

Shrimp Remoulade in Avocado Shell
Snapper Anastasia with Mango Curry
White Rice
Steamed Asparagus
Amaretto Pecan Ice Cream

Crab Stuffed Mushrooms
Tamari Salad
O'Steen's Shrimp Perlo
Steamed Vegetables
Fresh Fruit Tart

NORTH FLORIDA SEASONAL MENUS

Fall And Winter Menus

St. Augustine Minorcan Clam Chowder
Mama's Deviled Crabs
Champagne Battered Onion Rings
Sunflower Bread
Old-Fashioned Lemon Meringue Pie

Oyster and Artichoke Soup
French Bread
Salad with Creole Vinaigrette
Red Beans and Rice
Bread Pudding

Dixie Ham
A Pot of Lima Beans
Old-Fashioned Collard Greens
Rooster Spur Pepper Sauce
Cracklin Pone Corn Bread
Sweet Potato Pie

Oysters Wakulla
Bruce Creek Venison Stew
Swamp Cabbage Deluxe
Skillet Cornbread
Creamy Rice Pudding

Bern's Caesar Salad
Beef Tenderloin With Béarnaise Sauce
Steamed New Potatoes
Steamed Asparagus
Silky Smooth Flan

Fresh Spinach Salad
Grilled Dove with Smoked Bacon
Rutabaga and Wild Watercress
Potatoes Anna
The King's Favorite Cake
with Strawberry Topping

Oysters Bienville
Wood Duck Gumbo
White Rice
French Bread
Peanut Butter Custard Pie

Oysters Rock-a-Damn-Fella
Trophy Buck Chili with
Guacamole Dip
Hospitality Pineapple Fluff

Oyster Artichoke Soup
Gypsy Chicken
Steamed Vegetables
New Potatoes
Tawee's Favorite Chocolate Pie

Smoked Mullet Dip
Barbecue Ribs with Oriental Sauce
Granny's Green Rice
Wilted Lettuce Salad with Bacon
Rise and Shine Biscuits
Sweetie Pie

Gulf Coast Seafood Gumbo
Our Favorite Salad with Creamy
Dressing
Yardbird Perlo
Skillet Squash and St. Augustine Sweets
The Queen's Cheese Cake

Collard Green Soup
Cuban Pork Roast
Fried Sweet Potatoes
A Mess of Greens
Silky Smooth Flan

Artichoke Dip
Crabby Mushroom Soup
Salad with Creole Vinaigrette
Shrimp Creole
Pineapple Fluff

Oysters on the Half Shell with
Oyster Dipping Sauce
Salad with Creamy French Dressing
Pecan Crusted Catfish
Brabant Potatoes
Spinach Timbales
Old-Timey Egg Custard

Special Gatherings Menus

Thanksgiving Feast
Hickory Smoked Turkey
Hickory Smoked Ham
Skillet Corn Bread Dressing with
Giblet Gravy
Crookneck Squash Casserole
Field Peas and Speckled Butter Beans
A Mess of Greens
Old-Fashioned Collard Greens
Thanksgiving Brown Rice Casserole
Orange Sweet Potatoes
Campbell's Shrimp Ring
Ambrosia
Homemade Yeast Rolls
The Queen's Lemon Cheese Cake
The Chocolate Cake
Southern Pecan Pie
Fresh Pumpkin Pie

Chautauqua Day
Smoked Ribs & Chicken with Rib Rub
Calico Beans
Wayne's Wilted Slaw
Granny's Green Rice
Rise and Shine Biscuits
Terre's Dewberry Cobbler

Christmas Breakfast
Freshly Squeezed Florida Orange Juice
Creamy Scrambled Eggs
Cheddar Cheese and Datil Pepper Grits
Fried Smoked Ham and Sausage
Mother's Buttermilk Biscuits
Daddy's Hoecake
Tupelo Honey, Daddy's Fig Preserves,
Mayhaw Jelly, Blackberry Jelly

Summer Seafood Boil
Smoked Mullet Dip
Cold Zucchini Soup
Panhandle Seafood Boil
Boiled Crabs, Shrimp. Sausage, Potatoes,
Onions and Corn
Ice Cold Watermelon
Old-Fashioned Lemon Meringue Pie

Spring Picnic
Boarding House Fried Chicken
A Dozen Deviled Eggs
Pimento Cheese Sandwiches
Bacon, Egg and Olive Sandwiches
Ruby's Secret Oatmeal Cookies

Fall Fish Fry
Apalachicola Oysters on the half Shell
Datil "Bottled Hell" Pepper Sauce
Ingram's Fried Fish
Moccasin Branch Coleslaw
Old-Fashioned Potato Salad
Southern Hushpuppies
Florida Key Lime Pie

Winter Barbecue
Barbecue Pork Shoulder with
three Sauces
Minorcan Perlo
Rosin Potatoes
Plantation Fried Corn
Moccasin Branch Coleslaw

Florida-Georgia Tailgate
Boarding House Fried Chicken
Dixie Ham
Old-Fashioned Potato Salad
Tabbouleh
Bean Dip "Hummus"
A Dozen Deviled Eggs
Icebox Pickles
Datil Pepper Jelly with Cream Cheese
and Crackers
Ultimate Fudgy Brownies
Miss Lillie's Whisky Cakes

Macho Dinner For The Boys
T-Bone Steak a la Carte
with Macho Gravy
Tomato and Iceberg Lettuce with
Store-bought mayonnaise dressing
Italian Spaghetti with
Store-bought Tomato Sauce
Apple Uglies (from the bakery)

Glossary

APALACHICOLA OYSTER-Oysters grown in the waters of Apalachicola Bay, considered by connoisseurs as one of the best tasting oysters in the world.

ARMADILLO-Possum on the half-shell. Small edible animal that visited from the west and never went home. Maybe we should call it a damn armadillo.

AVOCADO-Alligator pear. Tasty pear-shaped fruit, excellent for salads and appetizers.

BARBECUE-Method of slow cooking meat and fowl over wood-burning coals, usually served with a spicy homemade sauce.

BATTEN ISLAND-Home of the Batten Island Gourmet Sauce.

BIRDS-EYE PEPPER-Small round peppers favored for pepper sauce.

BOTTLED HELL-Spicy hot sauce made with the fiery datil peppers.

BROWN TURKEY FIGS-Favored fig in North Florida for fig preserves.

CAST-IRON SKILLETS-Preferred cooking pans for Southern-style food.

CHAUTAUQUA-Cultural events held throughout the North and South at the turn of the century.

CHAYOTE-Pear shaped vegetable that grows on vines in the South.

CHORIZO-Spicy sausage, popular in Spanish and Cuban cooking.

CLABBER-Thick part from the souring of unpasteurized milk.

CONCH-Large snail-like creatures found in waters of the Florida Keys and islands, popular in fritters and salads.

COOTER-Local name for fresh water turtles, soft-shell or alligator.

CORNMEAL-Essential ingredient for North Florida cooking. Stone-ground medium grind is preferred. Our favorite brand is Fink's.

CRACKERS-Early North Florida settlers, many moved down from the Carolinas.

CRACKER CATTLE-A breed of cows brought to the New World by the Spanish in the 1500's.

DAMN YANKEES-Northern visitors who fail to return home.

DATIL PEPPER-Small fiery peppers grown around St. Johns County. Most popular in pepper sauces.

DEMI-GLACE-reduction of beef stock, intense in flavor.

DUTCH OVEN-cast-iron pot with lid, favored by our forefathers for outdoor cooking. Wonderful for our cookouts.

FATBACK-Pork fat with rind, fried and eaten with beans.

FILÉ-powdered sassafras, popular for thickening gumbos.

FLAN-Creamy custard popular in Cuban and Spanish cooking.

FLOUR-Southern wheat flour, Pillsbury or White Lily are preferred.

FROMAJARDIS-Cheesy pastry popular with St. Augustine Minorcan families.

GARFISH-Prehistoric looking fish found in lakes and rivers along the Gulf Coast.

GASPACHE-Salad popular with Spanish families in old Pensacola.

Glossary

GATOR TAIL-Meat from the tail section of the alligator, considered a delicacy by many gourmets.
GREENS-One or more leafy vegetables; turnips, mustard, kale or collards.
GUAVA-Small fruit popular for jelly.
GUMBO-Thick stew made with seafood, fowl, or vegetables thickened with filé or okra.
GUINEA HEN-Grey or white yard bird with dark meat.
GOPHER-Small land tortoise popular with our forefathers for stews and gumbos.
HOECAKE-Our version of a large biscuit cooked on a cast-iron griddle.
HOMINY-the corn kernel treated with lye to remove the outer husk.
HOMINY GRITS-Coarse stone-ground is our preference.
HUGUENOTS-French settlers that settled parts of Coastal Florida and Georgia.
KEY LIME-Small round limes popular in the Keys. Typically orange-yellow in color.
KIWIS-New fruit introduced from New Zealand, grows well in North Florida.
KUDZU- Prolific vine with edible root. Introduced from the Orient during the Depression to control erosion in the deep South.
MANGO-Sweet tropical fruit with flavor between peach and melon.
MARSH HENS-Small wild birds found in the marshes along the Atlantic Coast.
MAYHAW-Small crab apple like fruit native to North Florida. Treasured by our Granny for jelly and butter.
MINORCAN-Indentured servants brought from Minorca to North Florida to work on Indigo plantations. Descendants are now prominent citizens of St. Johns County.
MOON PIES- Round sweet cakes with rich chocolate icing popular with children and some adults in the Deep South.
MULLET-Tasty fish found on all of North Florida's coastlines.
MULLET ROE-Eggs of the prolific fish, popular breakfast dish in Coastal Florida homes.
OKRA-Small vegetable popular for frying or for thickening stews and gumbos.
ORANGE FLOWER WATER-flavor produced from the blossoms of sour orange trees.
PASTA MACHINE-Wonderful machine which produces various widths of pasta for spaghetti, fettuccine, and lasagne.
PEANUTS-Popular ground nut served boiled when green but also may be parched when dry.
PECANS-Large Southern nut, eaten raw, toasted or cooked in various dishes including the sinful Pecan Pie.
PERLO-Local term for rice dishes also known as pilafs.
PINEAPPLE PEAR- Hard pear used in relish and preserves.

Glossary

PINEY WOODS ROOTERS-Wild pigs, descendants of the Spanish pigs brought over by De Soto.

POT LIQUER-Flavorful liquor obtained from cooking fresh greens, traditionally eaten with corn bread.

REDHORSE SUCKER-Fresh water fish prized for its flavor.

ROAST NEERS-Whole ears of corn eaten off the cob.

ROOSTER SPUR PEPPER SAUCE-Vinegar based pepper sauce typically served with greens.

ROUX-Thickening agent made by browning equal amounts of flour in oil or butter.

PINEAPPLE PEAR-Hard pear used in relish and preserves.

SALT MULLET-mullet salted to preserve, before refrigeration.

SAND PEAR-Hard-grainy pear, popular for canning and preserves.

SANGRIA-Popular Spanish drink made with wine, soda water and fruit.

SATSUMA-Small citrus fruit with a thin peel.

SCUPPERNONG-Sweet grapes grown on vines, planted on arbors or fences. Popular for jellies, pies and eating off the vine.

SOUR ORANGE-Old type of orange favored for marmalade and jam.

STONE-GROUND-Local method used to process dried corn into grits and cornmeal.

SWAMP CABBAGE-The heart of the cabbage palm, eaten raw or cooked in stews.

SWEET POTATOES-Popular potatoes in the South served as a vegetable and also dessert.

TABBOULEH-Middle Eastern salad made with parsley and cracked wheat.

TAMARI-unsalted soy sauce.

TUPELO HONEY-Unique honey produced from the blossom of the Tupelo Gum trees which grow in the river swamps along the Gulf Coast.

VINE-RIPE TOMATOES-Tomatoes grown in home gardens picked in pink or red state.

YARD BIRDS-Domestic birds common in yards; chicken, geese, ducks, guineas, etc.

YARD EGG-Laid by yard birds who roam around grassed areas with diet of bugs and such. It has a rich yellow yolk.

FOOD FESTIVALS in NORTH FLORIDA

JANUARY
Great Southern
   Gumbo Cook Off   Destin   1-800-822-6877

FEBRUARY
Hoggetown Medival Faire   Gainesville   (904)-334-2197
Mardi Gras Street Festival   Pensacola   (850)-434-6211

MARCH
Cracker Day   Bunnell   (904)-437-7464
Crawfish Festival   Jacksonville Beach   (904)-384-5694
Scratch Ankle Festival   Milton   (850)-623-9418

APRIL
Sidewalk Art Festival   Cedar Key   (904)-543-5249
Cabbage and Potato Festival   Hastings   (904)-692-1420
Tupelo Honey Festival   Wewahitchka
Catfish Festival   Crescent City   (904)-698-1644
Chautauqua Festival   DeFuniak Springs   (850)-892-9494
Cracker Day   Deland   (904)-822-5778
Seafood Festival   Ft. Walton   (850)-244-5317
Winefest   San Destin
Taste of Jacksonville   Jacksonville   (904)-396-4900
Seafood-Minorcan
   Fromajardis Serenade Festival   St. Augustine   (904)-829-6545
Seafood Festival   Steinhatchee   (850)-578-2161
Railroad Days   Waldo   (904)-468-1001
Shrimp Festival   Amelia Island   (904)-261-3248
Clabber Girl Cook Off   Live Oak
Springing the Blues   Jacksonville Beach   (904)-247-4242
Down Home Days   Madison   (850)-973-2788
Walk Through Time   Micanopy   (850)-466-4100
Old Time Havana Days   Havana   (850)-539-5017

FOOD FESTIVALS, FARMERS MARKETS AND U-PICK'EMS

MAY

Isle of Eight Flags Shrimp Festival	Amelia Island	(904)-261-4212
Heritage Day	Deland	(904)-738-0649
Historic Day	Chipley	(850)-638-6130
Kuumba	American Beach	(904)-353-2270
Blue Crab Festival	Panacea	(904)-984-2722
Blue Crab Festival	Palatka	(904)-325-4406
Seafood Festival	Port St. Joe	(904)-229-8466
Florida Folk Festival	White Springs	(904)-397-2192
Zucchini Festival	Windsor	(904)-378-8671
Mayfest	Destin	(850)-832-6241
Catfish Festival	Blountstown	(904)-674-4519

JUNE

Fiesta of Five Flags	Pensacola	(850)-433-6512
Watermelon Festival	Chiefland	(904)-493-2210
Panhandle Watermelon Festival	Chipley	(850)-638-6268
Watermelon Festival	Monticello	(904)-997-5552
Watermelon Festival	Newberry	(904)-472-3361
Billy Bowlegs Festival	Ft. Walton	(850)-862-7141

JULY

Greater Jacksonville Kingfish and Seafood Festival Tournament	Jacksonville Beach (Mayport)	(904)-241-7127

AUGUST

B.B.Q. Rib Burn Off	Pensacola	(850)-432-0800
Possum and Fun Day Festival	Wausau	(850)-638-1271
Seafood Festival	Destin	(850)-837-6241
Pioneer Day	Mayo	(850)-294-2536

SEPTEMBER

Native American Heritage Festival	Tallahassee	(850)-575-8684
Seafood Festival	Pensacola	(850)-433-6512
Greek Festival	Jacksonville	(904)-396-5383
Seafest Restaurants	Jacksonville	(904)-396-4900
Festival of the Arts	Starke	(904-372-1976
Wine and Jazz Festival	Seaside	(850)-231-4224
Pioneer Day	Mayo	(904)-294-2536

OCTOBER

Good Life Jubilee	Alachua	(352)-642-8005
Boggy Bayou Mullet Festival	Niceville	(850)-678-1615
Seafood Festival	Panama City Beach	(850)-234-0292
Florida Forest Day	Perry	(904)-584-3227
Cracker Day Celebration	St. Augustine	(904)-824-4564
Ham Jam	Green Cove Springs	(904)-282-4444
Seafood Festival	Destin	(850)-837-6241
Ameliafest	Amelia Island	(904)-837-6241
Seafood Festival	Cedar Key	(904)-543-5308
Jazz Festival	Jacksonville	(904)-353-7770

NOVEMBER

Seafood Festival	Apalachicola	(850)-653-9419
Fall Harvest Festival	Micanopy	(352)-446-3540
Peanut Festival	Williston	(352)-528-6169
Collard Festival	Ponce deLeon	(850)-836-5208
Seafood Festival	Apalachicola	(850)-653-9419
Chowder Cook-off	Cedar Key	(352)-543-5600
Fall Festival	Cross Creek	(352)-466-4068
Greek Festival	Daytona	(904)-252-6012
Down Home Days	Trenton	(352)-463-6327
Suwanee River Olden Days	White Springs	(904)-397-2385
Museum	Tallahassee	(850)-575-8684
Rural Folk Life Fiesta	White Springs	(904)-397-2733

DECEMBER

Farm Days Syrup Making	Tallahassee	(850)-578-8684
Farm Days Syrup Making	Gainesville	(352)-374-2170
Historic Tours	Eden-Seagrove	(850)-231-4214

FARMER'S MARKETS IN NORTH FLORIDA

Chipley Farmers' Market
7th and Railroad Ave., Daily 8-5, (850) 638-6340

Alachua County Farmers' Market, Gainesville
U.S. 441 at N.W. 34th St., Tues., Thurs., Sat., Aug.-April, (352) 371-8236

Clay County Farmers' Market, Green Cove Springs
2463 Rt.16 West, June-July, Tues. and Sat., (904) 284-6355

Jacksonville Farmers' Market
1780 W. Beaver St., Daily, (904) 354-2821

Suwannee County Farmers' Market, Live Oak
Downtown, Tues., Fri., May-November, (904) 362-4002

Bay County Farmers' Market, Panama City
2234 E. 15th St., daily, May-October, (850) 784-6105

Pensacola Growers' Retail Market
Gonzalas at Desota under I-10, Tues., Thurs., Sat., May-Oct. (850)-986-7798

Jackson County County Growers', Marianna
Elks Lodge Parking Lot, Wed, and Sat.

Fort Walton Beach Farmers' Market, Fort Walton Beach
Okaloosa County Fair Grounds, Tues., Thurs., and Sat.

Quincy Farmers' Market
Gadsden County State Farmers' Market, Saturday Mornings

Santa Rosa County Growers' Market
Behind County Auditorium, Milton, May-August, Tuesday and Friday

Tallahassee Farmers' Market, Market Square Shopping Center, Tallahassee
Tuesday, Thursday and Saturday

St. Augustine Farmers' Market, St. Augustine Ampitheater, Anastasia Island,
Saturdays 8:30-12:30

U-PICK'EMS

This is a partial list of U-Pick'Em growers in North Florida. For a current listing in your area contact your county extension agent.

Take advantage of freshness and quality by taking your family and friends to these locations.

APPLES
Crawfordsville	Just Fruits	(904) 926-5644

BLUEBERRIES
Cross Creek	Southmoon Farm	(352) 466-4244
Brooker	Thomas Burton	(904) 485-1954
Earlton	Hartman's Blueberry Pinta	(904) 468-2087
Hampton	Hank Williams	(904) 468-2327
Hawthorne	Bluestar Nursery	(352) 481-3300
Gainesville	Hatchett Creek Farm	(352) 373-7589
Gainesville	The Blue Jillion Corp.	(352) 485-2669
High Springs	Barker's Blueberry Patch	(352) 454-3004
LaCrosse	Country Blue's Farm	(904) 376-0511
Glen St. Mary	Watson's Blueberry Farm	(904) 259-6299
Cook's Bayou	Daulphin's Blueberry Farm	(904) 763-9341
Lake City	Stafford's Blueberry Farm	(904) 758-0525
Dixie County	Our Fantasy Farm	(904) 542-7083
Jacksonville	Lou Clark's Blueberries	(904) 771-503
Cantonment	Touchablue	(904) 587-5072
Fouraker	Fouraker Farms	(904) 397-2083
White Springs	Quintero Farms	(904) 397-4212
Bonifay	Tison's Blueberry	(850) 547-4696
Tallahassee	Golden Oaks Orchard	(850) 878-2306
Tallahassee	Windy Hill Vineyard	(850) 893-4229
Callahan	Mrs. C. Ellis	(904) 879-3845
Hilliard	Wyatt Crawford	(904) 845-3655
Yulee	Mrs. L. Flood	(904) 225-520
Milton	Lundy's Blueberry Farm	(850) 623-0652
Milton	Gulf Coast Blueberry	(850) 623-0273
St. Augustine	Bruce Farms	(904) 797-4713
Live Oak	Sivyer U-Pick Farm and Nursery	(904) 362-7108
Wellborn	Muller's Suwannee Blue Berry Farm	(904) 963-5419
Hampton	U-Pick Blueberries	(904) 468-2327
Crawfordville	Just Fruits	(904) 926-5644

FOOD FESTIVALS, FARMERS MARKETS AND U-PICK'EMS

BLACKBERRIES

Tallahassee	Golden Oaks Orchard	(850) 878-2306
Tallahassee	Windy Hill Vineyard	(850) 893-4229
Crawfordville	Just Fruits	(904) 926-5644

GRAPES-SCUPPERNONGS

Alachua	Spencer's Vineyard	(352) 462-1329
Gainesville	Grandma's Vineyard	(352) 377-2678
Gainesville	Gulledge's Vineyard	(352) 332-1288
Hawthorne	Florigon Vineyard	(352) 481-4022
Earleton	Longnecker's Farm	(904) 468-2483
LaCrosse	John Hargrave	(904) 462-1076
Youngstown	Sweatmore Ranch	(904) 722-4819
Jacksonville	Jeff May	(904) 781-1301
Jacksonville	Donnie Cason	(904)-781-1314
Quincy	James F. Eckhart	(850) 539-6973
Fouraker	Fouraker Farms	(904) 397-2083
St. Augustine	Nadeau Vineyard	(904) 772-6765

PEACHES

Bonifay	Mill's Peach Farm	(850) 547-2817
Ponce de Leon	Padgett Farm's	(850) 956-2140
Tallahassee	Golden Oaks Orchard	(850)-878-2306
Madison	Bishop's Orchards	(850)-973-2476

STRAWBERRIES

Earleton	Santa Fe Berry Farm	(904) 468-1790
Youngstown	Sweatmore Ranch	(904) 722-4819
Lawtey	Leon Starling	(904) 782-3419
Century	Band J. Farms	(904) 256-4010
Quincy	Thomas B. Smith Farms	(850) 856-5193
Jennings	Reynold's Farm	(904) 938-4313
Milton	Greg Penton Farms	(850) 623-6586
Milton	James McDonald	(850) 957-4188
Crawfordsville	Just Fruits	(904)-926-5644

FOOD FESTIVALS, FARMERS MARKETS AND U-PICK'EMS

MELONS

Archer	A-Country Garden	(352) 495-2470
Bear Creek	Register's U-Pick	(904)-722-9341
Mayo	Talmadge Lawson	(904) 294-1674
Grand Ridge	Tommy Jackson	(904) 592-9530
Chipley	U-Pick Vegetables	(850) 638-4663

ORGANICALLY GROWN VEGETABLES

Bonifay	Tony's Produce	(850) 547-4656
Jennings	How-Well Organics	(904) 938-2046

VEGETABLES

Archer	A-Country Garden	(352)-495- 2470
Orange Heights	Roy Brown	(904) 475- 2015
Earleton	Santa Fe Berry farm	(904) 468-1790
Baker	Gerald Brook's Farm	(904) 537-4521
Bear Creek	Register's U-Pick	(904) 772-9341
Lake City	Wendell Bailey	(904) 752-3970
Dixie County	Romia's U-Pick	(904) 542-7648
Wewahitchka	J.C. Morgan	(904) 639-2898
Fouraker	Fouraker Farms	(904) 397-2083
Ponce de Leon	Padgett Farms	(850) 956-2140
Grand Ridge	Tommy Jackson	(850) 592-9530
Grand Ridge	Donald Hamilton	(850) 592-8977
Mayo	Talmadge Lawson	(904) 294-1674
Tallahassee	Julian Billingsley	(850) 877-4902
Okaloosa	Escambia Farms	(850) 537-9301
Baker	Charlie Day's Pea Patch	(850) 537-3102
Crestview	Sam Love	(850) 682-3510
Bonifay	Chestnut Farms	(850) 638-4663
Blackman	Raymond Cook Farm	(904) 537-5571
Chipley	U-Pick Vegetables	(850) 638-4663
Chipley	Guettier Farms	(850) 638-0437

TOMATOES

LaCrosse	Rodger's Farm	(904) 464-2406
Quincy	Thomas B. Smith Farms	(850) 856-5193
Jennings	Reynold's Farm	(904) 938-4313
Grand Ridge	Tommy Jackson	(850) 592-9530
Grand Ridge	John Stone	(850) 592-6701
Ponce de Leon	Padgett Farms	(850) 956-2140

ACKNOWLEDGEMENTS

Editing:

Cameron Manning	Daisy Helms	Judi and Joseph Angelerie	Cathy Mooney
Tom Wright	Beth Dees	Patti Winberry	

Graphics: Graphics Artist, Randy Taylor
Computer Graphics, Trey Manning, Carole Newton

Touring the Backroads adapted from article from Florida State Chamber of Commerce

Photos and Illustrations:
The photographs and illustrations reproduced in this book were provided with the permission and courtesy of the following: Gino, Charles and Helen Litrico, 18, George T. Davis, 180, 303, Sammy Salem, 156, Keith Newby, 406, David Butler, 6, St. Augustine Sweet-Frankie John, 159
Florida State Archives, Photographic Collection: Pages 8, 13, 14, 28, 31, 39, 43, 49, 71, 72, 85, 86, 89, 103, 108, 126, 142, 143, 172, 174, 175, 177, 191, 202, 208, 209, 210, 211, 230, 233, 234, 246, 258, 316, 321, 327
St. Augustine Historical Society, 83, Pensacola Historical Society, 171, 183, Hayden Burns Library, 261, 283, P.K. Yonge Historical Collection, 147, 310 , McElwee & McElwee, 282, Glen St. Mary Nursery, 351
Chautauqua Winery, 159, 240, San Sebastian Winery, 201, 252, Forestry Museum, 25, Greyfield Inn, 408, Elizabeth Pointe Lodge, 408

Contributing Cooks:

Carolyn Herring, Geneva, Alabama
Mildred Tillman, Pensacola
Ann Barnes, Ponce deLeon
Doris McDonald, DeFuniak Springs
Ruby Southard, DeFuniak Springs
Elizabeth Bishop, DeFuniak Springs
Tawee Calay, Tallahassee
Linda Schur, Ponte Vedra
Lynda Sparkman, Lakeland
Velora Withers, San Antonia, Texas
Ellen Bulan, Jacksonville
Millie Smith, Tallahassee
Glenda Dees, DeFuniak Springs
Debbie Werner, Jacksonville
Barbara Zuber, Fernandina
Carolyn Zimmerle, Atlanta, Georgia

Peggy Browning, Tallahassee
Susan Sincler, Delray Beach
Ruby Burdashaw Williams, Bonifay
Lucille Williams Manning, Ponce deLeon
Mary Elizabeth Manning, Ponce deLeon
Sarah Elizabeth Ingram, DeFuniak Springs
Leola Ingram McDonald, DeFuniak Springs
Aubrey McDonald, DeFuniak Springs
Ingram McDonald, DeFuniak Springs
Ann Fairchild, Jacksonville
Genny Van Slate, DeFuniak Springs
Ann Manning, Tampa
Lillian Torrey, Blue Mountain Beach
Joyce Nolin, Tallahassee
Carrie Ingram, DeFuniak Springs

Contributing Restaurants:
Gypsy Cab Company, St. Augustine
O'Steen's, St. Augustine
Whiteway Delicatessen, Jacksonville
Bern's Steak House, Tampa
Criolla's, Grayton Beach
R.P. Mc Murphy's, Jacksonville Beach
Captain Anderson's, Panama City

Contributing Bed and Breakfast Inns:
Elizabeth Pointe Lodge, Amelia Island
Island Hotel, Cedar Key
Greyfield Inn, Cumberland Island
Old City House Inn, St. Augustine
Chalet Suzanne Country Club, Lake Wales

INDEX

A

Amaretto,
    Cheese Cake, 341
        Pecan Ice Cream, 372
Ambrosia, 46
Anchovies, Vinaigrette Salad with, 151
APPETIZERS AND TAILGATE FOOD, 83
Apple Torte, 359
Apricot Scones, 363
Artichoke
    Dip, 96
    and Oyster Soup, 119
    Stuffed, 92
Asparagus
    Filling, 77
    Tom's Roasted, 307
Avocado,
    Shrimp Remoulade with, 100
    Dip "Guacamole", 97

B

Back Bone and Rice, 37
Backyard Barbecue Party, 281
Bacon,
    Smoked with Pasta "Carbonara", 297
    Wilted Lettuce with, 164
Baloney Sandwiches, 107
Banana,
    Betty, 385
    Bread, 63
    Pudding, Granny's, 365
    Sandwich, 106
    Tart, with Fresh Blueberry, 358
Barbecue,
    Dry Rubs, 265
    Essentials, 271
    Marinades, 266
    Party, 281
    Sauces, 267-269
    Sopping Shrimp, 184
Bass Welatka, Chowder, 138
Basil,
    Mayonnaise, 176
    Pesto Sauce, 296
    Shrimp with Pasta, 182
Bean(s),
    A Large Pot of Dried Lima, 32
    Bubba's Black, 276
    Calico, 278
    Dip "Hummus", 97
    Green String, with Ham Hock, 309
    Red, and Rice, 391
    Fresh Field Peas and Speckled Butter, 32
    Speckled Butter, with Gravy, 309
Béarnaise Sauce, 75
BED AND BREAKFAST INNS, 411
Beef,
    Fried Steak with Tomato Gravy, 68
    Mother's Roast, with Gravy, 253
    Scottish Rib Roast, 255
    Sloppy Jo, 400
    Steak Dianne, 385
    Steak Salteado, 252
    Steak Tartare, 94
    Stock, 23
    T-Bone Steak a la Carte w/ Gravy, 256
    The Children's, Bourguignon, 146
Beer Can Yardbird, 280
Bell Peppers,
    Roasted Red, 254
    Stuffed, 393
Biscuits,
    Mother's Buttermilk, 52
    Pudding, 401
    Rise and Shine, 54
    Sweet Potato, 43
BISCUITS, BREAKFAST AND BRUNCH, 49
Bisque,
    Cedar Key Clam, 122
    Crab and Corn, 123
    Tomato, 123
    Rock Shrimp, 122
Black Beans,
    Bubba's, 276
    Soup, 125
Black-Eyed Peas, with Hog Jowls, 30
Bloody Mary, Low-Country, 403
Blueberry
    Muffins, 57
    Fresh, and Banana Fruit Tart, 358
Blue Crabs,
    Boiled with Pita Toast, 190
    Fried with Hushpuppy Stuffing, 188
    Fried Soft-Shell, 189
    Mama's Deviled, 186
    Minorcan Deviled, 187
Boiled,
    Panhandle Seafood, 191
    Blue Crabs with Pita Toast, 190
    Fernandina Shrimp, 180
    Peanuts, 39
Bodacious Brunch Dishes, 74
Bouillabaisse, Florida, 195
Brains and Eggs, 38
Bran, Muffins, Honey, 56
Bread,
    and Butter Pickles, 110
    Banana, 63
    Cracker Hoecake, 40
    Cracklin' Pone Corn, 41
    Daddy's Crusty Pone Corn, 41
    Fromajardis, 55
    Hypocrite Rolls, 59
    Lacey Edge Corn Cakes, 40
    Lunchroom Yeast Rolls, 43
    Orange Blossom Special, 65
    Orange, Elizabeth Pointe Lodge, 413
    Pudding, 366

INDEX

Rise and Shine Biscuits, 54
Skillet Corn, Cake, 41
'Simmon, 62
Southern Hushpuppies, 42
Sunflower, 61
Sweet Potato Biscuits, 43

Breakfast
    Casserole, 69
    Frittata, 76

Broccoli,
    Creamy , Soup, 121
    Sautéed, 322
    Soufflé, 324

Brownies, The Ultimate Fudgy, 357

Butter,
    Beans, Field Peas, 32
    Homemade, 26
    Rosemary, 195
    Tupelo Honey, 59

Buttermilk,
    Fried Okra, 325
    Mother's Biscuits, 52
    Pie, 344

Butterscotch Pudding, 364
Buerre Blanc, Greyfield Inn, 415
Burgers, Jo's Pub, 392

C

Cabbage,
    Skillet Red, 321
    Steamed, 34
    Swamp, 326
    Swamp Deluxe, 325

Cakes,
    Almond, 339
    Carrot, 408
    Coconut, 406
    Fig Preserve, 339
    Hickory Nut, 369
    German Chocolate, 409
    Icebox, Inn Keeper's, 416
    Italian Wedding, 389
    Jimmy's Sponge, 335
    Johnny's Feud, 335
    Lafayette Grill, 334
    Mama's White, 399
    Molton Lava, 356
    Lane, 409
    Peach Upside Down, 337
    Pound, Lois Hillard's, 407
    Prize Winning Peanut, 336
    Robert E. Lee, 331
    Strawberry Short, 338
    The Chocolate, 330
    The Best Rum, Ever 282
    The King's Favorite, 332
    The Queen's Lemon Cheese, 333
    White Fruit , 340

Calico Beans, 278

Candy,
    Divinity, 46
    Peanut Brittle, 39
    Pecan Pralines, 369
    Sugar Peanuts, 39
    Sister's Fabulous Fudge, 356

Cane Syrup, 25
    Old-Fashioned Tea Cakes, 45
"Carbonara", Pasta with Smoked Bacon, 297
Carrots, Sautéed, 306

Catfish,
    Pecan Crusted, 198
    Suwannee, Head Stew, 143

Cauliflower Au Gratin, 311
Chantilly Cream Sauce, 337
Charlotte, Old-Timey, 366
Chayote, Stuffed, 308

Cheddar,
    Cheese, Beer, 99
    Grits, 28

Cheese Cake,
    Amaretto, 341
    Black Forrest, 342
    Key Lime, 341

Cheese,
    Bubba's Beer, 99
    Blue, Dressing, 152
    Fried Mozzarella, 99
    Hog's Head, 37
    Morrison's Macaroni and, 299
    Parmesan, Toast, 93
    Spicy, Dip, 98
    Spread, Green Derby, 155
    The Ultimate Mac n', 393

Chicasaw Plum Jam, 79

Chicken,
    Beer Can, 280
    Boarding House Fried, 218
    Coq Au Vin, 222
    Creole, on Pasta, 219
    Deviled, 221
    N' Dumplings, 216
    Filipino Adobo, 225
    Florida, Salad, 165
    Gypsy, 228
    Hunters Style, 226
    Lemon, 224
    Mama's, and rice, 221
    Marabella, 224
    Moutarde, 227
    Perlo (Yardbird), 289
    Piccata, 227
    Popcorn, 280
    Roasted, 217
    Southern Fried, 399
    Spanish, and Rice, 220
    Stock, 22
    Tallulah's, Pie, 381
    Portabella, 225
    Valdosta, 223

Chili,
    Jailhouse, 239
    Trophy Buck, 238

Chit'lin's, 37
Choron Sauce, 189

Chowder,
    Clam, Minorcan, 137
    Snapper Cheek, 139
    Welatka Fish, 138

Chutney, Mango, 111
Cinnamon Rolls, 60
Clabber, 26
Clotted Cream, 26
Cobblers,
    Libby Love's Pieberry, 360
    Mary Lizzie's Lazy Day, 362
    Terre's Dewberry, 361
Coleslaw,
    Moccasin Branch, 279
    Wayne's Wilted, 279
Collard Greens, 30
Cookies,
    Almond Cakes, 339
    Ginger Bread Persons, 46
    Grayton Sand Tarts, 370
    Hickory Nut, 369
    Miss Lillie's Whiskey Cakes, 363
    Old-Fashioned Cane Syrup Teacakes, 45
    Ruby's Secret Oatmeal, 370
Conch,
    Ann's, Salad, 161
    Cracked, 390
    Fritters, 104
Cooter,
    Cross Creek, 208
    Soup, 120
Corn,
    and Tomatoes, 33
    Fritters, Kapok Tree, 105
    Grilled, 276
    Lacey-Edged, Cake, 40
    Plantation Fried, 278
    Roast-Neers, 33
    Skillet Fried, 33
Cornmeal Coush, 223
Cornbeef Hash, 69
Corn Bread,
    Cajun, 391
    Cracklin Pone, 41
    Daddy's Crusty Pone, 41
    Skillet Cake, 41
    Skillet, Dressing, 42
Corncob Jelly, 82
Crab,
    and Corn Bisque, 123
    Boiled Blue, with Pita, 190
    Cracked, Salad, 163
    Crabby Mushroom Soup, 118
    Florida Lobster Stuffed with, 193
    Fried Blue, Hush Puppy Stuffing, 188
    Fried Soft-Shell, 189
    Lafitte, 75
    Mama's, Goulash, 140
    Mama's Deviled, 186
    Minorcan Deviled, 187
    Sand Fleas' Shrimp Stuffed with, 103
    Soft Shell, Greyfield Inn, 415
    Stock, 22
    Stone, Claws, 105
    Stuffed Mushrooms, 98
Crawfish, A, Dish, 185
Cream,
    Devonshire, 363
    Cheese, 26
Creamy Salad Dressings, 153
Creme Fraiche, 125
Creole,
    Chicken on Pasta, 219
    Dry Rub, 265
    Eggplant, 317
    Filling, 77
    Gumbo YaYa, 132
    Sauce, 75
Crust,
    Cookie Crumb, 44
    Graham Nut, 44
    Perfect Pie, 44
Cucumber(s),
    Bread and Butter Pickles, 110
    Icebox Pickles, 109
    Marinated, 35
    Sissified, Sandwich, 107
    Smothered, 323
    Yogurt, 32

D

Daddy's Crusty Pone, 41
    Fig Preserves, 78
    Hoecake, 53
Datil,
    "Bottled Hell" Pepper Sauce, 31
    Cocktail Sauce, 174
    Pepper, Cheese Grits with, 28
    Pepper Jelly, 112
Demi-glace, 23
Dessert Crepes, 371
Dessert Sauces,
    Blackberry, 371
    Chantilly Cream, 337
    Hot Fudge, 372
    Lemon, 371
    Orange, 371
    Raspberry, 371
    Whiskey, 366
DESSERTS AND SWEET THANGS, 327
Deviled Crab,
    Mama's, 186
    Minorcan, 187
Dewberry Cobbler, 361
Dips,
    Artichoke, 96
    Avocado "Guacamole", 97
    Bean "Hummus", 97
    Jewel's Tailgate, 98
    Smoked Mullet, 96
    Spicy Cheese, 98

INDEX

Divinity, 46
Doves, Grilled, with Smoked Bacon, 245
Dressing,
    Granny's Hen and, with Giblet Gravy, 214
    Skillet Corn Bread, 42
    Walnut, 226
Dried Beans, 32
Dry Rubs,
    Carolina, 265
    Creole, 265
    Florida, 265
    Fish, 265
    Pork Ribs, 265
Duck,
    Tupelo Teal, 249
    Wood, Gumbo, 130
Dumplings,
    Granny's Chicken and, 216
    Pot Likker, 29

E

Egg(s),
    A Dozen Deviled, 108
    Bacon, N' Olive Sandwich, 106
    Boiled, 27
    Brains and, 38
    Bread, 366
    Breakfast Casserole, 69
    Breakfast Frittata, 76
    Chautauqua, 74
    Country Fried Yard, 27
    Crab Lafitte, 75
    Custard Pie, 407
    Lafitte, 75
    Nassau, 74
    Ode to the Omelets, 77
        Asparagus, 77
        Creole, 77
        Florentine, 77
        Pesto, 77
        Seafood, 77
    Poached, 27
    Scrambled, 27
    Scottish, 108
    Toad-in-the Hole, 76
Eggnog, 47
Eggplant,
    Creole Stuffed, 317
    Fried, with Kudzu Sauce, 306
English Peas,
    Fresh, 319
    New Potatoes, 314

F

Fettuccine Cream Sauce, 297
Figs,
    Daddy's, Preserve, 78
    Orange, Muffin, 58
    Quail's Stuffed with, 247
FINGER LICKIN' SOUTHERN
        BARBECUE, 261
Fish,
    Bahamian Salt, 395
    Catfish, Pecan Crusted, 198
    Cobia with Dill Sauce, 203
    Dolphin, Grilled with Creole
        Seasoning, 204
    Flounder, Black Creek Stuffed, 205
    Grouper , Gulf, Victor, 197
    Ingram's Fish Fry, 194
    Kingfish, Mayport Galvanized, 196
    Pompano, Grecian Style Broiled, 206
    Redfish, Blackened, 198
    Red Snapper Vera Cruz, 199
    Salmon Croquettes wTartar Sauce, 207
    Scamp, Grilled, with Wine Sauce, 201
    Smoked Mullet, Choctawhatchee, 96
    Snapper Anastasia, Mango Curry, 200
    Stock, 22
    Sucker, Red Horse, 194
    Trigger, w/ Shrimp Centre Street, 202
    Trout, Amandine, 197
    Tuna Steaks on the Grill, 195
Flan, Silky Smooth, 367
Florida,
    Bouillabaisse, 145
    Chicken Salad, 165
    Citrus Sauce, 268
    Dry Rub, 265
    Key Lime Pie, 352
    Lobster Stuffed with Crabmeat, 193
    Lobster Thermador, 193
    Sweet Rib Sauce, 268
Flounder, Black Creek Stuffed, 205
FOOD FESTIVALS, FARMERS' MARKETS
        & U-PICK'EMS, 432
FOREWORD, 4
Freezer Jam, 79
Frittata, Breakfast, 76
Fritter's,
    Conch, 104
    Corn, Kapok Tree. 105
Frog Leg's, Oklawaha with Curry Sauce, 209
Fromajardis, 55
Fudge,
    Hot, Sauce, 372
    Sister's Fabulous, 356

G

Garfish Balls, 95
Gator Tail,
    Grilled, 92
    Fried, 210
Game Hens with Walnut Stuffing, 226
Gazpacho, 144
Giblet Gravy, 214
Gingerbread,
    Persons, 46
    with Cream Cheese Icing, 46
Goat, Jamaican Jerk, 395
Gopher, Grandpa's, Gumbo, 134

INDEX

Grapefruit, Broiled, Chalet Suzzane, 417
Gravy,
- Amelia Island Shrimp, 179
- Bacon, Old City House, 421
- Chicken, 218
- Giblet, 214
- Ham and Red-Eye, 67
- Marsh Hens with, 244
- Meat, 24
- Macho, T-Bone Steaks with, 256
- Mother's Roast Beef and, 253
- New Potatoes and Cream, 314
- Sawmill, 72
- Speckled Butter Beans with, 309
- Squirrel, Seahorse Stable, 250
- Milk, 24
- White, 24

Greek Salad, 157
Green Derby,
- Cheese Spread, 155
- Salad, 155

Green Tomatoes
- Fried Green Tomatoes, 34
- Green Tomato Pickles, 110

Griddle Cakes, Whole Grain, 64
Grilled,
- Cobia with Dill Sauce, 203
- Dolphin with Creole Seasoning, 204
- Doves and Smoked Bacon, 245
- Gator Tail, 92
- Corn, 276
- Doves with Bacon, 245
- Shrimp with Herbs, 176
- Scamp with Wine Sauce, 201
- Vegetables, 311
- Venison Backstrap, 240

Grits,
- Cheddar Cheese, 28
- Cheddar Cheese with Datil Pepper, 28
- Fried, Old City House, 421
- Nassau, 66
- Old-Fashioned, 28

"Guacamole", Avocado Dip, 97
Guinea with the Light Brown Flair, 232
Gumbo,
- Creole Ya Ya, 132
- Filé, 131
- Grandpa's Gopher, 134
- Grave Yard, 135
- Gulf Coast Seafood, 133
- Original Oyster, 128-129
- Okra, 136
- Wood Duck, 130
- Z'Herbs, 136

H

Ham,
- Country, Red-eye Gravy, 67
- Fresh, 38
- Dixie, 258
- Hock, Green String Beans, 319
- Smoked Biscuits, 67
- Stock, 23

Heart of Palm Salad, 158
Hen,
- Granny's, and Dressing, 214
- Marsh, with Gravy, 244

Hoecake, Daddy's, 53
Hog Jowls, Black-eyed Peas with, 30
Hog's Head Cheese, 37
Hog Killings, 37
Hog N' Hominy, 71
Homemade,
- Basil Mayonnaise, 176
- Fresh, Pasta, 294
- Horseradish Sauce, 253
- Mashed Potatoes, 36
- Mayonnaise, 152
- Rich Vanilla Ice Cream, 372

,Hot Fudge Sauce, 372
"Hummus" Bean Dip, 97
Hushpuppies, Southern, 42
Hush Puppy, Fried Blue Crabs with, Stuffing, 188

I

Ice Cream,
- Amaretto Pecan, 372
- Fresh Peach, 372
- Rich Vanilla Homemade, 372

Iced Tea, Southern, 47
IN PURSUIT OF FRESH FLAVOR, 7

J

Jack Daniel Sauce with, Venison Chops, 241
Jam,
- Freezer, 79
- Scuppernong, 81
- Chicasaw Plum, 79

Jelly,
- Corncob, 82
- Datil Pepper, 112
- Mayhaw, 80
- Prickly Pear, 112

K

Kabobs,
- Oyster, 91
- Shark, 91

Key Lime,
- Cheesecake, 341
- Pie, Florida, 352

L

Lamb,
- Leg of, 379

INDEX

Rack of, 383
Shanks, 257
Shepherd's Pie, 380
Lasagne,
    for a Crowd, 300
    Mayport Seafood, 301
Lemon,
    Old-Fashioned, Meringue Pie, 354
    Sauce, 371
    Squares, 368
Lemonade/Limeade, 47
Lima Beans, A Pot of Dried, 32
Lime, Florida Key, Pie, 352
Limeade, 47
Linguini,
    Basil Pesto Sauce, 296
    with Clam Sauce, 299
Liniment, Grandmother's, 48
Liver a L' Orange, 243
Lobster,
    Florida, Thermidor, 193
    Florida, Stuffed with Crabmeat, 193

M

Macaroni,
    College Inns', Salad, 169
    Morrison's, and Cheese, 299
    The Ultimate, and cheese, 393
Macho Gravy, T-Bone Steak a la Carté with, 256
Mama's,
    Chicken N' Rice, 221
    Crab Goulash, 140
    Deviled Crab, 186
    Pear Salad, 402
Mandarin Orange Pie, 351
Mango
    Chutney, 111
    Curry, Snapper Anastasia with, 200
    Salsa, 198
    Sorbet, 373
    Sudae, 335
Map of North Florida, 10
Marinades,
    Cuban Mojo Criollo, 259
    Oriental, 266
    Poultry, 266
    Venison, 266
Mayhaw Jelly, 80
Mayonnaise,
    Basil, 176
    Homemade, 152
Marsh Hens with Gravy, 244
Matchstick Vegetables, 322
Meat Gravy, 24
Meringue, 45
Mess of Greens, 29
Milk Cow, 26
    Gravy, 24

Minorcan, Deviled Crab, 187
Mojo Sauce, 259
Molé Olé, Turkey, 231
Mother's
    Buttermilk Biscuits, 52
    Carrot Cake, 408
    German Chocolate Cake, 409
    Lane Cake, 409
    Roast Beef with Gravy, 253
Muffins,
    Blueberry, 57
    Orange Fig, 58
    Honey Bran, 56
Mull, Fernandina Shrimp, 127
Mullet,
    Boggy Bayou, Stew, 141
    Roe, 73
    Smoked, Choctawhatchee, 96
    Smoked, Dip, 96
Mushrooms,
    Stuffed with Crabmeat, 98
    Crabby, Soup, 118
Mustard Greens, 29

N

Navy Bean, Dried, 32
    Soup, 124
New Potatoes,
    en Papillote, 315
    Spud's, Salad, 167
    String Beans with Ham Hock, 319
    with Cream Gravy, 314
NORTH FLORIDA COOKERY, 7
NORTH FLORIDA FARMERS' MARKETS, 435
Northern Bean Salad, Tuna and, 162

O

Oatmeal, Ruby's Secret, Cookies, 370
Okra,
    Buttermilk Fried, 325
    Fried, 34
    Gumbo, 136
    Pickled, 35
    Salad, 168
    Skillet, 308
    Tomatoes, 34
OLD-TIMEY FAVORITES, 19
Omelet,
    Ode to the, 77
    Asparagus, 77
    Creole, 77
    Florentine, 77
    Pesto, 77
    Seafood, 77
Onion,
    Baked, 310
    Battered, Rings, 310
    Soup, Huguenot, 116
Orange,
    Blossom Special, 65
    Fig Muffins, 58
    Liver a L', 243

Mandarin, Pie, 351
Peel, Candied, 351
Sweet Potatoes, 316
Oyster(s),
And Pig Roast, 272-275
Andy Jackson, 87
Apalachicola, on the Half Shell, 86
Apalachicola, Stew, 144
Artichoke Soup, 119
Bienville, 90
Criolla's Curried, 419
Dipping Sauce, 86
Fried Apalachicola, 174
Kabob, 91
Original, Gumbo, 128
Original, Rockefeller, 87
Rock-a-Damn Fellow, 88
Pan Roast, 175
Wakulla, 89
Yano's, Dipping Sauce, 86

P

Palm,
Heart of, Salad, 158
Swamp Cabbage, 325
Swamp Cabbage Deluxe, 326
Pancakes,
Gabby's, 64
Libby's Heavenly Hots, 63
Whole Grain Griddle, 64
Pancit, Philippine, 302
Panna Cotta, Tupelo, 367
Parmesan Cheese Toast, 93
Pasta,
Cream Sauce "Alfredo", 297
Creole Chicken on, 219
Fresh Homemade, 294
Ho-Style, "Puttanesca", 296
Potato, with Creamy Tomato Sauce, 295
with Smoked Bacon "Carbonara", 297
Peanut(s)
Brittle, 39
Butter Custard Pie, 242
Butter N' Jelly Sandwich, 107
Boiled, 39
Cake, Prize Winning, 336
Homemade, Butter, 342
Parched, 39
Sugar, 39
Peach(es),
Fresh, Ice Cream, 372
A Peck of Pickled, 109
Upside Down, Cake, 337
Pear,
Bartlett, Pie, 354

Mama's, Salad, 402
Pudding, 354
Relish, 31
Sand, Preserves, 81
Wine, Charlie's, 404
Peas,
Black-Eyed, with Hog Jowls, 30
Fresh English, 319
Fresh Field, with Butter Beans, 32
Pigeon, and Rice, 394
Pecan(s),
Amaretto, Ice Cream, 372
Crusted Catfish, 198
Mocha, Pie, 346
Pralines, 369
Roasted, 62, 346
Southern, Pie, 346
Sweet Potato, Pie, 346
Wild Rice with Wild, 291
Pepper, Datil, Jelly, 112
Sauce, Datil "Bottled Hell", 31
Sauce, Rooster Spur, 30
PERLOS, RICE DISHES AND PASTA, 283
Perlo,
Savannah, 288
Seafood, 285
Smoked Sausage, 287
Minorcan, 277
O'Steen's Shrimp, 286
Palm Valley Pig, 289
Panther Creek, 288
Yardbird, 289
Philippine Pancit, 302
Pickled,
Bread and Butter, 110
Green Tomato, 110
Icebox, 109
Okra, 35
Panhandle Shrimp, 99
Peaches A Peck, 109
Watermelon Rind, 111
Pickles, Bread and Butter, 110
Lime, 35
Sweet Dill, 35
Watermelon Rind, 111
Zucchini/Squash, 35
Pie(s)
AppleTorte, 359
Blackberry, 344
Blackbottom, 345
Buttermilk, 344
Cherry O, 353
Chocolate Icebox, 355
Crust, Southern, 44
Florida Key Lime, 352
Fresh Pumpkin Pie, 350
Granny Smith's Apple, 349
Half Moon, 45
Jeff Davis, 352
Libby Love's, Berry, 360
Mandarin Orange, 351
Mary Lizzie's Lazy Day Fruit, 362
Mocha Pecan, 346

    Old-Timey Lemon Meringue, 354
    Old-Timey Egg Custard, 407
    Peanut Butter Custard, 342
    Pecan, 346
    Pecan Sweet Potato, 346
    Pear, 354
    Pinto Bean, 348
    Scuppernong, 353
    Strawberry, 350
    Spanish Bakery Turnover, 349
    Sweetie, in the '55 Chevy, 347
    Sweet Potato, 348
    Sweet Potato Pecan, 346
    Tawee's Favorite Chocolate, 355
    Terre's Dewberry Cobbler, 361
    Watkins Coconut Cream, 343
Pie Crust,
    Perfect, 44
    Cookie Crumb, 44
    Graham/Nut, 44
Pig and Oyster Roast, 272-275
Pineapple
    Fluff, Hospitality, 368
    Sandwich, 107
Pinto Bean Pie, 349
Plum Jam, Chickasaw, 79
Poached, Perfect, Eggs, 27
Pompano, Grecian Style, 206
Potato(es),
    Anna, 312
    Baked Sweet, 36
    Brabant, 312
    Fried Sweet, 36
    Garlic Mashed, 36
    Hashbrown Casserole, 320
    Hellenthal's German, 315
    Homemade Mashed, 36
    New, with Cream Gravy, 314
    New, with English Peas, 314
    New with String Beans, 319
    en Papillote, 315
    Old-Fashioned, Salad, 36
    Orange Sweet, 316
    Oven roasted, 313
    Pasta with Creamy Tomato Sauce, 295
    Rhett's Turnip Root and, Purée, 318
    Rosin, 277
    Spuds New, Salad, 167
    Twice Baked, 313
Pork,
    Backbone N Rice, 37
    Charleston, Red Gravy, 402
    Cuban, Roast, 259
    Sausage, 71
Possum and Taters, 260
Pound Cake,
    Lois Hillard's, 407
    The King's Favorite, 332

Preserves,
    Daddy's Fig, 78
    Sand Pear, 81
Pralines, 369
Pudding(s),
    Banana Betty, 385
    Bread, 366
    Butterscotch, 364
    Creamy Rice, 364
    Granny's Banana, 365
    Granny's Biscuit, 401
    Pear, 364

Q

Quail,
    Plantation, 246
    Southern Fried, 247
    Stuffed with Figs, 247
Queen's Lemon Cheese Cake, 333

R

Rabbit,
    Dijon, 248
    Liver Paté, 94
    N'Rice, 248
    Smothered Fried, 70
Raspberry Sauce, 371
Red, Beans and Rice, Lillian's, 391
Relish, Sand Pear, 31
    Tomato, 31
Remoulade, Shrimp with, Sauce, 100
Rice,
    Brown, Thanksgiving, 293
    Cameron's Nutty, 290
    Creamy, Pudding, 364
    Dirty, 290
    Green, 292
    Pudding, Old-Fashioned, 46
    Rabbit N', 248
    Red Beans and, 391
    Savannah Red, 292
    Spanish Chicken and, 220
    Spanish Yellow, 293
    Spanish, 159
    Risotto Milanese, 386
    Wild, with Wild Pecans, 291
Wild, Casserole, 291
    White, 28
Roast(ed),
    Mother's, Beef and Gravy, 253
    -Neers, 33
    Pecans, 62
    Pork, Cuban, 259
    Scottish Rib, 255
    The Ultimate, Chicken, 217

INDEX

Rock Shrimp,
    Bisque, 122
    Smothered, 183
Roe, Fried Mullet, 73
Rolls,
    Cinnamon, 60
    Hypocrite, 59
    Lunchroom Yeast, 43
Rooster Spur Pepper Sauce, 30
Roux, Brown, 24
Rutabaga, 34
    Wild Watercress, 321

S

Salad(s)
    Ann's Conch, 161
    Bern's Caesar, 154
    Chicken, 165
    College Inn's Macaroni, 169
    Crab Boats, 164
    Cracked Crab, 163
    Fresh Spinach, 156
    Fresh Salsa, 169
    Fried Okra, 168
    Greek, 157
    Green Derby, 155
    Gulf Coast Shrimp, 161
    Heart of Palm, 158
    Mama's Pear, 402
    Marinated Tomato, 156
    Old-Fashioned Potato, 36
    Our Favorite Creamy Dressing, 152
    Our Favorite Vinaigrette, 150
    Pensacola Gaspache, 168
    Perfection 1905, 170
    Shrimp, 161
    Spanish, 159
    Spud's New Potato, 167
    Tabbouleh, 166
    Tamari, 160
    Tuna and Northern Bean, 162
    Vinaigrette with Anchovies, 151
    West Indies, 163
    Wilted Lettuce with Bacon, 164
Salad Dressings,
    Basil, 151
    Balsamic, 151
    Creamy French, 153
    Creole, 153
    Honey Mustard, 153
    Kevin's Cowboy, 152
    Louie, 153
    Oriental, 151
    Ranch, 153
    Thousand Island, 153
    Vinaigrettes, 151
Salmon Croquettes, 207
Salsa,
    Fresh, 169
    Mango, 198
Sand Pear
    Preserves, 81
    Relish, 31
Sandwiches,
    Bacon, Egg, Olive, 106
    Banana, 106
    Fried Baloney, 107
    Meatloaf, 107
    Parkway Bar-B-Q, 107
    Peanut Butter N' Jelly, 107
    Sissified Cucumber, 106
    Pimento Cheese, 106
    Pineapple, 107
    Tuna Fish, 106
    Tomato, 106
    Sardine, 107
Sauce(s),
    Barbecue, 267-269
        Bubba's, 267
        Carolina Clear, 267
        Carolina Red, 267
        Florida Sweet, 268
        Georgia Red, 268
        North Florida Mustard, 268
        Florida Citrus, 268
        Texas, 269
        Minorcan, 269
        Quick, 269
    Basil, Pesto, 296
    Béarnaise, 75
    Choron, 189
    Clam, 299
    Cream, 297
    Creamy Tomato, 295
    Creole, 75
    Curry, 209
    Datil Cocktail, 174
    Datil Pepper, 31
    Dijon, 95
    Dill, 203
    Hollandaise, 75
    Jezebel, 67
    Key Lime, 104
    Marchand de Vin, 240
    Marinara, 228
    Mojo Criolla, 259
    O'Steen's Shrimp, 177
    Peanutty, 101
    Pesto, Basil, 296
    Remoulade, 100
    Rooster Spur Pepper, 30
    Salsa, 169
    Salsa, Mango, 200
    Seafood Cocktail, 102
    Stone Crab Mustard, 105
    Tartar, 207
    White, 24
    Wine, 201
    Yano's Oyster Dipping, 86
Sangria,
    Red, 252
    White, 159
Sauces Sweet, 371
    Blackberry, 371
    Lemon, 371
    Orange, 371
    Raspberry, 371
Sausage, Link, 38
SAVORY SOUPS, GUMBOS AND CHOWDERS, 113

INDEX

Scallops,
    Marinated Calico, 93
    Seared with Peanutty Sauce, 101
Scones,
    Apricot, 363
    Scottish, 379
Scottish,
    Eggs, 108
    Trifle, 374
Scuppernong,
    Jam, 81
    Pie, 353
SEAFOOD, FISHES AND POND CRITTERS, 171
Seafood,
    Casserole, 192
    Cocktail Sauce, 102
    Gulf Coast Gumbo, 133
    Newburg. 192
    Perlo, 285
SEASONAL MENUS, 424-427
Shark, Black Tip, Kabobs, 91
Shrimp,
    Amelia Island, Gravy, 179
    Campbell's, Ring, 102
    Cocktail, 102
    Creole, 181
    Curry, 181
    Fernandina Boiled, 180
    Fernandina, Mull, 127
    Grecian, 178
    Grilled with Herbs, 176
    Gulf Coast, Salad, 161
    O'Steen's, Perlo, 286
    Panhandle Pickled, 99
    Paste, 73
    Remoulade, 100
    Rock, Bisque, 122
    Salad, 161
    Sopping Barbecue, 184
    St. Augustine Fried, 177
    Smothered Rock, 183
    Sand Fleas' Stuffed, 103
    Toast, 100
Skillet,
    Corn Bread, 41
    Corn Bread Dressing, 42
    Fried Corn, 33
    Okra, 308
    Squash and St. Augustine Sweets, 324
Slaw,
    Wayne's Wilted, 279
    Moccasin Branch, 279
Sloppy Jo, 396
Smokehouse, 38
Snapper,
    Anastasia w/ Mango Curry, 200
    Cheek Chowder, 139
    Vera Cruz, 199
    Snails, Snips and, 382
Sorbets,
    Blackberry, 373
    Fruit, 373
    Mango, 373
    Pear, 373
    Raspberry, 373
    Satsuma, 373
    Strawberry, 373
    Watermelon, 373
Soufflé,
    Broccoli, 324
    Sweet Potato, 316
Soup,
    Beef and Barley, 116
    Black Bean, 125
    Collard Green, 126
    Cold Zucchini, 121
    Cooter, 120
    Crabby Mushroom, 118
    Creamy Broccoli, 121
    du Jour, 390
    Florida Bouillabaisse, 145
    Gazpacho, 144
    Ham and Split Pea, 125
    Huguenot Onion, 116
    Jimmy's Peanut, 119
    Leek and Potato, 378
    Navy Bean, 124
    Oyster Artichoke, 119
    Red Bean, 124
    She Crab, 399
    Summertime Vegetable, 117
    Wintertime Vegetable Beef, 117
SOUTHERN GARDEN VEGETABLES, 303
Spaghetti
    Fisherman's Style, 298
    Ho-Style, "Putanesca", 296
    Smoked Bacon"Carbonara", 297
    with Garlic and Olive Oil, 298
Spanish,
    Chicken and Rice, 220
    Yellow Rice, 293
    Salad, 159
Spinach,
    Creamed, 317
    Fresh, Salad, 159
    Sautéed with Garlic, 318
    Timbales, 323
    Zucchini Sautéed with, 322
Squash,
    Casserole, Crookneck, 307
    Skillet, and St. Augustine Sweets, 324
Squirrel,
    Brunswick, Stew, 142
    Seahorse Stable, Gravy, 250
Steak,
    a la Carte, T-Bone, with Macho Gravy, 256
    Dianne, 385
    Country Fried with Tomato Gravy, 68
    Salteado, 252
    Tartare, Bern's, 94
Stews,
    Apalachicola Oyster, 144
    Boggy Bayou Mullet, 141
    Bruce Creek Venison, 237

Brunswick Squirrel, 142
Ingram's Camp, 405
Jo's Camp, 405
Raymond Gunn's Swamp Cabbage, 326
Suwannee Catfish Head Stew, 143
Swamp Cabbage, 326

Stocks,
- Beef, 23
- Chicken, 22
- Crab, 22
- Demi-glace, 23
- Fish, 22
- Ham, 23
- Shrimp, 23

Stone Crab Claws with Mustard, 105

Strawberry,
- Pie, 350
- Shortcake, 338

String Beans with New Potatoes, 319

Swamp Cabbage
- Deluxe, 325
- Raymond Gunn's, Stew, 326

Sweet Potatoes, Baked, 36

Syrup,
- Cane, 25
- Simple, 373

T

Tabbouleh, Whiteway, 166
Tamari Salad, 160
Tart, Fresh Fruit, 358
Tartar Sauce. 207
Teacakes, Old-Fashioned Syrup, 45

Tea,
- Black, 47
- Sassafras, 47
- Southern Iced, 47

Toast,
- Shrimp, 100
- Parmesan Cheese, 93
- Pita, 190

Tomato(es),
- Bisque, 123
- Fried Green, 34
- Green, Pickles, 110
- Marinated, Salad, 156
- Okra and, 34
- Relish, 31

Torte, Apple, 359
TOURING THE BACKROADS, 11
Trigger Fish, with Shrimp, 202
Trifle, Scottish, 374
Trout, Speckled, Amandine, 197

Tuna,
- and Northern Bean Salad, 162
- Grilled, Steaks, 195
- Ring with Almonds, 101

Tupelo Honey,
- Butter, 59
- Panna Cotta, 367
- Teal, 249

Turnovers, Sweet Potato, 349

Turkey,
- Florida Wild, 251
- Molé Olé, 231
- Tetrazinni, 230

Turnip,
- A Mess of Greens, 27
- Rhett's, Root Purée, 318

U

U-PICK'EMS, 432

V

Veal
- Camille, 254
- King Ferdinand, 390
- Osso Bucco, 387
- "Saltimbocca", 255
- Stuffed, Chops, 388

Vegetable(s)
- Matchstick, 322
- Summertime Soup, 117
- Wintertime, Soup, 117
- on the Grill, 311

Venison,
- Bruce Creek Stew, 237
- Chicken Fried, 242
- Chili, Trophy Buck, 238
- Chops, with Jack Daniel Sauce, 241
- Grilled Backstrap, 240
- Jailhouse Chili, 239
- Loaf, 242

Vinaigrette Salad Dressings, 151

W

Waffles, Tomorrow's, 65
Watercress, Rutabaga and Wild, 321
Watermelon Rind Pickles, 111
Wine, Charlie's Pear, 404
WILD GAME, CRACKER CATTLE AND PINEY WOODS ROOTERS, 233
Wild Boar Stew, 243

Wild Rice
- Casserole, 291
- with Wild Pecans, 291

Wood Duck Gumbo, 130

Y

YARDBIRDS AND OTHER FOWL, 211
Yeast Rolls. Lunchroom, 43

Z

Zucchini,
- Cold, Soup, 121
- Fried, 320
- Sautéed with Spinach, 322

See 'ya later, alligator!

That's all ya'll!

Original Secret Recipe

Original Secret Recipe

Original Secret Recipe

Seasonal Florida
P.O. Box 1694
Ponte Vedra Beach, Florida 32004
(904) 285-4410

Please send _____ copies of Seasonal Florida @ $29.95 each $_____
Add postage and handling @ $ 4.00 each $_____
Florida residents add 6% sales tax @ each $_____
seasonalfloridacookbook.com

Name _____

Address _____

City State Zip _____

Seasonal Florida
P.O. Box 1694
Ponte Vedra Beach, Florida 32004
(904) 285-4410

Please send _____ copies of Seasonal Florida @ $29.95 each $_____
Add postage and handling @ $ 4.00 each $_____
Florida residents add 6% sales tax @ each $_____
seasonalfloridacookbook.com

Name _____

Address _____

City State Zip _____

Seasonal Florida
P.O. Box 1694
Ponte Vedra Beach, Florida 32004
(904) 285-4410

Please send _____ copies of Seasonal Florida @ $29.95 each $_____
Add postage and handling @ $ 4.00 each $_____
Florida residents add 6% sales tax @ each $_____
seasonalfloridacookbook.com

Name _____

Address _____

City State Zip _____